The Handbook of Rhetoric and Public Address

Handbooks in Communication and Media

This series aims to provide theoretically ambitious but accessible volumes devoted to the major fields and subfields within communication and media studies. Each volume sets out to ground and orientate the student through a broad range of specially commissioned chapters, and also to provide the more experienced scholar and teacher with a convenient and comprehensive overview of the latest trends and critical directions.

The Handbook of Children, Media, and Development, *edited by Sandra L. Calvert and Barbara J. Wilson*

The Handbook of Crisis Communication, *edited by W. Timothy Coombs and Sherry J. Holladay*

The Handbook of Internet Studies, *edited by Mia Consalvo and Charles Ess*

The Handbook of Rhetoric and Public Address, *edited by Shawn J. Parry-Giles and J. Michael Hogan*

Forthcoming

The Handbook of Critical Intercultural Communication, *edited by Rona Halualani and Thomas Nakayama*

The Handbook of Global Communication and Media Ethics, *edited by Robert Fortner and Mark Fackler*

The Handbook of Global Research Methods, *edited by Ingrid Volkmer*

The Handbook of International Advertising Research, *edited by Hong Cheng*

The Handbook of Rhetoric and Public Address

Edited by

Shawn J. Parry-Giles and J. Michael Hogan

A John Wiley & Sons, Ltd., Publication

Library of Congress Cataloging-in-Publication Data

The handbook of rhetoric and public address / edited by Shawn J. Parry-Giles and J. Michael Hogan.
   p.   cm. – (Handbooks in communication and media)
   Includes bibliographical references and index.
   ISBN 978-1-4051-7813-6 (hardcover : alk. paper)   1. Rhetorical criticism.   2. Speeches, addresses, etc. – History and criticism–Theory, etc.   3. Speeches, addresses, etc., American–History and criticism.   4. English language–Rhetoric–Research–Methodology.   I. Parry-Giles, Shawn J., 1960– II. Hogan, J. Michael, 1953–
   PN4096.H36 2010
   809.5'1–dc22

                                                    2010001890

A catalogue record for this book is available from the British Library.

Set in 10/13pt Galliard by SPi Publisher Services, Pondicherry, India
Printed and bound in Malaysia by Vivar Printing Sdn Bhd

01   2010

*To David Zarefsky upon his retirement – a mentor
and inspiration to all public address scholars*

Contents

Notes on Contributors

Karlyn Kohrs Campbell is Professor of Communication Studies at the University of Minnesota. She is a rhetorical theorist and critic whose primary interests are the public discourse of women and US presidents. She is the author or editor of eight books. Her research has appeared in such journals as *Quarterly Journal of Speech*, *Philosophy & Rhetoric*, *Communication and Critical/Cultural Studies*, and *Rhetoric & Public Affairs*. She has received the Francine Merritt Award for contributions to women, the National Communication Association Distinguished Scholar Award, the Ehninger Award for Distinguished Rhetorical Scholarship, the Winans–Wichelns Book Award, and the University of Minnesota Distinguished Woman Scholar Award.

Bonnie J. Dow is Associate Professor and Chair of Communication Studies and Associate Professor of Women's and Gender Studies at Vanderbilt University. She is the author of *Prime-Time Feminism: Television, Media Culture, and the Women's Movement Since 1970* (University of Pennsylvania Press, 1996), and the co-editor (with Julia T. Wood) of *The Sage Handbook of Gender and Communication* (2006). She is also a co-editor of *The Aunt Lute Anthology of US Women Writers, Volume One: 17th–19th Centuries* (Aunt Lute Books, 2004). Dow's research interests include the rhetoric and representation of the first and second waves of US feminism.

Cara A. Finnegan is Associate Professor of Communication at the University of Illinois at Urbana-Champaign. Her research explores the visual politics of US rhetorical history. She is the author of *Picturing Poverty: Print Culture and FSA Photographs* (Smithsonian, 2003) and co-editor of *Visual Rhetoric: A Reader in Communication and American Culture* (Sage, 2008). Her essays on visual rhetoric have appeared in such journals as *Rhetoric & Public Affairs*, *Quarterly Journal of Speech*, and *Rhetoric Society Quarterly*. She is a past recipient of the National Communication Association's Diamond Anniversary Book Award and its Golden Monograph Award.

Robert N. Gaines is a Professor of Communication at the University of Maryland. His interests in text authentication have developed in connection with his participation in two NEH-funded research initiatives, the *Voices of Democracy* Project at the University of Maryland and the Philodemus Translation Project at the University of California, Los Angeles. His textual scholarship has appeared in *Advances in the History of Rhetoric, Cronache Ercolanesi, Hermes: Zeitschrift für klassische Philologie, Papers on Rhetoric, Rhetoric & Philosophy, Transactions of the American Philological Association*, and the Oxford Text Archive.

J. Michael Hogan is Professor of Rhetoric and Co-Director of the Center for Democratic Deliberation at the Pennsylvania State University. He is a scholarly advisor to the National Constitution Center and co-director of *Voices of Democracy*, an NEH-funded online educational initiative. Hogan is the author, co-author, or editor of six books and nearly 50 articles, book chapters, and reviews. He has won a number of scholarly awards, including the NCA Distinguished Scholar Award and the Douglas W. Ehninger Distinguished Rhetorical Scholar Award. He earned his PhD at the University of Wisconsin-Madison. Before moving to Penn State, he taught at the University of Virginia and at Indiana University in Bloomington.

Davis W. Houck is Associate Professor of Communication at Florida State University. He is the author or editor of nine books, including *In Her Words: The Rhetoric of Fannie Lou Hamer 1963–1976* (with Maegan Parker-Brooks, University Press of Mississippi), and *Rhetoric, Religion, and the Civil Rights Movement 1954–1965* (with David E. Dixon, Baylor University Press). He is the founding book series editor of *Race, Rhetoric, and Media* with the University Press of Mississippi.

James Jasinski is Professor of Communication Studies at the University of Puget Sound. He is the author of *Sourcebook on Rhetoric* (Sage, 2001) and numerous essays and book chapters that examine early American as well as African American public address. He is at work on a project which will explore the role of prudential argument in Supreme Court decisions on race and educational policy (from *Brown* to *Parents Involved in Community Schools v. Seattle School District*).

Sarah Jedd earned her doctoral degree in rhetoric from the Department of Communication Arts at the University of Wisconsin-Madison in 2009. Her dissertation is titled "Reproducing Families: The Rhetoric of the Planned Parenthood Association of America, 1942–1973." Jedd's research focuses on the twentieth-century birth control movement, abortion discourse, and parenting ideology. Jedd is Associate Director of the Basic Public Speaking course at the University of Wisconsin-Madison. In addition, she teaches an advanced-level course on the Rhetoric of Reproductive Rights.

Cheryl R. Jorgensen-Earp is Professor of Communication Studies at Lynchburg College in Lynchburg, Virginia. Her primary research interests include violence as a rhetorical tool, public memory as it functions in planned and spontaneous memorials, and the British women's suffrage movement. She is the author of *The*

Transfiguring Sword: The Just War of the Women's Social and Political Union (University of Alabama Press) and editor of *Speeches and Trials of the Militant Suffragettes* (Fairleigh Dickinson University Press). Her most recent book is *In the Wake of Violence: Image and Social Reform*, published by Michigan State University Press.

Martin J. Medhurst is Distinguished Professor of Rhetoric and Communication, and Professor of Political Science, at Baylor University in Waco, Texas. He has taught at the University of California, Davis, and Texas A&M University. Medhurst is the author or editor of 13 books, including *Words of a Century* (with Stephen E. Lucas), *Before the Rhetorical Presidency*, and *The Prospect of Presidential Rhetoric* (with James Arnt Aune). He has authored more than 85 refereed articles and chapters, and has won several awards for teaching and research, including the NCA Distinguished Scholar Award.

Jennifer R. Mercieca is an Associate Professor in the Department of Communication at Texas A&M University. She combines public address, history, and political theory scholarship to analyze the rhetorical construction of American citizenship. Her book *Founding Fictions* (University of Alabama Press, 2010) examines how America's republican and democratic political fictions have constituted American citizens as romantic heroes, tragic victims, and ironic partisans. Her work has been published in the *Quarterly Journal of Speech*, *Rhetoric & Public Affairs*, *Presidential Studies Quarterly*, and *Argumentation and Advocacy*.

Charles E. Morris III is an Associate Professor in the Department of Communication at Boston College. He is editor of *Queering Public Address: Sexualities in American Historical Discourse* and co-editor (with Stephen H. Browne) of *Readings on the Rhetoric of Social Protest*. His queer history and criticism has regularly appeared in the *Quarterly Journal of Speech*, as well as *Rhetoric & Public Affairs*, *Communication and Critical/Cultural Studies*, and the *Southern Communication Journal*. He has received several awards from the National Communication Association, most recently the Randy Majors Memorial Award from the Caucus on LGBTQ Concerns.

John M. Murphy is an Associate Professor in the Department of Communication at the University of Illinois. His research has appeared in the *Quarterly Journal of Speech*, *Rhetoric & Public Affairs*, *Presidential Studies Quarterly*, and elsewhere. A former book review editor of the *Quarterly Journal of Speech*, Murphy is also a recipient of the National Communication Association's Golden Anniversary Monograph Award and the NCA Public Address Division's Wrage–Baskerville Award.

Shawn J. Parry-Giles is a Professor of Communication and the Director of the Center for Political Communication and Civic Leadership at the University of Maryland. She teaches and studies rhetoric and politics. Her research has appeared in the *Quarterly Journal of Speech*, *Presidential Studies Quarterly*, *Rhetoric & Public Affairs*, and elsewhere. She is the author of *The Rhetorical Presidency, Propaganda, and the Cold War, 1945–1955* (named a *Choice* "Outstanding Academic Title"), the co-author of *Constructing Clinton: Hyperreality and Presidential Image-Making in Postmodern Politics*, as well as *The Prime-Time Presidency: The West Wing and US Nationalism*. She is also a co-editor of the *Voices of Democracy* online journal.

Mary E. Stuckey is a Professor of Communication and Political Science at Georgia State University and the editor of *Southern Communication Journal*. She is the author, editor, or co-editor of nine books, including *Defining Americans: The Presidency and National Identity*, and *Jimmy Carter, Human Rights, and the National Agenda*. Her work has appeared in *Quarterly Journal of Speech*, *Presidential Studies Quarterly*, and a variety of other venues. Her book on Jimmy Carter was honored with the Public Address Division's Marie Hochmuth Nichols Award.

Eric King Watts is an Associate Professor in the Department of Communication Studies at the University of North Carolina at Chapel Hill. Watts's scholarship explores the conditions in which rhetorical voice can be invented, performed, consumed, mutated, and suppressed. In particular, he examines how the endowment of African American voices intervenes in the manner in which the public deliberates on a vision of the civic good and social justice. He is finishing a book on the rhetoric, aesthetics, and ethics of the New Negro Renaissance. His work has appeared in such venues as *Quarterly Journal of Speech*, *Rhetoric & Public Affairs*, *Critical Studies in Media Communication*, and *New Media and Society*. Watts is the current editor of *Critical Studies in Media Communication*.

Kirt H. Wilson is a critic and theorist of public address and African American rhetoric. An Associate Professor, he teaches for the University of Minnesota's Communication Studies Department. Winner of the National Communication Association's New Investigator Award (2001), the Karl R. Wallace Memorial Award (2002), and the James A. Winans–Herbert A. Wichelns Memorial Award (2003), he is the author of *The Reconstruction Desegregation Debate*. He is currently working on two book manuscripts – first, a study of the theory and practices of imitation in the nineteenth century and, second, a study of the sentimental aesthetics in contemporary commemorations of the civil rights movement.

Susan Zaeske is Professor and Chair of the Department of Communication Arts at the University of Wisconsin-Madison. Her research focuses on rhetoric, gender, religion, and political culture. She is the author of *Signatures of Citizenship: Petitioning, Antislavery, and Women's Political Identity* as well as articles and chapters analyzing the public discourse of Presidents Washington, Van Buren, and Lincoln along with studies of the rhetoric of congressional debates and women activists. Zaeske has received the National Communication Association's Golden Anniversary Monograph Award, its James A. Winans–Herbert A. Wichelns Memorial Award, and the Marie Hochmuth Nichols Award.

David Zarefsky is Owen L. Coon Professor Emeritus of Argumentation and Debate and Professor Emeritus of Communication Studies at Northwestern University. His research concerns the history and criticism of US public discourse, with a special focus on the pre-Civil War period and on the 1960s. He is the author of *President Johnson's War on Poverty: Rhetoric and History* and *Lincoln, Douglas, and Slavery: In the Crucible of Public Debate*, both of which received the National Communication Association's Winans–Wichelns Award for Distinguished Scholarship in Rhetoric and Public Address, as well as seven other books and over 100 scholarly articles. He is a recipient of the NCA's Distinguished Scholar Award and is a former president of both the NCA and the Rhetoric Society of America.

Acknowledgments

We came up with the idea for this volume as we were working on *Voices of Democracy: The US Oratory Project* (www.voicesofdemocracy.umd.edu), an NEH-funded educational website focusing on great speeches and debates. As we reflected on the importance of studying our rhetorical heritage, we thought it might be a good time to take stock of the scholarly discipline that historically had claimed speeches as its unique subject matter – the discipline of rhetoric and public address. As will be evident from this volume, that discipline has evolved well beyond a narrow focus on platform orators, but it remains committed to understanding how rhetoric and public address – now more broadly defined – has shaped history and the human experience. In taking stock of the discipline at the start of the twenty-first century, we hope to reinvigorate the historical and critical study of public address and inspire a new generation of scholars in the field.

Elizabeth Swayze of Wiley-Blackwell helped us to envision the volume and bring the project to completion. We are very grateful for Elizabeth's support and patience throughout the entire process. We also thank Margot Morse for her helpful and positive guidance as we moved the manuscript through production. We also are grateful to Annie Jackson and Brigitte Lee Messenger for their attention to detail in the final stages of the *Handbook*'s publication. The professionalism and collegiality of the Wiley-Blackwell team has been evident throughout the development and publication of this handbook.

From the outset, we envisioned the project as bringing together some of the most thoughtful and influential scholars in the field to reflect on the state of the art, including working critics spanning different generations who were identified with various approaches to public address or who had carved out distinctive areas of specialization. We were pleased when almost everybody we invited to contribute agreed, and the resulting volume is, of course, largely the product of their labors. All of these authors devoted considerable time and energy to the project, despite their very busy schedules. Their devotion to the discipline is evident in the final result, and we are inspired and thankful for their commitment to the project.

We especially want to thank three people who devoted enormous time and energy to the project as advisors and research assistants. Una H. Kimokeo-Goes, a PhD student at the Pennsylvania State University, and Belinda Stillion-Southard, a PhD graduate of the University of Maryland, contributed countless hours to the project proofreading, copy-editing, and otherwise helping to get the chapters into shape. Una also prepared a style sheet for the volume, compiled the bibliography, and created the index. The selfless commitment of these two research assistants was invaluable, and the volume could never have been completed without their help. We also want to thank Alyssa Samek, a PhD student at the University of Maryland, who stepped up to provide editorial assistance as the manuscript neared completion. These three young scholars testify to the exciting promise of rhetoric and public address in the next generation.

Finally, we wish to acknowledge all of those scholars of rhetoric and public address who came before us and whose vision of the discipline we seek to perpetuate and extend. That list of scholars is too long to include here, but the reflections contained within these pages suggest a few of the more prominent names from the past: Herbert Wichelns, William Norwood Brigance, Marie Hochmuth Nichols, and Edwin Black, to name just a few. We also would like to give special thanks to a few teachers and role models who have shaped our own careers, some of whom contributed to this volume: Lloyd Bitzer, Stephen E. Lucas, James R. Andrews, David Zarefksy, Martin J. Medhurst, Karlyn Kohrs Campbell, and Richard J. Jensen. Without their support and inspiration, there would be no *Handbook of Rhetoric and Public Address*.

The editors and publisher gratefully acknowledge permission for use of the following material:

Portions of Chapter 1 appear in Martin J. Medhurst, "William Norwood Brigance and the Democracy of the Dead: Toward a Genealogy of the Rhetorical Renaissance," in *Rhetoric and Democracy: Pedagogical and Political Practices*, ed. Todd F. McDorman and David M. Timmerman (East Lansing: Michigan State University Press, 2008), 3–38.

Portions of Chapter 6 appear in Shawn J. Parry-Giles, "Dwight D. Eisenhower: 'Atoms for Peace' (December 8, 1953)," *Voices of Democracy* 1 (2006): 118–129; and Shawn J. Parry-Giles, "John F. Kerry: Vietnam Veterans Against the War, Speech Before the US Senate Committee on Foreign Relations (April 22, 1971)," *Voices of Democracy* 2 (2007): 99–125 (www.voicesofdemocracy.umd.edu).

Portions of Chapter 12 appear in Mary E. Stuckey, *Jimmy Carter, Human Rights, and the National Agenda* (College Station: Texas A&M University Press, 2008), 24, 25, 48–49, 56–59, portions of ch. 4.

Portions of Chapter 17 appear in J. Michael Hogan, "Rhetorical Pedagogy and Democratic Citizenship: Reviving the Traditions of Civic Engagement and Democratic Deliberation," in *Rhetoric and Democracy: Pedagogical and Political Practices*, ed. Todd F. McDorman and David M. Timmerman (East Lansing: Michigan State University Press, 2008), 75–97.

Introduction
The Study of Rhetoric and Public Address

Shawn J. Parry-Giles and J. Michael Hogan

On November 4, 2008, the United States elected its first African American president. The key to President Barack Obama's victory, many commentators noted, was the power of his oratory – his mastery of the spoken word. Electronic mass media have dramatically changed our conception of "eloquence" over the years,[1] but Obama showed that the ability to deliver stump speeches that resonate with the American people still matters. "As much as anything else," Henry Allen of the *Washington Post* observed, "Obama won the presidency with words. He is an orator, a rare thing in a time when educated people, a lot of them Obama supporters, have been taught to distrust old-fashioned eloquence."[2] Richard O'Mara of the *Christian Science Monitor* agrees, puzzling over Obama's style but still placing him in the company of a small number of presidents remembered as great speakers: "He can be a bit professorial, but he's part Reagan, part FDR, and may be a lot of Teddy Roosevelt."[3]

Obama's election reminds us of several important points. First, oratory still matters in US politics. Obama rose from political obscurity to the highest office in the land largely on the strength of his platform oratory. At the same time, many Americans harbor a certain distrust of speakers who seem *too* skilled or *too* adept at arousing the passions of a crowd. Within some circles, at least, Obama's very success as a speaker served as evidence that he was "all talk" and no substance.[4] Finally, of course, Obama's appeal illustrates just how dramatically our conception of "eloquence" has changed over time. Bordering at times on the "professorial," as O'Mara observed,[5] Obama's cool, televisual style is a far cry from the arm-waving, podium-thumping style of the "spellbinders" of the early twentieth century. His unique story – and his very ascendance to the "bully pulpit" – may well signal a revolution in our conception of what constitutes a "great speech."

Obama's election thus provides an opportune moment to reflect upon the American tradition of rhetoric and public address – how it has evolved over the years, the impact of new technologies, and the very meaning of "public address." It inspires us to reconsider our conception of "eloquence" and to reflect anew on the pragmatic and ethical principles of public speaking. It forces us to revisit the canon of "great speeches" – those touchstones we hold up as models of eloquence – and to reconsider the methods and criteria we employ as historians and critics of American public address. In short, Obama's election not only marks a watershed moment in American political history, but also raises new questions and challenges for the study of rhetoric and public address.

The theoretical and critical study of rhetoric is, of course, centuries old. Since Plato and Aristotle wrote about rhetoric in ancient Greece, the discipline has been at the center of the liberal arts and integral to education for citizenship – at least in those times and places where democracy flourished. As George Kennedy explains, "Aristotle was primarily concerned with public address on the occasions offered by civic life in Greece," where speakers sought to "persuade or influence action or belief and thus to impose their own ideas and values on others."[6] For Aristotle, rhetoric was an essential practical art in a democratic society – an art that empowered people "to deliberate among themselves."[7]

America's founders were well schooled in the classical rhetorical tradition. Thomas Jefferson's library included some 33 volumes on rhetoric, including works by Aristotle and Cicero. From 1806 to 1809, John Quincy Adams served as a professor of rhetoric and oratory at Harvard University. He later published his *Lectures on Rhetoric and Oratory*, which were firmly grounded in the classical texts.[8] In the first half of the nineteenth century, Daniel Webster, Henry Clay, and John Calhoun forged a golden age of American oratory, and the study of classical rhetoric and great speeches flourished in US colleges and universities. During the Gilded Age, rhetoric declined both as an art and as an academic subject, but as the new century approached, a young academic named Woodrow Wilson joined with other Progressive reformers in forging a revival of teaching and scholarship on rhetoric and debate. As "spellbinders" and "muckrakers" stimulated public participation in politics, Progressive educators and reformers looked for ways to address what John Dewey would later call the "problem of the public": the need for improvements in "the methods and conditions of debate, discussion, and persuasion."[9] These efforts helped inspire many of the institutions and programs that still promote debate and deliberation today, including civic organizations, debate and forensics clubs, and student government and student newspapers.

Out of this rhetorically vibrant era – a period that Robert Kraig has labeled the "second oratorical renaissance"[10] – emerged the modern discipline of rhetoric and public address. Over the twentieth century, that discipline would evolve far beyond its founders' emphasis on "great" speakers and speeches. Yet it would remain, at its core, a discipline concerned with how public discourse has shaped the American democratic experience – whether for good or ill. As such, the study of rhetoric and public address remains important to education for citizenship. Not only does it contribute to the historical and civic literacy of our citizenry, it also cultivates the habits and skills of engaged citizenship.

Traditionally, the term "public address" has been used to describe both a canon of great speeches and a field of scholarly inquiry, even a critical perspective or a research paradigm. For most early public address scholars, the subject matter was platform oratory and their method was what Edwin Black would later call "Neo-Aristotelianism."[11] Treating speech as the strategic art of discovering the "available means of persuasion," public address scholars focused narrowly upon particular speakers, speeches, and audiences, and they typically asked questions about the invention and disposition of the speaker's ideas, style and delivery, and the effects of a given speech on its immediate audience. A few early scholars took a wider view, touting the study of public address as a means of illuminating the "social and intellectual history" of our culture. As Ernest J. Wrage explained, the study of speeches could illuminate those ideas that either explained or rationalized human behaviors; it could provide "an index to the history of man's values and goals, his hopes and fears, his aspirations and negations."[12] Yet even Wrage focused rather narrowly on "great speakers and speeches," and few early public address scholars imagined theoretical alternatives to the classical tradition.

Since the late 1960s, the field of public address has expanded dramatically in terms of both subject matter and critical perspectives. While some public address scholars continue to focus on great speakers and speeches, others have embarked upon recovery projects, giving voice to those who have historically been marginalized or excluded from the canon of great speakers.[13] Still others have emphasized the need to broaden the scope of public address beyond platform orations or to invent new critical paradigms or new standards of critical judgment. Most public address scholars still focus on persuasion in the public sphere, but studies in public address now encompass a broader range of voices and a greater variety of written and mass mediated texts, including advertisements, autobiographies, cartoons, films, manifestoes, memorials, photographs, television and print news, and many other forms of discourse.[14] In addition, public address scholars have embraced a variety of new critical vocabularies and methodologies, ranging from genre and social movement studies to an "ideological turn" emphasizing issues of race, gender, sexuality, and class. More and more scholars now turn to the study of American public address for insights into contemporary problems and controversies. In search of "lessons of history" relevant to today's political issues, these scholars find important parallels between the past and the present.[15]

Not surprisingly, all of these developments have inspired spirited debates, forcing public address scholars to revisit fundamental questions about the purposes, scope, methods, and contributions of their scholarship. Today, scholars of rhetoric and public address study a wide variety of "texts," and the discipline has matured into a broader, more inclusive, and more theoretically sophisticated scholarly enterprise. *The Handbook of Rhetoric and Public Address* represents an effort to take stock of that progress, reflecting on the history of the discipline and some of the trends and challenges it faces at the start of a new century. It both showcases the historical traditions and reflects on the future possibilities of scholarship in rhetoric and public address. With contributions from many of the most prolific and influential scholars in the field, it reminds us of the importance of reflecting on where we have been and where we are going.

Celebrating the traditions of the discipline, *The Handbook of Rhetoric and Public Address* reaffirms the value of studying important texts in context and identifying rhetorical motives, strategies of argument and style, and the effects of public discourse on particular audiences. Reflecting the earliest trends in public address, the volume explores the relationship between rhetoric and history and considers the value of archival research, textual recovery and authentication, and "complex and nuanced" interrogations of texts and their "contextual dynamics."[16] At the same time, the *Handbook* gives voice to scholars who have criticized those very traditions or who have taken the ideological turn, focusing instead on the role of power and politics in history and putting the study of public address in the service of contemporary causes. In several chapters of the volume, scholars reflect on the role of race, class, gender, and/or sexuality in research on public address and explore the relevance of those historical moments to ongoing political and social debates.

Despite differences over purpose, subject matter, and critical perspective, public address scholars do share some common ground. First, they all agree that rhetoric matters – that is, they believe rhetoric is a force in history and that the study of public address can shed light on the human condition. Whether studying a great speech, the influence of rhetoric on "human action and reaction" over time,[17] or the general "rhetorical climate of an age,"[18] students of rhetoric and public address believe that their work can illuminate how rhetoric shapes human understanding and action. Second, public address scholars share a commitment to free speech and our democratic way of life, whether that commitment manifests itself in the recovery of marginalized voices or in critiques of those who deceive or manipulate the public. While some public address scholars continue to discover important new primary texts through archival research, others focus on authenticating texts, reinterpreting canonical texts, assessing the contributions of public texts to the history of ideas, or revising our theoretical concepts and critical standards. Still others identify with the so-called "deliberative democracy movement,"[19] emphasizing the relationship between research, teaching, and a commitment to revitalizing public deliberation.

These shared commitments distinguish rhetorical scholarship from other academic disciplines, yet they also dictate an interdisciplinary perspective. Sharing interests with scholars in history, English, American studies, media studies, political science, and other disciplines, rhetorical scholars are no longer alone in their interest in the art of public persuasion. Indeed, disciplines across the humanities and social sciences have taken a "rhetorical turn," and scholars interested in rhetoric now may be found across the university. While some might consider that a threat to our discipline, it also affirms the importance of our work and opens up exciting new opportunities for interdisciplinary collaboration. *The Handbook of Rhetoric and Public Address* is written in that spirit: we view the growing interdisciplinary interest in rhetoric as an opportunity to contribute to larger conversations about rhetoric and democracy.

If scholars of rhetoric and public address hope to make a difference in those larger scholarly conversations, they must have clear answers to two important questions: What defines rhetoric and public address as a scholarly discipline? And what are the most promising and productive areas of research in the field? This volume represents at least a preliminary effort to answer these questions with reflections from some of the most accomplished scholars in the field.

The Past and Future of Rhetoric and Public Address

Historically, there have been a number of key moments when scholars of rhetoric and public address have reflected on the state of their art, debated their purposes and critical practices, and published works that redefined the field or showcased its best work. One such moment actually unfolded over more than a decade between 1943 and 1955: the publication of the three-volume set of critical studies, *A History and Criticism of American Public Address.*[20] A second came in 1970, when a number of leading rhetoric scholars gathered at the Wingspread Conference Center in Wisconsin to reflect upon the past and future of the discipline. The result was a volume that radically redefined what it meant to do rhetorical criticism: *The Prospect of Rhetoric: Report of the National Development Project.*[21] Nearly 20 years later, the first Biennial Public Address Conference convened in Madison, Wisconsin, and the result was a volume edited by Michael Leff and Fred Kauffeld that touted close textual analysis as the wave of the future: *Texts in Context: Critical Dialogues on Significant Episodes in American Political Rhetoric.*[22] Subsequent Public Address Conferences also produced volumes, each with its own unique theme or emphasis,[23] and other "boutique" conferences in rhetoric and public address were launched as well, including a conference on "Rhetorical History" in 1995 and a biennial Presidential Rhetoric Conference at Texas A&M University. All of this activity resulted in still more volumes reflecting on the state of the art and showcasing the work of public address scholars, including *Doing Rhetorical History: Concepts and Cases* (1998), *Presidential Speechwriting: From the New Deal to the Reagan Revolution and Beyond* (2003), *Who Belongs in America? Presidents, Rhetoric, and Immigration* (2006), and *The Prospect of Presidential Rhetoric* (2008).[24] In 2002, Texas A&M University Press published the first in a continuing series of volumes on notable presidential speeches; the Library of Presidential Rhetoric now includes studies of Thomas Jefferson, Woodrow Wilson, Franklin D. Roosevelt, John F. Kennedy, and Ronald Reagan, among others.[25] And in 2003, the first of an ambitious ten-volume series, *A Rhetorical History of the United States*, was published by the Michigan State University Press.[26] Three more of these volumes have since appeared.[27]

The Handbook of Rhetoric and Public Address has neither the same ambitions nor the scope of some of these earlier projects. Instead, it picks up where they left off, addressing issues and controversies that have arisen in the first decade of the new century and situating new directions in public address scholarship within the scholarly traditions of the discipline. The volume reflects an understanding of public address as both a subject matter and a critical perspective, mindful of the connections between the study of public address and the history of ideas. The chapters in this book include in-depth discussions of such basic issues as textual recovery and authentication, the purposes and complexities of archival research, and the role of historical context in public address scholarship. Yet the book also delves into complex methods of interpreting written and spoken texts as well as visual artifacts, the role of theory and ideology in public address research, and the various methods for assessing the effects of public discourse. With multiple scholars addressing many of the same issues and debates, the book reflects both the common ground and the diversity of views among public address scholars, advancing ongoing discussions and debates over the goals and character of rhetorical scholarship.

The Handbook of Rhetoric and Public Address was conceptualized at the same time as *Voices of Democracy: The US Oratory Project* (*VOD*) – an NEH-funded website devoted to the study of significant speeches and debates in US history.[28] Providing authenticated texts and an online journal of critical essays, *VOD* was designed to encourage the study of speeches in the undergraduate classroom. Organized around such persistent themes as war and peace, economic and social justice, civil rights, and religion in public life, *VOD* aims to promote historical and critical literacy, as well as a better understanding of the ethical and pragmatic principles of rhetoric and public address. By studying great speeches, we believe that students not only equip themselves to become more engaged citizens, but also find inspiration to "speak out" themselves.

The Handbook of Rhetoric and Public Address probes more deeply into both the rationale for studying public address and some of the theoretical and methodological issues that underlie the study of public discourse. It also provides readers with a better understanding of some of the critical perspectives employed by rhetorical critics. The goal of the *Handbook* is to stimulate discussion about the key purposes and methods of public address scholarship in the twenty-first century. By encouraging deeper reflection on the goals, methods, and contributions of public address scholarship, we hope to further the revival of interest in rhetoric and public address, not only as a scholarly pursuit but as education for citizenship.

Part I: The History and Prospects of Rhetoric and Public Address

Part I of the *Handbook of Rhetoric and Public Address* includes three major essays assessing the state of the art in the discipline. Chapter 1, authored by Martin J. Medhurst (Baylor University), provides an in-depth examination of the field's history, with an emphasis on the historical commitments and controversies that have defined the study of oratory since the sixteenth century. In tracing that history, Medhurst situates the study of public address in Hugh Blair's *Lectures on Rhetoric and Belles Lettres* (1783), as well as in the elocutionary movement of the nineteenth and early twentieth centuries. Medhurst also recounts the history of college courses in public speaking and the split between English and Speech departments in the early twentieth century. Locating the origins of the modern discipline in that split, Medhurst touches on the formation of the National Speech Arts Association and the Eastern Public Speaking Conference, as well as the debut of the *Quarterly Journal of Public Speaking*. Medhurst also reviews subsequent debates over the development of the traditional paradigm, the relationship between theory and criticism, and the role of ideology in rhetorical criticism. He also reflects on the place of ethical judgment in the criticism of public discourse and the connections between public address and democratic governance. Assessing the current status of rhetoric and public address, Medhurst concludes optimistically: "One hundred and ten years later, the study of public address is alive and well in all three of its senses: the teaching of public speaking, the analysis of discrete texts, and the evaluation and criticism of discourses – oratorical and nonoratorical – that create, find, or address a public."

Chapter 2, by David Zarefsky (Northwestern University), also reflects on the history of public address scholarship and its prospects for the future. Zarefsky celebrates the accomplishments of public address studies but also notes some anxieties about where the field is headed. Reflecting on the paradox of a discipline with a rich history of scholarly achievement yet persistent worries about its place in rhetorical studies, Zarefsky offers a blueprint for the future: "By examining historical situations on their own terms … we can engage in a rich and meaningful dialogue between the past and the present, strengthening our understanding of where our public culture came from and how it got from there to here." That "dialogue" between the past and the present, Zarefsky concludes, is "one of the great rewards of studying public address."

In Chapter 3, Karlyn Kohrs Campbell (University of Minnesota) attends specifically to the role of method in rhetorical criticism, narrating the history of the field's development through a review of literature, as well as reflections on her own academic career. Arguing that pre-established "methods" tend to "become screens through which we view this symbolic world," Campbell concludes that "in most cases" those "screens distort, alter, or damage what they are intended to explain and reveal." In making that argument, Campbell reaffirms the wisdom of Edwin Black, who in his influential 1965 book, *Rhetorical Criticism*, took aim at overly rigid critical methodologies, particularly the Neo-Aristotelian paradigm so dominant at the time. "Black was right," Campbell concludes. "There are no methods – only language and critics."

With Part I providing historical perspective and reflections on the state of the discipline, Parts II through V of the volume probe more deeply into the challenges and controversies surrounding particular approaches to rhetoric and public address. Each chapter reflects on the author's own interests and perspectives, and each illustrates particular theoretical or methodological arguments with case studies from the author's own research.

Part II: Basic Research in Rhetoric and Public Address

Part II of this volume focuses on some of the basic issues in research on rhetoric and public address. The authors provide an overview of the issues and challenges involved in textual recovery, textual authentication, and archival research. All of the authors ground their discussion in extended examples from their own scholarly projects.

Chapter 4, authored by Davis W. Houck (Florida State University), explores the complications and processes of textual recovery. He expands the notion of textual recovery to include textual *discovery*, or bringing to light texts long lost, forgotten, or deemed unimportant. While the work of recovery is ongoing, Houck demonstrates how public address scholars, because of their training and recent advancements in technology, are uniquely positioned to discover new and profoundly important cultural texts. In the process of detailing the principles and complications of textual recovery, he discusses his own recovery of some 180 African American civil rights speeches – speeches that might have been lost to history without the sort of recovery efforts he champions.

In Chapter 5, Robert N. Gaines (University of Maryland) addresses the complexities and processes of textual authentication. Given that texts represent the object of study for public address inquiry, Gaines argues that reliable, authenticated texts are just as crucial to public address scholars as rigorous and disciplined data collection is to any other venue of knowledge production. Recalling how textual authentication was once an important part of public address scholarship, Gaines laments that we no longer take it so seriously. He offers both a rationale and a method for reviving textual authentication as a central concern in rhetorical inquiry. With public address texts now including not just spoken but also written, acoustic, and even visual and multimedia texts, the challenges of textual authentication are greater than ever before. Gaines offers guidance for authenticating radically different sorts of texts with three unique case studies: Abraham Lincoln's "Gettysburg Address"; Jimi Hendrix's performance of the "Star Spangled Banner" at Woodstock; and the iconic image known as "Old Glory Goes Up on Mt. Suribachi," from the battle for Iwo Jima during World War II.

Chapter 6, authored by Shawn J. Parry-Giles (University of Maryland), discusses the role of archival research in the study of presidential rhetoric. Illuminating the historical development and controversies surrounding the preservation of presidential papers, Parry-Giles elaborates on the contributions of archival research to the study of public address, focusing on issues of rhetorical motives, the behind-the-scenes production of public discourse, the complications of historical context, and the assessment of rhetorical strategies at work in public texts. Parry-Giles turns to Dwight D. Eisenhower's "Atoms for Peace" campaign and the Nixon administration's response to protests by the Vietnam Veterans Against the War to illustrate her arguments about how archival sources might enhance our understanding of public texts. In the process, she also sheds light on the relationship between presidential rhetoric and the US news media, raising questions about the manipulation of the press that are still relevant today.

Chapter 7, co-authored by Susan Zaeske (University of Wisconsin) and Sarah Jedd (University of Wisconsin), focuses on archival research on women and gender in the history of American public address. After recalling how some of the earliest public address scholars engaged in ground-breaking archival research, the authors contemplate "contemporary issues in archival research facing scholars of gender and women's public address." Describing some of the challenges of such research, the authors note that the archives of women are generally less accessible and less well organized than those of male political figures, and they call upon public address scholars to broaden the scope of their archival research beyond traditional notions of what constitutes a relevant rhetorical text. Urging public address scholars to both continue the effort to recover women's voices and to broaden their search for evidence of how gender functions in public discourse, they illustrate their contentions by examining the role of gender in the congressional debates over women's antislavery petitions from 1835 to 1840.

Part III: Text and Context in Rhetoric and Public Address

In this part of the *Handbook*, the chapters focus on the key characteristics and controversies of critical scholarship on spoken, written, and visual texts. In addition, the role of theory in textual analysis and public address scholarship is addressed. In the process, the authors attend to the relationships between text and context, between the public and the private, and between the author/producer and the text itself. These chapters also discuss the role of authorial intent and other persistent issues in rhetorical analysis.

Chapter 8, written by Kirt H. Wilson (University of Minnesota), assesses the obstacles that scholars face when contextualizing discourses of race – discourses often overlooked in earlier histories of US public address. Wilson "views public address as an expansive field in which US race relations are negotiated, sometimes violently but always with and through discourse," leading him to conclude that "context may be the most important conceptual category in public address criticism today." His chapter addresses the theoretical, methodological, and critical challenges facing scholars interested in discourses of race, and he argues that the subject inevitably requires creative and politicized acts of textual recreation. Thus, Wilson attends to issues of biography, context, and social conflict throughout the chapter, and he illustrates his argument about the importance of context with a study of how different interpretive communities responded to racial violence in the aftermath of the Civil War.

Cheryl R. Jorgensen-Earp (Lynchburg College) is the author of Chapter 9, which examines conceptions of public and private in the historical study of women's discourse. Using archival research to cast new light on women's political activities during the early twentieth century, Jorgensen-Earp asserts that "private documents, such as letters and diaries, take on greater importance in understanding the rhetoric of women" because women were still largely excluded from political venues. In developing her argument, Jorgensen-Earp describes three ways that the public/private distinction might inform criticism: (1) by investigating how "private interactions bolster public rhetoric," (2) by advancing a conception of the public and private that "intertwines the two in a manner more reflective of women's lives," and

(3) through an approach that "moves the concept of private to an interior realm and considers those archival materials that reveal the subject's deepest thoughts and emotions." She then turns to the British suffrage movement to illustrate the ways in which the distinction between the public and the private "retains its usefulness" in rhetorical analysis, at least "when applied in a flexible manner."

Chapter 10, authored by Cara A. Finnegan (University of Illinois), examines visual texts from a public address perspective. Finnegan centers attention on strategies for conducting close "readings" of images and visual artifacts, addressing five different aspects of images that invite rhetorical analysis: production, composition, reproduction, circulation, and reception. Finnegan contends, importantly, that the visual represents "a potent mode of public address which should be studied in ways that recognize images' political, cultural, and historical specificity, as well as their fluidity as circulating objects in public culture." Finnegan illustrates her approach to the rhetorical analysis of visual texts with an examination of a Lewis Hine poster published in a 1915 edition of the *Child Labor Bulletin* entitled "Making Human Junk."

Chapter 11, authored by John M. Murphy (University of Illinois), reflects on the role of theory in public address studies. In this chapter, Murphy details "four modes of theoretical reflection that public address scholars use in order to realize the possibilities of rhetoric: classification, generalization, subversion, and abduction." Murphy contends that "rhetorical theories organically grow from our discursive times," thereby situating the "relationships between rhetorical theory and public address in the context of political and moral challenges." Murphy turns to President George W. Bush's Second Inaugural Address to illustrate how various theoretical modes of inquiry work in critical practice. In the process, he offers an intriguing analysis of how John F. Kennedy's Inaugural Address functions as a "shadow text" that "haunts" Bush's speech.

Part IV: Questions of Effect in Rhetoric and Public Address

This section grapples with questions of effect in public address scholarship, including both traditional notions of instrumental effect and more contemporary, "constitutive" understandings of rhetorical influence.

Chapter 12, authored by Mary E. Stuckey (Georgia State University), employs an instrumental approach to presidential rhetoric. Challenging those who have suggested that presidential rhetoric falls on "deaf ears," Stuckey argues that presidential words do matter, although she complicates the question of rhetorical effects, calling for attention to "a combination of more subtle, indirect, and long-term effects," including how presidential rhetoric might set the national agenda, "frame" issues in particular ways, or influence "the national understanding of an issue over time." To illustrate her conception of instrumentality, Stuckey turns to the case of Jimmy Carter's human rights policies, illustrating how Carter's rhetoric may have had little immediate effect but nevertheless contributed to an important, ongoing conversation by placing Carter's conception of human rights on the national and international political agenda.

James Jasinski (University of Puget Sound) and Jennifer R. Mercieca (Texas A&M University) explore constitutive renderings of rhetorical force in Chapter 13. A constitutive approach is centered on the representational capacity of language, where texts invite audiences to experience the world in particular ways. In exploring the capacity of discourse "to constitute identity," Jasinski and Mercieca urge "critics to consider how texts invite listeners and readers to modify the meaning of a culture's key terms, to reconceptualize a culture's experience of public time, ... to reaffirm or reconfigure accepted demarcations of social space, and to affirm as well as challenge established sources of cultural authority, bonds of affiliation, and institutional relationships." Additionally, Jasinski and Mercieca distinguish between interior and exterior modes of constitutive critical inquiry, urging critics to attend more to "textual exteriors by tracing the text's reception, circulation, and articulation." This perspective is then illustrated in an extended discussion of the Virginia and Kentucky *Resolutions* drafted in 1798. Noting the initial, instrumental failure of those resolutions to rally states against the Alien and Sedition Acts (1798), Jaskinski and Mercieca show how, in the long run, the resolutions were canonized as the "principles of '98" and significantly influenced later debates over the powers of the federal government and states' rights.

Part V: The Politics of Rhetoric and Public Address

The chapters in this section address the role of ideology and practical politics in the study of public address. In the process, these authors grapple with controversies over the role of race, gender, and sexuality in rhetorical scholarship, as well as questions about the connections between research and teaching in public address and the challenges of deliberation and citizenship in our democratic society.

Chapter 14, authored by Bonnie J. Dow (Vanderbilt University), assesses the place of feminist politics in public address studies. Dow recalls how the "second wave" created new possibilities for the study of women's public address, and she reviews "several overlapping threads in feminist public address scholarship" that emerged during that time, "including the recovery of women's and feminist public address, feminist critique of contemporary (increasingly mass-mediated) political discourse, and public address scholars' engagement with feminist and critical theories." Calling for heightened attention to mass-mediated and visual texts, along with further explorations of the concept of masculinity in public address studies, Dow illustrates her arguments with a case study in media constructions of gender, focusing on a three-part series on the feminist movement broadcast by CBS News in 1970.

In Chapter 15, Eric King Watts (University of North Carolina) offers another perspective on the importance of race in public address scholarship. Watts explores the character of the dominant ideology in public address scholarship and considers how ideas about race have been defined, contested, and deployed. Watts charges that while early attention to race in public address scholarship expanded the canon to include voices of African Americans, such efforts "left largely unexamined the basic character of 'race' as a political/economic discursive formation and an unstable trope." Watts concludes his chapter with reflections on the public discourse of W. E. B. Du Bois during the Harlem Renaissance, which he argues demonstrates "how the concept of voice may help public address scholars contend with the instabilities constitutive of the trope of 'race.'"

Charles E. Morris III (Boston College), author of Chapter 16, explores the role of sexuality in public address scholarship, showcasing the growing prominence of gay, lesbian, bisexual, transgendered, and "queer" studies in public address. The founding premise of this work is that sexuality constitutes a key domain in the construction of human experience, identity, knowledge, community, culture, and politics. Equally foundational is the belief that sexuality historically has constituted a chief motive and means of oppression, diminishing the lives and livelihoods of millions. Morris offers a genealogy of sexuality within rhetoric and public address, charting its conditions of silence. Morris concludes that "queer inducements and interrogations constitute not the end of history and memory, but an impetus to queer world-making that must ultimately be deepened by its ineluctable and intractable historicity." Morris illustrates his arguments by pursuing his "ongoing effort to queer Abraham Lincoln."

In Chapter 17, J. Michael Hogan (Pennsylvania State University) suggests how the study of rhetoric and public address might contribute to broader efforts to revive civic culture in the United States. Reviewing evidence of the decline in civic literacy and political participation over the past 50 years, he explores the connections between the health of our democracy and the character and quality of our public discourse. He then argues that research and teaching in rhetoric and public address have important contributions to make to the growing interdisciplinary movement for civic renewal in America. Drawing upon his own research, teaching, and outreach initiatives, Hogan suggests a number of ways that students of rhetoric and public address might educate for engaged citizenship, uphold higher standards of public discourse, and illuminate the lessons of history implicit in the American rhetorical tradition. Emphasizing both the practical skills of engaged citizenship and the ethical foundations of our discipline, Hogan concludes with an optimistic vision of engaged, reform-minded public scholarship in rhetoric and public address.

The Handbook of Rhetoric and Public Address is designed to meet an important need in the field. Combining reverence for the traditions of rhetoric and public address with reflections on some of the latest trends in the discipline, it pauses to take stock of the purposes and character of research and teaching in public address at the start of a new century. We do not pretend that the chapters in this volume exhaust the subject, nor do we offer a definitive roadmap to the future. We do hope, however, that the hard work that went into this volume will inspire a new generation of scholars to take up the charge and sustain the study of rhetoric and public address into the next millennium.

Notes

1 See Kathleen Hall Jamieson, *Eloquence in an Electronic Age: The Transformation of Political Speechmaking* (New York: Oxford University Press, 1988), 1–16.

2 Henry Allen, "His Way With Words: Cadence and Credibility," *Washington Post*, January 20, 2009, www.washingtonpost.com/wp-dyn/content/article/2009/01/17/AR2009011701429.html (accessed September 12, 2009).

3 Richard O'Mara, "Deconstructing Obama's Oratorical Skills," *Christian Science Monitor*, April 26, 2009, www.csmonitor.com/2009/0426/p02s03-usgn.html (accessed September 12, 2009).

4 "Democrats Make Their Cases in Wisconsin," *Los Angeles Times*, February 17, 2008, articles.latimes.com/2008/feb/17/nation/na-wisconsin17 (accessed October 5, 2009). The same critique was often leveled by conservative opponents. See Dean Barnett, "The Blathering Storm," *Weekly Standard*, March 25, 2008, www.weeklystandard.com/Content/Public/Articles/000/000/014/919gxfus.asp (accessed October 5, 2009).

5 O'Mara, "Deconstructing Obama's Oratorical Skills."

6 George A. Kennedy, "Introduction," in Kennedy, ed., *Aristotle: A Theory of Civic Discourse* (New York: Oxford University Press, 1991), 7.

7 Aristotle, *On Rhetoric*, 1.1356b11.

8 John Quincy Adams, *Lectures on Rhetoric and Oratory Delivered to the Classes of Junior and Senior Sophisters in Harvard University*, 2 vols. (Cambridge, MA: Hilliard and Metcalf, 1810).

9 John Dewey, *The Public and Its Problems* (Athens, OH: Swallow Press, 1991), 208.

10 Robert Kraig, "The Second Oratorical Renaissance," in *Rhetoric and Reform in the Progressive Era*, ed. J. Michael Hogan (East Lansing: Michigan State University Press, 2003), 1–48.

11 Edwin Black, *Rhetorical Criticism: A Study in Method* (Madison: University of Wisconsin Press, 1965/1978).

12 Ernest J. Wrage, "Public Address: A Study in Social and Intellectual History," *Quarterly Journal of Speech* 33 (1947): 451.

13 See Davis W. Houck and David E. Dixon, *Women and the Civil Rights Movement, 1954–1965* (Jackson: University Press of Mississippi, 2009); and Davis W. Houck and David E. Dixon, *Rhetoric, Religion and the Civil Rights Movement, 1954–1965* (Waco, TX: Baylor University Press, 2006). See also Stephen E. Lucas and Martin J. Medhurst, *Words of a Century: The Top 100 American Speeches, 1900–1999* (New York: Oxford University Press, 2009), which reflects the tradition of great speeches and the expansion of the canon to include more multicultural voices.

14 See, for example, Bonnie J. Dow, *Prime-Time Feminism: Television, Media Culture, and the Women's Movement Since 1970* (Philadelphia: University of Pennsylvania Press, 1996); Cara A. Finnegan, *Picturing Poverty: Print Culture and FSA Photographs* (Washington, DC: Smithsonian Institution Press, 2003); Lester C. Olson, *Emblems of American Community in the Revolutionary Era: A Study in Rhetorical Iconology* (Washington, DC: Smithsonian Institution Press, 1991); Lester C. Olson, *Benjamin Franklin's Vision of American Community: A Study in Rhetorical Iconology* (Columbia: University of South Carolina Press, 2004); and Trevor Parry-Giles and Shawn J. Parry-Giles, *The Prime-Time Presidency: The West Wing and US Nationalism* (Urbana: University of Illinois Press, 2006).

15   See, for example, Karlyn Kohrs Campbell, *Man Cannot Speak For Her*, vol. 2: *Key Texts of the Early Feminists* (Westport, CT: Praeger, 1989); Charles E. Morris III, ed., *Queering Public Address: Sexualities in American Historical Discourse* (Columbia: South Carolina University of Press, 2007); and Susan Zaeske, *Signatures of Citizenship: Petitioning, Antislavery, and Women's Political Identity* (Chapel Hill: University of North Carolina Press, 2003).

16   Davis W. Houck, "On or About June, 1988," *Rhetoric & Public Affairs* 9 (2006): 136.

17   Kathleen J. Turner, "Rhetorical History as Social Construction: The Challenge and the Promise," in *Doing Rhetorical History: Concepts and Cases*, ed. Kathleen J. Turner (Tuscaloosa: University of Alabama Press, 1998), 8.

18   David Zarefsky, "Four Senses of Rhetorical History," in *Doing Rhetorical History*, ed. Turner, 31.

19   See John Gastil and William M. Keith, "A Nation That (Sometimes) Likes to Talk: A Brief History of Public Deliberation in the United States," in *The Deliberative Democracy Handbook*, ed. John Gastil and Peter Levine (San Francisco: Jossey-Bass, 2005), 3–19.

20   See William Norwood Brigance, ed., *A History and Criticism of American Public Address*, 2 vols. (New York: McGraw-Hill, 1943); and Marie Hochmuth, ed., *A History and Criticism of American Public Address*, vol. 3 (New York: Longmans, Green, 1955).

21   Lloyd F. Bitzer and Edwin Black, eds., *The Prospect of Rhetoric: Report of the National Developmental Project* (Englewood Cliffs, NJ: Prentice Hall, 1971).

22   Michael C. Leff and Fred J. Kauffeld, eds., *Texts in Context: Critical Dialogues on Significant Episodes in American Political Rhetoric* (Davis, CA: Hermagoras Press, 1989).

23   These include Thomas W. Benson, ed., *Rhetoric and Political Culture in Nineteenth-Century America* (East Lansing: Michigan State University Press, 1997); J. Michael Hogan, ed., *Rhetoric and Community: Studies in Unity and Fragmentation* (Columbia: University of South Carolina Press, 1998); and Shawn J. Parry-Giles and Trevor Parry-Giles, eds., *Public Address and Moral Judgment: Critical Studies in Ethical Tensions* (East Lansing: Michigan State University Press, 2009).

24   Turner, *Doing Rhetorical History*; Kurt Ritter and Martin J. Medhurst, eds., *Presidential Speechwriting: From the New Deal to the Reagan Revolution and Beyond* (College Station: Texas A&M University Press, 2003); Vanessa B. Beasley, ed., *Who Belongs in America? Presidents, Rhetoric, and Immigration* (College Station: Texas A&M University Press, 2006); and James Arnt Aune and Martin J. Medhurst, eds., *The Prospect of Presidential Rhetoric* (College Station: Texas A&M University Press, 2008). Other books emerging out of the Presidential Rhetoric Conference at Texas A&M University include: Martin J. Medhurst, ed., *Beyond the Rhetorical Presidency* (College Station: Texas A&M University Press, 1996); Martin J. Medhurst and H. W. Brands, eds., *Critical Reflections on the Cold War: Linking Rhetoric and History* (College Station: Texas A&M University Press, 2000); Leroy G. Dorsey, ed., *The Presidency and Rhetorical Leadership* (College Station: Texas A&M University Press, 2002); Tarla Rai Peterson, ed., *Green Talk in the White House: The Rhetorical Presidency Encounters Ecology* (College Station: Texas A&M University Press, 2004); James Arnt Aune and Enrique D. Rigsby, eds., *Civil Rights Rhetoric and the American Presidency* (College Station: Texas A&M University Press, 2005); and Martin J. Medhurst, ed., *Before the Rhetorical Presidency* (College Station: Texas A&M University Press, 2008).

25   See Ira Chernus, *Eisenhower's Atoms for Peace* (College Station: Texas A&M University Press, 2002); Davis W. Houck, *FDR and Fear Itself: The First Inaugural Address*

(College Station: Texas A&M University Press, 2002); Stephen Howard Browne, *Jefferson's Call for Nationhood* (College Station: Texas A&M University Press, 2003); Thomas W. Benson, *Writing JFK: Presidential Rhetoric and the Press in the Bay of Pigs* (College Station: Texas A&M University Press, 2004); Mary E. Stuckey, *Slipping the Surly Bonds: Reagan's Challenger Address* (College Station: Texas A&M University Press, 2006); J. Michael Hogan, *Woodrow Wilson's Western Tour: Rhetoric, Public Opinion, and the League of Nations* (College Station: Texas A&M University Press, 2006); Amos Kiewe, *FDR's First Fireside Chat: Public Confidence and the Banking Crisis* (College Station: Texas A&M University Press, 2007); Garth E. Pauley, *LBJ's American Promise: The 1965 Voting Rights Address* (College Station: Texas A&M University Press, 2007); Richard J. Jensen, *Reagan at Bergen-Belsen and Bitburg* (College Station: Texas A&M University Press, 2007); Denise M. Bostdorff, *Proclaiming the Truman Doctrine: The Cold War Call to Arms* (College Station: Texas A&M University Press, 2008); and Steven R. Goldzwig, *Truman's Whistle-Stop Campaign* (College Station: Texas A&M University Press, 2008).

26 J. Michael Hogan, ed., *Rhetoric and Reform in the Progressive Era* (East Lansing: Michigan State University Press, 2003).

27 Thomas W. Benson, ed., *American Rhetoric in the New Deal Era, 1932–1945* (East Lansing: Michigan State University Press, 2006); James R. Andrews, ed., *Rhetoric, Religion, and the Roots of Identity in British Colonial America* (East Lansing: Michigan State University Press, 2007); and Martha S. Watson and Thomas R. Burkholder, eds., *The Rhetoric of Nineteenth-Century Reform* (East Lansing: Michigan State University Press, 2008).

28 *Voices of Democracy: The US Oratory Project*, online at www.voicesofdemocracy.umd.edu/.

Part I

The History and Prospects of Rhetoric and Public Address

I

The History of Public Address as an Academic Study

Martin J. Medhurst

[I]f modern methods of study are to be applied to the art, the science, or the philosophy of public address, something like a connected narrative of its beginning and growth, its decadences and revivals is necessary.

Lorenzo Sears, *The History of Oratory* (1895)

The history of public address is a complex subject. As traditionally used within the Communication discipline, public address can refer to a practice (the giving of speeches), the product of that practice (speech texts), or the analysis of both the practice and its product (speech criticism). Implicit is an interest in speakers, speeches, and audiences. While the term public address has expanded since the 1960s to include media other than public speeches, it is important to keep in mind that the origins of the field lay in the studies which, at the beginning of the nineteenth century, usually went by the moniker Rhetoric and Oratory. We cannot understand how we got to where we are today without first understanding from whence we came.

The Nineteenth-Century Seedbed of Public Address

Perhaps no single event was more consequential for the development of public address studies than the publication of Hugh Blair's *Lectures on Rhetoric and Belles Lettres* in 1783. Blair's book was the catalyst that began the movement away from Rhetoric and Oratory in the late eighteenth and early nineteenth centuries. In 1800, Rhetoric and Oratory still dominated American education, which, it must be remembered, was education for the elite. Courses in Rhetoric and Oratory emphasized declamations, disputations, commonplace speeches, the reading of dramatic dialogues, the translation of Greek and Roman orations, and public speaking. The new belles lettres tradition subordinated all of that to written rhetoric, placing a heavy emphasis on style, composition, criticism, taste, grace, charm, wit, and various forms of literary rhetoric. Although other rhetorics were available – John Holmes's *The Art of Rhetoric* (1755), John Ward's *A System of Oratory* (1759), George Campbell's *Philosophy of Rhetoric* (1776), John Witherspoon's *Lectures on Moral Philosophy and Eloquence* (1800–1801), John Quincy Adams's *Lectures on Rhetoric and Oratory* (1810), and Richard Whately's *Elements of Rhetoric* (1828) – Blair's ideas quickly came to dominate the American academy and held the preeminent place in higher education for more than half a century. One result of this domination was a rising interest in literary forms of rhetoric – essays, poems, letters, and dialogues – and a concomitant decrease of academic interest in oral rhetoric as the centerpiece of higher education. Shortly after the so-called Golden Age of American Oratory – the age of Webster, Calhoun, Clay, and Lincoln – the teaching of oratorical forms of rhetoric slowly began to give way to the teaching of written rhetoric.[1]

As mainstream rhetorical education moved away from the oratorical ideal, another stream of thought with European origins – the elocution movement – began to fill the vacuum. Elocution traced its origins to the Europe of 1762 and the teachings of Thomas Sheridan. But by the second quarter of the nineteenth century it had firmly established roots in America with the publication of James Rush's *The Philosophy of the Human Voice* (1827). Elocutionists emphasized voice and delivery, to the exclusion of any serious thought about invention or arrangement. Style was important only as adornment – a way to make an impression on an audience. Memory was practiced but not theorized. Delivery was everything. With the English translation of François Delsarte's *The Art of Oratory, System of Delsarte* (1882), elocution became the predominant way to teach oral delivery, whether of a speech, poem, play, or interpretive reading. For students interested in oratory, the elocution movement was about as close to systematic education as one could find in the mid-to-late nineteenth century. Some of that education was given in colleges and universities, some provided by private schools of elocution, some by independent teachers, and some by churches, schools, and civic organizations. Herman Cohen captured the ubiquity of elocution when he noted:

> By the middle of the nineteenth century, Elocution books were in abundance and almost every middle class home contained at least one such volume. The books were often adapted to very specific audiences; some contained material included for children who had just begun to read; others were designed to be read by young people and adults. The selections in the books included many of the "classics" of literature; many of them contained "morally uplifting" selections advocating chastity, temperance and religion. Most of the books also contained physical and breathing exercises, as well as vocal exercises.[2]

There was even a sort of natural symbiosis between the belles lettres tradition, with its emphasis on writing and literature, and the elocution movement, with its emphasis on speaking for an audience. Both used literary works to achieve performative ends.

By the last third of the nineteenth century, the belles lettres tradition was being challenged by the rise of the German research university, with its emphasis on research, specialization, and language studies. Beginning in the 1860s, many American scholars traveled to Germany to obtain the PhD degree, something not yet offered in most American universities.[3] The emphasis in the German universities was on language, logic, and philology. Soon academic departments in America, which had displayed a wide variety of titles throughout most of the nineteenth century, came to be called departments of English Language and Literature, eventually shortened to simply English. The title was meant to signify that the departments were research oriented and devoted to the "scientific" study of language and literature. It was also a way of distinguishing themselves from the earlier educational traditions of Rhetoric and Oratory on the one hand, and Rhetoric and Belles Lettres on the other, both of which were primarily interested in pedagogy, not research.

Just as this German ideal of a research university was emerging in Europe, another branch of scholarship started to appear in America. This was the movement toward Composition and Rhetoric. Represented by works such as Alexander Bain's *English Composition and Rhetoric* (1866), Adams Sherman Hill's *Principles of Rhetoric* (1878), John Franklin Genung's *Practical Elements of Rhetoric* (1886), and Barrett Wendell's *English Composition* (1891), this branch of scholarship grew out of those parts of the Rhetoric and Oratory as well as the Rhetoric and Belles Lettres traditions concerned with the principles of composition. Orators had been concerned with the composition of speeches. Scholars in the belles lettres tradition had been concerned with the composition of poems and letters and essays. But both of these traditions were now being challenged – and in many places would soon be supplanted – by the philological emphasis spawned by the German research university.

By 1890, these three distinct branches of human learning were discernible in American universities. In a way, these branches represented the reinvention of the ancient trivium of rhetoric, grammar, and dialectic. The old Rhetoric and Oratory branch, which never disappeared entirely but which, by the 1890s, existed primarily in its bastardized form of Elocution, represented ancient rhetoric. That part of the belles lettres tradition that emphasized written composition and criticism had been incorporated into the Composition and Rhetoric branch, and bore some similarities to medieval grammar. And the new emphasis on philology, logic, and language structures bore a resemblance to some branches of ancient dialectic. The analogy is not perfect, but it underscores the fact that each of these branches represented the basic ways of striving for knowledge that had represented humanistic inquiry since the time of Cicero. By the end of the nineteenth century, all three of these branches were growing – uncomfortably – in the academic soil of the English department.

The Emergence of Public Speaking

The act of speaking in public had, of course, continued unabated throughout the nineteenth century. But the theory of speaking in public to influence an audience – what the ancients called rhetoric – was no longer taught on a systematic basis in most institutions of American higher education by the end of the nineteenth century. Indeed, there had been little systematic instruction in the whole art of rhetoric since the middle 1820s. Rhetorical instruction had been broken up into parts and taught by people who were primarily interested in something else – literature, language, philology, grammar, composition, criticism, drama – almost anything but rhetoric proper. To the extent that training in oral rhetoric existed at all, it did so primarily in the schools of elocution, the student-sponsored literary society, or the extracurricular debate club. Space does not allow a complete explication of each of these sources, but two events of the 1890s seem to warrant comment: the founding in 1892 of the National Association of Elocutionists, and the publication in 1895 of George Pierce Baker's *The Principles of Argumentation*.

The National Association of Elocutionists was a trade organization that counted private teachers, professional speakers and actors, seekers of self-help and personal improvement, and academic educators as members. It is important to our history because (1) several of the early members of what will become the National Association of Academic Teachers of Public Speaking – Thomas C. Trueblood, Robert I. Fulton, S. S. Hamill, and others – were trained as elocutionists and studied under some of the famous elocutionary teachers of the late nineteenth century,[4] and (2) the National Association of Elocutionists would morph into the National Speech Arts Association in 1906. This association would number among its members such figures as James A. Winans, Charles H. Woolbert, Joseph Searle Gaylord, Binney Gunnison, and Haldor Gislason – all founding members of the National Association of Academic Teachers of Public Speaking, the organization now called the National Communication Association.[5]

The publication of Baker's book in 1895 is also important for two reasons: (1) it was the first textbook to articulate the rhetorical principles of argumentation, and (2) it gave a theoretical basis for a practice that had been going on at the literary society and club level for decades and that would shortly become a staple of the university curriculum – competitive debating. In short, Baker's work helped to make debating an acceptable part of the university curriculum by giving the practice a theoretical rationale. Intercollegiate debating had been going on for more than a decade, but the 1892 debate between Harvard and Yale drew widespread attention to the activity. Debating in the 1890s was purely a club sport, not a part of the university curriculum. Baker's book helped to move debate into the curriculum. With the growth of debate as an "official" university activity, the demand for qualified faculty to direct the activity grew. But with rare exceptions, there were few qualified faculty.

By the middle 1890s, there were fewer than 60 colleges and universities across the nation with a department that focused on oral rhetoric, and those that did exist were mostly in the Midwest, with DePauw (1884), Earlham (1887), Michigan (1892), Chicago (1892), and Ohio Wesleyan (1894) leading the way. The main exceptions to this geographical density were Cornell (1889) in the East and Southern California (1895) in the West. When James A. Winans arrived at Cornell in the fall of 1899, he joined a department of English that had three internal divisions: English literature, rhetoric and English philology, and elocution and oratory. Winans's initial job was to teach declamation – the oral presentation of selected pieces of literature and oratory, usually from memory.[6] Throughout the last third of the nineteenth century and well into the twentieth, declamation was the chief way of teaching oral rhetoric.

But starting around 1900, Winans sought and received permission to begin teaching students how to conceive and deliver original speeches. Today, we usually call such courses public speaking, but that was a locution that had only recently come into use – and not widespread use at that. Indeed, the first textbooks to use the words "public speaking" in their titles did not appear until the mid-to-late 1890s.[7] Even if such courses or books had existed, they would not have connoted to most academics the kind of course that we call "public speaking" today. In 1900, "public" meant a work intended to be performed, usually at a public recital or an elocutionary display. It was more akin to our contemporary notion of public entertainment. And the "speaking" part did not necessarily mean – indeed, it usually did not mean – a public speech. It typically meant a reading, a declamation, a dramatic dialogue, or a poem, often rendered from memory and given as a performance. The first "public address" book of the twentieth century – George Pierce Baker's *The Forms of Public Address* (1904) – was a collection of written (letters and editorials) and spoken (speeches) rhetoric, intended to be read aloud by the students, who could memorize selections as needed. Correspondingly, the first page following the copyright is labeled "Choice Readings."[8]

Public speeches were, of course, still being given, but they were primarily the domain of public leaders – legislators, politicians, judges, ministers, and lawyers. Since the publication in Philadelphia of James Burgh's *The Art of Speaking* (1775) and of Caleb Bingham's *The American Preceptor* (1794), Americans from various walks of life had busied themselves with publishing speech compilations, extracts, abridgments, readers, and anthologies. Early works included *The Columbian Orator* (1797), *The Pulpit Orator* (1804), *The Forum Orator, or, The American Public Speaker* (1804), *The American Orator* (1807), *The Virginia Orator* (1808), *The British Cicero* (1810), *The American Orator* (1817), and *The American Orator* (1819). This early body of work culminated with the publication in 1827 of the five-volume work, *Eloquence of the United States*, compiled by Ebenezer Bancroft Williston. Ironically, Williston's collection of American speeches appeared the same year as Rush's *The Philosophy of the Human Voice*, the first American elocution text. The titles of books thereafter began to reflect the growing influence of elocution: *The New American Speaker: Comprising Elegant Selections in Eloquence and Poetry, Intended for Exercises in Declamation and Elocution* (1835), *The Little Orator for Boys and Girls: In Progressive Lessons: Part I: Founded on Nature as Investigated by Dr. Rush* (1837), and *Russell's American Elocutionist* (1851).

Elocution was not, of course, the only tradition represented. The older Rhetoric and Oratory tradition was seen in such titles as *Specimens of American Eloquence* (1837), *The American Orator's Own Book* (1840), *Library of Oratory: Embracing Selected Speeches of Celebrated Orators of America, Ireland, and England* (1845),

The Eloquence of the Colonial and Revolutionary Times (1847), *Living Orators in America* (1849), and *The Book of Oratory* (1851). Even during their lifetimes, orators such as Webster, Everett, Clay, Calhoun, Benton, and Corwin were celebrated and anthologized. Many of their individual speeches were reproduced in pamphlet form and widely distributed. The one work of the mid-nineteenth century that would have a profound influence on the subsequent development of the public address tradition was Chauncey Allen Goodrich's *Select British Eloquence* (1852). Goodrich, Professor of Rhetoric at Yale, brought an Aristotelian mindset to bear on his critical analysis of the speaking of such figures as Pitt, Fox, Chatham, and Burke. And it was to that analysis that one of the founders of the modern public address tradition, Herbert A. Wichelns, would turn in 1925. But that event was still far in the future.

The immediate situation for orators and oratory as an academic subject in post-Civil War America was none too bright. As written forms of rhetoric came to supplant oral discourse in college classrooms, and as elocutionary theory challenged both the oratorical and belles lettres traditions for dominance, the older tradition of Rhetoric and Oratory was divided both theoretically and practically. Theories of rhetoric were taught by professors of Composition and Rhetoric who focused mostly on invention, arrangement, and style, with style understood primarily as correctness and clarity. There was no need for the classical canons of memory and delivery if the basic rhetorical form was an essay or letter. At the same time, the elocutionary movement, with its emphasis on voice and gesture, seemed to supply what the teachers of Composition and Rhetoric were lacking. But most elocutionists were not interested in the one thing that had distinguished the early teachers and practitioners of the oratorical tradition – political oratory. To the contrary, by the latter third of the nineteenth century the elocutionists' primary field of activity had become popular oratory, understood as public readings and recitations, the oral rendering of poetry and verse, declamation of short speech extracts from famous orators, and the performance of dramatic dialogues. Their primary venues were not politics and statesmanship, but rather public performances at churches, schools, the Lyceum and Chautauqua lecture circuits, and at private schools of elocution established to promulgate particular theories and techniques of oral performance.[9] The titles told the tale: *The Exhibition Speaker Containing Farce Dialogue and Tableaux with Exercises for Declamation in Prose and Verse* (1856), *The Perfect Gentleman, or, Etiquette and Eloquence: A Book of Information and Instruction … Containing Model Speeches for All Occasions* (1860), *The American Union Speaker: Containing Standard and Recent Selections in Prose and Poetry, for Recitation and Declamation, in Schools, Academies, and Colleges: With Introductory Remarks on Elocution, and Explanatory Notes* (1865), *One Hundred Choice Selections; A Rare Collection of Oratory, Sentiment, Eloquence and Humor* (1875). In short, elocutionists were interested in oral discourse for the sake of a performance, and the end of speaking in public was the entertainment of an audience.

The serious study of political oratory was thus left without an advocate in the halls of academia. It was not that political oratory suddenly disappeared or vanished from public sight – quite to the contrary. In the years 1884–1910, numerous editors produced multi-volume sets of oratory, almost all of it political in nature. More sets were produced during these years than in any other era in American history. But the sponsors of these volumes were not usually academicians, but rather the keepers of the civic culture – statesmen, politicians, newspaper editors, and lawyers. Between the Williston volumes of 1827 and the publication in 1884 of Alexander Johnston's *Representative American Orations to Illustrate American Political History*, there had been only three multi-volume sets published – the *Library of Oratory* (1845), Frank Moore's two-volume *American Eloquence* (1857), and the six-volume (and nonpolitical) *The Speaker's Garland and Literary Bouquet* (1880–1885). But all of that changed, starting in 1884. Between 1884 and 1910 there were no fewer than 13 multi-volume sets of orations published in America, virtually all of them political in nature.[10] Yet only two of those sets – the 1884 volumes by Johnston and the 1899–1901 volumes by Guy Carleton Lee – had an academician as the lead editor. Others were compiled by statesmen such as William Jennings Bryan, Thomas B. Reed, Chauncey M. Depew, and Henry Cabot Lodge. One was put together by a Justice of the Supreme Court, David J. Brewer. Newspaper editors such as Mayo W. Hazeltine and Alexander K. McClure produced multi-volume sets, as did librarians such as Richard Garnett. Even men of letters such as Julian Hawthorne, the son of Nathaniel Hawthorne, compiled collections of speeches. If academicians were involved in any of these productions they generally served in secondary editorial roles or as project consultants. In the scholarly world of the late 1900s, the serious study of speech texts had not yet arrived, and the fight for the right to teach public speaking as an art that involved invention, disposition, style, and memory – as well as delivery – had only just begun.

James A. Winans would be a central leader in that fight, along with James Milton O'Neill and Charles H. Woolbert. By 1904, Winans had become head of the new Department of Oratory and Debate at Cornell, following in the footsteps of Brainard Gardner Smith and Duncan Campbell Lee. He had successfully moved the department from focusing on elocution and declamation to public speaking and debate. The same movement was slowly taking place at other institutions around the country – at Michigan, under the direction of Thomas C. Trueblood; at Illinois, under the direction of Charles H. Woolbert; at Iowa, under the direction of Henry E. Gordon and Glenn N. Merry; and at Wisconsin, under the direction of James Milton O'Neill, following in the footsteps of David B. Frankenburger and Rollo L. Lyman. But at most colleges and universities around the country, public address was still being taught by professors with appointments in the English department. Indeed, even Woolbert was still in an English department at Illinois. Few had been able to make the move to separate departmental status, even though Winans, O'Neill, and others were convinced that public speaking could only flourish once the ties to English had been severed.

In 1906, the National Association of Elocutionists became the National Speech Arts Association. The name change was, in part, an effort to cleanse the organization of the opprobrium that had come to be associated with the term "elocutionist."[11]

It was also an effort to redirect the organization from one concerned primarily with practitioners of the elocutionary arts – performers, actors, professional readers, and the like – to one more congenial to educators. But just as the nascent speech professors felt constrained within a department of English, they also felt that they were out of place in an association started by, and existing primarily on behalf of, elocutionists. Consequently, in 1910, Paul M. Pearson, Wilbur Jones Kay, and Winans founded the Public Speaking Conference of the New England and the North Atlantic States, known colloquially as the Eastern Public Speaking Conference – what is today the Eastern Communication Association. It was the first academic association dedicated entirely to public address, understood as the theory and practice of public speaking.

The moving force behind the Eastern Public Speaking Conference was Paul M. Pearson. A professor of public speaking at Swarthmore College since 1902, Pearson had graduated from Baker University, and studied at both Harvard and Northwestern. In 1904, he produced *Pearson's Irish Reciter and Reader*. In 1905, he founded the quarterly publication *The Speaker: A Collection of the Best Orations, Poems, Stories, Debates, and One Act Plays for Public Speaking and Voice Training*. The publication ran from 1905 through 1913. In 1909, Pearson compiled *Intercollegiate Debates: Being Briefs and Reports of Many Intercollegiate Debates*. That same year he wrote *The Humorous Speaker: A Book of Humorous Selections for Reading and Speaking*. Thus, by 1910, Pearson was one of the best known – perhaps the best known – public speaking instructor in America. He was also a Chautauqua speaker. In 1912, he founded the Swarthmore Chautauqua Association. It was so successful that Pearson eventually resigned his position as professor of public speaking to spend full-time on the Chautauqua circuit, where he was already a renowned reader and reciter. In 1912, the *New York Times* reported: "Prof. Paul M. Pearson has left for his annual recital tour of the West. He is one of the most sought-after reciters on the lecture platform to-day, and has many more offers than he can spare the time for."[12] Today we tend to draw a strict line between the elocutionists and the academic teachers of public speaking. But in the period from 1895–1915, those two groups were often one and the same, with many of those who would go on to become leaders in the emerging field of Speech having studied with elocutionists or having been professional readers themselves. Many of these individuals studied at the Cumnock School of Oratory at Northwestern, including Pearson.[13]

Having founded their own eastern regional association, it was perhaps inevitable that Pearson and his colleagues would want a broader national association. Some thought that such a broader association had come into being in December 1911, with the founding of the National Council of Teachers of English (NCTE). Indeed, Winans himself was one of the 35 charter members of the NCTE, whose creation was inspired by a report from the National Education Association.[14] Most of the NCTE's early members were also affiliated with the larger Modern Language Association, which had been in existence since 1883. The new organization came as a direct result of the clash between those in English departments who taught literature and literary criticism and those who taught written and oral composition – freshman writing and public speaking. But just as the composition teachers had found themselves treated as second-class citizens by their literary colleagues, so the speech teachers soon found themselves marginalized by teachers of composition. The NCTE was fine for those who taught written composition, but it did not meet the needs of public speaking teachers, some of whom, by 1912–1913, had decided that only a separate national organization would suffice. Their reasons for so thinking were multiple.

In a fiery resolution introduced at the March 1913 conference of the Eastern Public Speaking Conference, O'Neill noted that the teaching of public speaking around the country was unorganized and chaotic, that courses in public speaking were treated as less important than courses in English composition, that professors who taught public speaking were often overlooked at promotion time, that the principles of oral composition were different from those of written composition, that students deserved teachers who were trained in the specific subject matter, that the standards of scholarship in public speaking were simply different than those recognized by the German model of research, that public speaking classes were often assigned to the lowest-ranking instructors and to people who were unqualified to deliver the course, and that public speaking teachers were regularly treated with contempt and often abused by their English department colleagues.[15] He then moved that the conference support a resolution in favor of the complete separation of public speaking courses from English departments. The resolution passed.

Eight months later, at the November 1913 meeting of the NCTE, the Public Speaking Section decided to send out a nationwide questionnaire to teachers of public speaking, seeking to ascertain their preferences about departmental structure – whether public speaking should remain part of the English department or whether it should be a separate, stand-alone department. The questionnaire also asked the speech teachers whether they favored a separate national organization. The results of that survey were presented at the 1914 NCTE meeting where, after several ballots, it became clear that the group was hopelessly divided between those who wished to remain within the NCTE orbit and those who wished to form a separate organization. It was at this point that 17 of those in favor of a new organization, led by O'Neill and Winans, met separately on the second floor of the Auditorium Hotel in Chicago and proceeded to form the National Association of Academic Teachers of Public Speaking, the organization now known as the National Communication Association.[16]

The new association was incorporated in 1914 and published the first issue of its new journal – the *Quarterly Journal of Public Speaking* (*QJPS*) – in April 1915. Almost immediately there arose a significant difference of opinion as to what "research" in the field of public speaking should accomplish. The influence of the German university model had made research the god-term of American higher education – what Winans characterized as "the standard way into the sheepfold."[17] For Winans, such research was to be focused on the psychology of the entire public speaking situation. His 1915 public speaking textbook, based on the psychology of William James, was the model for such an approach.[18] For Woolbert, on the other hand, research should be devoted to discovering the facts, laws, and principles that would set the teaching of public speaking on an equal footing with the emerging social sciences of psychology, sociology, and political science.[19] But for Everett Lee Hunt, a young instructor at Huron College in South Dakota, research ought to be focused on the development of character and broad, liberal learning of the sort recommended by Cicero and the ancient rhetoricians. Education in speaking should be education for life, Hunt believed, with as much focus on the content of what was said – the issues – as on the techniques used to say it or the effects of the saying on an audience.[20] Hunt's first book, *Persistent Questions in Public Discussion* (1924), underscored his focus on content.

The differences of opinion, as represented most dramatically in the exchanges between Woolbert and Hunt between 1915 and 1920, are of interest to the history of public address for several reasons. The Woolbert approach considered public speaking to be part of the broader science of "speech," including speech production, speech correction, and language behavior, as well as public speaking. His 1916 *QJPS* article – "The Organization of Departments of Speech Science in Universities" – included a chart illustrating how the various aspects of "speech sciences and arts" could be conceptualized. Woolbert clearly placed the "scientific" dimensions of speech at the center of his conceptual universe. Tellingly, the "Literature of Public Address" and "Criticism" were placed *outside* of the circle of "speech sciences and arts," and wholly within the realm of English. This was the first great challenge faced by scholars of rhetoric, oratory, and public address: Was the field of Public Speaking to be a strictly scientific enterprise or was it to include humanistic approaches to knowledge generation?[21]

From Woolbert's point of view, Hunt and those like him were simply stuck in a mythical past, uncomprehending of the great advances of the previous decades. With what appeared to be a bit of condescension, Woolbert wrote,

> Mr. Hunt and I are of different epochs and countries. He is of a romantic golden age, I, of the common, ignoble now. He is from Greece, I am from Germany(!) – he probably by choice, I perforce. He cries out for the glory that was Greece and the grandeur that was Rome; I am surrounded by laboratories and card catalogues. Consequently when we talk about the problems of public speaking, we aren't talking about the same thing at all.[22]

Yet, from the outset, the teaching of public speaking had, for many members, included the teaching of public address – understood as the study of orators and oratory. In the very first volume of the *Quarterly Journal of Public Speaking*, the organization's research committee listed among the needed research:

> An interpretive study in the light of modern methods of great orators and orations of the past.…
> A first-hand study of the methods and technique of living orators.…
> A study of the history of public speaking and of methods of teaching it.[23]

In outlining his vision for a college-level curriculum in public speaking, Trueblood suggested an entire course on "great orators," writing:

In this course a few representative ancient orators and a few modern orators of Continental Europe should be studied, but chiefly English-speaking orators – ten or twelve English and about as many American orators. Lectures should be given on the qualifications and sources of power of the orator, the construction and style of the speech, the kinds of oratory, etc.[24]

There was more than a little irony in the fact that the proposal to study "great orators" came from Trueblood. With his partner, Robert Fulton, Trueblood had run one of the most prominent schools of elocution in the country, starting in 1878 and continuing well into the twentieth century. He and Fulton were a veritable publishing and educational empire unto themselves and represented the very kind of instruction that many members of the new organization perceived themselves to be fighting against.[25]

Hence, there was from the very beginning of the National Association of Academic Teachers of Public Speaking a basic disagreement as to the purpose and direction of the field. All were agreed that public address – in the sense of public speaking – was central to the enterprise. Many, though not all, believed that public address – in the sense of the study of orators and oratory – was an important part of the field, even when such study was seen primarily as a resource for learning techniques that could then be emulated by students in their own public speaking. Great orators or famous speeches were most often seen as educational models that were studied for the sake of something else – giving good speeches of one's own or providing material for oral reading – rather than as ends in themselves or objects of critical analysis. Examination of the books produced between 1900 and 1915 shows considerable interest in public address as a source of historical knowledge.[26] There was even one book – *The Battle of Principles: A Study of the Heroism and Eloquence of the Anti-Slavery Conflict* (1912), by Newell Dwight Hillis, D.D. – that might be described as a rhetorical history, by which I mean a history told through the lens of the great speeches, arguments, and debates of the era.[27]

From Public Speaking to Speech

The battle between those who, like Woolbert, wanted the field of public speaking to become a scientific enterprise and those who, like Hunt, wanted it to become a liberal arts discipline was never fully resolved. In the end, it was the views of men such as O'Neill and Merry that prevailed, with the adoption of "speech" as a covering term that included both the scientific enterprise and the liberal arts courses. Most of the early departments of public speaking offered course work in both science and art, and this mixed model became the standard of the early graduate programs at places such as Iowa, Minnesota, Southern California, and Wisconsin.

The earliest issues of *QJPS* show that the study of orators and oratory was present, but not a major focus of published scholarship. Indeed, in the period from 1915 to 1920, the journal published only five articles – out of a total of 187 – that represented the emerging public address tradition, understood as the critical examination and analysis of speakers, speeches, audiences, occasions, and the interactions among them. In 1916, J. M. Doyle published an analysis of "The Style of Wendell Phillips"; in 1917, H. B. Gislason published "Elements of Objectivity in Wendell Phillips"; in 1918, Edwin Du Bois Shurter published "The Rhetoric of Oratory and How to Teach It"; in 1919, Charles F. Lindsley published "George William Curtis: A Study in the Style of Oral Discourse"; and, in 1920, Lindsley published another article on "Henry Woodfin Grady, Orator." But the simple fact that such studies could appear so soon after the founding of the association was a sign that public address studies had been going on for some time.

As early as 1884, newspaper editor C. M. Whitman had published a book on *American Orators and Oratory* that was comprised of "biographical sketches of the representative men of America, together with gems of eloquence upon leading questions that have occupied public attention from the foundation of the republic to the present time."[28] In 1894, Cornelius Beach Bradley, Professor of Rhetoric at the University of California, published *Orations and Arguments by English and American Statesmen*. This book might well be considered the first scholarly textbook on public address, as that term would come to be understood in the Speech discipline. Not only did Bradley reprint complete speech texts, but he also appended substantive notes to each speech that explained the context and annotated the content. This was followed, in 1895, by the mistitled but nonetheless substantive *History of Oratory from the Age of Pericles to the Present Time*, by Lorenzo Sears, Professor of English Literature at Brown University. Sears's book was, in fact, a history of rhetorical precepts, not oratory. As such, it was the most authoritative text of its day. In 1898, Ralph Curtis Ringwalt, Lecturer in Rhetoric at Columbia University, produced *Modern American Oratory* in which he discussed deliberative, forensic, demonstrative, and pulpit oratory, and provided examples of each.

Several individuals who would play a role in the early years of the national association were also active at the turn of the century. In 1899, A. H. Craig and Binney Gunnison published *Pieces for Prize Speaking Contests*. In 1901, Edwin Du Bois Shurter, Professor of Oratory at the University of Texas, produced *The Modern American Speaker*, followed in 1903 by *Public Speaking: A Treatise on Delivery, with Selections for Declaiming*, and *Masterpieces of Modern Oratory* in 1906. In 1907, Robert I. Fulton, Thomas C. Trueblood, and Edwin P. Trueblood edited *Standard Selections*, a collection of readings for use in the classroom. In 1908, Shurter produced *Oratory of the South, from the Civil War to the Present Time*, which reprinted significant speeches, and followed that in 1909 with *The Rhetoric of Oratory*, a college-level textbook. In his introductory essay, Shurter noted:

> Oral discourse has a rhetoric of its own which should not be neglected in the work of instruction in English composition. Many schools and colleges, where no separate department of oratory exists, have recognized the distinction by establishing chairs of "rhetoric and oratory." But oral discourse receives scant attention in treatises on

rhetoric; the subject of Persuasion is usually treated in a single chapter, or not at all; and in the schools generally oratorical composition finds little or no part in the work of instruction in English composition.[29]

This complaint would, of course, become one of the central arguments on behalf of forming a new scholarly organization only a few years later. In 1910, Shurter produced *American Oratory To-day* and edited *The Complete Orations and Speeches of Henry W. Grady.* Fulton and Trueblood edited *British and American Eloquence* in 1912, a collection that in addition to reprinting speech selections also included extended biographical portraits of each speaker. As many of these titles indicate, most of these works were intended as models for oral reading. The critical impulse was not yet much in evidence, but it was beginning to form. As early as 1913, Fulton, who taught at Ohio Wesleyan, presented a paper at the NCTE that envisioned courses in "Oratory," "Rhetorical Criticism," and an "Oratorical Seminar."[30] Fulton may, in fact, have been the first person in the field to use the term "rhetorical criticism," a locution that surfaced occasionally over the first 50 years of the association, but which did not come into widespread usage until the 1960s.

The story of the period between 1899 (when Winans went to Cornell) and 1914 (when the national association was founded) is a narrative with multiple plots – the rise of the English department as the custodian of Oral English, the reduction of rhetorical instruction to matters of grammar and composition, the widespread influence of the elocutionary movement, the beginnings of intercollegiate debate as a curricular offering, the interest in speeches primarily as models for emulation or source material for elocution, and the movement away from declamation and toward public speaking. It would, in fact, be the need to theorize and teach public speaking and argumentation that would drive the field for the next two decades. Most of the publication that took place between 1914 and 1934 was in the form of textbooks. Space does not allow a detailed description of those works, even though many were penned by the founders of the public address tradition, including Winans, Woolbert, and O'Neill.[31] Until 1920, the term "public address" usually referred to the teaching of public speaking, the study of model speeches, or the oral declamation of great literature, only some of which was oratorical. After the 1920s, the term would have an entirely different connotation, taking on the sense of critical analysis and evaluation of spoken discourse. The beginning of that transformation can be traced to a single course offered at Cornell.

Cornell University and the Classical Seminar of 1920–1921

By 1920, the name "Speech" was beginning to emerge from the plethora of departmental titles as the preferred name for the field that had previously been known as Oral English or Public Speaking. The first evidence of this change came in 1918, when the journal changed its title from the *Quarterly Journal of Public Speaking* to the *Quarterly Journal of Speech Education*. In 1923, the organization would follow by changing its name to the National Association of Teachers of Speech. Speech was seen as a broader term than Public Speaking – broad enough to encompass speech correction, phonology, speech science, language behavior, persuasion, argumentation, dramatic arts, oral reading, rhetoric, public address, and more – and university education (not the public platform) was understood as the primary arena of action. By 1920, departments associated with the national organization were in existence at scores of colleges and universities around the country, but graduate education was severely limited. Only a handful of programs had awarded the MA degree before 1920.[32] There were no PhDs being offered in the field of Speech.

Although the first PhD in Speech would be awarded in 1922 at the University of Wisconsin, that degree was in speech science, not public address.[33] The doctorates held by the founders of the public address tradition were earned in fields other than Speech, and several of them were inspired by a single graduate seminar held at Cornell University in the 1920–1921 academic year. That seminar, believed to be the first graduate course on classical rhetoric ever held in twentieth-century America, involved at least five people: Alexander M. Drummond, Everett Lee Hunt, Hoyt H. Hudson, Harry Caplan, and Herbert A. Wichelns.[34] These five men became the progenitors of what would come to be called the Cornell School of Rhetoric. Drummond had earned his PhD in 1918 in the field of English, with an emphasis in drama; Hunt earned an MA in Philosophy from the University of Chicago in 1922, never earning the PhD; Hudson earned the PhD at Cornell in 1923 under the classicist Lane Cooper in the department of English Literature; Harry Caplan also studied under Cooper, earning his PhD in Classics in 1921; and Wichelns took his PhD in English Literature in 1922.

Although the teachers and graduates of Cornell were primarily noted for their contributions to the history and theory of rhetoric, with Hunt, Hudson, and Caplan making major contributions to this area, one of the members of this early seminar, Herbert Wichelns, would make his mark in the tradition of public address. That tradition had, by the mid-1920s, been represented only sporadically within the pages of the *Quarterly Journal of Speech Education*, primarily by the work of Charles F. Lindsley of the University of Minnesota. While the early 1920s found very few published studies that could be considered part of the public address tradition, several MA theses were being written that clearly reflected the mounting interest in public address. At Cornell, theses were completed on "Edmund Burke, The Rhetorician" (Robert Hannah, 1922), "The Rhetorical Practice of Abraham Lincoln" (Marvin Bauer, 1924), "The Rhetorical Practice of John Donne in His Sermons" (Charles Kenneth Thomas, 1924), and "A Study of the Structure of a Selected Group of Webster's Speeches" (Howard Bradley, 1927). At Illinois, in 1923, Florence G. Weaver became the first woman to complete an MA thesis in public address on "John Randolph of Roanoke." Ironically, the study was directed by Woolbert, the leading advocate of a "scientific" approach to speech.

By 1923, Wichelns was calling for more research and suggesting the need for comprehensive bibliographies for each part of the field. There had been no effort to conceptualize a method for the study of public address beyond Wichelns's observation that "Gayley and Scott's *Methods and Materials in the Study of Criticism* is, after twenty years, still a useful, indeed an indispensable work."[35] The book by Charles Mills Gayley and Fred Newton Scott to which Wichelns referred was one of the early textbooks on literary criticism, published in 1899. Literary criticism and history were coming into their own in the latter part of the nineteenth century, with major works by such figures as Matthew Arnold, Henry Home of Kames, and William Dean Howells being widely read. By the 1890s textbooks in literary criticism were beginning to appear, and the text by Gayley and Scott was part of that trend.[36] Doubtless spurred on by the Gayley and Scott volume, Wichelns first turned to the literary critics, only to find them wanting. They were concerned with literature, seldom with oratory. So Wichelns set about the task of doing for oratory what Gayley and Scott had done for the study of literature. It would start in 1925 with the publication of "The Literary Criticism of Oratory," penned by Wichelns as his contribution to a *Festschrift* honoring James A. Winans. The book, *Studies in Rhetoric and Public Speaking in Honor of James Albert Winans*, was edited by Alexander M. Drummond, with contributions from Hunt, Caplan, Hannah, Hudson, Theodore Thorson Stenberg, Wichelns, Wayland Maxfield Parrish, Lee S. Hultzen, Smiley Blanton, Margaret Gray Blanton, and William E. Utterback. But it was the chapter by Wichelns that would lay the foundation for a whole field of study – public address criticism.

Much has been written about Wichelns's famous essay. It has been analyzed, critiqued, and reproduced in numerous anthologies. Wichelns began his chapter by pointing out that there had not been "much serious criticism of oratory." His survey of nineteenth-century literary critics found few who dealt at all with oratory, fewer still who treated oratory as something qualitatively different than literature, and only a handful of works whose standards of judgment seemed to him appropriate for an activity that was "partly an art, partly a power of making history, and occasionally a branch of literature."[37] This state of affairs he sought to correct. His goal was to put rhetorical studies on a par with literary studies as an arena of academic interest and research.

Wichelns believed that for oratory to be taken seriously as an academic subject, it had to be treated in a serious manner. Seriousness meant, among other things, that it had to be subjected to criticism and analysis in much the same manner as enduring works of literature. But Wichelns understood that while the tools of literary analysis were necessary – and perhaps even sufficient – for the student of oratory, the ends of great literature and the means of judging imaginative works were insufficient for the analysis of public speech. Because oratory was "intimately associated with statecraft," it could be understood and appreciated "only by the careful student of history."[38] In short, oratory operated in the real world, not the imaginative; it dealt with real people and events, not characters and plots; it had real and sometimes enduring consequences for the lives of people, not merely momentary flights into fantasy or make-believe. While oratory was a language art, it was also more. It was a power used to shape decision-making and influence decision-makers. It was, as Aristotle had said about rhetoric, part of the ethical branch of politics, the branch concerned with making decisions about the nature of the good in community.

Wichelns had precious little upon which to build. Among nineteenth-century commentators, he found only the work of Chauncey Goodrich to have "critical significance" for the analysis of oratory. Hence his task was to construct a framework within which scholars of public address could subject oratory to the same sort of analysis that literary scholars accorded to works of fiction. Wichelns held that "the man, his works, his times" were the necessary "common topics" of criticism, and that "no one of them can be wholly disregarded by any critic." Working from this foundational principle, Wichelns sought to distinguish oratorical or rhetorical criticism from its literary counterpart. "Rhetorical criticism," he wrote, "is not concerned with permanence, nor yet with beauty. It is concerned with effect. It regards a speech as a communication to a specific audience, and holds its business to be the analysis and appreciation of the orator's method of imparting his ideas to his hearers."[39] These three sentences, which would become the source of much misunderstanding and misapplication of Wichelns's ideas, became the theoretical stance from which 40 years of work in public address criticism flowed. But this was not all that Wichelns offered. He also articulated a 15-point scheme for what "a rhetorical study includes." This scheme included:

1 The speaker's personality as a conditioning factor.
2 The public character of the man – what he was thought to be.
3 A description of the audience.
4 The leading ideas with which he plied his hearers.
5 The topics he drew upon.
6 The motives to which he appealed.
7 Proofs offered in his speeches.
8 The relation of surviving texts to what was actually uttered.
9 The adaptation to two audiences – that which heard and that which read.
10 The speaker's mode of arranging ideas.
11 The speaker's mode of expression.
12 The speaker's habits of preparation.
13 The manner of delivery from the platform.
14 The speaker's style, especially diction and sentence movement.
15 The effect of the discourse on its immediate hearers.[40]

It is unclear from Wichelns's essay whether he expected every rhetorical study to touch upon all 15 of these points. What is clear is that he never intended to reduce the study of oratory to the single question of its effect on the immediate audience. Indeed, had there been a systematic development of Wichelns's 15 points, the practice of oratorical criticism might have evolved in significantly different directions than it did.

From 1925 to 1934, there was little advance in either the theory or practice of rhetorical criticism, but there was a major development. In 1925, Professor A. Craig

James Otis
John Adams
Patrick Henry
Thomas Jefferson
Alexander Hamilton
Fisher Ames
John Randolph

Henry Clay
John C. Calhoun
Daniel Webster
James Buchanan
Edward Everett
Rufus Choate
William H. Seward
Ralph Waldo Emerson
William Lloyd Garrison
Jefferson Davis
Abraham Lincoln
Wendell Phillips
Henry Ward Beecher
Stephen A. Douglas
Charles Sumner
George W. Curtis
Carl Schurz
James G. Blaine
Ralph G. Ingersoll
Grover Cleveland
Thomas B. Reed
Elihu Root
Henry W. Grady

Henry Cabot Lodge
Woodrow Wilson
Theodore Roosevelt
Booker T. Washington
William Jennings Bryan
William E. Borah

Figure 1.1

Baird of Bates College moved to the University of Iowa. Baird had earned the MA in 1912 from Columbia University in English Literature, his thesis on Chaucer.[41] But under his leadership, the study of public address would blossom, and Iowa, along with Cornell and Wisconsin, would become a major center of rhetorical studies. The list of graduate students advised by Baird reads like a *Who's Who* of rhetorical studies in the middle part of the twentieth century – William Norwood Brigance, Lester W. Thonssen, Loren Reid, Carroll Arnold, Waldo Braden, Earnest Brandenburg, Laura Crowell, Gregg Phifer, and Robert C. Jeffrey, to mention only the most prominent. In 1926, Baird published "A Selected Bibliography of American Oratory," thus fulfilling one of Wichelns's 1923 recommendations. Baird divided the bibliography into General References, which included several of the multi-volume works noted earlier, and works on 36 specific orators (see Figure 1.1).

Unsurprisingly, the list was dominated by powerful white males, mostly from the nineteenth century. This bibliography was the first sort of "to do" list produced by scholars of public address. It was noteworthy in several ways, not the least of which was its focus on speakers rather than speeches, events, movements, or genres. Public address was, from 1925 to 1950, to be primarily the study of orators.[42]

In 1928, Warren Choate Shaw, Professor of Public Speaking at Knox College, produced a *History of American Oratory*. This was the first comprehensive history of oratorical practice produced by a member of the Speech field. In his preface,

Shaw noted "the urgent necessity of providing for teachers and students of oratory just such a background of history as is provided so lavishly for teachers and students of composition and English literature in its written form."[43] To accomplish this goal, Shaw organized each chapter by speaker, with short sections on the general background of the period, the biography of the speaker, the historical setting of a particularly important speech, the reprinting of that speech text – sometimes in full, often only in part – and a comprehensive bibliography. Shaw's 713-page tome covered Patrick Henry, Alexander Hamilton, Fisher Ames, John Randolph, Henry Clay, Daniel Webster, John C. Calhoun, Thomas Corwin, Theodore Parker, Rufus Choate, Stephen A. Douglas, Charles Sumner, Wendell Phillips, Abraham Lincoln, Henry Ward Beecher, Robert G. Ingersoll, Henry W. Grady, William Jennings Bryan, Albert J. Beveridge, Theodore Roosevelt, and Woodrow Wilson. There was little evidence that Shaw had been influenced by Wichelns's essay on critical method. His list of notable orators does, however, bear a striking resemblance to the list produced by Baird two years earlier, perhaps suggesting the emergence of a sort of widely accepted canon of orators by the late 1920s. This canon would have a profound effect on one of Baird's first PhD students, William Norwood Brigance.

Setting the Agenda

Having earned his MA degree in history in 1920 from the University of Nebraska, Brigance began his career as a speech teacher in 1922 at Wabash College in Crawfordsville, Indiana. Although he had minimal formal training in speech, Brigance believed that he could fill the bill and began what would be a 38-year career as a Speech professor. Like many professionals of his day, he was told that he needed to complete the PhD if he wanted to be promoted. In 1929, he left Crawfordsville and journeyed to Iowa City, where he spent the next nine months taking coursework and completing his dissertation on Jeremiah Sullivan Black, under the direction of A. Craig Baird. His degree was awarded in June 1930, making Brigance the second person to earn the PhD in Speech at Iowa, and the first to do so in public address.[44]

Brigance led a decade in which some of the leading scholars of public address would emerge, most of them coming out of Iowa, Wisconsin, Cornell, or Michigan – Lester Thonssen (1931), Loren Reid and Henry Lee Ewbank (1932), Lionel Crocker and Karl R. Wallace (1933), Horace Rahskopf and James H. McBurney (1935), Marvin Bauer (1936), Robert T. Oliver and Kenneth G. Hance (1937), Dallas C. Dickey and Dayton David McKean (1938), among others. The numbers were small – very small. Between 1930 and 1945, the three schools that produced the most MA and PhD students in Speech were Iowa, Wisconsin, and Cornell.[45] Yet, close examination of the theses and dissertations produced in this 15-year period reveals a startling fact: As a percentage of graduate degrees completed, studies in public address never comprised more than 13 percent of the whole. Most of

Iowa, 1930–1945	Wisconsin, 1930–1945	Cornell, 1930–1945
409 MA degrees in Speech	170 MA degrees in Speech	107 MA degrees in Speech
45 theses on Public Address	21 theses on Public Address	2 theses on Public Address
66 PhD degrees in Speech	64 PhD degrees in Speech	36 PhD degrees in Speech
17 dissertations on Public Address	18 dissertations on Public Address	2 dissertations on Public Address

Figure 1.2

the graduate degrees completed in this era were in dramatic arts, speech correction, and language behavior. Even within the world of rhetorical studies, there were far more theses and dissertations dealing with some aspect of rhetorical theory or the history of rhetoric than there were those examining public address. Figure 1.2 is illustrative.

As these numbers clearly show, the study of public address was a small part of a much larger whole. Throughout the period from 1930 to 1945, most universities that taught Speech employed only one specialist in public address. Consequently, most of the PhDs produced during this period can be traced back to a single advisor – A. Craig Baird at Iowa, Henry Lee Ewbank at Wisconsin, or Herbert A. Wichelns at Cornell. These three men produced the vast majority of the dissertations noted above, which is to say that they produced most of the next generation of leaders in public address scholarship. No single person was more crucial to the development of that scholarship than W. Norwood Brigance.

Brigance wrote the most important article following Wichelns's 1925 masterpiece when, in 1933, he published "Whither Research?" In that article, Brigance set forth an agenda, the complete fulfillment of which has not been accomplished to this day. His article foreshadowed the treatment of speeches as a form of rhetorical literature, and his understanding of the audience – and particularly of rhetorical constraints – foreshadowed Lloyd Bitzer's explication in 1968. He also was concerned with textual authenticity, insisted on primary source research, and called for an understanding of speech content as ideas that have force in history and through time. Not all of these ideas were developed in depth, but they were all present in this one article.

Brigance began by stating that he was "writing this article in an attempt to hasten the coming out [from the intellectual wilderness] and to suggest one of several possible directions which research should next take." He then wrote, "I think we ought to recognize that there is a great body of rhetorical or oratorical literature almost untouched by scholars in our field. Of it, I think we might safely say that this literature can do without our scholarship, but that our scholarship cannot do without that literature."[46]

Brigance also concerned himself with the rhetorical situation, writing, "The statesman who must dominate a crisis, or the advocate who must mold the mind of a court or jury … must seize the hour, strike the iron at white heat, adapt himself to the mind, mood, and temperature of the audience and occasion. It is impossible ever to read their speech apart from the hopes, fears, prejudices, and passions that beset the hearers at the moment of delivery."[47] Even more clearly than Wichelns, Brigance located rhetoric as the contingent art of adapting discourse to audiences in the immediate situation. Many would repeat Brigance's ideas after 1933, but few would put them into practice.

Brigance closed "Whither Research?" by noting, "Commonly we are content to edit what other biographers and essayists have said. But this is mere rewriting. We must, if we expect recognition of our scholarship, go to the records themselves. We must examine first-hand the manuscripts, letters, documents, and read again the newspapers, periodicals and memoirs of that period."[48] This was the culmination of all the calls for research, making of bibliographies, and reporting of individual projects that occupied the pages of the journal between 1925 and 1930. In the end, it all came down to the admonition to do research in primary sources – something that virtually no one in the area of public address was doing in 1933. But that was about to change.

In the fall of 1934, Brigance was appointed to lead the association's Committee on Joint Research in the History of American Oratory.[49] Over the course of the next nine years, Brigance and his committee would strive to give form to many of the ideas he had expressed in "Whither Research?" The result, both for better and for worse, was the first two volumes of *A History and Criticism of American Public Address*, published by McGraw-Hill in 1943. At the time of his appointment, Brigance was 38 years old, making him one of the youngest members of the editorial committee. But his appointment was more than justified, for not only had he set forth the agenda in his 1933 article, but he had also published, in 1934, one of the first scholarly books produced by a member of the Speech profession, a rhetorical biography titled *Jeremiah Sullivan Black: Defender of the Constitution and the Ten Commandments*.[50]

That a concerted effort was needed to advance oratorical and public address scholarship was clear. From the publication of Wichelns's essay in 1925 through the publication of *A History and Criticism of American Public Address* in 1943, virtually no progress had been made in refining what it meant to be a public address scholar, even though the field had established a second journal, *Speech Monographs*, in 1932, with Wichelns as editor. During this period, there was a handful of articles that merited attention, but most of those were concerned with only three figures – Abraham Lincoln, Woodrow Wilson, and Franklin D. Roosevelt.[51] The vast storehouse of "oratorical literature" of which Brigance wrote in 1933 remained largely untouched. But that would soon change.

Using Baird's bibliographical listing of 1926 as well as his own study of orators, Brigance and his committee identified "The Twenty-Eight Foremost American Orators."[52] Each of these 28 was then assigned to a scholar. Six synthetic essays on particular eras were also assigned, making a total of 34 chapters in volumes one and two of *A History and Criticism of American Public Address*. This was the first big, multi-volume project undertaken by the national association. In many ways the sheer execution of the project – the conceptualization, planning, editing, and publishing – was an achievement unto itself, quite apart from the quality of the contents. Although later scholars would criticize these volumes as too historical in orientation, too methodologically monolithic, too focused on white males, too reliant on secondary sources, too concerned with the speaker's biography to the neglect of textual criticism, too committed to mainstream speakers and speeches, and too wed to effects on the immediate audience, the fact remains that these volumes represented the best public address scholarship published through 1943. Virtually all of those who published multiple public address studies in the 1930s – Mildred Freburg Berry, Lionel G. Crocker, Dayton David McKean, Wayland Maxfield Parrish, and Earl W. Wiley, chief among them – also appeared in this multi-volume set.

We must also remember what it meant to be a member of the Speech profession at this time. From its founding in 1914 through the publication of the Brigance volumes in 1943, the profession was far broader and considerably more flexible than it is today. We remember Brigance primarily as a public address scholar, but he also published widely in persuasion theory, language behavior, and speech correction. Early members of the field often specialized in several different aspects of Speech. Some members who made important contributions to public address when the field was young ended up making their primary reputations in other areas of the discipline. Mildred Freburg Berry and Wayland Maxfield Parrish were two such scholars. Berry wrote one of two chapters on Lincoln for *A History and Criticism of American Public Address*, but her scholarly reputation was made in the area of speech correction. Parrish was a Cornell-trained rhetorician who completed his 1929 dissertation on Whately's *Elements of Rhetoric*, but he made his reputation in the area of oral reading. In later years, Russell Wagner, Carroll Arnold, Ernest Bormann, and Edwin Black would do ground-breaking work in discussion; Robert T. Oliver would be the first in the field to do serious work in intercultural communication; and Walter Emery, who wrote the chapter on Samuel Gompers for the Brigance volumes, made his career as a scholar of media. There were very few scholars who specialized *only* in public address from 1914 to 1943.

Even so, the 1940s was a time of great advance in public address scholarship, starting with the publication of Bower Aly's *The Rhetoric of Alexander Hamilton* (1941). The number of MA and PhD degrees started to increase, as did the quality of the people completing their doctoral degrees – Bower Aly, Glen Mills, and Ernest J. Wrage (1941), Carroll Arnold, William Behl, and Waldo Braden (1942), Marie Hochmuth (1945), S. Judson Crandell and Robert D. Clark (1946), J. Jeffrey Auer and Eugene E. White (1947), Earnest S. Brandenburg, Laura Crowell, Rollin Quimby, Barnet Baskerville, Frederick Haberman, Robert G. Gunderson (1948), and Gregg Phifer (1949). The nature of what constituted a public address study also began to expand. From the focus on single orators in *A History and Criticism of American Public Address*, scholarship started to appear on such topics as debates in Congress, multiple speeches across a single topic, the rhetorical characteristics of democracy, critical analysis of written rhetoric, examination of single speeches, and criticism of rhetorical campaigns. The Brigance volumes were a high point in public address scholarship, but it is important to remember that even as they appeared in 1943, they were both a culmination of work that had gone on during the preceding decade (1934–1943) and a model for much of the work that would be undertaken for the next two decades (1944–1964). As such, they were in some senses anachronistic even as they were published.

Even in the immediate wake of publication, not everyone was enamored with the approach taken in the Brigance volumes. Two such critics were Loren Reid and Ernest Wrage. Writing in 1944, Reid warned of "The Perils of Rhetorical Criticism." One such peril was the tendency merely to report historical and biographical data rather than to criticize the content of the speeches. "Although the reader needs to know what the speaker *said*," wrote Reid, "he really seeks a critical judgment *about* the ideas of the speech." Such critical judgment was to be based on detailed research of the speaking situation, research "not likely to come from a college history text-book, but from letters, diaries, memoirs, and periodicals, and sometimes from spe-cialized monographs." In short, Reid called for research in primary sources – the same call that Brigance had made in 1933. Reid also noted that from a methodo-logical point of view, "Aristotelian rhetoric cannot be made to cover every aspect of all types of speaking."[53] To produce good critical studies of public discourse was a demanding task. Neither second-hand history nor narrowly circumscribed rhe-torical theory could produce the type of critical research needed to establish public address scholarship as significant. Reid closed by noting,

> Rhetorical criticism is an exacting type of research. The critic must know what is com-monly called rhetoric, but to know rhetoric is not enough. He must know historical methods, but to know historical methods is not enough. He must have infinite patience in the search for details. ... He must have the imagination to recreate events and movements long since passed into time. And he must take to heart his primary and inescapable responsibility as a critic: to interpret, to appraise, to evaluate; to say here the speaker missed, here he hit the mark.[54]

While Reid's critique of traditional public address studies was implicit, Ernest Wrage's critique, written three years later in 1947, was explicit. Wrage attacked head-on the traditional paradigm of public address studies. "The prevailing approach to the history and criticism of public address appears to consist of a study of individual speakers for their influence upon history," he wrote. "If one may judge from studies available through publication, they fall short of that ambitious goal."[55] Instead of the traditional speaker-centered studies, Wrage argued for an "idea-centered" approach to public address. Such an approach would focus "upon the speech and its content" and yield "knowledge of more general interest in terms of man's cultural strivings and heritage." Wrage's call for the serious study of speech content echoed a topic first broached by Hunt in 1922. Wrage was clearly correct in his judgment that "the rich vein of literature in speaking has hardly been tapped."

But his call for "a wide investigation of sermons, lectures, and speeches related to issues, movements, and periods" was not immediately forthcoming. Wrage's vision of studies in public address becoming "a kind of anthropological approach to a segment of cultural history" found few disciples before the mid-1960s, in part because the dominant paradigm had, in fact, become established not as *a* way of doing public address criticism, but as *the only way*.[56]

The paradigm established by the Brigance studies was given formal explication in a 1947 article by Baird and Thonssen in the *Quarterly Journal of Speech*. One year later, they published the first textbook on critical analysis of public address – *Speech Criticism* – a text that would have a corner on the market until the mid-1960s, and go into a second edition in 1970. In their article, Baird and Thonssen took an expansive view of the scope of public address criticism, reflecting some of the changes since the early 1940s. They wrote:

> The critical judgment may limit itself to a single speech, one that was delivered either last week or last century. Or the critic may enlarge the scope of his inquiry to encompass the entire speaking career of the orator; to evaluate a speaking movement, such as temperance reform; or to interpret a period of the history of public speaking. The problem, in any case, is that of pronouncing judgment.[57]

As expansive as Baird and Thonssen's views were, they did not envision an expansion of public address beyond the confines of public speech or didactic written prose. Neither did they envision any kind of methodological advance beyond the traditional paradigm that characterized most of the studies in the Brigance volumes. That paradigm, broadly construed as historical-rhetorical in orientation, resulted in a standard pattern followed by most analysts of public address from 1943 to 1964. In outline form, the paradigm looked like this:

   I. The speaker's background
  II. The speaker's ideas and their support
      A. Premises and lines of argument
      B. Proofs and refutation
 III. Speech Composition
      A. Speech preparation
      B. Organization
      C. Language and style
 IV. Delivery

The widespread adoption of this procedure for analyzing public address had mixed results. On the one hand, it produced a great deal of information and, if properly pursued, virtually guaranteed that the researcher would be well versed in the topic at hand. Those earning degrees under Baird at Iowa, Wichelns at Cornell, Ewbank at Wisconsin, James McBurney or Wrage at Northwestern, or Kenneth Hance at Michigan were well-educated people, many of whom went on to distinguish themselves through their scholarship. On the other hand, in less well-trained hands, the historical-rhetorical method could become mechanical, categorical, and wooden. It could substitute method for thought, and discourage innovation and insight by limiting the kinds of questions one might ask about a speaker, or text, or situation. Even as this paradigm was being enshrined by the Brigance volumes and the Thonssen and Baird textbook, it started to come under scrutiny by scholars eager to expand both the scope and methods of rhetorical analysis.

With the publication in 1947 of S. Judson Crandell's essay on "The Beginnings of a Methodology for Social Control Studies in Public Address," serious thought started to be given to social movements, persuasive campaigns, and cultural ideals – and how such phenomena might best be studied by students of rhetoric and public address.[58] Judson's essay was followed, in 1952, by Leland Griffin's path-breaking article, "The Rhetoric of Historical Movements." While Crandell and Griffin led the way into what would blossom into a long series of articles on various movements in the 1960s and early 1970s, Marie Hochmuth and Virginia Holland were introducing the field to the thought of Kenneth Burke, I. A. Richards, and other practitioners of what was called the "New Rhetoric." The old paradigm had positioned itself as grounded in Aristotle, even though many of the critical studies owed as much or more to Cicero than to the Stagirite. Now both the theoretical foundations and the analytical methods employed by the traditional paradigm were being challenged.

Even the effects standard of evaluation, ostensibly erected by Wichelns and practiced faithfully by public address critics thereafter, came under scrutiny. Wayland Maxfield Parrish, in an introductory essay to *American Speeches* (1954) titled "The Study of Speeches," argued that "rhetoric, strictly speaking, is not concerned with the effect of a speech, but with its quality, and its quality can be determined quite apart from its effect." Speeches, Parrish held, were to be judged by their internal artistic qualities, not their external effects. He noted that "many of the great speeches of history have been made in lost causes," and argued that "a speaker's success in achieving a desired response from his audience is not necessarily proof that he has spoken well, or his failure, that he has spoken ill."[59] Public address was an art and had to be evaluated by the standards of excellence peculiar to the art. That such internal artistic standards were poorly understood in the 1950s was a direct outcome of the failure to seriously analyze individual speech texts. Although the field had been called Speech for more than 30 years, almost no one studied discrete speeches. Instead, they studied speakers and speaking careers. The speeches themselves were often incidental to the criticism.

This problem can be seen even in volume three of *A History and Criticism of American Public Address*, edited by Marie Hochmuth in 1955. Even though scholars were starting to expand the scope of public address studies and were beginning to question the dominant paradigm, there was little evidence of this ferment in the Hochmuth volume. There were no Burkean or dramatistic studies, nothing informed by General Semantics or Richards's theory of metaphor, and no studies of social or historical movements. In short, there was little to distinguish volume three from its earlier predecessors. Some of the essays were exemplary for their time – Carroll Arnold's article on George William Curtis and Martin Maloney's chapter on Clarence Darrow stood out. But the fact remained that every essay dealt with an individual speaker, most employed some brand of traditional, if not explicitly Aristotelian analysis, and all spent as much or more space on history and biography as in the act of speech criticism.

Even as the Hochmuth volume was replaying the past, other scholars were pushing the boundaries of public address criticism. For the first time, detailed studies of rhetorical texts, some oratorical and some nonoratorical, began to appear in print. Foremost among these were studies by Laura Crowell on Roosevelt's "Four Freedoms" speech, Donald C. Bryant on Edmund Burke's *Present Discontents*, and Eugene E. White on Cotton Mather's *Manuductio ad Ministerium*. In addition to textual studies, 1955–1964 was the germination period for studies in the rhetoric of social movements generally and social protest rhetoric particularly. Genre studies of various sorts became more prominent as was the examination of speakers who were not white, Anglo-Saxon males, which had long been the preferred subject of analysis for the "Great Man" school of criticism. The traditional paradigm was beginning to show signs of weakening.

In 1956, Thomas R. Nilsen and Albert J. Croft called into question various aspects of the paradigm. For Nilsen, it was not the emphasis on the speech's effect that was problematic, but the related assumption that effect was to be defined only in terms of the speaker's purported purpose or aim. "It is the viewing of the social act, the speech, so predominantly from the point of view of the individual – the speaker and his purposes – rather than from the point of view of society and its purposes," wrote Nilsen, "that has led to much of the conflict and confusion about effects as an object of criticism."[60] Nilsen wanted to retain the effects criterion, but to redefine effect to refer to that which society viewed as good or desirable, not what the individual speaker sought to achieve. He thus offered "criteria for judgment" drawn from "the assumptions upon which our society is based."[61] By relocating the locus of judgment from the individual to the collective and reconfiguring criticism as an essentially ethical act of judgment rather than a pragmatic act, Nilsen sought to establish social effect as the central criterion of speech criticism.

Albert Croft saw matters differently. To him, the problems of the traditional paradigm were considerably more severe than those identified by Nilsen. "Perhaps the chief problems of research in public address," Croft wrote, "is that we have thought of it all as 'criticism' when some is really theory, some is history, and some is criticism which has not evaluated the speeches studied."[62] The theory–criticism relationship was particularly problematic in the traditional paradigm, Croft held, because "criticism cannot alter theory; it can only use the existing forms." Such criticism was static and treated rhetorical theory "as a closed, fixed system." Such a view of the theory–criticism relationship led to a sort of cookie-cutter criticism, with the role of the critic being reduced to "finding illustrations of standard, preconceived forms."[63] As unproductive as the standard theory–criticism relationship had been, Croft found the interaction of history and criticism even more delimiting.

The challenge was to bring history and criticism into proper relationship, one to the other, so that the central question of "audience adaptation" could be explored. Croft observed,

> It is not enough to talk separately about the make-up of an audience at one point, about the main propositions of the speaker at another point, and about the speaker's use of traditional rhetorical techniques at still another point. The main function of history and criticism is to show how propositions and audiences are *connected*: how a speaker uses techniques to adapt his ideas to his audiences.[64]

These criticisms, though ostensibly derived from examination of graduate theses, were also a telling indictment of critical scholarship as practiced in professional journals and textbooks.

Opposition to the reigning paradigm continued when, in 1957, Wrage edited a special issue of *Western Speech* on the subject of "Criticism and Public Address." Essays by Thomas R. Nilsen, Joseph L. Blau, Donald C. Bryant, Robert D. Clark, Marie Hochmuth, W. Charles Redding, and Barnet Baskerville called into question several dimensions of the traditional paradigm – the focus on single speakers, the critical standard of effect on the immediate audience, the separation of pragmatic from ethical judgment, the bowdlerized Aristotelianism, the lack of symmetry between judgments of internal artistic integrity and external political results, and other equally problematic areas.[65]

Even as these debates were proceeding, the practice of public address criticism scored some significant advances. Griffin followed his path-breaking 1952 article on "The Rhetoric of Historical Movements" with an equally stunning application of that theory in "The Rhetorical Structure of the Antimasonic Movement," published as a chapter in *The Rhetorical Idiom* (1958), a collection of essays edited by Donald C. Bryant and featuring graduates of the Cornell School of Rhetoric. Eugene E. White contributed a series of articles on George Whitefield and the Great Awakening. Robert T. Oliver wrote about the rhetoric of diplomacy and published books about his experiences in Korea as an advisor to Syngman Rhee. Ross Scanlan contributed a series of articles on Hitler and the Nazi Party, while Laura Crowell and Earnest Brandenburg continued their studies of Franklin D. Roosevelt. The decade from the mid-1940s through the mid-1950s also saw the publication of several books grounded in the analysis of public address, including Dallas C. Dickey's *Seargent S. Prentiss, Whig Orator of the South* (1945), Robert T. Oliver's *Four Who Spoke Out: Burke, Fox, Sheridan, Pitt* (1946), Robert D. Clark's *The Life of Matthew Simpson* (1956), and Robert Gray Gunderson's *The Log-Cabin Campaign* (1957).

By the end of the 1950s, the traditional paradigm was in deep trouble even as the practice of public address criticism was beginning to broaden. In addition to the programs at Iowa, Wisconsin, Cornell, and Michigan, other doctoral programs – some of which had been in existence for many years – started to produce graduates in public address, with Louisiana State, Northwestern, Illinois, and

Minnesota chief among them. Such outstanding scholars as Leland M. Griffin (1950), Donald K. Smith (1951), Paul H. Boase and Gordon L. Thomas (1952), Ernest G. Bormann and Anthony Hillbruner (1953), Ronald F. Reid and Wayne E. Brockriede (1954), Malcolm O. Sillars, Howard H. Martin, and Robert L. Scott (1955), Robert P. Newman (1956), Hermann G. Stelzner and Robert C. Jeffrey (1957), and Russel Windes, Jr. (1959) joined the ranks of those from the previous three decades to form a significant cadre of public address leadership. It was, in fact, from the ranks of those earning their degrees in the 1950s and 1960s that the new theories, methods, and practices of public address criticism would emerge. Even as the traditional paradigm was dying, the early 1960s saw several works published that drew heavily from that tradition. In 1961, Loren Reid edited *American Public Address: Studies in Honor of Albert Craig Baird*. This was followed by Marie Hochmuth Nichols's *Rhetoric and Criticism* (1963) and *Antislavery and Disunion, 1858–1861* (1963), edited by J. Jeffrey Auer. In 1965, Robert Oliver published *History of Public Speaking in America*, the first comprehensive survey of American public address since Shaw's 1928 volume. All of these works were outstanding examples of the traditional paradigm at its peak. But the tradition which had been monolithic from 1925 to 1955 had reached its zenith. By 1965, it would start its descent.

Edwin Black and *Rhetorical Criticism: A Study in Method*

Although Black's *Rhetorical Criticism* carries a copyright date of 1965, it is important to remember that the book was originally a dissertation completed at Cornell University in 1962, under the direction of Herbert A. Wichelns. It thus represented the thinking of the late 1950s and early 1960s, as revised for publication in 1965.[66] The book had an immediate – and in some ways devastating – influence on both the theory and practice of public address criticism. Yet the disease had already been diagnosed and various prescriptions for cure offered before the publication of Black's book. In a sense, Black reaped where others had sown. He did so for several reasons. His was the first book-length analysis of (some would say assault on) the tradition. He not only diagnosed the problems, he also offered potential solutions. And he did this in a writing style that was at once incisive, witty, clear, and logically compelling. Newly hooded, Dr. Black took scalpel in hand and proceeded to dissect 40 years of public address scholarship. That he did this under the influence and guidance of Wichelns was a historical irony of no small note.

Rhetorical Criticism was a small book that carried a huge impact. In six brief chapters, Black laid out his definition of criticism, his view of how rhetorical criticism had been practiced traditionally, the relation of rhetoric to criticism, the uses of Aristotle's *Rhetoric* in the practice of criticism, an "alternative" frame of reference, and a final chapter on "the Genre of Argumentation." Black wasted no time in pointing out the faults of what he called "neo-Aristotelianism":

> The neo-Aristotelians ignore the impact of the discourse on rhetorical conventions, its
> capacity for disposing an audience to expect certain ways of arguing and certain kinds
> of justifications in later discourses that they encounter, even on different subjects.
> Similarly, the neo-Aristotelian critics do not account for the influence of the discourse
> on its author: the future commitments it makes for him, rhetorically and ideologically;
> the public image it portrays to which he must adjust.[67]

Black went even further, chastising the traditional critics for viewing discourses as
discrete entities, for their interest in immediate effects only, for the linearity of
conception – from speaker's background to message construction to audience
effect – implied in traditional analysis, for the tendency to reduce the realm of
rhetoric to oratory only, and for the assumption of audience rationality implicit in
the traditional paradigm.

The extent to which the traditional paradigm influenced the field, even as late as
1965, is revealed by Black's attempt to describe two other extant approaches to rhetorical texts – movement criticism and psychological criticism. Movement studies
had made some small degree of progress by 1965, due largely to the work of another
Cornell graduate, Leland Griffin. The so-called psychological study, however, was
barely discernible, even in outline. Black cited but one instance of a psychological
criticism in the speech literature and even that instance seems, in retrospect, suspect.
Nevertheless, Black was on to something. He realized that psychological criticism
could be a potent tool in the arsenal of the rhetorical critic if it could be made to
comment on the "discourse-as-communication" rather than on the "discourse-as-
symptom" of some hidden reality. Black noted that there was "no system of analysis
or body of techniques available to the critic for the reliable psychological examination of argumentative strategies or discursive texture," yet he was convinced that
precisely that kind of examination was necessary for "full disclosure" – the goal of all
criticism.[68] Previewing what such a system of analysis might look like, Black wrote,

> We are compelled to believe in the existence of relationships between a man's deepest
> motives and his discourses. Such a conviction is bound up with the very ways we have
> of talking about human motives. The mystery lies in the identification of those char-
> acteristics of discourse which reveal motive, for we know that motive only rarely
> receives a full and direct expression.[69]

Black would spend the next 40 years working out an approach to rhetorical criticism
that revealed "those characteristics of discourse which reveal motive," but in 1965 it
was only a vision of a type of criticism that did not then exist in the field of Speech. But
it would not take forty years for Black's influence to be felt. In the wake of *Rhetorical
Criticism: A Study in Method*, public address scholars suddenly found themselves in a
world where not only the historical-rhetorical method was challenged, but the very
assumptions about language, thought, discourse, and audiences upon which that
method had been erected were challenged as well. The results of this change included
a movement from speech to rhetoric (as controlling term), from history to criticism
(as type of scholarly activity), from one monolithic method to multiple methods or
perspectives (each with potentially equal credibility), from conscious attempts to

achieve critical objectivity to conscious celebration of critical subjectivity (as acknowledgment of the radical situatedness of all knowledge claims), from reporters and compilers of data to interpreters and analyzers of data (with a radical expansion of what counted as "data" for the rhetorical critic), and from a predominant focus on style and delivery to a primary focus on strategy (or movement from a focus on the text or speaker to a focus on the critic and his or her interpretive powers).

Toward Critical Pluralism

The fact that the traditional paradigm was already in the process of crumbling helped to explain the immediate impact of Black's book. So, too, did the historical moment of its appearance – in the middle of the most tumultuous decade of the twentieth century. It was a moment of change on many fronts as antiwar, women's liberation, black power, civil rights, and gay liberation movements all converged between 1965 and 1970. For public address scholars such changes and movements were reflected in the topics studied, the methods of analysis employed, and the sense of release or freedom from what was increasingly viewed as an anachronistic and flawed critical tradition.

The pages of the *Quarterly Journal of Speech* and *Speech Monographs* reflected these forces. Topics became more diverse. Studies of persuasive discourses other than speeches and didactic essays began to appear. Movement studies became more frequent, and names other than Leland Griffin started to be associated with movement criticism. The rhetoric of contemporary social protest – observable every day in the streets of America – started to be studied as an academic specialty, with critics such as Franklyn S. Haiman, Parke Burgess, Robert L. Scott, Donald K. Smith, James R. Andrews, and Richard B. Gregg writing major essays during the late 1960s and early 1970s. In 1971, John Waite Bowers and Donovan J. Ochs produced *The Rhetoric of Agitation and Control*, the first book-length theoretical treatment of protest rhetoric. Of equal importance, the methods of analysis started to change. Spurred on, in 1968, by a wide-ranging essay on "The Anatomy of Critical Discourse" by Lawrence W. Rosenfield and a clear articulation of "The Rhetorical Situation" by Lloyd F. Bitzer, critics began to find or invent new ways of analyzing rhetorical discourse: genre criticism, analog criticism, mythic criticism, phenomenological criticism, psychological criticism, metaphoric and archetypal criticism, stylistic criticism, dramatistic criticism, fantasy-theme analysis, model criticism, structuralist criticism, feminist criticism, and the list goes on. Suddenly, there seemed to be no end to available critical approaches and few boundaries as to what constituted a study in "public address."

Vestiges of the old paradigm remained, but they were few. Anthony Hillbruner published *Critical Dimensions: The Art of Public Address Criticism* (1966), the most complete statement on the traditional paradigm since Thonssen and Baird's *Speech Criticism* in 1948. Lionel Crocker contributed *Rhetorical Analysis of Speeches* (1967). And Loren Reid produced a masterful rhetorical biography on *Charles James Fox: A Man for the People* (1969). But even the titles betrayed a tradition now past. DeWitte Holland made an important contribution by editing volumes on *Preaching in American History* (1969), *Sermons in American History* (1971), and *America in Controversy* (1973), while Waldo Braden added a volume on *Oratory in the Old South, 1828–1860* (1970). But merely applying the traditional understanding to new eras or artifacts was not enough to save it. As the decade of the 1970s dawned, several new textbooks and anthologies on criticism appeared, each eschewing the old paradigm for more contemporary approaches. Chief among these were Karlyn Kohrs Campbell's *Critiques of Contemporary Rhetoric* (1972), Robert L. Scott and Bernard L. Brock's *Rhetorical Criticism: A Twentieth-Century Perspective* (1972), and a critical anthology, *Explorations in Rhetorical Criticism* (1973), edited by G. P. Mohrmann, Charles J. Stewart, and Donovan J. Ochs. These books featured multiple perspectives, including mythic and archetypal criticism, dramatistic criticism, social movement criticism, stylistic criticism, argumentative analysis, fantasy-theme analysis, and more. In 1974, Carroll Arnold tried to revive the Aristotelian tradition with *Criticism of Oral Rhetoric*, but the field was not much interested in thinking about the distinctions between orality and literature – the very distinction that had led to its birth 60 years earlier.

The period from 1965 to 1980 was one of unprecedented growth and change, both in terms of the objects of criticism and in terms of the methods or approaches used by critics to analyze and evaluate those objects. Before the middle 1960s, scholars engaged in what they called "speech criticism" or the "criticism of public address"; after 1965, the term of choice became "rhetorical criticism." The change was meant to connote several things, not the least of which was that prior to 1965 it was unusual to find a study concerned with anything other than oratory or didactic literature – pamphlets, tracts, broadsides, instruction manuals, and the like. After 1965, such studies became commonplace, with analyses of various "non-oratorical forms" regularly appearing in print. The leaders of this sea change in public address studies were an amazing cohort of scholars, most of whom earned their doctoral degrees between 1960 and 1970. This group included Wil A. Linkugel and Walter R. Fisher (1960), Herbert W. Simons and Jane Blankenship (1961), Edwin Black, Harry P. Kerr, and G. P. Mohrmann (1962), Richard B. Gregg, Michael Osborn, Lawrence W. Rosenfield, and Charles J. Stewart (1963), Theodore O. Windt (1965), Thomas W. Benson, Ronald Carpenter, and James R. Andrews (1966), Cal Logue (1967), Karlyn Kohrs Campbell, Philip C. Wander, and Andrew A. King (1968), Martha Solomon and Craig R. Smith (1969), and Roderick P. Hart and Bruce E. Gronbeck (1970). So rapidly did this change overtake the field that as early as 1970, conferees at the National Developmental Conference on Rhetoric could conclude:

> Rhetorical criticism is to be identified by the kinds of questions posed by the critic. . . . The critic becomes rhetorical to the extent that he studies his subject in terms of its suasory potential or persuasive effect. So identified, rhetorical criticism may be applied to any human act, process, product, or artifact which, in the critic's view, may formulate, sustain, or modify attention, perceptions, attitudes or behavior.[70]

Clearly this view of criticism's scope and responsibilities went far beyond anything contemplated by traditional scholars of public address. Yet it was precisely the limitations imposed by the tradition that motivated the conferees. As they noted in the same report: "Much of our theory has presupposed formal platform speaking and has thereby ignored a multitude of presentational and transactional possibilities."[71] Starting in the late 1960s and extending throughout the decades of the 1970s and 1980s, those "possibilities" were thoroughly explored. In 1968, Philip K. Tompkins explored the rhetoric of novelist James Joyce; in 1969, James R. Andrews looked at "Confrontation at Columbia"; in 1970, Robert Rutherford Smith examined the radio broadcasts of Raymond Swing, and John Angus Campbell wrote about Darwin's *Origins of Species*; in 1971, Jimmie Rogers and Theodore Clevenger examined the CBS television documentary "The Selling of the Pentagon," while Roderick P. Hart was writing about the "Rhetoric of the True Believer"; in 1972, Malcolm O. Sillars studied the "Rhetoric of the Petition in Boots"; in 1973, Karlyn Kohrs Campbell analyzed the "Rhetoric of Women's Liberation"; and, in 1974, Thomas W. Benson explored autobiography as a form of rhetoric, using *The Autobiography of Malcolm X* as a case study. No longer were speeches the privileged – or even preferred – focus of scholarly study. Critics could study virtually any symbolic form – and they did.

All of this was too much for some of the more established scholars, particularly those committed to the traditional paradigm. Two voices, in particular, stood out. Donald C. Bryant had earned his PhD at Cornell in 1937. By the 1970s, Bryant had long been one of the true giants of the field, having published ground-breaking articles on the nature and scope of rhetoric and on Edmund Burke.[72] In 1973, Bryant published *Rhetorical Dimensions in Criticism*. In this slim volume, he criticized the expansion of the scope for rhetorical studies and explicitly noted, "I do not find it fruitful, even if plausible, to enlarge the rhetorical to comprehend all symbolic interaction, by whatever vehicle communicated. Nor do I find it fruitful or plausible to extend the rhetorical dimensions to encompass all kinds of study of all kinds and vehicles of symbolic interaction."[73] Bryant's concern was for an over-extension of the traditional domain of rhetoric – the fear that if every symbolic form was now rhetorical, then rhetoric as a distinct kind of discourse would no longer be recognized or appreciated. Also lamenting some of the changes that had come upon the field was Barnet Baskerville. Baskerville had earned his PhD in 1948 at Northwestern under the direction of Ernest Wrage. In 1979 he published a book titled *The People's Voice*, which was a traditional analysis of American oratorical practice. Two years earlier, Baskerville had published an article in the *Quarterly Journal of Speech* titled, "Must We All Be 'Rhetorical Critics'?" In this article Baskerville noted that the study of rhetoric and public address had always been broader than criticism per se and that the recent enthusiasm for criticism and new critical methods risked the loss of those other aspects of public address scholarship. "What then is my concern?" asked Baskerville. "It is that in our enthusiasm for rhetorical criticism … we may neglect important scholarly responsibilities. As the literary scholar has made himself custodian of a body of imaginative writings, so should we be the custodians of a body of purposive, public discourse in which the literary man for various reasons has not shown much interest."[74] In short, Baskerville asked the field to take seriously the study of rhetorical history, the history of oratory, rhetorical biography, and other aspects of the public address tradition that were seemingly being overwhelmed by the new-found focus on criticism. *The People's Voice* was Baskerville's attempt to revive what some people saw as a dying tradition. He was not alone. Books and anthologies of the late 1970s and early 1980s by Waldo Braden, Cal Logue, Paul Boase, Howard Dorgan, and others also tried to revive the tradition, but it was not to be.[75]

While it is true that some scholars abandoned oratory altogether in the 1970s, others invented new and exciting ways to understand public discourse. And they did so by a method that had been little employed in public address criticism – the close study of a single speech text. Between 1970 and 1972, four public address critics published individual analyses of President Nixon's November 3, 1969, "Vietnamization" address. Never before had any single address been the subject of such sustained critical interest. Equally important, each of these four critics – Robert P. Newman, Hermann G. Stelzner, Forbes I. Hill, and Karlyn Kohrs Campbell – took a decidedly different view of the rhetorical action instantiated in the text.[76] This event was one source of what would become in the 1980s a full-scale school of public address criticism based on the "close reading" of oratorical texts. For the early 1970s, four competing readings of a single speech, even though they came about by happenstance rather than design, was a unique, and to the surprise of many, highly illuminating exercise.

But there were other significant moments as well. Edwin Black began to flesh out his notion of a true psychological criticism with a brilliant essay on "The Second Persona." Arthur L. Smith (now Molefi Kete Asante) made the first contribution toward a theoretical understanding of black oratory, one that would lead, in time, to his theory of Afrocentricity. Karlyn Kohrs Campbell and Brenda Hancock illuminated oratorical features of the women's liberation movement, thus planting seeds for the serious study of women's discourse, an interest that can be traced all the way back to 1912 when Edwin Shurter published a short booklet on *Woman Suffrage*. Critics such as G. P. Mohrmann and Michael Leff sketched the outlines of a new traditionalism with a pair of essays on "Lincoln at Cooper Union." This new traditionalism merged the insights of classical and contemporary rhetoric in new and interesting ways, becoming yet another source for the close reading of the 1980s. Debate over the role, purpose, and methods of criticism proceeded apace as Philip Wander and Michael Calvin McGee laid the theoretical bases for what would become, in the 1980s, two different schools of ideologically driven criticism. Wayne Brockriede set forth the dimensions of argument as applied to critical analysis. Significant studies of public address in the older sense of oratory were conducted by Stephen E. Lucas, Richard B. Gregg, and Halford Ross Ryan. In 1976, Lucas produced a book-length study, based on his Penn State dissertation, titled *Portents of Rebellion*. It became a model of public address scholarship, foreshadowing the rise of a scholarly book culture within public address studies, something that was, at best, sporadic prior to 1976.

Scholars of public address were often textbook writers, but they seldom produced a scholarly book. When Lucas's book was followed in quick succession by Hart's *The Political Pulpit* (1977), Campbell and Jamieson's *Form and Genre: Shaping Rhetorical* Action (1978), and a series of short studies by Barbara A. Larson, Ronald Reid, and Kurt Ritter and James R. Andrews (1978), commissioned by the national association as "centennial monographs," it signaled that a book culture was on the horizon.[77] In the 1980s and early 1990s that horizon would come into full view. And it would do so largely because of a handful of scholars who earned their degrees in the 1970s: Roderick P. Hart, John C. Hammerback, and Bruce E. Gronbeck (1970), Halford Ryan (1971), Michael Leff, Kathleen Hall Jamieson, and Robert L. Ivie (1972), Stephen E. Lucas (1973), David Zarefsky, Richard J. Jensen, Thomas B. Farrell, and Michael Calvin McGee (1974), Randall L. Bytwerk (1975), David Henry and Janice Hocker Rushing (1976), G. Thomas Goodnight (1977), Kathleen J. Turner and Barry Brummett (1978), and Robert Hariman and Christine Oravec (1979) chief among them.

The Rise of the Rhetorical Renaissance

From a historical point of view, the decade of the 1980s was the moment that public address studies came to full intellectual maturity. That maturity was marked by multiple and competing theories of criticism, an interest in all forms of symbolic inducement, a commitment to primary source research, and the commitment to study texts – both oratorical and nonoratorical – in context. The 1980s produced the scholarship that set the agenda for the next 30 years. From James Chesebro's path-breaking work on *Gayspeak* (1981) to Karlyn Kohrs Campbell's *Man Cannot Speak for Her* (1989), the 1980s was a decade of innovation and expansion of the scope and domain of public address studies. The trend toward book publishing that began with Lucas's 1976 book continued in the early 1980s with Bitzer's *Carter vs. Ford: The Counterfeit Debates of 1976* (1980), William R. Underhill's *The Truman Persuasions* (1981), Bytwerk's *Julius Streicher: The Man Who Persuaded a Nation to Hate Jews* (1983), and Ronald Hatzenbuehler and Robert Ivie's *Congress Declares War* (1983). This focus on political rhetoric expanded with Hart's *Verbal Style and the Presidency* (1984), Jamieson's *Packaging the Presidency* (1984), Turner's *LBJ's Dual War: Vietnam and the Press* (1985), J. Michael Hogan's *The Panama Canal in American Politics* (1986), Zarefsky's *President Johnson's War on Poverty* (1986), Hart's *The Sound of Leadership* (1987), Solomon's *Emma Goldman* (1987), Robert E. Denton's *The Primetime Presidency of Ronald Reagan* (1988), Jamieson's *Eloquence in an Electronic Age* (1988), Jamieson and David S. Birdsell's *Presidential Debates* (1988), Ryan's *The Rhetorical Presidency of Franklin D. Roosevelt* (1988), and Craig R. Smith's *Freedom of Expression and Partisan Politics* (1989).

Alongside this focus on political rhetoric was the continued expansion of public address to encompass media other than public speech. Representative of this expansion was Thomas W. Benson's studies of documentary film, Medhurst and Benson's *Rhetorical Dimensions in Media* (1984), Bruce Gronbeck's studies of television criticism and political advertising, Medhurst and Michael A. DeSousa's studies of political cartooning, and Thomas S. Frentz and Janice Hocker Rushing's extension of Jungian and mythic analysis to the medium of film. The rhetorical renaissance was marked by several factors unique in the history of American public address: Books started to be written on a regular, rather than occasional, basis; journals started to reflect a growing interest in the study of various symbolic forms, including speech texts – something the field had long professed but seldom undertaken; book series were launched devoted largely or entirely to rhetoric and public address; rhetorical biographies that took seriously the interrelationships between history and criticism were published; anthologies devoted to practical criticism became commonplace; and a rotating conference devoted to the theory and criticism of public address was established. All of this happened in the 1980s.

In 1987, Bernard K. Duffy and Halford R. Ryan edited the first multi-volume set on public address since the Brigance volumes of 1943. *American Orators Before 1900: Critical Studies and Sources* and *American Orators of the Twentieth Century: Critical Studies and Sources* were part of the larger effort led by Duffy and Ryan to restore rhetorical history, and especially rhetorical biography, to its rightful place in public address. Ryan followed these volumes in 1988 with *Oratorical Encounters: Selected Studies and Sources of Twentieth-Century Political Accusations and Apologies.* As editors of the "Great American Orators" series at Greenwood Press, Duffy and Ryan oversaw the production of four volumes in the series in 1989 alone, with production continuing into the twenty-first century. Also of significance was the founding of the "Rhetoric and Communication" series at the University of South Carolina Press in 1984, under the editorial direction of Carroll C. Arnold. Although focused initially on rhetorical and communication theory, the South Carolina series eventually came to publish public address studies as well. Likewise, the "Political Communication" series at Praeger, under the editorship of Robert E. Denton, Jr., produced several volumes informed by public address scholarship.

Parallel to these events and part of the driving force behind some of them was the articulation of a theory of public address criticism that came to be known as "close reading." The chief sponsor of this theory was Michael Leff. Starting with a 1980 essay on "Interpretation and the Art of the Rhetorical Critic," Leff identified the central problem in public address criticism as "a thorough preoccupation with abstract theories and methods … [that] dulls the critic's sensitivity to the problem of interpretation. Thus, we obtain a proliferation of critical methods, without any of these methods solving the problem that lies at their collective origin – the neo-Aristotelian tendency to impose mechanical categories on texts." Because "we have erred so long in the direction of the abstract," Leff argued, "it now seems reasonable to encourage efforts that begin with the particular."[78] In short, Leff proposed that the field start to give serious study to speeches and other symbolic texts as sites of rhetorical action. The fullest explanation of this approach to public address criticism was his 1986 essay, "Textual Criticism: The Legacy of G. P. Mohrmann."

In "Textual Criticism," Leff pointed to the speech text as a complex artistic construction in need of expert analysis and evaluation, a construction involving "a formidable number of elements":

> The close reading and rereading of the text, the analysis of the historical and biographical circumstances that generate and frame its composition, the recognition of basic conceptions that establish the co-ordinates of the text, and an appreciation of the way these conceptions interact within the text and help determine its temporal movement.[79]

For Leff, the "well constructed oration possesses a high degree of artistic integrity and density, and its proper understanding requires careful interpretative work." Following the logic laid out by Lucas in his 1981 essay "The Schism in Rhetorical Scholarship,"[80] Leff observed that:

> To rely exclusively either upon a formal/intrinsic or a representational/extrinsic criterion is to distort the rhetorical integrity of the discourse. Though critical analysis can separate these dimensions, the fact is that they occur simultaneously and work cooperatively within the fabric of the discourse.[81]

Leff then proceeded to formulate what he called a "theory of the text." Rather than bring a theory such as neo-Aristotelianism or dramatism or structuralism to bear on a text, Leff argued that the critic must discover the theory that lay hidden in the fabric of the text itself. Thus one worked from text to theory rather than from theory to text. Since every text "retains an internal history of its own," to "experience the text is to be coached to experience the world as the text constructs it."[82]

This reformation of the theory–text relationship led to two different responses: debate over Leff's "theoretical" approach, and attempts to validate that approach in the form of practical criticism. The theoretical debate took place in journals and conferences, with Michael Calvin McGee leading the opposition to close reading and advocating, in its stead, his own theory of ideological rhetoric. McGee claimed that there was no such thing as "the" text, and that all so-called discrete texts were better understood as fragments of cultural residues. It was cultural and ideological formations that rhetorical critics should be studying, McGee held.[83] Others joined in the debate, with Celeste Condit, John Angus Campbell, J. Robert Cox, and Dilip Goankar making major statements regarding the nature of rhetorical criticism.[84] While the theoretical debate continued, other scholars tried to put the tenets of close reading into practice. One of the best examples of this second response was Stephen Lucas's 1988 essay on "The Renaissance of American Public Address: Text and Context in Rhetorical Criticism." In this essay, Lucas illustrated many of the theoretical premises articulated by Leff. In so doing, he also provided an example of the kind of study that could not easily be classified as history or criticism, for it was both.

Lucas began his essay by noting that the field's "persistent neglect of major texts in the history of American oratory is nothing short of astonishing." He went on to argue that:

> Oratory is an art form with its own special criteria, constraints, and potentialities. Judgments about an oration as a literary production or an ideological pronounce-ment, legitimate and important as they may be, are tangential to its "rhetorical integ-rity" and cannot yield adequate assessment of it as a work of rhetoric. Such assessment can only be reached by radical attention to the internal dynamics of the text itself.[85]

Lucas then proceeded to demonstrate exactly what he meant by conducting a rhe-torical examination of the preamble to the Declaration of Independence. He later expanded this critique to include the whole of the Declaration in a chapter for *American Rhetoric: Context and Criticism* (1989), edited by Thomas W. Benson. Having demonstrated with practical criticism the efficacy of close reading, Lucas concluded,

> The ideal is to combine full and penetrating comprehension of the rhetorical situation with a sensitive and discerning reading of the text as an evolving, temporal phenom-enon that creates its own internal context even as it is leavened by the social and lin-guistic context. This is a very different exercise from the kind of artful paraphrase of a speech that often passes for textual analysis in rhetorical criticism. The purpose of the critic is not simply to retell the speech in his or her own words, but to apprehend it fully from the inside out – to break down its rhetorical elements so completely as to determine how they function individually and to explain how they interact to shape the text as a strategic, artistic response to the exigencies of a particular situation.[86]

The movement that had begun in the early 1970s to reclaim oratory as a legitimate and valued site of rhetorical investigation reached a crucial milestone with the con-vening in June 1988 of the First Biennial Public Address Conference at the University of Wisconsin, Madison. The results of that conference were published the next year under the title *Texts in Context: Critical Dialogues on Significant Episodes in American Political Rhetoric* (1989), edited by Michael C. Leff and Fred J. Kauffeld. This was the first in what would become an ongoing series of conferences that would carry the fruits of the rhetorical renaissance into the new millennium and, along the way, produce several important volumes of public address criticism.[87]

It is more than a little ironic that the "renaissance" of public address studies in the 1980s was powered by the discovery of a basic unit of analysis – the discrete speech text – which should, by all rights, have been discovered within the field's first decade. Yet it was not. Furthermore, this historical irony led to a seeming paradox: a theory of the case that operated within the confines of the particular textual site to generate critical understanding of issues that transcended the case.Even so, the renaissance proceeded to spread. Scholars of the 1980s – James Arnt Aune and Martin J. Medhurst (1980), Celeste Michelle Condit (1982), J. Michael Hogan and Robert C. Rowland (1983), John Louis Lucaites (1984), Steven R. Goldzwig,

Kenneth S. Zagacki, and James Darsey (1985), James Jasinski, Stephen Howard Browne, and John M. Murphy (1986), Mari Boor Tonn, Mark Lawrence McPhail, Kathryn M. Olson, and Denise M. Bostdorff (1987), James M. Farrell (1988), and others – continued the expansion of public address studies, both conceptually and methodologically. Aune brought the insights of Marxist analysis, first proposed by Wander, to bear on rhetorical texts. Medhurst, following in the footsteps of Benson, applied rhetorical precepts to films and cartoons. Condit, inspired by Gronbeck and McGee, investigated the argumentative and ideological structure of the debate over abortion.

From an intellectual endeavor that barely existed in 1900 to the dynamic enterprise of 1990 and beyond, public address scholarship worked to established itself as a center of humanistic learning. Along the way, as David Zarefsky noted in *Texts in Context* (1989),

> We have enlarged the meaning of "public address" from a mode to a function of discourse. … By embracing a broader conception of public address and not reducing the term to formal oratory, our studies have enhanced the potential for understanding historical or rhetorical situations and for formulating theoretical generalizations.[88]

By adopting this "broader conception of public address," the 1990s would prove to be the most productive decade of the century, seeing the production of more scholarly books than the previous 100 years combined. The final decade would also bring more book series dedicated to scholarship in rhetoric and public address, a new scholarly journal, the launching of a ten-volume rhetorical history, the establishment of topical conferences, and the continued success of the biennial public address conference. It would also produce one of the largest cohorts of public address scholars, several of whom have authored the chapters that comprise this volume.

Today, studies of how discourses address publics range from the traditional focus on oratory and public speech to analysis of film, television, literature, popular culture, advertising, and the Internet, as well as such nontraditional venues as body art, museums, graveyards, and monuments.[89] Wherever there is symbolic inducement being practiced, the scholar of public address is not far behind.

When James A. Winans took that position in the English department at Cornell in 1899, he could scarcely have imagined what he and his colleagues would ultimately create. One hundred and ten years later, the study of public address is alive and well in all three of its senses: the teaching of public speaking, the analysis of discrete texts, and the evaluation and criticism of discourses – oratorical and non-oratorical – that create, find, or address a public.

Notes

1   See Elizabethada A. Wright and S. Michael Halloran, "From Rhetoric to Composition: The Teaching of Writing in America to 1900," in *A Short History of Writing Instruction: From Ancient Greece to Modern America*, ed. James J. Murphy, 2nd ed. (Mahwah, NJ: Lawrence

Erlbaum, 2001), 213–246; Donald C. Stewart, "The Nineteenth Century," in *The Present State of Scholarship in Historical and Contemporary Rhetoric*, ed. Winifred Bryan Horner, rev. ed. (Columbia: University of Missouri Press, 1990), 151–185; Gregory Clark and S. Michael Halloran, "Transformations of Public Discourse in Nineteenth-Century America," in *Oratorical Culture in Nineteenth-Century America: Transformations in the Theory and Practice of Rhetoric*, ed. Gregory Clark and S. Michael Halloran (Carbondale: Southern Illinois University Press, 1993), 1–26; William N. Denman, "Rhetoric, the 'Citizen-Orator,' and the Revitalization of Civic Discourse in American Life," in *Rhetorical Education in America*, ed. Cheryl Glenn, Margaret M. Lyday, and Wendy B. Sharer (Tuscaloosa: University of Alabama Press, 2004), 3–17; Thomas P. Miller, "Lest We Go the Way of Classics: Toward a Rhetorical Future for English Departments," in *Rhetorical Education in America*, 18–35. There is ongoing debate over the extent to which the oratorical ideal was abandoned in the latter third of the nineteenth century. For a point of view that differs from my own, see Nan Johnson, *Nineteenth-Century Rhetoric in North America* (Carbondale: Southern Illinois University Press, 1991). However, careful study of Johnson's own Appendix A, "Sample College and University Calendar Descriptions of Rhetoric Courses, 1824–1900," clearly shows a diminution in the role of oratory and a concomitant increase in written and literary forms of rhetoric.

2   Herman Cohen, *The History of Speech Communication: The Emergence of a Discipline, 1914–1945* (Annandale, VA: Speech Communication Association, 1994), 2.

3   Yale University granted the first earned PhD in America in 1861. According to Bruce A. Kimball, "Before 1870, the total number of non-medical doctorates granted in the United States amounted to 16. In 1880 alone, 54 were awarded; in 1890, 149; in 1900, 382." See Kimball, *Orators and Philosophers: A History of the Idea of Liberal Education* (New York: Teacher's College, Columbia University, 1986), 161–163. Quote on 163.

4   There were numerous schools of elocution spread throughout America. The more prominent ones included the National School of Elocution and Oratory (1874), which was located in Philadelphia; the Monroe Conservatory (1880), which became the Emerson College of Oratory in 1891, both of which were located in Boston; the School of Expression (1885), also located in Boston; the Columbia School of Oratory, Physical Culture, and Dramatic Art (1890), which was located in Chicago; and the School of the Spoken Word (1904), located in Boston. On the elocutionary movement see Mary Margaret Robb, "The Elocutionary Movement and Its Chief Figures," in *History of Speech Education in America: Background Studies*, ed. Karl R. Wallace (New York: Appleton-Century-Crofts, 1954), 178–201; Lester L. Hale, "Dr. James Rush," in *History of Speech Education in America*, 219–237; and Edith Renshaw, "Five Private Schools of Speech," in *History of Speech Education in America*, 301–325. To view the 1893 catalogue of the Columbia School of Oratory, Physical Culture, and Dramatic Art see www.lib.colum.edu/archives/1893catalog.pdf (accessed July 27, 2009).

5   Elocution is important to the history of public address not only because it was one of the streams that fed into the academic study of Speech, but also because numerous members of the National Association of Academic Teachers of Public Speaking had studied under one or more elocutionists. In particular, the teaching of James E. Murdoch and S. S. Curry was highly valued. Even those early members who opposed the elocution movement sometimes studied under elocutionists, including James A. Winans, who spent one summer studying with S. S. Curry. See James Albert Winans, *Public Speaking: Principles and Practice* (Ithaca, NY: Sewell Publishing Co., 1915), xii.

6   Most of the information about Winans is derived from his own writings or from Cohen, *The History of Speech Communication*. Also helpful are Thomas W. Benson, "The Cornell School of Rhetoric: Idiom and Institution," *Communication Quarterly* 51 (2003): 1–56; Lionel Crocker, "The Break with Elocution – The Origins of James A. Winans' *Public Speaking*," *Today's Speech* 6 (April 1958): 23–26; Herbert A. Wichelns, "James Albert Winans," *Speech Teacher* 10 (1961): 259–264.

7   Examples of such early textbooks include George Jacob Holyoake, *Public Speaking and Debate: A Manual for Advocates and Agitators*, 2nd rev. ed. (Boston: Ginn, 1896); and Guy Carleton Lee, *Principles of Public Speaking* (New York: G. P. Putnam, 1899).

8   George Pierce Baker, ed., *The Forms of Public Address* (New York: Henry Holt and Company, 1904).

9   On elocution and popular oratory see Nan Johnson, "The Popularization of Nineteenth-Century Rhetoric: Elocution and the Private Learner," in *Oratorical Culture in Nineteenth-Century America*, 139–157.

10 These multi-volume sets included: Alexander Johnston, ed., *Representative American Orations to Illustrate American Political History*, 3 vols. (New York: G. P. Putnam's Sons, 1884); Alexander Johnston with James Albert Woodburn, eds., *American Orations: Studies in American Political History*, 4 vols. (New York: G. P. Putnam's Sons, 1896–1898); *A Library of Universal Literature in Four Parts Comprising Science, Biography, Fiction and the Great Orations: Part Three – Orations* [vols. 6, 7, 8], 8 vols. (New York: P. F. Collier and Son, 1897–1900); Guy Carleton Lee, et al., eds., *The World's Orators: Comprising the Great Orations of the World's History, with Introductory Essays, Biographical Sketches and Critical Notes*, 10 vols. (New York: G. P. Putnam's Sons, 1899–1901); David J. Brewer, ed., *The World's Best Orations, from the Earliest Period to the Present Time*, 10 vols. (St. Louis: Ferd. P. Kaiser, 1899); Richard Garnett, ed., *Masterpieces of Oratory*, 8 vols. (New York: Fifth Avenue Press, 1900); Julian Hawthorne, ed., *Orations of British Orators* [vol. 1] and *Orations of American Orators* [vol. 2] *Including Biographical and Critical Sketches* (New York: Colonial Press, 1900); Thomas B. Reed, ed., *Modern Eloquence*, 15 vols. (Philadelphia: John D. Morris, 1900); Guy Alexander K. McClure, ed., *Famous American Statesmen and Orators Past and Present, with Biographical Sketches and Their Famous Orations*, 6 vols. (New York: F. F. Lovell Publishing, 1902); Chauncey M. Depew, ed., *The Library of Oratory, Ancient and Modern, with Critical Studies of the World's Great Orators by Eminent Essayists*, 15 vols. (New York: A. L. Fowle, 1902); Mayo W. Hazeltine, ed., *Orations from Homer to William McKinley*, 25 vols. (New York: P. F. Collier, 1902); William Jennings Bryan, ed., *The World's Famous Orations*, 10 vols. (New York: Funk and Wagnalls, 1906); and John Vance Cheney, ed., *Memorable American Speeches*, 4 vols. (Chicago: The Lakeside Press, R. R. Donnelley and Sons, 1907–1910).

11 It is important to note that the terms "elocution" and "elocutionist" did not take on negative connotations until after 1880. See Giles Wilkeson Gray, "What Was Elocution?" *Quarterly Journal of Speech* 46 (1960): 1–7. According to Gray, there were four sources of the opprobrium that attached to the terms in the later nineteenth and early twentieth centuries: (1) elocution became associated primarily with the vocal and stylistic dimensions of oral reading; (2) as such, it lost all contact with the other canons of rhetoric; (3) it came to emphasize form and style over content; and (4) in some cases elocution became associated with the mystical doctrines that grew out of Delsarte's theories of elocution. According to Gray, "One result was that much of the elocution of the late

nineteenth and early twentieth centuries degenerated into statue-posing, bird-calls, and imitations of children" (7). There appear to have been other factors as well. One involved the role of emotion in persuasion. Elocutionists based their theories on arousal of the passions, thus making topical invention and logical analysis moot. One of the reasons that the founders of the field of Speech laid their foundations in Aristotelian rhetoric was to separate themselves from the elocutionists' emphasis on emotion. Another factor was the crossing of the line between speaking and acting. This was facilitated by the fact that many actors sought out elocutionists to help them with their craft. Elocutionists were committed to the performance of (mostly) fictive works. Speech professors were committed to logical and psychological argumentation on (mostly) social and political topics. Finally, the end of elocutionary displays was entertainment, while the end of academic speech was enlightenment or education.

12 "Swarthmore College. Prof. Paul M. Pearson Off On Recital Tour – Fraternity Teas," *New York Times*, November 17, 1912. Pearson's travels, and his Quaker connections, brought him into contact with many prominent people, including Herbert Hoover. In 1931, Hoover nominated Pearson as the first civilian governor of the Virgin Islands. Pearson was confirmed by the Senate and served from 1931–1935. From 1935 until his death in 1938, Pearson served as Assistant Director of Housing in the Department of the Interior. Swarthmore College holds the Paul M. Pearson Papers, including a manuscript on Pearson's life, written by his daughter: *Man of Chautauqua and His Caravans of Culture: The Life of Paul M. Pearson* (2001), by Barbara Pearson Lange Godfrey.

13 Robert McLean Cumnock taught elocution at Northwestern from 1868–1913. In 1878, he founded the Cumnock School of Oratory, which was a private school that he operated under contract with Northwestern. In 1921, the Cumnock School became the School of Speech, which, in 2002, became the School of Communication. Cumnock was a renowned teacher and his school drew many students who would later play major roles in the founding of the Speech profession, including Glenn N. Merry, Frank Rarig, and Paul M. Pearson.

14 For the original charter members of the NCTE go to ncte.org/history. Winans's signature appears as number twelve on the list.

15 This list of miseries is adapted from Frank M. Rarig and Halbert S. Greaves, "National Speech Organizations and Speech Education," in *A History of Speech Education in America*, 490–517.

16 For a more complete rendering of the founding of the National Association of Academic Teachers of Public Speaking, see Cohen, *A History of Speech Communication*; J. M. O'Neill, "The National Association," *Quarterly Journal of Public Speaking* 1 (1915): 51–58; Andrew Thomas Weaver, "Seventeen Who Made History – The Founders of the Association," *Quarterly Journal of Speech* 45 (1959): 195–199; Giles Wilkeson Gray, "The Founding of the Speech Association of America," *Quarterly Journal of Speech* 50 (1964): 342–345; and Robert C. Jeffrey, "History of the Speech Association of America, 1914–64," *Quarterly Journal of Speech* 50 (1964): 432–444. The most recent attempt to assay the founding of the Speech field is William Keith, "On the Origins of Speech as a Discipline: James A. Winans and Public Speaking as Practical Democracy," *Rhetoric Society Quarterly* 38 (2008): 239–258. Although based on primary source research, Keith's article is marred by several errors of fact, including the number of scholars who founded the new field (17, not 10); the date and name of what would become the National Speech Arts Association (the National Association of Elocutionists

was founded in 1892, not 1890, and didn't become the National Speech Arts Association until 1906); the "Speech Arts teachers" were, contrary to Keith's claim, at least somewhat interested in both public speaking and debate, which is why Winans, Woolbert, O'Neill, and others became members after the name change; the NCTE came into existence in December 1911, not 1910. These are relatively minor errors in an otherwise enlightening article.

17   James A. Winans, "The Need for Research," *Quarterly Journal of Public Speaking* 1 (1915): 17.

18   Winans used a local printer in Ithaca to issue the 1915 version of his book. When it began to sell, he was able to negotiate a contract to his liking with a major publisher. See James Albert Winans, *Public Speaking*, rev. ed. (New York: Century Co., 1917).

19   See C. H. Woolbert, "A Problem in Pragmatism," *Quarterly Journal of Public Speaking* 2 (1916): 264.

20   See Everett Lee Hunt, "General Specialists," *Quarterly Journal of Public Speaking* 2 (1916): 253–263. For further insight into Hunt's thinking during this period see Theodore Otto Windt, Jr., *Rhetoric as a Human Adventure: A Short Biography of Everett Lee Hunt* (Annandale, VA: Speech Communication Association, 1990); and Theodore Otto Windt, Jr., "Everett Lee Hunt and the Humanistic Spirit of Rhetoric," in *Twentieth-Century Roots of Rhetorical Studies*, ed. Jim A. Kuypers and Andrew King (Westport, CT: Praeger, 2001), 1–30.

21   See C. H. Woolbert, "Theories of Expression: Some Criticisms," *Quarterly Journal of Public Speaking* 1 (1915): 127–143; Charles H. Woolbert, "The Organization of Departments of Speech Science in Universities," *Quarterly Journal of Public Speaking* 2 (1916): 64–77; Woolbert, "A Problem in Pragmatism"; Charles H. Woolbert, "Suggestions as to Methods in Research," *Quarterly Journal of Public Speaking* 3 (1917): 12–26; Charles H. Woolbert, "Conviction and Persuasion: Some Considerations of Theory," *Quarterly Journal of Public Speaking* 3 (1917): 249–264; Charles H. Woolbert, "The Place of Logic in a System of Persuasion," *Quarterly Journal of Speech Education* 4 (1918): 19–39; Charles H. Woolbert, "Old Terms for New Needs," *Quarterly Journal of Speech Education* 3 (1918): 296–303; Charles H. Woolbert, "Persuasion: Principles and Methods," *Quarterly Journal of Speech Education* 4 (1919): 12–25; Charles H. Woolbert, "Persuasion: Principles and Methods," *Quarterly Journal of Speech Education* 4 (1919): 101–19; Charles H. Woolbert, "Persuasion: Principles and Methods," *Quarterly Journal of Speech Education* 4 (1919): 212–238; Hunt, "General Specialists"; Everett Lee Hunt, "Academic Public Speaking," *Quarterly Journal of Public Speaking* 3 (1917): 27–36; Everett Lee Hunt, "An Adventure in Philosophy," *Quarterly Journal of Public Speaking* 3 (1917): 297–303; Everett Lee Hunt, "Creative Teaching in War Time," *Quarterly Journal of Speech Education* 4 (1918): 386–397; and Everett Lee Hunt, "Plato on Rhetoric and Rhetoricians," *Quarterly Journal of Speech Education* 6 (1920): 35–56.

22   Woolbert, "A Problem in Pragmatism," 265.

23   The Research Committee, "Research in Public Speaking," *Quarterly Journal of Public Speaking* 1 (1915): 30.

24   Thomas C. Trueblood, "College Courses in Public Speaking," *Quarterly Journal of Public Speaking* 1 (1915): 262–263.

25   The relationship of the elocutionary movement to the founding of the modern field of Speech, and especially to the study of Public Address, is fascinating – and complex.

Some of the earliest founders of the field were clearly elocutionists – Robert Fulton, Thomas Trueblood, Binney Gunnison, and Robert Cumnock chief among them. Other founders studied at the various schools of elocution, though whether they should be considered elocutionists is debatable. Even so, the influence of elocution on scholars such as Haldor Gislason, Joseph Searle Gaylord, James A. Winans, Charles H. Woolbert, Glenn N. Merry, Frank Rarig, and a host of others is undeniable. Still others, like Paul Pearson, were public readers and reciters, with varying relationships to the schools of elocution. The relationship between reading out loud and giving a formal speech was the chief link of elocution to the field of Speech. Declamation was the middle passage between elocution and public speaking. Winans is often considered the father of modern public speaking, not because he wrote a textbook in 1915 (many others wrote earlier textbooks) but because he was one of the first to make the transition from declamation (which was heavily influenced by theories of elocution) to public speaking (which relied more on audience psychology and thus the need for rhetorical invention as the main engine of audience adaptation). Yet, even as public speaking sought to separate itself from elocution, another part of the emerging field of Speech – that which would come to be called oral interpretation of literature – continued to draw heavily from the elocutionary past. So, in a sense, the field of Speech simultaneously abandoned (public address) and absorbed (oral interpretation) elocution.

26   Important volumes of public addresses compiled by academicians who taught public speaking included: Edwin Du Bois Shurter, ed., *Masterpieces of Modern Oratory* (New York: Ginn and Company, 1906); Shurter, ed., *Oratory of the South* (New York: Neale, 1908); Shurter, ed., *American Oratory of To-day* (New York: Hinds, Noble, and Eldridge, 1910); and Robert Fulton and Thomas Trueblood, eds., *British and American Eloquence* (Boston: Ginn and Company, 1912).

27   Hillis also edited *Lectures and Orations by Henry Ward Beecher* (New York: Fleming H. Revell Company, 1913). It is interesting to note that A. Craig Baird reported that one of the ministers whose sermons he made a point of attending while a student at Columbia University and Union Theological Seminary was none other than Newell Dwight Hillis. See Orville A. Hitchcock, "Albert Craig Baird," in *American Public Address: Studies in Honor of Albert Craig Baird*, ed. Loren D. Reid (Columbia: University of Missouri Press, 1961), xiv. Several scholars who wrote on rhetoric and oratory in the late nineteenth and early twentieth centuries also produced biographies of noted statesmen. Lorenzo Sears, for example, produced several of these books, including works on Wendell Phillips (1909), John Hancock (1912), and John Hay (1914).

28   C. M. Whitman, ed., *American Orators and Oratory* (St. Louis: T. N. James and Co., 1884), preface. It appears as though there are several distinct stages through which the study of orations or speech texts has developed. In the first stage, from approximately 1800 to 1875, orations or extracts were reprinted primarily as resources for the development of eloquence. By studying eloquent passages, the reader could learn to become eloquent himself. In the second stage, from approximately 1875 to 1920, the reprinting of speeches became more a source of historical knowledge and pride of country than models of eloquence. In this second stage, the speeches were used to teach patriotism and served as models of great actions in history, which the reader was encouraged to emulate. In the third stage, from approximately 1920 to 1950, orations (now usually labeled speeches) were reprinted as models of rhetorical excellence in the public speaking classroom. The speeches, now organized by type or occasion, were used as exem-

plars for students to emulate in their own speaking. Hence the proliferation during this period of textbooks using the locution "classified models." Examples include James Milton O'Neill, *Classified Models of Speech Composition* (New York: D. Appleton-Century Co., 1921) and William Norwood Brigance, *Classified Speech Models of Eighteen Forms of Public Address* (New York: F. S. Crofts, 1928). In the fourth stage, from approximately 1950 to the present, speech collections were compiled not just for historical knowledge or rhetorical excellence, but as texts to be studied in their own right. One way to distinguish this last phase from its predecessors was the care that scholars used in reproducing an accurate and complete text, not just excerpts or passages. Notable collections from 1950 through 1989 included Harold F. Harding, ed., *The Age of Danger: Major Speeches on American Problems* (New York: Random House, 1952); Wayland Maxfield Parrish and Marie Hochmuth, eds., *American Speeches* (New York: Longmans, Green, 1954); A. Craig Baird, ed., *American Public Addresses 1740–1952* (New York: McGraw-Hill, 1956); Ernest J. Wrage and Barnet Baskerville, ed., *American Forum: Speeches on Historic Issues, 1788–1900* (New York: Harper and Brothers, 1960); Ernest J. Wrage and Barnet Baskerville, eds., *Contemporary Forum: American Speeches on Twentieth-Century Issues* (New York: Harper and Brothers, 1962); Robert T. Oliver and Eugene E. White, eds., *Selected Speeches from American History* (Boston: Allyn and Bacon, 1966); Bower Aly and Lucile Folse Aly, eds., *American Short Speeches: An Anthology* (New York: Macmillan, 1968); Wil A. Linkugel, R. R. Allen, and Richard L. Johannesen, eds., *Contemporary American Speeches* (Belmont, CA: Wadsworth, 1965); James H. McBath and Walter R. Fisher, eds., *British Public Addresses, 1828–1960* (Boston: Houghton Mifflin, 1971); Frederick W. Haberman, ed., *Peace*, 3 vols. (Amsterdam, NY: Elsevier, 1972); Ronald F. Reid, ed., *Three Centuries of American Rhetorical Discourse: An Anthology and Review* (Prospect Heights, IL: Waveland Press, 1988); James R. Andrews and David Zarefsky, eds., *American Voices: Significant Speeches in American History, 1640–1945* (White Plains, NY: Longman, 1989); and Karlyn Kohrs Campbell, ed., *Man Cannot Speak for Her*, 2 vols. (New York: Praeger, 1989).

29 Edwin Du Bois Shurter, *The Rhetoric of Oratory* (New York: Macmillan, 1911), vi–vii.

30 See Robert I. Fulton, "College Courses in Public Speaking," *Public Speaking Review* 3 (1914): 205–209.

31 Winans, *Public Speaking*; James Milton O'Neill, Craven Laycock, and Robert Leighton Scales, *Argumentation and Debate* (New York: Macmillan, 1917); Charles Henry Woolbert, *The Fundamentals of Speech: A Behavioristic Study of the Underlying Principles of Speaking and Reading* (New York: Harper and Brothers, 1920); and James Milton O'Neill and Andrew Thomas Weaver, *The Elements of Speech* (New York: Longmans, Green, 1926).

32 According to Donald K. Smith, there had been only seven MA degrees awarded in the field of Speech prior to 1910. Three of those seven were granted by the University of Iowa, three by the University of Utah, and one by Ohio Wesleyan University. See Smith, "Origin and Development of Departments of Speech," in *History of Speech Education in America*, 466. Two of the early theses completed at Iowa were almost certainly in the public address tradition. See Thomas Farrell, "Transition in American Oratory, or the Rise of the Lawyer," MA Thesis, University of Iowa, 1903; and Jesse Resser, "The Second Transition in American Oratory," MA Thesis, University of Iowa, 1904.

33 The first dissertation completed in the field of Speech was Sara Mae Stinchfield, "The Formulation and Standardization of a Series of Graded Speech Tests," PhD Diss., University of Wisconsin, 1922.

34   All of the sources agree that these five men were in the seminar. Other sources suggest that William E. Utterback was also part of the seminar.

35   Herbert A. Wichelns, "Research," *Quarterly Journal of Speech Education* 9 (1923): 233. The book that Wichelns referenced was Charles Mills Gayley and Fred Newton Scott, *An Introduction to the Methods and Materials of Literary Criticism, the Bases in Aesthetics and Poetics* (Boston: Ginn, 1899).

36   Other late nineteenth- and early twentieth-century texts on literary criticism include Lorenzo Sears, *Principles and Methods of Literary Criticism* (New York: G. P. Putnam's Sons, 1898); Charles Frederick Johnson, *Elements of Literary Criticism* (New York: Harper and Brothers, 1898); Barrett Wendell, *A Literary History of America* (New York: Scribner's Sons, 1900); and George Saintsbury, *A History of Criticism and Literary Taste in Europe from the Earliest Texts to the Present Day* (Edinburgh: W. Blackwood and Sons, 1900–1904).

37   Herbert A. Wichelns, "The Literary Criticism of Oratory," in *Studies in Rhetoric and Public Speaking in Honor of James Albert Winans*, ed. A. M. Drummond (New York: Century Co., 1925), 181–216. Quote on 207.

38   Herbert A. Wichelns, *Landmark Essays on Rhetorical Criticism*, ed. Thomas W. Benson (Davis, CA: Hermagoras Press, 1993), 2.

39   Wichelns, *Landmark Essays on Rhetorical Criticism*, 26.

40   These 15 points are abstracted from pages 212–213. Only 400 copies of the original book were printed. It was reprinted by Russell and Russell in 1962. Wichelns's chapter has been reprinted many times. It is easily accessed in Martin J. Medhurst, ed., *Landmark Essays on American Public Address* (Davis, CA: Hermagoras Press, 1993), 1–32. The discerning reader will note that much of the analysis in this chapter is borrowed from my earlier essay, "The Academic Study of Public Address: A Tradition in Transition," which is the introductory chapter to *Landmark Essays on American Public Address*.

41   The title of Baird's 1912 thesis was "The Sources of Chaucer's Man-at-Laws Tale." The thesis was directed by Harry Emerson Ayers, who was a Professor of Middle English at Columbia. Two years earlier, in 1910, Baird had earned a Bachelor of Divinity degree from Union Theological Seminary. His BA degree was from Wabash College in 1907.

42   See Albert Craig Baird, "A Selected Bibliography of American Oratory," *Quarterly Journal of Speech Education* 12 (1926): 352–356. There was at least one person thinking about speeches during this period. See Hugo E. Hellman, "The Greatest American Oratory," *Quarterly Journal of Speech* 24 (1938): 36–39.

43   Warren Choate Shaw, *History of American Oratory* (Indianapolis: Bobbs-Merrill, 1928), preface.

44   The first PhD in Speech at Iowa was awarded in 1926. There were two dissertations completed at Iowa in 1930 under the direction of A. Craig Baird. One was by Brigance and the other was Floyd W. Lambertson, "Survey and Analysis of American Homiletics Prior to 1860." I have chosen to give Brigance pride of place. For a detailed rendering of Brigance's time at Iowa, see David George Burns, "The Contributions of William Norwood Brigance to the Field of Speech," PhD Diss., Indiana University, 1970. For an overview of Brigance's contributions to the academic study of public address, see Martin J. Medhurst, "William Norwood Brigance and the Democracy of the Dead: Toward a Geneaology of the Rhetorical Renaissance," in *Rhetoric and Democracy: Pedagogical and Political Practices*, ed. Todd F. McDorman and David M. Timmerman (East Lansing: Michigan State University Press, 2008), 3–38. I have drawn several paragraphs from this earlier work.

45 This statement is based on close examination of the Knower Index, prepared under the guidance of Professor Franklin H. Knower and published yearly in *Speech Monographs* from 1935 to 1969. Several of the other early graduate programs – Louisiana State, Northwestern, Columbia, and Southern California, for example – simply did not produce many theses or dissertations in public address until the late 1940s or 1950s. According to the Knower Index, Louisiana State, Northwestern, Columbia, and Southern California *combined* produced only eight dissertations in public address between 1930 and 1945. The earliest of these was Doris G. Yoakam, "An Historical Study of the Public Speaking Activities of Women in America from 1828 to 1860," PhD Diss., University of Southern California, 1935.

46 W. Norwood Brigance, "Whither Research?" *Quarterly Journal of Speech* 19 (1933): 552–561. Quote on 556.

47 Brigance, "Whither Research?" 556–557.

48 Brigance, "Whither Research?" 558–559.

49 In addition to Brigance, the original members of the committee were A. Craig Baird (Iowa), C. C. Cunningham (Northwestern), Giles W. Gray (Louisiana State), Louis M. Eich (Michigan), Frank M. Rarig (Minnesota), Grafton P. Tanquary (Southern California), Herbert A. Wichelns (Cornell University), and W. Hays Yeager (George Washington University). Later additions to the committee were Lionel Crocker (Denison), Dallas C. Dickey (Louisiana State), Henry Lee Ewbank (Wisconsin), and Lester Thonssen (College of the City of New York).

50 Two other scholarly public address books were also published in 1934. See Lionel G. Crocker, *Henry Ward Beecher's Art of Preaching* (Chicago: University of Chicago Press, 1934); and Willard Hays Yeager, *Chauncey Mitchell Depew, the Orator* (Washington, DC: George Washington University Press, 1934).

51 There were 16 articles published in the speech literature on Lincoln, Wilson, and Roosevelt between 1925 and 1943. Most of these were written by Mildred Freburg Berry, Dayton David McKean, Earl W. Wiley, and Robert T. Oliver.

52 William Norwood Brigance, "The Twenty-Eight Foremost American Orators," *Quarterly Journal of Speech* 24 (1938): 376–380.

53 Loren D. Reid, "The Perils of Rhetorical Criticism," *Quarterly Journal of Speech* 30 (1944): 416–422. Quotes on 417 and 421.

54 Reid, "The Perils of Rhetorical Criticism," 422.

55 Ernest J. Wrage, "Public Address: A Study in Social and Intellectual History," *Quarterly Journal of Speech* 33 (1947): 451–457. Quotes on 454.

56 Wrage, "Public Address," 452, 456.

57 A. Craig Baird and Lester Thonssen, "Methodology in the Criticism of Public Address," *Quarterly Journal of Speech* 33 (1947): 134–138. Quote on 134.

58 In a personal letter to the author on August 11, 1993, Carroll C. Arnold noted: "I think few people know that 'movement studies' were promoted by Wichelns (and Henry Ewbank at Wisconsin) well before they became a 'fashion.' Ewbank directed studies on the neutrality debates prior to WW II, I remember (and there were others). Wichelns was more insistent on that tack. He directed Griffin's study of the Anti-Masonic movement and Arthur Barnes's (later Head of Journalism at Penn State) study of the Civil Service Reform movement – and there are others that I can't now remember. The trouble was that neither Wichelns nor Ewbank *wrote* about this as a mode of research, so when Griffin came along in publication about movement study, one couldn't tell where the notion had really started." Further research seems to indicate

that movement studies did, indeed, start in the 1930s. See, for example, Dallas C. Dickey, "The Movement for the Conservation of Natural Resources, 1900–1912," MA Thesis, University of South Dakota, 1932.

59   Wayland Maxfield Parrish, "The Study of Speeches," in *American Speeches*, ed. Parrish and Hochmuth, 7.

60   Thomas R. Nilsen, "Criticism and Social Consequences," *Quarterly Journal of Speech* 42 (1956): 173–178. Quote on 175.

61   Nilsen, "Criticism and Social Consequences," 177.

62   Albert J. Croft, "The Functions of Rhetorical Criticism," *Quarterly Journal of Speech* 42 (1956): 283–291. Quote on 284.

63   Croft, "The Functions of Rhetorical Criticism," 285.

64   Croft, "The Functions of Rhetorical Criticism," 286.

65   The articles from the special issue of *Western Speech* (Spring 1957) were published in book form, along with a few other essays, in 1968. See Thomas R. Nilsen, ed., *Essays in Rhetorical Criticism* (New York: Random House, 1968).

66   For a discussion of Black's relationship with Wichelns and a comparison of the dissertation to the book, see Thomas W. Benson, "Edwin Black's Cornell University," *Rhetoric & Public Affairs* 10 (2007): 481–488. Benson's article is part of a section "Celebrating the Life of Edwin Black, 1929–2007," which includes remembrances from Martin J. Medhurst, John Angus Campbell, Kathleen Hall Jamieson, Lloyd F. Bitzer, James Darsey, and Stephen E. Lucas.

67   Edwin Black, *Rhetorical Criticism: A Study in Method* (New York: Macmillan, 1965), 35.

68   Black, *Rhetorical Criticism*, 111, 104. "Disclosure" would become a central term for Black as he worked out his program of psychological criticism. It received its fullest treatment in his essay, "Secrecy and Disclosure as Rhetorical Forms," *Quarterly Journal of Speech* 74 (1988): 133–150.

69   Black, *Rhetorical Criticism*, 110.

70   Thomas O. Sloan et al., "Report of the Committee on the Advancement and Refinement of Rhetorical Criticism," in *The Prospect of Rhetoric*, ed. Lloyd F. Bitzer and Edwin Black (Englewood Cliffs, NJ: Prentice Hall, 1971), 220.

71   Sloan, "Report," 222.

72   See Donald C. Bryant, "Some Problems of Scope and Method in Rhetorical Scholarship," *Quarterly Journal of Speech* 23 (1937): 182–189; Bryant, "Rhetoric: Its Functions and Its Scope," *Quarterly Journal of Speech* 39 (1953): 401–424. Bryant's books included *Edmund Burke and His Literary Friends* (St. Louis: Washington University Studies in Language and Literature, 1939) and *An Historical Anthology of Select British Speeches*, edited with Carroll C. Arnold, Frederick W. Haberman, Richard Murphy, and Karl R. Wallace. His articles and chapters on Burke included "Edmund Burke on Oratory," *Quarterly Journal of Speech* 19 (1933): 1–18; "Edmund Burke's Opinions of Some Orators of His Day," *Quarterly Journal of Speech* 20 (1934): 241–254; "Some Notes on Burke's Speeches and Writings," *Quarterly Journal of Speech* 25 (1939): 406–409; "Edmund Burke's Conversation," in *Studies in Speech and Drama in Honor of Alexander H. Drummond* (Ithaca, NY: Cornell University Press, 1944), 354–368; "Edmund Burke: New Evidence, Broader View," *Quarterly Journal of Speech* 38 (1952): 435–445; "Burke's *Present Discontents*: The Rhetorical Genesis of a Party Testament," *Quarterly Journal of Speech* 42 (1956): 115–126; "The Contemporary Reception of Edmund Burke's Speaking," in *Historical Studies of Rhetoric and Rhetoricians*, ed. Raymond F. Howes (Ithaca, NY: Cornell University Press, 1961),

271–293; "Edmund Burke: The New Images," *Quarterly Journal of Speech* 52 (1966): 329–336; "The Rhetorical Art of Edmund Burke: Wilkes and the Middlesex Election, 1769," "British Voices for America, 1765–1780," and "The Rhetorical Art of Edmund Burke: *A Letter to the Sheriffs of Bristol,* 1777," all in his *Rhetorical Dimensions in Criticism* (Baton Rouge: Louisiana State University Press, 1973), 44–66, 67–90, 91–118. Bryant was the first person in the area of rhetoric and public address to pursue a systematic research agenda, which he worked out over the course of five decades.

73 Bryant, *Rhetorical Dimensions in Criticism,* 40.

74 Barnet Baskerville, "Must We All Be 'Rhetorical Critics'?" *Quarterly Journal of Speech* 63 (1977): 112.

75 See, for example, Waldo W. Braden, ed., *Oratory in the New South* (Baton Rouge: Louisiana State University Press, 1979); Paul H. Boase, ed., *The Rhetoric of Protest and Reform, 1870–1898* (Athens: Ohio University Press, 1980); Cal M. Logue and Howard Dorgan, eds., *The Oratory of Southern Demagogues* (Baton Rouge: Louisiana State University Press, 1981); Waldo W. Braden, *The Oral Tradition in the South* (Baton Rouge: Louisiana State University Press, 1983); and Calvin M. Logue and Howard Dorgan, eds., *A New Diversity in Contemporary Southern Rhetoric* (Baton Rouge: Louisiana State University Press, 1987). Howard Dorgan later produced a series of interesting books on religious rhetoric in Appalachia, the first two of which were *Giving Glory to God in Appalachia: Worship Practices of Six Baptist Subdenominations* (Knoxville: University of Tennessee Press, 1987) and *The Old Regular Baptists of Central Appalachia: Brothers and Sisters in Hope* (Knoxville: University of Tennessee Press, 1989).

76 See Robert P. Newman, "Under the Veneer: Nixon's Vietnam Speech of November 3, 1969," *Quarterly Journal of Speech* 56 (1970): 168–178; Hermann G. Stelzner, "The Quest Story and Nixon's November 3, 1969 Address," *Quarterly Journal of Speech* 57 (1971): 163–172; Karlyn Kohrs Campbell, "An Exercise in the Rhetoric of Mythical America," in *Critiques of Contemporary Rhetoric* (Belmont, CA: Wadsworth, 1972); and Forbes I. Hill, "Conventional Wisdom – Traditional Form: The President's Message of November 3, 1969," *Quarterly Journal of Speech* 58 (1972): 373–386. These four critiques, along with the subsequent debate between Hill and Campbell, were reprinted in James R. Andrews, *The Practice of Rhetorical Criticism,* 2nd ed. (New York: Longman, 1990) and thus reached a much larger audience.

77 The bicentennial monographs all focused on the revolutionary period. See Barbara A. Larson, *Prologue to Revolution: The War Sermons of the Reverend Samuel Davies* (Falls Church, VA: Speech Communication Association, 1978); Ronald F. Reid, *The American Revolution and the Rhetoric of History* (Falls Church, VA: Speech Communication Association, 1978); and Kurt W. Ritter and James R. Andrews, *The American Ideology: Reflections of the Revolution in American Rhetoric* (Falls Church, VA: Speech Communication Association, 1978). Other public address scholars were also examining revolutionary rhetoric. See G. Jack Gravlee and James R. Irvine, eds., *Pamphlets and the American Revolution: Rhetoric, Politics, Literature, and the Popular Press* (Delmar, NY: Scholars' Facsimiles and Reprints, 1976).

78 Michael C. Leff, "Interpretation and the Art of the Rhetorical Critic," *Western Journal of Speech Communication* 44 (1980): 346.

79 Michael Leff, "Textual Criticism: The Legacy of G. P. Mohrmann," *Quarterly Journal of Speech* 72 (1986): 380.

80 Stephen E. Lucas, "The Schism in Rhetorical Scholarship," *Quarterly Journal of Speech* 67 (1981): 1–20.

81   Leff, "Textual Criticism," 169.

82   Leff, "Textual Criticism," 175.

83   Michael Calvin McGee, "Text, Context, and the Fragmentation of Contemporary Culture," *Western Journal of Speech Communication* 54 (1990): 274–289.

84   See the special issue on rhetorical criticism in the *Western Journal of Speech Communication* 54 (1990): 249–376.

85   Stephen E. Lucas, "The Renaissance of American Public Address: Text and Context in Rhetorical Criticism," *Quarterly Journal of Speech* 74 (1988): 189.

86   Lucas, "The Renaissance of American Public Address," 197.

87   In addition to *Texts in Context*, the volumes produced to date from the biennial public address conferences include Thomas W. Benson, ed., *Rhetoric and Political Culture in Nineteenth-Century America* (East Lansing: Michigan State University Press, 1997); J. Michael Hogan, ed., *Rhetoric and Community: Studies in Unity and Fragmentation* (Columbia: University of South Carolina Press, 1998); and Shawn J. Parry-Giles and Trevor Parry-Giles, eds., *Public Address and Moral Judgment: Critical Studies in Ethical Tensions* (East Lansing: Michigan State University Press, 2009).

88   David Zarefsky, "The State of the Art in Public Address Scholarship," in *Texts in Context: Critical Dialogues on Significant Episodes in American Political Rhetoric*, ed. Michael C. Leff and Fred J. Kauffeld (Davis, CA: Hermagoras Press, 1989), 304.

89   For a sampling of rhetorical criticism applied to these various symbolic forms, see Martin J. Medhurst and Thomas W. Benson, eds., *Rhetorical Dimensions in Media: A Critical Casebook*, 2nd rev. ed. (Dubuque, IA: Kendall/Hunt, 1991); Janice Hocker Rushing and Thomas S. Frentz, *Projecting the Shadow: The Cyborg Hero in American Film* (Chicago: University of Chicago Press, 1995); Bonnie J. Dow, *Prime-Time Feminism: Television, Media Culture, and the Women's Movement Since 1970* (Philadelphia: University of Pennsylvania Press, 1996); Thomas W. Benson and Carolyn Anderson, *Reality Fictions: The Films of Frederick Wiseman*, 2nd ed. (Carbondale: Southern Illinois University Press, 2002); Barbara Warnick, *Critical Literacy in a Digital Age: Technology, Rhetoric, and the Public Interest* (Mahwah, NJ: Lawrence Erlbaum, 2002); Cara A. Finnegan, *Picturing Poverty: Print Culture and FSA Photographs* (Washington, DC: Smithsonian Institution Press, 2003); Lester C. Olson, *Benjamin Franklin's Vision of American Community: A Study in Rhetorical Iconology* (Columbia: University of South Carolina Press, 2004); Barry Brummett, *Rhetoric in Popular Culture* (Thousand Oaks, CA: Sage, 2006); Lawrence J. Prelli, ed., *Rhetorics of Display* (Columbia: University of South Carolina Press, 2006); Robert Hariman and John Louis Lucaites, *No Caption Needed: Iconic Photographs, Public Culture, and Liberal Democracy* (Chicago: University of Chicago Press, 2007); Barbara Warnick, *Rhetoric Online: Persuasion and Politics on the World Wide Web* (New York: Peter Lang, 2007); Thomas W. Benson and Brian J. Snee, eds., *The Rhetoric of the New Political Documentary* (Carbondale: Southern Illinois University Press, 2008); and Lester C. Olson, Cara A. Finnegan, and Diane S. Hope, eds., *Visual Rhetoric: A Reader in Communication and American Culture* (Thousand Oaks, CA: Sage, 2008).

2

Public Address Scholarship in the New Century
Achievements and Challenges

David Zarefsky

Never has there been as rich an array of scholarship in public address as at the present, yet this unprecedented scholarly productivity coexists with uncertainty about future directions and anxiety about the status of the field of study. Attempting to unravel this paradox is the goal of this essay.

How We Got Here

Approximately 75 years have passed since modern studies of public address began. To be sure, the orations of antiquity had been studied for centuries, emulating models of public discourse was a prominent mode of instruction in rhetoric during the nineteenth century, and orations were assembled in massive multi-volume anthologies edited by politicians as well as by scholars in the early years of the twentieth century. But the goals were appreciation and imitation, not analysis; improved artistic performance, not understanding and explanation. Not until after the publication in 1925 of Herbert Wichelns's "The Literary Criticism of Oratory" can we find what today would be recognized as studies of public address.[1]

Wichelns regarded oratory as a species of literature and therefore as a fit object for criticism. The objectives, as with any species of criticism, were understanding, interpretation, and assessment. But the special feature of oratory was its pragmatic character; it was intended to produce effects in particular situations. Of course, there were many examples of eloquence that remained meaningful long after the moment of delivery had passed. Nevertheless, the principal goal of an oration was to achieve intended effects with a given audience on a given occasion. Although he sometimes has been misunderstood, Wichelns was not calling for empirical studies to identify or measure the actual effects of an oration, but for critical studies that both explained and evaluated *how* the oration achieved its effects. This agenda implicitly assumed that the effects of the oration were known and uncontroversial, and it reasoned backwards to account for them by reference to factors in the speaker, the speech, and the audience.

Precursors to today's studies of public address can be found in the 1930s. A few were book-length, such as William Norwood Brigance's rhetorical biography of Jeremiah Sullivan Black (President James Buchanan's Attorney General) and Bower Aly's study of Alexander Hamilton.[2] Most, however, took the form of articles appearing in communication journals alongside articles recovering elements of classical rhetorical theory or offering pedagogical advice about public speaking. In general, they focused on orators rather than orations, highlighting the major rhetorical moments in a speaker's career but not focusing intensively on any one text. They concentrated heavily on preachers and politicians, these being the occupational categories in which oratory figured most prominently. And their method can be described as elementary biography combined with the application of categories derived from Aristotle's *Rhetoric*. A stimulus to scholarship, as well as a marker of what had been achieved to date, was the publication of the two-volume *A History and Criticism of American Public Address*, edited by William Norwood Brigance and published under the auspices of the National Association of Teachers of Speech (now the National Communication Association).[3] The method of neo-Aristotelianism, as it was called – originally with respect, later with ridicule – was codified by Lester Thonssen and A. Craig Baird in 1948,[4] and a third volume of the anthology was published under the editorship of Marie Hochmuth in 1955.[5]

The subsequent history of public address studies has been charted comprehensively in a series of essays by Martin Medhurst[6] and in a brief overview by David Zarefsky.[7] Although Medhurst's concept of "generations" of study may be forced (he divides 90 years of scholarship into six 15-year generations), and although his application of Tom Brokaw's phrase "the greatest generation" should apply only until the next generation comes along, his argument that the field of study has progressed qualitatively over time is fundamentally sound. Zarefsky writes not about generations but about studies before and after 1965. The year 1965 is chosen as a dividing point not because it saw the publication of Edwin Black's *Rhetorical Criticism: A Study in Method*,[8] which was a fundamental challenge to neo-Aristotelianism, but rather because it marked a division between studies reflecting a single paradigm of the object, method, and goals of study and studies reflecting a multiplicity of perspectives on each of these dimensions.

Prior to about 1965, most studies were of individual orators, whether historical or contemporary, and most employed the biographical and analytical methods known together as neo-Aristotelianism. Neither generalization would hold for the later years, when so many different approaches would be used that it would be impossible to identify any single one as dominant. To be sure, the distinction is imprecise. Leland Griffin pioneered the study of the rhetoric of social movements during the 1950s,[9] Ernest Wrage introduced the idea-centered study of public address during the 1940s,[10] Loren Reid challenged the dominance of neo-Aristotelianism during the 1940s,[11] Marie Hochmuth introduced the field to Burkean criticism during the 1950s,[12] and Wayland Maxfield Parrish and Marie Hochmuth questioned the seemingly simple-minded focus on effects and called instead for more intensive study of speech texts.[13] In retrospect, though, these and similar works are significant mainly as harbingers of the profusion of paradigmatic approaches that characterized the field beginning in the 1960s.

Simply to catalogue some of the major developments makes one aware of the geometric growth of the field of study. First, studies of social movements took their place alongside studies of individual orators. These studies focused on the role of public discourse in mobilizing masses of people, usually lacking in institutional power, in support of a cause. Prompted by the social forces of the time, most of these studies examined contemporary movements, although some addressed movements of the past.

Second, other studies of public discourse also focused not on orators who traditionally held positions of power but instead on the marginalized and underrepresented. In these studies, public discourse was seen as a means of empowerment, in some measure offsetting the disadvantage of a subordinate position in a hierarchy of power. During the early 1970s, Karlyn Kohrs Campbell undertook what would be a rich and sustained research program on the public discourse of US women.[14] Other scholars examined confrontations on college campuses, street protests and demonstrations, and the discourse of other marginalized groups such as Native Americans, African Americans, and gays and lesbians.[15] There is no single method or focus to these studies except for their common concern for the relationship between discourse and power.

Third, the field of study broadened considerably beyond oratory. Formal public speeches continue to be studied, of course, but other genres of rhetorical texts also have been acknowledged as a means of addressing publics. Pamphlets, tracts, and formal written documents are the most obvious examples, but nonverbal and visual modes of interaction, such as iconic photographs and popular film, television, and music, have been studied as well.[16] This broadening of the concept of text calls into question the very definition of "public address," introducing a source of confusion that will be considered later in the essay.

Fourth, even the idea that studies of public address examine a discrete text or set of texts has been called into question, as scholars have examined society and culture as if they were "enacted texts."[17] On this view, social and cultural practices are themselves means of conveying messages to audiences and of producing effects. Following this orientation, scholars have investigated such diverse modes as ritual practices, monuments, collective memory, and public culture.[18]

Fifth, alongside these moves away from studying individual orations, there also has been a new emphasis on intensive study of significant texts. Even canonical texts covered briefly in earlier neo-Aristotelian analyses are being given careful and close readings, often for the first time. Although there are exceptions, these studies usually concern works already well recognized for their historical significance and seek to describe their underlying rhetorical dynamics. There have been many book-length as well as article-length studies of significant texts, including several written by historians and others from disciplines other than rhetorical studies.[19] In addition to studies of specific texts, there also are more sophisticated rhetorical biographies.[20]

Sixth, studies have been devoted to the public discourse of specific institutions – sometimes corporate discourse[21] but more often the discourse of political bodies, especially the US presidency.[22] There also has been lively attention to the discourse of science.[23] The underlying premise of these studies is that institutional context, more than the idiosyncrasies of any particular rhetor, shapes the public address emerging within the institution. In a related move, a growing body of scholarship addresses the role of public discourse in the making of public policy. Both historical and contemporary policy controversies are examined, and topics include constitutional ratification, slavery, civil rights, social welfare policy, and defense and foreign policy.[24]

Seventh, public address studies, along with other fields in the humanities, have examined issues of identity, with special consideration to race, gender, sexual orientation, and class. One approach, as noted above, is to recover discourse traditions previously neglected, such as speeches by women, the oral traditions of African Americans, and the vernacular discourses of labor. Another approach is to assume that questions of identity inflect public discourse generally, in interesting and fundamental ways, and to describe and assess the nature of those inflections. There is now a significant literature reflecting feminist perspectives on public discourse, and growing numbers of studies elaborating a queer perspective or treating race as an underlying feature of public discourse.[25]

Others might construct a different list, but these seven topics suggest how, over the past 45 years, public address studies have moved beyond their earlier monochromatic character. Read from the culture of the early twenty-first century, the studies of the 1950s seem to be highly restricted in scope, method, and purpose. The increase in the volume and quality of scholarship has been a geometric, not arithmetic, progression.

Where Are We Now?

The explosion of scholarly output and its increased sophistication are dazzling features of the contemporary moment. There are more conference papers and journal articles. There is now an interdisciplinary journal, *Rhetoric & Public Affairs*, devoted largely to studies of public address. And there are several book series published by distinguished university presses. A twenty-first-century counterpart to the Brigance anthologies is the ten-volume *A Rhetorical History of the United States*, published by Michigan State University Press; at this writing four of the volumes have appeared. And scholars in fields other than rhetorical studies have joined in the celebration of the vitality of public address. These are heady achievements about which the field should feel a collective sense of pride.

One could identify various exemplars of public address scholarship. From my own perspective, with interests centering on political rhetoric, these works stand out as representative of the best: (1) Stephen Lucas's 1976 study, *Portents of Rebellion*, which examines the changing rhetorical culture of Philadelphia during the winter of 1775–1776 to uncover how public discourse helped to move public attitudes in the direction of independence; (2) Kenneth Cmiel's 1990 study of the emergence in the early nineteenth century of a distinctive American discourse that he calls "democratic eloquence"; (3) the 1993 history by Celeste Michelle Condit and John Louis Lucaites of the uses of the term "equality" by both European Americans and African Americans as an index of changing attitudes about race; (4) the study by Andrew Robertson in 1995 comparing how democracy affected public discourse in Great Britain and the United States; (5) Stephen Hartnett's 2002 account of cultural artifacts of the mid-nineteenth century as conveyors of public discourse and indicators of cultural values; (6) Angela Ray's 2005 volume exploring how the lyceum was a site of discourse that both ratified and modified the public culture of the age; and (7) Michael William Pfau's 2005 book exploring the use of conspiracy arguments in the public address of Charles Sumner, Salmon P. Chase, and Abraham Lincoln to discover under what circumstances the conspiracy argument is the province of cranks and fanatics, and when it becomes credible in "mainstream" public discourse.[26]

Except for a portion of the Pfau book, this list does not even include the voluminous output of Lincoln scholarship that has appeared in time for the bicentennial of his birth. That corpus includes studies of particular speeches, such as the 1854 Peoria address, the 1860 Cooper Union address, the Gettysburg Address, and the Second Inaugural Address.[27] The body of recent Lincoln studies also includes works by John Channing Briggs, Ronald C. White, Jr., Douglas L. Wilson, and Fred Kaplan that present the development of Lincoln's rhetorical skills through careful study of a series of speeches.[28] And there is a recent biography by White that pays significant attention to Lincoln's public discourse.[29]

Even omitting this substantial body of recent Lincoln scholarship, though, the list of exemplars is impressive. The entries in the list have several features in common. First, they develop complex and nuanced arguments that warrant book-length treatment. Compared to journal articles, they offer a far more textured view of their subject and provide a wider array of supporting material. Second, they rely heavily on primary source materials and make sophisticated use of archival research. Third, their claims are potentially interdisciplinary in scope. They are not concerned primarily with insular matters regarding the nature of rhetoric or methods of rhetorical criticism – although they do have things to say that are relevant to such topics. Rather, their principal focus is the artifacts or rhetorical objects the authors have selected for analysis. Scholars from a variety of disciplines or vantage points will be attracted to them. Fourth, these works are addressed broadly to concerns of civic discourse and the public sphere. These have been rhetoric's traditional interests, but as the boundary between public and private has blurred, rhetorical scholars find themselves examining issues and topics that previously had escaped their notice. These books provide reassurance that the field's original interests continue to warrant study. Fifth, these books, for the most part, concentrate on the nineteenth century. That focus may reflect the specific interest of these authors or the fact that it was I who made the choices. But in a field of study that so often seems oriented to the present moment, it is a welcome sign that studies of the era sometimes called the "golden age of oratory" continue to attract a readership. Sixth, with the exception of Cmiel and Robertson, the authors are trained in rhetoric and public address, and they write with awareness of the rhetorical tradition. In the hands of these and other like-minded scholars, "public address" as a field of study has become far more sophisticated.

Perhaps the most striking feature of this collection of works, however, is the breadth that the authors attribute to the concept of "public address," ranging from the individual political oration to the large-scale study of social formations and controversy. Lucas, for example, examines the circulation of the idea of independence, whereas Ray explores the institutional characteristics of the lyceum as they related to the phenomenon of public discourse. Condit and Lucaites trace the evolution of meanings of a particular term, "equality," as it reverberated through the discourses of different ethnic and religious traditions. Pfau demonstrates how political ideology and public discourse interpenetrate in ways that make conspiracy arguments seem more or less probable. Robertson uses evidence of language and verbal style to deepen understanding of the rhetorical commitments that are entailed in different political systems.

Taken together, these books illustrate how studies of public address have evolved from mechanical application of rhetorical categories to individual speeches, to the situated study of rhetorical practice. This evolution would be even more obvious if the list of exemplars extended beyond the public sphere to examine discourses in scientific and professional fields and the discourses of popular culture. Today the term "public address" can refer to virtually any form of situated rhetorical practice.

Current Predicaments

Definition and scope

Yet for many, the term "public address" still is taken to mean the oration, pure and simple. With such a view, it is easy to see why the study of public address might be sidelined, since – with a few exceptions such as Barack Obama – oratory is not the principal means of discourse or of rhetorical influence. This complaint is sometimes difficult to answer. On the one hand, one does not wish to be on the defensive with regard either to the power of oratory or to the value of historical study. The spoken word retains power to express aspirations and hopes, to index values and beliefs, and to move people to act. And the study of the past continues to inform our understanding of the contemporary moment as rooted in a rich and meaningful tradition.

On the other hand, one does not wish to be pigeonholed into a narrow or reductionist version of one's intellectual project, just as a clergyperson's task should not be reduced to delivering a weekly sermon or a lawyer's to appearing in court. Like them, public address scholars should not be reduced to historians of oratory. The challenge is to understand and to describe public address studies in their richness and complexity without seeming to reject their still-vital roots. The organization of the contemporary communication discipline does not facilitate this broader understanding. Subfields such as political communication, argumentation, religious communication, visual communication, and environmental communication, to name but a few, occupy parts of the domain of public address, leaving public address in many people's minds with the "remainder" of formal oratory. Not only is such reductionism harmful for our understanding of public address, but thinking of the communication discipline as organized into such discrete silos also limits the ability to advance strong claims and arguments about any communication practice.

Priorities for study

If general agreement existed that the scope of public address studies was as broad as is suggested here, then a second question would present itself: Given such breadth, how should one decide what is most important to study? In one sense this is a silly question. Scholars will study what interests them, just as they always have. And what interests them will be determined sometimes by theoretical reflection, sometimes by the desire to supply a missing piece in the historical record, sometimes because something presents an analytical puzzle, and sometimes because something idiosyncratically has piqued their curiosity. Attempts to prescribe an agenda for scholarship or to define scholarly priorities will be resisted as acts of hubris and may well be ignored. After all, anyone who sets out to tell someone else what to study is not likely to get very far.

If the strategy of allowing a thousand flowers to bloom is sensible at the level of the individual scholar, however, it is problematic for public address studies as a whole. As is true of the communication discipline generally, the number of public address scholars is relatively small when compared either to the vastness of the object of study or to the numbers of scholars in related disciplines. The result is that the number of scholars qualified on any given topic will be small and the field as a whole will be broad but not deep.

The vitality of the public address subfield depends both on enriching the study of paradigm cases, so that they do not become stale, and on "pushing the envelope," expanding the scope of our studies so that our subject matter does not become overly constricted. To be sure, there are many points along a continuum between these two poles, but for simplicity's sake I will focus on these seeming extremes.

Currently, we are doing well at "pushing the envelope." A large percentage of our studies deal with the contemporary world, with the recovery of under-studied speakers and marginalized voices, and with a broadening of topics and forms of public address. While this is all to the good, the field would be healthier if there were *also* greater scholarly attention devoted to the paradigmatic, even canonical, cases of public address. This is a plea for recalibrating the balance.

It is surprising in some cases how little attention has been given to canonical speeches. A body of work is emerging on Lincoln's speeches, including the works mentioned above. These works hardly exhaust what can be said about the texts they examine, and there are many other Lincoln speeches that largely escape scholarly attention. And Lincoln is the rhetor who is *most* studied by scholars both within and outside the communication discipline. There are books on Kennedy's Inaugural Address and King's "I Have a Dream" speech,[30] but few others, and there are articles offering serious analysis and criticism of canonical speech texts – but, again, many escape attention. The Library of Presidential Rhetoric being published by Texas A&M University Press will redress this deficiency to some extent, but only with respect to presidents, and predominantly contemporary ones. There are still few studies of such noted rhetors as Franklin D. Roosevelt, William Jennings Bryan, or the Senate triumvirate of Henry Clay, Daniel Webster, and John C. Calhoun. (There are exceptions, of course.)

Moreover, even if there was a body of extant scholarship, it needs to be refreshed from time to time in light of new insights, new evidence, and new ways of thinking. Historical insight is continually revised, and historical studies of public address should be no exception. Andrew Jackson's attack on the Bank of the United States reads differently in the wake of the banking and financial crisis of 2008 and 2009, just as the founders' warnings about the risk of corruption in government read differently in the aftermath of Watergate. And, early Cold War rhetoric reads differently in the context of the terrorist attacks of September 11, 2001. Not every new publication offers new insight, of course, and not every new perspective will be more valuable than the old. But the fact that cases of public address have been studied before is hardly a reason to avoid subjecting them to renewed attention. This is especially so for the paradigm cases, those widely regarded as models of the genre as well as instances of its application. New views may modify not only our understanding of the cases but our understanding of public address more broadly.

While this reasoning argues for renewed attention to well-known orations – recalibrating the balance between the well known and the newly studied, as noted above – it does not propose them as the exclusive focus of our studies. Many scholars will be attracted to other instances of public address or will have research questions that cannot be answered well by recourse to paradigm cases of oratory. The last thing we need is to constrain our inquiry by restricting our objects of study. The key point, rather, is that one's object of study should be dictated by one's interests and questions, not by the false belief that everything worth saying about the well-known cases already has been said.

One frequent objection to focusing on canonical texts is that the canon is systematically restrictive. With relatively few exceptions, the orators studied are white males (usually dead), the topics studied are politics and religion, the medium studied is verbal public discourse. Each of these limitations, it is alleged, deprives us of important knowledge and insight, limits our ability to generalize, and impoverishes our understanding of public address as significant human activity. Conversely, pushing our studies beyond traditional limitations can enrich us in each of these respects.

Although sometimes overstated, this criticism is well founded. It is the reason the field must continue to "push the envelope" even as I hope it renews interest in canonical texts. The rich understanding gained by broadening our sights can be illustrated by three successful research programs. The best known is Karlyn Kohrs

Campbell's project of the past four decades, to recover and analyze the speaking of US women. This work involved locating and transcribing largely fugitive records, recreating the surrounding context, and subjecting the materials to analysis and criticism. The long-standing cultural norm of separate spheres and the belief that it was inappropriate for women to speak in public marginalized their voices and obscured their contributions to public dialogue. In working to redress this imbalance, Campbell has not just filled in gaps in the record. Rather, her work has enhanced understanding of such topics as the genesis and evolution of social movements, the historical grounding of contemporary issues of woman's rights, the process of rhetorical invention in the face of severe social and cultural constraints, and similarities and differences in how men and women approach rhetorical problems.[31] To cite one small example, our understanding of abolitionist public discourse of the 1830s is richer because we can do comparative studies of Wendell Phillips's well-known 1837 address on the murder of Elijah Lovejoy and Angelina Grimké's less well-known 1838 address at Pennsylvania Hall.

More recently, James Darsey, Charles E. Morris III, and other scholars have exposed the heteronormativity of traditional scholarship in public address. This project is newer than Campbell's and it has a somewhat different objective. Although it is yielding studies of the history of the gay rights movement and accounts of discourse produced by people who are gay, lesbian, bisexual, transgendered, or queer, that does not appear to be its only purpose. More significantly, this work is identifying sexuality as a topic and characteristic of public discourse more generally. Long obscured, even repressed, as a purely private matter and one about which variance from norms was thought sinful, sexuality can inflect our understanding of public discourse in new and important ways. The previously cited volume of essays edited by Morris, *Queering Public Address*,[32] is aptly titled, because these studies demonstrate how viewing public address through the prism of sexuality yields different but productive insights when compared to those obtained through the prism of politics or religion, the traditional topics associated with the field. The result is to see public address as a richer and more complex human interaction than we might have thought.

The third example of a research program that productively pushes against canonical boundaries is the growing interest in visual rhetoric, reflecting the obvious realization that – especially in the contemporary world – a substantial part of public "discourse" is nondiscursive but visual. Among the many scholars exploring visual rhetoric, the work of Cara Finnegan, Lester Olson, and Robert Hariman and John Louis Lucaites is especially noteworthy because of its sustained and programmatic character. Finnegan's studies of photography during the Depression make clear how visual representations conveyed attitudes and influenced understanding of those years. Olson's studies of Revolutionary-era iconography reveal how colonists envisioned intercolonial relationships. And Hariman and Lucaites's studies of iconic photographs explore how these pictures condense meaning and emotion, and how their successive transcription can reappropriate meanings. Their methods of close reading of images and historical study of their transformations are analogous to the close reading of verbal texts and longitudinal studies of their reception.[33]

Significantly, Hariman and Lucaites refer to iconic photographs as cases of public address.[34] Their work illustrates (pardon the pun) the rich insight that is yielded by regarding public address as situated rhetorical practice rather than identifying it exclusively with a particular medium of discourse.

A much-needed effort to "push the envelope" would be to internationalize public address studies. With few exceptions, including Cheryl R. Jorgensen-Earp's books on the British suffrage movement,[35] most extant scholarship focuses on public address in the United States. Teaching and research in British public address and classical public address, once mainstays of rhetoric curricula, have virtually disappeared. The Robertson book cited above illustrates the potential for comparative studies of democracy in Britain and the United States that would be possible if scholarship in British public address were revitalized. And from the study of classical public address should emerge insights into the conflict between liberalism and civic republicanism that is one of the major themes of American public discourse. But beyond studies of British and classical discourse, it is important that we learn more about public address in today's emerging democracies to explore similarities and differences between newer and older democracies. We need to learn more about how public address functions in nondemocratic societies without a culture of deliberation. And in the contemporary world, we need to study global public address – the discourses of commerce, diplomacy, and politics that transcend national and cultural boundaries.

It is clear, then, that studies of paradigm cases of oratory are valuable, as are studies challenging the boundaries of the traditional canon. We need both. It is also clear, though, that the burdens of proof are different. For the scholar reexamining paradigm cases, the burden is to demonstrate that there is "news": that the new study truly adds to the available knowledge and insight, so that it warrants the allocation of scarce resources such as journal pages. For the scholar pushing the envelope, the burden is to demonstrate the broader significance of the new texts, showing that they warrant the attention of a wider audience rather than merely gratifying the scholar's personal interest.

I have spoken of a continuum between studying paradigm cases and "pushing the envelope." This continuum, however, should not be seen as synonymous with a continuum between "tradition" and "innovation." Innovative methods and approaches should be brought to the study of traditional texts, and vice versa. The choice between adding depth to well-examined texts and broadening our understanding of significant texts is not a conflict to be resolved but a tension to be managed productively.

Case studies or theory building

The preceding discussion raises yet another significant issue – the competing demands of disciplinarity and interdisciplinarity. That issue can perhaps be discussed in different terms, as the distinction between studying a specific case of public address and building broader generalizations. One option is the in-depth study of a specific case – an oration, persuasive campaign, social movement, or whatever other form it may take. The result is a richly textured understanding and analysis of the case, which is produced by a close reading of the text and careful grounding of the text in its historical context. What is produced might be regarded as a "theory of the case," a better understanding of a specific instance of rhetorical practice. The public address scholar who proceeds in this fashion engages in abductive reasoning – an inference from the facts of the case to what is proffered as the best explanation for them.[36]

Who will be interested in such a study? Beyond the scholar who conducts it, the project should be of interest to other scholars, perhaps from multiple disciplines, who are interested in the particular case. For example, a study of Lincoln's Second Inaugural Address might draw the attention of historians, political scientists, literary critics, theologians, philosophers, and compositionists, as well as scholars of public address. What the public address scholar contributes to this interdisciplinary community is an account of the text in *interaction* with the historical context, a unique kind of reading. On the strength of that contribution, the public address scholar is welcomed by that broader community and his or her work gains legitimacy and respect. Of course, this requires that the public address scholar become immersed in the extant scholarship on the case, from multiple disciplinary perspectives, so that the contribution is made from a strong knowledge base. The burden of this preparatory research is above and beyond the obligation to be competent in one's own discipline. It is the price of appealing to an interdisciplinary audience.

Yet within the discipline of rhetoric and communication, or even the specific subdiscipline of public address, the number of scholars with intrinsic interest in Lincoln's Second Inaugural (or any other specific case) is relatively small. An essay on Lincoln's Second Inaugural that is submitted to the *Quarterly Journal of Speech* or *Rhetoric & Public Affairs* must therefore intervene in a different conversation from the one imagined to occur among readers of the *Journal of the Abraham Lincoln Association* or *Civil War History*. What about the study should be of interest to scholars in the discipline who do not focus on this particular case? Answers might include that the study suggests models, exemplars, or normative standards of rhetorical practice, or that it offers perspective by incongruity that aids the understanding of more typical quotidian cases, or that it offers insight that may apply by analogy to other specific cases. Usually, though, the typical answer is that the study makes a contribution to theory. The scholar who proceeds in this fashion is reasoning by example, whether applying a generalization to a particular case or inferring from a specific example to a more general conclusion. For example, Lincoln's Second Inaugural might be offered as an instance of the Inaugural Address genre; a study of this text might confirm, modify, or challenge generalizations about the genre that have been put forward by others. Or it might be used as evidence from which to infer broader generalizations about American civil religion or the role of the president as a kind of "healer-in-chief." What is common to both approaches – applying and inferring generalizations – is that they connect the specific case to something broader than itself. The reason for doing so is to warrant the attention of readers interested in the broader issues but presumably not focused on the specific case.

The claim that public address studies should contribute to theory is sometimes misunderstood in an overly mechanistic way: that one should take a general theory such as Kenneth Burke's theory of dramatism or Richard Weaver's theory that sound rhetoric is grounded in a preceding dialectic,[37] map the terms and categories of the theory onto a specific case, and conclude that the theory applies to the case. This finding is neither surprising nor profound because these general theories offer broad world-views about how discourse works. Precisely because they are so general, they will apply across a very broad range of cases, so confirming them is not particularly noteworthy. More valuable contributions to theory will be made by studies of public address that extend or limit the reach of lower-level, falsifiable theoretical claims (for example, that ambiguity is harmful to rhetors in the long run).

Often, the demands of studying the specific case and of contributing to theory will pull the scholar in opposite directions. The temptation is great to slight one or the other – either to rely entirely on a few secondary sources for the historical context, focusing only on a theoretical issue, or else to assume that the significance of the case is self-evident so that no broader theoretical connection is needed, focusing only on the specific context. Either of these shortcuts will weaken the study and likely render it unpublishable. It is of no use to complain that needing to meet both demands is unfair. To be sure, there are some species of scientific research that simply take a theory and reaffirm it by applying it to an additional set of data. And there are some species of humanities research in which appreciation of the particular case is the end in itself. The predicament of public address (as well as other fields investigating situated practice) is that it sits astride both of these traditions and must speak to both. Rather than regard it as a burden or an albatross, however, we should see it as an opportunity for studies of public address to achieve both disciplinary and interdisciplinary impact.

Accounting for effects

A final example of a contemporary predicament is the need to understand and account for how public address achieves effects. Instinctively, we are convinced that public address does matter. Yet studies sometimes find that individual instances of public address make no difference. Even with respect to the US president, who presumably enjoys the greatest influence of anyone because of the bully pulpit, George C. Edwards III has assembled voluminous and impressive evidence to cast doubt on the claim that public discourse affects citizens' attitudes or behavior.[38] To be sure, these results may be consequences of examining only a single message or of defining "effects" too narrowly. We know that almost no one-shot attempt at persuasion will have much effect, and we know that the kinds of effect that messages can have are not limited to providing information and changing attitudes. But scholars of public address have not done much to advance a constructive argument about effects, even though they have been vocal in objecting to Edwards's criticisms. Worse, we have been sloppy in application of causal reasoning. Sometimes we infer both intent and effect merely from inspecting a text. Committing the intentional fallacy with abandon, we may describe textual characteristics as an "invitation" for an audience to respond in a particular fashion, and if we like the text, we may go on to assume that the "intended" or "invited" effects actually were achieved. And sometimes scholars engage in post hoc reasoning, knowing that certain things happened and inferring that they happened because of the public address that advocated them.

In explaining how messages have effects, we must come to a more sophisticated understanding of human agency. The expectation that individual messages could have significant effects is grounded in the assumption of nearly unlimited agency: Within very broad limits, a speaker or writer has the ability to influence how an audience understands a situation and acts upon it. The proclamation that public address makes no difference is grounded in the opposite assumption: that society is governed by large impersonal forces and that people play the parts assigned to them but are relatively powerless to influence things in any fundamental way. Most likely, the truth lies somewhere between these views and is an amalgam of both. The study of public address rests upon faith in human agency, in the belief that individuals make choices about how to represent themselves and their ideas in appealing to others, and in the conviction that these choices make a difference. Yet it is also true that over time, societies have been more the result of the working of complex systems than of unbridled individual choice. The ability to influence a complex system by an individual action is limited – though not altogether absent – and to believe otherwise may be to succumb to false consciousness. It is unlikely that the boundaries of human agency can be defined in advance; they will need to be worked out through prudential judgment in the analysis of individual cases. Public address scholars should neither absolve rhetors of responsibility for their individual actions by assuming that the course of events was completely predetermined, nor fault rhetors for failing to make choices that were not realistically available to them. Instead, we must develop a richer case-based understanding of *how* public address achieves effects – and what the scope of "effects" might be.

There are at least two promising examples of efforts in this direction. In an under-examined aspect of his exploration of fantasy-theme criticism, Ernest G. Bormann postulated that successful themes (heroes and villains, plot structure, and the like) "chain out" among an increasingly larger audience, eventually becoming generally accepted and serving as a filter through which individuals will understand and respond to their world.[39] For example, during the summer of 2009, the Obama administration suddenly found itself on the defensive with regard to the issue of health care. Opponents had spoken of the measure, probably inaccurately, as government takeover of health care, removing individuals' choice of doctors and insurance plans. These apparently false statements gained traction because of the strong suspiciousness of government that has deep resonance in American culture. A significant number of Medicare beneficiaries who were quite satisfied with their coverage reconciled the dissonance between supporting and opposing government programs of health care by contending, erroneously, that Medicare was not a government program. It is easy to see in this case how public discourse had effects. Rhetors used themes that resonated with audience values; listeners picked them up and conveyed them to others; and the ground of the health care debate seemed to change. One need not subscribe to all the tenets of fantasy-theme criticism to notice that the skillful selection of themes and touchstones can affect how people understand a complex situation.

Another promising approach, though there are yet few exemplars to which to point, is reception studies. Rather than make assumptions about effects from the text itself, reception studies are empirical or quasi-empirical reconstructions of how actual audiences understood and reacted to a text. Focus groups, questionnaires, interviews, letters to the editor, inspection of correspondence, and blogs are among the materials that reception studies employ. This is an obvious advance over the earlier practice of taking one or two editorials in elite newspapers as evidence of a response that is assumed to be widespread. Though they of course are easier to conduct for contemporary than for historical cases of public address, reception studies are not out of the question even for nineteenth-century discourse. One's understanding of Lincoln's Second Inaugural Address, for example, is enhanced by realizing that the speech was harshly criticized by some contemporaries because of its absence of specific proposals for Reconstruction.[40]

Failure to understand how discourse has effects is aggravated by a tendency among scholars to use causal language even though they are not establishing a causal claim. It is this misuse of language that Edwards rightly condemns, because it makes the public address scholar appear to be advancing claims on the basis of unsupported assertions. More precise language, confining claims to what can be supported, would enhance the credibility of public address scholarship.

The Paths Ahead

This essay began with a paradox: Despite a record of impressive achievement in public address scholarship, there is anxiety about the future. The discussion of current predicaments may make it easier to understand why doubt and uncertainty surround public address studies. They are fraught with seemingly fundamental questions for which there are no clear and definite answers. These are substantial predicaments but they should be sources of challenge, not discouragement. Too often, however, the response to them is either to let others narrowly define the scope of the field so that it is but a shadow of its real self and seemingly irrelevant to broader concerns, or else to divide the community of public address scholars by regarding the unresolved issues as binary choices separating what is appropriate scholarship from what is not. Instead, they should be seen as tensions to be managed on a case-by-case basis. It is simply not true that the field must choose between historical and contemporary topics, or between the reexamination of canonical texts and the recovery of the voices of the marginalized, or between historical and critical scholarship, or between individual texts and recurrent forms and genres, or between verbal and nonverbal discourse, or between locating agency in the speaker or the audience or the situation. Scholars of public address should follow their instincts and their intellectual curiosity down all of these paths.

As noted above, however, the scope of the field is vast and our numbers are relatively small. We cannot do everything. But our priorities should not be determined a priori but by the compellingness of the case – both the case we select for study and the case we make for studying it. If we shoulder the burden of arguing that there is "news" in a reexamination of the familiar or significance in "pushing the envelope," we can assess the value of specific projects and choose our topics accordingly. If we commit ourselves to research *programs* rather than unconnected individual studies, then we can hope for greater depth of development and the ability to make assertions with confidence. If our writing is accessible to interested others as well as to ourselves, and if our scholarly infrastructure makes others aware of our work, then we can augment our own numbers with the attention of like-minded colleagues in other fields and also bring to our work the additional rigor that results from scrutiny by an interdisciplinary as well as a disciplinary audience. Guideposts such as these should help us manage our contemporary predicaments while producing scholarship of increasing strength.

One caveat is needed, however, to this call for a wide-ranging pluralistic approach to reinvigorating public address scholarship. Since the 1960s, at least, the communication discipline has shown a marked preference for contemporary issues.[41] This has led to an imbalance in research topics that should be addressed by weighting the scale a bit more in the direction of the historical. This can be done collectively through such means as assuring that graduate seminars acquaint students with historical topics and exemplars, both for their own value and for the light they shed on contemporary issues. Incentives to produce strong historical scholarship can be provided through special issues of journals, conference presentation opportunities, rewards and recognition for such scholarship – all without denigrating the value of contemporary studies. This is not just a matter of keeping our roots alive, important as that may be. It also gives depth and comparative perspective to our observations about the contemporary. It involves us in an important interdisciplinary conversation. And as students invariably discover, the past is not as different from the present as we sometimes assume. History does not exactly repeat itself, but rhetorical situations come close to doing that. By examining historical situations on their own terms – as if we did not know how they would turn out, as though the issues were live controversies and contested terrain – we can engage in a rich and meaningful dialogue between the past and the present, strengthening our understanding of where our public culture came from and how it got from there to here. Engaging in that dialogue is one of the great rewards of studying public address.

Notes

1   Herbert A. Wichelns, "The Literary Criticism of Oratory," in *Studies in Rhetoric and Public Speaking in Honor of James Albert Winans*, ed. A. M. Drummond (New York: Century Co., 1925), 181–216.

2   William Norwood Brigance, *Jeremiah Sullivan Black: A Defender of the Constitution and the Ten Commandments* (Philadelphia: University of Pennsylvania Press, 1934);

and Bower Aly, *The Rhetoric of Alexander Hamilton* (1941; rpt. New York: Russell and Russell, 1965).

 3 William Norwood Brigance, ed., *A History and Criticism of American Public Address*, 2 vols. (New York: McGraw-Hill, 1943).

 4 Lester Thonssen and A. Craig Baird, *Speech Criticism: The Development of Standards for Rhetorical Appraisal* (New York: Ronald Press, 1948).

 5 Marie Hochmuth, ed., *A History and Criticism of American Public Address*, vol. 3 (New York: Longmans, Green, 1955).

 6 Martin J. Medhurst, "The Academic Study of Public Address: A Tradition in Transition," in *Landmark Essays in American Public Address*, ed. Martin J. Medhurst (Davis, CA: Hermagoras Press, 1993), ix–xliii; Martin J. Medhurst, "William Norwood Brigance and the Democracy of the Dead: Toward a Genealogy of the Rhetorical Renaissance," in *Rhetoric and Democracy: Pedagogical and Political Practices*, ed. Todd F. McDorman and David M. Timmerman (East Lansing: Michigan State University Press, 2008), 3–38; and Martin J. Medhurst's chapter within this volume, entitled "The History of Public Address as an Academic Study."

 7 David Zarefsky, "History of Public Discourse Studies," in *The Sage Handbook of Rhetorical Studies*, ed. Andrea Lunsford, Kirt H. Wilson, and Rosa A. Eberly (Thousand Oaks, CA: Sage, 2009), 433–459.

 8 Edwin Black, *Rhetorical Criticism: A Study in Method* (New York: Macmillan, 1965).

 9 Leland M. Griffin, "The Rhetoric of Historical Movements," *Quarterly Journal of Speech* 38 (1952): 184–188.

10 Ernest J. Wrage, "Public Address: A Study in Social and Intellectual History," *Quarterly Journal of Speech* 33 (1947): 451–457.

11 Loren Reid, "The Perils of Rhetorical Criticism," *Quarterly Journal of Speech* 30 (1944): 416–422.

12 Marie Hochmuth, "Kenneth Burke and the 'New Rhetoric,'" *Quarterly Journal of Speech* 38 (1952): 133–141.

13 Wayland Maxfield Parrish and Marie Hochmuth, "The Study of Speeches," in *American Speeches*, ed. Wayland Maxfield Parrish and Marie Hochmuth (New York: Greenwood Press, 1954), 1–20.

14 The first publication in this program was Karlyn Kohrs Campbell, "The Rhetoric of Women's Liberation: An Oxymoron," *Quarterly Journal of Speech* 59 (1973): 74–86. Her best known work is the two-volume *Man Cannot Speak for Her* (New York: Praeger, 1989).

15 See, for example, James R. Andrews, "Confrontation at Columbia: A Case Study in Coercive Rhetoric," *Quarterly Journal of Speech* 55 (1969): 9–16; Franklyn S. Haiman, "The Rhetoric of the Streets: Some Legal and Ethical Considerations," *Quarterly Journal of Speech* 53 (1967): 99–114; Robert L. Scott and Donald K. Smith, "The Rhetoric of Confrontation," *Quarterly Journal of Speech* 55 (February 1969): 1–8; Randall A. Lake, "Enacting Red Power: The Consummatory Function in Native American Protest Rhetoric," *Quarterly Journal of Speech* 69 (1983): 127–142; Molefi K. Asante [Arthur L. Smith], *The Rhetoric of Black Revolution* (Boston: Allyn and Bacon, 1969); and James Darsey, "From 'Gay is Good' to the Scourge of AIDS: The Evolution of Gay Liberation Rhetoric, 1977–1990," *Communication Studies* 42 (1991): 43–66.

16 See, for example, Robert Hariman and John Louis Lucaites, *No Caption Needed: Iconic Photographs, Public Culture, and Liberal Democracy* (Chicago: University of Chicago

Press, 2007); Gary L. Gumpert and Robert Cathcart, *Inter/Media* (New York: Oxford University Press, 1982); Martin J. Medhurst and Thomas W. Benson, eds., *Rhetorical Dimensions in Media: A Critical Casebook* (Dubuque, IA: Kendall/Hunt, 1984); Barry Brummett, *Rhetorical Dimensions of Popular Culture* (Tuscaloosa: University of Alabama Press, 1991); Robert J. Branham and Stephen John Hartnett, *Sweet Freedom's Song: "My Country 'Tis of Thee" and Democracy in America* (New York: Oxford University Press, 2002); Lester C. Olson, *Benjamin Franklin's Vision of Rhetorical Community: A Study in Rhetorical Iconology* (Columbia: University of South Carolina Press, 2004); and Irving Rein, Philip Kotler, and Martin Stoller, *High Visibility* (New York: Dodd, Mead, 1987).

17 See especially Richard Harvey Brown, *Society as Text: Essays in Rhetoric, Reason, and Reality* (Chicago: University of Chicago Press, 1987).

18 On ritual practices, see, for example, Marsha Houston Stanback and W. Barnett Pearce, "Talking to 'The Man': Some Communication Strategies Used by Members of 'Subordinate' Social Groups," *Quarterly Journal of Speech* 67 (1981): 21–30. For a study of monuments, see Victoria J. Gallagher, "Displaying Race: Cultural Projection and Commemoration," in *Rhetorics of Display*, ed. Lawrence Prelli (Columbia: University of South Carolina Press, 2006), 177–196. On collective memory, see Kendall Phillips, ed., *Framing Public Memory* (Tuscaloosa: University of Alabama Press, 2004). Concerning public culture, see Gerard A. Hauser, *Vernacular Voices: The Rhetoric of Publics and Public Spheres* (Columbia: University of South Carolina Press, 1999).

19 For example, Garry Wills, *Lincoln at Gettysburg: The Words that Remade America* (New York: Simon and Schuster, 1992); Harold Holzer, *Lincoln at Cooper Union: The Speech that Made Abraham Lincoln President* (New York: Simon and Schuster, 2004); Richard J. Tofel, *Sounding the Trumpet: The Making of John F. Kennedy's Inaugural Address* (Chicago: Ivan R. Dee, 2005); and Eric J. Sundquist, *King's Dream* (New Haven, CT: Yale University Press, 2009). There are many other examples.

20 Examples include Stephen Howard Browne, *Angelina Grimké: Rhetoric, Identity, and the Radical Imagination* (East Lansing: Michigan State University Press, 1999); Gregory P. Lampe, *Frederick Douglass: Freedom's Voice, 1818–1845* (East Lansing: Michigan State University Press, 1998); Robert Alexander Kraig, *Woodrow Wilson and the Lost World of the Oratorical Statesman* (College Station: Texas A&M University Press, 2004); and Robert E. Terrill, *Malcolm X: Inventing Radical Judgment* (East Lansing: Michigan State University Press, 2004).

21 For example, see Richard E. Crable and Steven L. Vibbert, "Mobil's Epideictic Advocacy: 'Observations' of Prometheus-Bound," *Communication Monographs* 50 (1983): 380–394; and William L. Benoit and James J. Lindsey, "Argument Strategies: Antidote to Tylenol's Poisoned Image," *Argumentation and Advocacy* 23 (1987): 136–146.

22 Representative examples include Jeffrey K. Tulis, *The Rhetorical Presidency* (Princeton, NJ: Princeton University Press, 1987); Richard J. Ellis, ed., *Speaking to the People: The Rhetorical Presidency in Historical Perspective* (Amherst: University of Massachusetts Press, 1998); Vanessa B. Beasley, *You the People: American National Identity in Presidential Rhetoric* (College Station: Texas A&M University Press, 2004); and Mary E. Stuckey, *Defining Americans: The Presidency and National Identity* (Lawrence: University Press of Kansas, 2004). There has been far less work on Congress and the Supreme Court, representing the legislative and judicial branches.

23   Examples include Alan G. Gross, *The Rhetoric of Science* (Cambridge, MA: Harvard
      University Press, 1990); and Leah Ceccarelli, *Shaping Science with Rhetoric: The Cases
      of Dobzhansky, Schrödinger, and Wilson* (Chicago: University of Chicago Press, 2001).

24   For example, see Michael Allen Gillespie and Michael Lienesch, eds., *Ratifying the
      Constitution* (Lawrence: University Press of Kansas, 1989); William Lee Miller, *Arguing
      about Slavery: The Great Battle in the United States Congress* (New York: Knopf, 1996);
      Garth E. Pauley, *The Modern Presidency and Civil Rights: Rhetoric on Race from
      Roosevelt to Nixon* (College Station: Texas A&M University Press, 2001); David
      Zarefsky, *President Johnson's War on Poverty: Rhetoric and History* (Tuscaloosa:
      University of Alabama Press, 1986); Robert Asen, *Invoking the Invisible Hand: Social
      Security and the Privatization Debates* (East Lansing: Michigan State University Press,
      2009); Gordon R. Mitchell, *Strategic Deception: Rhetoric, Science, and Politics in Missile
      Defense Advocacy* (East Lansing: Michigan State University Press, 2000); and Martin J.
      Medhurst et al., *Cold War Rhetoric: Strategy, Metaphor, and Ideology* (Westport, CT:
      Greenwood, 1990).

25   Examples of studies reflecting feminist perspectives are Susan Zaeske, *Signatures of
      Citizenship: Petitioning, Antislavery, and Women's Political Identity* (Chapel Hill:
      University of North Carolina Press, 2003), and John Sloop, *Disciplining Gender:
      Rhetorics of Sex Identity in Contemporary US Culture* (Amherst: University of
      Massachusetts Press, 2004). The essays in Charles E. Morris III, ed., *Queering Public
      Address: Sexualities in American Historical Discourse* (Columbia: University of South
      Carolina Press, 2007) reflect queer perspectives. On race as a fundamental category,
      see, for example, Thomas K. Nakayama and Robert L. Krizek, "Whiteness: A Strategic
      Rhetoric," *Quarterly Journal of Speech* 81 (1995): 291–309.

26   Stephen E. Lucas, *Portents of Rebellion: Rhetoric and Revolution in Philadelphia, 1765–
      1776* (Philadelphia: Temple University Press, 1976); Kenneth Cmiel, *Democratic
      Eloquence: The Fight Over Popular Speech in Nineteenth-Century America* (New York:
      Morrow, 1990); Celeste Michelle Condit and John Louis Lucaites, *Crafting Equality:
      America's Anglo-African Word* (Chicago: University of Chicago Press, 1993); Andrew
      W. Robertson, *The Language of Democracy: Political Rhetoric in the United States and
      Britain, 1790–1900* (Ithaca, NY: Cornell University Press, 1995); Stephen John
      Hartnett, *Democratic Dissent and the Cultural Fictions of Antebellum America* (Urbana:
      University of Illinois Press, 2002); Angela G. Ray, *The Lyceum and Public Culture in
      the Nineteenth-Century United States* (East Lansing: Michigan State University Press,
      2005); and Michael William Pfau, *The Political Style of Conspiracy: Chase, Sumner, and
      Lincoln* (East Lansing: Michigan State University Press, 2005).

27   Lewis E. Lehrman, *Lincoln at Peoria: The Turning Point* (Mechanicsburg, PA:
      Stackpole, 2008); Holzer, *Lincoln at Cooper Union*; Wills, *Lincoln at Gettysburg*; James
      Tackach, *Lincoln's Moral Vision: The Second Inaugural Address* (Jackson: University
      Press of Mississippi, 2002); and Ronald C. White, Jr., *Lincoln's Greatest Speech*
      (New York: Simon and Schuster, 2002).

28   John Channing Briggs, *Lincoln's Speeches Reconsidered* (Baltimore: Johns Hopkins
      University Press, 2005); Ronald C. White, Jr., *The Eloquent President* (New York:
      Random House, 2005); Douglas L. Wilson, *Lincoln's Sword: The Presidency and the
      Power of Words* (New York: Knopf, 2006); and Fred Kaplan, *Lincoln: The Biography of
      a Writer* (New York: HarperCollins, 2008).

29   Ronald C. White, Jr., *A. Lincoln: A Biography* (New York: Random House, 2009).

30 Tofel, *Sounding the Trumpet*; and Sundquist, *King's Dream*.

31 Representative of Campbell's many works are Karlyn Kohrs Campbell, "Stanton's 'Solitude of Self': A Rationale for Feminism," *Quarterly Journal of Speech* 66 (1980): 304–312; Karlyn Kohrs Campbell, "Gender and Genre: Loci of Invention and Contradiction in the Earliest Speeches by US Women," *Quarterly Journal of Speech* 81 (1995): 479–495; and Karlyn Kohrs Campbell, "Agency: Promiscuous and Protean," *Communication and Critical/Cultural Studies* 2 (2005): 1–19.

32 See Morris, ed., *Queering Public Address* (cited in note 25 above).

33 Cara A. Finnegan, *Picturing Poverty: Print Culture and FSA Photographs* (Washington, DC: Smithsonian Institution Press, 2003); Olson, *Benjamin Franklin's Vision*; and Hariman and Lucaites, *No Caption Needed*. For summaries of visual rhetoric scholarship, see especially Lester C. Olson, "Intellectual and Conceptual Resources for Visual Rhetoric: A Reexamination of Scholarship Since 1950," in *Sizing Up Rhetoric*, ed. David Zarefsky and Elizabeth Benacka (Long Grove, IL: Waveland Press, 2008), 118–137; and the special issues of *Argumentation and Advocacy* devoted to visual argument edited by David S. Birdsell and Leo Groarke: Summer 1996, Fall 1996, and Winter/Spring 2007.

34 Hariman and Lucaites set out to prove, in part, that iconic photographs "can operate as a legitimate form of public address." See Hariman and Lucaites, *No Caption Needed*, 40.

35 Cheryl R. Jorgensen-Earp, *The Transfiguring Sword: The Just War of the Women's Social and Political Union* (Tuscaloosa: University of Alabama Press, 1997); and Cheryl R. Jorgensen-Earp, *In the Wake of Violence: Image and Social Reform* (East Lansing: Michigan State University Press, 2008).

36 See Douglas Walton, *Abductive Reasoning* (Tuscaloosa: University of Alabama Press, 2004). Walton traces the concept of abductive reasoning to Charles Sanders Peirce.

37 Kenneth Burke, "Dramatism," in *International Encyclopedia of the Social Sciences* (New York: Macmillan, 1968), 445–452; and Richard Weaver, *The Ethics of Rhetoric* (Chicago: Henry Regnery, 1953), esp. 3–26.

38 George C. Edwards III, *On Deaf Ears* (New Haven, CT: Yale University Press, 2003). For an earlier statement of his position, focusing especially on rhetorical scholarship, see George C. Edwards III, "Presidential Rhetoric: What Difference Does It Make?" in *Beyond the Rhetorical Presidency*, ed. Martin J. Medhurst (College Station: Texas A&M University Press, 1996), 199–217.

39 Ernest G. Bormann, "Fantasy and Rhetorical Vision: The Rhetorical Criticism of Social Reality," *Quarterly Journal of Speech* 58 (1972): 396–407.

40 The reception of the Second Inaugural is examined briefly in White, *Lincoln's Greatest Speech*, 180–199; and Leah Ceccarelli, "Polysemy: Multiple Meanings in Rhetorical Criticism," *Quarterly Journal of Speech* 84 (1998): 400–402.

41 This preference is reflected, for example, in the call for contemporary scholarship in Lloyd F. Bitzer and Edwin Black, eds., *The Prospect of Rhetoric* (Englewood Cliffs, NJ: Prentice Hall, 1971), 222, 226. The committee report containing this recommendation noted, however, that the emphasis on the contemporary "is in no way meant to denigrate historical scholarship which is simply [*sic*] aimed at forming perspectives on the past" (225).

3

Rhetorical Criticism 2009
A Study in Method

Karlyn Kohrs Campbell

Yes, the title of my chapter is presumptuous. No, I do not promise a work of significance equal to the original. What I claim is that the persistent issue in rhetorical criticism today remains the same as it was in 1965 – method. Before I turn to the alternative Edwin Black proposed and offer a critique of current pedagogy, I want to rehearse part of our disciplinary history.

Disciplinary History

Rhetorical criticism is a relatively recent development in our disciplinary history,[1] linked to the trajectory of my professional career, so I shall make some personal references. The history of rhetorical criticism is important in understanding the problem of method. When I was a graduate student in the late 1950s and 1960s, courses in rhetorical criticism did not exist. We studied US and British public address, but speeches were not analyzed as texts; we focused on the speaker's biography and the historical impact of his – and I do mean his – speeches. Chauncey Goodrich's comments on great British parliamentary orators included some material on style and argument,[2] but the instructions for doing criticism derived from essays by A. Craig Baird,[3] Marie Hochmuth,[4] and Wayland Maxfield Parrish.[5] These essays reinforced the idea of speeches as works that emerged out of the lives and talents of individual speakers and in response to events of their times. They were worthy of study because of their impact on the controversies and events of the period in which they were delivered. The conception of oratory in the works by Herbert Wichelns[6] and the authors of essays in *A History and Criticism of American Public Address* was assumed,[7] and the accepted theory and methods were those described by Lester Thonssen and A. Craig Baird.[8] The publication in 1966 of the first textbooks on rhetorical criticism, by Robert Cathcart and Anthony Hillbruner, marked the emergence of courses in rhetorical criticism in our curriculum.[9]

Early scholarship was part of establishing a disciplinary identity differentiating speech communication from English and of gaining recognition and stature in academia for an area disparaged as practical and atheoretical – the teaching of public speaking. These works carved out a distinctive area of scholarship – oratory or public discourse – and described methods drawn from such revered classical authors as Aristotle, Cicero, and Quintilian, methods that were vital to justifying our disciplinary existence, providing communication with a historical pedigree, and responding to the attacks on rhetoric by philosophers influenced by the Platonic dialogues. These methods eschewed the close textual analysis that increasingly was dominating literary criticism.

If fledgling rhetorical critics learned textual analysis at this time, they learned it in literature courses, which had been transformed by the principles of *explication de texte*, a kind of criticism associated with John Crowe Ransom's *The New Criticism*.[10] Ransom proposed close readings based on I. A. Richards's studies of language and T. S. Eliot's critical essays; his perspective was spread by such textbooks as Cleanth Brooks and Robert Penn Warren's *Understanding Poetry* and Brooks's *Modern Rhetoric*.[11] These "New Critics" treated historical and biographical studies as extrinsic to the literary work and urged an intrinsic approach to texts as artistic works. They warned against the intentional fallacy, interpreting a work by the author's intent, and the affective fallacy, evaluating a work by its effects on an audience. In *Explication as Criticism,* W. K. Wimsatt asserted the textualist position: "explication *is* criticism; it *is* the evaluative account of the poem."[12]

Textual analysis also had roots in rhetorical scholarship. In one of the classics of nineteenth-century rhetorical theory, *The Philosophy of Rhetoric*, George Campbell captured the essence of textualism when he defined rhetoric as "that art or talent by which discourse is adapted to its end."[13] This definition identified the critic's task as analysis of the relationship between form – the choices that shape a literary or rhetorical work – and function – what that text is designed to achieve. Accordingly, rhetorical criticism could be applied to literary as well as other kinds of discourse, as illustrated by Wayne Booth's *Rhetoric of Fiction* and John Ciardi's *How Does a Poem Mean?*[14]

Edwin Black's *Rhetorical Criticism: A Study in Method* emerged in the midst of that conversation,[15] and it aroused mixed reactions from rhetoricians. Black identified the assumptions underlying the dominant paradigm, using as data the essays in the three volumes of *A History and Criticism of American Public Address*, which were published under the aegis of the Speech Communication Association. Black concluded that established methods consisted of classifying speeches into the Aristotelian genres, analyzing content in terms of the Aristotelian modes of proof, and assessing speeches in terms of the Greco-Roman canons of invention, disposition, style, and delivery. The primary evaluative criterion at the time was the effect of a speech on its immediate audience, consistent with Herbert Wichelns's injunction that rhetorical criticism "is not concerned with permanence, nor yet with beauty. It is concerned with effect. It regards a speech as a communication to a specific audience, and holds its business to be the analysis and appreciation of the orator's method of imparting his ideas to his hearers."[16] Black's conclusions were consistent with other critical and theoretical works.[17] The text, as an artistic work, was of lesser importance than the context, as illustrated by Marie Hochmuth Nichols's study of Abraham Lincoln's First Inaugural, which recreated the historical moment in vivid detail but offered little analysis of the speech itself beyond historical work documenting Lincoln's choices in creating the text.[18]

Black identified three fundamental constraints inherent in such methods: They prevented contemporary critics from fresh engagement with a speech from another era; they limited critics historically to the time of a speech's original delivery; and they limited evaluation to responses of the immediate audience. These limitations were challenged in Black's critique of John Chapman's address at Coatesville, Pennsylvania, on August 18, 1912, a speech heard only by a few, that lacked discernible immediate effects, and that was delivered by a man of quixotic character. Nonetheless, the speech was still able to speak powerfully to modern readers, a capacity that could be captured only by close analysis of the text, which Black described in generic terms as a morality play, an oratorical version of the earliest extant works of Western drama, such as "Everyman."[19]

Exposure to the theoretical and critical works of Kenneth Burke reinforced impulses toward intrinsic, eclectic, comparative, hermeneutic, and transformative studies involving bodies of discourse.[20] For Burke, all symbolic action is rhetoric, a conception that fostered rhetorical analysis of mediated texts, music, art, literature, photography, and film, as well as more traditional forms of symbolic action. Although Burke contended that his theory was an extension of, not a substitute for, Aristotle's works, dramatism offered an alternative mode of analysis that privileged language or symbols as more fundamental than argument and the identification or divisions prompted by symbols as more fundamental than overt efforts at persuasion. The possibilities of dramatism were illustrated in Burke's prescient analysis of Hitler's *Mein Kampf*.[21] Subsequently David Ling appropriated one element of dramatism, the pentad, to analyze Senator Edward Kennedy's apologia for the events at Chappaquiddick.[22] David Birdsell used the elements of the pentad to show how President Ronald Reagan's speech reframed the martyrdom of US marines in Lebanon through its conjunction with the invasion of Grenada.[23] The insights made possible by viewing events through a Burkean lens are apparent in studies of symbolic transformations by which a hunter in Maine was exonerated by a communally created mediated narrative after he had shot a woman hanging up clothes behind her home.[24] Similarly, Brian Ott and Eric Aoki traced the narrative by which Matthew Shepard's murder was similarly transformed into a story more palatable to a general audience.[25] Nathaniel Cordova used Burke's explication of the dialectic of constitutions to explain the constitutive character of the *Catecismo del Pueblo* as a covenanting document in the 1938–1940 senatorial campaign of the Partido Popular Democratico in Puerto Rico.[26] Similarly, Burke's notions of pure persuasion informed Lin-Lee Lee's analysis of "Women's Script" discourses in China.[27] Although dramatism offered an alternative mode of criticism based on language and its role in fostering the identification that unifies communities and energizes conflicts among different communities, I believe that relatively few critics adopted it as a perspective, in part, because of the complexity of Burke's theory and the originality required in its application.

The report of the 1970 Wingspread conference echoed Burke's enlarged view of rhetoric by asserting that "rhetorical criticism may be applied to any human act, process, product, or artifact which, in the critic's view, may formulate, sustain, or modify attention, perceptions, attitudes, or behavior."[28] Despite the report's emphasis on the importance of studying contemporary rhetorical action, on examining the transactional nature of rhetoric, and on expanding the range of objects for rhetorical analysis, the conference reflected the divisions in the discipline. As Marie Nichols observed, "one wonders if a sufficient amount of consensus existed among conferees about the reality of the present and of the possibilities of rhetoric for transforming it."[29] A powerful presumption in favor of civility and decorum persisted, but the power of symbolic transformations would come to be recognized in studies of rhetorics of dissent, confrontation, and difference.[30]

The trajectory of rhetorical criticism was changed by the turmoil of the 1960s. In 1966, I began teaching in Los Angeles at a school that was populated predominantly by students of color – chiefly African Americans, with significant numbers of Latinos and Asian Americans. The draft threatened my male students, and issues raised by the Vietnam War, Black Power rhetoric and the rise of the Black Panthers in California, and the counterculture were unavoidable. Accordingly, my students and I began to do analyses of contemporary discourse and, quite by accident, I became a public critic.

I shared an office with the program director of KPFK-Pacifica Radio, who overheard me working with students and invited me to present a rhetorical criticism as the editorial segment on the evening news hour. I offered a critique of President Richard Nixon's 1971 State of the Union address, and I was invited to continue that practice weekly. Eventually, 13 programs aired analyzing such diverse rhetoric as Jean-Paul Sartre's opening speech to the War Crimes Tribunal in Stockholm, George Wald's speech at the one-day work stoppage of scientists protesting the war, Vice President Spiro Agnew's attacks on the news media's criticism of presidential speeches, Nixon's State of the World message, Nixon's Vietnamization address of November 3, 1969, the Black Power rhetoric of Stokely Carmichael and others, and Paul Ehrlich's apocalyptic rhetoric on environmental threats. Subsequently, in *Critiques of Contemporary Rhetoric*,[31] I combined some of these with chapters on language, the critical process, and three broad critical approaches: deliberative rationalism (the dominant paradigm); psychological analysis emphasizing audience adaptation and effects; and dramatism. I focused on identification through language, ethical assessment of long-term effects, and genre as an interpretive way to identify similarities among discourses.

Eventually my published critique of Nixon's Vietnamization speech precipitated a dialogue with Forbes Hill about the role of the critic. The central issues addressed whether a scholarly critic, like me, should make political judgments about a rhetorical work or should instead follow a reading of Aristotle's *Art of Rhetoric* that confined the critic to the speaker's parameters (e.g., Nixon's choice of target audience and purpose).[32] The issue was never resolved between us; because rhetorical scholarship demonstrates over and over again that words have great power, no critic can avoid these issues. Are the material effects of discourse to be ignored, described, evaluated? Are we obligated to make moral judgments? Is it our critical responsibility to analyze issues, including assessments that call into question the claims of one or both sides?

Partly in response to this debate, I attempted to distinguish between what I called ephemeral and enduring criticism.[33] I conceived of my editorials on KPFK as ephemeral – that is, as responding with immediacy as a public critic to contemporary rhetorical acts. Influenced by issues about the relationship between criticism and theory, I defined enduring criticism, not by the objects analyzed, but as scholarship that was conceptual and contributed to theory – to larger understandings of how discourse works to achieve its ends. I now think those are tenuous distinctions; all criticism rests on a conceptual base and illuminates some dimension of symbolic action, whether it be the value of stock issue analysis of deliberative rhetoric or an exploration of the protean character of agency.[34] James Klumpp and Thomas Hollihan, Philip Wander, Michael McGee, Raymie McKerrow, Dana Cloud, and Stephen Hartnett,[35] among others, have contributed to this debate, and current attacks by David Horowitz and others on academics who participate in public debate keep this issue alive. Nonetheless, the analysis of contemporary political discourse remains a central part of critical practice, as illustrated by recent critiques of George W. Bush's rhetoric surrounding the Iraq War, and Barack Obama's keynote address at the 2004 Democratic National Convention,[36] among others.

During the late 1960s and early 1970s, I also gathered the scattered and ephemeral materials of second-wave feminism. My analysis of that rhetoric reinforced my discomfort with assumptions underlying traditional approaches that emphasized political leadership, celebrated logic, denigrated strategies with emotional impact, and failed to acknowledge audience differences in the reception of arguments.[37] That audiences differed dramatically was underscored by the year I spent teaching at City College, CUNY, in Harlem, where my students were overwhelmingly African American. My scholarship on women's liberation rhetoric, the rhetoric of Black Power, and anti-Vietnam War rhetoric convinced me that each movement for social change is distinctive, that no formula can be adapted to describe their differing dynamics, stages, structure, or leadership. Each such effort needs to be approached intrinsically to identify its distinctive challenges, membership, and internal workings, illustrated vividly by the special character of the American Indian Movement, and others.[38]

At the University of Kansas, Wilmer A. Linkugel invited me to co-teach the class he developed on women's rights rhetoric, and my exposure to woman's rights/ woman suffrage rhetoric was transformative, in part because none of my education had included my own history. Moreover, except for essays by Doris Yoakam and Linkugel and a book by Lillian O'Connor that had been all but forgotten,[39] there had been no critical response to the rhetoric of early women speakers. Ten years of research were needed to produce what became *Man Cannot Speak for Her*,[40] in which I integrated intrinsic readings of key works into a broad social movement analysis that included essential historical and biographical background. During this period I was the principal investigator on a grant to collect oral histories and other materials from members of the Kansas Association of Colored Women's and Girls' Clubs, many of which had been formed in response to the anti-lynching lectures of Ida B. Wells. That, in turn, made me aware of my ignorance of the civil rights activism of African American women, as well as of their participation in woman's rights and woman suffrage efforts.

Studying the rhetoric of the early women's movement and the second wave of feminism led me to develop concepts to describe the distinctive challenges women speakers face, challenges ignored in our critical history and challenges that persist. In the early movement, I identified a congeries of strategies that I called the "feminine style," strategies that attempted to diminish the hostility of audiences who believed that women should not speak in public, especially on controversial political issues.[41] These are, in effect, patterns of adaptation by which women speakers signal their adherence to traditional notions of femininity while violating those norms in rhetorical action. In describing the rhetoric of second-wave feminism as oxymoronic,[42] I noted the special problems of reception faced by women activists, observing that efforts to obtain basic citizenship rights were often transformed by audiences into scenarios imagining feminists making radical demands that threatened the foundations of society. Reactions to the vice presidential candidacy of Geraldine Ferraro,[43] and to the Senate and presidential campaigns of Hillary Rodham Clinton, provided further evidence of the persistence of this phenomenon. On January 9, 2008, for example, after Clinton had won the New Hampshire primary, Chris Matthews of MSNBC's *Hardball* disparaged her by stating, "The reason she's a US Senator, the reason she's a candidate for president, the reason she may be a front-runner, is her husband messed around."[44] As these instances demonstrate, all women political candidates face challenges arising out of a long tradition of sexism.[45]

Closely related to those challenges affecting women in politics are issues of sexuality. A significant addition to our critical literature is *Queering Public Address*, a collection of essays that explores the many ways in which "queer" experience has been suppressed and distorted in biographical work, psychological research, and historical studies, as well as the ways in which the intersection of race and sexuality results in erasure and oppression.[46] The anthology is notable for enlarging the circumference of our gaze conceptually and critically. These essays should prompt greater attention to the gendered and sexualized character of language in the public discourse of politicians and the media, including the repeated use of such terms as "wimps" and "girlie-men" to "feminize" ("queer"?) politicians (usually Democrats) by portraying them as incapable of tough decisions, particularly on security issues.[47]

Although much remains to be done in studies of language in US culture, our critical work is weakest where our linguistic competence and cultural knowledge are limited. Studies of race and culture, of intercultural dynamics, and of non-Western rhetoric and theory are poorly represented in our scholarship. Gerry Philipsen's analysis of a speech by Mayor Daley, Janice Watson's African American reading of Nelson Mandela's speech to the US Congress,[48] and Lin-Lee Lee's analysis of Zhao Ziyang's speech to the students in Tiananmen[49] are powerful evidence of the significance of cultural differences in interpretation and audience response.[50] Since Robert Oliver's early work on Syngman Rhee, the first president of the Republic of Korea,[51] only one essay on Korean rhetoric has appeared.[52] Xiaosui Xiao has published analyses of Chinese cultural reception of Western ideas.[53] Essays by Mary Garrett[54] and Lin-Lee Lee[55] have analyzed Chinese rhetoric from different periods produced by different groups, and Xing Lu has analyzed the rhetoric of the Chinese Cultural Revolution.[56] All of these works demonstrate the importance of linguistic and cultural competence in analyzing the public discourse in other languages.

In 1971, as largely white and male critics were struggling to respond to the assaults of civil rights, feminist, and antiwar activists, I made another attempt to define the essence of criticism, which I claimed was intrinsic to communication. I described the relationship between the activity of criticism and the discourse analyzed as "cannibalistic," and in what now sounds a bit like postmodernism, I suggested that criticism was the serpent in our communicative Eden that confounds our human desire for total spontaneity and transparency.[57] In effect, no symbolic act is complete without the critical role of another, suggesting that the symbolic act comes into being in the act of critical apprehension; we cannot act symbolically alone. Accordingly, I held that criticism was pervasive because human symbolization inevitably is reflexive – that as human symbols users, we are perpetually engaged in critical acts.

I identified two stages in the critical act, initial exposure to the symbolic act, which I described as pre-critical and linear, the sense in which we do not immediately apprehend wholes but experience symbolic action in sequence, encountering symbolic acts as they unfold, watching a film, or listening to a piece of music or a speech. From such serial encounters, critics then move toward a second stage, an apprehension of the whole enriched progressively by the knowledge that an experienced critic brings to it. In effect, we can recognize and interpret only what we already know. Through wide exposure critics train themselves to respond in ever more complex ways to works of art, pieces of music, films, television programs, photographs, speeches, and other forms of symbolic action. The critical act begins as perception of a pattern that emerges out of the details and coheres into some kind of interpretive structure or perspective. In some critical works, the perceived pattern is generic – a perceived version of the jeremiad,[58] a recognition of covenanting rhetoric,[59] identification of a eulogy for dead warriors, or the like. It can be conceptual – an illustration of the protean character of agency,[60] an illustration of the dynamics of political judgment,[61] or a group of metaphors that coheres into a scenario or that informs a movement for change.[62] It may be the confluence of strategies of enactment reinforced by repetition that produce enthymematic refutation, illustrated by the refrain in President Kennedy's "Ich bin ein Berliner."[63] It may be the recognition of a prophetic persona that makes sense of the choices of a particular rhetor.[64] On the most basic level, criticism is pattern recognition and creation.

The second stage, the cognitive dimension of criticism, is the sensitivity critics develop via experience and training that makes it possible to see what is distinctive, allowing for the creation of complex perspectives. Much of what critics need to know must be taught by repeated exposure to rhetorical acts and their interpretation. What Burke called "occupational psychosis" emerges in using methods that are fixed perspectives and formulas. Simplified ways of approaching texts that ease critical analysis become dangerously attractive. In effect, criticism must be polymorphous because rhetoric is polysemous; that is, rhetorical acts mean in many different ways and on many different levels. Differing analyses of the same rhetorical act are the clearest evidence for that claim. Cognitively, criticism always involves some level of evaluation, the most fundamental of which is the quality of performance. Was it fitting? How well did its form match its function? That process is facilitated by touchstones, outstanding exemplars by which we come to realize the possibilities of symbolic action. In sum, critical activity is at the heart of rhetorical studies, a view I still hold. Accordingly, my final efforts involve such evaluation.

All my professional experience has contributed to three conclusions: that our challenge is to enlarge our conceptual perspectives in order to incorporate the dynamics of gender, sexuality, culture, ethnicity, and race; that an emphasis on and privileging of methods is the enemy of insightful rhetorical criticism; and that the alternative to the dominant paradigm proposed by Black is one that ought to be considered seriously. In the remainder of this essay, I address the last two of these conclusions.

A Question of Method

In a 2001 special issue of the *Western Journal of Speech Communication* on the state of the art of rhetorical criticism, James Jasinski quotes Sonja Foss, who asserts: "Methods have been of central concern to rhetorical critics from the beginning of our discipline."[65] William Nothstine, Carole Blair, and Gary Copeland agree: "Method has been and continues to be of primary concern to most critics," adding that "many critics treat them [critical methods] as if they were equivalent to the analytic methods and instruments of science … as if they provided a direct and universal access bridge for the critic between 'data' and theoretical generalizations."[66] Jasinski demurs, disagreeing with claims "regarding the continued significance of method in rhetorical criticism" but agreeing that "method still dominates critical pedagogy."[67] The emphasis on methods is part of clinging to the status conferred by our classical heritage and a response to the milieu in which rhetorical criticism emerged, a period in which scientific advances were celebrated, and interpersonal communication scholars were attempting to develop theory and research that adopted procedures similar to those in the sciences. Humanistic impulses pushed us away from literary methods – we wished to be distinct from English departments and studies of literature – and toward formulas with the imprimatur of classical sources and toward imagining the critical process as analogous to the methods of science. Jasinski is correct in saying that an emphasis on method in critical practice has diminished, but he also is correct in his assessment that method still dominates critical pedagogy.

Accordingly, I would argue that there is a significant disjunction between the texts we choose to teach criticism and the kinds of critical practice we find praiseworthy. As humans, we seek to organize our worlds into categories, but the organization of textbook collections is at odds with the diversity of perspectives and the originality of the approaches evident in our critical practice. As an illustration, consider the tables of contents of the several editions of the widely used *Readings in Rhetorical Criticism*.[68] Even in the contents proposed for the new fourth edition, the opening section on the purposes of rhetorical criticism includes Wichelns's 1925 essay, Wrage's 1947 argument for rhetorical history, Parrish's 1954 survey of traditional lore, Bitzer's 1968 three-part formula for parsing rhetorical situations, and Black's 1965 analysis of the problems of the dominant paradigm and his analysis of Chapman's speech. These are followed by Black's 1970 essay on the ideological power of the metaphor "cancer of communism" and the audience it implies, Philip Wander's essay on the ideological turn to the critical study of ideas, McKerrow's essay on critical rhetoric as a means to undermine dominant discourses, and Thomas Nakayama and Robert Krizek's essay on the interrogation of whiteness. This is an odd selection of ways to parse the purposes of criticism. Are students to conclude that purposes change? Except for the works by Black, none of these is a model of criticism at work.

In a general sense, this collection concerns me primarily because its structure privileges methods and discourages recognition of the difficulties in viewing critical practice from this perspective. Instead of organizing critical works by category, as I see it, the ideal approach in a pedagogical anthology would be to introduce exemplary essays by calling attention to the many different critical traditions in which each participates. Let me illustrate. Much of what has been categorized as feminist criticism, for example, is really just analysis of works by or about women. For example, my own analysis of Elizabeth Cady Stanton's "Solitude of Self," included in earlier editions of the Burgchardt anthology, is a close textual reading that identifies the unusual lyrical structure of the speech, its apparently tragic perspective on human experience, and its existential and humanistic emphasis on creating those conditions that enable all to realize their capabilities. Yes, the speech was part of the rhetorical and political efforts for woman suffrage, but this does not make the critical perspective feminist. By contrast, Bonnie Dow's analysis of television coverage of the 1970 Women's Strike for Equality, not included in any edition of Burgchardt's volume, *is* a feminist critique because it views coverage of the march through a feminist lens. Dow shows the ways that journalists diminished the goals of the march by treating it as sheer spectacle, framed the march as absurdist rather than reasoned protest, and treated feminist goals as attacks on femininity, represented primarily by comments about women's bodies as a source of visual pleasure for males.[69] Even my much-praised essay on the rhetoric of women's liberation, now in a section of the Burgchardt text titled "Gender Criticism," is equally well described as a movement study, particularly in its claims that each movement's discourse is distinctive. It is also an attack on traditional theory as unable to capture the symbolic dynamics of this particular effort for social change (so why not include it in traditional criticism as a critique of that perspective?).

The new gender category of the Burgchardt anthology now includes Chuck Morris's essay on J. Edgar Hoover's sex crime panic, which prompts the question why Brian Ott and Eric Aoki's essay on media framing of Matthew Shepard's murder is not included here – or, given its focus on media narratives, why it is not in the section on narrative criticism?[70] The shifting of Dana Cloud's essay on biographies of "Oprah" from the feminist category to the category of critical/cultural studies underscores the problems of organizing by "method." Cloud's essay deals with myth and mythic narrative, the genre of tokenist biography in which individuals become personae as "tokens," and the ways in which such biographies contribute to liberal hegemony – a point significant for analyzing Barack Obama's autobiography and his keynote address at the 2004 Democratic National Convention as well.[71]

In the first edition of Burgchardt's anthology, the neoclassical category included Carroll Arnold's study of the forensic discourse of Lord Thomas Erskine, which I consider an outstanding example of generic criticism. Based on Erskine's practice, Arnold identifies highly praised forensic discourse as those speeches which invite juries and judges to make law, not just interpret it, a critical insight that helps to explain praise for some of the trial speeches of Clarence Darrow or for the outstanding forensic address of Susan B. Anthony in defense of her vote.

Also in that category, which now omits Arnold and is renamed "Traditional Criticism," is Forbes Hill's critique of Nixon's Vietnamization speech of November 3, 1969, an essay claiming that ethical evaluation of long-term effects or evaluation of the accuracy of claims are inappropriate, based on Hill's reading of Aristotle's *Art of Rhetoric*. Isn't this an important statement about the purposes of criticism, suggesting that it might be included in the opening section? Hill's critique is classical in the sense that its method is derived from the works of Aristotle, but only in its focus on immediate effects does it follow neo-Aristotelian method as described by Edwin Black.[72] In Hill's hands, the best rhetoric is a matter of skillful adaptation, selecting those arguments best suited to achieve one's goals with an immediate audience selected by the speaker. It is a form of criticism that focuses on adaptation to a specific target audience, aligning it most closely to studies of advertising, for example. These differences are an ideal venue for asking questions about the dominant paradigm historically and what shifts make some criticism *neo*classical or traditional.

The usefulness of making that move becomes even clearer with the inclusion under "traditional criticism" of Michael Leff and Gerald Mohrmann's analysis of

Lincoln's speech at Cooper Union, a close textual analysis of the speech, which the authors argue is best characterized as a campaign oration. Since the authors themselves state that identification of genre is basic to their analysis, it might be used either to discuss the purposes of criticism or categorized with other genre studies as an alternative to the "traditional" approach.

In earlier editions, the Burgchardt anthology included a section on ethical criticism, which included my original essay on Nixon's Vietnamization address and Black's essay on "the second persona," which is now in the opening section on purposes. Black begins his essay discussing the problems of moral judgment in criticism; in his analysis, however, he identifies a "verbal token of ideology" that "can be taken as implying an auditor who shares that ideology." The example developed is the "cancer of communism," as used in "the discourses associated with the Radical Right in American politics."[73] The essay includes a detailed analysis of the meanings of that metaphor as a horrible and incurable pregnancy, based on a view of the state as an organism, and inducing guilt by linking a terrifying affliction to the culpability of the diseased. Here, a metaphorical analysis that is also focused on ideology is obscured by its categorization in the Burgchardt collection.

In my view, the category of close textual analysis ought to encompass every essay to be studied as an example of criticism, and why this section was relegated to the penultimate position in earlier editions was puzzling. Now it is placed after traditional criticism. A candidate for this section is Hermann Stelzner's analysis of FDR's response to the bombing of Pearl Harbor, which deserves a special place here because it is a model of close textual analysis that considers carefully the impact of specific word choices on a speech's artistry, as well as its immediate and long-term effects. It also helps us to understand the speech's role in fostering attitudes that led to the incarceration of Japanese immigrants and citizens during World War II.[74] The essays by Michael Leff on Lincoln's Second Inaugural, which emphasizes the temporal/linear experience of a speech as delivered, and by Stephen Lucas on the style and argument of the Declaration of Independence, are also excellent examples of close textual analysis.[75] It appears that these essays are treated as examples of close textual analysis because they fit nowhere else, yet Leff's analysis is a study of the management of disposition, and Lucas's critique helps to explain why the argumentative structure of the Declaration made it such an attractive template for so many other manifestoes, including those of the abolitionists and early woman's rights advocates.[76]

A section on dramatism in the Burgchardt text implies that it is a distinctive method, yet Burke's analysis of Hitler's *Mein Kampf* is an ideological study that postulates that all totalizing ideologies adopt the essential forms of religion.[77] Both the study of the hunting incident in Maine and of the murder of Matthew Shepard focus attention on symbolic transformations, but both equally reveal the power of narrative – of the ways in which the communal, mediated shaping of a narrative can expunge guilt. The Ott and Aoki essay might usefully be paired with Black's analysis of the Coatesville Address as a morality play, a generic move in the Coatesville Address that attempts to preempt the trajectory of the narratives described in these essays. That, in turn, calls into question the rationale behind Burgchardt's separate section on narrative criticism.

My reactions to other categories follow similar lines. A critical essay focusing on the use of metaphor should be called into being by rhetorical works that pivot on the use of – or the challenge posed to – one set of metaphors by another set, such as occurred in Mario Cuomo's keynote address to the Democratic National Convention in 1984.[78] Kathleen Hall Jamieson's comparison of the metaphors used by Pope Paul VI with those used by Edmund G. "Jerry" Brown in his presidential primary campaign illustrates a way to understand institutional constraints and the discursive reach of archetypal metaphors in contrast to those drawn from contemporary popular culture.[79] By studying works in which a particular strategy is salient – enactment in President Kennedy's "Ich bin ein Berliner" or in Angelina Grimké's 1838 speech in Pennsylvania Hall, for example – students come to recognize such possibilities and see examples of their power. Still, critiques that call attention to these elements do not constitute a critical category of "enactment criticism."

One of the problems of categorizing is that whatever does not fit into currently fashionable categories is excluded. There are no essays in the Burgchardt anthology that focus on the rhetoric of the body,[80] and none that look at photography, although the essays and book by Robert Hariman and John Lucaites on iconic photographs have been significant in helping us to understand how such nonverbal forms work rhetorically.[81] Cara A. Finnegan's award-winning essay, "Recognizing Lincoln: Image Vernaculars in Nineteenth-Century Visual Culture,"[82] links photography to studies of vernacular discourse by Kent Ono and John Sloop[83] and by Samuel McCormick.[84] Catherine Palczewski's perceptive essay on the visual rhetoric of anti-suffrage postcards[85] would be enhanced if placed in dialogue with Nathan Stormer's analysis of the transformation of the body in E. C. Stanton's "The Solitude of Self."[86] No essays are included in the Burgchardt volume that feature the role of stylistic choices.[87] None call attention to imitation, the problems of satire, or the possibilities of irony; none focus on performativity as rhetorical action.[88] Obviously, anthologies are limited in size, but these omissions are significant.

I make these comments about Burgchardt's anthology precisely because it is the best available, and it is an attractive choice for a criticism text. Is it possible to imagine a pedagogical anthology or textbook that is not driven by method? Is it possible to create teaching materials that do not invite students to see methods as the essence of critical practice? I believe that it is, and in the final section of this chapter, I elaborate on that alternative conception of rhetorical criticism.

An Alternative

As a way to open an alternative conception of criticism, Edwin Black, like Kenneth Burke, turned to language. Underlying Black's book was this claim: "There will be a correspondence among the intentions of a communicator, the characteristics of his [*sic*] discourse, and the reactions of his auditors to that discourse ... to deny

that is to deny the possibility of language as we ordinarily understand that term."
As he described an alternative perspective, Black wrote that "when we find three
factors – strategies, situations, and effects – coinciding, this is a tolerably good
reason for suspecting that the three factors ... are really just three aspects of the
same thing. Rhetorical strategies refer to characteristics of the discourse; rhetorical
situations refer to extralinguistic influences on the audience; audience effects refer
to responses to the strategies in the situations." For Black, the rhetorical transaction was a synthesis of these three constituents.[89]

What has this to do with method and what might it mean? What we call language
requires a vocabulary, a syntax for combining these elements, and a community of
users among whom norms have arisen about usage, including notions of what is fitting and how best to express certain ideas and feelings. Situations, broadly understood, are all the conditions of human life that evoke symbolic responses, from the
simplest to the most abstract and complex.[90] Presumably, there is a significant amount
of recurrence in a linguistic community – of situations in which discourse is needed
and appropriate, of competent individuals producing such discourse, and of community members knowing how to interpret what is symbolized based on their linguistic competence and their understanding of community practices and norms.

Black invites us to think of all rhetorical action in these terms – which, of course,
is the basis for our recognition of the elements that prompt critical attention to
what is different: personae, arguments, structures, tropes, strategies, styles, and the
like. Presumably, situations will arise that evoke prophets and prophecy, that permit
enactment, that enable enthymemes, that call for eulogistic discourse, and so on.
The possibilities for symbolic action are legion, yet our capacity to recognize – even
to perceive what is being enacted – depends on comparison and requires a frame of
reference that enables us to discern when a particular kind of argument, a strategy,
or a metaphor is being used. On one level, then, criticism is, as Wimsatt claimed,
explication, decoding the complex message encrypted in a memorial, a speech, a
photograph.[91] On another level, of course, critics create symbolic castles out of
symbolic thin air – Lincoln's control of time, La Follette's melodramatic scenario,
Grimké's use of the personae of the prophet and of the biblical Esther, tokens of
ideology, and so on.[92] On the basic level, however, we are all practicing criticism
continuously; we are critics whose interpretations are tested daily against those of
our peers. Critics engaged in rhetorical scholarship are skillful artists whose creations are tested by a disciplinary community of peers who, based on shared *techne* –
talent and training – judge whether the castle is a mirage or a useful way to perceive
an instance of complex symbolic architecture.

Two terms complicate our understanding of Black's alternative. One is situation,
a term now so linked to Lloyd Bitzer's materialistic conception that understanding
"situation" in other senses becomes difficult. Situations are real, at least in the
sense that they are shared perceptions by groups of people. In some cases, they are
widely shared and their meanings are commonly held, but never entirely (recall, for
example, the intense disputes among Americans about the meaning of the events
of 9/11). Equally, they are unreal, conceptual, a product of a symbolic world that

we have created. Raymie McKerrow's critical rhetoric is intended as an attack on these unreal but hegemonic rhetorical creations by which we live our lives. Situation needs to be understood broadly as a symbolic context grounded in a community, whose limits we come to understand whenever our cultural incapacities are made evident, as when Gerry Philipsen unpacks the council speech by Mayor Daley that confounds us, or when Lin-Lee Lee helps us to comprehend why Zhao Ziyang's speech to the hunger-striking students in Tiananmen had such an impact.[93]

The other term is genre. Black's critique of the Coatesville Address and his descriptions of rhetorical transactions as responses to recurring situations were the beginnings of a way to think generically about rhetorical criticism.[94] Black defended such an emphasis, saying: "The neo-Aristotelians ignore the impact of the discourse on rhetorical conventions, its capacity for disposing an audience to expect certain kinds of justifications in later discourses that they encounter, even on different subjects."[95] What Black proposed combined close readings of texts with a kind of generic sensitivity based on repeated rhetorical transactions that emphasized a form–function relationship. Black claimed that within a linguistic community, situations recur, and rhetors will act in similar ways in order to achieve appropriate ends. The genres he proposed were loosely defined clusters scattered along a continuum, but his analysis of Chapman's address at Coatesville, which attributed its continuing power to its form as a morality play, proposed a distinctive understanding of generic analysis.

The recurrence of rhetorical transactions produces clusters that constitute genres. Black was very general in describing them, rightly recognizing the chasms of misunderstanding that concept makes possible. Plausibly, those clusters appear at points marking particularly disturbing communal events – transitions in leadership, births and deaths, war and peace. At base, recognizable types of discourse, like all other symbolic forms, enable us to interpret the behavior of others. The names given them become shorthand labels for certain kinds of symbolic moves – covenanting, jeremiadic warning, responding to accusations with an apologia, eulogizing the dead, sermonically interpreting sacred texts, and so on. In institutions, they are shorthand for the kinds of symbolic moves needed to maintain them.

As I read Black, rhetorical criticism is a more complex form of the interpretations we make of the symbolic action that surrounds us. We recognize questions, commands, requests, evasions. What attracts us as critics are the more complex symbolic acts, those that emerge under conditions of stress or transition in the community. Because these are the symbolic inheritance we seek to claim, we return to them again and again. The critical enterprise claiming the symbolic inheritance of Lincoln seems to be inexhaustible precisely because the challenges of claiming that inheritance are so great. That is true of all great writers and speakers, of iconic photographs, and of memorials, such as Maya Lin's Vietnam Memorial, which transcends the contentious debates of a particular historical moment to honor those who sacrificed for some larger cause.

Interpreting symbolic behavior in terms of a perceived form or type is a natural development because all criticism, whatever its theoretical bent, is based on comparison. Our ability to recognize any element of discursive practice relies on familiarity with other instances – of types of argument (e.g., a fortiori), kinds of structure (e.g., method of residues), strategies (e.g., refutation, enactment), forms of evidence (authority, testimony), tropes (metaphor, metonymy), and so on. Accordingly, criticism based on analogues, comparisons of similar types of speeches, such as the eulogies for warriors by Pericles and Abraham Lincoln,[96] or Reagan's ceremonial speeches at Bitburg and Bergen-Belsen compared to those at Omaha Beach and on D-Day,[97] are the natural outcome of the comparative foundations of critical analysis. Evaluation is, likewise, based on comparison. We derive norms for judging immediate and long-term effects from familiarity with the successes and failures of past efforts. We judge the artistry of rhetorical works by comparing them to those we consider models of excellence. We assess the ethical value of different works by weighing the principles espoused in comparison to others that might have been chosen, and we judge the truth and propriety of rhetorical works through comparison to outstanding exemplars. Moreover, the complex relationships between form and content at different levels of abstraction are essential to the ways in which we make meaning. Carolyn Miller explains that our ability to understand the form–content relationships created in communal practice is an aspect of our social competence. She writes:

> [W]hat we learn when we learn a genre is not just a pattern of forms. … We learn, more importantly, what ends we may have: that we may eulogize, apologize, recommend one person to another, instruct customers on behalf of a manufacturer, take on an official role, account for progress in achieving goals. We learn to understand better the situations in which we find ourselves and the potentials for failure and success in acting together. As a recurrent, significant action, a genre embodies an aspect of cultural rationality.[98]

Her conclusion emphasizes the ways in which social knowledge and language competence teach us how to adopt personae and to perform symbolic acts, both of which are essential elements in creating and interpreting the generic acts that are part of our daily life as well as our lives as critics.

Northrop Frye linked genre to such forms as "typical recurring images," "associative clusters," and "complex variables." He compared them to the *topoi* of rhetorical commonplaces and called them "communicable units" through which our experiences and feelings can be made intelligible to others.[99] Metaphors, repetition of key words or phrases, strategies of all kinds, and types of argument are all means by which we communicate our beliefs and values to others. The history and possibilities of generic rhetorical criticism as understood in 1978 were explored in the introduction to *Form and Genre: Shaping Rhetorical Action*,[100] the proceedings of a conference sponsored by the SCA Research Board. Subsequently, Kathleen Hall Jamieson and I began to study US presidential inaugural addresses, the speeches of ascendant vice presidents, and, finally, the recurrent types of discourse through which the US presidency is sustained and develops.[101] As critics were quick to point out, this kind of critical analysis was as vulnerable to cookie-cutter applications as were the neo-Aristotelian methods it was designed to replace. John Patton and Thomas Conley argued forcefully that generic analysis was reductive and formulary.[102] They were right; any critical procedure applied rigidly as a method becomes just that – reductive and formulary.

Generic analysis is not a method as that term is ordinarily understood. It is a kind of interpretive frame based on the ways in which language works in human interaction. What might become generic analysis begins with close readings of texts. These can be texts widely understood to be somehow importantly similar, such as eulogies, with the critic in a search of the key symbolic moves they share. Or a close textual analysis might lead to a generic claim, as occurs in Black's analysis of Chapman's Coatesville Address. That speech emphatically is not a morality play, but it works symbolically in ways that are similar to the transformations effected in and through morality plays. Once "seen" or interpreted in those terms, we can understand why and how the address is still able to speak to us.

Conclusion

As I view the current scene, there are two competing assessments of the state of criticism. On the one hand, there is good reason for pride in published critiques and in the excellence of the books that expand the range of criticism beyond what is possible in article-length works. In the area of presidential studies, I am impressed by works in the Library of Presidential Rhetoric series published by the Texas A&M University Press. I particularly commend the books on FDR's First Inaugural Address,[103] Jefferson's First Inaugural Address,[104] Kennedy's rhetoric following the Bay of Pigs crisis,[105] FDR's first fireside chat,[106] LBJ's 1965 voting rights address,[107] Reagan's speeches at Bergen-Belsen and Bitburg,[108] Reagan's eulogy for the crew of *Challenger*,[109] and the speeches delivered on Woodrow Wilson's Western tour.[110] They exemplify public address criticism that combines historical, contextual, and biographical information with close readings of texts, comparing such texts with related works. Although some elements of traditional methods appear in them, they avoid reductive and formulary perils because their focus is first and foremost on a specific presidential speech, which concentrates critical attention on the text rather than on any particular method of analysis. By contrast, as journal editors and reviewers acknowledge, there is a paucity of critical essays in our journals and the overall quality of submissions is low. One reason may be our critical pedagogy which, even at its best, privileges methods.

What I have tried to argue is that there are no methods other than the recurring patterns that inhere in and constitute our language and its use in human communities and cohere into complex symbolic works that amaze, delight, and sometimes horrify us. Our critical task is to possess these riches. Methods, as usually understood, become screens through which we view this symbolic world, and in most cases, these screens distort, alter, or damage what they are intended to explain and reveal. Black was right. There are no methods – only language and critics.

Notes

1 Although the earliest works presupposed rhetorical criticism as public address scholarship, some have argued that the historical study of public address was distinct from its critical analysis. See, for example, Barnet Baskerville, "Must We All Be 'Rhetorical Critics'?" *Quarterly Journal of Speech* 63 (1977): 107–116.

2 Chauncey A. Goodrich, *Select British Eloquence* (1853; Indianapolis: Bobbs-Merrill, 1963).

3 A. Craig Baird, "The Study of Speeches," in *American Public Addresses, 1740–1952*, ed. A. Craig Baird (New York: McGraw-Hill, 1956), 1–14.

4 Marie Hochmuth, "The Criticism of Rhetoric," in *A History and Criticism of American Public Address*, vol. 3, ed. Marie Hochmuth (New York: Longmans, Green, 1955), 1–23.

5 Wayland Maxfield Parrish, "The Study of Speeches," in *American Speeches*, ed. Wayland Maxfield Parrish and Marie Hochmuth (New York: Greenwood Press, 1954), 1–20.

6 Herbert A. Wichelns, "The Literary Criticism of Oratory," in *Studies in Rhetoric and Public Speaking in Honor of James Albert Winans*, ed. A. M. Drummond (New York: Century Co., 1925), 181–216.

7 William Norwood Brigance, ed., *A History and Criticism of American Public Address*, vols. 1 and 2 (New York: McGraw-Hill, 1943); vol. 3, ed. Hochmuth.

8 Lester Thonssen and A. Craig Baird, *Speech Criticism: The Development of Standards for Rhetorical Appraisal* (New York: Ronald Press, 1948).

9 Robert Cathcart, *Post Communication: Criticism and Evaluation* (Indianapolis: Bobbs-Merrill, 1966); and Anthony Hillbruner, *Critical Dimensions: The Art of Public Address Criticism* (New York: Random House, 1966).

10 John Crowe Ransom, *The New Criticism* (Norfolk, CT: New Directions, 1941).

11 Cleanth Brooks and Robert Penn Warren, *Understanding Poetry* (New York: H. Holt and Co., 1938); and Cleanth Brooks, *Modern Rhetoric* (New York: Harcourt Brace, 1949). Both works went through a number of editions.

12 W. K. Wimsatt, *Explication as Criticism* (New York: Columbia University Press, 1963), ix.

13 George Campbell, *The Philosophy of Rhetoric* (1841; Carbondale: Southern Illinois University Press, 1963), 1.

14 Wayne Booth, *Rhetoric of Fiction* (Chicago: University of Chicago Press, 1961); John Ciardi, *How Does a Poem Mean?* (Boston: Houghton Mifflin, 1957); and M. H. Abrams, *A Glossary of Literary Terms*, 3rd ed. (New York: Holt, Rinehart, and Winston, 1971), 147–149.

15 Edwin Black, *Rhetorical Criticism: A Study in Method* (New York: Macmillan, 1965).

16 Wichelns, "The Literary Criticism of Oratory," 212.

17 See also Marie Hochmuth Nichols, "Approaches to the Study of Public Address," in her *Rhetoric and Criticism* (Baton Rouge: Louisiana State University Press, 1963), 49–78.

18 "Lincoln's First Inaugural," in *American Speeches*, ed. Parrish and Hochmuth, 60–100.

19 *Everyman: A Morality Play* (New York: J. F. Taylor & Co., 1903).

20 A paperback that combined *A Grammar of Motives* and *A Rhetoric of Motives* (Cleveland & New York: Meridian Books, 1962) was particularly influential.

21 Kenneth Burke, "The Rhetoric of Hitler's 'Battle,'" in *The Philosophy of Literary Form*, 2nd ed. (1941; Baton Rouge: Louisiana State University Press, 1967), 191–220.

22 David A. Ling, "A Pentadic Analysis of Senator Edward Kennedy's Address to the People of Massachusetts, July 25, 1969," *Central States Speech Journal* 21 (1970): 81–86.

23 David S. Birdsell, "Ronald Reagan on Lebanon and Grenada: Flexibility and Interpretation in the Application of Kenneth Burke's Pentad," *Quarterly Journal of Speech* 73 (1987): 267–279.

24 Mari Boor Tonn, Valerie A. Endress, and John N. Diamond, "Hunting and Heritage on Trial in Maine: A Dramatistic Debate over Tragedy, Tradition, and Territory," *Quarterly Journal of Speech* 79 (1993): 165–181.

25 Brian L. Ott and Eric Aoki, "The Politics of Negotiating Public Tragedy: Media Framing of the Matthew Shepard Murder," *Rhetoric & Public Affairs* 5 (2002): 483–505.

26 Nathaniel Cordova, "The Constitutive Force of the *Catecismo del Pueblo* in Puerto Rico's Popular Democratic Party Campaign of 1938–1940," *Quarterly Journal of Speech* 90 (2004): 212–223.

27 Lin-Lee Lee, "Pure Persuasion: A Case Study of *Nüshu* or 'Women's Script' Discourse," *Quarterly Journal of Speech* 90 (2004): 403–421.

28 Lloyd F. Bitzer and Edwin Black, eds., *The Prospect of Rhetoric* (Englewood Cliffs, NJ: Prentice Hall, 1971), 220.

29 Marie Hochmuth Nichols, in Robert E. Nebergall and Marie Hochmuth Nichols, "Two Windows on 'The Prospect of Rhetoric,' " *Quarterly Journal of Speech* 58 (1972): 88–96. Quoted material on 96.

30 See, for example, Parke B. Burgess, "The Rhetoric of Black Power: A Moral Demand?" *Quarterly Journal of Speech* 54 (1968): 122–133, and "The Racial Crisis: Intolerable Conflict Versus Democratic Violence," *Quarterly Journal of Speech* 55 (1969): 318–324; Robert L. Scott and Donald K. Smith, "The Rhetoric of Confrontation," *Quarterly Journal of Speech* 55 (1969): 1–8; and Molefi K. Asante [Arthur L. Smith], *Rhetoric of Black Revolution* (Boston: Allyn and Bacon, 1969).

31 Karlyn Kohrs Campbell, *Critiques of Contemporary Rhetoric* (Belmont, CA: Wadsworth, 1972).

32 Forbes Hill, "Conventional Wisdom – Traditional Form: The President's Message of November 3, 1969," *Quarterly Journal of Speech* 58 (1972): 373–386; also *Forum* 58 (1972): 451–454. See also Robert P. Newman, "Under the Veneer: Nixon's Vietnam Speech of November 3, 1969," *Quarterly Journal of Speech* 56 (1970): 168–178.

33 Karlyn Kohrs Campbell, "Criticism: Ephemeral and Enduring," *Speech Teacher* 23 (1974): 9–14.

34 Karlyn Kohrs Campbell, "Agency: Promiscuous and Protean," *Communication and Critical/Cultural Studies* 2 (2005): 1–19.

35 James F. Klumpp and Thomas A. Hollihan, "Rhetorical Criticism as Moral Action," *Quarterly Journal of Speech* 75 (1989): 84–97; Philip Wander, "The Ideological Turn in Modern Criticism," *Central States Speech Journal* 34 (1983): 1–18; Michael Calvin McGee, "The 'Ideograph': A Link Between Rhetoric and Ideology," *Quarterly Journal of Speech* 66 (1980): 1–18; Raymie McKerrow, "Critical Rhetoric: Theory and Praxis," *Communication Monographs* 56 (1989): 91–111; Dana Cloud, " 'To Veil the Threat of Terror': Afghan Women and the 'Clash of Civilizations' in the Imagery of the US War on Terrorism," *Quarterly Journal of Speech* 90 (2004): 285–306; Stephen Hartnett and D. Larson, " 'Tonight Another Man Will Die': Crime, Violence, and the Master Tropes of Contemporary Arguments about the Death Penalty," *Communication and Critical Cultural Studies* 3 (2006): 263–287.

36 Denise Bostdorff, "George W. Bush's Post-September 11 Rhetoric of Covenant Renewal," *Quarterly Journal of Speech* 89 (2003): 293–319; special issue guest edited by Herbert Simon on rhetoric and the war in Iraq, *Rhetoric & Public Affairs* 10 (Summer 2007); Robert C. Rowland and John M. Jones, "Recasting the American Dream and American Politics: Barack Obama's Keynote Address to the 2004 Democratic National Convention," *Quarterly Journal of Speech* 93 (2007): 425–448.

37 See Leah Ceccarelli, "Polysemy: Multiple Meaning in Rhetorical Criticism," *Quarterly Journal of Speech* 84 (1998): 395–415.

38 Randall Lake, "Enacting Red Power: The Consummatory Function in Native American Protest Rhetoric," *Quarterly Journal of Speech* 69 (1983): 127–142; Kevin DeLuca and Jennifer Peeples, "From Public Sphere to Public Screen: Democracy, Activism, and the 'Violence' of Seattle," *Critical Studies in Media Communication* 19 (2002): 125–151.

39 Doris Yoakam, "Woman's Introduction to the American Platform," in *A History and Criticism*, ed. Brigance, 1: 153–193; "Susan B. Anthony," in *A History and Criticism*, ed. Hochmuth, 3: 97–132; Lillian O'Connor, *Pioneer Women Orators: Rhetoric in the Antebellum Reform Movement* (New York: Columbia University Press, 1954); and Wil A. Linkugel, "The Woman Suffrage Argument of Anna Howard Shaw," *Quarterly Journal of Speech* 49 (1963): 165–174.

40 Karlyn Kohrs Campbell, *Man Cannot Speak for Her*, 2 vols. (Westport, CT: Praeger, 1989).

41 See Campbell, *Man Cannot Speak for Her*; and Bonnie J. Dow and Mari Boor Tonn, "'Feminine Style' and Political Judgment in the Rhetoric of Ann Richards," *Quarterly Journal of Speech* 79 (1993): 286–302.

42 Karlyn Kohrs Campbell, "The Rhetoric of Women's Liberation: An Oxymoron," *Quarterly Journal of Speech* 59 (1973): 74–86.

43 Karlyn Kohrs Campbell and E. Clair Jerry, "Woman and Speaker: A Conflict in Roles," in *Seeing Female: Social Roles and Personal Lives*, ed. Sharon Brehm (Westport, CT: Greenwood Press, 1988), 123–133.

44 *Minneapolis Star Tribune*, January 10, 2008, A15.

45 Kathleen Hall Jamieson, *Beyond the Double Bind: Women and Leadership* (New York: Oxford University Press, 1995).

46 Charles E. Morris III, ed., *Queering Public Address: Sexualities in American Historical Discourse* (Columbia: University of South Carolina Press, 2007).

47 Rebecca A. Kuehl, "Wimps, Wusses, and Girlie-Men: The Democratic Party as Feminized 'Other' in Post 9/11 US Politics," paper presented at the NCA Convention, 2007.

48 Janice Watson, "In Search of a Hero: An African American Interpretation of Nelson Mandela's Address to Congress," in *Critiques of Contemporary Rhetoric*, 2nd ed., ed. Karlyn Kohrs Campbell and Thomas R. Burkholder (Belmont, CA: Wadsworth, 1997), 241–265.

49 Lin-Lee Lee, "Zhao Ziyang's Plea to the Students in Tiananmen Square," in *Critiques of Contemporary Rhetoric*, 2nd ed., ed. Campbell and Burkholder, 216–233.

50 Gerry Philipsen, "Mayor Daley's Council Speech: A Cultural Analysis," *Quarterly Journal of Speech* 72 (1986): 247–260; see notes 41 and 42.

51 Robert T. Oliver, *Syngman Rhee: The Man and the Myth* (New York: Dodd, Mead, 1954).

52 Sangchul Lee and Karlyn Kohrs Campbell, "Korean President Roh Tae-woo's 1988 Inaugural Address: Campaigning for Investiture," *Quarterly Journal of Speech* 80 (1994): 37–52.

53 Xiaosui Xiao, "China Encounters Darwinism: A Case of Intercultural Rhetoric," *Quarterly Journal of Speech* 81 (1995): 83–99; and "The 1923 Scientistic Campaign and Dao Discourse: A Cross-Cultural Study of the Rhetoric of Science," *Quarterly Journal of Speech* 90 (2004): 469–494.

54 Mary Garrett, "*Pathos* Reconsidered from the Perspective of Classical Chinese Rhetorics," *Quarterly Journal of Speech* 79 (1993): 19–39.

55 Lin-Lee Lee, "Pure Persuasion."

56 Xing Lu, *The Rhetoric of the Chinese Cultural Revolution* (Columbia: University of South Carolina Press, 2004).

57 In "The Rhetorical Situation," *Philosophy & Rhetoric* 1 (1968): 1–14, Lloyd Bitzer concludes: "In the best of all possible worlds, there would be communication perhaps, but no rhetoric" (14).

58 See John M. Murphy, "A Time of Shame and Sorrow: Robert F. Kennedy and the American Jeremiad," *Quarterly Journal of Speech* 76 (1990): 401–414.

59 See Bostdorff, "George W. Bush's Post-September 11 Rhetoric of Covenant Renewal."

60 Campbell, "Agency: Promiscuous and Protean."

61 John M. Murphy, "The Light of Reason: Robert F. Kennedy on Vietnam," in *Critiques of Contemporary Rhetoric*, 2nd ed., ed. Campbell and Burkholder, 168–189.

62 Carl R. Burgchardt, "Discovering Rhetorical Imprints: La Follette, 'Iago,' and the Melodramatic Scenario," *Quarterly Journal of Speech* 71 (1985): 441–456. See also Sara Hayden, "Family Metaphors and the Nation: Promoting a Politics of Care through the Million Mom March," *Quarterly Journal of Speech* 89 (2003): 196–215; and James P. McDaniel, "Figures for New Frontiers: From Davy Crockett to Cyberspace Gurus," *Quarterly Journal of Speech* 88 (2002): 91–111.

63 Karlyn Kohrs Campbell and Kathleen Hall Jamieson, "Introduction," in *Form and Genre: Shaping Rhetorical Action* (Falls Church, VA: Speech Communication Association, 1978), 18–19.

64 James Darsey, *The Prophetic Tradition and Radical Rhetoric in America* (New York: New York University Press, 1997); and Phyllis Japp, "Esther or Isaiah? The Abolitionist-Feminist Rhetoric of Angelina Grimké," *Quarterly Journal of Speech* 71 (1985): 335–348.

65 Sonja K. Foss, "Constituted by Agency: The Discourse and Practice of Rhetorical Criticism," in *Speech Communication: Essays to Commemorate the 75th Anniversary of SCA*, ed. Gerald M. Philips and Julia T. Wood (Carbondale: Southern Illinois University Press, 1990), 36–37.

66 William L. Nothstine, Carole Blair, and Gary A. Copeland, *Critical Questions: Invention, Creativity, and the Criticism of Discourse and Media* (New York: St. Martin's Press, 1994), 39–40.

67 James Jasinski, "The State of Theory and Method in Rhetorical Criticism," *Western Journal of Speech Communication* 65 (2001): 249–270. Quoted material on 268 n.22.

68 Carl Burgchardt, ed., *Readings in Rhetorical Criticism* (State College, PA: Strata, 1995, 2000, 2005). Three editions have been published; I also have received the proposed contents of a fourth edition.

69 Bonnie J. Dow, "Spectacle, Spectatorship, and Gender Anxiety in Television News Coverage of the 1970 Women's Strike for Equality," *Communication Studies* 50 (1999): 143–157.

70 Ott and Aoki, "The Politics of Negotiating Public Tragedy."

71 Rowland and Jones, "Recasting the American Dream and American Politics."

72 Hill notes that he is attempting "a critique that re-interprets neo-Aristotelianism slightly" (374). If, as Hill notes, "neo-Aristotelian criticism does not warrant us to estimate the truth of Nixon's statements or the reality of the values he assumes as aspects of American life" (385), then how, if at all, does Aristotle's approach to rhetoric differ from that of the sophists as attacked by Plato and Isocrates? Consider whether this reading is consistent with the treatment of the *pisteis* in Thonssen and Baird, *Speech Criticism*, or in the critical essays in the three volumes of *A History and Criticism of American Public Address*.

73 Edwin Black, "The Second Persona," *Quarterly Journal of Speech* 56 (1970): 109–119. Quoted material on 191, 192.

74 Hermann G. Stelzner, " 'War Message,' December 8, 1941: An Approach to Language," *Communication Monographs* 33 (1966): 419–437.

75 Michael Leff, "Dimensions of Temporality in Lincoln's Second Inaugural," *Communication Reports* 1 (1988): 26–31; and Stephen E. Lucas, "The Stylistic Artistry of the Declaration of Independence," *Prologue: Quarterly of the National Archives* 22 (1990): 25–43.

76 See Philip S. Foner, ed., *We, the Other People: Alternative Declarations of Independence by Labor Groups, Farmers, Woman's Rights Advocates, Socialists, and Blacks, 1829–1975* (Urbana: University of Illinois Press, 1976).

77 Burke, "The Rhetoric of Hitler's 'Battle.' "

78 David Henry, "The Rhetorical Dynamics of Mario Cuomo's 1984 Keynote Address: Situation, Speaker, Metaphor," *Southern Speech Communication Journal* 53 (1988): 105–120.

79 Kathleen Hall Jamieson, "The Metaphoric Cluster in the Rhetoric of Pope Paul VI and Edmund G. Brown Jr.," *Quarterly Journal of Speech* 66 (1980): 51–72. For a study of audience reception, see Celeste M. Condit et al., "Recipes or Blueprints for our Genes: How Contexts Selectively Activate Multiple Meanings of Metaphors," *Quarterly Journal of Speech* 88 (2002): 303–325.

80 See, for example, Nathan Stormer, "In Living Memory: Abortion as Cultural Memory," *Quarterly Journal of Speech* 88 (2002): 265–283.

81 See Robert Hariman and John Lucaites, *No Caption Needed: Iconic Photographs, Public Culture, and Liberal Democracy* (Chicago: University of Chicago Press, 2007).

82 Cara A. Finnegan, "Recognizing Lincoln: Image Vernaculars in Nineteenth-Century Visual Culture," *Rhetoric & Public Address* 8 (2005): 31–58.

83 Kent A. Ono and John M. Sloop, "The Critique of Vernacular Discourse," *Communication Monographs* 62 (1995): 19–46.

84 Samuel McCormick, "Earning One's Inheritance: Rhetorical Criticism, Everyday Talk, and the Analysis of Public Discourse," *Quarterly Journal of Speech* 89 (2003): 109–131.

85 Catherine H. Palczewski, "The Male Madonna and the Feminine Uncle Sam: Visual Argument, Icons, and Ideographs in 1909 Anti-Woman Suffrage Postcards," *Quarterly Journal of Speech* 91 (2005): 365–394.

86 Nathan Stormer, "Embodied Humanism: Performative Argument for Natural Rights in 'The Solitude of Self,' " *Argumentation and Advocacy* 36 (1999): 51–64.

87 See, for example, Stephen Hartnett, "Fanny Fern's 1855 *Ruth Hall*, The Cheerful Brutality of Capitalism, and the Irony of Sentimental Rhetoric," *Quarterly Journal of Speech* 88 (2002): 1–18.

88 See, for example, Susan Zaeske, "Signatures of Citizenship: The Rhetoric of Women's Antislavery Petitions," *Quarterly Journal of Speech* 88 (2002): 209–227.

89   Black, *Rhetorical Criticism*, 16, 134, 135.

90   In particular, see Carolyn Miller, "Genre as Social Action," *Quarterly Journal of Speech* 70 (1984): 151–167.

91   Wimsatt, *Explication as Criticism*, ix.

92   Leff, "Dimensions of Temporality in Lincoln's Second Inaugural"; Burgchardt, "Discovering Rhetorical Imprints"; Japp, "Esther or Isaiah"; and Black, "Second Persona."

93   Lin-Lee Lee, "Zhao Ziyang's Plea to the Students in Tiananmen Square."

94   In practices that preceded Black's book, generic criticism had coincided with close readings of texts, even when the genres were Aristotelian. Harold Zyskind, for example, attempted to determine whether the Gettysburg Address was best understood as epideictic or deliberative rhetoric. He asserted that the value of generic classification could be tested by asking, "Are the meaning and purpose of the Address – in its uniqueness – in any way illuminated by an analysis of it as belonging to that genre?" "A Rhetorical Analysis of the Gettysburg Address," *Journal of General Education* 4 (1950): 202–212. Quoted material on 202.

95   Black, *Rhetorical Criticism*, 35.

96   Garry Wills, *Lincoln at Gettysburg: The Words that Remade America* (New York: Simon and Schuster, 1992), 41–62.

97   Richard J. Jensen, *Reagan at Bergen-Belsen and Bitburg* (College Station: Texas A&M University Press, 2007).

98   Miller, "Genre as Social Action," 165.

99   Northrop Frye, *Anatomy of Criticism: Four Essays* (Princeton, NJ: Princeton University Press, 1957), 99; see also 95–115, 245.

100 Campbell and Jamieson, *Form and Genre*.

101 Karlyn Kohrs Campbell and Kathleen Hall Jamieson, *Deeds Done in Words: Presidential Rhetoric and the Genres of Governance* (Chicago: University of Chicago Press, 1990); and Campbell and Jamieson, *Presidents Creating the Presidency: Deeds Done in Words* (Chicago: University of Chicago Press, 2008).

102 John H. Patton, "Generic Criticism: Typology at an Inflated Price," *Rhetoric Society Quarterly* 6 (1976): 5; and Thomas M. Conley, "Ancient Rhetoric and Modern Genre Criticism," *Communication Quarterly* 27 (1979): 53. See also his review of *Form and Genre* in *Communication Quarterly* 26 (1978): 71–75.

103 Davis W. Houck, *FDR and Fear Itself: The First Inaugural Address* (College Station: Texas A&M University Press, 2002).

104 Stephen Howard Browne, *Jefferson's Call for Nationhood* (College Station: Texas A&M University Press, 2003).

105 Thomas W. Benson, *Writing JFK: Presidential Rhetoric and the Press in the Bay of Pigs Crisis* (College Station: Texas A&M University Press, 2004).

106 Amos Kiewe, *FDR's First Fireside Chat: Public Confidence and the Banking Crisis* (College Station: Texas A&M University Press, 2007).

107 Garth E. Pauley, *LBJ's American Promise: The 1965 Voting Rights Address* (College Station: Texas A&M University Press, 2007).

108 Jensen, *Reagan at Bergen-Belsen and Bitburg*.

109 Mary E. Stuckey, *Slipping the Surly Bonds: Reagan's Challenger Address* (College Station: Texas A&M University Press, 2006).

110 J. Michael Hogan, *Woodrow Wilson's Western Tour: Rhetoric, Public Opinion, and the League of Nations* (College Station: Texas A&M University Press, 2006).

Part II

Basic Research in Rhetoric and Public Address

4

Textual Recovery, Textual Discovery
Returning to Our Past, Imagining Our Future

Davis W. Houck

On a cold, dark night in January 2006, I sat in a church parking lot in Indianola, Mississippi, with a graduate student from Florida State University. We were just a bit apprehensive as we watched parishioners head to their cars following Wednesday evening services. Slowly, perhaps cautiously, a middle-aged black woman approached our vehicle. "Could I help you?" she asked. "Yes, ma'am," I replied, "we're here to meet with Charles McLaurin. We were supposed to meet him here at 7 o'clock." Her countenance softened noticeably. "Oh, Mr. Mac, I just saw his wife. I'm sure he'll be here soon." With that she was off with a car full of kids.

As we exited our car and began to unload our recording equipment, I noticed a stocky black man walking purposefully toward us. We met in the middle of the parking lot: "Mr. Mac?" I asked. He didn't bother to shake my outstretched hand; instead, he gave me a bear hug: "Hey brother, it's good to finally meet you." A legendary organizer and field secretary for the Student Nonviolent Coordinating Committee (SNCC) embracing me as his "brother"? The man who was Fannie Lou Hamer's personal escort around the Mississippi Delta? Brother!?

The town of Indianola sits in the heart of the Mississippi Delta, a fertile alluvial plain stretching famously from the lobby of the Peabody Hotel in Memphis, south and west to Vicksburg, Mississippi. This football-shaped and pancake-flat area, flooded ritually by the Mississippi River to the west and the Yazoo River to the east, is home to some of the most fertile soil in the world. The swampy plain was cleared and drained following the Civil War to make way for one crop – cotton. And with King Cotton and the sharecropping system came both fabulous wealth and extreme poverty. "Croppers" famously worked "from cain't to cain't" ("can't see till can't see"). Children of any age who could wield a hoe or haul a sack were put to work in the stifling heat of the cotton fields. Most sharecropping families, however large, white or black, struggled to make even a subsistence living. Demographically, the Delta was home to a black majority; in fact, in some Delta counties blacks outnumbered whites nearly two to one.

That ratio and attendant political calculus got a young Charles McLaurin's attention. Picked up one afternoon while hitchhiking in his hometown of Jackson, Mississippi, McLaurin met the National Association for the Advancement of Colored People's (NAACP) Medgar Evers, and got a quick lesson in civil rights mathematics: If blacks in Mississippi exercised their right to vote (ensured, after all, by the Fifteenth Amendment to the Constitution), they could wield enormous electoral power. The civics lesson persuaded McLaurin: By 1962 he was organizing voter registration drives for SNCC in the small town of Ruleville, just 18 miles north of the Sunflower County seat of Indianola.

At that time, Fannie Lou Hamer was, in her words, "existing" in Ruleville as a 44-year-old black sharecropper. The youngest of 20 children, Hamer had endured dreadful deprivation as she came of age in the Delta. Forced to quit school at age 12, the inquisitive and bright young girl learned the lessons of the Bible from her mother – and the daily indignities of Jim Crow and white supremacy from life on the Brandon Plantation. Through the timely intervention of a family friend, Hamer attended a local civil rights meeting on August 27, 1962. Her life would never be the same.[1]

Four days after that meeting, Hamer and 17 other black volunteers from Sunflower County traveled by bus to the county courthouse in Indianola. Organizing this voter registration attempt was 20-year-old Charles McLaurin. Met with hostility both inside and outside of the courthouse, Hamer was fearless as she courageously agreed to be the first one to take the test. As part of her application, she was forced to disclose where she worked. She also had to pass a literacy test and then make a "passable" interpretation of a section of the state's vexing and lengthy constitution.[2] She failed the test. On the way back to Ruleville, police pulled over their bus. The driver was charged with driving a bus that was the wrong color; it was too yellow. He was driven back to Indianola while the others remained on the bus and stewed over the day's many injustices. And just when Charles McLaurin thought he was losing all control, a powerful voice rang out among the group; it was a church song led by Fannie Lou Hamer, and it quickly eased the anxiety on the bus.

After paying a fine and returning to Ruleville, the bad news got worse: Before Hamer had even made it back to her family's plantation shack, D. W. Marlow, the plantation's patriarch, paid a personal visit to her husband, "Pap" (Perry). His warning was clear: Either Fannie Lou would withdraw her voter registration application, or she would be forcibly removed from the plantation. That very night, August 31, Hamer left a home and a job she'd had for 18 years, as well as her two adopted daughters and her husband. But she did not withdraw her voter registration application.

Charles McLaurin told the story of the bold, middle-aged sharecropper to Robert Moses, the leader of SNCC's Mississippi project headquartered in Greenwood. Hers was the type of unflinching and indigenous leadership that SNCC hoped to find and cultivate. Later that fall, Moses instructed McLaurin to find the brave woman who so willingly sacrificed everything for the dignity of registering to vote. He finally found her in a small shack in Tallahatchie County. She quickly dropped everything to head north for a SNCC conference at Fisk University in Nashville. By December 1962 she was organizing full-time for the movement.

Nearly 50 years later, Fannie Lou Hamer has become one of the most famous women of the entire civil rights movement. Much of that fame dates to a short speech she delivered before the Credentials Committee at the 1964 Democratic National Convention – a speech that was televised live to the entire nation. Wearing a simple print dress, and with her husky voice and unlettered grammar, she took America to task for its hypocrisy. Surely the "land of the free and the home of the brave" could do better than beating and torturing Mississippi blacks seeking only the prospect of "becoming first-class citizens." Fannie Lou Hamer spoke to the nation in 1964 without a manuscript and without any notes. Her speech survives only because television cameras were present. Fannie Lou Hamer likewise survives in American public memory, to a considerable extent, because of the television cameras.[3]

Back to that cold, gray January night in Indianola. We were hoping to conduct an oral history interview with Charles McLaurin. But we were also there because he needed to do a bit of interviewing himself. I was just then in the process of gathering speeches and seeking permission to reprint them for what would become *Rhetoric, Religion, and the Civil Rights Movement, 1954–1965.*[4] My colleague David E. Dixon and I had gathered nearly 200 speeches from archives around the country. The finding proved to be the easy part. Far more difficult was the process of determining who owned a given speech, where and how that person or persons might be contacted, and the conditions under which we might publish it.

In the early phase of our project, we'd found a remarkable address by Fannie Lou Hamer at the Smithsonian National Museum of American History. The speech had been captured on audiotape as it was delivered in the summer of 1964 before a hometown audience in Indianola, Mississippi. In my estimation, it was the gem of the entire collection. But who owned it? After emailing the staff at the Fannie Lou Hamer Institute at Jackson State University, we were advised to approach Charles McLaurin about securing copyright permissions. We were also duly advised that many SNCC veterans were wary of responding to such requests. And so while "Mr. Mac" had been most gracious and kind on the telephone, and while he had gratefully accepted a transcribed text and an audio copy of the address, our meeting in Indianola was much on my mind. As it turned out, our embrace in a dark church parking lot on a cold January night ensured the text's inclusion.

The happy ending to this story should not blind us to the many complexities involved in any act of textual recovery. As it turns out, many of those complexities have a deep and abiding history in the study of American public address. They are bound up with issues of canonicity, gender, class, and race, and they also involve questions about the role of the researcher, the politics and economics of preservation, disciplinary legitimacy, and computer technologies. They even relate to two of the most challenging issues in public address scholarship – the question of effect and the conundrum of delivery. In the first half of the essay, I argue that despite disciplinary traditions that favored speeches by what one scholar deemed "the biggest man," other scholars ran against the grain and argued for a far more "local" view of American public address, one that eventually resulted in far more inclusive scholarly practices. In the second half of the essay, I offer advice based on my own successes and failures in locating speeches and other primary historical materials. With the multiplication of computer and Internet technologies, the possibilities for public address scholars are truly legion.

Founding a Discipline, Finding a Speech

Textual recovery and discovery is the process of locating and evaluating primary source documents – in this case speeches – which have the *potential* to advance our knowledge of public address generally and a significant person, event, genre, and rhetorical situation more specifically.[5] Those speeches can take several forms: We may recover an audiotape or a televised recording of an address, or we may find a reading copy of a speech. Or we may recover a speech as transcribed by a reporter or a member of the audience. Many speeches were later reprinted as pamphlets, while others were reprinted in newspapers, periodicals, and magazines. *Recovering* a speech is an act of finding it – again; it is to confirm that a speech already deemed significant does, in fact, exist. This is not to say that the text in question is well known or accurate, only that its rhetorical value has already been noted. The value of a speech may be a function of many factors, including authorship, historical context, strategic adaptations, generic characteristics, artistry, and/or impact. Importantly, the value of a speech is never fixed, but always fluid. *Discovering* a speech is something entirely different; it is to locate *and* evaluate; it is to argue that a heretofore unknown speech demands attention. Ideally, the recovered or discovered speech then moves from the entombed archive to the published article, chapter, book, or website.

Of course any act of recovery or discovery is bound up with complex disciplinary traditions – traditions that strongly influence how we evaluate the worth of a speech. As a discipline initially grounded in Aristotle's *On Rhetoric*, for example, we for many years favored the civic address – the politically consequential speech delivered by a white male, typically well educated and upper class. At the same time, we typically overlooked speeches by women, gays and lesbians, blacks, and other ethnic minorities, speeches of only local or regional concern, and those delivered in a local, regional, or ethnic vernacular. In short, our disciplinary traditions limited the scope of speeches we thought worthy of preservation and serious study.

In a revealing survey of public address scholars and teachers conducted by Robert J. Brake in 1967, respondents were asked to identify the women speakers who they thought "most significant in American and foreign history."[6] Of the 500 surveys Brake sent out, only 96 were returned – nine of which were left blank. Perhaps not surprisingly, Eleanor Roosevelt was singled out as the most significant female speaker by a nearly two-to-one margin over Susan B. Anthony. Others mentioned included Margaret Chase Smith, Aimee Semple McPherson, Elizabeth Cady

Stanton, Lucy Stone, Angelina Grimké, Frances Wright, and Frances Willard. Of the "foreigners," Indira Gandhi, Madame Chiang Kai-shek, Lady Astor, and Queen Elizabeth I and Queen Elizabeth II were deemed most significant. Far more interesting were the "reactions" to the survey itself. "It looks like 'pretty thin pickin' to me," wrote one respondent. Another replied, "Women generally (I regret to say) are very poor speakers primarily because they cannot forget themselves when speaking." A third spoke for his immediate colleagues: "This department would be hardpressed to name one." Such responses left Robert J. Brake rather nonplussed: The discipline, he concluded, needed to do "some hard thinking" about the "question" of women's oratory.[7]

Interestingly, Brake was not the only one giving hard thought to whose voices were valued by public address scholars. As early as 1933, for example, William Norwood Brigance opined, "I think we ought to recognize that there is a great body of rhetorical or oratorical literature almost untouched by scholars in the field."[8] Brigance's recognition is somewhat ironic given that the "field" of rhetorical criticism had effectively been "founded" only eight years prior with Herbert Wichelns's book chapter, "The Literary Criticism of Oratory." As Martin J. Medhurst has noted, the very first published study of a single speech was still four years away, in 1937. Moreover, Brigance did not specify who he thought might be included in that "great body of rhetorical or oratorical literature."[9] Ten year later, however, Dallas C. Dickey did, at least in a limited sense. Writing in the *Quarterly Journal of Speech*, Dickey noted, "we are yet studying what may be called the more obvious speakers. There is nothing wrong with this. The advice of the major professor to the graduate student, 'study the biggest man you can find,' has been good. Very likely, though, this counsel will not be given so often in the future."[10]

By "the biggest man," of course, Dickey was referring to the size of the stage upon which the "man" spoke, his reputation, and his influence upon history. While acknowledging the value of such advice, Dickey called upon speech scholars to broaden their view: "[W]e need most of all in the next few years to take up the study of speakers who are just as truly neglected, but who are either completely unknown to many of us, or unassociated with effectiveness in public address." Explaining why he thought the field should attend to such "neglected" and "unknown" speakers, Dickey noted that such speakers often created the rhythms of history: "*Great movements of history begin in obscure places and gather momentum only when leaders arise who can speak for the wants of many. It may be given to one speaker to speak for a nation, to another for a region, and to a third for a small locality.*"[11]

Dickey thus envisioned what Steven R. Goldzwig would much later call "critical localism," or the careful examination of discourse as it gets articulated to local audiences.[12] Such a critical preference, though, typically butted up against one very stubborn fact: What if a "neglected" or "unknown" speaker's words were never recorded, transcribed, translated, or otherwise preserved? If Alan Ribback had not lugged his cumbersome recording equipment to Indianola, Mississippi, in 1964, for example, Fannie Lou Hamer's speech, for all intents and purposes, would simply not exist.[13] In other words, Dickey's preference for the "obscure speaker" remains just that – a preference, however well intentioned – in the absence of a recording or transcript of that "unknown" or "neglected" speech.

In a forum in the *Quarterly Journal of Speech* just three years later, Wayne N. Thompson again addressed some of the problems of textual access and preservation. Whether he wrote in response to Dickey is not clear, but he did grasp some of the challenges and complications of studying obscure speakers. Urging public address scholars to "see and hear" more speakers, Thompson identified the recording and archiving of more speeches as an important priority for public address scholars – both to inform their own studies and to create a readily accessible library for future scholars. In addition to articles, monographs, and books, Thompson urged public address scholars to create speech "reports," or documents that recorded key details about a speaker, a speech, and its reception by the audience. Instead of advocating a respectable scholarly distance, Thompson argued for closeness and immediacy, urging public address scholars to experience more speeches first hand.[14]

Thompson's scholarly agenda was underscored by his insistence that public address scholars "must study language *as it is heard*," assess its effects "*at the time of delivery*," and judge "the ethical power of the speaker *as he stands before the audience*." In other words, he urged an emphasis on (1) oral delivery and (2) the effects of a speech on its immediate audience. As Thompson explained, "Speech is a living subject … It is the spoken word, not the written page."[15] Thus, he urged attention to those aspects of speech that most distinguished it from literature: its performance at a specific place and time before a live audience. In the process, he articulated two major challenges to early students of public address: How does a critic study the delivery of a speech not actually witnessed or recorded at the time of its delivery? And how does a critic measure and assess the "effect" of a speech?

One very early and influential "critic" of speech was bedeviled by the canon of delivery. In book three, chapter one of *On Rhetoric*, an unusually perturbed Aristotle referred to delivery as a "vulgar matter" and devoted a terse two pages to the subject.[16] On his account, delivery exerted too great a power on audiences easily swayed by the emotions conveyed by the human voice.[17] That power, conceptualized as an important dimension of "effect" by Wichelns as he distinguished the oratorical from the literary in his seminal 1925 essay, has long engaged our discipline.[18] In 1916, just two years after the formation of the National Association of Academic Teachers of Public Speaking, for example, Charles H. Woolbert outlined a detailed and scientific research program involving the measurement of the effects of the human voice on an audience.[19] That program, though vastly more sophisticated theoretically and methodologically, remains a vibrant core of communication pedagogy and nonverbal communication – but not among public address scholars. Despite Thompson's call, echoed more recently by Frank E. X. Dance and Joshua Gunn, written symbols rather than spoken words have long held sway in the field.[20]

As mentioned, the field's interest in rhetorical *effect* can be traced back to Wichelns, who famously declared that rhetorical criticism was "concerned with effect. It regards a speech as a communication to a specific audience, and holds its business to be the analysis and appreciation of the orator's method of imparting his ideas to his hearers."[21] Spoken rhetoric delivered to live audiences did things; it changed the world in ways written literature never could. David Zarefsky notes that many aspiring critics mistook Wichelns's critical counsel as a call for empirical investigation into causal factors, which resulted in "a usually futile quest that often produced bad scholarship."[22] But some of Wichelns's contemporaries grasped his advice: Early studies of Matthew Arnold and the Lincoln–Douglas debates, for example, noted the *probable* effects of certain rhetorical strategies and tactics on a given audience.[23]

Nonetheless, the emphasis on delivery and effect in early public address studies had an obvious impact on the speeches the field deemed important and worthy of study. Because the delivery and public reactions to an important political speech by a national leader might be recorded by major newspapers or duly noted by audience members in letters, telegrams, or diaries, the speeches of the "biggest men" were more likely to be preserved and subsequently analyzed.[24] Also, such speeches were more likely to be preserved in writing, which facilitated critical inter-rogation. Speeches by presidents or members of Congress, for example, have been routinely published by the Government Printing Office, albeit typically in edited form quite different from the versions actually delivered. Even before the advent of electronic recording devices, famous speakers often employed stenographers to record their speeches verbatim, and newspapers often published full transcripts of important addresses.

Certainly, the momentous speeches relating to the nation's civic affairs ought to be carefully preserved and examined by public address scholars. With that I have no quarrel. But if records concerning the delivery and effects of a speech, along with a reliable written text, become the *sine qua non* of critical investigation, that clearly limits the number and types of speeches deemed worthy of analysis. Little wonder that so many aspiring public address scholars have conveniently and eagerly focused on the "biggest man" and their "biggest speeches." This explanation may even mitigate suspicions of sexism, racism, and homophobia in the early history of the field, for the speeches of women and of ethnic and other minorities, along with evidence of how they were delivered and received, simply have not been available – or so one might argue.

"Old-Time Negro Preaching" as Exemplar

If the speeches selected and preserved for analysis in the early years of the field reflect a founding and overweening methodology, then it stands to reason that new, more creative methodological approaches might broaden the purview of American public address. Such new methods might inspire us to include the local or the largely unknown address, the speech not preserved as a written text, or the speech which produced no measurable or observable effects. Today, public address scholars continue to grapple with questions about delivery and audience reception.[25] Yet Wayne N. Thompson's early call for proximity, preservation, and the interrogation of delivery and effect might be interpreted more broadly, in ways that open up new possibilities for the recovery, discovery, and critical analysis of neglected voices.

One of the most fascinating and earliest manifestations of these possibilities is William H. Pipes's 1951 book, *Say Amen, Brother! Old-Time Negro Preaching: A Study in American Frustration*.[26] To my knowledge, this is the very first sustained and critical analysis of black public address.[27] Pipes, whose family claims he was the country's first African American PhD in speech, was raised in Inverness, Mississippi (in Sunflower County). He later attended Tuskegee Institute and the University of Michigan, where he completed his doctorate in 1943. Based on his dissertation, "An Interpretive Study of Old-Time Negro Preaching," Pipes examined the rhetorical patterns of eight sermons delivered by different "old-time" preachers in Macon County, Georgia. Employing a small team of researchers, Pipes recorded each sermon for accuracy. He and his wife also carefully detailed audience reactions to the sermons, as "old-time" preaching typically involved "call and response," or antiphonal patterns. All eight sermons were transcribed and analyzed in terms of their emotional appeals, style, and arrangement. Pipes also analyzed the ethos and the delivery of each of the eight preachers.[28]

Beyond his contributions in simply reproducing these eight vernacular addresses, Pipes foreshadowed the sort of ideological criticism that would become commonplace 30 years later. Reflecting on the larger political implications of the sermons, he did not care for what he saw: a rhetorical form that constrained the southern and rural black imagination to a rather primitive emotionalism, whose full release and redemption would only take place in the hereafter. To seek racial redress, let alone justice, was simply beyond the rhetorical pale; generic form and preaching precedent rendered such earthly concerns non-sequiturs. Yet by immersing himself in the local, vernacular, and impoverished speech communities of south Georgia, Pipes at least began to take the field in some of the scholarly directions urged by Brigance, Dickey, and Thompson; he was taking seriously speakers and speech forms that previously might have been dismissed as mere "entertainment."[29] In addition, he had shown how the discovery and preservation of such speeches was serious business, requiring expensive and unwieldy recording equipment – and the electricity to make it work.[30]

It would be misleading to suggest that Brigance, Dickey, Thompson, or Pipes ushered in a revolution in the field of American public address. As Medhurst has ably demonstrated, a number of factors contributed to the field's expansion beyond "great speakers and speeches," including the introduction of movement studies in the 1950s and the theoretical and critical possibilities offered by Kenneth Burke and I. A. Richards.[31] It is also clear that the political, social, cultural, and legal revolution brought about by the civil rights movement had a major impact not only on the field, but upon American society more generally. Still, the influence of Brigance, Dickey, Thompson, and Pipes is clearly discernible in scholarship such as Newsom and Gorden's 1963 study of a civil rights meeting in Atlanta two years earlier. At least one of the authors attended the fractious meeting – with recording equipment in tow. First-hand observations of speakers and audience were made and post-speech interviews were conducted. At once a case study in group decision-making, an ethnography of a meeting, and a critical account of the speeches made therein, Wayne N. Thompson seems ever-present in the essay.[32]

Several other race-related articles quickly followed Newsom and Gorden's lead, including Gorden in 1964, Ferris in 1965, and Jefferson and Phifer and Taylor in 1967.[33] What was an oddity in 1951 had, by the early 1970s, become something of a cliché as public address scholars published the *Rhetoric of Racial Revolt* (1964), *The Rhetoric of the Civil-Rights Movement* (1969), *The Rhetoric of Black Power* (1969), *The Oratory of Negro Leaders* (1969), *The Negro Speaks* (1970), *The Voice of Black Rhetoric* (1971), *The Rhetoric of Black Americans* (1971), and *Speeches by Black Americans* (1971).[34] With this very conspicuous recognition of the civil rights movement, public address scholars had finally recovered and discovered the black man.[35] Not yet the black woman.

Six years after Brake's 1967 essay on women orators, he and Robert D. Neuleib conducted another survey of public address scholars. Their results suggested that much had changed in just six years. While women were still significantly underrepresented in speech anthologies, the women's movement and a more gender-inclusive public address curriculum had "increased awareness." Whereas only 60 notable American women had earlier been identified by the 96 respondents, 100 such women were deemed "significant" by more than 150 respondents in 1973.[36] Contemporary women, including Gloria Steinem, Shirley Chisholm, Coretta Scott King, and Angela Davis, were singled out alongside Mary Harris "Mother" Jones, Harriet Tubman, Susan B. Anthony, and Elizabeth Cady Stanton. Indeed, it appeared that the field had done some "hard thinking" about women speakers; Brake and Neuleib did not report any of the egregious sexism so apparent in their earlier survey responses.

By the 1980s, women were no longer anomalous in the study of American public address. Anthologies such as Kennedy and O'Shields's *We Shall Be Heard: Women Speakers in America* began to appear, and individual studies were also published, including critical studies of the speeches of "Mother" Jones and Maria W. Stewart.[37] Pioneered largely by Karlyn Kohrs Campbell, whose two-volume *Man Cannot Speak For Her* represented a massive project of recovery and discovery, women's rhetoric, especially as reflected in reform movements, moved from the margins to the center of the discipline.[38] Following Campbell were anthologies such as *Women at the Podium* (2000), *Available Means: An Anthology of Women's Rhetoric(s)* (2001), and *From Megaphones to Microphones: Speeches of American Women, 1920–1960* (2003).[39] More narrowly focused anthologies also appeared, featuring black American women, nineteenth-century American black women, and individual black rhetors such as Barbara Jordan.[40] Predictably, these efforts to recover and discover primary sources also engendered a large corpus of critical, historical, and theoretical studies outside of the field.

In like fashion, as America continues to come to terms with (if not celebrate) its multiethnic, multiracial, and multicultural heritage, a varied array of speeches representing the country's ethnic, religious, and sexual diversity has become available. These include Deborah Gillan Straub's *Voices of Multicultural America* (1995), Ronald K. Burke's *American Public Discourse* (1992), Barbara Alice Mann's *Native American Speakers of the Eastern Woodlands* (2001), Richard J. Jensen and John C. Hammerback's *The Words of Cesar Chavez* (2002), and Josh Gottheimer's *Ripples of Hope* (2003).[41] And while public address scholars have gone to great lengths to flesh out their discipline, even the "old" contains something of the new: Stephen E. Lucas and Martin J. Medhurst's highly anticipated *Words of a Century: The Top 100 American Speeches, 1900–1999* features for the first time carefully authenticated texts of each address as well as extensive in-text annotations.[42]

Some might be inclined to say that indeed we've come a long way, from a field that once privileged the "biggest man" to one whose boundaries know few limits. Such a progressive view has plausible warrants. Considering Brake's survey work and the types of speeches and speakers preserved and critically examined early in the field's history, it is clear that much progress has been made. But my admittedly partial survey here suggests some other possibilities: While the work of recovery and discovery might have been initially constrained by *methodological* limitations, some disciplinary agenda-setters did argue forcefully for a radically inclusive view of what and who might be studied, and at least one trailblazing black scholar – William Harrison Pipes – made good on some of those possibilities – and won the approval of a doctoral committee, a journal editor, and a book publisher's editorial board. In short, the field bought it, even found it "fascinating," back in an era presumably concerned principally with the "big men" of history.

Recovery and Discovery in the Twenty-First Century

What are the prospects for recovery and discovery work in the field of public address – today and tomorrow? Does our past in any way inform our present and our future? In some ways, yes, we will continue to be constrained by our history and traditions. In at least one important way, however, our future will be very different from our past and present, as new technologies have opened up exciting possibilities for the study of public address.

In 1988, Stephen E. Lucas noted that the study of public address was "in the midst of a remarkable renaissance."[43] But perhaps even Lucas could not have anticipated just how remarkable and enduring that renaissance would be. Even today, as the field continues to recover and discover new speeches and as new publication outlets emerge for both those documents and our critical work, Lucas never could have imagined what his Reagan-era 14.4 baud external modem and analogue phone line would soon become – nor what those technological advancements could do to sustain the renaissance in public address.[44]

There has never been a better time to be a public address scholar. Thanks to extensive public and proprietary database technologies, it will no longer be so common that scholars in other disciplines will say, "Well, I wasn't aware of this literature."

In the digital age, our work will not only be more accessible to scholars in other disciplines; it also will be easier to do the work of recovery and discovery in the first place. With wireless Internet access, powerful integrated networks, broadband technologies, and massive storage and retrieval capacities, we have entered an age when finding things is exponentially easier. For example, I can rapidly locate those once-obscure sermons recorded by William H. Pipes back in 1943 by conducting an "Advanced Search" in Google. Furthermore, when Google eventually scans the book – which for better and worse it will – I will have nearly instant access to those fascinating texts. Similarly, by logging on to Florida State University's proxy server, I have instant off-campus access to every page ever published by the *New York Times* – from 1851 to the present. If I know generally what I'm looking for and when, I can search that database efficiently. As a newspaper that once routinely published the full texts of speeches, the *Times* is an excellent archive for recovery work. Other newspapers are rapidly following suit, as are magazines and periodicals. AmericanRhetoric.com features hundreds of complete video and audio recordings of speeches, which for a generation weaned on the visual makes for an important classroom resource. Similarly, the *Voices of Democracy* project includes authenticated speech texts, critical essays, and teaching and learning materials. As for secondary scholarly materials, the databases are getting bigger and better by the hour: Sites such as JSTOR, Lexis-Nexis Academic, Project Muse, Expanded Academic ASAP, and WorldCat, to name just a few, now provide full-text access to generations of scholarly research. Even the National Communication Association now archives and indexes its national publications online.

I'm not saying anything new in suggesting that the computer revolution will greatly facilitate our work of recovery and discovery. Nor have I mentioned any research sites that public address scholars do not already use on a regular basis. But I would like to dwell for a moment on some of the processes involved in the work of discovery and recovery – processes that I've learned about the hard way over the past five years in completing two very challenging speech anthologies. In so doing, I'm aware that much of what I say might soon be obsolete, but I nevertheless offer the following observations in the spirit of sharing some of the joys and professional satisfactions unique to the work of recovery and discovery.

First, chances are that someone else has already trod at least part of the research path you'll be walking. I've often heard colleagues and graduate students lament this fact, fearing that an idea has already been "stolen," source material "exhausted," or the whole research enterprise generally redundant. I encourage just the opposite sensibility, for one scholar's find can – and often does – lead to several more. Not long ago I read with great interest Janice D. Hamlet's essay on Fannie Lou Hamer.[45] I dutifully and eagerly consulted her endnotes, as I was unaware of the speeches from which she was quoting. The repository that held her primary sources was new to me: the Moses Moon audio archive at the Smithsonian National Museum of American History in Washington, DC. I checked for the archive at the Smithsonian's website: Did they have an online finding aid? (They didn't.) Did they describe the contents of the collection in any detail? (They didn't.) But they did list a contact – Wendy Shay – along with a phone number and email address. I called Wendy.[46] She grew rather animated during the course of our conversation as the archive had been rarely used. Remember, archivists' budgets and resources are often based on use of their collections, so most archivists are eager to help facilitate use of their materials. And the Moses Moon archive turned out to be quite a find: It contained more than 80 hours of recorded civil rights meetings, speeches, songs, prayers, and interviews. Included were such legendary and never-before-anthologized figures as Ella Baker, Ed King, Dave Dennis, Robert Moses, Allard Lowenstein, Aaron Henry, and Lawrence Guyot. In short, it contained a lot more than a few speeches by Fannie Lou Hamer.

There was one big problem, of course: How could I possibly listen to all the material, and then transcribe all the recordings I considered germane to my project? I'd be in Washington longer than Strom Thurmond. Many archives are also notoriously stingy about reproducing material from their collections – and with good reason. Too much duplicated material can rather quickly render an archive obsolete; they are especially reluctant if the product stands to generate revenue. So I was pleasantly surprised to receive permission to bring as many blank tapes as I wanted. Wendy also gladly set up the Smithsonian's recording equipment for me. Yes, acquiring more than 23 hours of recorded material was time consuming, but such large audio archives, I've since learned, are very rare. Unlike many speech texts, they also usually provide a verbatim record of what was actually said.[47] And converting cassette tapes to digital format is neither difficult nor prohibitively expensive.

Finding aids for archival collections – if they exist – range from the very general to the very specific, from series-level information ("outgoing correspondence") to folder-level details ("July 18, 1963, typescript speech"). Many finding aids are now online, accessible and key-word searchable under such headings as "special collections" or "archival holdings" on a library's web page. But even if a collection does not have an online finding aid, archivists are often amenable to sending an electronic or hard copy. Importantly, a finding aid is only as good as the person(s) compiling it. Moreover, as a collection acquires additional materials over the years, some of that new material might not be correctly catalogued. Hidden treasures often go unindexed, so every potentially relevant folder should be carefully examined. Recently, at the Amistad Library at Tulane University, I was browsing through Fannie Lou Hamer's papers, and judging by the finding aid, none of her speeches or letters were contained in the collection. But I happened to notice an unmarked folder contained in the first box of her papers. It turned out to include more than 20 of Hamer's handwritten letters donated to the collection in the late 1990s by Mrs. Rose Fishman, a friend and frequent correspondent from Massachusetts. Archivists had simply not updated the finding aid.

I've also learned that speeches are not necessarily always found in collections or series labeled "speeches" or "addresses" or "personal writings." Well-known figures often received unsolicited speech manuscripts, or they filed away collected speech materials in odd places, as "correspondence," "unpublished manuscripts," or "miscellaneous materials." In the Special Collections at the University of

Georgia, for example, several important and rare addresses by theologian, farmer, and civil rights activist Clarence Jordan are located in folders that simply could not have been found by relying on a finding aid.

Beyond a detailed finding aid, the best resource researchers have is a knowledgeable and helpful archivist. More often than not, that archivist is the person who inventoried and catalogued the collection and created the finding aid in the first place. While conducting research at the Jacob Marcus Rader Center of the American Jewish Archives, for example, I recently made the error of relying solely on an online finding aid. As a result, I mistakenly thought I had exhausted their holdings of civil rights speeches. Early one afternoon an archivist asked if I'd checked the card catalogue's listings under "civil rights." Surely, I thought, an online finding aid was more complete than anything in the card catalogue. And who uses card catalogues anymore? The archivist cured me of my misconceptions when she later brought me an entire collection of civil rights sermons. Each of them had been dutifully recorded nearly 50 years earlier – but only in the card catalogue.

Whether out of self-interest, pity, or just plain kindness, I've also found archivists to be remarkably generous in answering questions, locating related collections, searching collections, and copying material. Most archivists understand all too well the expenses and time of travel, but they still want to make material in their collections available to scholars. Ken Chandler, head archivist at the Bethune Council House in Washington, DC, for example, sent me scanned electronic files of an entire collection of the National Council of Negro Women's national conventions. It was a remarkably generous act, one I didn't even dare request, given its enormity. But there the collection sits in PDF files on my hard-drive. Not all archivists will go to such lengths, of course. But most will lend a generous hand, especially if time and expense preclude an on-site visit.

When happening upon an important document on-site, of course, the question of reproduction comes to the fore. Some archives try to discourage photocopying by charging a premium – as much as 50 cents per page in some cases. Other archives will do the job for you – for a price – because they do not want researchers unstapling, folding, bending, and in general roughly handling treasured documents. I once nearly lost an eardrum when a horrified archivist loudly complained that I was mishandling a treasured Roosevelt speech. Still other archives allow and encourage their patrons to do their own on-site photocopying at a reasonable cost. But at the Southern Historical Collection, housed at the University of North Carolina, researchers are encouraged to use the best method of all: taking digital photographs of documents using their own cameras. It's fast, relatively inexpensive, and easy to download to a CD-Rom. It also causes no wear to the documents, and the quality of the reproduction is generally excellent – especially when working with worn, faded, or poorly produced originals or copies.

Reproduction gets a bit more tricky with photographs, videotapes, and audiotapes. Some archives simply aren't equipped to make audiovisual copies, while others prohibit it. I recently learned, for example, that the very large and rare collection of audiotapes from the Highlander Folk School, housed at the Wisconsin Historical

Society and featuring recorded speeches and meetings with civil rights stalwarts such as Myles Horton, Rosa Parks, Septima Clark, and Fred Shuttlesworth, are not available for reproduction. Interested scholars must transcribe audio material on-site if they want texts of those speeches and meetings. Can such tedious, time-consuming, and expensive work be avoided and/or circumvented? One possibility that I've begun exploring with several archivists is a swap: If you send me or my special collections department copies of the audio or videotapes, I'll provide you with transcriptions. Everybody wins in this sort of exchange, including student transcribers who can learn much by working with primary sources.

There is of course no substitute for on-site archival work; for many reasons it's simply the best way to discover important primary sources. But we would also do well not to sell our own libraries short. With the present availability of many collections on microfilm, interlibrary loan has become a tremendously important resource in the recovery and discovery process.[48] Furthermore, with the publication of extensively detailed finding aids, small parts of large collections can be borrowed from other libraries and examined more efficiently on the new generation of scanning equipment. Many collections, of course, remain unfilmed or non-circulating, but in many cases, organizational and individual papers are available for purchase or loan.

In stepping away from the library and the special collections room for a moment, it goes without saying that these are places for sources that are already collected and catalogued. What of the uncollected sources, the ones sitting idly in people's attics, garages, storage facilities, and file cabinets? Many – in fact most – living veterans of the civil rights movement have neither donated nor sold their papers to a library. Some, such as the minister and mentor to Martin Luther King, Jr., James Lawson, guard them rather jealously. Others, such as Ed King, share their documents readily. But whatever their attitude, how would one go about contacting such people in the first place? How does one cultivate a personal and professional relationship with such historical actors?

I'm a bit embarrassed to admit that an undergraduate informed me about a website – and he did it in class, before a large audience no less – that has facilitated a great deal of my discovery and recovery work. At www.zabasearch.com, researchers can find phone numbers, addresses, ages, and dates of birth for almost anyone in any state – for free. Of course, none of us is anonymous in the wired age, and zabasearch proves it in some rather eerie ways. I have located scores of "minor" and "major" participants in the civil rights movement – from ministers, housewives, businessmen, journalists, professors, sons, and daughters, to regional and national leaders – with just a few keystrokes and mouse clicks. I write first – always on departmental letterhead – to explain the nature of my research, and I promise to share any documents that might be of personal interest to them. Then I wait. More times than not, they write back or call. Some send documents. Others share their stories from the movement. Many children express warm thanks for somebody taking an interest in an aging or departed parent. And, of course, I sometimes hear nothing. The point is to try – politely – to begin a conversation about the past and to convey a sincere interest in a movement that helped change the nation for the better. To hear Will D. Campbell talk about the threat of being murdered in the Homochitto Bottoms by his boyhood friends; to listen as Allan Levine, an octogenarian residing in Israel, recalls his 1962 arrest in Ruleville, Mississippi; to feel the anguish of Shelton Chappell as he tells the story of his mother's murder along a dark, lonely road in Jacksonville; to hear the Reverend Lawson's warm baritone as he describes why his friend "Martin" came to Memphis in 1968 – these are the rich and embodied cadences of a movement that changed history, a movement that still moves.

But in addition to the rare source materials that can surface from such encounters, researchers also can gain rare insight into the context behind those materials. Charles McLaurin, for example, informed me that Fannie Lou Hamer's recorded speech from the Moon archive was in fact a campaign speech, part of what would soon become a historic challenge to Mississippi's all-white congressional delegation. Ed King revealed the somewhat shocking detail that the NAACP's Roy Wilkins was indignant that Hamer had even been allowed to address the Credentials Committee in 1964; he believed that such a poorly dressed and unlettered woman should not command a national television audience when upper-class, educated, and more lettered black leaders were available. Former Vanderbilt faculty member Everett Tilson described in detail how he bailed theology student James Lawson out of jail, as well as Chancellor Harvey Branscomb's racist intransigence in expelling him. Even "failures" are instructive. Despite our best efforts, the widow of James Reeb, a Unitarian minister murdered before the famous Selma-to-Montgomery march in 1965, would not share his papers. But her granddaughter, Leah Reeb, corresponded with us about the pain and suffering endured by the family after their sacrifice for the cause of civil rights. In sum, direct contact with key people and/or their families often leads to invaluable materials and fascinating contextual details. Friendships, too.

As some of these prescriptions and processes suggest, recovery and discovery work is often tedious, slow, expensive, and contingent upon the whims of other people. But once in a while such work is simple, cheap, and primarily at our discretion. I'm talking specifically about government documents. Public address scholars have always relied on publications such as the *Public Papers of the President* to locate important state papers. Providing preferred and edited versions of speeches and press conferences, the publication of presidential papers is an invaluable resource. But, look deeper, much deeper. Prominent issues, events, and legislation are often accompanied by public hearings and careful transcription. Some of the rarest speech material I've ever discovered was found in dusty bound volumes of congressional subcommittee hearings. Furthermore, with the help of such electronic databases as Lexis-Nexis, the dates, places, and publications of many of those hearings have been carefully documented. Even Dorothy Tilly's personal papers, housed at Emory University, don't contain her important remarks before a 1959 Senate subcommittee on civil rights. Jane Schutt's impassioned plea for civil rights in her home state of Mississippi is nowhere to be found – except in a 1963 US Senate publication. The same is true of Gus Courts, a remarkably brave black grocer and voting rights activist from Belzoni, Mississippi. Nothing by Courts has been preserved to my knowledge, save for his riveting testimony before a very contentious and often racist Senate Judiciary Subcommittee hearing on constitutional rights, which occurred on the morning of February 28, 1957. I recently discovered nearly 3,000 pages of transcribed depositions given by Mississippi blacks in 1965 in response to the challenge to unseat the state's elected and white congressional delegation. Similarly, state and even local governments often transcribe the testimony and statements of leaders, witnesses, and government officials. All of this material has the added advantage of being in the public domain, thus rendering permission and copyright issues moot.

A final bit of counsel on recovering and discovering primary source documents: Be sure to contact other scholars working in the area; they are often eager to share stories, swap resources, offer counsel, or even send boxes of documents. I can never repay Mary Stuckey for sending me, while I was an MA student, a large box full of Ronald Reagan's pre-presidential speeches – speeches that she had gone to great time and expense to secure during her dissertation research. In my civil rights work, scholars across the country have generously shared their archival treasures, as well as their address books, promising leads, and suggested readings – and of course their latest scholarship.

In no way does the preceding exhaust the possibilities of recovery and discovery work, nor its many contingencies. In fact, I've really only scratched a considerable surface. What about the archives at local, regional, and national radio and television stations? What about the millions of small-circulation periodicals, bulletins, newspapers, pamphlets, proceedings, and newsletters? What about the thousands of churches, synagogues, dioceses, businesses, schools, museums, county libraries, historical societies, trade unions, and trade associations? And what about the many large and small collections, awaiting resources, family permission, litigation or death, held in storage facilities? The possibilities for recovery and discovery are truly limited only by our imagination and determination, and yes, sometimes our financial resources.

"What's Going On Here? And What About It?"

All of this leads us, at long last, to that all-important question: So what? Who cares about the congressional testimony of Gus Courts and his small, middle-of-nowhere grocery store? Why should we concern ourselves with some random recordings of an uneducated black female sharecropper? What difference does it make if we find Ed King's eulogy to James Chaney at the Pacifica Radio Archives? Maybe some things are better off lost than found. As a community of academics, after all, we're not in the business of sponsoring garage sales or flea markets. Sometimes rhetorical junk is just rhetorical junk.

These are precisely the concerns, although stated in a different manner, raised two and three generations ago by William Norwood Brigance, Dallas C. Dickey, and

Wayne N. Thompson. The same concerns have been addressed by public address scholars for decades. In David Zarefsky's most apt and concise expression, our recovery and discovery work really boils down to this: "What's going on here?" And "What about it?"[49] Minus a compelling and persuasive answer to these two important questions, our efforts at recovery and discovery are much ado about nothing, and we are but antiquarians with a manifestly odd Jones for the rhetorical.

Zarefsky's questions, though, speak rather eloquently to an important point for public address scholars: Beyond our seemingly limitless technological possibilities, we live and work in an age in which we still struggle with old moral questions – questions about race, social justice, and our ideals as a nation. Critical invention, careful argument, and convincing evidence, adjudicated by our peers, will continue to constitute our disciplinary ideals. But in our disciplinary past, visionaries such as William Harrison Pipes, who went to the great trouble of recording and transcribing eight nobody-cares sermons in nobody-cares Georgia for a nobody-cares dissertation, also remind us that the study of rhetoric raises those important moral questions that cannot be answered by studying only the "big men," the "big speeches," and the "big effects." Sometimes, perhaps most times, the little men of Macon, Georgia, and the little women of Ruleville, Mississippi, can teach us much about the ethics of rhetoric – and about how to care, and what to care about.

If only we can hear them.

Acknowledgments

The author thanks Abe Khan, Mary Stuckey, Amos Kiewe, Ulla Bunz, and David Dixon for their helpful comments on an earlier draft of this chapter. Thanks also to Shawn Parry-Giles and Mike Hogan, who have improved this essay immeasurably with their patient reading and sagacious comments.

Notes

1 Biographical details on Fannie Lou Hamer come from two excellent biographies; see Kay Mills, *This Little Light of Mine: The Life of Fannie Lou Hamer* (New York: Plume, 1994); and Chana Kai Lee, *For Freedom's Sake: The Life of Fannie Lou Hamer* (Urbana: University of Illinois Press, 1999). For a fascinating anthropological account of Indianola's racial dynamics, see Hortense Powdermaker, *After Freedom: A Cultural Study in the Deep South* (New York: Viking, 1939).

2 In 1954 Mississippi voters passed, by a five-to-one majority, an amendment to the state's constitution that forced would-be registrants to give a "reasonable interpretation" of a section of the state's byzantine constitution. See John Dittmer, *Local People: The Struggle for Civil Rights in Mississippi* (Urbana: University of Illinois Press, 1994), 52–53.

3 An audio recording of Hamer's famous address is available from AmericanRhetoric. com, americanradioworks.publicradio.org/features/sayitplain/flhamer.html (accessed August 2, 2009).

4   Davis W. Houck and David E. Dixon, eds., *Rhetoric, Religion, and the Civil Rights Movement, 1954–1965* (Waco, TX: Baylor University Press, 2006).

5   Of course this process can include a host of primary source materials, from letters and diaries to memoranda and transcribed notes of meetings and conversations.

6   Robert J. Brake, "Women Orators: More Research?" *Today's Speech* 15 (November 1967): 22.

7   Robert J. Brake and Robert D. Neuleib conducted a similar survey in 1973 and received a far greater response rate (154 out of 500), and a far greater number of women were mentioned as significant (100 compared with 60), including several black women. See "Famous Women Orators: An Opinion Survey," *Today's Speech* 21(1973): 33–37.

8   William Norwood Brigance, "Whither Research?" *Quarterly Journal of Speech* 19 (1933): 556.

9   Martin J. Medhurst, "The Academic Study of Public Address: A Tradition in Transition," in *Landmark Essays on American Public Address*, ed. Martin J. Medhurst (Davis, CA: Hermagoras Press, 1993), xviii.

10 Dallas C. Dickey, "What Directions Should Future Research in American Public Address Take?" *Quarterly Journal of Speech* 29 (1943): 301.

11 Dickey, "What Directions Should Future Research in American Public Address Take?" 301, 303 (emphasis in original).

12 Steven R. Goldzwig, "Multiculturalism, Rhetoric and the Twenty-First Century," *Southern Communication Journal* 63 (1998): 273–290.

13 Ribback, later known as Moses Moon, owned and operated a well-known bar in Chicago, and came south with his recording equipment in the spring of 1963. According to SNCC Executive Secretary James Forman, with whom I spoke at a chance meeting at his office in June 2004, Ribback was invited by Forman to record the music of the movement at civil rights meetings throughout the south. Those recordings, made in places such as Selma, Greenwood, Danville, Indianola, Jackson, Hattiesburg, and Washington, DC, are archived at the Smithsonian National Museum of American History.

14 Wayne N. Thompson, "Contemporary Public Address as a Research Area," *Quarterly Journal of Speech* 33 (1947): 274, 278.

15 Thompson, "Contemporary Public Address as a Research Area," 278, 277. Emphasis in original.

16 Aristotle, *On Rhetoric: A Theory of Civic Discourse*, trans. George A. Kennedy (New York: Oxford University Press, 1991), 218.

17 This is much the same critique made of oral rhetoric by both the Platonic Socrates in the dialogue *Phaedrus* and Gorgias in his "Encomium to Helen."

18 Herbert A. Wichelns, "The Literary Criticism of Oratory," reprinted in *Landmark Essays on American Public Address*, 1–32.

19 Charles H. Woolbert, "Suggestions as to Methods in Research," *Quarterly Journal of Public Speaking* 3 (1917): 12–26. For an early call to speech scholars to prioritize the study of the human voice, see Clara Kathleen Rogers, "The Voice as a Revelation of the Individual," *Quarterly Journal of Public Speaking* 2 (1916): 229–235.

20 For a very suggestive analysis of the disciplinary consequences for studying the symbol, see Carole Blair, "'We Are All Just Prisoners Here of Our Own Device': Rhetoric in Speech Communication after Wingspread," in *Making and Unmaking the Prospect for Rhetoric: Selected Papers from the 1996 Rhetoric Society of America Conference*, ed.

Teresa Enos (Mahwah, NJ: Lawrence Erlbaum, 1998), 29–36. For arguments urging communication scholars return to the study of voice and speech, see Frank E. X. Dance, "Speech and Thought: A Renewal," *Communication Education* 51 (2002): 355–359; and Joshua Gunn, "Speech is Dead; Long Live Speech," *Quarterly Journal of Speech* 94 (2008): 343–364.

21 Wichelns, "The Literary Criticism of Oratory," 26.

22 David Zarefsky, "Reflections on Rhetorical Criticism," *Rhetoric Review* 25 (2006): 384.

23 See Everett Lee Hunt, "Matthew Arnold: The Critic as Rhetorician," *Quarterly Journal of Speech* 20 (1934): 483–507; and Marvin G. Bauer, "Persuasive Methods in the Lincoln–Douglas Debates," *Quarterly Journal of Speech* 13 (1927): 29–39.

24 As early as 1938, public address scholars had begun compiling lists of the "greatest oratory" and the "foremost orators." See Hugo E. Hellman, "The Greatest American Oratory," *Quarterly Journal of Speech* 24 (1938): 36–39; and William Norwood Brigance, "The Twenty-Eight Foremost American Orators," *Quarterly Journal of Speech* 24 (1938): 376–380. In compiling his list, Brigance essentially farmed out the work of determining the "foremost" to a "group of distinguished historians" who could apparently adjudicate the "effects" question better than any rhetorician. See also Elwood Murray, "An Historiometric Study of the Early Traits of Great Orators," *Quarterly Journal of Speech* 14 (1928): 502–508.

25 Audience reception is again being taken very seriously. See, for example, Amos Kiewe, *FDR's First Fireside Chat: Public Confidence and the Banking Crisis* (College Station: Texas A&M University Press, 2007); Davis W. Houck and Mihaela Nocasian, "FDR's First Inaugural Address: Text, Context, and Reception," *Rhetoric & Public Affairs* 5 (2002): 649–678; Carole Blair, "Reflections on Criticism and Bodies: Parables from Public Places," *Western Journal of Communication* 65 (2001): 288; and Michael C. Leff, "Lincoln at Cooper Union: Neo-Classical Criticism Revisited," *Western Journal of Communication* 65 (2001): 240, 246. For a fine survey of recent work on voice and speech as well as a call to return to those subjects, see Gunn, "Speech is Dead; Long Live Speech."

26 William H. Pipes, *Say Amen, Brother! Old-Time Negro Preaching: A Study in Frustration* (New York: William Frederick, 1951).

27 An earlier article from Pipes's dissertation appeared in 1945. See William Harrison Pipes, "Old-Time Negro Preaching: An Interpretive Study," *Quarterly Journal of Speech* 31 (1945): 15–21. While the book's content was certainly novel to scholars of American public address during that era, perhaps even more remarkable is the book's shelf life: It remains in print with Wayne State University Press. This qualifies it as one of the longest in-print, single-authored books in the field.

28 Just to give the reader a flavor of how preachers addressed their congregations, here is part of Pipes's transcription of sermon number eight: "I done been in de pulpit for four weeks; I been preachin' fer 'em. (You know I ain't lazy – 'till I git lazy.) [*Laughter.*] It don't take all dat hard preaching ter be saved. I sed to dem Friday night, 'De Lord's gettin' ti'ed of our wicked ways.' Don't you know, nobody come to de mournin' bench now but little chillun? I feel lack de mothers and fathers, mothers expecially, send 'em outta de way, look lack to me. Dey is comfort' seats; won't be worried wid 'em back yonder. It's lack dat everywhere I been." Pipes, *Say Amen, Brother!*, 46.

29 For his immersion in these religious communities and for his prophesying, Pipes was impugned for being less than "objective" by Thomas D. Pawley. See his review in the

Quarterly Journal of Speech 37 (1951): 498–500. In spite of this comment, Pawley deemed Pipes's book "highly readable, even fascinating."

30   Perhaps the most important factor in determining which sermons Pipes recorded and then transcribed and analyzed was which rural churches actually had electricity. See Pipes, *Say Amen, Brother!*, 6.

31   Medhurst, "The Academic Study of Public Address," xxiv.

32   Lionel Newsom and William Gorden, "A Stormy Rally in Atlanta," *Today's Speech* 11 (1963): 18–21.

33   William Gorden, "An Antiphonal Negro Sermon," *Today's Speech* 12 (1964): 17–19; Maxine Schnitzer Ferris, "The Speaking of Roy Wilkins," *Central States Speech Journal* 16 (1965): 91–98; Pat Jefferson, "The Magnificent Barbarian at Nashville," *Southern Speech Journal* 33 (1967): 77–87; and Elizabeth Flory Phifer and Dencil R. Taylor, "Carmichael in Tallahassee," *Southern Speech Journal* 33 (1967): 88–92.

34   Roy L. Hill, ed., *Rhetoric of Racial Revolt* (Denver, CO: Golden Bell, 1964); Haig A. Bosmajian and Hamida Bosmajian, eds., *The Rhetoric of the Civil-Rights Movement* (New York: Random House, 1969); Robert L. Scott and Wayne Brockriede, eds., *The Rhetoric of Black Power* (New York: Harper and Row, 1969); Marcus H. Boulware, *The Oratory of Negro Leaders: 1900–1968* (Westport, CT: Negro Universities Press, 1969); Jamye Coleman Williams and McDonald Williams, eds., *The Negro Speaks: The Rhetoric of Contemporary Black Leaders* (New York: Noble and Noble, 1970); Molefi K. Asante [Arthur L. Smith] and Stephen Robb, eds., *The Voice of Black Rhetoric: Selections* (Boston: Allyn and Bacon, 1971); James L. Golden and Richard D. Rieke, eds., *The Rhetoric of Black Americans* (Columbus, OH: Merrill, 1971); and Daniel J. O'Neill, ed., *Speeches by Black Americans* (Encino, CA: Dickinson, 1971).

35   Critical essays on "black oratory" or "black rhetoric" also proliferated during this same time period. Though not an exhaustive listing, they include Karl W. Anatol and John R. Bittner, "Kennedy on King: The Rhetoric of Control," *Today's Speech* 16 (1968): 31–34; Harry W. Bowen, "Does Non-Violence Persuade?" *Today's Speech* 11 (1963): 10–11; Harry W. Bowen, "The Future of Non-Violence," *Today's Speech* 11 (1963): 3–4; Wayne Brockriede and Robert L. Scott, "Stokely Carmichael: Two Speeches on Black Power," *Central States Speech Journal* 19 (1968): 3–13; R. D. Brooks, "Black Power: The Dimensions of a Slogan," *Western Speech* 34 (1970): 108–114; P. G. Burgess, "The Rhetoric of Black Power: A Moral Demand?" *Quarterly Journal of Speech* 54 (1968): 122–133; P. G. Burgess, "The Racial Crisis: Intolerable Conflict Versus Democratic Tolerance," *Quarterly Journal of Speech* 55 (1969): 318–323; Karlyn Kohrs Campbell, "The Rhetoric of Radical Black Nationalism: A Case Study in Self-Conscious Criticism," *Central States Speech Journal* 22 (1971): 151–160; M. Dickens and R. E. Schwartz, "Oral Argument Before the Supreme Court: *Marshall vs. Davis* in the School Segregation Cases," *Quarterly Journal of Speech* 57 (1971): 32–42; Wayne Flynt, "The Ethics of Democratic Persuasion and the Birmingham Crisis," *Southern Speech Journal* 35 (1969): 50–53; Richard B. Gregg and A. Jackson McCormack, " 'Whitey' Goes to the Ghetto: A Personal Chronicle of a Communication Experiment with Black Youths," *Today's Speech* 16 (1968): 25–30; Richard B. Gregg, A. Jackson McCormack, and Douglas J. Pedersen, "The Rhetoric of Black Power: A Street-Level Interpretation," *Quarterly Journal of Speech* 55 (1969): 151–160; David M. Jabusche, "The Rhetoric of Civil Rights," *Western Speech* 30 (1966): 176–184; Pat Jefferson, " 'Stokely's Cool': Style," *Today's Speech* 16 (1968): 19–24; Patrick Kennicott and Wayne E. Page, "H. Rap Brown:

The Cambridge Incident," *Quarterly Journal of Speech* 57 (1971): 325–334; Andrew A. King, "The Rhetorical Legacy of the Black Church," *Central States Speech Journal* 22 (1971): 179–185; Charles U. Larson, "The Trust-Establishing Function of the Rhetoric of Black Power," *Central States Speech Journal* 21 (1970): 52–56; Gladys Ritchie, "The Sit-In: A Rhetoric of Human Action," *Today's Speech* 18 (1970): 22–25; Robert L. Scott, "Justifying Violence: The Rhetoric of Militant Black Power," *Central States Speech Journal* 19 (1968): 96–104; Robert L. Scott and Donald K. Smith, "The Rhetoric of Confrontation," *Quarterly Journal of Speech* 55 (1969): 1–8; Molefi K. Asante [Arthur L. Smith], "Socio-Historical Perspectives on Black Oratory," *Quarterly Journal of Speech* 56 (1970): 264–269; Molefi K. Asante [Arthur L. Smith], "Markings of an African Concept of Rhetoric," *Today's Speech* 19 (1971): 13–18; Donald H. Smith, "Social Protest ... and The Oratory of Human Rights," *Today's Speech* 15 (1967): 2–8; Donald H. Smith, "Martin Luther King, Jr.: In the Beginning at Montgomery," *Southern Speech Journal* 34 (1968): 8–17; John H. Thurber and John L. Petelle, "The Negro Pulpit and Civil Rights," *Central States Speech Journal* 19 (1968): 273–278; Philip C. Wander, "Salvation Through Separation: The Image of the Negro in the American Colonization Society," *Quarterly Journal of Speech* 57 (1971): 57–67; Richard L. Weaver II, "The Negro Issue: Agitation in the Michigan Lyceum," *Central States Speech Journal* 22 (1971): 196–201; and Ronald Williams, "Race and the Word," *Today's Speech* 19 (1971): 27–33. For a more complete and multi-disciplinary survey of race and rhetoric scholarship, see Robert W. Glenn, ed., *Black Rhetoric: A Guide to Afro-American Communication* (Metuchen, NJ: Scarecrow, 1976).

36   Brake and Neuleib, "Famous Women Orators: An Opinion Survey," 34–35.

37   Patricia Scileppi Kennedy and Gloria Hartmann O'Shields, eds., *We Shall Be Heard: Women Speakers in America* (Dubuque, IA: Kendall/Hunt, 1983); Philip S. Foner, ed., *Mother Jones Speaks: Speeches and Writings of a Working-Class Fighter* (New York: Pathfinder, 1983); and Marilyn Richardson, ed., *Maria W. Stewart, America's First Black Woman Political Writer: Essays and Speeches* (Bloomington: Indiana University Press, 1987).

38   Karlyn Kohrs Campbell, ed., *Man Cannot Speak For Her: Key Texts of the Early Feminists* (Westport, CT: Praeger, 1989); and Karlyn Kohrs Campbell, *Man Cannot Speak For Her: A Critical Study of Early Feminist Rhetoric* (Westport, CT: Praeger, 1989).

39   S. Michele Nix, ed., *Women at the Podium* (New York: Harper, 2000); Joy Ritchie and Kate Ronald, eds., *Available Means: An Anthology of Women's Rhetoric(s)* (Pittsburgh: University of Pittsburgh Press, 2001); and Sandra J. Sarkela, Susan Mallon Ross, and Margaret A. Lowe, eds., *From Megaphones to Microphones: Speeches of American Women, 1920–1960* (Westport, CT: Praeger, 2003).

40   Robbie Jean Walker, ed., *The Rhetoric of Struggle: Public Address by African American Women* (New York: Garland, 1992); Shirley Wilson Logan, ed., *We Are Coming: The Persuasive Discourse of Nineteenth-Century Black Women* (Carbondale: Southern Illinois University Press, 1999); and Barbara A. Holmes, ed., *A Private Woman in Public Spaces: Barbara Jordan's Speeches on Ethics, Public Religion, and Law* (Harrisburg, PA: Trinity, 2000).

41   Deborah Gillan Straub, ed., *Voices of Multicultural America: Notable Speeches Delivered by African, Asian, Hispanic, and Native Americans, 1790–1995* (New York: Gale, 1995); Ronald K. Burke, ed., *American Public Discourse: A Multicultural Perspective*

(Lanham, MD: University Press of America, 1992); Barbara Alice Mann, ed., *Native American Speakers of the Eastern Woodlands* (Westport, CT: Greenwood Press, 2001); Richard J. Jensen and John C. Hammerback, eds., *The Words of Cesar Chavez* (College Station: Texas A&M University Press, 2002); and Josh Gottheimer, ed., *Ripples of Hope: Great American Civil Rights Speeches* (New York: Basic Books, 2003). In 2007 the field published its first anthology of critical essays on "queer" public address. See Charles E. Morris III, ed., *Queering Public Address: Sexualities in American Historical Discourse* (Columbia: University of South Carolina Press, 2007).

42   Stephen E. Lucas and Martin J. Medhurst, eds., *Words of a Century: The Top 100 American Speeches, 1900–1999* (New York: Oxford University Press, 2009).

43   Stephen E. Lucas, "The Renaissance of American Public Address: Text and Context in Rhetorical Criticism," *Quarterly Journal of Speech* 74 (1988): 241.

44   While trade presses Greenwood and Praeger were on the leading edge of the publication outlets fueling the renaissance in the 1980s and 1990s, other academic and trade presses have begun to feature the fruits of recovery and discovery efforts; these include Baylor University Press, the University Press of Mississippi, Syracuse University Press, Texas A&M University Press, Southern Illinois University Press, the University of Pittsburgh Press, Waveland, St. Martin's, and Lawrence Erlbaum. I would call particular attention to Texas A&M University Press's new Landmark Speeches series, which will publish several short volumes of speeches that highlight seminal rhetorical moments of a particular movement or epoch. In addition, the award-winning journal *Rhetoric & Public Affairs*, founded in 1998 by Martin J. Medhurst and published by Michigan State University Press, is an important, nationally recognized outlet for public address scholarship.

45   Janice D. Hamlet, "Fannie Lou Hamer: The Unquenchable Spirit of the Civil Rights Movement," *Journal of Black Studies* 26 (1996): 560–576.

46   Always call ahead to notify archivists of impending visits. Not only can they begin gathering germane materials, but they will also notify researchers of any restrictions placed on an archive's collections. In addition, many archives store their collections off-site, so it is imperative that archivists are carefully consulted at least one week in advance of a research trip.

47   There are, however, some important drawbacks to audiotapes: breaks in a tape caused by equipment failure or running out of recording material during a speech; a microphone that works intermittently or a speaker who strays from speaking into it; poor acoustics; and audiotapes whose sound quality has been compromised by age, preservation conditions, or both.

48   There are several civil rights-related collections available through interlibrary loan, including the Papers of the NAACP, the Papers of the Southern Christian Leadership Conference, the Papers of the American Missionary Association's Race Relations Conference, the Papers of the Southern Regional Council, the Papers of the Congress of Racial Equality (with addenda), the Papers of the Student Nonviolent Coordinating Committee, KZSU's (Stanford University) Project South, 1965, Civil Rights During the Kennedy Administration, and Civil Rights During the Johnson Administration. Personal papers include Mary McLeod Bethune, Horace Mann Bond, W. E. B. Du Bois, Modjeska Simkins, and Fannie Lou Hamer.

49   Zarefsky, "Reflections on Rhetorical Criticism," 384.

5

The Processes and Challenges of Textual Authentication

Robert N. Gaines

In 1994, Edwin Black offered a new interpretation of Abraham Lincoln's "Gettysburg Address."[1] The essay began with a full presentation of the text, and Black's analysis of that text initially considered "audiences." On this subject Black observed that Lincoln's first two paragraphs were concerned with universal, national, and local audiences (lines 1–9 in Black's text).[2] Black then proceeded to analyze Lincoln's third paragraph as follows:

> "But" (10) begins a decisive shift in perspective. The "larger sense" (10) that will now inform the discourse is a sense no longer merely of appropriateness, but, more encompassing, of moral adequacy. "But" also crystallizes a shift of the object of the Address to the audience at Gettysburg. The immediate audience had been discussed (6–9) only in its relation to the larger historical account. Beginning with "but," its capacities and obligations occupy the speech. The focus remains arrested on the cemetery at Gettysburg for awhile, reinforced by six references to "here" – six references in five lines (12, 14, 15, 16, 17).
>
> The word "here" tolls like a bell through that period of fixation on the present moment. It appears a total of eight times in the speech. Two functions, at least, can be attributed to the repetition of "here," in addition to the enhancement of the rhythmic solemnity of the Address. One is the pointing these repetitions do of the occasion … During the section of the speech when the audience's attention is fastened on the occasion, "here" serves to remind them not only of that occasion, but also of how bounded the occasion is, and of the co-existence with the "here" of a "there": a different and less bounded time and place. … The other function of the repetition of "here" – a subtler function – relates to the pun on "hear," a recurrent command issued to the audience to attend. Faintly, allophonically, Lincoln directs his audience to listen.
>
> The first-person plural references during the middle of the speech (6–14) all have the audience at Gettysburg at their center. With the instruction to "us the living" (15), however, the synecdochal character of the first-person plural begins re-emerging to a point of unmistakable clarity (21) that "we" stand in deputy to the whole nation and

act on its behalf. The audience, then, transcribes a movement through the speech from unspecified universal (1–3) to national (4) to local (6–14), back to national again.[3]

Black's comments in this passage bristle with the sort of insight that earned his textual readings much admiration across several decades. In this case, though, there is a difficulty. The text that Black reads is not the one that Lincoln delivered at Gettysburg. In fact, Black's reading-text did not exist until three months after the cemetery dedication had passed.[4] Throughout Black's analysis, his employment of an anachronistic text of the "Gettysburg Address" involves him in four references to language that did not exist in Lincoln's actual speech performance.[5] The methodological problem associated with such references is obvious: Black makes scholarly assertions about Lincoln's speech performance at Gettysburg using evidence from a different speech text, one that was composed and published much later and for a different purpose.[6] In the passage just quoted, for example, the anachronistic text leads Black to count one too many instances of "here" in the space of "five lines" of the speech.[7] At this point and elsewhere, the anachronistic text insinuates itself inextricably into Black's argument, and the result is that Black's conclusions cannot generally be accepted as advancing knowledge of Lincoln's actual address at Gettysburg.

I offer the example of Black's analysis to raise an important consideration. Historical and critical knowledge claims about rhetorical discourse depend inherently upon the texts employed as objects of scholarly inquiry. Insofar as such texts are anachronistic, inaccurate, or otherwise misrepresentative, then the arguments to which they give rise must necessarily fall short of the disciplinary standards applicable to public address scholarship. The implication is that public address scholars are obliged to ensure the reliability of texts that figure in their disciplinary arguments.

Text authentication is the method whereby the reliability of texts may be ensured, and the present essay is designed to historicize and explicate the method of text authentication as it relates to public address inquiry. I shall begin with a brief sketch of the engagement of text authentication with American public address scholarship from the nineteenth century until now. In consideration of this engagement, the remainder of my remarks will consider text authentication as a theoretical and procedural matter. I shall first describe recent developments in public address inquiry that affect text authentication, not the least of which is the extension of the term "text," which now includes linguistic, acoustic, and visual performances and artifacts. I shall then explain five authentication activities that should be used to establish and document texts of rhetorical discourses, specifically (1) collection of texts, (2) analysis of texts, (3) selection of a composition-text, (4) refinement of the composition-text, and (5) explanation of the refined text. To the extent possible, my remarks on these activities will be accompanied by illustrations connected with three well-known rhetorical discourses, Abraham Lincoln's "Gettysburg Address," Jimi Hendrix's Woodstock performance of the "Star Spangled Banner," and the photographic image known as "Old Glory Goes Up on

Mt. Suribachi, Iwo Jima."[8] I have chosen these discourses for special attention because they offer instructive examples of linguistic, acoustic, and visual texts.

Historical Background

The problem of text authentication was recognized in American public address inquiry by the early nineteenth century. Nathaniel Chapman prefaced his *Select Speeches* of 1808 with the following critical observations:

> In the collation of the contents of these volumes, the editor, rejecting vague reports, and newspaper authority, has been particularly solicitous to select such orations and pleadings, as have undergone the revision, or been published under the superintend-ance of the author. He has been sedulous to follow with fidelity the text, nor ever presumed foolishly, if not flagitiously, to interpolate the copy; a practice, which of late, has become a sort of fashion in America, to the confusion of authors, and to the prejudice of learning.[9]

Some later scholars expressed similar concerns,[10] but, in general, early public address inquiry demonstrated little interest in text authentication.[11] Where the problem was considered at all, scholarly approaches were typically anecdotal, point-ing out discrepancies between printed texts and spoken words,[12] or cautionary, illustrating difficulties posed by forms of evidence for delivered speeches.[13] Within this context, the development of critical theory to guide textual authentication processes was very limited.

The earliest systematic attempt to theorize text authentication for public address inquiry came in Lester Thonssen and A. Craig Baird's *Speech Criticism* of 1948, where the scope of text authentication study was specified as follows:

> Investigations into the authenticity of texts are of two principal types. The first attempts to answer the question, "Did the specified orator actually deliver the speech, or is it spurious?" The second searches out the answer to this query, "Admitting that the speaker gave the speech, is this the way he said it?" ... Modern critics are con-cerned, in the main, with the second type of investigation, seeking to answer the question as to whether the available text mirrors the words originally spoken by the orator.[14]

Thonssen and Baird offered two sorts of advice regarding the principles of textual authentication. They stressed the importance of bibliographical research to find "the most authentic texts" before proceeding to criticism.[15] They also insisted, "The best method of getting an authentic text is ... to make a recording of the speech while it is being delivered."[16] In the absence of a recording, they advised, the critic should turn to collation or comparison.[17] Thonssen and Baird's summary position on text authentication was that "[i]t is the critic's obligation to determine textual authenticity – to establish the best possible text through such processes of investigation and collation as may be open to him."[18]

The doctrine of text authentication proposed by Thonssen and Baird was consistent with text-critical theories of the time, though it fell short of them in a crucial respect. Where a "recording of the speech" did not exist, Thonssen and Baird offered no methical procedure to establish texts suitable for scholarly purposes. Specific methods for text establishment had been available in modern literary studies for almost half a century,[19] and the omission of analogous methods by Thonssen and Baird may partly explain why text authentication research after *Speech Criticism* generally continued along anecdotal and cautionary lines of inquiry.[20]

In other ways, mid-twentieth-century scholarship on text authentication of speeches was more advanced. By the 1940s, it was widely acknowledged that elite speakers collaborated with ghostwriters in the preparation of their speeches, and beginning in the 1950s public address studies interrogated the significance of the ghostwriting phenomenon as a problem in criticism of rhetorical discourse.[21] One upshot of such studies was the recognition that many speeches could not be attributed to an individual speaker; rather, "authorship" had to be distributed among multiple contributors in a composition process.[22] By 1960 multiple authorship was recognized as a problem for text authentication of rhetorical discourse,[23] and in this respect public address inquiry anticipated textual studies in literature by more than two decades.[24]

A method for establishing reliable texts of speeches was eventually proposed by James Cleary and Herbert Hildebrandt in 1961.[25] Their recommendations were designed to assist in preparing critical editions of speeches and other texts, and they covered bibliography, collation, selection of the copy-text, modification of the copy-text, and clarification of the edited text. Bibliography accounted for extant manuscripts and all published editions.[26] Collation involved comparison of texts to identify differences.[27] In light of collation, editors considered the kinds of texts available, then selected a copy-text (i.e., the particular text instance on which the editor would base a critical edition). Cleary and Hildebrandt recommended that the copy-text should be the one "which best approaches the final revision the author intended for publication and which best accommodates the special interests of the editor."[28] Copy-text modification – when employed – was for modernizing type style, spelling, and syntax.[29] Finally, clarification of the edited text documented departures from the copy-text as well as text variations existing within copies of the copy-text edition and among other editions.[30]

Cleary and Hildebrandt's method offered a useful expansion of text authentication theory. However, this expansion was not well adapted to the practical needs of public address scholars because it was based on text-critical theories designed for establishment of literary artworks.[31] Consequently, Cleary and Hildebrandt neglected types of text instances that were relevant to authentication of speeches (e.g., stenographic transcriptions). They also ignored the complexities of choosing among different types of text instances for differing critical purposes (e.g., oral and published speeches are often different and destined for different audiences). Finally, they did not address problems of text establishment that were especially acute in cases of oral speech, including spelling, word division, capitalization, punctuation, and paragraphing of stenographic transcriptions; correction of flawed copy-texts; and documentation of editorial intervention in corrected texts.

Some deficiencies in Cleary and Hildebrandt's method of text authentication were addressed by later studies. Writing in 1965, Richard Murphy discussed types of speech text instances and the necessity for text correction even in the best available texts.[32] Murphy recognized six forms of speech text instances: pre-delivery texts, electronically recorded texts, stenographic texts, texts constructed by reporters and observers, post-delivery texts, and texts revised and published after delivery.[33] Of particular importance were Murphy's remarks on electronic recordings and published texts of speeches. Before Murphy, the standard view in public address inquiry had been that electronically recorded speeches were the best source of authentic texts.[34] However, Murphy discussed two ways in which even electronically recorded text instances might require editorial intervention, namely, when the speaker pronounced the text inarticulately or committed a mistake in phrase or diction.[35] Concerning published texts of speeches, Murphy insisted that these were "real" speeches quite apart from their oral manifestations, because they were composed in speech form and called speeches by their composers, even when they had not been delivered.[36] Thus, Murphy conceptualized published speech editions as rhetorical discourses in their own right.[37] Additional development of text authentication theory came in 1972 from Robert Smith's discussion of special problems related to oral–aural texts.[38] Smith noted that editors of oral–aural texts must concern themselves with spelling, capitalization, punctuation, and paragraphing (because these are not obvious from delivered speech), and he suggested collation with written text instances as a means of justifying editorial decisions regarding these textual features.[39] Further, he elaborated Murphy's observations that speaker articulation and error posed problems for the critic.[40]

The advances in text authentication theory initiated by Cleary and Hildebrandt, Murphy, and Smith provided public address scholars with a workable method for establishing and documenting speeches and other linguistic forms of rhetorical discourse. Nevertheless, public address inquiry proceeded almost independently of this method. Studies with a focus on textual authentication itself generally persisted along anecdotal and cautionary lines.[41] Publication of speeches in anthologies did not typically involve editors in establishment and documentation of the texts they presented.[42] And critical studies of rhetorical discourse routinely relied on published editions without any deliberate consideration of the authenticity of the text.[43]

More recently, text authentication has almost disappeared in public address inquiry. In the last decade or so, only a handful of studies in public address have seriously entertained text authentication as a theoretical or methodological concern.[44] Moreover, text authentication is ignored in all three encyclopedic treatments of rhetoric published since the mid-1990s.[45] Finally, as a pedagogical matter, it appears that public address inquiry could completely lose touch with text authentication inasmuch as standard sources for teaching rhetorical criticism omit any treatment of the subject.[46] In this circumstance, there is both need and urgency to reconsider text authentication and its methodological relation to contemporary public address inquiry.

Theory and Method in Text Authentication

Rhetorical discourses are the objects toward which public address inquiry is directed, and accordingly, the texts of such discourses constitute foundational data for historical and critical knowledge claims that arise in public address studies. On this account, the establishment and documentation of reliable texts for rhetorical discourses – that is, text authentication – has been conceived and necessarily remains as a necessary step in public address scholarship. Of course, the project of text authentication has changed somewhat over time as public address scholars have taken an increasingly complicated perspective on rhetorical transactions and the forms of interpretation that are germane to their explanation. Therefore, as a prerequisite to any contemporary account of method in text authentication, it is necessary to consider these complications at least insofar as they affect the scope and resources of textual investigation.

Of particular importance to the method of text authentication have been advances in conceptual thinking about discourses and texts, authors, audiences, and contexts. What constitutes a rhetorical *discourse*, for instance, has changed since the 1950s to include not just speaking and writing,[47] but also photographs, films, television programs, video clips, Internet pages and sites, graphic and plastic artworks and illustrations, cartoons, monuments, landscapes, music, public demonstrations, personal gestures, and many other means of generating meaning.[48] Consistent with this expansion of rhetorical discourse, the notion of *text* pertinent to discursive phenomena has been extended to include not only linguistic, but also acoustic and visual performances and artifacts.[49] Similarly, the standard conception of *speaker* or *author* for some time referred exclusively to composer-performers of rhetorical discourses;[50] however, since the 1940s, scholars have increasingly recognized that authorship of rhetorical discourse is a social and cultural practice that often depends upon collaboration.[51] Accordingly, the term *author* now refers to the complex of individuals who are creatively involved in the construction, presentation, or publication of a given discourse (including, for example, speakers, writers, performers, ghostwriters, advisors, technicians, editors, directors, organizers, producers, publishers, and discourse consumers). At least through the 1960s, rhetorical *audiences* were conceived mainly as groups of decision-makers or change-mediators that could be influenced by discourse.[52] These days, the standard view of *audiences* emphasizes their capacities for multiplicity, for separation in space and time, and for divergence in reception and use of discourses.[53] Such developments require that an *audience* be conceived as any collection of one or more hearers, readers, or spectators of any rhetorical discourse or representative text within any circumstance, moment, or location. Finally, the scholarly notion of *context* was long defined by the situational elements that surrounded and inspired the creation and transmission of rhetorical discourse.[54] However, beginning in the 1990s, *context* was extended to incorporate the full range of circumstances attendant to the production, reproduction, and reception of rhetorical discourse, including its immediate environment of presentation or display (i.e., placement and relation to proximate discourse).[55] As a consequence, the *context* of a given rhetorical discourse can be multiple and can arise at any moment or location associated with any phase of a rhetorical transaction.

I now turn to the method of establishing and documenting texts of rhetorical discourses. As indicated above, my comments will be concerned with five authentication activities: collection of texts, analysis of texts, selection of the composition-text, refinement of the composition-text, and explanation of the refined text. These activities are designed on analogy with standard procedures for editing rhetorical and literary texts.[56] However, I have modified the activities to accommodate current circumstances of public address inquiry insofar as these affect text authentication. As represented here the activities of text authentication have two main applications. In their narrow application, they can be used to create independent critical editions of rhetorical texts; in their broad application, they can be used to ensure that texts subjected to public address research are sufficiently reliable to support scholarly inquiry.

Collection of texts

The first activity in text authentication is to collect instances of the text. The main purpose of text collection is to learn what forms of the text exist; therefore, collection should continue until the authenticator believes that further collection will not capture additional forms.[57] Deciding that text collection is sufficient involves the authenticator in some preliminary analysis of text instances, which points to the fact that the activities of textual authentication are not entirely independent of one another. Still, collection of text instances is an identifiable and necessary activity in its own right, one that involves the authenticator in a broad-ranging investigation concerned with the nature of the discourse and the historical circumstances of its performance, production, or reception. For example, collection of text instances for the photographic image known as "Old Glory Goes Up on Mt. Suribachi, Iwo Jima" would presumably identify at least the original film negative,[58] publicly held prints,[59] published prints,[60] publicly held negatives of the wirephoto,[61] publications of the wirephoto,[62] and representations in other media of the photographic image that have the same general form.[63] Likewise, collection of text instances for Jimi Hendrix's Woodstock performance of the "Star Spangled Banner" would conceivably include the Woodstock concert documentary films[64] and sound recordings,[65] the extant video recordings of Hendrix's performance set at Woodstock,[66] and the performance-set sound recordings.[67] Similarly, collection of text instances for Abraham Lincoln's "Gettysburg Address" would assuredly acknowledge pre-delivery holographic drafts,[68] stenographic representations of the delivered speech,[69] newspaper publications,[70] documentary publications,[71] post-delivery holographic representations,[72] and numerous literary editions of the speech in several media.[73]

The scholarly value of a text instance identified in text collection depends upon the degree to which it constitutes or documents a performance or artifact at stake in the inquiry. Some artifacts (e.g., a painting or a pamphlet) constitute enduring text instances in themselves, and documentary representations of such artifacts may also serve as text instances.[74] However, many performances of speech, visual display, music, or vernacular discourse (including demonstrations and individual gestures[75]) are ephemeral and do not constitute enduring text instances in themselves; these performances – if they are to be represented as texts – must be documented by audio and/or visual recording, stenographic and/or historical report, or methodical description.[76]

Analysis of texts

Once text instances have been collected, they must be compared with one another through collation. Collation is crucial to text authentication, because it allows the authenticator to apprehend how many forms of the text are represented among the instances and to determine which forms of the text represent different versions.[77] Collation involves comparison of texts with respect to their elements or characteristics. Where linguistic texts are at stake, collation normally involves inspection of words, surface features (i.e., spelling, word division, capitalization, punctuation, paragraphing, indications of emphasis[78]), medium, and environment of presentation or display.[79] Acoustic texts can be compared based on their duration, content, acoustic properties, medium, and environment of presentation or display.[80] Visual texts are subject to comparison with respect to dimensions, proportions, contents, resolution, color range, medium, and environment of presentation or display.[81] Live performances as well as films, videos, and Internet pages and sites may combine linguistic, acoustic, and visual information; accordingly, their collations can involve all the forms of comparison already mentioned.[82] Also, many rhetorical discourses are instantiated by texts in multiple modes of representation (linguistic, acoustic, visual); for example, Dwight D. Eisenhower's "Atoms for Peace" speech is instantiated in printed, audio, film, and video texts.[83] In such cases, corresponding textual elements and/or characteristics can be collated across all text instances.

The objective of collation is to discover differences among text instances. If the elements or characteristics of two text instances are not identical, they represent different forms of the text. Where differences between forms of the text cannot be explained by changes that are incidental to processes of representing the text, then they may be said to constitute separate versions. In this connection, a version is a distinct rhetorical discourse. Thus, the photographic representation of the Iwo Jima flag-raising on the cover of *Time* magazine on March 5, 1945 is a different rhetorical discourse from the analogous representation of the Iwo Jima flag-raising on US Treasury war bond posters later in the same year. These images differ with respect to dimensions, proportions, color range, and environment of presentation. So too, different rhetorical discourses are distinguishable in the acoustic/visual representations of Jimi Hendrix's "Star Spangled Banner" provided by *Woodstock* (1970) and by *Jimi Hendrix Live at Woodstock* (2005). The two recordings differ in duration, content, recording properties, color range, medium, and environment of presentation. Likewise, Abraham Lincoln's speech performance at Gettysburg on November 19, 1863 is a different rhetorical discourse from that represented by the text published in the New York State Education Department's *Selections for Study and Memorizing* (1910); the two texts differ at least in terms of words, medium, and environment of presentation. In these cases and more generally, the recognition of versions allows an authenticator to assess variation both within and across versions to determine what – if any – relationships exist among the pertinent texts. Such information may be useful, especially when the development of a text over time is of critical interest. Identification of versions also permits an authenticator to consider the range of texts available as the basic foundation for the text(s) that shall later be subjected to scholarly inquiry.

Selection of the composition-text

From among all versions of a text, and for each version that will be subjected to scholarly inquiry, the authenticator selects one text instance to serve as the composition-text.[84] The purpose of the composition-text is to provide a concrete exemplar of the text that may serve as the basis for a refined text suited to scholarly purposes. A variety of specific factors may influence the selection of a composition-text, but the chief criterion is that the version selected must be appropriate to the objectives of the scholarly inquiry to which the text will be subjected. As a practical rule, the authenticator should select the version of the text that is most closely associated with the rhetorical phenomenon of interest in the particular study at hand.

For example, a study which related the visual text of the Iwo Jima flag-raising to US public opinion concerning military success in the Pacific in early 1945 should almost certainly select the text's presentation on the front page of an American newspaper on Sunday, February 25, 1945. After all, it was in this reception context that most Americans first encountered and responded to the image.[85] However, a study that attempted to explain the establishment of the Iwo Jima flag-raising image as an icon in American political consciousness might reasonably choose – instead or as well – from more enduring or more ubiquitous versions of the image as composition-texts; for instance, the study might focus on the US Treasury war bond drive poster, *Now ... All Together* (1945) or the US postage stamp, *Marines at Iwo Jima* (1945).[86] Again, a study concerned with the popular iconicity of Jimi Hendrix's "Star Spangled Banner" at Woodstock might arguably adopt its representation in the film documentary *Woodstock* (1970) as the composition-text, because this was the version that crystallized Hendrix's performance as a compressed symbol of the hippie movement and youth protest against the war in Vietnam.[87] However, a study attempting to explain the reception of Hendrix's performance among scholarly critics might sensibly include the 1989 reissue of the *Woodstock* soundtrack as a composition-text, inasmuch as this version of the performance seems to have precipitated an enthusiastic reassessment of its musical and cultural significance.[88] In the case of Lincoln's "Gettysburg Address," a study that attempted to understand reception of the speech by the audience at the Gettysburg cemetery could reasonably turn to the Associated Press stenographic transcription for its composition-text. This text provides direct evidence of the words that Lincoln's audience heard; moreover, Lincoln himself relied upon the Associated Press report when he attempted to reconstruct his speech for purposes of documentation.[89] Accordingly, the Associated Press transcript would furnish a firm foundation for investigating how the Gettysburg audience interpreted Lincoln's speech.[90] A study that aimed to explain how Lincoln's speech became an icon in American political culture might reasonably look for multiple composition-texts among the several hundred versions eventually presented in biographical, educational, historical, literary, reference, and monumental publications.[91]

Text authentication is a critical endeavor, and this fact is nowhere more evident than in the selection of composition-texts. Each selection is based on the authenticator's judgment of what constitutes an appropriate text to examine in a particular case of inquiry. Such judgments may be open to question, but they are not merely subjective. Every selection of a composition-text must be based on a rationale, and such rationales are subject to the same disciplinary scrutiny that attaches to all scholarly arguments. For this reason, acceptable rationales provide disciplinary justifications for the scholarly study of selected composition-texts.

Refinement of the composition-text

Refinement of a composition-text involves correcting, emending, or otherwise improving that text, based on pertinent textual and historical information. Many composition-texts do not require refinement prior to their scholarly use. For example, the Iwo Jima flag-raising photograph as presented on the front page of the *New York Times*, February 25, 1945, could be used, without refinement, as the composition-text in a rhetorical study of public opinion formation during World War II. Likewise, Jimi Hendrix's performance of the "Star Spangled Banner" as represented in the film *Woodstock* (1970) could be used as the composition-text, again without refinement, in a rhetorical study of Hendrix's reception in popular culture. In cases such as these, the composition-text and refined text are identical. However, many composition-texts do need refinement, and such needs arise – in the main – from defects, errors, and limitations in their contents.

Defective texts contain at least one passage that is unintelligible or incomplete. Refinement of a defective text may be effected through restoration or supplementation. For example, in editing Mayor Daley's Chicago City Council speech of July 21, 1971, Gerry Philipsen followed an audio recording of the speech as his composition-text.[92] The tape recording itself was of poor quality and included numerous passages that were inaudible or undecipherable.[93] However, based on comparison of the recording with fragmentary newspaper reports of Daley's comments, Philipsen was able to restore words that were unintelligible in the audio recording alone.[94]

An erroneous text contains information that is inconsistent with the factual or intended rhetorical performance or artifact that it represents. Textual errors commonly arise in linguistic representations of speech performances. The main sources of these errors are mistakes incidental to the mechanics of representation (e.g., omission, misspelling, duplication) and mistakes of report (e.g., deletion, substitution, insertion). The means of discovering such errors are close reading and collation of texts, and the first recourse to remedy these errors should always be the adoption of readings from text instances and versions outside of the composition-text. For example, collation of the Associated Press report of Lincoln's "Gettysburg Address" with other stenographic transcriptions shows that where the Associated Press report uses the plural "Governments," other transcriptions use the singular.[95] In this case, the text of the Associated Press report would appear to be erroneous, and presumably it should be refined with the singular form. However, emendation of composition-texts based on variant readings ought to be performed very cautiously, taking care that the text instances and versions employed are appropriate for the purposes to which they are being applied. For instance, in the attempt to represent Lincoln's speech performance at Gettysburg, changes in the Associated Press report based on subsequently published editions of the speech would be inappropriate, because we know such editions incorporated substantial revisions. Where alternative text instances and versions are silent or in agreement with the composition-text, the authenticator should suggest conjectural emendations only when these are necessary to create an intelligible text and, then, only when both the source of error and its specific correction are obvious (e.g., where the only available version of a text contains a typographical error).[96]

Textual errors can also arise in rhetorical performances and artifacts themselves, where rhetorical performers unintentionally misperform their discourses or deviate sporadically from their planned performance to accommodate audience participation in the transaction. These misperformances and deviations are usually obvious in audio and video representations of rhetorical discourse, and their handling requires a principled decision as to whether they constitute a substantial element of the performance or a mistake of representation incidental to the performance. Based on this decision, these textual features can either be retained or refined.[97]

Even complete and accurate texts may be affected by limitations that require improvement. Stenographic reports as well as audio and video recordings of speech performances do not contain all the information that is required for linguistic representation, particularly in relation to surface features; accordingly, in constructing linguistic representations of speech performances from such texts, authenticators must adopt some methodical approach to the establishment of these features. Where authoritative linguistic versions of the speech performance are available, as in the case of Lincoln's speech at Gettysburg, the authenticator should select a suitable version as the surface-feature exemplar and generally follow this exemplar throughout the linguistic representation of the speech performance.[98] Where authoritative linguistic versions of the speech are not available, as in the case of Mayor Daley's speech of July 21, 1971, the authenticator should introduce surface features according to explicitly stated principles. In constructing such principles, the authenticator should be guided by practices exhibited elsewhere by the author and/or by conventional editing practices for discourses of the sort represented.[99]

Explanation of the refined text

Refinement of a composition-text establishes a text that is suitable for scholarly inquiry. However, in order to demonstrate the reliability of such a text for research applications, it is necessary to document the text with explanations of what linguistic, acoustic, or visual performance or artifact is the subject of authentication, what source materials have been used in the authentication process, and what procedures the authenticator has followed.

Explaining what text is the subject of authentication should identify and contextualize the performance or artifact that is in question. This may involve a historical or interpretive account of the text, a discussion of the circumstances and textual environment in which it was presented or displayed, and a summary of its contents. However, at minimum, this sort of explanation need only specify the performance or artifact, its context of occurrence, and where necessary, evidence of its existence. Explanation of source materials should specify the textual evidence that is relevant to the establishment of the refined composition-text. This sort of explanation should at least document every text instance or version that figures in the established text; it may also identify and document additional texts of significance in previous authentications. Explanation of the procedures followed by the authenticator should at least (a) specify the authenticator's rationale for selection of the composition-text, (b) specify the method used in establishing surface features of the text, (c) specify and justify any departure from the composition-text, and (d) where necessary, annotate text elements, persons, entities, or events and/or explicate specific textual decisions of the authenticator.[100]

The authenticator's explanation of the refined composition-text may be presented systematically or distributed throughout the report of a research study.[101] However, it is crucial that every authentication should specify its text, identify its sources, and document both the design and application of its procedures. The reason is that the reliability of a scholarly text is inherently dependent upon the explanation that accompanies it. The Modern Language Association's *Guidelines for Editors of Scholarly Editions* articulate the principle in this way:

> The scholarly edition's basic task is to present a reliable text … Reliability is established by accuracy, adequacy, appropriateness, consistency, explicitness – accuracy with respect to texts, adequacy and appropriateness with respect to documenting editorial principles and practice, consistency and explicitness with respect to methods.[102]

In line with this principle, it is only through explanation of a refined text that an authenticator's text collection, analysis, selection, and refinement become visible and subject to scholarly assessment. Accordingly, explanation of the refined composition-text is the final and most important activity in establishing and documenting reliable texts for public address inquiry.

Conclusion

Few scholars of public address would deny that the textual performances and artifacts to which they devote their research should be reliable. Nevertheless, for some time there has been little attention to text authentication in public address research and instruction. This conflict between principle and practice is explicable, I think, as a consequence of three problems. First, despite a gradual development of text authentication method from the 1940s to the 1970s, it never addressed the full range of technical problems associated with rhetorical discourse in its linguistic, acoustic, and visual forms. Second, text authentication method did not contemplate the complexities posed by different critical outlooks on the rhetorical transaction; for example, outlooks focused on audience reception or processes of text production and placement as opposed to author intentions and strategies. Third, text authentication method was not systematically adjusted over time to address conceptual advancements in rhetorical studies concerning authors, texts, audiences, and contexts. Arguably, then, text authentication method was ignored and eventually abandoned because it was incapable of direct application to existing and developing lines of inquiry.

The present essay has been designed to reposition text authentication in public address studies. Reliable texts are essential to the enterprise of historical and critical research on rhetorical discourse, and text authentication is here proposed as a methodical way of ensuring reliable texts. As I have described it, text authentication method involves the scholar in as many as five activities: collection of texts, analysis of texts, selection of a composition-text, refinement of the composition text, and explanation of the refined text. The purpose of these activities is to assist scholars in identifying, assessing, and documenting texts that are appropriate to their scholarly approach and specific research objectives. In explicating a text authentication method, I have tried to make its principles sensitive to the great diversity of performances and artifacts, critical perspectives, and theoretical commitments that are characteristic to contemporary public address studies. Nonetheless, I recognize that this statement on text authentication is neither exhaustive nor likely to endure long before it needs revision. A number of issues concerning authentication practice could not be addressed in a general essay. For instance, I was not able to provide specific principles for methodical documentation of acoustic and visual discourse contents. It may be added that rapid development of scholarly theory and practice in public address will inevitably require revision of this statement in the near future. Of course, developments in knowledge-making about rhetorical transactions are difficult to predict. Still, in whatever circumstance rhetorical discourse becomes an object of scholarly inquiry, it will always be possible to ensure by rational means that texts are as reliable as possible. Inasmuch as reliability is a criterion for the adequacy of texts in public address scholarship, the application, elaboration, and eventual extension of text authentication method would seem to be worth the effort.

Appendix

Documented Authentication of Abraham Lincoln's Speech Performance at the Consecration of the National Cemetery at Gettysburg, Pennsylvania, November 19, 1863

[1] Four score and seven years ago our fathers brought forth, upon this continent, a new nation, conceived in Liberty, and dedicated to the proposition that all men are created equal.

[2] Now we are engaged in a great civil war, testing whether that nation, or any nation, so conceived, and so dedicated, can long endure. We are met on a great battle-field of that war. We are met to dedicate a portion of it as the final resting place of those who here gave their lives that that nation might live. It is altogether fitting and proper that we should do this.

[3] But in a larger sense we can not dedicate – we can not consecrate – we can not hallow this ground. The brave men, living and dead, who struggled here, have consecrated it far above our power to add or detract. The world will little note, nor long remember, what we say here, but it can never forget what they did here. It is for us, the living, rather to be dedicated here to the unfinished work that they have, thus far, so nobly carried on. It is rather for us to be here dedicated to the great task remaining before us – that from these honored dead we take increased devotion to that cause for which they here gave the last full measure of devotion – that we here highly resolve that these dead shall not have died in vain; that the nation shall under God have a new birth of freedom, and that government of the people, by the people, for the people, shall not perish from the earth.

Text specification

This text represents Abraham Lincoln's speech performance at Gettysburg, Pennsylvania, November 19, 1863. The speech performance and its immediate environment of presentation are documented in Everett and Lincoln, *Address of Hon. Edward Everett*, 22–88.

Source materials

A = Associated Press report; H = Hale report; L = Hay Copy.[103]

Authentication procedures

This text offers a minimal authentication of Lincoln's speech performance at Gettysburg. Sources are limited to those required to establish the text, and source variants other than departures from the composition-text are not systematically documented.

Rationale for composition-text selection: The composition-text is the Associated Press report (= A). A is a stenographic transcription of the speech and so offers direct evidence of Lincoln's spoken words. Also, A was considered to be generally accurate by Lincoln who consulted it when asked to document his delivered speech (Nicolay, "Lincoln's Gettysburg Address").

Establishment of surface features. Spelling, word division, capitalization, punctuation, and paragraphing follow the Lincoln holographic manuscript known as the Hay Copy (= L); there are no ambiguous end-of-line hyphenations in this version of the text. Consistent with paragraphing in L, paragraph numbers have been introduced in the text within square brackets.

Departures from the composition-text. L evidently precedes Lincoln's speech performance; and of the two pre-speech holographs, L is closer than the Nicolay Copy to stenographic reports A and H (Boritt, *The Gettysburg Gospel*, 94, 272–286). Accordingly, L is used as evidence of Lincoln's intentions for words to be delivered in the speech. This evidence is employed to corroborate departures from the composition-text that follow the stenographic transcription of Hale (= H). The following represent departures from the composition-text (= A): 3 unfinished HL: refinished A 3 thus far so nobly HL: thus so far nobly A 3 that these dead HL: that the dead A 3 government HL: Governments A 3 by the people, for the people HL: by the people and for the people A.

Annotations. Some scholars claim that in paragraph 3 Lincoln's speech performance text should read "our poor power" based on stenographic transcriptions published in *The Philadelphia Inquirer* ("our poor attempts") and *Chicago Tribune* ("our poor power").[104] This claim is based on the supposition that "poor" in the transcripts is inexplicable unless Lincoln said it; see, e.g., Roy P. Basler, ed., *The Collected Works of Abraham Lincoln*, 9 vols. (New Brunswick, NJ: Rutgers University Press, 1953–1955), 7: 19n.19; Boritt, *The Gettysburg Gospel*, 331, 371. In my view, this argument is not cogent. Appearance of "poor" might easily be the result of an insertion error in both transcriptions. At mid-nineteenth century there was a common figure of speech in American English involving the phrase "poor power," often in the sense of humble understatement; see, e.g., "deserves a higher encomium than it is in our poor power to bestow" ("Scriptural Anthology, or Biblical Illustrations, with Extracts," *The Gentlemen's Magazine* 2 [1838]: 66); "I am heartily willing, to my poor power, to serve you in his education" (Matthew Henry, *Memoir of the Rev. Philip Henry*, ed. J. B. Williams [New York: American Tract Society, 1853], 195); "I could wish to do what lay in my poor power to comfort 'em" (Mary Cowden Clarke, *The Iron Cousin; or, Mutual Influence*, [New York: Appleton, 1863], 459). Contemporary circulation of "poor power" as an artful form of expression could easily have influenced the transcriptions in *The Philadelphia Inquirer* and *Chicago Tribune*; moreover, the general likelihood of an insertion error in these transcriptions is high, since both are affected by numerous *other* insertion errors.

Notes

1   Edwin Black, "Gettysburg and Silence," *Quarterly Journal of Speech* 80 (1994): 21–36.
2   Black, "Gettysburg and Silence," 22–23.
3   Black, "Gettysburg and Silence," 23–24.
4   Black offers no source for his text of the "Gettysburg Address"; however, a detailed comparison of Black's text against known versions of the speech discloses that he unquestionably resorts to the so-called Bliss Copy (Gettysburg Address, Lincoln Room, White House, Washington, DC). In fact, the text Black publishes is identical with the Bliss Copy except in its omission of the comma where the Bliss Copy reads "whether that nation, or any nation ..." On the distinctive language of the Bliss Copy of Lincoln's "Gettysburg Address," see, e.g., Garry Wills, *Lincoln at Gettysburg: The Words that Remade America* (New York: Touchstone, 1993), 203; and Gabor Boritt, *The Gettysburg Gospel: The Lincoln*

Speech that Nobody Knows (New York: Simon and Schuster, 2006), 151–152). The Bliss Copy was composed sometime after the letter of Alexander Bliss to John G. Nicolay, March 7, 1864, 42772, Abraham Lincoln Papers, Library of Congress.

5   Here and elsewhere, for Lincoln's speech performance at the dedication of the National Cemetery at Gettysburg, I follow the text established and documented in the accompanying appendix. Substantive differences between the performance text (pt) and the Bliss Copy (B) to which Black resorts may be summarized as follows (by paragraph): **2** (a) pt We are met to dedicate: B We have come to dedicate (b) pt portion of it: B portion of that field (c) pt as the final: B as a final (d) pt resting place of: B resting place for **3** (e) pt above our power: B above our poor power (f) pt unfinished work that: B unfinished work which (g) pt they have, thus: B they who fought here have thus (h) pt nobly carried on: B nobly advanced (i) pt they here gave the last: B they gave the last (j) pt that the nation: B that this nation. The three language differences numbered (b), (g), and (h) figure explicitly in Black's analysis (at pages 25, 23, and 27); also the conjunction of differences in language (and word division) leads Black to count 272 words in B (at page 26), whereas the accurate word count in pt is 264.

6   The purpose of the Bliss Copy was to support fund-raising efforts associated with the Maryland State Fair for US Soldier Relief, April 18–May 2, 1864 (see, e.g., John Mason Potter, "The Gettysburg Address," *Cornell Library Journal* 1 [1966]: 25–26; and Robert W. Schoeberlein, "A Fair to Remember: Maryland Women in Aid of the Union," *Maryland Historical Magazine* 90 [1995]: 473–474). Following the original request of George Bancroft (on behalf of Alexander Bliss), Lincoln agreed to produce a holographic copy of his Gettysburg speech for publication (see *Autograph Leaves of Our Country's Authors*, comp. John Pendleton Kennedy and Alexander Bliss [Baltimore: Cushings and Bailey, 1864], 3–5).

7   In paragraph 3, the phrase (as read by Black) "who fought here" did not exist in the historical speech performance (see appendix).

8   On the rhetorical nature of these three discourses, see, e.g., Black, "Gettysburg and Silence"; Eric F. Clarke, "Jimi Hendrix's 'Star Spangled Banner," in *Ways of Listening: An Ecological Approach to the Perception of Musical Meaning* (Oxford: Oxford University Press, 2005), 48–61; and Robert Hariman and John Louis Lucaites, "Performing Civic Identity: The Iconic Photograph of the Flag Raising on Iwo Jima," *Quarterly Journal of Speech* 88 (2002): 369–392.

9   Nathaniel Chapman, *Select Speeches, Forensick and Parliamentary, with Prefatory Remarks*, 5 vols. (Philadelphia: Hopkins and Earle, 1808), 1: 13.

10 See, e.g., Chauncey Goodrich, *Select British Eloquence: Embracing the Best Speeches Entire of the Most Eminent Orators of Great Britain for the Last Two Centuries* (New York: Harper, 1852), 75.

11 Authenticity of texts figures significantly in only six of the 34 public address studies published in William Norwood Brigance, *A History and Criticism of American Public Address*, 2 vols. (New York: McGraw-Hill, 1943).

12 E.g., Robert D. King, "Franklin D. Roosevelt's Second Inaugural Address: A Study in Textual Authenticity," *Quarterly Journal of Speech* 23 (1937): 439–444; and Paul M. Angle, "Four Lincoln Firsts," *Papers of the Bibliographical Society of America* 36 (1942): 1–17; cf. *A History and Criticism*, ed. Brigance, 1: 353–356, 407–408n.2, 479–480; 2: 721–772.

13 E.g., Loren Reid, "Factors Contributing to Inaccuracy in the Texts of Speeches," in *Papers in Rhetoric*, ed. Donald C. Bryant (St. Louis: Rhetoric Section, National Association of Teachers of Speech, 1940), 39–45; and Zon Robinson, "Are Speeches

in Congress Reported Accurately?" *Quarterly Journal of Speech* 28 (1942): 8–12; cf. *A History and Criticism*, ed. Brigance, 2: 593–594, 631.

14 Lester Thonssen and A. Craig Baird, *Speech Criticism: The Development of Standards for Rhetorical Appraisal* (New York: Ronald Press, 1948), 305.

15 Thonssen and Baird, *Speech Criticism*, 307.

16 Thonssen and Baird, *Speech Criticism*, 308.

17 Thonssen and Baird, *Speech Criticism*, 311.

18 Thonssen and Baird, *Speech Criticism*, 311.

19 See, e.g., Ronald Brunlees McKerrow, ed., *The Works of Thomas Nashe* (London: Bullen/Sidgwick and Jackson, 1904–1910); and Ronald Brunlees McKerrow, *An Introduction to Bibliography for Literary Students* (Oxford: Clarendon Press, 1927).

20 Among anecdotal studies, see, e.g., Gregg Phifer, "Andrew Johnson at Cleveland and St. Louis, 1866: A Study in Textual Authenticity," *Quarterly Journal of Speech* 37 (1951): 455–462; and Jerald L. Banninga, "James Otis on The Writs of Assistance: A Textual Investigation," *Speech Monographs* 27 (1960): 351–352; cautionary studies include Ray H. Sandefur, "Logan's Oration – How Authentic?" *Quarterly Journal of Speech* 46 (1960): 289–296; and Earl Cain, "Obstacles to Early Congressional Reporting," *Southern Speech Journal* 27 (1962): 239–247.

21 For a review and critique of public address scholarship on ghostwriting from 1956 to 1986, see Martin J. Medhurst, "Ghostwritten Speeches: Ethics Isn't the Only Lesson," *Communication Education* 36 (1987): 241–249.

22 See, e.g., Robert Ray, "Ghostwriting in Presidential Campaigns," *Today's Speech* 4 (1956): 15.

23 Ernest G. Bormann, "Ghostwriting and the Rhetorical Critic," *Quarterly Journal of Speech* 46 (1960): 286.

24 In literary studies, the view that *authorship* is complex – involving social relations between authors and institutions of literary production – was originally proposed in Jerome J. McGann's *A Critique of Modern Textual Criticism* (Chicago: University of Chicago Press, 1983).

25 James W. Cleary and Herbert W. Hildebrandt, "The Critical Edition in Rhetorical Scholarship: A Guide to Its Preparation," *Speech Monographs* 28 (1961): 29–38.

26 Cleary and Hildebrandt, "The Critical Edition," 31.

27 Cleary and Hildebrandt, "The Critical Edition," 31, 35.

28 Cleary and Hildebrandt, "The Critical Edition," 35.

29 Cleary and Hildebrandt, "The Critical Edition," 35.

30 Cleary and Hildebrandt, "The Critical Edition," 36.

31 Cleary and Hildebrandt follow the text-critical theory presented in André Morize, *Problems and Methods of Literary History, with Special Reference to Modern French Literature: A Guide for Graduate Students* (Boston: Ginn, 1922); McKerrow, *Bibliography* [repr. 1948]; and Chauncey Saunders, *An Introduction to Research in English Literary History. With a Chapter on Research in Folklore, by Stith Thompson* (New York: Macmillan, 1952).

32 Richard Murphy, "Problems in Speech Texts," in *Papers in Rhetoric and Poetic*, ed. Donald C. Bryant (Iowa City: University of Iowa Press, 1965), 27–86.

33 Murphy, "Problems," 74, 75, 82.

34 See, e.g., Ernest G. Bormann, *Theory and Research in the Communicative Arts* (New York: Holt, Rinehart, and Winston, 1965), 176.

35 Murphy, "Problems," 75, 78.

36 Murphy, "Problems," 80–81, 83.

37 Cf. Murphy's "The Speech as Literary Genre," *Quarterly Journal of Speech* 44 (1958): 117–127.

38 Robert W. Smith, "The Textual Critic: Hung-Up On Trivia?" *Southern Speech Communication Journal* 37 (1972): 424–437.

39 Smith, "The Textual Critic," 428–429.

40 Smith, "The Textual Critic," 429–430.

41 Anecdotal studies include Judy Hample, "The Textual and Cultural Authenticity of Patrick Henry's 'Liberty or Death' Speech," *Quarterly Journal of Speech* 63 (1977): 298–310; and Haig Bosmajian, "The Inaccuracies in the Reprintings of Martin Luther King's 'I Have a Dream' Speech," *Communication Education* 31 (1982): 107–114; cautionary studies include David F. Quadro, "The Congressional Record: Another Look," *Western Journal of Speech Communication* 41 (1977): 253–259; and G. Jack Gravlee, "Reporting Proceedings and Debates in the British Commons," *Central States Speech Journal* 32 (1981): 85–99.

42 Concerning practices prevailing up to 1965, see Murphy, "Problems," 71. Examples of recent practice are W. Stuart Towns, *Oratory and Rhetoric in the Nineteenth-Century South: A Rhetoric of Defense* (Westport, CT: Praeger, 1998); and Davis W. Houck and David E. Dixon, eds., *Rhetoric, Religion, and the Civil Rights Movement, 1954–1965* (Waco, TX: Baylor University Press, 2006). For a general critique of text authentication in speech anthologies, see Stephen E. Lucas and Martin J. Medhurst, eds., *Words of a Century: The Top 100 American Speeches, 1900–1999* (New York: Oxford University Press, 2009), xx.

43 See, e.g., Stephen H. Browne, *Jefferson's Call for Nationhood: The First Inaugural Address* (College Station: Texas A&M University Press, 2003); and Angela G. Ray, "The Rhetorical Ritual of Citizenship: Women's Voting as Public Performance, 1868–1875," *Quarterly Journal of Speech* 93 (2007): 1–26.

44 E.g., Terry Desch Croy, "The Crisis: A Complete Critical Edition of Carrie Chapman Catt's 1916 Presidential Address to the National American Woman Suffrage Association," *Rhetoric Society Quarterly* 28 (1998): 49–73; Garth E. Pauley, *LBJ's American Promise: The 1965 Voting Rights Address* (College Station: Texas A&M University Press, 2007); and Lucas and Medhurst, *Words of a Century*, esp. xx–xxxi.

45 Theresa Enos, ed., *Encyclopedia of Rhetoric and Composition: Communication from Ancient Times to the Information Age* (New York: Garland, 1996); Thomas O. Sloane, ed., *Encyclopedia of Rhetoric* (Oxford: Oxford University Press, 2001); and James Jasinski, *Sourcebook on Rhetoric: Key Concepts in Contemporary Rhetorical Studies* (Thousand Oaks, CA: Sage, 2001).

46 See, e.g., Sonja K. Foss, *Rhetorical Criticism: Exploration and Practice*, 3rd ed. (Long Grove, IL: Waveland Press, 2004); Roderick P. Hart and Suzanne M. Daughton, *Modern Rhetorical Criticism*, 3rd ed. (Boston: Pearson/Allyn and Bacon, 2005); and Carl R. Burgchardt, comp., *Readings in Rhetorical Criticism*, 3rd ed. (State College, PA: Strata, 2005).

47 Donald C. Bryant, "Rhetoric: Its Functions and Its Scope," *Quarterly Journal of Speech* 39 (1953): 407.

48 See, e.g., Lawrence J. Prelli, ed., *Rhetorics of Display* (Columbia: University of South Carolina Press, 2006); Theo van Leeuwen and Carey Jewitt, eds., *Handbook of Visual Analysis* (Thousand Oaks, CA: Sage, 2001); Foss, *Rhetorical Criticism*; and Barbara Warnick, *Rhetoric Online: Persuasion and Politics on the World Wide Web* (New York: Peter Lang, 2007).

49 For justifications of this extension, see, e.g., D. F. McKenzie, *Bibliography and the Sociology of Texts: The Panizzi Lectures 1985* (London: British Library, 1986), 5–6; G. Thomas Tanselle, *A Rationale of Textual Criticism* (Philadelphia: University of Pennsylvania Press, 1989), 18–33; and Yuri M. Lotman, *Universe of the Mind: A Semiotic Theory of Culture*, trans. Ann Shukman (London: Tauris, 2001), 36–37. The definition of text I employ here is analogous to McGee's notion of "finished text," and it is not meant to preclude conceptualization of realized performances and artifacts as intertextual composites or as fragments of larger discourse formations (see Michael Calvin McGee, "Text, Context, and the Fragmentation of Contemporary Culture," *Western Journal of Speech Communication* 54 [1990]: 279).

50 See, e.g., Thonssen and Baird, *Speech Criticism*, 301; and Cleary and Hildebrandt, "The Critical Edition," 31–32.

51 See, e.g., Ray, "Ghostwriting," 15; McGann, *A Critique*, 81; and McGee, "Text, Context, and the Fragmentation," 287–288.

52 Lloyd F. Bitzer, "The Rhetorical Situation," *Philosophy & Rhetoric* 1 (1968): 7–8; cf. Bryant, "Rhetoric," 404–407.

53 See, e.g., Craig R. Smith, "Richard Nixon's 1968 Acceptance Speech as a Model of Dual Audience Adaptation," *Today's Speech* 19 (Fall 1971): 15; Leah Ceccarelli, "Polysemy: Multiple Meanings in Rhetorical Criticism," *Quarterly Journal of Speech* 84 (1998): 399–409; and Hariman and Lucaites, "Performing Civic Identity," 363–364, 376–377.

54 See, e.g., David Zarefsky, "Four Senses of Rhetorical History," in *Doing Rhetorical History: Concepts and Cases*, ed. Kathleen J. Turner (Tuscaloosa: University of Alabama Press, 1998), 30; and Bitzer, "The Rhetorical Situation," 8.

55 See, e.g., David D. Perlmutter, "Visual Historical Methods: Problems, Prospects, Applications," *Historical Methods* 27 (1994): 172–173; Mieke Bal, *Double Exposures: The Subject of Cultural Analysis* (New York: Routledge, 1996), 128; Gillian Rose, *Visual Methodologies: An Introduction to the Interpretation of Visual Materials* (Thousand Oaks, CA: Sage, 2001), 88; and Hariman and Lucaites, "Performing Civic Identity," 366–368.

56 The account I offer is inspired partly by rhetorical scholarship on textual authentication and partly by literary scholarship on textual criticism, especially James Thorpe, *Principles of Textual Criticism* (San Marino, CA: Huntington Library, 1972); McGann, *A Critique* (1983); D. C. Greetham, *Textual Scholarship: An Introduction* (New York: Garland, 1994); and Peter L. Shillingsburg, *Scholarly Editing in the Computer Age: Theory and Practice*, 3rd ed. (Ann Arbor: University of Michigan Press, 1996).

57 Truncation of text collection can lead to incomplete or inaccurate texts. For example, in collecting texts for her edition of Carrie Chapman Catt's speech "The Crisis," September 7, 1916, Karlyn Kohrs Campbell neglected two major sources, a contemporary publication of the speech ("The Crisis," *The Women's Journal and Suffrage News*, September 16, 1916, 299–303) and a partial typescript of the speech (Untitled, Carrie Chapman Catt Papers, Box 11, Manuscript Division, Library of Congress); this led Campbell to print slightly more than half of the discourse as a complete text of the speech (*Man Cannot Speak for Her*, 2 vols. [Westport, CT: Praeger, 1989], 2: 483–502). Terry Croy uncovered the neglected sources, found corroboration of their relationship in the *New York Times*, September 8, 1916, and combined known sources to produce an authenticated text ("Complete Critical Edition").

58 "Old Glory Goes Up on Mt. Suribachi, Iwo Jima," Joe Rosenthal, February 23, 1945, APA6201490-L, The Associated Press Collection, Limited Editions, New York.

59   E.g., "Old Glory Goes Up on Mt. Suribachi, Iwo Jima," 1945, GEH NEG: 11438, George Eastman House International Museum of Photography and Film, Rochester, NY.

60   E.g., "Marines Raise Flag Atop Mt. Suribachi," *Life*, March 26, 1945, 17.

61   E.g., "Photograph of Flag Raising on Iwo Jima, 02/23/1945," Joe Rosenthal, Photographer, Naval Photographic Center, NAIL Control Number NWDNS-80-G-413988, ARC 520748, National Archives and Records Administration, College Park, MD.

62   "Old Glory Goes Up Over Iwo," *New York Times*, February 25, 1945, 1; and "Old Glory on Mt. Suribachi, Feb. 23, 1945," *Time*, March 5, 1945, 1.

63   E.g., war bond drive poster: *Now ... All Together*, C. C. Beall. (36 3/4″ × 26″) US Treasury (Washington, DC: US Government Printing Office, 1945); stamp: Marines at Iwo Jima (3 cents), Washington, DC, July 11, 1945; commemorative coin: 2005 Marine Corps 230th Anniversary Silver Dollar, July 20, 2005, US Mint; and veterans' memorial: Marine Corps War Memorial, dedicated November 10, 1954, Rosslyn, Virginia.

64   *Woodstock*, directed by Michael Wadleigh, film (ca. 16,560 ft), Warner Brothers, 1970; *Woodstock, Three Days of Peace and Music*, directed by Michael Wadleigh, VHS, 2 videocassettes (184 min.), Warner Home Video, 1987, 1970; *Woodstock, Three Days of Peace and Music: The Director's Cut*, directed by Michael Wadleigh, film (ca. 20,160 ft), Warner Brothers, 1994, 1970; *Woodstock, Three Days of Peace and Music: The Director's Cut*, directed by Michael Wadleigh, VHS, 2 videocassettes (225 min.), Warner Home Video, 1994, 1970; and *Woodstock, Three Days of Peace and Music: The Director's Cut*, directed by Michael Wadleigh, DVD, 1 videodisc (225 min.), Warner Home Video, 1994, 1970.

65   John B. Sebastion et al., *Woodstock*, analogue, 3 sound discs (33 1/3 rpm, stereo; 12 in.), SD 3-500, Cotillion, 1970; John B. Sebastion et al., *Woodstock*, CD, 2 sound discs, SD 500-2, Atlantic, 1989, 1970; and Richie Havens et al., *Woodstock, Three Days of Peace and Music: Twenty-Fifth Anniversary Collection*, CD, 4 sound discs, 82636-2, Atlantic, 1994, 1969.

66   Jimi Hendrix et al., *Jimi Hendrix Live at Woodstock*, VHS, 1 videocassette (57 min.), MCAV-11989, Experience Hendrix/MCA, 1999; Jimi Hendrix et al., *Jimi Hendrix Live at Woodstock*, DVD, 1 videodisc (57 min.), MCADV-11988, Experience Hendrix/MCA, 1999; Jimi Hendrix et al., *Jimi Hendrix Live at Woodstock*, DVD, 2 videodiscs, B0005283-09, Experience Hendrix LLC, 2005; and Jimi Hendrix et al., *Jimi Hendrix Live at Woodstock*, Blu-Ray DVD, 1 videodisc (60 min.), B0011668-59, Experience Hendrix LLC, 2008.

67   Jimi Hendrix et al., *Jimi Hendrix Woodstock*, analogue, 1 sound cassette, MCAC-11063, MCA, 1994; Jimi Hendrix et al., *Jimi Hendrix Woodstock*, CD, 1 sound disc, MCAD-11063, MCA, 1994; Jimi Hendrix et al., *Live at Woodstock*, analogue, 3 sound discs (33 1/3 rpm, 12 in.), MCA3-11987, Experience Hendrix/MCA Records, 1999; and Jimi Hendrix et al., *Live at Woodstock*, CD, 2 sound discs, MCAD2-11987, Experience Hendrix, 1999.

68   Abraham Lincoln, Gettysburg Address: Nicolay Copy, November 1863, 43565, Abraham Lincoln Papers, Library of Congress; and Gettysburg Address: Hay Copy, November 1863, 43566, Abraham Lincoln Papers, Library of Congress. In categorizing the Hay Copy as a pre-delivery text, I follow Boritt, *The Gettysburg Gospel*, 94, particularly his argument that Lincoln would not have produced a post-delivery holograph without the words "under God."

69   E.g., the Associated Press report in "Heroes of July," *New York Times*, November 20, 1863, 1, and the Hale report in *Address of His Excellency John A. Andrew, to the Two*

Branches of the Legislature of Massachusetts, January 18, 1864 (Boston: Wright and Potter, 1864), lxxii.

70   E.g., " 'Gettysburg' Celebration," *The Philadelphia Inquirer*, November 20, 1863, 1; and "The Consecration of the Battle Cemetery," *Chicago Tribune*, November 21, 1863, 1. Newspaper reports of the speech were generally based – directly or indirectly – on transcriptions of the speech from its live performance. Such transcriptions, as in the case of the examples offered here, were often of questionable quality (see William H. Lambert, "Variations in the Reports of the Gettysburg Address," *The Century Illustrated Monthly Magazine* 47 (November 1893–November 1894): 637; Wills, *Lincoln at Gettysburg*, 392n.1). The most frequently published (and most reliable) newspaper texts were derived from the Associated Press report.

71   E.g., Abraham Lincoln, "Dedicatory Speech of President Lincoln," in *Address of Hon. Edward Everett, at the Consecration of the National Cemetery at Gettysburg, 19th November, 1863, with the Dedicatory Speech of President Lincoln, and the Other Exercises of the Occasion; accompanied by An Account of the Origin of the Undertaking and of the Arrangement of the Cemetery Grounds, and by a Map of the Battle-field and a Plan of the Cemetery* (Boston: Little, Brown and Company, 1864), 84.

72   Edward Everett holograph of the Gettysburg Address (Everett Copy), LR 926, Henry Horner Lincoln Collection, Abraham Lincoln Presidential Library, Springfield, IL; Gettysburg Address: Manuscript Presented to George Bancroft with Accompanying Letter, February 29, 1864, Kroch Library Rare & Manuscripts, E173.N95 pt.5 Address, Division of Rare and Manuscript Collections, Cornell University Library; and Gettysburg Address (Bliss Copy), White House.

73   John G. Nicolay and John Hay, eds., *Abraham Lincoln: A History*, 10 vols. (New York: Century Co., 1890), 8: 202; New York State Education Department, *Selections for Study and Memorizing: Poetry and Prose. Prescribed by the New York State Education Department in the Course of Study and Syllabus for Elementary Schools* (Boston: Houghton Mifflin, 1910), 111; Isaac Newton Arnold, *The History of Abraham Lincoln, and the Overthrow of Slavery* (Chicago: Clarke, 1866), 423–424; Charles Francis Richardson, *American Literature, 1607–1885* (New York: Putnam's Sons, 1887), 241; William Vincent Byars, ed., *The Cyclopedia of Oratory: A Handbook of Authorities on Oratory as an Art and of Celebrated Passages from the Best Orations from the Earliest Period to the Present Time* (Indianapolis: Bobbs-Merrill, 1901), 419; Lincoln Speech Memorial (cast bronze plaque), dedicated January 1912, National Cemetery, Gettysburg National Military Park, Gettysburg, Pennsylvania; and Lincoln Memorial (marble engraving), dedicated May 30, 1922, Washington, DC.

74   Cf. Kathleen Weil-Garris Brandt, "The Grime of the Centuries is a Pigment of the Imagination: Michelangelo's Sistine Ceiling," in *Palimpsest: Editorial Theory in the Humanities*, ed. George Bornstein and Ralph G. Williams (Ann Arbor: University of Michigan Press, 1993), 266–268.

75   Vernacular discourses are instances of popular symbolic activity that generally arise apart from authoritative or institutional discourse practices (see Gerald A. Hauser, *Vernacular Voices: The Rhetoric of Publics and Public Spheres* [Columbia: University of South Carolina Press, 1999]; "Demonstrative Displays of Dissident Rhetoric," in *Rhetorics of Display*, ed. Prelli, 229–254).

76   See, e.g., Karen A. Foss and Kathy L. Domenici, "Haunting Argentina: Synecdoche in the Protests of the Mothers of the Plaza de Mayo," in Foss, *Rhetorical Criticism*, 431–454, where a photograph documents a demonstration (at page 442). For general

discussion of ephemeral text documentation practices (performance of speech and gesture), see Beverly J. Sauer, *The Rhetoric of Risk: Technical Documentation in Hazardous Environments* (Mahwah, NJ: Lawrence Erlbaum, 2003), 219–235.

77 Insufficient analysis of text instances can lead to anachronism and inaccuracy; for instance, Rebecca Brooks Edwards, *Angels in the Machinery: Gender in American Party Politics from the Civil War to the Progressive Era* (Oxford: Oxford University Press, 1997), 155–156, discusses Theodore Roosevelt's address of 1899, "The Strenuous Life," with recourse to a paragraph that was inserted into a literary edition of the speech published in 1901 (see "Speech by Gov. Roosevelt," *Chicago Tribune*, April 11, 1899, 1, 3; Theodore Roosevelt, *The Strenuous Life: Essays and Addresses* [New York: Century, 1901], 1–21); cf. Leroy G. Dorsey, ed., "'The Strenuous Life,' A Machine-Readable Edition, by Theodore Roosevelt," *Voices of Democracy* 3 (2008): 1–16.

78 I follow Greetham (*Textual Scholarship*, 333) in using the term "surface features" to refer to spelling, word division, capitalization, punctuation, paragraphing, and indicators of emphasis. Such features of texts are also called "accidentals" (Modern Language Association [MLA], *Guidelines for Editors of Scholarly Editions*, September 25, 2007, www.mla.org/cse_guidelines#d0e1937 [accessed August, 6, 2009]).

79 For large-scale comparisons of words and surface features of linguistic texts, computer collation systems may be employed; see, e.g., Susan Hockey, *Electronic Texts in the Humanities: Principles and Practice* (Oxford: Oxford University Press, 2000), 130–131.

80 On acoustic properties and computer-assisted means of collation, see, e.g., Pedro Cano, Eloi Batlle, Emilia Gómez, Leandro de C. T. Gomes, and Madeleine Bonnet, "Audio Fingerprinting: Concepts and Applications," in *Computational Intelligence for Modelling and Prediction*, ed. Saman K. Halgamuge and Lipo Wang (Berlin: Springer, 2005), 233–245.

81 Cf. Philip Bell, "Content Analysis of Visual Images," in *Visual Analysis*, ed. van Leeuwen and Jewitt, 10–34.

82 Video and film collation is complicated by the large number of visual images at stake in such texts; regarding applicable technologies, see Dajun He and Quibin Sun, "Multimedia Authentication," in *Multimedia Security Technologies for Digital Rights Management*, ed. Wenjun Zeng, Heather Yu, and Ching-Yung Lin (Amsterdam: Elsevier, 2006), 111–137.

83 Linguistic text: Dwight D. Eisenhower, "Address Before the General Assembly of the United Nations on Peaceful Uses of Atomic Energy, New York City," in *Public Papers of the Presidents of the United States: Dwight D. Eisenhower. Containing the Public Messages, Speeches, and Statements of the President: January 20 to December 31, 1953* (Washington, DC: Government Printing Office, 1960), 813–822; audio text: Dwight D. Eisenhower, "'Atoms for Peace' Address," Audiovisual Department, EL-D16-24 (RA) part 1, EL-D16-25 (RA) part 2 (45 min.), The Dwight D. Eisenhower Presidential Library, Abilene, KS; film text: Dwight D. Eisenhower, "Atomic Power for Peace: A Statement of United States Policy, Atoms for Peace Address, New York, New York, December 8, 1953," film (B&W, sound), United States Information Agency, 1953 (10 min.), Audiovisual Collection, EL-MP16-50, Dwight D. Eisenhower Library, Abilene, KS; and video text: Dwight D. Eisenhower, "Atoms for Peace," VHS, *Great Speeches. Volume III: An Alliance Video Production*; Director, Susan Cook (Greenwood, IN: Educational Video Group, 1987). Cf. Martin J. Medhurst and Belinda Stillion Southard, eds., "'Atoms for Peace,' a machine-readable edition," by Dwight D. Eisenhower, *Voices of Democracy*, www.voicesofdemocracy.umd.edu [accessed September 8, 2009].

84 In diachronic reception studies of rhetorical discourse it may be necessary to select and investigate multiple composition-texts derived from an original linguistic, acoustic, or visual performance or artifact.

85 See, e.g., Hal Buell, *Uncommon Valor, Common Virtue: Iwo Jima and the Photograph that Captured America* (New York: Berkley, 2006), 132.

86 Charles V. Kinter, "The Changing Pattern of the Newspaper Publishing Industry," *American Journal of Economics and Sociology* 5 (1945): 49, estimates the aggregate circulation of US newspapers in 1944 as 45,954,838; this may be considered a rough approximation for the frequency of publication of the Iwo Jima flag-raising image in newspapers on February 25, 1945 (and in the days immediately thereafter). The Iwo Jima flag-raising image was employed by the US Treasury Department on approximately 3.5 million posters and 175,000 street-car cards for its Seventh War Bond Drive (Phillip Knightley, *The First Casualty: The War Correspondent as Hero and Myth-Maker from the Crimea to Iraq* [Baltimore: Johns Hopkins University Press, 2005], 323); the drive extended from May 14 through June 30, 1945 (James J. Kimble, *Mobilizing the Home Front: War Bonds and Domestic Propaganda* [College Station: Texas A&M University Press, 2006], 101), during which time the posters and street-car cards were displayed in a wide range of public venues. The first-class US postage stamp, *Marines at Iwo Jima* (3 cents), was released July 11, 1945 with an issue size of 137,321,000 (1847usa.com/identify/YearSets/1945.htm [accessed January 17, 2008]). Hariman and Lucaites, "Performing Civic Identity," 368–370, select the wirephoto of the Iwo Jima flag-raising photograph by Joe Rosenthal as the composition/interpretation-text in explaining the iconic significance of the visual image. This choice seems questionable insofar as the wirephoto has no environment of presentation. Because public access to the image occurred almost without exception within an environment of presentation (e.g., in the pages of newspapers, in war bond posters, in postage stamps), and because environment of presentation affects the meaning/reception of visual images (Perlmutter, "Visual Historical Methods," 172–173; Bal, *Double Exposures*, 128; Rose, *Visual Methodologies*, 88), it seems unlikely that the reception of the visual image by the American audience can be explained adequately without considering the immediate environment(s) of presentation within which the image was encountered.

87 Cf. Mike Daley, "Land of the Free. Jimi Hendrix: Woodstock Festival, August 18, 1969," in *Performance and Popular Music: History, Place and Time*, ed. Ian Inglis (Burlington, VT: Ashgate, 2006), 52–53. Viewers of the documentary film *Woodstock* (1970) may be estimated as numbering about 10 million through 1979 based on box office receipts (R. Serge Denisoff and William D. Romanowski, *Risky Business: Rock in Film* [Edison, NJ: Transaction, 1991], 715) and ticket prices (Aniko Bodroghkozy, "Reel Revolutionaries: An Examination of Hollywood's Cycle of 1960s Youth Rebellion Films," *Cinema Journal* 41.3 [2002]: 52, 54).

88 Sebastion et al., *Woodstock*, CD, SD 500-2, 1989; regarding critical reevaluation coincident with the reissue of this soundtrack, see Daley, "Land of the Free," 56–57.

89 David Wills (Agent for the National Cemetery) asked Lincoln for the original manuscript of his "dedicatory remarks" on November 23, 1863, with a view toward placing them "with the correspondence and other papers connected with the project" (David Wills to Abraham Lincoln, November 23, 1863, 28203, Abraham Lincoln Papers, Library of Congress). In complying with Wills's request, Lincoln resorted to his original draft, the Associated Press report, and his own "fresh recollection" (John G. Nicolay, "Lincoln's Gettysburg Address," *Century Magazine* 47 [November 1893–April 1894]: 604–605). The results of Lincoln's reconstruction of the speech are very likely

represented in the text of his "Dedicatory Speech" published in Everett and Lincoln, *Address of Hon. Edward Everett*, 84 (cf. Wills, *Lincoln at Gettysburg*, 195–198).

90   Special care is needed in selecting composition-texts for use in reception studies. Leah Ceccarelli, "The Ends of Rhetoric Revisited: Three Readings of Lincoln's Gettysburg Address," in *The Viability of the Rhetorical Tradition*, ed. Richard Graff, Arthur E. Walzer, and Janet M. Atwill (Albany: State University of New York Press, 2005), 47–60, discusses the editorial reception of Lincoln's address in the *Chicago Times* on November 23, 1863, but she does not observe the differences between the text of Lincoln's address published in the *Chicago Times* (see Boritt, *The Gettysburg Gospel*, 165–272) versus the text published in the more widespread Associated Press report to which she refers. Arguably, differences in the *Chicago Times* publication of Lincoln's address accounted for elements of its editorial reception in the same newspaper; therefore, Ceccarelli's use of the Associated Press report instead of the *Chicago Times* text is problematic.

91   Possible composition-texts in these categories are documented in note 73 above.

92   Gerry Philipsen, "Mayor Daley's Council Speech: A Cultural Analysis," *Quarterly Journal of Speech* 72 (1986): 241–260.

93   Philipsen, "Council Speech," 248.

94   Philipsen, "Council Speech," 248–250.

95   See Boritt, *The Gettysburg Gospel*, 271.

96   Compare the principles of emendation applied by Lucas and Medhurst in establishing texts from audio and video recordings (*Words of a Century*, xxvii).

97   Lucas and Medhurst offer useful guidance for authenticating texts of speech performances that contain performer errors (*Words of a Century*, xxvi–xxvii).

98   The Lincoln holograph manuscript known as the Hay Copy is used as a surface-feature exemplar in the documented authentication of the "Gettysburg Address" provided as an appendix to this essay.

99   Consistent with his ethnographic inquiry, Philipsen tacitly adopted conventions of discourse analysis in his representation of Daley's speech ("Council Speech," 248–250). For principles more suited to the requirements of public address scholarship, see Lucas and Medhurst, *Words of a Century*, xxvi–xxix.

100 Additional guidance on procedures for explaining a refined text may be found in Martin L. West, *Textual Criticism and Editorial Technique. Applicable to Greek and Latin Texts* (Berlin: de Gruyter, 1973); and G. Thomas Tanselle, "Some Principles for Editorial Apparatus," *Studies in Bibliography* 25 (1975): 41–88.

101 Systematic explanation of a refined text is illustrated in the appendix – a documented authentication of Lincoln's speech performance at Gettysburg (headers in the authentication correspond to elements of refined-text explanation). Procedures involved in distributed explanation of refined texts are illustrated throughout this essay in passages where I discuss collection of texts, analysis of texts, selection of composition-texts, and refinement of composition-texts pertinent to Jimi Hendrix's Woodstock performance of the "Star Spangled Banner" and the photographic image known as the "Old Glory Goes Up on Mt. Suribachi, Iwo Jima."

102 MLA, *Guidelines for Editors*, www.mla.org/cse_guidelines#d0e198 (accessed August 3, 2009).

103 For full documentation, see notes 68 and 69 above.

104 For full documentation, see note 70 above.

6

Archival Research and the American Presidency
The Political and Rhetorical Complexities of Presidential Records

Shawn J. Parry-Giles

As George Washington prepared to leave the presidency, he shipped his papers to his family home in Mount Vernon, Virginia. Even though he wanted to build a library that would house his presidential and military documents at Mount Vernon, he died before his vision was realized, ultimately willing the papers to his nephew, Bushrod Washington. Over the next century, his papers would be reviewed by many interested in writing biographies or simply publishing the papers of the nation's first president. One such biographer, Tobias Lear – Washington's friend and secretary – ultimately turned over the personal correspondence between the first lady and the president to Martha Washington, who opted to burn the documents prior to her own death (only two of those letters are known to have survived). The remaining presidential papers went to Chief Justice John Marshall, who compiled a three-volume edition of the president's papers in collaboration with Washington's nephew. By the time the collection was published in the 1820s, however, the documents had suffered extensive damage from rat infestations and damp conditions. Upon his death, Bushrod Washington willed the papers to his own nephew, George Corbin Washington, who sold them to the US Department of State for $55,000. In 1904, what was left of Washington's papers were transferred from the Department of State to the Library of Congress, which also continued to collect papers that Washington's heirs had kept or sold to private collectors and historical societies.[1]

The story of Washington's papers typifies the complicated and erratic process of preserving presidential documents prior to the twentieth century. Some presidents, like Thomas Jefferson, James Madison, and James Monroe, meticulously preserved their papers, which were turned over to the US Congress in the 1830s and 1840s. More commonly, however, such papers were sold for profit by the heirs of the various presidents. Still other presidential papers were destroyed by the presidents themselves (Martin Van Buren, Franklin Pierce, Chester A. Arthur, Ulysses S. Grant) or by their family members (Millard Fillmore, Warren G. Harding). A large portion of Abraham Lincoln's papers were nearly destroyed by his son Robert

Todd Lincoln in the aftermath of his father's assassination; fortunately, they were ultimately sealed and made available to scholars in 1947. Still other presidential papers were lost to fire: John Tyler's papers burned in a fire in Richmond during the Civil War; large portions of other president's papers (William Henry Harrison, John Tyler, Zachary Taylor, and Andrew Johnson) also burned. Calvin Coolidge's papers might not have survived if an assistant had not ignored his wishes. Today, the papers of 23 presidents – the majority of which were acquired either by purchase or by gift – are held in the collections of the Library of Congress. Some of the papers of at least eight presidents are also preserved in historical societies or special libraries, including records from the presidencies of John Adams, John Quincy Adams, Millard Fillmore, Franklin Pierce, James Buchanan, Abraham Lincoln, Rutherford B. Hayes, and Warren G. Harding.[2]

The lack of a settled process for collecting and preserving the papers of early American presidents resulted from the widespread view that White House records were the private property of the president and his heirs. The dispute over property and privacy rights that surrounded such papers foreshadowed later constitutional debates over the ownership of presidential documents, such as the controversy over Richard Nixon's papers during the Watergate scandal. Deliberations over presidential records ultimately involve questions about the constitutional balance of power, executive privilege, national security, personal privacy rights, and public access. They involve all three branches of government, as well as journalists, scholars, and the American people themselves in political and legal disputes. These debates not only influence our understanding of the presidency, but also affect the ways in which we understand the distinction between public and private discourse within US political culture.

Archival records hold particular salience for scholars of public address. Charles E. Morris III refers to archival depositories as "chief among the inventional sites of rhetorical pasts."[3] As David Zarefsky argues, archival research also aids the public address scholar in comprehending the "historical situation," which gave rise to or constrained the interpretation and impact of particular rhetorical texts.[4] Concerning presidential archives in particular, Mary E. Stuckey suggests that such primary documents offer an understanding of "individual presidencies and the presidency as an institution in ways that are simply impossible without them,"[5] particularly for those scholars interested in the rise of the so-called "rhetorical presidency."[6]

This chapter traces the historical and constitutional controversies surrounding the preservation of presidential papers, focusing on disputes over access to the private documents of particular presidents. In the process, I explore the important relationship between presidential archives and the study of public address by illuminating the limitations and benefits of archival research on the early Cold War presidents. The chapter ends with a discussion of how archival research might lead to a fuller understanding of the Nixon administration's response to protests by the Vietnam Veterans Against the War. Revealing the behind-the-scenes collusion between a presidential administration and the news media, the analysis sheds light on why many presidents seek to control access to the most hidden or covert activities of their presidencies. In the end, the chapter suggests how archival research can lead to a more robust understanding of the rhetorical presidency by complicating our understanding of the rhetorical context, enhancing analysis of public texts, and contributing to more informed arguments about presidential strategies and motives. The chapter also reveals that presidential archives are not just for scholars of the presidency. Much also is to be gained by those studying US foreign policy, US domestic policy, news coverage of politics and political leaders, and even the rhetorical actions of activist groups seeking to produce social and political change.

The History of Presidential Archives

For nearly 200 years, the papers of presidents were treated as each president's personal property. The handling of the president's papers was largely determined by the individual presidents themselves, since they were neither obliged to keep records during their time in office nor required to turn them over to the federal government once they left office.[7] Between 1873 and 1915, more than 250 fires damaged various federal records, and a fire at the Department of Commerce in 1921 prompted the development of a national archives project to help preserve the nation's political records. Construction of the national archives began in 1926 and its doors were opened in 1934.[8] During this same period, President Franklin D. Roosevelt (FDR) began planning for the first presidential library, which would set a precedent for future presidents but also usher in a new era of political controversy surrounding the preservation of presidential documents.

The first presidential libraries

FDR's commitment to document preservation is well established. He signed the act creating the National Archives as an independent agency answerable to the president (after President Herbert Hoover commissioned the project); he also helped develop the concept of presidential libraries, which were to be constructed with private money and operated as a branch of the National Archives. FDR chose Hyde Park in his home state of New York as his library's location because of fears that if war broke out, the concentration of federal documents in Washington, DC, could prove disastrous. Part of the president's motivation was his reluctance to burden his family with the management of his extensive records. FDR, nevertheless, still conceived of such papers as his own property to be *donated* to the archives. He further assumed that a large portion of the documents would remain closed to the public, with the museum holding the greatest public appeal.[9]

Not coincidentally, the move toward the enhanced preservation of presidential documents paralleled the growth of the presidency and an increase in the magnitude of presidential records. Over the next several decades, the practices and assumptions involving presidential records would evolve. The National Archives, for example, lost its status as an independent agency in 1949 and was merged with the General Services Administration (GSA) as the National Archives and Records Service, granting supervisory authority to the GSA administrator.[10] By 1955, presidential libraries were institutionalized with the Presidential Libraries Act (PLA), which allowed the federal government to accept the documents of future government officials without additional legislation. The act also allowed the government to accept "any land, buildings, and equipment offered as a gift to the United States for the purposes of creating a Presidential archival depository."[11] After its passage, Herbert Hoover created a presidential archive in West Branch, Iowa – a practice that continued for each subsequent president. In 1964, the Office of Presidential Libraries was established as a permanent feature of the National Archives.[12] Presidents, though, were still not required to create libraries or to donate their papers to a federal agency. This assumption that presidential records were the personal property of the president would become the subject of intense controversy in the aftermath of Watergate and President Richard Nixon's resignation.

Presidential archives in the wake of Watergate

Just prior to Nixon's resignation over the Watergate scandal, the Supreme Court ruled in *US v. Nixon* that the Nixon administration was required to release the tapes requested by the Watergate special prosecutor, Leon Jaworski. In an 8–0 decision, the court declared in a precedent-setting case that "Neither the doctrine of separation of powers nor the generalized need for confidentiality of high-level communications … can sustain an absolute, unqualified Presidential privilege of immunity from judicial process under all circumstances."[13] After the release of the "smoking gun" tape that revealed the president's involvement in the Watergate cover-up, Nixon still assumed that his presidential papers, including his presidential tapes, represented his private property. Attorney General William Saxbe concurred with Nixon, especially given the historical precedents and the lack of definitive court rulings on such matters. Such a perspective was codified by the Ford administration on September 8, 1974, when Nixon entered into an agreement with Arthur Sampson – the administrator of the General Services Administration – that Nixon would ultimately have full control over the documents.[14] Once the agreement became public, members of the US House of Representatives expressed outrage that Nixon could destroy incriminating evidence of his legal misconduct during the Watergate scandal. Subsequently, Congress passed the Preservation of Presidential Recordings and Materials Act (PPRMA), which gave the GSA Administrator "complete possession and control" over Nixon's presidential documents from January 20, 1969 through August 9, 1974.[15]

Nixon's lawyers immediately issued what would be one of numerous legal challenges over the preservation and control of his presidential records. In *Nixon v. Administrator of General Services* (1977), for example, the Supreme Court denied Nixon's constitutional argument involving separation of powers and the presidential prerogative of executive privilege but simultaneously confirmed that "control over the materials remains in the Executive Branch."[16] Interpreting the significance of the decision, Bruce P. Montgomery explains: "It is remarkably ironic that this Supreme Court case, which Nixon lost, would serve as the fundamental rationale for presidential attempts to reclaim control over their White House materials" in subsequent years.[17]

The uncertainty about presidential records was resolved, at least in part, with the passage of the Presidential Records Act (PRA) of 1978. Even though the act did not define executive privilege or require presidents to keep records, it did specify for the first time that the *future* "ownership" of such "presidential records" would belong to the US government: "The United States shall reserve and retain complete ownership, possession, and control of Presidential records," with greater authority given to the archivist of the United States.[18] The president was still granted authority to restrict access in terms of "national defense or foreign policy" for at least 12 years. The act took effect at the beginning of Ronald Reagan's presidency; his records and subsequent presidential documents were treated as the property of the federal government, which were to be held "in trust" by the National Archives. As Peter Sezzi explains, the PRA was the "most noticeable effort at asserting public ownership of and access to the records of … the president of the United States."[19] Apart from denying private ownership, the US Congress also legislated control over the papers of the president while preserving the practice of private ownership of their own congressional papers – an irony not lost on later presidential administrations.

The PRA, not surprisingly, triggered new rounds of legal battles and executive orders. In 1984, the National Archives regained its independence from the GSA in a hard-fought battle.[20] Independent status, however, did not shield the agency from presidential scrutiny and control, especially since the National Archives still existed as part of the executive branch. Two days before leaving office, President Reagan issued an executive order (12667), which gave "incumbent and former Presidents" the authority of "Executive privilege" over the "release of Presidential records by the National Archives and Records Administration,"[21] linking executive privilege to national security. President George H. W. Bush likewise sought to erode the PRA's authority on the eve of his own departure from office when Don Wilson, US archivist and the person who ultimately served as the Executive Director of the George H. W. Bush Presidential Library Foundation, signed an agreement that awarded the president exclusive control over the computerized records of his presidency – a position supported by the Clinton administration. The agreement granted the former president the power to require the archivist of the United States to destroy computerized records, which like the Nixon–Sampson agreement, treated the presidential papers more as their private property. Ultimately, Judge Charles R. Richey of the United States District Court in Washington, DC, overturned the "Bush–Wilson agreement" as a violation of the PRA and cited the Clinton administration with a "civil contempt order" for providing insufficient means by which to preserve federal records. Richey's decision helped determine that the preservation of electronic records was, in fact, covered under the PRA.[22]

Although Executive Order 12667 gave the incumbent president greater control over current records, government archivists still maintained authority over the records of a former president. This too would change, however, when George W. Bush signed the highly controversial Executive Order 13233. Signed on November 5, 2001, in the wake of the 9/11 terrorist attacks, EO 13233 overturned the PRA by awarding a "former President or the incumbent President" the authority to prevent "access to any such privileged records unless and until the incumbent President advises the Archivist that the former President or the incumbent President agree to authorize access to the records or until so ordered by a final and nonappealable court order." The order also extended to communication between the president and his advisors, even if national security issues were not involved.[23] In defending the order, the Bush administration relied on the failed arguments of Nixon's legal team in an attempt, Nancy Kassop contends, "to return to the pre-PRA" period by giving control over such records back to the presidents and to "deny public access permanently."[24] Bush subsequently slowed or blocked the release of papers from the Reagan administration, as well as his father's vice presidential and presidential records.[25]

Bush's executive order not surprisingly produced legal and political challenges that are still underway. On November 28, 2001, the American Historical Association, Public Citizen, and other groups teamed up to bring a law suit against the National Archives and Records Administration. Among its complaints, the Plaintiffs claimed that EO 13233 violated "the PRA by instructing the Archivist, after the expiration of the 12-year restriction period, to withhold the release of records that are not restricted under the Act and that are not subject to a valid claim of constitutional privilege."[26] Members of Congress were also alarmed by the Bush order and initiated a series of hearings. While the US Senate has yet to release its report, the House Committee on Government Reform held hearings in 2002 and released its Report (107–790) on November 22. The committee condemned the executive order as a violation of the spirit if not the letter of the PRA:

> The Executive Order 13233 converts the Act's [PRA] presumption of disclosure into a presumption of non-disclosure. It forces the Archivist of the United States to automatically accept any claim of executive privilege by a former President, regardless of merit, which is in clear violation of the Archivist's duties under the Act. It allows friends, relatives and descendants of a former President to claim executive privilege – an approach lacking in any legal or historical precedent. Perhaps most serious … is that it allows an incumbent or former President to prevent indefinitely the public disclosure of records under the Act simply by inaction – without ever having to assert a claim of executive privilege.[27]

Similarly, the US District Court for the District of Columbia ruled in *American Historical Association v. National Archives and Record Administration* (2007) that EO 13233 violated that section of the PRA which required a president's records to be released as rapidly as possible. Yet the court did not rule on the right of former presidents to exercise an unlimited veto power over the release of documents, declaring that this portion of the case was "unripe" for legal consideration because no former president had attempted to exert that right.[28]

As President George W. Bush prepared to leave office in January of 2009, the issue of his presidential records was still on the minds of many, including the editors of the *New York Times*, who wanted to "remind President Bush ... that his White House records are not his personal property. They belong to the nation."[29] The newly inaugurated president, Barack H. Obama, boldly concurred with the *Times'* sentiments and promptly issued an executive order on day one of his presidency, revoking Executive Order 13233.[30] When signing the order, President Obama proclaimed that, "Starting today ... every agency and department should know that this administration stands on the side not of those who seek to withhold information, but those who seek to make it known."[31] The president justified his actions on the grounds that, "The Government should not keep information confidential merely because public officials might be embarrassed by disclosure, because errors and failures might be revealed, or because of speculative or abstract fears."[32] Reflecting the sentiments of many troubled by EO 13233, the *New York Times* concluded that "the new president had traded a presumption of secrecy for a presumption of disclosure."[33]

Thus, the meaning of the Presidential Records Act of 1978 and the ownership of presidential papers continue to inspire disagreement and debate. President Obama's decision to reenforce the 1978 act "carries great symbolism,"[34] yet it too will likely provoke legal challenges and will be difficult to enforce. Despite these ongoing controversies surrounding public access to the inner workings of the nation's executive branch, the presidential libraries nevertheless provide an immense resource for public address scholars – resources, however, that also must be viewed through politicized lenses.

Archival Research and Public Address Scholarship

As rhetorical scholars approaching the presidential archives, we need to understand that such depositories are, as Benjamin Hufbauer reminds us, "sites of memory" with an "ideology that attempts to reify reverence for the presidency."[35] While archival records can offer considerable insight into the context, production, motives, and strategic thinking behind presidential discourse, they simultaneously magnify the self-interestedness of presidential administrations and provide inevitably partial and politicized views of their actions.

The reminders and limitations of presidential archival research

Much has been written about the expansion of presidential power, culminating in what some refer to as the "imperial presidency."[36] In an important sense, the creation of presidential libraries serves to magnify this modern expansion of presidential power. Writing in the *Chronicle of Higher Education*, historian Joan Hoff argues: "the libraries themselves 'are a bad idea.' Their very existence represents an attempt to organize the historical record into president-size units, implicitly encouraging scholars to portray US history as a grand procession of chief executives." In the process, she concludes, they elevate "political history over social and cultural history."[37] Hufbauer conceives of presidential libraries as part of the nation's "civil religion," as they "are meant to be sacred national places where pilgrimages can be made to see relics and reconstructions of presidential history, all in order to elevate in the national consciousness presidents who ... are represented as worthy of patriotic veneration."[38]

Presidential archives thus should be recognized as reflections of US identity, power, and ideology rather than passive receptacles of factual material. Barbara A. Biesecker challenges scholars to move beyond the view that any archive features "material proof of the past" or sites "of a singular discovery." Instead, she claims, archives "serve as [an] ultimate arbiter of identity, history, practice, criticism, and theory."[39] Similarly, Charles E. Morris III has emphasized how archives can function "ideologically and politically," sometimes "insidiously." Concerned with how some archival administrators have suppressed "archival holdings of a queer nature,"[40] Morris calls attention to the larger ideologies of race, ethnicity, gender, sexuality, and class that potentially can be masked, silenced, or reframed by archival practices.

Because presidents often attempt to limit public access to their administration's records, or because they wish to cast their administration in the most positive light, presidential archives inevitably provide only a partial and politicized vision of history. At the Harry S. Truman Presidential Library, for example, archivists acknowledge that more than half of the documents relating to the Psychological Strategy Board (PSB) – a presidentially appointed group that secretly coordinated national security and "psychological warfare" operations during the Truman and Eisenhower administrations[41] – remain classified, providing a very incomplete view of Cold War propaganda efforts. And even though the Freedom of Information Act (FOIA) in 1966 was designed to protect the public's "right to know,"[42] certain FOIA restrictions circumvent the declassification of such classified material. The 1974 amendment to FOIA, which passed in spite of President Ford's veto, sought to ensure that the president and the intelligence community could no longer delay or thwart public access to such presidential records.[43] Nevertheless, further obstructions were erected by the Bush administration during the post-9/11 era.[44] A president can still refuse to declassify anything on national security grounds; short of litigation, such documents can be kept secret indefinitely. In January 2009, President Obama directed the Attorney General to create new FOIA guidelines "reaffirming the commitment to accountability and transparency."[45] Yet restrictions remain, which means that any historical account is at best partial and potentially inaccurate. As Mary E. Stuckey explains, "When scholars are forced to guess, to piece together narratives from inadequate source material, the chances of error are vastly increased."[46]

Consequently, we need to continue to fight for access to presidential records, and we need to understand the politics of archives. Like any other text we encounter as critics, a document from the archives is not to be automatically celebrated or revered, but rather interrogated, challenged, and taken apart in search of its political or ideological implications. And while archivists are often extremely helpful in that process, some may have a vested interest in ensuring that the president whose memory they help to create is viewed in a more positive light. According to Hufbauer, one case in point is the presentation of the Watergate controversy at the Nixon presidential library and museum, which, he claimed, featured a voiceover that suggested "the entire [Watergate] scandal boils down to the misinterpretation of a few words."[47]

Still, there is much to be gained from analyzing presidential records – insight not only into the rhetorical activities of the presidents, but also into the media coverage of their presidencies, the policies they supported and opposed, and even the activist groups who protested against them. And despite all the restrictions on public access, there are still more records available on the inner workings of the presidency than for any other governmental office in the United States. As Hufbauer concedes, "In no other nation can citizens so easily obtain access to previously secret, sensitive, personal, as well as banal, documents and collections as one can in a presidential library."[48] Presidential libraries remain a treasure-trove of information and insight, especially for students of rhetoric and public address.

The contributions of presidential archives: Interrogating the rhetorical presidency

The contributions of presidential records are varied and vast. Obviously, a key feature for public address scholars is the study of the rhetorical presidency. In the process, such records can offer a more complex rendering of the rhetorical context of those involved in the practice of politics and policy formation. Presidential documents can likewise provide greater insight into the discourse that was produced by the presidents and their staffs, including the processes involved in drafting important public texts. And, such records provide additional evidence for the assessment of rhetorical motives and strategies. In order to illustrate these potential contributions, the presidential papers relating to President Dwight D. Eisenhower's "Atoms for Peace" campaign will be examined.

As noted, presidential records can provide a richer understanding of the rhetorical context of particular rhetorical acts, shedding light on the historical development of ideas and providing critical insights into the discourse itself. In establishing the "setting" of a particular speech, as Loren D. Reid recognized as early as 1944, "letters, diaries, memoirs, and periodicals" can help the rhetorical critic "interpret the circumstances leading up to the delivery of the speech."[49] Forty years later, David Zarefsky noted that, as a discipline, we still have not become "as skilled as we ought to be at knowing how to identify and locate the relevant primary sources, how to assess them, and how to use them as evidence for claims that we might advance" in terms of both "historical and critical methods."[50] Yet as Ronald H. Carpenter has argued, archival research is crucial to sound "rhetorical history," as it allows us to "reconstruct communication mosaics surrounding particular texts we study, to situate that discourse more firmly in the *total process* of persuasion."[51]

Put another way, archival research allows us to transport our readers to another time and place, to recreate the historical context of a rhetorical act. Done well, as William Norwood Brigance contended in 1933, good historical criticism can bring the "past before our eyes as though it were the living present."[52]

Students of rhetoric and public address historically have made extensive use of archives not only for primary sources, but also for establishing the historical context and the influence of important presidential speeches. In *A History of Criticism of American Public Address*, for example, rhetorical scholars often cited public laws, speech texts, Supreme Court cases, congressional debates, and newspaper accounts from primary rather than secondary sources to enhance the depth and credibility of their research.[53] In his essay on Abraham Lincoln's political rhetoric, for example, Earl W. Wiley surveyed more than 40 different newspaper and magazine periodicals published throughout the nineteenth century, personal letters from eight collections, including the Illinois Historical Society, and historical and contemporary biographies about Lincoln from the nineteenth throughout the twentieth centuries. Wiley's extensive review of primary and secondary resources allowed him to provide a more informed analysis of Lincoln's rhetorical texts, as well as chart the advancement and circulation of his ideas and ideology.[54]

Similarly, my own archival research at the Truman and Eisenhower libraries provided me with a more nuanced understanding of how those administrations approached Cold War propaganda. In addition to the secondary literature, I examined presidential diary entries, departmental minutes, memos that were exchanged between cabinet officials and members of Congress, secret directives passed down from agencies like the PSB, speech drafts, and letters sent by the president to political officials and members of the media. These primary source materials gave me a richer sense of the rhetorical context from the perspective of those who were most deeply involved in Cold War policymaking. And they contributed to what I believe were new and unique insights about the politics of the Cold War. As Brigance suggested more than 70 years ago, we should not be "content" to accept what other "biographers and essayists have said" about the past because that sort of research represents "mere rewriting."[55] By locating and making use of primary source materials, we can offer richer interpretations in our rhetorical analysis and make more original contributions to historical knowledge.

Specifically, my archival research on the Eisenhower administration's "Atoms for Peace" campaign revealed how the PSB, under presidential direction, embraced a very different understanding of "peace" than the president championed publicly. In his "Atoms for Peace" speech, Eisenhower called for the "peaceful use[s] of atomic energy" as a means to reverse "this greatest of destructive forces" in order to "move forward toward peace and happiness."[56] Behind the scenes, however, members of Eisenhower's own administration were arguing that "no good policy was ever made with either peace or compromise as its main ingredient,"[57] and that "to balk at action because of an uncertain fear of precipitating war is to increase the risk of defeat in the world struggle."[58] Without delving into the recently declassified documents from the time period, I might have missed this apparent contradiction between the public and the private rhetoric of the Eisenhower administration, and I would have had a severely limited understanding of the assumptions, the tensions, and the conflicts within the administration that provided the context for Eisenhower's speech.

A second key contribution of archival research is recovering the evolutionary processes that gave rise to public discourse. Although the president's public papers are published, archival research can still provide insight into how particular speeches, public campaigns, and policy initiatives evolved over time. The "Atoms for Peace" speech, for instance, involved several speechwriters and multiple drafts. One of those speechwriters, Eisenhower's World War II aide, C. D. Jackson, was also deeply involved with the PSB and served as Special Assistant to the president for Cold War strategy. Other key contributors to the speech included Lewis Strauss, Chair of the Atomic Energy Commission, and Robert Cutler, Eisenhower's national security advisor. As Charles J. G. Griffin argues, Eisenhower was both "willing and well qualified to involve himself in the speechwriting process."[59] He also closely edited drafts of the "Atoms for Peace" speech, as evidenced by his handwriting on those drafts. Martin J. Medhurst explains that Eisenhower's editing was significant as the speech progressively took on "a much more conciliatory tone" and as "the themes of peace and hope, always present," came into greater prominence.[60] Knowing how the speech evolved and how Eisenhower deployed a rhetoric of "peace" as a rhetorical and political strategy complicates our understanding of the speech beyond what we might learn from the public discourse alone. In other words, the archival work allows for a more nuanced interpretation of the speech. And, as Davis W. Houck suggests, "archival sources that speak directly to interpretive claims catch a reader's attention."[61]

Reviewing primary sources can also help rhetorical scholars understand the decision-making processes and the rhetorical motives behind a president's policies and public discourse.[62] Arguments relating to rhetorical "intent" are often disparaged by scholars more focused on questions of ideology, or the power dynamics and cultural commitments reflected in rhetorical texts. Yet as Zarefsky argues, a president functions "as the chief inventor and broker of the symbols of American politics," and as such his intentions and motives are important. Some of those motives, as Zarefsky argues, "may be revealed to the sensitive critic through the discourse itself,"[63] but arguments about motives are greatly strengthened by behind-the-scenes evidence of how such discourse came about. By reading only Eisenhower's "Atoms for Peace" speech, for example, one might miss the complicated mixture of motives behind the administration's larger Cold War propaganda campaign.[64] By 1954, the Eisenhower administration's program of nuclear testing seemed clearly inconsistent with the themes of its "Atoms for Peace" campaign. Consequently, the administration opted to delay its announcements about the results of those tests while continuing to speak of the country's commitment to an "enduring peace," portraying nuclear weapons as a key "*defense shield* of the free world."[65] Clearly, there was more to the administration's Cold War policy than the promulgation of peaceful uses of atomic energy, as emphasized in the president's public pronouncements.

Ultimately, primary source materials can reveal the hidden or covert side of presidential policy in both foreign and domestic affairs. For example, C. D. Jackson, Eisenhower's expert in psychological warfare and a principal architect of the "Atoms for Peace" campaign, returned to his career in journalism in 1954, yet he continued as an *informal* advisor to Eisenhower until he left office. In addition to submitting drafts of speeches and ideas for new campaigns to further promote the themes of the "Atoms for Peace" campaign, Jackson repeatedly advised the president on "psychological warfare" against the Soviets and public relations at home. In one letter to Eisenhower in the days leading up to Nikita Khrushchev's visit in 1960, for example, Jackson wrote: "If ever there was a moment for incisiveness, boldness, and virile action, it is now. Furthermore, this is the time for what I call effective 'orchestration' of *our* psychological warfare plans."[66] Jackson also sent Eisenhower copies of *Time* editorials in advance of their publication; in one such editorial, the news magazine praised Eisenhower's "superb Geneva performance." In the accompanying letter, Jackson exclaimed that it was "now up to the American people to back your play, and up to American journalism to inform the American people as to what was the play."[67] Jackson's letter portended the more active role the American press would play in promulgating the administration's Cold War ideology in the years to come and the complicated mix of motives behind the relationship between the Eisenhower administration and the press.

As more of the Eisenhower administration's papers became open to the public in the 1980s and beyond, the memory of his presidency began to shift. In *The Hidden-Hand Presidency*, Fred I. Greenstein explains that prior to the late 1970s, one prevailing perception among "president watchers" of the thirty-fourth president was that of an "aging hero" – a "nonpolitical" leader whose personal popularity transcended politics. Greenstein argues, however, that Eisenhower was in fact a very effective leader who "went to great lengths to conceal the political side of his leadership."[68] As Eisenhower's presidential records became more available, the conventional wisdom shifted.

No doubt the same will be true of Eisenhower's former vice president, Richard M. Nixon. As more of his contested presidential records become public (in spite of concerted efforts to block their release), we stand to learn much about what went on behind the scenes during that administration's two terms in office.[69] But more than that, we also can learn much about the relationship between the modern rhetorical presidency and the news media and activist organizations that seek to support or discredit presidents in power. In the analysis that follows, I look specifically at the archival records documenting the Nixon administration's response to the Vietnam Veterans Against the War (VVAW). The analysis illustrates the ways in which presidential archives can complicate our understanding of rhetorical context, the modes of production involved in news coverage, and strategies of presidential discourse designed to disrupt political opposition.

The Nixon Administration and the Vietnam Veterans Against the War

One manifestation of the discord over the nation's involvement in the war in Vietnam was the formation of a prominent antiwar group composed of returning veterans, the Vietnam Veterans Against the War. The formation of this group, according to Gerald Nicosia, "would put Richard Nixon into a panic, provoke FBI Director J. Edgar Hoover into breaking the law in order to destroy it ... and bring to prominence at least one leader of national stature, John Kerry."[70] For many returning soldiers, the decision to denounce the war represented a "search for redemption" – "a struggle to find meaning ... in the human experience" and to "narrow the gap between the ideals and the reality of American society."[71]

Because returning veterans had more credibility than the typical antiwar protester, they complicated public deliberations over the war and the patriotism of those who opposed it. Donald A. Ritchie explains the complications: "commentators often tend to portray those who fought in Vietnam as proponents of the war, and those who eluded the draft and military service as demonstrators against the war. Yet some of the most outspoken hawks never served in uniform, while some of the most passionate doves were Vietnam veterans."[72] The veterans of the VVAW entered the political fray over the war in Vietnam with an "authority of experience,"[73] yet in the eyes of the Nixon administration, the group was just another disloyal and unpatriotic voice advocating surrender in Vietnam. According to one planning document in the White House Special Files, the VVAW supported the "People's Peace Treaty," which according to the unknown author of the document was "the Hanoi version of a peace settlement for Vietnam." The writer went on to conclude: "It's not too difficult to figure whose side this group is on."[74]

In response, the Nixon administration embarked upon a rhetorical campaign to discredit the VVAW by questioning their war experiences and political views. As Charles W. Colson, Special Counsel to the President (Nixon), emphasized, there are "a number of articles published which question the authenticity of the [VVAW] veterans."[75] In response to the VVAW's calls to end the US involvement in the Vietnam War, the Nixon administration worked to infiltrate the organization, disrupt its political power, and ultimately to challenge its authenticity as a veterans' group. Archival resources offer a glimpse into these strategies and the motives behind them, and they also shed light on the collusion between some members of the news media and the Nixon administration in efforts to discredit the dissenting veterans. Framing their actions with a rhetoric of patriotism, of course, put a positive public face on the administration's campaign to stifle the dissent of the anti-VVAW campaign and provided a plausible rationale in the event that the covert campaign became public.

The Vietnam Veterans Against the War

The genesis of the VVAW is rooted in the interactions of six returning Vietnam veterans in the spring of 1967.[76] From the outset, the organization faced hostility not only from the Nixon administration, but also from others within the antiwar movement who considered all returning vets tainted by allegations of US war atrocities against the civilians of Vietnam. Many of the organization's activities were designed to raise awareness over what the VVAW itself considered US war crimes. Operation Raw (Rapid American Withdraw) – the organization's first major protest in September of 1970 – involved a four-day walk from Morristown, New Jersey, to Valley Forge, Pennsylvania, reenacting a march that George Washington made between the two battlefields during the Revolutionary War.[77] Operation Raw was John Kerry's first public involvement with the VVAW.[78] Kerry quickly assumed a leadership role within the group, determined to carry the VVAW's message to a broader audience.

Kerry's profile helped explain his rapid rise to prominence within the VVAW. Kerry attended boarding school in Switzerland before entering Yale University and graduating in June of 1966 with a BA in political science. He also possessed strong communication skills. Most significantly, he served as an officer in the US Navy from November 1968 through April of 1969, where he was the recipient of three purple hearts, a bronze star, and a silver star. He was also, by many accounts, politically motivated from a young age.[79]

Following Operation Raw, Kerry and the VVAW continued trying to focus attention on alleged US war atrocities, co-sponsoring the Winter Soldier Investigation with the Citizens' Commission of Inquiry on US War Crimes in Vietnam (CCI). Andrew E. Hunt suggests that "[t]he Winter Soldier Investigation would be but a beginning in rousing America's conscience and healing its veterans."[80] The CCI launched the investigation into the US war atrocities in Washington, DC, on December 1, 1970; the investigations continued with VVAW-sponsored public inquiries in Detroit, Michigan, from January 31 through February 2, 1971. In Detroit, more than 100 veterans gave eyewitness accounts of war crimes, and some even testified to their own involvement in such crimes.[81] In total, war crime investigations were held in 13 cities across the country, offering still more veterans the opportunity to provide eyewitness testimony. VVAW member Joe Urgo explained the goal of the public investigation: "[W]e had to prove that what was done in Vietnam – in terms of the torture, murder, massacres, rape – was not individual decisions by individual GIs but in fact policy that had been worked out by the centers of the United States government, through its think tanks, war colleges, Pentagon …"[82]

Building on the successes of the Winter Soldier Investigations, the VVAW planned their next event: Dewey Canyon III, a five-day veterans' protest in Washington, DC. Among other activities, the event included marches, an encampment on the national mall, guerilla theater performances, and the symbolic return of war medals. It was during this event that Kerry delivered his famous speech of April 22, 1971, before a subcommittee of the Senate Foreign Relations Committee.[83] Dewey Canyon III not only "triggered a nationwide organizing drive," but it attracted considerable media coverage and, of course, the attention of the Nixon administration.[84] Prior to the rise of the VVAW, both the Johnson and Nixon administrations had effectively portrayed war protesters as unpatriotic rich kids from college campuses who were merely acting out against authority and lacking in genuine conviction.[85] The presence in Washington of Vietnam veterans protesting against the war significantly undermined that image of the antiwar movement.

The Nixon administration counters the VVAW

The VVAW came under surveillance by the Nixon administration from the start. The FBI allegedly began keeping files on the VVAW as early as the fall of 1967 as part of a Counter-Intelligence Program (COINTELPRO) designed to track antiwar activities and infiltrate antiwar groups, particularly those suspected of ties to the Communist Party. The US government reportedly used paid informants and undercover plants to infiltrate the VVAW and to encourage violent acts by its members. The US government also was accused of wiretapping the VVAW's telephones and of attempting to have its tax-exempt status revoked.[86] The Nixon administration kept tabs on the daily activities of Dewey Canyon III as part of the Internal Security Division's intelligence-gathering operations. The documents from these efforts were marked "Secret – Eyes Only," and were linked with secret service investigations and sent to H. R. Haldeman, Nixon's Chief of Staff, and John D. Ehrlichman, Assistant to the President for Domestic Affairs.[87] These records clearly document the administration's efforts to disrupt the VVAW's political activities through covert means, ultimately complicating our understanding of the rhetorical context and the impact of antiwar protest.

Some within the news media aided the administration's efforts to damage the credibility of Kerry and the VVAW. The *Detroit News*, for example, contrasted Kerry with Melville L. Stephens, a former Vietnam Navy Lieutenant, who argued before the same Senate hearing that the United States should not abandon its South Vietnamese allies, emphasizing instead the enemy's war atrocities.[88] The *Detroit News*, in contrasting the two veterans – one who supported the war effort and one who did not – noted that Kerry was "wealthy" and "slept in a clean bed at one of Georgetown's most fashionable addresses" during Dewey Canyon III. Stephens, on the other hand, "spent every night on the damp ground of the Mall, risking arrest." J. F. Ter Horst, the author of the news article (and President Gerald Ford's future press secretary), also raised questions of Kerry's authenticity, charging that Adam Walinsky (former Robert Kennedy speechwriter) admitted that "he had helped Kerry put together his eloquent presentation," while Stephens supposedly "wrote his own statement" for the Senate committee – an allegation that Walinsky denied.[89] *Newsday* also emphasized Kerry's wealth and his political ambitions: "Kerry comes from a rich, privileged background, has excellent social and political connections and is frankly ambitious."[90] The *Boston Evening Globe* charged that Kerry intentionally modeled his political career, including his naval service, after John F. Kennedy – the two even shared the same initials. Paraphrasing one of Kerry's classmates, the reporter alleged "that Kerry even as far back as his pre-college days was recognized by his classmates as modeling himself on JFK, and harboring unconcealed ambitions to become President."[91]

There is at least some evidence that the news media were complicit in the administration's efforts to damage the credibility of Kerry and the VVAW. As part of its efforts to promote this counter-strategy, the Nixon administration created a media team to target news outlets with competing visions of Kerry and the VVAW. Documents in the Nixon papers reveal that Colson, Nixon's Special Counsel, worked directly with journalists to shape news stories about the VVAW. He knew about the impending publication of Ter Horst's negative feature on Kerry, noting in a memo that "the terHorst piece" was being "done about Kerry this weekend."[92] According to Douglas Brinkley, Ter Horst represented a "Nixon boosting … columnist" who "failed to mention" that Stephens "was a paid operative of the Nixon administration, working for Chuck Colson."[93] Whether or not Stephens functioned as a Nixon administration informant when he opted to join the antiwar veterans on the mall is unclear. Yet, there is evidence of collaboration between Stephens and the Nixon administration when the latter is identified as a "White House Staff" member in a memo from the President's Office Files that summarized a meeting between Nixon, Henry Kissinger, Stephens, and John O'Neill.[94] Even more than Stephens, O'Neill would subsequently lead the Nixon administration's efforts to counter Kerry's media image as a heroic veteran. As head of a pro-war veterans' group, the Vietnam Veterans for a Just Peace, O'Neill challenged Kerry's claim to speak for Vietnam veterans on a number of fronts.

Evidence of O'Neill's connections to the White House includes another memo from Colson setting up a meeting between O'Neill and Ter Horst in June of 1971. Colson urged Ter Horst to interview O'Neill because "we want to build him up" given that he "is a very charismatic guy."[95] In another memo written only a week later, Colson urged his colleagues to discredit Kerry in "as many sources as possible," even though he believed they already had "Kerry on the run." He was "beginning to take a tremendous beating in the press," Colson wrote, "but let's not let up, let's destroy this young demagogue before he becomes another Ralph Nader."[96] Colson summarized his mission in a memo dated May 14, 1971, in the following way: "the more effectively we discredit him [Kerry] the better."[97]

O'Neill played a major role in this effort to discredit John Kerry. In a summary of the meeting between Nixon, Kissinger, Stephens, and O'Neill, Colson wrote the following to Haldeman: "O'Neill went out charging like a tiger, has agreed that he will appear anytime, anywhere that we program him and was last seen walking up West Executive Avenue mumbling to himself that he had just been with the most magnificent man he had ever met in his life."[98] In public appearances, O'Neill often championed Nixon's Vietnamization plan, yet his connections with the White House were not always transparent, especially at first, when O'Neill championed such policies in a debate with Kerry on the *Dick Cavett Show* on June 30, 1971. By the 1972 presidential campaign, O'Neill's alliance with the Nixon administration had become obvious, as he actively campaigned for Nixon as the public face of the group, Concerned Veterans for Nixon.[99] More recently, O'Neill reemerged as a member of the Swift Boat Veterans for Truth, challenging the veracity of Kerry's claims about his war record during the 2004 presidential campaign. In a book that he co-authored that year, *Unfit for Command*, O'Neill charged that "the real John

Kerry of Vietnam was a man who filed false operating reports, who faked Purple Hearts, and who took a fast pass through the combat zones."[100]

Of course, John Kerry was not the only target of the Nixon administration's attempts to discredit antiwar protesters. In a *UPI* wire story on April 21, 1971, an anonymous White House official minimized the role of veterans at Dewey Canyon III, charging that "fewer than 30 per cent of protesters were veterans" and that "not all of them had served in Vietnam." Following up on the charge, the *UPI* reporter approached participants on the mall and asked to see their discharge papers. While some were prepared for the request and displayed their discharge papers, others were not able to do so. VVAW leaders stepped in to show their own discharge papers, and they claimed that 95 percent of those camping were veterans – arguing that a "large majority" were veterans of the Vietnam War. Colson considered the story a victory for his efforts, boasting to Haldeman of their efforts to "expose the non-veterans demonstration" and asking him to assure the president that he would be "continuing the effort." Concerning the same effort, DeVan L. Shumway bragged to Colson about his success in persuading journalists to question the credentials of the protesting veterans, concluding: "I await the medal which you said the President would pin on my chest personally." Shumway would later become the chief spokesperson for the Committee to Re-Elect the President (CREEP) during the period when other members of the committee were being investigated for their role in the Watergate break-in.[101]

Finally, the Nixon administration worked to counter the impact of the VVAW by cultivating support for the war from other veterans' groups. As early as February of 1971, the White House created a preliminary blueprint to map out that part of the strategy, responding to the Winter Soldier Investigation with a plan entitled "Mobilization of Vietnam Veterans." With the goal of obtaining "highly visible support for the President's Indochina policy from Vietnam Veterans," the plan called for public statements by President Nixon and Don Johnson, the head of the Veterans Administration, addressing the concerns of returning Vietnam veterans with issues like unemployment. Administration officials also planned to work with the Veterans of Foreign Wars (VFW) and the American Legion to garner more support for the war effort.[102] Reflecting the administration's concern with media coverage of the veterans' attitude toward the war, Colson wrote that syndicated columnist Nick Thimmesch would be "doing some pieces about Kerry running away from the debate" with Tony MacDonald of the VFW, who Colson called "superb" and someone he planned to "get ... on some of the talk shows."[103] In the aftermath of Dewey Canyon III, other veterans' groups, under the banner of Vietnam Veterans for a Just Peace, organized a counter-protest in support of Nixon's Vietnamization policies. And in a letter trying to recruit still more veterans to the administration's cause, the president of the Fleet Reserve Association (FRA), Robert L. Bastian, wrote that while 1,000 veterans may have protested at the VVAW's event, "two and a half million other Veterans did not" and they were "damn mad at being called *War Criminals* by that thousand."[104]

The themes of patriotism and sacrifice for one's country permeated the anti-VVAW discourse of the Nixon administration and its allies. In a confidential "Plan to Counteract Viet Nam Veterans Against the War" found in Colson's papers, the administration envisioned "Veterans' organizations" issuing statements "disavowing the VVAW as not being representative of veterans and stating that they are offended by their actions and allegations."[105] In his letter denouncing the VVAW, Bastian wrote about giving "the South Vietnamese the opportunity to be free of outside or Communist domination" and emphasized his hope that thousands of American troops had not died in vain: "DON'T WASTE OUR BLOOD." The salutation of his letter read, "I remain in Loyalty, Protection, and Service."[106] Bruce N. Kessler, a member of the Vietnam Veterans for a Just Peace, wrote in a *New York Times* column that "We are proud of our nation and its exertions in defense of freedom in the world"; and he went on to brand the VVAW as "un-American."[107]

All of this effort to undermine the credibility of the VVAW and its allies was part of a broader effort to rally public opinion behind the administration's war policies. In a taped telephone conversation between Larry Higby, an aide to H. R. Haldeman, and Tom Benham of the Opinion Research Cooperation, Benham noted: "You know the public doesn't like the demonstrations and somehow they can be made to symbolize the sort of UnAmerican–Unpatriotic approach to this damn thing." Higby then reported to Colson that Haldeman strongly agreed with Benham, and he instructed Colson's "planning group to formulate some activity, posture or ideas of what we can be doing to turn the upcoming demonstrations into an opportunity."[108] The reach of this strategy to shape public opinion extended into the 1972 presidential election, becoming part of the motive for the break-in at the Democratic Party headquarters at the Watergate building. Among other things, CREEP sought to link George McGovern and the Democratic National Committee with the VVAW and its "un-American" activities.[109] In the portrait of the protesters painted by the administration, none of the protesting veterans had sincere, reasonable objections to the war; they were simply "trying to compensate for some guilt feeling or psychological defect by participation in this organization."[110]

Conclusion

The archival records of the presidential administrations represent important resources for public address scholars seeking to gain greater insight into the rhetorical presidency. Through archival research, scholars can gain a fuller understanding of the historical context, reconstruct the processes through which private and public texts were produced, and offer richer interpretations of the rhetorical strategies and potential motives involved in the public deliberations over US foreign and domestic policies. Yet, presidential archives are not of interest only to scholars of the presidency. Because presidents grapple with a host of issues, scholars should not overlook the potential of presidential records to shed light on an array of political topics involving Supreme Court cases, congressional debates, news media coverage, and opposition groups seeking to promote political and social change. As more and more archival sources become available online, the utility of such presidential records will continue to expand for rhetorical scholars.[111]

Of course, the complications involving the preservation and release of such documents remain. In terms of preservation, the expense associated with operating presidential libraries continues to grow as more presidents leave office and build new libraries. Even though the presidents raise private funds for their libraries, the upkeep and operation of the libraries fall to the US government; the cost of operating the George H. W. Bush library, for example, was approximately $3 million in 2004, and the Clinton library costs on average $4 million annually. With the addition of President George W. Bush's library, there will soon be 13 presidential libraries to fund.[112] The scope of the holdings simultaneously has grown exponentially, which increases the operating costs. In 2007, the Office of Presidential Libraries reported that it will take up to 100 years for the papers of the most recent presidents to become available. Roosevelt's library, for example, holds some 17 million documents, while the Clinton library houses more than 76 million records.[113] The number of archivists at each library, however, does not always keep pace with the size of the holdings.

Additional concerns relate to the fragility of the documents and changes in technology. Even as document preservation supposedly becomes more technologically sophisticated, William Honan explains that the "tapes, disks, drives and software that make electronic records accessible keep being modified, updated, worn out and replaced." New storage technologies can quickly become obsolete, which adds to the expense of keeping up with cutting-edge preservation techniques. Archivists are discovering that some CD-Roms are already decaying and that electromagnetic tapes are beginning to "melt."[114] And while such technologies can store larger amounts of data, only a small percentage of NARA's 9 billion documents – to cite just one example – has been digitized and made available online.[115]

Of course, apart from the issues of preservation and costs associated with document storage, the question of access poses an ongoing challenge. The Obama administration's FOIA executive order represents a new attitude of openness that should help ensure that more documents become available for scholarly inspection. It is only a matter of time, however, before Obama's executive order will be challenged in the courts, which could further delay the release of documents from past administrations. In addition, the next administration may not share President Obama's propensity for openness. Thus, the constitutional issues surrounding the papers of the presidency – the proper balance between public access and executive privilege – will continue to be debated. Hopefully, that balance will be tilted more toward open access, as the availability of such materials is critical to our understanding of the rhetorical presidency and a broad range of issues concerning the other branches of government and the American people. Nancy Kassop summarizes the importance of public access:

> As a public officer who can expect his actions to come under intense scrutiny, a president bears a heavy responsibility for what is said and decided behind closed doors; but when those doors are flung open and the sunshine flows in, there is no better illustration of a system that prides itself on open government and official accountability than easy access to the public records belonging to all of us.[116]

Acknowledgments

The author wishes to thank archivists at the Dwight D. Eisenhower Presidential Library and the National Archives and Records Administration at College Park.

Notes

1   See Benjamin Hufbauer, *Presidential Temples: How Memorials and Libraries Shape Public Memory* (Lawrence: University Press of Kansas, 2005), 25–26; and Frank L. Schick, Renée Schick, and Mark Carroll, *Records of the Presidency: Presidential Papers and Libraries from Washington to Reagan* (Phoenix, AZ: Oryx Press, 1989), 1, 41–44.

2   Some documents for these presidents are housed in the Library of Congress and more specialized libraries. See Hufbauer, *Presidential Temples*, 26; Bruce P. Montgomery, *Subverting Open Government: White House Materials and Executive Branch Documents* (Lanham, MD: Scarecrow, 2006), 11; "Presidential Papers, Manuscript Division, Library of Congress," Manuscript Division, Library of Congress, memory.loc.gov/ammem/ presprvw/23pres.html (accessed January 8, 2009); Schick, Schick, and Carroll, *Records of the Presidency*, 1–10, 20; and Fritz Veit, *Presidential Libraries and Collections* (New York: Greenwood Press, 1987), 2–5, 107–125.

3   Charles E. Morris III, "The Archival Turn in Rhetorical Studies; Or, the Archives Rhetorical (Re)turn," *Rhetoric & Public Affairs* 9 (2006): 113.

4   David Zarefsky, "The State of the Art in Public Address Scholarship," in *Texts in Context: Critical Dialogues on Significant Episodes in American Political Rhetoric*, ed. Michael C. Leff and Fred J. Kauffeld (Davis, CA: Hermagoras Press, 1989), 24.

5   Mary E. Stuckey, "Presidential Secrecy: Keeping Archives Open," *Rhetoric & Public Affairs* 9 (2006): 138.

6   The concept of the rhetorical presidency refers to the process by which presidents have gone over the heads of members of Congress in an attempt to sway public opinion, a practice that has historically been linked to the early twentieth-century presidents. See James W. Ceaser, Glen E. Thurow, Jeffrey Tullis, and Joseph M. Bessette, "The Rise of the Rhetorical Presidency," *Presidential Studies Quarterly* 11 (1981): 158–171; Martin J. Medhurst, ed., *Beyond the Rhetorical Presidency* (College Station: Texas A&M University Press, 1996); and Martin J. Medhurst, ed., *Before the Rhetorical Presidency* (College Station: Texas A&M University Press, 2008). Barbara Hinckley explains the importance of the bully pulpit to presidential power by arguing that the "public record becomes … a beginning point for the study of the office" because presidents present "themselves and the office in speeches to the nation." See Barbara Hinckley, *The Symbolic Presidency: How Presidents Portray Themselves* (New York: Routledge, 1990), 16–17. I also demonstrate how archival research surrounding the US official propaganda programs showcased the modes of production surrounding the rhetorical presidencies of the Truman and Eisenhower administrations. See Shawn J. Parry-Giles, *The Rhetorical Presidency, Propaganda, and the Cold War, 1945–1955* (Westport, CT: Praeger, 2002).

7   Peter Sezzi, *Personal Versus Private: Presidential Records in a Legislative Context – A Bibliographic Exploration* (Lanham, MD: Scarecrow, 2005), 4; and Veit, *Presidential Libraries and Collections*, 3.

8   See Pamela Kessler, "At the Archives, the Inside Story," *Washington Post*, July 27, 1984, online at Lexis-Nexus Academic, November 19, 2007; and Schick, Schick, and Carroll, *Records of the Presidency*, 7.

9   See Hufbauer, *Presidential Temples*, 29–34; and Sezzi, *Personal Versus Private*, 12–14.

10   Schick, Schick, and Carroll, *Records of the Presidency*, 14.

11   *Presidential Libraries Act of 1955*, US Public Law 84–373, August 12, 1955, 695.

12   Schick, Schick, and Carroll, *Records of the Presidency*, 11.

13   *United States v. Nixon, President of the United States*, 418 US 683 (1974), 684.

14   Montgomery, *Subverting Open Government*, 5.

15   *Preservation of Presidential Records and Materials Act*, US Public Law 93–526, December 19, 1974, 1695.

16   *Nixon v. Administrator of General Services*, 433 US 425 (1977), 441.

17   Montgomery, *Subverting Open Government*, 146.

18   *Presidential Records Act*, US Public Law 95–591, November 4, 1978, 2523–2526.

19   Sezzi, *Personal Versus Private*, 4, xi.

20   Robert M. Warner, *Diary of a Dream: A History of the National Archives Independence Movement, 1980–1985* (Metuchen, NJ: Scarecrow, 1995), viii.

21   Ronald Reagan, "Presidential Records," Executive Order 12667, January 18, 1989, 1748.

22   See Montgomery, *Subverting Open Government*, 100–106; and *Armstrong, et al. v. Executive Office of the President, et al.* (Civil Action No. 89cv00142), May 21, 1993.

23   George W. Bush, "Further Implementation of the Presidential Records Act," Executive Order 13233, *Federal Register* 66, no. 214 (November 5, 2001): 56025–56026.

24   Nancy Kassop, "Not Going Public: George W. Bush and the Presidential Records Act," in *In the Public Domain: Presidents and the Challenges of Public Leadership*, ed. Lori Cox Han and Diane J. Heith (Albany: State University of New York Press, 2005), 271.

25   See Charlie Savage, "Presidential Dynasties Can Add Layer of Secrecy; Executive Privilege Allows For Keeping Documents Sealed," *Boston Globe*, November 13, 2007, online at Lexis-Nexus Academic, November 19, 2007.

26   "American Historical Association v. National Archives and Records Administration," *Public Citizen*, November 28, 2001, www.citizen.org/litigation/briefs/FOIAGovtSec/PresRecords/articles.cfm?ID=6515 (accessed November 19, 2007). See also *American Historical Association, et al., v. National Archives and Records Administration, et al.*, 516 F. Supp. 2d 90 (2007).

27   US House of Representatives, Report of the Committee on Government Reforms, *Presidential Records Act Amendments of 2002*, 107 Cong., 2nd Sess., November 22, 2002, Library of Congress, Thomas.gov., thomas.loc.gov/cgi-bin/cpquery/?sel=DOC&&item=&r_n=hr790.107&&&sid=cp107M6VRe&&refer=&& (accessed January 12, 2009).

28   *American Historical Association, et al., v. National Archives and Records Administration, et al.*

29   "Who Owns White House History?" *New York Times*, January 10, 2009, www.nytimes.com/2009/01/10/opinion/10sat3.html?hp (accessed January 10, 2009).

30   Barack H. Obama, "Presidential Records," Executive Order, January 21, 2009, www.whitehouse.gov/the_press_office/ExecutiveOrderPresidentialRecords/ (accessed January 21, 2009).

31 As cited in Sheryl Gay Stolberg, "On Day One, Obama Sets a New Tone," *New York Times*, January 22, 2009, www.nytimes.com/2009/01/22/us/politics/22obama.html?th&emc=th (accessed January 22, 2009).

32 "Memorandum for the Heads of Executive Departments and Agencies," Freedom of Information Act, White House Office of the Press Secretary, January 21, 2009, www.whitehouse.gov/the_press_office/ExecutiveOrderPresidentialRecords/ (accessed January 22, 2009).

33 Stolberg, "On Day One."

34 Stolberg, "On Day One."

35 Hufbauer, *Presidential Temples*, 25.

36 Arthur M. Schlesinger, Jr., *The Imperial Presidency* (Boston: Houghton Mifflin, 1973).

37 Michael Nelson, "Presidential Libraries Are Valuable Reflections of Their Eras," *Chronicle of Higher Education* 51 (November 12, 2004), online at Lexis-Nexus Academic, November 19, 2007.

38 Hufbauer, *Presidential Temples*, 5, 7.

39 Barbara A. Biesecker, "Of Historicity, Rhetoric: The Archive as Scene of Invention," *Rhetoric & Public Affairs* 9 (2006): 124.

40 Charles E. Morris III, "Archival Queer," *Rhetoric & Public Affairs* 9 (2006): 146.

41 Parry-Giles, *The Rhetorical Presidency, Propaganda, and the Cold War, 1945–1955*, 55–56. The PSB was referred to as the Operations Coordinating Board during much of the Eisenhower administration.

42 *Freedom of Information Act (FOIA)*, 5 US C. 552 (1966).

43 *1974 Amendments to the Freedom of Information Act*, US Public Law 93–502, November 21, 1974. See also Montgomery, *Subverting Open Government*, 130–131.

44 *Freedom of Information Act as Amended in 2002*, 5 US C. 552, December 23, 2002.

45 "Memorandum for the Heads of Executive Departments and Agencies," Freedom of Information Act, White House Office of the Press Secretary, January 21, 2009, www.whitehouse.gov/the_press_office/ExecutiveOrderPresidentialRecords/ (accessed January 22, 2009).

46 Stuckey, "Presidential Secrecy," 143.

47 Hufbauer, *Presidential Temples*, 2.

48 Hufbauer, *Presidential Temples*, 34.

49 Loren D. Reid, "The Perils of Rhetorical Criticism," *Quarterly Journal of Speech* 30 (1944): 417.

50 Zarefsky, "The State of the Art in Public Address Scholarship," 24.

51 Ronald H. Carpenter, "A Disciplinary History of Rhetorical History: Retrospect and Prospect," in *Doing Rhetorical History: Concepts and Cases*, ed. Kathleen J. Turner (Tuscaloosa: University of Alabama Press, 1998), 231 (emphasis in original).

52 William Norwood Brigance, "Whither Research?" *Quarterly Journal of Speech* 19 (1933): 559.

53 Ultimately three volumes were produced. Two were edited by Brigance and the third by Marie K. Hochmuth. See, for example, William Norwood Brigance, ed., *A History and Criticism of American Public Address*, vol. 1 (New York: McGraw-Hill, 1943).

54 Earl W. Wiley, "Abraham Lincoln: His Emergence as the Voice of the People," in *A History and Criticism of American Public Address*, ed. William Norwood Brigance (New York: Russell and Russell, 1960), 2: 859–877.

55   Brigance, "Whither Research?" 559.

56   Dwight D. Eisenhower, "Address before the General Assembly of the United Nations on Peaceful Uses of Atomic Energy," *Public Papers of the Presidents of the United States, Dwight D. Eisenhower, 1953* (Washington, DC: Government Printing Office, 1960), 817–821.

57   "Notes for a General Policy Approach to the Lodge Project," July 1953, White House Office, NSC Staff: Papers, 1953–1961, PSB Central Files Series, Box 23, Dwight D. Eisenhower Presidential Library (here after cited DDEPL), 14–15. For a greater explication of how the Truman and Eisenhower administrations conceptualized the role of propaganda in the Cold War, see Parry-Giles, *The Rhetorical Presidency, Propaganda, and the Cold War, 1945–1955.*

58   Psychological Strategy Board, August 26, 1953, Policy Paper for the Lodge Project, White House Office, NSC Staff: Papers, 1948–1961, OCB Secretariat Series, Lodge's Human Rights Project, Box 4, DDEPL, 17–20.

59   Charles J. G. Griffin, "Dwight D. Eisenhower: The 1954 State of the Union Address as a Case Study in Presidential Speechwriting," in *Presidential Speechwriting: From the New Deal to the Reagan Revolution and Beyond*, ed. Kurt Ritter and Martin J. Medhurst (College Station: Texas A&M University Press, 2003), 86. For more on the "Atoms for Peace" campaign, see Shawn J. Parry-Giles, "Dwight D. Eisenhower, 'Atoms for Peace,'" *Voices of Democracy* 1 (2006): 118–129. See also Ira Chernus, *Eisenhower's Atoms for Peace* (College Station: Texas A&M University Press, 2002).

60   Martin J. Medhurst, "Ghostwritten Speeches: Ethics Isn't the Only Lesson," *Communication Education* 36 (1987): 241–249.

61   Davis W. Houck, "On or About June 1988," *Rhetoric & Public Affairs* 9 (2006): 137.

62   For further discussion on the role of intent and archival research, see Carpenter, "A Disciplinary History of Rhetorical History," 221–242; and Houck, "On or About June 1988," 132–137.

63   David Zarefsky, *President Johnson's War on Poverty: Rhetoric and History* (Tuscaloosa: University of Alabama Press, 1986), 6, 8.

64   For a greater explication of the "Atoms for Peace" speech, see Martin J. Medhurst, "Eisenhower's 'Atoms for Peace' Speech: A Case Study in the Strategic Use of Language," *Communication Monographs* 54 (1987): 204–220.

65   Operations Coordinating Board, "Overseas Reaction to the AEC Report on the Effects of High Yield Nuclear Explosions," March 1955, White House Office, NSC Staff: Papers, 1948–1961, OCB Central Files Series, Box 9, DDEPL, 2–3 (emphasis added).

66   C. D. Jackson, Letter to President Eisenhower, September 1960, Presidential Papers of Dwight D. Eisenhower (Ann Whitman File), Box 22, DDEPL, 2–3 (emphasis added). For more information on the relationship between the Truman and Eisenhower administrations' relations with the US media, see Shawn J. Parry-Giles, "'Camouflaged' Propaganda: The Truman and Eisenhower Administrations' Covert Manipulation of News," *Western Journal of Communication* 60 (1996): 146–167.

67   C. D. Jackson, Letter to President Eisenhower, July 1955, Presidential Papers of Dwight D. Eisenhower (Ann Whitman File), Box 22, DDEPL, 1.

68   Fred I. Greenstein, *The Hidden-Hand Presidency: Eisenhower as Leader* (New York: Basic Books, 1982), viii, 5.

69   The Richard Nixon Presidential Library and Museum opened in Yorba Linda, California, on July 11, 2007. His presidential records that have been housed with the National Archives and Records Administration under the guidelines of the PPRMA of 1974 are

gradually being transferred to Nixon's presidential library. Many of Nixon's private papers were donated to the federal government and will be housed in the presidential library as well. See "The National Archives Opens Federal Nixon Library, Releases Previously-Restricted Documents and Tapes," National Archives and Records Administration, July 11, 2007, www.archives.gov/press/press-releases/2007/nr07-114.html (accessed January 30, 2009).

70 Gerald Nicosia, *Home to War: A History of the Vietnam Veterans' Movement* (New York: Crown Publishers, 2001), 5. For a more extended analysis of John Kerry and the VVAW, see "John Kerry, 'Statement Before the Senate Committee on Foreign Relations,'" *Voices of Democracy* 2 (2007): 99–125.

71 Andrew E. Hunt, *The Turning: A History of Vietnam Veterans Against the War* (New York: New York University Press, 1999), 4.

72 Donald A. Ritchie, "Foreword," in *Winter Soldiers: An Oral History of the Vietnam Veterans Against the War*, ed. Richard Stacewicz (New York: Twayne, 1997), ix.

73 Richard Stacewicz, ed., *Winter Soldiers: An Oral History of the Vietnam Veterans Against the War* (New York: Twayne, 1997), 316.

74 Vietnam Veterans Against the War, n.d., Nixon Presidential Materials Project (hereafter cited NPMP), White House Special Files (hereafter cited WHSF), Staff Member and Office Files (hereafter cited SMOF), H. R. Haldeman, Alpha Name Files (April–May 1971), Chuck Colson, April 1971–Don Rumsfeld, April 1971, Box 77, National Archives and Records Administration – College Park, Maryland (hereafter cited as NARA – CP), 1. W. Richard Howard served as Staff Assistant to Charles W. Colson in the Nixon White House. Howard communicated directly with media and public opinion outlets to bolster positive public images of the president and his policies. See "Special Files: W. Richard Howard," NPMP, NARA – CP, nixon.archives.gov/find/textual/presidential/special/staff/howard.html.

75 Charles Colson to Dick Howard, May 3, 1971, NPMP, WHSF, SMOF, Charles W. Colson, Vietnam – Various Groups, Vietnam Veterans Against the War (VVAW), Box 123, NARA – CP, 1. Charles Colson often worked as a liaison between the Nixon administration and various special interest groups (veterans, labor, farmers) in an attempt to gain their support on presidential policies. He also targeted media outlets to garner additional public support for Nixon administration policies. See "Special Files: Charles W. Colson," NPMP, NARA – CP, nixon.archives.gov/find/textual/presidential/special/staff/colson.html#note.

76 See Hunt, *The Turning*, 2; and Milton Viorst, *Fire in the Streets* (New York: Simon and Schuster, 1979), 187.

77 For more on Operation Raw, see Hunt, *The Turning*, 44–54; and Nicosia, *Home to War*, 58–67.

78 David Halbfinger, "Kerry Role in Antiwar Veterans is Delicate Issue in His Campaign," *New York Times*, April 24, 2004, 4, online at Lexis-Nexus Academic, May 24, 2006.

79 Hunt, *The Turning*, 48. For more on Kerry's war background, see Douglas Brinkley, *Tour of Duty: John Kerry and the Vietnam War* (New York: William Morrow, 2004), 27–34, 459–463.

80 Hunt, *The Turning*, 55. The name, Winter Soldiers, represented an inversion of Thomas Paine's concept of the sunshine patriot or the summer soldiers who shrank from duty.

81 See Hunt, *The Turning*, 55–76; and Stacewicz, *Winter Soldiers*, 5.

82 Joe Urgo, "The Winter Soldier Hearings," in *Winter Soldiers*, 235.

83 John F. Kerry, "Statement of John Kerry, Vietnam Veterans Against the War," *Legislative Proposals Relating to the War in Southeast Asia*, United States Senate Committee on

Foreign Relations, 92d Congress, lst sess., April 22, 1971 (Washington, DC: US Government Printing Office, 1971), 180–185.

84   See Hunt, *The Turning*, 77–84; and Richard R. Moser, *The New Winter Soldiers: GI and Veteran Dissent During the Vietnam Era* (New Brunswick, NJ: Rutgers University Press, 1996), 112. The name Dewey Canyon III was inspired by the code name of a military excursion into Laos in 1971.

85   Hunt, *The Turning*, 57.

86   See Hunt, *The Turning*, 5, 84, 167; Nicosia, *Home to War*, 251; and Stacewicz, *Winter Soldiers*, 314–315, 318, 331.

87   See Ronald H. Walker to W. Dewey Clower, April 6, 1971, NPMP, WHSF, SMOF, H. R. Haldeman, Alpha Name Files, Coverage of Presidential Activities – Decorating/ Construction, Box 121, NARA – CP, 1–2; and "Veterans' Actions Against the War," April 8, 1971, NPMP, WHSF, SMOF, H. R. Haldeman, Alpha Name Files, Coverage of Presidential Activities – Decorating/Construction, Box 121, NARA – CP, 1–2. For more information on John D. Ehrlichman, see "Special Files: John D. Ehrlichman," NPMP, NARA – CP, nixon.archives.gov/find/textual/presidential/special/staff/ehr-lichman.html.

88   Nicosia, *Home to War*, 150.

89   J. F. Ter Horst, "2 Vets with Medals, 1 with Silver Spoon," *Detroit News*, May 1, 1971, n.p. The article was found in the file, NPMP, WHSF, SMOF, Charles W. Colson, Larry Higby to Steve Karalekas, Box 8, NARA – CP, 2. See also Brinkley, *Tour of Duty*, 401.

90   Nick Thimmesch, "Playing Fair: Another Side," *Newsday*, June 3, 1971, n.p. The article was found in the file, NPMP, WHSF, SMOF, Charles W. Colson, Memorandum File, HRH Memos 1969–1970 to HRH Memos 1971, January–June 1971, Box 2, NARA – CP, 1.

91   George Frazier, "Blend of Calm and Crusader," *Boston Evening Globe*, June 9, 1971, n.p. The article was found in the file, NPMP, WHSF, SMOF, Charles W. Colson, Memorandum File, Van Shumway [1972] to Ron Ziegler [1971], Van Shumway [2 of 3] [1971], Box 12, NARA – CP, 2. Van Shumway's full name is DeVan L. Shumway. The documents within the Nixon papers refer to him as Van Shumway or DeVan L. Shumway.

92   See Charles W. Colson to Dick Howard, May 3, 1971, NPMP, WHSF, SMOF, Charles W. Colson, Vietnam – Various Groups, Vietnam Veterans Against the War (VVAW), Box 123, NARA – CP, 1.

93   Brinkley, *Tour of Duty*, 393, 401. Brinkley refers to Melville "Stevens" rather than Melville "Stephens." Other sources collaborate the Nixon records that the name of the person in question is spelled "Stephens" rather than "Stevens" See Nicosia, *Home to War*, 150. (Nicosia, however, refers to him as "Melvin" rather than "Melville.")

94   See Memo for the President's File, June 16, 1971, NPMP, WHSF, POF, Memoranda for the President, May 2, 1971–August 15, 1971, Box 85, NARA – CP, 1.

95   Charles Colson to Van Shumway, June 8, 1971, NPMP, WHSF, SMOF, Charles W. Colson, Memoranda File, Van Shumway [1972] to Ron Ziegler [1971], Box 12, NARA – CP, 1.

96   Charles Colson to Van Shumway, June 15, 1971, NPMP, WHSF, SMOF, Charles W. Colson, Memoranda File, Van Shumway [1972] to Ron Ziegler [1971], Box 12, NARA – CP, 1.

97   Charles Colson to Van Shumway, May 14, 1971, NPMP, WHSF, SMOF, Charles W. Colson, Memoranda File, Van Shumway [1972] to Ron Ziegler [1971], Box 12, NARA – CP, 1.

98 See Memo for the President's File, June 16, 1971, 1; and Charles Colson to H. R. Haldeman, June 17, 1971, A–Z June–July 1971, Lyndon K. Allin June, 1971–Bruce Kehrli June, 1971, Charles Colson, June 1971, Box 80, NARA – CP, 1.

99 See summary of a *UPI* story: DeVan L. Shumway to Herbert G. Klein, June 28, 1971, in press coverage of O'Neill's speech, NPMP, WHSF, SMOF, Charles W. Colson, Memoranda File, Van Shumway [1972] to Ron Ziegler [1971], Box 12, NARA – CP, 2. See also "Vets," *UPI*, June 28, 1971, n.p. The article was found in the file, NPMP, WHSF, SMOF, Charles W. Colson, Memorandum File, Van Shumway [1972] to Ron Ziegler [1971], Van Shumway [2 of 3] [1971], Box 12, NARA – CP, 2. The *UPI* reports that "O'Neill … said his organization is not tied to President Nixon or the Republican Party." Finally, see "Press Release – Concerned Vietnam Veterans for Nixon," July 26, 1972, NPMP, WHSF, SMOF, Charles W. Colson, Larry Higby to Steve Karalekas, Dick Howard, Box 8, NARA – CP, 1.

100 John E. O'Neill and Jerome R. Corsi, *Unfit for Command: Swift Boat Veterans Speak Out Against John Kerry* (Washington, DC: Regnery, 2004), 12.

101 DeVan L. Shumway to Mr. Colson, April 22, 1971, NPMP, WHSF, SMOF, H. R. Haldeman, Alpha Name Files, A–Z March–April 1971, Jonathan Rose March, 1971–Chuck Colson April 1971, Chuck Colson April 1971 [Part 1 of 2], Box 76, NARA – CP, 1–3. Concerning Shumway's connection to CREEP, see Carl Bernstein and Bob Woodward, "FBI Finds Nixon Aides Sabotaged Democrats," *Washington Post*, October 10, 1972, www.washingtonpost.com/wp- srv/national/longterm/water-gate/articles/101072–1.htm (accessed November 19, 2007). See also Patricia Sullivan, "Nixon Aide DeVan Shumway, 77," *Washington Post*, April 26, 2008, www.washingtonpost.com/wp dyn/content/article/2008/04/25/AR2008042503538_pf.html (accessed August 21, 2009).

102 See "Tentative Plan – Vietnam Veterans," n.d., NPMP, WHSF, SMOF, Charles W. Colson, Memoranda File, HRH Memos 1969–1970 to HRH Memos – 1971, January–June 1971, Box 2, NARA – CP, 1; and Colson to Haldeman, February 23, 1971, NPMP, WHSF, SMOF, Charles W. Colson, Memoranda File, HRH Memos 1969–1970 to HRH Memos – 1971, January–June 1971, Box 2, NARA – CP, 1–2.

103 Charles Colson to H. R. Haldeman, May 28, 1971, NPMP, WHSF, SMOF, Charles W. Colson, Memoranda File, HRH Memos 1969–1970 to HRH Memos – 1971, January–June 1971, Box 2, NARA – CP, 1.

104 National President to National Mailing List, F.R.A., May 27, 1971, NPMP, WHSF, SMOF, Charles W. Colson, Memoranda File, HRH Memos 1969–1970 to HRH Memos – 1971, January–June 1971, Box 2, NARA – CP, 1–3 (emphasis in original).

105 "Plan to Counteract Viet Nam Veterans Against the War," n.d., NPMP, WHSF, SMOF, Charles W. Colson, Vietnam – Various Groups, Vietnam Veterans Against the War (VVAW), Box 123, NARA – CP, 1.

106 National President to National Mailing List, F.R.A., 1–3 (emphasis in original).

107 Bruce N. Kessler, "Veterans for Vietnam," *New York Times*, May 13, 1971, 45.

108 Larry Higby to Chuck Colson, April 13, 1971, NPMP, WHSF, SMOF, H. R. Haldeman, Alpha Name Files, A–Z April–May 1971, Chuck Colson April, 1971–Don Rumsfeld April, 1971, Chuck Colson April 1971 [Part 2 of 2], Box 77, NARA – CP, 1–6.

109 Hunt, *The Turning*, 164–166; and Nicosia, *Home to War*, 263–264.

110   "Vietnam Veterans Against the War," n.d., NPMP, WHSF, SMOF, H. R. Haldeman, Alpha Name Files, A–Z April–May 1971, Chuck Colson April, 1971–Don Rumsfeld April, 1971, Dick Howard April 1971, Box 77, NARA – CP, 1.

111   Benjamin Hufbauer, "Archives of Spin," *New York Times*, January 20, 2007, online at Lexis-Nexus Academic, November 19, 2007.

112   Fred A. Bernstein, "Who Should Pay for Presidential Posterity?" *New York Times*, June 10, 2004, online at Lexis-Nexus Academic, November 19, 2007.

113   Hufbauer, "Archives of Spin."

114   William H. Honan, "At the National Archives, Technology Has a Flip Side," *New York Times*, October 1, 1995, online at Lexis-Nexus Academic, November 19, 2007.

115   Katie Hafner, "History, Digitized (and Abridged)," *New York Times*, March 11, 2007, online at Lexis-Nexus Academic, November 19, 2007.

116   Kassop, "Not Going Public," 274.

7

From Recovering Women's Words to Documenting Gender Constructs
Archival Research in the Twenty-First Century

Susan Zaeske and Sarah Jedd

"No documents, no history," intoned Mary R. Beard in *Woman as a Force in History*, a volume that inspired scholars in multiple disciplines to study women's lived experiences and their contributions to humanity.[1] What Beard wrote about history in general rings true in particular for the study of women's public address. Documents, more precisely texts, have been and continue to be the field's *sine qua non*. The importance of primary sources was no more clearly evident than when those who contemplated writing a history of women's oratory were told that the very idea was folly. Indeed, when in the mid-1940s Lillian O'Connor proposed to write a dissertation about speeches made by US women between 1828 and 1861, at least one member of her doctoral advising committee expressed grave reservations. "If women had made any speeches in public during those years," the Columbia University faculty member told her, "we historians would have found them."[2] To the archives went O'Connor to gather primary sources to prove the existence of women who spoke in public throughout American history and thus to establish the very possibility of researching and teaching women's public address. These initial efforts succeeded, and subsequent generations of scholars returned to the archives with a different yet parallel purpose of recovering, authenticating, and publishing the texts of women's public address. Throughout its founding decades, then, archival research proved to be an absolute necessity for scholars of what would emerge as women's public address, feminist public address, and gender analysis of public discourse.

This chapter takes as its focus archival practices employed by scholars of gender and women's public address. Rather than offering a historiography of the study of women's and feminist public address,[3] it centers on the archival element of the enterprise, drawing on representative examples instead of weaving an inclusive narrative. After exploring why and how early women's public address scholars practiced archival research, the chapter contemplates contemporary issues in archival research facing scholars of gender and women's public address. Just as archival research was a defining and necessary feature of early women's public address, so, too, must present-day scholars seek out primary sources using both traditional and new research strategies. At the same time, we must broaden the scope of our archival research beyond the borders of the United States and beyond limited notions of what constitutes a rhetorical text. Most pressingly, we must adapt our archival practices to serve theoretical and methodological changes, continuing the recovery of women's rhetoric while also locating archival resources to analyze how gender functions in public discourse. An analysis of how gender functioned in congressional debates over women's antislavery petitions demonstrates how archival practices aimed at both recovery and gender analysis can work hand in hand.

A History of Archival Research on Women Political Activists

During the nascent phase of the study of American women's public address from the 1930s through the 1960s, archival research proved an absolute necessity. This was because while the words of presidents, clergymen, and many male reformers were readily available in published anthologies, the speeches and writings of women remained hidden in archives. So unknown were artifacts of women's rhetorical activity, in fact, that their apparent absence warranted the conclusion that in the past women did not give speeches or write about matters of political import. Consequently, the archival efforts of the earliest scholars of American women's public address were driven not so much by a desire to make the texts of women's speeches available as they were to provide evidence that, in the past, women did in fact speak publicly on matters of political importance. To that end, not one of the early scholars who wrote a master's thesis, dissertation, article, or book on the political discourse of past women published a single text she had recovered from the archives. Instead, these emergent women's public address scholars, such as Armella Helen Bersch, engaged in archival research to prove that women had spoken and that the scholarly study of historical women speakers was indeed possible.[4] As their archival research efforts underscored, dispelling the myth that women historically had been silent on political issues was a crucial first step in early studies of women's public address. The second step involved demonstrating that what historical women said about political issues possessed sufficient intellectual, social, and aesthetic richness to warrant scholarly attention. Doris G. Yoakam mined archives for primary sources that documented the significance of women orators and their impact on US history.[5] Likewise, O'Connor analyzed texts that she had retrieved from archives to demonstrate women's mastery of prevailing rhetorical norms.[6]

That is not to say, however, that these scholars were driven entirely by the desire to refute their critics. On the contrary, as early as 1967, O'Connor articulated a humanistic if not feminist rationale for conducting archival research. "The vast bulk of recorded history will give us very little encouragement, but there have been splendidly endowed women in every nation who thought great thoughts," she declared. "We must develop scholars who will delve into original documents and winnow out the essential: the great, warm, humanitarian ideas so that girls tomorrow will not be lured aside by the trivia of personal idiosyncrasy." O'Connor concluded her call to an international audience of Catholic women by charging, "Let us now seek out the records and contributions by women already made in the realm of ideas, and, joining together all efforts, go forward confidently, unafraid, secure in our humanity, so that our children can better manage in an insecure world because of the *contributions of their mothers to the realm of ideas.*"[7] For O'Connor, then, archival research served the crucial function of harvesting primary sources to yield evidence of women's contributions to humanity. This evidence, she implied, would safeguard children, Christians, Catholics, and their compatriots against the Cold War ravages of insecurity, inhumanity, ungodliness, and communism.

Whether motivated by ideologies of humanism, feminism, or otherwise, the goal of demonstrating that women of the past spoke in public on political topics influenced the strategies early scholars of women's public address employed in their archival research. They cast their nets widely, over expansive periods of time and an impressive number of libraries to seine from the archival depths primary and secondary evidence that demonstrated the very existence of a history of women's oratory in early America. In her 1932 master's thesis, "Who's Who of Women Orators in America from 1634 to 1865," for example, Bersch dug deep into secondary sources to identify 143 women who spoke in public from the colonial period to the end of the Civil War. Bersch's main sources during the first stage of her study were eight biographical reference works, including *Woman's Who's Who of America* and the *Dictionary of American Biography.* After working through these sources to identify women speakers, she used not only the reference works but also biographies and the *History of Woman Suffrage* to compose biographical sketches of all 143 of the female speakers. These are presented in alphabetical order, from "Miss Jessie A. Ackerman" to "Miss Elizabeth Yates." In addition to providing information about each woman's background, education, and the causes that led her to the platform, many of the biographical entries include titles and dates of the speeches the women delivered.[8]

While Bersch's thesis provides evidence that women gave speeches throughout all of US history, it also draws upon the available evidence to engage in critical judgment. Bersch assigned each speaker a rating, not of her rhetorical performance per se, but rather of her reputation as an orator. That is, Bersch used secondary sources, most of which had drawn upon primary sources, to assess the oratorical reputation of each speaker. A rating of three stars meant that the woman, according to the sources consulted, had developed a reputation for possessing great oratorical ability. Two stars meant that she had a mediocre reputation as a speaker, while one star meant either that she was known to be a poor speaker or that a lack of information precluded judgments about her reputation as a speaker. Reflecting on the significance of her study, Bersch concluded, "These pioneer platform speakers made it possible for the modern feminist to appear on a lecture program unmolested, with dignity and social approval, and to speak on nearly any subject."[9]

In like manner, Bersch herself proved a pioneer in the effort to use available sources to construct a history of American women's oratory. As the presence of her signature on the lending page dated April 5, 1947, attests, O'Connor consulted Bersch's thesis a decade and a half later when she conducted dissertation research at the University of Wisconsin Library for what would become *Pioneer Women Orators: Rhetoric in the Ante-Bellum Reform Movement* (1954).

Like Bersch, Yoakam sought to compose a history of early American women's oratory, a goal that led her as well to focus on the context in which women spoke rather than on the recovery or the analysis of speech texts. Indeed, after searching the archives, she concluded that "a dearth" of speeches, letters, and memoirs of women orators greeted the "bibliographer" of women's speech. Women speakers were so opposed publicly, she explained, that they "burned personal materials, had little use or time for the popular custom of keeping journals, and very infrequently recorded the content of their speeches." Accordingly, Yoakam's ground-breaking chapter in *A History and Criticism of American Public Address* (1943), "Women's Introduction to the American Platform," chronicles the history of American women's public speaking, describing the challenges they faced, offering biographies of key speakers, describing speech settings, and documenting reactions to female orators. While the topics and general arguments made by women speakers are mentioned, Yoakam's goal was to construct a narrative history of women speakers rather than to recover and analyze specific texts. In the course of this effort, she studied more than 90 nineteenth-century periodicals, including, in her words, "practically every variety from penny dailies to religious monthlies." These included *The Liberator, The Free Enquirer*, and *Frederick Douglass's Paper*. These papers printed proceedings of meetings at which women had spoken, and *The Liberator* in particular recognized the efforts of women speakers. By contrast, Yoakam reported, "The more conservative newspapers often followed the policy that to ignore women's speaking was one highly effective weapon of opposition."[10] In addition, Yoakam turned to autobiographies, letters, lectures, and reminiscences of prominent male reformers, such as William Lloyd Garrison, Henry B. Stanton, and Wendell Phillips. These sources also provided her with important information about women speakers.

Inspired by reading Yoakam's unpublished dissertation about the struggles of women speakers, O'Connor set out to learn what it was that they had fought so hard to say.[11] In her formidable efforts to recover the words of pioneering women orators, O'Connor conducted research at 42 libraries throughout the United States. These included archives in all regions of the country, including the American Antiquarian Society in Worcester, Massachusetts, the Los Angeles Public Library, the Chicago Historical Society, and the New Orleans Public Library. As revealed by her bibliography, O'Connor's *Pioneer Women Orators* drew upon 20 manuscript collections containing speeches by female reformers or their male colleagues. The collections included the Letters of Abby Kelley at the Huntington Library, the Samuel Maye Papers and the Gerrit Smith Papers at Cornell University, and the Amelia Bloomer Collections at the Seneca Falls Historical Society. O'Connor also consulted 46 newspapers ranging from the feminist tract entitled *The Una* to the *Workingman's Advocate*, and from the mainstream New York *Sun* to Frederick Douglass's the *North Star*.[12]

In addition to printed or handwritten documents, a significant part of O'Connor's research involved conducting interviews and visiting sites where women delivered speeches. She traveled to Cambridge, Massachusetts, for example, to interview Alice Stone Blackwell, daughter of abolitionist feminist Lucy Stone. During their discussion, Blackwell, who was more than 90 years old, recalled "some of the exciting events of her own early youth" and spoke about friends of her mother, including the Grimkés, Ernestine Rose, and Paulina Wright Davis. O'Connor also traveled to New Harmony, Indiana, to see the building where Frances Wright spoke in 1828 and to visit the reformer's grave. While it is unclear how this research trip might have garnered information used in the book, it is certain that the excursion proved inspirational. Wrote O'Connor, "This writer felt a glow of pride in the old, red-brick structure that had been the Town Hall in 1828."[13]

Unlike Yoakam, who bemoaned the dearth of speeches recorded by women and left extant, O'Connor recovered 145 texts of speeches delivered by women. O'Connor explained that the majority of the speech texts she found were printed in newspapers, magazines, or publications of reform organizations, especially convention proceedings. Leading metropolitan newspapers, by contrast, maintained what she described as "a conspiracy of silence," refusing to print public speeches by women.[14] While the vast majority of the speeches she recovered were published, ten were in the form of handwritten manuscripts, a few others were privately printed, and two were drawn from *The History of Woman Suffrage*. O'Connor subjected these speeches to analysis and judgment employing criteria derived from rhetoric treatises of the time. Apparently preoccupied with the goal of demonstrating that pioneer women orators met neo-Aristotelian standards of eloquence, O'Connor chose not to print the texts she had found.

Key to the success of O'Connor's archival project, as she indicates in her acknowledgments, was the assistance of librarians and archivists at the institutions where she conducted her research. At the Seneca Falls Historical Society, she gained access to private files on nineteenth-century ladies' magazines, thanks to curator Eleanor Thompson, who also shared manuscripts and explored the countryside to locate materials. Not only that, but Thompson "generously joined in the thrilling exploration of literally barrels of manuscripts by and about Amelia Bloomer, a treasure that had arrived a short time before from Arizona." Among others mentioned in her acknowledgments, O'Connor singles out for special thanks "Mrs. Dorothy Porter" of the Library of Howard University, a fellow Columbia graduate who in 1932 became the first African American woman to earn a master's degree in library science from that school. Not only did Porter provide important assistance to O'Connor, but from 1930 to 1973 she played a key role in expanding the collections at the Moorland-Spingarn Research Center to make possible the study of black culture and history. In addition, Porter improved the collection's classification scheme, thereby rendering it more accessible to researchers like O'Connor.

Porter also compiled authoritative bibliographies and developed a wide variety of research tools to facilitate the study of primary sources relevant to the lived experiences of African Americans.[15]

As Porter retired in 1973, historian Barbara Welter lamented that only a "handful" of her colleagues had "actually done research in primary materials relating to women in this country's history, and written about it."[16] One of those historians was Gerda Lerner, who recalls that when she was conducting research for her dissertation on the Grimké sisters in the early 1960s, she had "the great good fortune" to work with the best collection of printed sources on women's history. This collection was to be found not at a leading academic institution, but in the private library of Miriam Y. Holden, a member of the National Woman's Party who had worked closely with both Alice Paul and Margaret Sanger. Holden had dedicated herself to collecting printed sources on women of all nations. These were housed in her brownstone on New York's East Side. "Miriam Holden opened her superb library to a few scholars working on Women's History topics," wrote Lerner in *The Majority Finds its Past: Placing Women in History* (1979). She recalled, "I spent many weeks and months there, able to browse freely in works about women and by women spanning 300 years. In this library the history of women was a reality; the possibilities of comparative and inter-disciplinary approaches were evident."[17]

Subsequently, Lerner embarked on a project to make available primary documents related to the lives of women. Though an historian rather than a scholar of public address, Lerner recovered texts of interest to feminist rhetoricians, a good number of which were speeches. Her archival efforts, moreover, are representative of endeavors to recover women's texts that occurred during the 1970s and 1980s in history, literary studies, and related fields. These efforts provided inspiration and examples for feminist public address scholars. In 1972, for example, Lerner published *Black Women in White America: A Documentary History*, which offered important texts for historians and rhetoricians alike.[18] Lamenting the "double invisibility" of black women whose "records lie buried, unread, infrequently noticed and even more seldom interpreted," Lerner collected and called attention to primary sources about African American women. Her explicit goal was to make available primary documents by and about black women. Lerner winnowed down the hundreds of documents she had collected to 162 texts, some of which she excerpted and others she published in full. "It is difficult to find black women in primary sources," Lerner wrote in 1979. "Only a very few libraries have arranged their resources in such a way as to make material on black women easily accessible to the researcher." She explained that card catalogues of most manuscript collections keep no listing for "Negro women," that the papers of outstanding black women remained unedited and scattered in various libraries, and that there was no collection of the records of black women's clubs comparable to those for the white women's club movement. "Many libraries have primary sources on black women hidden among family papers, general organizational records, and educational and religious organization files," Lerner reported. She concluded: "The women's history sources at the Schomburg Collection of the New York Public Library and those at Howard University and Fisk University, merely illustrate the wealth of material awaiting the work of archivists, librarians, and scholars."[19]

Influenced by Lerner's work as well as recovery efforts in cognate fields such as literary studies, rhetoricians focused their attention on recovering the texts of women's speeches from primary sources and making them accessible to scholars and students. Publication of anthologies of women's speech texts, such as Judith Anderson's *Outspoken Women* (1983), Patricia S. Kennedy and Gloria Hartmann O'Shields's *And We Shall Be Heard* (1984), and Karlyn Kohrs Campbell's *Man Cannot Speak for Her* (1989), marked a significant change in the purpose and strategies of archival research on women speakers.[20] Whereas previous scholars of women's public address had entered the archives to search for evidence of the existence of women speakers and to demonstrate their significance and rhetorical mastery, scholars in the 1980s emphasized the recovery of key texts of various women's movements. While reconstructing the rhetorical context was important to this recovery effort, archival research was aimed first and foremost at locating and authenticating texts in order to gain an understanding of women's rhetorical experiences and women's public address on its own terms. As Campbell wrote in the introduction to *Man Cannot Speak for Her*, "The works discussed and anthologized in these volumes are basic documents through which to understand the history of what became a large and complex social movement culminating in the enfranchisement of women." Her primary goal, she explained, was "simply to make these works available."[21]

Campbell's stated purpose and resultant research strategy illustrate changes afoot in the study of women's public address, as well as more broadly in the humanistic study of minority public discourse. With one volume making available the texts of 26 important speeches, and the other providing context and critical analyses, Campbell sought "to rescue the works of great women speakers from the oblivion to which most have been consigned." She also hoped that publication of the speech texts would "prompt re-examination of US rhetorical literature and the inclusion of some of these works in courses that survey the history of rhetoric and that explore artistic excellence in speaking." In order to do so, Campbell developed a set of principles that guided her archival efforts and consequent selection of texts. She decided to focus on "the central women's movement rather than examining its branches or movements that worked for related goals."[22] Thus in *Man Cannot Speak for Her*, all the speeches are from the early women's rights movement rather than from related campaigns, such as various labor movements, the settlement house movements, or the anti-suffrage movement. Likewise, Campbell kept her research focused on orators associated with national suffrage organizations rather than activists at the local level. Along the same lines as Lerner, Campbell made a critical choice to focus her archival efforts on recovering speeches by African American women, and she also devoted a chapter to analyzing those speeches in her volume of critical essays.[23]

Most importantly, in terms of both the content of the collection and understanding the role of archival research in her work, Campbell acknowledged the power as well as the limitations of working with primary sources. "The accidents of history have compelled me to direct my attention primarily to those who left an extensive rhetorical record," Campbell noted. While she could say a great deal about Elizabeth Cady Stanton or Mary Church Terrell because they prepared, published, and retained texts of their speeches, little could be written about the rhetoric of Lucy Stone, who left behind few texts. Thus, the emphasis in the book, as Campbell conceded, was "not wholly a function of the impact individuals had on the early movement but also the extant rhetorical evidence."[24] Campbell searched for representative speeches of nationally known women's rights advocates, and she found substantial collections in the Carrie Chapman Catt Papers at the New York Public Library, Wilmer A. Linkugel's volume of speeches by Anna Howard Shaw,[25] and various manuscript collections at the Schlesinger Library, the Kansas State Historical Society, and the Library of Congress. She stated clearly that her goal was not, however, to recover and anthologize the texts of lesser-known women speakers.

While Campbell and other rhetoric scholars have searched existing archives to recover the words of American women activists, historians extended the enterprise to international and transnational contexts.[26] Notable among the collections published in the late 1970s and early 1980s is the two-volume collection edited by Susan Groag Bell and Karen M. Offen, *Women, the Family, and Freedom: The Debate in Documents*. These volumes explore the ongoing debate in Western nations "over women, their relationship to the family, and their claims to freedom," with the first volume covering the years 1750 to 1880 and the second volume chronicling 1880 to 1950. When doing their research, Bell and Offen sought texts generated not only by major female figures, but also by ordinary women. Moreover, the editors wished to represent various positions in debates over women and their rights, which led to the inclusion of statements by men as well. In order to include the voices of women and men from France, Britain, Germany, Russia, Norway, Finland, the United States, Austria, Switzerland, and Sweden, the authors drew upon archives from throughout Europe, including the Bibliothèque Marguerite Durand (Paris), the Millicent Fawcett Library (London), the British Library (London), and others.[27] Their task required the ability to do archival work in multiple languages and to translate documents in order to make them accessible in English.

No comparable anthology of international or transnational public address by and about women has been published, though a few scholars in the field have done critical work that entailed archival research beyond the borders of the United States.[28] It is crucial that scholars concerned with gender, feminism, and women's public address broaden the scope of recovery and criticism to these wider contexts. This is necessary in order to remain relevant in conversations with cognate disciplines that have responded to modern globalization by interrogating the notion of the nation-state. As well, greater attention to the transnational in the analysis of public address would productively complicate prevailing critical methods by emphasizing comparison across national boundaries and the permeability of those boundaries. By destabilizing the notion of the nation and understanding it as a rhetorical construct, a transnational approach would also lead public address scholars to interrogate the complex interactions of gender, race, and ethnicity in the interpellation of identity.[29] Such studies, of course, would require public address scholars to conduct research in archives that house discourses that cut across national boundaries and, perhaps, multiple languages.

Contemporary Issues in Archival Research on Women and Gender

Since the beginning of recovery efforts in the 1930s, tremendous advances have been made in the archiving and availability of women's texts. Rhetorical and historical researchers have developed astute methods for accessing materials buried in old collections and unaccounted for in finding aids. Honor R. Sachs describes these methods, writing that doing women's history involves "reading the subtexts of card catalogs and online database entries for evidence of what they conceal." This reading strategy, she explains, involves probing finding aids for what they elide more than for what they reveal. It also means searching for collections and documents that have been dismissed as irrelevant or unimportant. Most importantly, Sachs advises, doing archival research on women requires a reliance on librarians and archivists "to provide roadmaps to rich and complex collections."[30] Librarians, most of whom are women, have been a major force in making documentary evidence of women's words and lives more available to researchers. Heavily influenced by the feminist movement, librarians and archivists have led the charge to save important documents, prepare better finding aids, and make those collections more accessible. Taking seriously the contributions of women, as Sachs has explained, these library workers have "created a new landscape" that values rather than obscures documents by and about women.[31] Notable among the early efforts to improve accessibility to women's documents was the publication in 1979 of the two-volume *Women's History Sources: A Guide to Archives and Manuscript Collections in the United States.* This survey of more than 11,000 repositories and 18,000 manuscript collections, edited by Andrea Hinding, "transformed the nature of research for the next generation of women's historians."[32]

The improvement in collection practices and the development of new archives of women's documents over the last two decades have significantly increased the availability of texts for rhetorical analysis and pedagogy. The Gerritsen collection, for example, which is available on microfilm and in digital form, contains more than 4,700 books and periodicals pertaining to the movements for and against women's rights in Europe and the United States from 1543 to 1945. The Sophia Smith Collection consists of more than 10,000 linear feet of manuscript, print, and audiovisual artifacts related to the lives of American women from the colonial era to the present. Likewise, the Arthur and Elizabeth Schlesinger Library on the History of Women in America at Harvard University holds more than 2,500 unique manuscript collections and 80,000 books and periodicals documenting women's history. Not only does the Schlesinger Library house manuscripts and other print documents, but it also holds an extensive audiovisual collection of both still and moving images, including more than 90,000 photographs. This collection is of particular interest as the study of rhetoric moves from its traditional focus exclusively on the spoken and written word to visual forms of communication. Other leading archives important to research on women and gender include the American Antiquarian Society, the Boston Public Library, the New York Public Library, the Rare Books and Special Collections at the Sallie Bingham Center for Women's History and Culture at Duke University, and the Wisconsin Historical Society.[33]

In addition to collections housed in brick and mortar, the availability of women's rhetorical artifacts has increased tremendously with the growth of digital publishing. The Internet affords scholars who recover authoritative and even multiple versions of women's speeches from archives to partner with digitization projects to mount the speeches, along with annotations and contextual comments. Many academic libraries have such projects, which represent cooperative efforts among scholars, librarians, and archivists. Noteworthy among these digital collections is the Archive of Women's Political Communication, run by the Carrie Chapman Catt Center for Women and Politics at Iowa State University. The Women's Political Communication project involves two archives, both of which have a digital component. The first is an online speech archive, which has posted hundreds of speech texts delivered over the past two centuries by women from all over the world. The second is a videotape collection of television commercials for women who have run for political office in the United States as well as in other countries. These, too, will eventually be available online.[34]

Internet speech archives such as this have made it possible for schoolchildren, college students, scholars, and the wider public to easily access the spoken words of political women. Such accessibility has led to wider study and appreciation of women's speeches at multiple levels, as evidenced by comments posted on the websites themselves.[35] Yet, in their haste to make women's speeches available, some of these sites post texts without taking the time to authenticate them or even note their source, much less discuss them. Nor do these websites discuss important issues related to why one version of a text is preferred over another, as in the case of Sojourner Truth's "Ain't I a Woman," a speech for which multiple differing transcripts are extant.[36] Neither do they make clear why some of the speeches have been radically abridged, leading readers to think, for example, that Susan B. Anthony defended her act of voting illegally with a rather short speech of only 536 words (History Place Great Speeches Collection)[37] or 2,424 words (Gifts of Speech).[38] Given that Anthony's speech was actually 10,123 words long,[39] the History Place website presents only about 5 percent of the speech, with no source citation and no acknowledgment that most of the speech has been cut. The Gifts of Speech website also cites no source, but a careful reading of the note below the text reveals that the speech was abridged by the editors of the volume from which it was taken.[40]

A positive effect of the Internet for scholars of gender and women's public address is that it provides access to finding aids for collections located throughout the world. For her dissertation on Planned Parenthood from 1942 to 1973, for example, Sarah Jedd scoured the organization's papers in the Sophia Smith Collection at Smith College. While neither the Planned Parenthood collection nor any of the Sophia Smith holdings are available online, Jedd was able to access comprehensive finding aids for processed collections on the Internet. These detailed finding aids allowed Jedd to maximize her time onsite at the Smith archives by doing important pre-visit research work and locating specific files of interest. She also made use of email and telephone contacts with archivists to focus her search. While Smith's unprocessed collections may be inspected only in person and have less detailed finding aids, Jedd also was able to better plan research trips with the help of these aids. Likewise, she employed an online finding aid to the Schlesinger Library to locate relevant documents and to request that they be copied and sent to her.[41]

While there have been vast improvements in the accessibility and availability of primary texts, the recovery project in women's public address is far from complete. Archival research remains crucial to scholarship on women political activists, as well as research on gender in general. As literary scholar Jennifer Bernhardt Steadman and her colleagues have written, "It is imperative that we work against the increasing tendency of many to theorize or teach American women writers and American women's lives as if all data has now been recovered and the existing 'canon' of texts, interpretations, and women's traditions and innovations is complete enough."[42] Relying on anthologies and failing to engage in additional archival work leaves us with a closed set of texts that circumscribe the critical conversation. Another undesirable effect of relying too much upon existing anthologies is that errors in textual authentication and historical context may be perpetuated. After archival research that uncovered multiple, differing versions of Sojourner Truth's "Ain't I a Woman" speech, for example, Nell Irvin Painter called into question not only what Truth had said, but also how abolitionists and others had crafted her legacy and constructed her public memory.[43] Similarly, Kathryn Palmer and Stephen E. Lucas returned to the archives to investigate the provenance of Emma Goldman's "Address to the Jury." Their painstaking archival research enabled them to demonstrate that Goldman produced multiple versions of the speech, each of which differed in important ways. Ultimately, by recovering and authenticating multiple versions of the speech, Palmer and Lucas illuminated rhetorical complexities of the speech that had been overlooked previously and shed new light on Goldman's rhetorical artistry.[44]

Finally, archival practices have become dramatically more inclusive, yet gender biases persist in some archives. Proquest's American Periodical Series Online, for example, offers Internet access to more than a thousand newspapers from 1741 to 1940. One can read the long-running abolitionist journal, *The Liberator*, as well as *The Pioneer* (a literary and critical magazine) and *The Plough Boy*, both of which were published for less than a year. However, *The Lily*, a temperance and women's emancipation newspaper edited by Amelia Bloomer that played a significant role in the women's movement from 1849 to 1856, was left out of the online collection. Likewise, the words of Reverend Martin Luther King, Jr., Stokely Carmichael, and other male speakers in the civil rights struggle are widely available, but few speeches by women civil rights activists are readily accessible. Maegan Parker Brooks has recently recovered dozens of Fannie Lou Hamer's speeches by traveling to more than a dozen archives and transcribing audio recordings made available by movement veterans.[45] The absence of key sources such as *The Lily* from readily accessible digital collections, as well as the small number of available texts representing racial minorities and workers, underscores the necessity for continued research in physical as well as digital archives.

Gender as a Theoretical and Methodological Issue: The Case of Antislavery Petitions

While recovery of rhetorical texts by and about women remains important, recent theoretical and methodological developments that shift the focus from women as a subject of research to gender as a category of analysis have necessitated changes in archival collection and research practices. Elsewhere in this volume, Bonnie J. Dow urges feminist rhetoricians to expand their critical practice to encompass the construction and performance not only of femininity, but also of masculinity. She argues that by exploring gender only when the rhetor is female, critics further naturalize the universal subject as masculine.[46] Such conflation reinforces the notion that the "true" political subject, the "real" citizen is and always has been male. Gender criticism is a useful method for feminist public address scholars, we agree, because it untethers masculinity and the universal subject by revealing how gender has been employed to naturalize this relation. Indeed, attending to masculinity as well as femininity enables critics to expose how gender is employed to naturalize inequality and maintain relationships of power.

Adoption of a gender approach throughout the humanities and social sciences has changed the nature of critical practice as well as practices of the researcher and archivist. Sachs observes that the emergence of gender as a theoretical and critical framework has made the work of researchers and archivists at once more difficult and more liberating. While it can be difficult to unearth women from collections of primary sources, it is not impossible. But the need to archive relationships of power resulting from recent scholarly attention to gender has created significant challenges for librarians and archivists. As Sachs explains, these challenges proved liberating for archivists and librarians because the new methods of analysis called for expansion of their collections. She cites as an example the Schlesinger Library, long considered one of the premiere repositories in the United States of documents relating to women, which now collects artifacts related to "masculinity," "technology," and "parenting." Simultaneously, the Schlesinger has continued to collect materials pertaining to categories more central to the original recovery project, such as women's social activism, reproductive rights, and women's work.[47]

In the same way that the Schlesinger has changed its collection practices to both preserve and expand, so too may recovery efforts and gender criticism flourish side by side and in a mutually reinforcing manner in public address scholarship. Kathleen J. Ryan comes to the same conclusion in her historiography of discussions that occurred in the early 1990s about the future of feminist rhetorical scholarship. She writes, "Recovery in anthologies and edited collections provides openings for gender critique by bringing new texts, locations, and approaches to rhetoric to light because of the ways gender issues inform, enable, and constrain women's rhetorical contributions."[48] The following case study, a discussion of archival research practices employed to conduct an analysis of gender performances in congressional debates over women's antislavery petitions, illustrates the compatibility of archival practices for recovering women's public address and locating primary sources needed to analyze gender performance.

In February 1835, a correspondent for the *New York Commercial Advertiser* reported that the presentation of abolitionist petitions in the House of Representatives "struck the sensitive nerve which pervades and vibrates throughout the entire South." The reporter described this "sensitive nerve" as "the absorbing, controlling and vital principle which animates the whole South – electrifies the South – *unites* the South – in their morals, habits, feelings, religion, politics – nullification – PRESIDENTIAL CANDIDATES." As the petitions, many of them sent by women, poked the Southern nerve, "it thrilled and twinged, like the agonies of a decayed tooth." According to the reporter, Northern representatives looked surprised and alarmed as "the South arose as one man."[49] Among the spokesmen for slaveholders was Representative James W. Bouldin of Virginia, who complained that Northerners "took a swaggering stand over the South, and proposed a kind of guardianship over [our] morals."[50] Bouldin expressed the pervasive sentiment that the petitions had provoked more than a challenge between Northern petitioners and slaveholders or between their representatives in Congress. And he perceived the attack as animated by more than words – Northerners, he said, had taken "a swaggering," in-your-face, physical stance over the South. Thus, this debate surpassed disagreement over interpretations of the First Amendment right of petition. For Bouldin and the majority of his slaveholding colleagues in the House of Representatives, the antislavery petitions inflamed the jealous pride of Southern members and entangled them in debates over slavery.

Provoking discussion of slavery on the floor of Congress was a major accomplishment. During the first 50 years of the young republic, American statesmen of all sorts had studiously avoided public disputation on this delicate subject. Yet, as Susan Zaeske maintains in an article in *Rhetoric & Public Affairs*, congressional debates over the reception of antislavery petitions were monumental in another respect: They provoked the first sustained discussion of women's political rights and their status as citizens in the history of the United States Congress.[51] She argues further that the intense disputation over the antislavery petitions was fired in no small part by competing notions of gender. Analyzing antislavery petitions sent by females and the speeches by congressmen from both sections, she finds that each questioned the womanhood and manhood of their political opponents. As a result, the debates overflowed the argumentative category of constitutionality and escalated in ferocity as rhetors perceived their very way of life under attack. After examining how women and men on various sides of the debates argued, she concludes that the House debate over women's antislavery petitions from 1835 to 1840, waged as it was through a rhetoric of gender, amounted to a battle about the very question of who rightfully could be considered a citizen of the United States.

This study required archival work both to recover the long-ignored role that women played in the House debates over slavery and to understand performances of masculinity on the floor and in the petitions. That is to say that Zaeske's essay both extends the project of writing women's rhetorical history and employs gender analysis to advance the critical practice of disentangling hierarchies of power. These larger goals required a combination of archival practices and choices, some of which are commonly associated with recovery efforts and others of which are more common to recent studies of gender, such as locating texts of men's discourse and searching for primary sources that offer clues about the construction of masculinity as well as femininity.

Previous studies of the debates over slavery had focused on the arguments made by members of Congress, especially those related to the First Amendment and, of course, slavery itself. As Zaeske pictured the debate in her mind, she recognized that even though women were not present on the floor of the House to debate face to face with their representatives, their petitions were in fact there on the desks and in the aisles, leaving the moral specter of abolitionist women lingering over the chamber. Thus, the mounds of their petitions made women virtually present during the debate, and the rhetoric of their petitions sparked the anger of Southern members consequently shaping the representatives' oratorical responses. In order to know what women said in their antislavery petitions, she engaged in extensive archival research. After deciding to narrow her focus to the federal rather than state level, she consulted with a government documents librarian. From him she learned that the petitions were located in the National Archives and were administered by the Center for Legislative Archives, which maintains the unpublished records of Congress (Record Groups 233 and 46). At this point she also obtained a guide to research in the National Archives, which proved to be extremely helpful for purposes of understanding the organization of government records and for proper citation.

Next, Zaeske wrote to the Center for Legislative Archives and described her research project and the documents she hoped to obtain, namely, antislavery petitions sent by women. She received a response that informed her that "Our finding aids do not index petitions by the name of the petitioner. As such you will need to review all of the petitions dealing with slavery in order to find those submitted by women." The archivist then explained that for early Congresses (1790 to 1836), the finding aids did not index slavery petitions separately, though they were indexed from 1836 to 1841. Within that series alone, she informed Zaeske, there were approximately 30 trays of House records and ten trays of Senate records. The archivist gave her information that was crucial to locating petitions, which was that the gag rule was in effect from 1836 to 1844 and therefore the antislavery petitions were filed separately in a series entitled "Petitions and Memorials, Resolutions of State Legislatures, and Related Documents Which Were Tabled." The archivist also gave Zaeske another important piece of information: The Outreach Branch of the Center for Legislative Archives was currently surveying House and Senate records to find women's petitions to be used in an educational publication.[52]

Upon her arrival at the National Archives, Zaeske met with an archivist to discuss her project and research needs. After gaining more guidance from him, she set to work in the reading room, sifting through thousands of petitions. This task required multiple research trips to Washington, DC, over the course of several years. The number of records that needed to be surveyed, the lapse of many months between research visits, and the fact that the same petition was often sent by signers in the same or different states, meant that it was crucial to develop a system to organize the documents she had found. It was impossible to photocopy all the petitions signed by women – some were too fragile and there were simply too many. Thus, Zaeske developed a system whereby she kept track of the petitions submitted to Congress month by month. She gave each form of petition a title and charted when and from where it was sent, along with how many were received (or at least how many were extant). Zaeske made photocopies of petitions that were both representative and unique. On each photocopy as well as on the chart, she recorded the full government document citation so that she could return to the document if necessary or cite it in her study.

While scholars of women's public address have traditionally engaged archival work to recover the words of women, few have done the archival work necessary for gender analysis – work that uncovers clues about constructions of masculinities as well as femininities. Reconstructing congressional debate over slavery, abolitionist petitions, and the gag rule involved going through transcripts of the proceedings of both the House and Senate. These nineteenth-century (and earlier) records are found in three separate publications: *Annals of Congress*, which covers 1789–1824; *Gales and Seaton's Register of Debates in Congress*, which covers 1824–1837; and the *Congressional Globe*, which covers 1833–1873. In most cases, the debates could be found by using the index to the record of debates and their appendices. Zaeske copied these debates in full and supplemented the debate transcripts by locating published versions of the speeches delivered by representatives such as Adams. In addition, she followed reportage of the debates in Congress in selected Northern, Southern, and abolitionist newspapers. Finally, in order to understand constructions of Southern and Northern masculinity, she sought nineteenth-century guides to gentlemanly conduct and dueling, which she found in archives and also in a South Carolina bookstore.

After acquiring the women's petitions and the congressmen's speeches, Zaeske reconstructed the debates along a variety of organizing principles. These included chronology, section, argument, style, and so forth. Looking at the discourse from various angles allowed her to see recurring imputations of manhood and womanhood and how these insults were refuted. By documenting the content of the women's petitions and the congressmen's statements, and by searching for cultural clues to why they said what they said, Zaeske was able to account for how the power dynamics played out over a field of gender in the debates over abolitionist petitions.

Conclusion

Archival research has long been the bedrock of scholarship on women's public address. Archival research that has recovered the texts of female speakers has quieted those who once contended that women had nothing to say. Yet while the field of women's public address is well established and women's discourse is more accessible, archival research must continue. Research into primary sources is crucial because while anthologies of women's rhetorical discourse exist, it remains difficult to locate for purposes of teaching or research the words of many women from any number of movements. Continued archival research, moreover, is necessary for projects that broaden the scope of published collections to include transnational voices as well as different forms of discourse such as visual images and songs. Public address scholars who study the rhetoric of women political activists, moreover, must continue the work of recovery and reinvigorate scholarship in this area by embracing theoretically informed practices of gender analysis. Public address scholarship employing gender analysis would extend rather than abandon the task of recovering women's voices and understanding how rhetoric affected the lived experience of women. Like the initial recovery project, it would require archival work to locate primary sources that provide insights to the construction of masculinities and other types of identities. Doing so will tremendously expand the critical imaginary of the subdiscipline known as women's public address by affording it more powerful analytical tools that yield keen, significant insights.

Acknowledgments

The authors wish to thank Phyllis Holman Weisbard, Women's Studies Librarian at the University of Wisconsin-Madison, for her expertise and guidance.

Notes

1 Mary R. Beard, *Woman as a Force in History: A Study in Traditions and Realities* (New York: Macmillan, 1946), 333. Beard began what she titled "An Illustrative Bibliography" with this quotation from the renowned French historian Numa Denis Fustel de Coulanges. Beard's influence on the study of women is articulated by Gerda Lerner, who recalls that during her interview for admission to the graduate program at Columbia University, she was asked why she wanted to study history. "Without hesitating I replied that I wanted to put women into history. No, I corrected myself, not put them into history, because they were already in it, what I want to do is make the study of women's history legitimate. I want, I said plainly, to complete the work begun by Mary Beard." Gerda Lerner, *The Majority Finds its Past: Placing Women in History* (New York: Oxford University Press, 1979), xix.

2 Maureen Haggerty, "The Wide, Wide World of CGA Member Lillian O'Connor," *CGA World*, March/April 1984, Lillian O'Connor Papers, Schlesinger Library, Radcliffe Institute, Harvard University.

3 For an analytical review of scholarship on feminist public address, see Bonnie J. Dow's chapter in this volume entitled "Feminism and Public Address Research: Television News and the Constitution of Women's Liberation."

4 Armella Helen Bersch, "Who's Who of Women Orators in America from 1634 to 1865" (MA thesis, University of Wisconsin-Madison, 1932).

5 Doris G. Yoakam, "Women's Introduction to the American Platform," in *A History and Criticism of American Public Address*, vol. 1, ed. William Norwood Brigance (New York: Russell and Russell, 1960), 153–192. This essay appeared in the first edition of *A History and Criticism of American Public Address* published in 1943 by McGraw-Hill, which was reissued in 1960.

6 Lillian O'Connor, *Pioneer Women Orators: Rhetoric in the Ante-Bellum Reform Movement* (New York: Columbia University Press, 1954).

7 Dr. Lillian O'Connor, "For A Better World Tomorrow," delivered before the 16th Congress of World Union Catholic Women's Organization, Rome, October 4, 1967, *Vital Speeches of the Day* (January 15, 1968), 217. Lillian O'Connor Papers, Schlesinger Library, Radcliffe Institute, Harvard University (emphasis in original).

8 Bersch, "Who's Who of Women Orators."

9 Bersch, "Who's Who of Women Orators," iv, ii.

10 Yoakam, "Women's Introduction to the American Platform." The quotations about sources are taken from Yoakam's "Critical Essay on Selected Authorities" at the end of her essay. See *A History and Criticism of American Public Address*, ed. Brigance, 1: 189.

11 In her preface, O'Connor explains that *Pioneer Women Orators* "stemmed from the enjoyment and interest engendered in me" when she read Doris G. Yoakam's unpublished doctoral dissertation "An Historical Survey of the Public Speaking Activities of American Women, 1828–1860," completed at the University of Southern California in 1935 (O'Connor, *Pioneer Women Orators*, vii–viii).

12 In her preface, O'Connor mentions that she searched for materials at "more than forty leading libraries of the nation." In her acknowledgments she lists 42 libraries. See O'Connor, *Pioneer Woman Orators*, viii, xiii.

13 O'Connor, *Pioneer Women Orators*, xi, xii.

14 O'Connor, *Pioneer Women Orators*, 125–130.

15 See O'Connor, *Pioneer Women Orators*, xii–xiii; Thomas C. Battle, "History of the Moorland-Spingarn Research Center," *Library Quarterly* 58 (1988), 143–163; and Eric Pace, "Dorothy Porter Wesley, 91, Black-History Activist," *New York Times*, December 20, 1995.

16 Barbara Welter, *The Woman Question in American History* (Hinsdale, IL: Dryden Press, 1973), 172.

17 Lerner, *Majority Finds its Past*, xxiv.

18 Gerda Lerner, *Black Women in White America: A Documentary History* (New York: Vintage Books, 1973), xvii–xviii. The first printing was in 1972.

19 Lerner, *Majority Finds its Past*, 64.

20 See Judith Anderson, ed., *Outspoken Women: Speeches by American Women Reformers, 1635–1935* (Dubuque, IA: Kendall/Hunt, 1984); Patricia Scileppi Kennedy and Gloria Hartmann O'Shields, eds., *And We Shall Be Heard: Women Speakers in America* (Dubuque, IA: Kendall/Hunt, 1983); Karlyn Kohrs Campbell, *Man Cannot Speak for Her: A Critical Study of Early Feminist Rhetoric*, vol. 1, and *Man Cannot Speak for Her: Key Texts of the Early Feminists*, vol. 2 (Westport, CT: Praeger, 1989).

21 Campbell, *Man Cannot Speak for Her*, 1: 9.

22 Campbell, *Man Cannot Speak for Her*, 1: 8–9.

23 Campbell, *Man Cannot Speak for Her*, 1: 8–9.

24 Campbell, *Man Cannot Speak for Her*, 1: 8–9.

25 Wilmer Albert Linkugel, "The Speeches of Anna Howard Shaw, Collected and Edited with Introduction and Notes," 4 vols. (PhD Diss., University of Wisconsin, 1961).

26 Key anthologies of European women's discourse published by historians include Patricia Hollis, ed., *Women in Public, 1850–1900: Documents of the Victorian Women's Movement* (London and Boston: G. Allen and Unwin, 1979); Erna Olafson Hellerstein, Leslie Parker Hume, and Karen M. Offen, eds., *Victorian Women: A Documentary Account of Women's Lives in Nineteenth-Century England, France, and the United States* (Stanford, CA: Stanford University Press, 1981); Susan Groag Bell and Karen M. Offen, eds., *Women, the Family, and Freedom: The Debate in Documents: Volume One, 1750–1880* (Stanford, CA: Stanford University Press, 1983); and Susan Groag Bell and Karen M. Offen, eds., *Women, the Family, and Freedom: The Debate in Documents: Volume Two, 1880–1950* (Stanford, CA: Stanford University Press, 1983).

27 In addition, notable international libraries for research on women and gender with holdings relevant to scholars of public address include Biblioteca Popular Francesca Bonnemaison (Barcelona); International Information Center and Archives for the Women's Movement (IIAV) (Amsterdam); Women's Library and Information Center, Istanbul, Turkey. Additional online resources are Genesis (women's history sources in the British Isles) www.londonmet.ac.uk/genesis/ and Mapping the World (an inventory of women's information services throughout the world) at www.iiav.nl/mapping-the-world/.

28 Good examples of studies about women's discourse that are international in focus are Cheryl R. Jorgensen-Earp's books, *The Transfiguring Sword: The Just War of the Women's Social and Political Union* (Tuscaloosa: University of Alabama Press, 1997) and parts of *In the Wake of Violence: Image and Social Reform* (East Lansing: Michigan State University Press, 2008).

29 This formulation of a transnational gender criticism of public discourse draws upon Mary Louise Roberts, "The Transnationalization of Gender History," *History and Theory* 44 (2005): 456–468.

30 Honor R. Sachs, "Reconstructing a Life: The Archival Challenges of Women's History," *Library Trends* 56 (2008): 651.

31 Sachs, "Reconstructing a Life," 651. The 83 percent of librarians are women figure comes from an interview with Phyllis Holman Weisbard, Women's Studies Librarian at the University of Wisconsin-Madison, January 2007. Weisbard indicated that while older collections may well be problematic, she detects no clear bias in current collecting of primary sources by and about women.

32 Sachs, "Reconstructing a Life," 662.

33 Other archival resources of interest to scholars studying women's public address and the rhetorical function of gender are American Women: A Gateway to Library of Congress Resources for the Study of Women's History and Culture in the United States, which can be found at memory.loc.gov/ammem/awhhtml/; American Women's History: A Research Guide, frank.mtsu.edu/~kmiddlet/history/women.html; and the website of the University of Wisconsin-Madison Women's Studies Librarian's Office, womenst.library.wisc.edu/.

34 Archive of Women's Political Communication, www.womenspeecharchive.org/.

35 See, for example, the guestbook on the Gifts of Speech website at books.dreambook.com/lizkent/main.html, Sweet Briar College, "Gifts of Speech," September 2009, www.giftsofspeech.org/ (accessed September 24, 2009).

36 For discussion of the competing extant versions of Truth's speech, see Nell Irvin Painter, "Representing Truth: Sojourner Truth's Knowing and Becoming Known," *Journal of American History* 81 (1994): 461–492; and Nell Irvin Painter, *Sojourner Truth, A Life, A Symbol* (New York: W. W. Norton, 1996).

37 Phillip Gavin, "The History Place," www.historyplace.com/speeches/anthony.htm (accessed September 24, 2009).

38 Sweet Briar College, "Gifts of Speech," September 2009, gos.sbc.edu/a/anthony.html (accessed September 24, 2009).

39 We determined the word count for the complete speech by first comparing the version in Campbell's *Man Cannot Speak for Her* with the version posted on a famous trials website hosted by the University of Missouri-Kansas City Law School. The famous trials site indicates that the text of the Anthony speech was drawn from the same primary source that was used by Campbell. With the exception of differences in paragraphing, the texts were the same and apparently complete.

40 See Gifts of Speech, gos.sbc.edu/.

41 Sarah Meinen Jedd, "Reproducing Families: The Rhetoric of the Planned Parenthood Federation of America, 1943–1973" (PhD Diss., University of Wisconsin-Madison, 2009).

42 Jennifer Bernhardt Steadman, Elizabeth Engelhardt, Frances Smith Foster, and Laura Micham, "Archival Survival Guide: Practical and Theoretical Approaches for the Next Century of Women's Studies Research," *Legacy* 19 (2002): 230.

43 Painter, "Representing Truth," and Painter, *Sojourner Truth, A Life, A Symbol.*

44 Kathryn Palmer and Stephen E. Lucas, "On Trial: Conflicting Versions of Emma Goldman's Address to the Jury," *Rhetoric & Public Affairs* 11 (2008): 47–88.

45 Maegan Parker Brooks, "From the Front Porch to the Platform: Fannie Lou Hamer and the Rhetoric of the Black Freedom Movement" (PhD Diss., University of Wisconsin-Madison, 2009); Maegan Parker Brooks and Davis W. Houck, *In Her Words: The Speeches of Fannie Lou Hamer, 1963–1976* (Jackson: University Press of Mississippi, 2010). Another recent archival recovery effort has culminated in Davis W. Houck and David E. Dixon, eds., *Women and the Civil Rights Movement, 1954–1965* (Jackson: University Press of Mississippi, 2009). See also Houck's chapter in this volume entitled "Textual Recovery, Textual Discovery: Returning to Our Past, Imagining Our Future."

46 As a consequence of failing to interrogate the construction of masculinity, Dow warns, feminist public address scholars "leave ourselves with an incompletely realized critique of the politics of gender in public address" (Dow, "Feminism and Public Address Research").

47 Sachs, "Reconstructing a Life," 663.

48 Kathleen J. Ryan, "Recasting Recovery and Gender Critique as Inventive Arts: Constructing Edited Collections in Feminist Rhetorical Studies," *Rhetoric Review* 25 (2006): 36–37.

49 *New York Commercial Advertiser*, correspondence from Washington, DC, dated February 16, 1835, quoted in *The Liberator*, March 7, 1835.

50 *Register of Debates*, 24th Cong., 1st Sess. (December 21, 1835), 2002–2004.

51 Susan Zaeske, "'The South Arose as One Man': Gender and Sectionalism in Antislavery Petition Debates, 1835–1845," *Rhetoric & Public Affairs* 12 (2009): 1–28.

52 Martha Wagner Murphy, Center for Legislative Archives, National Archives, to Susan Zaeske, April 7, 1994.

Part III

Text and Context in Rhetoric and Public Address

8

The Racial Contexts of Public Address
Interpreting Violence During the Reconstruction Era

Kirt H. Wilson

This chapter examines a question that is essential to my work and much of public address scholarship: How does one establish the meaning and significance of research, especially research of a past that seems distant to the political or cultural concerns of the present? Public address, as a subfield of rhetoric within communication studies, has advanced various justifications for its significance. I contend, along with Stephen Browne, that twenty-first-century scholars view public address as moments of articulation within rich temporal, spatial, and conceptual contexts. Further, "context is invoked" within criticism "as a necessary category for the work of interpretation and suggests how it can function to advance, enrich, and ultimately redeem the practice of rhetorical criticism."[1] It is the conceptual category of *context* that animates both critical practices in public address scholarship and the value of any given study.

From this initial hypothesis extends a series of additional claims pursued within this chapter. First, the role of context in contemporary research has precedents in the discipline's literature; nevertheless, its importance today departs from historic critical norms that prioritized knowledge about speakers, speech texts, strategies of rhetoric, ideologies, and methods of criticism. Second, the turn toward contexts began in earnest in the late 1960s and early 1970s as rhetoric scholars grappled with the history of racism in American public life. Third, the use of context as *a* dominant category of critical practice makes room for alternative modes of discursive action and the analysis of rhetoric by people who lack institutional power or access to the traditional spaces of public oratory. Fourth, the act of building or constituting a context for one's analysis is as important to criticism as the analysis of the object itself, because in an era of theoretical and methodological pluralism, public address scholars judge the significance of a study on the basis of how it contributes to the existing knowledge of culturally significant contexts. The case study herein examines the rhetoric of three distinct interpretive communities to demonstrate how the hermeneutic alignment of texts and contexts shaped social understandings of racial violence in the aftermath of the Civil War. By illuminating how

Americans made sense of Reconstruction-era violence, I conclude, the study of public address can help us comprehend the racial context of American life.

Speaker Biography, Social Conflict, and Racial Contexts

Because several exhaustive histories of rhetorical criticism and public address exist, including a lengthy chapter by Martin J. Medhurst in this volume,[2] it is unnecessary to offer a comprehensive narrative here. Nevertheless, an abbreviated history is useful to appreciate how context as a conceptual category influenced public address scholarship and the study of African American rhetoric. My purpose in this section is neither to provide an exhaustive explanation of how public address scholars have theorized context nor to explain the history of minority studies in public address. Rather, I will discuss first how the concern for speakers and speeches as statecraft prior to the 1960s is correlated to an absence of minority voices within the extant research. Second, I will explain how the civil rights movement pushed context to the forefront of scholarly attention. Third, I will detail my own struggle to negotiate the seemingly conflicting demands of textual and critical methods.

Speakers and speeches

In 1947, Ernest Wrage wrote an essay that encouraged rhetorical scholars to use their analyses of public addresses to understand the world of ideas and the intellectual histories that ideas establish.[3] According to Wrage, "the reach of an idea, its viability within a setting of time and place, and its modifications are expressed in a vast quantity of documentary sources."[4] The documentary sources were so broad that no single academic discipline could account for it all; therefore, he encouraged public address scholars to partner with historians to uncover the power and reach of human ideas as they were expressed in historical contexts. "When seen against a contextual backdrop," he affirmed, "speeches become at once a means of illustrating and testing, of verifying or revising generalizations offered by other workers in social and intellectual history."[5] Wrage offered a bold new vision for the study of public address, but his recommendation also was a critique of what David Zarefsky calls "rhetorical biography."[6] Wrage argued that neither a speaker's personal history nor his rhetorical career and style of speech exhausted the rich elements of context as he theorized it. He claimed that history, interpreted as a genealogy of ideas and social practices, was the most important contextual element of oratorical performances. If public address embraced his vision and expanded its criticism beyond a catalogue of oratorical techniques or a judgment of a speech's efficacy, Wrage promised that rhetoric scholars might secure new prestige in the humanities.

Disciplinary historians agree that Wrage's attempt to reorient rhetorical criticism was unsuccessful.[7] The "speaker-centered" model not only remained ascendant, but researchers increasingly perceived a chasm between studies that focused on history, which were devalued, and those that focused on important speakers and the techniques of their rhetoric.[8] This emphasis did not bode well for African American speakers. Prior to the 1960s, speech communication as a discipline paid only limited attention to minority orators.[9] These early studies are noteworthy, but when compared to the discipline's literature generally they are few in number. Further, they departed from the critical norms of public address at that time. Based solely on this evidence, one might conclude that either minority communities possessed few orators or that the major speeches of non-white speakers were inaccessible. Both conclusions would be incorrect.

Not only was oratory an important aspect of public life within minority communities, but evidence of their speeches existed at the time. Volume 5 of *The World's Best Orations* (1899) contained one speech by Frederick Douglass and one speech by Porfirio Díaz, while volume 7 contained a small section devoted to the "Indian Orators" Tecumseh, Logan, Red Jacket, and Old Tassel.[10] The *Modern Eloquence* anthology of 1903 contained two speeches by Wu Ting-Fan, the Chinese envoy to the United States, and two speeches by Booker T. Washington.[11] In 1925, the African American historian Carter G. Woodson published a large volume of speeches produced solely by African Americans titled *Negro Orators and Their Orations*.[12] A review of the anthology appeared the following year in the *Quarterly Journal of Speech Education*. Cornell Professor Russell Wagner demonstrated familiarity with black speakers when he noted with some disappointment that W. E. B. Du Bois was excluded from Woodson's collection. Nevertheless, Wagner conceded that after reading the volume's 75 distinct texts, he was "inclined to agree with the claim advanced by the editor that 'these Negro orators have furnished the only humanizing theme which has stimulated eloquence during the last generation.'"[13] These examples do not prove that scholars of public address had extensive or easy access to minority texts; nevertheless, they do suggest that researchers did not take advantage of the opportunities that did exist. Certainly it was possible, by 1943, for William Brigance to have included more than just a single study of Booker T. Washington in *A History and Criticism of American Public Address*.[14]

So why were black orators not more evident in public address studies between 1925 and the 1960s? Karlyn Kohrs Campbell and Zornitsa Keremidchieva contend that the absence of women, minorities, and labor issues in the discipline's early literature was a natural consequence of its critical methodology.[15] The criteria used to establish whose oratory mattered and what one could claim about that oratory seemed designed to exclude people of color and women. Brigance, for example, declared that his seminal two-volume publication contained studies of "men who have used words to direct the course of American history."[16] Lester Thonssen and A. Craig Baird explained that speech "criticism may thus be confined, as it unquestionably was in certain of Plato's works, to a philosophical determination of the role of speechcraft in a well organized society."[17] Marie Hochmuth Nichols affirmed that the speech anthologies published before 1963 were "designed to exemplify the substance of statecraft, inspire patriotism, implant ideals," and reveal the eloquence of British and American political oratory.[18] In short, the speeches most worthy of study were those uttered by men who had altered history through their public oratory in formally organized social or political situations. Because minorities and women existed in a state of relative alterity prior to the 1960s, it is no surprise that they failed to appear in studies that focused on those contexts.[19]

The civil rights movement and the "new" context of social conflict

Most accounts of the communication studies discipline identify Edwin Black's short volume, *Rhetorical Criticism* (1965), as a transformative work in the study of rhetoric.[20] Whether *Rhetorical Criticism* was the catalyst for or a reflection of the concurrent social and academic transformations of the 1960s, the text is instructive for how it reconfigures the possibilities of public address. Black writes, "The critic, on the other hand, studies the products of man [*sic*]. Whether in painting or city planning, poetry or pottery, music or mosaics, the subject of criticism is always some harvest of human imagination."[21] Black narrows the critic's duties considerably when he attends to rhetorical criticism; nevertheless, his words reflect a widespread reevaluation of criticism within speech communication during the mid- to late 1960s. The expanding horizon of rhetorical criticism is evident also in *The Prospect of Rhetoric* (1971), the book that summarized the conclusions of the Wingspread and Pheasant Run conferences. Rhetoric, according to this text, includes "any human transaction in which symbols and/or systems of symbols influence values, attitudes, beliefs, and actions."[22] One of the book's editors, Lloyd Bitzer, elaborated on the mood that generated this definition when he recalled an exchange between Larry Rosenfield and Richard McKeon at Wingspread. In the afternoon conference, explains Bitzer, Rosenfield "returned to that expansive notion [of rhetoric] and remarked, with seeming exasperation, 'So far as I can tell,' the notion of rhetorical phenomena 'includes everything but tidal waves.' McKeon's immediate quip was 'Why not tidal waves?' "[23]

Edward Schiappa explains the trend toward "big rhetoric" as the result of two forces: a shift in the discipline's philosophical foundations and the civil unrest of the 1960s.[24] As the "symbolic interactionist" and the "rhetoric as epistemic" perspectives attracted ever-increasing numbers of rhetorical critics, the need to expand rhetoric's scope beyond the speech became inescapable.[25] For example, a year before Black's *Rhetorical Criticism*, Malcolm Sillars argued that speeches were not "representations" of political behavior. Citing both Wrage and Kenneth Burke, Sillars defined public speeches as rhetorical acts in and of themselves, acts that transpired within a "confused and bewildering world of conflict and interaction."[26] Public address scholars should approach their subject as an explicitly political behavior, a rhetorical effort to gain advantage in a context of social conflict. Campbell and Keremidchieva suggest that the social conflict which influenced the discipline most profoundly in the 1960s was the civil rights movement.[27]

Social movement researchers produced some of the earliest scholarship on the civil rights movement in our discipline,[28] but a short essay in *Spectra* by Donald Hugh Smith (1966) provided the clearest explanation as to the importance of the movement for public address scholars. Smith explained, "The contemporary civil rights movement in America may best be understood when it is perceived and analyzed as an effort to establish communication between two dissonant groups: the have-nots and the haves."[29] He argued further that the obstacles to effective and mutually beneficial communication between white and black Americans were rooted in racist practices that public orators had tried to resolve for well over a century. According to Smith, the protests of Martin Luther King, Jr. were associated, historically and rhetorically, with the abolitionist rhetoric of William Lloyd Garrison, Wendell Phillips, and Frederick Douglass. Smith wrote that public address critics should consider how the civil rights movement existed in a larger discursive context that included not only the debate between accommodation and agitation as embodied in the rhetoric of Booker T. Washington and W. E. B. Du Bois, but also the forgotten oratory of Monroe Trotter, Charles Lennox Redmond, Congressmen John Willis Menard and John R. Lynch, Ida B. Wells, and Senator Blanche K. Bruce.[30]

Smith's 1966 essay established a series of presumptions that would guide studies of African American public address for some time. First, he affirmed the modern civil rights movement as a problem of communication, transforming the social conflict into a legitimate object of rhetorical analysis. Second, Smith argued that civil rights protests were important not only because of their immediate impact, but also because they existed within a larger temporal context; that is, they participated in centuries of political, social, and cultural conflict. Third, Smith implied that African American rhetoric should be understood, first and foremost, as an attempt to ameliorate the problems of racism. A convention address published in *Today's Speech* by Robert S. Browne illustrates this point well: "So, if in 1968 the nation finds itself in a racial crisis which may well destroy the entire fabric of society, we can hardly call the situation incomprehensible. The discontent has been seething beneath the surface for the full 350 years, during which it has erupted into view on more than one occasion."[31] Smith, Browne, and others had defined a new horizon of critical inquiry, a field spanning centuries that the discipline had ignored until that moment.

Evidence for this new area of study exists in the dissertations and early publications of several emerging scholars. Donald Smith's 1964 Wisconsin dissertation was on the rhetoric of Dr. King, and his early essays in *Southern* (1968) and *Today's Speech* (1967) focused on the civil rights movement.[32] Patrick C. Kennicott completed a dissertation on black abolitionists at Florida State University in 1967.[33] He published an essay from that dissertation in 1970 and a study of H. Rap Brown in 1972.[34] In 1968, Andrew A. King completed his dissertation at the University of Minnesota on metaphors in the civil rights movement.[35] He would publish several essays that either began with or were influenced by that research.[36] In 1968, Philip Wander graduated from the University of Pittsburg with a PhD thesis that examined the image of African Americans within the rhetoric of abolitionists, colonizationists, and pro-slavery advocates.[37] He would publish two essays from this dissertation in 1971 and 1972, respectively.[38] John C. Hammerback's 1970 dissertation at Indiana University employed a more traditional methodology, but even his person-centered study of George Washington Julian, a white abolitionist, considered how inequality and racism had structured the nineteenth century.[39] Finally, Raymond G. Fulkerson leveraged his University of Illinois dissertation (1971) on the rhetoric of Frederick Douglass into an essay in the *Quarterly Journal of Speech* examining the versatility of Douglass's rhetoric against the Kansas/ Nebraska Act.[40] Each of these studies contributed to a new context that the field suddenly believed important – the political and social history of racial injustice.

In the decade that followed Smith's call to study the civil rights movement, the rhetoric that generated the most attention was not that of Dr. King but the radical discourse of black revolutionaries. Between 1967 and 1973, a remarkable number of essays, books, and book reviews devoted to the rhetoric of Black Power appeared in *Today's Speech*, the *Quarterly Journal of Speech*, the *Central States Speech Communication Journal*, and similar outlets.[41] Rather than describe each essay, I would note how the 1968 article by Parke G. Burgess, "The Rhetoric of Black Power: A Moral Demand?," represented many of the characteristics that marked this scholarship generally. Burgess suggested that although most white Americans viewed "Black Power" rhetoric as "abhorrent," the movement was actually the democratic consequence of an immoral racist culture that hypocritically spoke of equality while simultaneously refusing to treat African Americans as equal citizens. For Burgess, neither the speaker nor the speech was of ultimate importance. He explained that his purpose was "to shift focus from rhetorical conflict itself to the motives that necessitated it."[42] Motives, for Burgess, were not tied to persons, but were instead the product of a specific political context that prompted speakers to protest. Burgess explained, "If a rhetoric of protest and disruption virtually represents the only means available to dissident citizens with a just claim, then one must ask whether the democratic order is justified in suppressing it."[43]

Robert L. Scott, Wayne Brockriede, Donald Smith, and Karlyn Kohrs Campbell offered perhaps the most important theoretical contributions of this literature by arguing that radical black protest could not be understood well through traditional public address methodologies. For Scott, Brockriede, and Smith, the issue was whether the "confrontational rhetoric" of Black Power challenged the discipline's theoretical assumptions about coercion and persuasion.[44] Extending the ideas of Sillars, they argued that sometimes the traditional distinction between persuasion and coercion, oratory and force, was difficult if not impossible to determine. The rhetoric of Black Power was an act of confrontation or a form of violence that sought personal liberation through the symbolic annihilation of one's enemies. While this discourse might make the public and even rhetorical critics nervous, it should not be ignored or deemed illegitimate. Likewise, Campbell argued that critics needed to be more self-aware of how different methodologies shaped their conclusions.[45] Using the rhetoric of black nationalism as a case study, she demonstrated how Burkean dramatism leveraged different interpretive conclusions when compared to the traditional modes of public address inquiry. The presumption across this research was that Black Power departed from the norms of rhetorical practice that had been the focus of public address studies; therefore, special effort was necessary to either interpret its meaning correctly or to reformulate rhetorical theory to account for its social impact.

Two public address scholars from this period established extensive careers researching the contexts of US race relations. The first of these was the black scholar Molefi Asante (then Arthur L. Smith). Asante spoke for a new young generation of black academics who experienced the racial conflicts of the civil rights movement first hand and who refused to separate activism and scholarship.[46] Asante would eventually establish an international reputation for his theories of Afrocentricity, but in his early career he led both black and white scholars to reconsider black oratory as public address. An important theme of his scholarship was that black oratory could not be distinguished from the fight for racial justice, on the one hand, or from distinctively African traditions on the other. The study of speeches by Henry Highland Garnet, for example, necessitated critical attention to the larger contexts of civil rights and the inventional and intertextual culture of black America. Martin Luther King was intimately connected to Ray Charles, explained Asante, and the oratorical cadence of a black sermon should not be separated from the legal arguments of an African American politician. Among African American speakers, the norms of an African heritage and the political realities of racism combined to create a unique rhetorical culture that traditional studies of black orators, their biographies, or their individual speeches could never uncover.[47]

Concurrent with Asante's research, Cal Logue began to publish about America's racial contexts. Whereas Asante championed an explicitly black perspective and an African discursive tradition, Logue wrote from the perspective of a white male who had grown up in the segregated South. His research illustrated both the personal and professional aspects of writing race into public address literature. In an essay discussing the merits of teaching black rhetoric, Logue described his experiences with race as a young white boy in Alabama and, later, as a member of the Marines.[48] The protests of the civil rights movement led him to personal introspection and shifts in his pedagogy.[49] His studies of nineteenth- and twentieth-century Southern oratory and, especially, his analysis of the Reconstruction era set a new standard for how one might approach rhetoric as a discursive force that shapes the lives of African and European Americans.[50] For Logue, interracial conflict was a defining characteristic of US history that shaped the rhetoric and the reception of even the South's white politicians.[51]

The decade of scholarship I've described above created both subtle and obvious shifts in public address research. First, the study of the civil rights movement and black protest rhetoric brought African American voices into the study of public address in an unprecedented manner. Second, public address researchers began to consider how songs, visual imagery, protest slogans, and written propaganda were rhetorical artifacts, in order to account more fully for the social conflict they wished to study. Third, theorists who tried to interpret the confrontational demands of black protesters were forced to rethink rhetoric's definition and functions, as well as the methods one might use to understand its significance. Most important, the idea that single speeches and speakers were sometimes less important than the sociopolitical contexts that both influenced and were then influenced by rhetoric became a warrant that sustained a new generation of scholars. Thus, the study of the civil rights movement between 1966 and 1975 revitalized public address, and it changed the accepted horizon of critical scrutiny. After 1975, the number of studies that considered African American rhetoric declined, but important articles would appear from time to time.[52] The authors who were writing during this period did so within a changed critical environment.

Text and context in hermeneutic criticism: My story

I began my career as a graduate student at Purdue University and Northwestern University between 1989 and 1995. Among public address scholars, this period is noteworthy because of the debate over "the text." The perspective of close textual analysis championed by Michael Leff seemed to regard the speech as a stable unified field of meaning, an aesthetic object with clear boundaries and a unified texture.[53] Michael McGee's insistence that critics examine ideology seemed to affirm that single speeches were but fragments.[54] What mattered, according to McGee, were the ideological practices that dictated which fragments sustained value and how audiences would stitch together the "texts" that comprised their reality. In Dilip Gaonkar's disciplinary narrative, the two sides of this debate seemed irreconcilable.[55] The "textual criticism"/"critical rhetoric" debate caused many graduate students of my generation to choose one side or the other; you either studied texts to appreciate the dynamic movement of form and content, or you studied discursive and cultural practices that privileged some communities while simultaneously oppressing others.[56]

As a doctoral candidate this choice seemed false to me. As a student at Northwestern working with Leff, I appreciated the explanatory power of close textual criticism when used by astute readers. As an African American male whose dissertation examined the Reconstruction era's debate over racial desegregation, I was interested in the cultural and political history of racial oppression in the United States. The orations of Senator Charles Sumner and Representatives Alonzo Ransier, Alexander Stephens, Robert Elliott, and John T. Harris were remarkable, but the dynamic texture of each speech was only a small part of their significance. The speeches interacted with one another, sustaining references and allusions that suggested an intertextual context. When combined they constituted several typologies – what I termed rhetorics of inequality, of equality, and of place. They reflected and influenced the public policies of the Reconstruction and Jim Crow eras. Finally, each speech participated in an intellectual history of race. In sum, each speech was a rich and dynamic rhetorical expression, yet it was imbricated within a matrix of additional contexts. Even after I expanded the dissertation for publication, I knew that some academics, historians in particular, would argue that the book underplayed the regional, state, biographical, and juridical contexts of the 1875 Civil Rights Act.[57]

While researching Lincoln's rhetorical leadership, I came to realize more fully why I was interested in the 1875 Civil Rights Act and in public address.[58] Public address provides an almost limitless opportunity to study the multilayered *contexts* of America's racial history, while, simultaneously, the study of this racial history is grounded in concrete moments of expression that have value as unique performances of human experience. Of necessity, I view public address as an expansive body of discursive action: the speeches of presidents and members of Congress;[59] the publicized research of scientists;[60] the recorded recollections of people who have experienced racial oppression and reconciliation.[61] Yet, despite the diversity of this object domain, public address as both a practice and a research endeavor remains a hermeneutic enterprise. Robert J. Branham and W. Barnett Pearce provide some useful language for the critical practice I envision for public address research.[62] Text and context are separable concepts but only within the act of human interpretation: "In any specific instance, 'text' and 'context' are constituted by the work of an interpretive community ... they are interactive, in that the meaning and, hence, substance of each derives from the other ... they are fully reflexive, in that each may function either as text or as context."[63] People, acting as human subjects embedded within an influential but not determinative interpretive community, create the texts and contexts that constitute meaning. There is no text without context and no context without text, because both are necessary for the hermeneutic process of understanding that is the most important (though not the sole) function of communication.

Approached in this fashion, I contend that public address criticism is not terribly distinct from the act of public address itself. The practice of public speech, understood broadly, is a hermeneutic production of meaning in which context is established to explain the meaning of an utterance (the what) and the value or valence of that utterance (its significance). The criticism of public address is also a hermeneutic production of meaning that may employ specialized language and terminology, but that nevertheless constitutes a context and a text in relation to one another. Thus, I characterize my own research as an attempt to "understand" the "rhetoric/hermeneutic" practices of particular communities, while always acknowledging that these practices construct social relations and systems of power and material interest. An example of how this criticism might proceed follows.

Interpreting the Violent Acts of Reconstruction

Simon Elder had lived in Clarke County, Georgia, for all of his 54 years. He was a farmer who raised cotton and wheat on land that he rented from the white family that lived about one and a half miles from his house. Simon, his wife Mary, and their son and daughter were good tenants; moreover, they were prosperous compared to sharecroppers of either race. In one season during the Reconstruction era, they harvested over 223 bushels of wheat and paid in cash to have it threshed. Simon did not consider himself to be political; he did not "go about making speeches." Nevertheless, he did vote the Republican ticket when given the opportunity. Then, one Saturday night in mid-November, Mary and Simon's lives changed forever. Around eleven o'clock they sat in front of a warm fire, resting after a full day that included the sale of cotton and the purchase of winter provisions. They had a hundred dollars left over, and as they relaxed they talked about their good fortune. Suddenly, the door erupted with sharp knocking that sounded, according to Simon, as though a "whole gang of rocks" had been thrown against it. Simon jumped to his feet, but the door threw him backward as it broke under the weight of the disguised men who rushed into the room. Two men immediately began to beat Simon on the head with clubs. Simon struggled, but the men shouted that if he continued they would "blow his brains out." Mary was shouting too until one of the men slapped her, informing her that they would "knock [her] brains out" as well. The robed assailants dragged Simon and Mary out the door and then forced them down the path away from their home. Simon testified, "They made me go into the thicket of woods, and there it looked almost like a judgment to me." The attackers told Simon to strip naked, but just as he began to remove his coat, he fled. "I thought I would as quick [*sic*] die with a quick pain as a slow fever, and I made a spring and ran off." His attackers fired three times at his back but only succeeded in putting a hole through his breeches. After Simon escaped, the men turned toward Mary, questioned her about Simon's probable whereabouts, and eventually released her. Before they let her go, they promised that she and her husband would be in hell before the following night was over. Simon and Mary left their house and most of their possessions to escape to Decatur in Dekalb County, Georgia.[64]

What is initially significant about this narrative as an object of public address criticism is that it is both radically particular and radically general. The particularity is evident in the fact that the narrative is the recorded personal testimony of the speaker, Elder's memories expressed in vernacular language. Moreover, the testimony speaks to a very specific set of interpersonal relationships; as we shall see later, Simon knew his "white robed" attackers and why they tried to kill him. That said, the story is just one of many hundreds of similar stories recorded by federal authorities investigating the Reconstruction Ku Klux Klan (KKK). Throughout the South after the Civil War, the KKK traveled country roads and town streets administering "justice" to those who violated its code. Judge Albion W. Tourgee counted 12 murders, nine rapes, 14 cases of arson, and over 700 beatings in his North Carolina district alone. Officials in Spartanburgh County, South Carolina, counted 227 instances of whippings, shootings, and stabbings in less than two years. In Jackson County, Florida, approximately 150 African Americans and one person of Jewish decent were murdered between 1866 and 1871.[65]

What makes the testimony of Simon Elder worthy of contemporary study, then, is that it exists within a complex matrix of overlapping *contexts* – contexts that are both unique to its historical moment and relevant to how Americans have struggled with race to this present day. The events of this narrative are emblematic of one set of experiences that constitute our shared history; they could have happened at any moment during the nineteenth century and for a significant portion of the twentieth century. Even today some feel justified in attacking those they believe to be racially inferior, as the murder of Stephen Tyrone Johns at the National Holocaust Museum on June 10, 2009 reveals.[66] Mark Potok, editor of the Southern Poverty Law Center's *Intelligence Report*, claims that contemporary instances of racial violence are not simply the result of mental illness; there is a "growing consensus" that "right-wing hate groups and radical ideas [are] spreading across the United States."[67] There is a continued contemporary relevance to Elder's story that makes it an especially productive field for hermeneutic analysis.

The wave of post-Civil War violence is well known among historians, but it is not the subject of research for rhetoric or public address scholars. A traditional definition of rhetoric as oratorical persuasion may even conclude that violence is beyond rhetoric's scope. Yet, when judged from the perspectives of those scholars who studied the civil rights movement in the late 1960s and early 1970s, one recognizes that the violence of the Reconstruction era implicates many important contexts about which rhetorical criticism can speak. For example, Reconstruction violence was a social phenomenon about which different speakers made competing claims. Among many white Southerners, violence was the natural result of rampant black lawlessness and a potential solution to their own powerlessness. For white Republican lawmakers, violence was a conspiratorial act, an organized attempt by former confederates to overturn Republican policies. For black Americans, violence was, quite literally, part of a historic communicative action that extended back to slavery. With ruthless efficiency, violence communicated and performed the message that one's white neighbors would not accept you as an equal partner in the South's systems of power. Evidence for these claims can be found in one of the richest (and most daunting) texts of the period – the Ku Klux Klan Conspiracy Hearings.

Interpreting violence as natural and necessary

It is difficult to imagine the world that Southern confederates faced at the end of the Civil War. General Sherman's March to the Sea, which began with the burning of Atlanta in mid-November of 1864, "brought the war home" to confederate wives and children. Sherman believed that war was a hell in which Georgia's civilians should share; therefore, they became the object of his violence. Sometimes at his direct command and sometimes on their own initiative, his troops destroyed miles of railroad track, acres of farmland, many private homes, and, eventually, the city of Columbia, South Carolina. Sherman's own estimate of the damage he caused was $100,000,000, $80,000,000 of which was solely destruction and waste. Of course, these numbers reflect the ruin of only a single campaign. The effect of this devastation on the psyche of many Southerners was even greater, and it undoubtedly contributed to how they described the challenges they faced after the war. Of particular importance here, however, is that many white Southerners told federal investigators that white Northerners and the former slaves took advantage of the war's destruction. Ambrose Wright, editor of the *Chronicle and Sentinel* in Augusta, Georgia, described those dark times as follows:

> Immediately after the war society was very much disorganized. Just after the close of the war the negroes were educated to regard the whites of the South as their enemies, and made to believe that southern native whites would put them back into slavery if they could. We had no courts; our judicial system was destroyed; we had nothing there but military government. The negroes, who had just been emancipated, were very lawless, thinking they would be supported by a class of men who had come down there to teach them – a class that we call carpet-baggers; and there was a great deal of crime at that time.[68]

Wright's comments illustrate how one community – Southern whites who desired local control through the Democratic Party – practiced their interpretive and rhetorical skills.

According to this interpretive production, attacks on black Americans, carpetbaggers, and scallywags were simply the result of a chaotic, lawless situation. It was not the violence of Klansmen that destabilized Southern society; it was the inversion of traditional systems of power. Carpetbaggers had persuaded the former slaves through political speeches and interpersonal argument that the same master who once had been their ally was now their enemy. The federally established military governments were complicit in this shift. Former Confederate General Wade Hampton argued that the army ruled the South without regard for the region's true leadership.[69] Attorney Robert Aldrich testified that in his experience the military "seemed to have the impression that the white citizens of the community were desirous of oppressing the colored citizens of the community. They exaggerated that impression, and seemed to officiate with a view of correcting what they considered a prevalent abuse."[70] The alleged bias of military courts in favor of African Americans led many whites to argue that black criminality was not punished, lawlessness was rampant, and "the peace of society was very much disturbed and property unsafe."[71]

Articulated from within a context that they described as chaotic, conservatives argued that violence was not only inevitable, it was also natural and necessary. On April 6, 1871, the *Yorkville Enquirer* declared:

> Our former slaves, headed by these carpet-baggers, have not only assumed all the civil powers of the State, but they are armed to the teeth as a military force, to the exclusion of any white militia. … Resistance on the part of individuals is the inevitable consequence of such outrages. Those who sow to the wind, let them take care lest they reap the whirlwind. Roused at midnight, by the repeated fires of incendiaries; threatened by the bayonets of our former slaves, insultingly and defiantly marching by night and by day, in squads, and by companies, through the peaceful county and in the thronged streets … retaliation must commence – it has commenced. The guilty perpetrators of crime and outrage have been overtaken and scourged. It was the result of their own aggression. If blood has been spilled by one race, let it not be forgotten that arson and robbery had first been committed by the other.[72]

The instrument of correction – the means by which the chaotic context would be rectified – was the Ku Klux Klan.

Interpreting violence as a political conspiracy

The exact date of the Klan's birth is lost to history, but it is believed that the organization was founded in May or early June of 1866 by six young confederate veterans in Polaski, Tennessee. The historian Allen Trelease writes that the term Ku Klux was "merely a corruption of the Greek world *kuklos*, meaning circle or band; 'Klan' was redundant but it added to the alliteration."[73] Throughout 1867, the

KKK seemed to transform from a localized phenomenon to a widespread secret army, dedicated to the old Democratic Party and the social order of the antebellum era. The ceremonial robes of private gatherings disguised gangs of men who traveled the countryside seizing the guns of people of color, disrupting Union League meetings, intimidating blacks at the polls, and "teaching lessons" to carpetbaggers, scallywags, and anyone who did not know their proper place in the social order. By April of 1868, the Ku Klux Klan had grown from six counties in the middle of Tennessee "to every Southern State between the Potomac and the Rio Grande."[74]

The violence performed by the Ku Klux Klan during this period took many forms; the testimony taken by the Joint Committee in South Carolina and Georgia includes details of shootings, rapes, the "exposure" of women, beatings, stabbings, burnings, and hangings. Unlike the lynching practices of the late nineteenth century, however, the dominant form of violence during the Reconstruction period was whipping. It is described well by the testimony of Isham McCary:

QUESTION: Go on and tell how they whipped you.

ANSWER: When they came in they broke down one of the doors, and they broke the hinge off the other one, and four came in the doors at once. It was about 2 o'clock at night, as nigh as I can tell you; and then they came in and shot twice over my head, and said they were going to kill me. ... After they had shot over my head twice when they asked me out, they told me now to say my prayers; that they were going to kill me. They asked for my arms too. I told them I had no arms. Then they asked me out the door. I went out. They told me to get down and say my prayers; that they were going to kill me. ... Then they commenced whipping me, calling the names by numbers. ... I got to understand the way they called; they called the number that they gave. They gave me twenty-five lashes apiece; four did, and the first that whipped me gave me three lashes after they were done whipping me, to make me take the hickories they had whipped me with down to show them to my friends.

QUESTION: Did they say anything to you?

ANSWER: Yes, sir; they asked me who I voted for; and said if I told a lie they would shoot me right off. I told them I would not lie; I voted for Mr. Scott [the Republican Governor] ... let a man be what he was; I would not know how to turn any other way; that is what I told them.

QUESTION: How many were there of them?

ANSWER: There were eight or nine; I cannot say exactly.

QUESTION: How were they dressed?

ANSWER: That had just a common – I thought it was cloth, and I reckon it was; anyhow it was white; some white and some black, and bound around with black; and you could see this far around; you could see the back of the eyes. The disguise was so that you could see the disguise over the mouth and eyes. ... Some of them had on – it looked like night-gowns.[75]

McCary's testimony contains remarkable details but it is banal in the sense that it narrates actions that were repeated often during this period. In almost every case of whipping described to federal investigators, the victim was attacked at night in his or her home by men on horseback who wore long robes and hoods. The most common piece of property destroyed in these raids, excluding the victim's door, was the family shotgun or pistol, the iconic representation of black autonomy and influence. The attackers typically knew their victims and often engaged them in conversations that explained the political rationale for the visit and the subsequent violence. The whipping was not haphazard; it was premeditated and orderly unless the victim or the victim's family disturbed the proceedings. The beatings were invariably severe, and the attackers seemed to make few distinctions with respect to age and sex. In many cases, the victims were incapacitated for days, and in some instances they died from the injuries. The KKK usually concluded the ritual sacrifice with specific instructions about how the victim should behave in the future. In McCary's example, they told him to change his vote or not vote at all, and they gave him the instruments of his torture as an object lesson for him and his friends.[76]

Given such events it is not surprising that Republican politicians believed that the Ku Klux Klan was an organized conspiracy led by former confederate soldiers. On May 31, 1870, Congress passed the first Enforcement Act, which made it a federal crime to bribe or intimidate voters during an election or to punish an individual for his vote. This measure proved ineffectual, so Congress passed a second Enforcement Act in February of 1871, but when that too made little difference a third law, the Ku Klux Act, was passed on April 20, 1871. This legislation made it a federal crime to "conspire together, or go in disguise upon the public highway, or upon the premises of another for the purpose ... of depriving any person or class of persons of the equal protection of the laws." It also gave the president broad powers to use military force to restore law and order in regions where violence was rampant. As one might imagine, the measure was extremely unpopular among Northern and Southern Democrats, but even Republicans who voted for the bill worried about its extension of federal power.[77]

These laws had one ironic though unintended consequence, however. They legitimized the Ku Klux Klan for those individuals who interpreted congressional legislation as an unrestrained violation of Southern white culture. After Reconstruction, the KKK itself would become a text that others transformed into a robust mythology. Thomas Dixon's popular 1905 novel, *The Clansman*, and D. W. Griffith's monumental film, *Birth of a Nation* (1915), are representative of reinterpretations that portrayed the Klan as the saviors of Southern white culture, a brave secret army that withstood the corruption of carpetbaggers, the treachery of scallywags, and the brutal domination of ignorant freedmen. Subsequent historians, the press, and communities of both races have condemned the Ku Klux Klan, but it is not difficult, even today, to find people who view the Reconstruction Klan in very different terms. Throughout the post-Reconstruction era and well into the twentieth century, the KKK would be remembered within some circles as a band of brave freedom fighters who stopped radical Republican tyranny in the South.

Interpreting violence as an intimate struggle among neighbors

The mythology that surrounds the Ku Klux Klan and its campaign during the Reconstruction era obscures the social and rhetorical functions of that period's violence; therefore, a new context is necessary. That context is explained well by the theories of René Girard.[78] Girard argues that sanctioned violence – violence that is interpreted by some community members as natural and necessary – usually results from a basic human impulse toward imitation. Mimesis, he argues, is the most common mode of learning and adaptation among human beings; furthermore, people transform themselves by modeling the habits, persona, and values of others. For Girard, mimesis is the primary vehicle of desire, because personal growth leads humans to appropriate not just the thoughts and ideas of others, but also their needs and wants. Consequently, mimesis results in envy, rivalry, and violence as two parties discover that they desire the same object.[79] The biblical admonition – "thou shalt not covet" – is perhaps the most important proscription of social order, but it is also the one command that cannot be obeyed, leading eventually to the transgression of "thou shalt not kill." What begins as a harmless attempt to pattern oneself after an exemplar shifts to something darker when the imitator and the exemplar lay claim to the same "object of desire."

In 2003, I argued that the freedmen and women of the post-Civil War era engaged in purposeful acts of mimesis, imitating the models of citizenship that they had witnessed during the antebellum period.[80] The former slaves defined freedom as the opportunity to pursue those privileges that European Americans took for granted. Henry Turner declared in the early years of the Reconstruction era, "If I cannot do like a white man I am not free," and another former slave said, "I see how the poor white people do. I ought to do so too, or else I am a slave."[81] Educated African Americans expressed more expansive desires and followed Maria Stewart's admonition:

> I see [the white people of America] thriving in the arts, and sciences, and in polite literature. Their highest aim is to excel in political, moral and religious improvement. ... The Americans have practiced nothing but head-work these 200 years, and we have done their drudgery. And is it not high time for us to imitate their examples, and practice head-work too, and keep what we have got, and get what we can?[82]

After the Civil War, many black leaders believed that they would take a position next to the white elite and, like their models, begin to direct the political and economic restructuring of the South. Most certainly Thomas Allen had these ambitions.

Allen was the pastor of the Baptist Church in Marietta, Georgia. A popular individual among whites and blacks, he was elected as a delegate to Georgia's constitutional convention (December 9, 1867 to March 15, 1868). The morning before Allen voted to ratify the constitution, he received the following letter:

> Tom, you are in great danger; you are going heedless with the radicals, against the interest of the conservative white population, and I tell you if you do not change your course before the election for the ratification of the infernal constitution, your days are numbered, and they will be but few. ... My advice to you, Tom, is to stay at home if you value your life, and not vote at all, and advise all of your race to do the same thing. You are marked and closely watched by K. K. K., (or in plain words Ku-Klux). Take heed; a word to the wise is sufficient. By order of Grand Cyclops.[83]

Allen ignored this threat and voted for the new constitution. His experiences at the constitutional convention also changed his aspirations; he sought and obtained the office of state legislator.

Sometime during the night of October 16 or 17, Allen's house was surrounded by disguised men who demanded to see him. His wife refused to let him go, but his brother-in-law Emanuel went to the door in a vain attempt to manage the situation. When he opened the door, he was shot by three separate shotguns. Emanuel died later that night in the arms of his wife and family. The next day, one of Allen's neighbors, Colonel James Wilson, came to the house and said, "By God, Allen, I told you six months ago that we would not submit to negroism in this State; did I not tell you they would kill you?" Allen replied, "Yes, but I did not believe it; I did not think anybody had anything against me; I preached for you all during the war, when you could not get a white preacher, for all had gone into the army; I did not think anybody would kill me for my political sentiments." Wilson then said, "I told you they would do it; you leave the county now or they will murder you, and your wife and children."[84]

From the perspectives of the two interpretive communities comprised of European Americans – Southern Democratic whites and Northern Republicans – Reconstruction violence was conducted by the anonymous and ultimately unknowable persona of the Ku Klux Klan. But for a third community, the African American victims of violence, each attack was yet another example of the intimate struggle among neighbors that had been fought since slavery's moment of origin. Colonel Wilson expressed a sincere concern for Allen's well-being, but as he put it, he would "not submit to negroism in this state." If people of color sought to obtain leadership in the community by holding public office, they would be denied. Mary and Simon Elder, the couple whose testimony began this brief analysis, testified that the men who attacked them were their neighbors. In fact, they were the very men that Simon and Mary had paid to thresh their wheat. During the attack, according to Simon, the robed men said that the black couple had become too prosperous for their own good, which was why they had to either leave the county or die. In case after case, the testimony of African Americans suggests that the context that explained Reconstruction violence was the same agonistic interpersonal relationships that they had hoped the Civil War would have abolished. These "rituals of violence" were messages from "friends" or acquaintances who selfishly denied the victims something that the attackers kept for themselves.

Conclusion

In this brief analysis I have tried to accomplish two tasks. First, I have worked within a tradition and perspective that began with the rhetorical analysis of the civil rights movement in the mid-1960s. This tradition views public address as an expansive field in which US race relations are negotiated, sometimes violently but always with and through discourse. Second, I have sought to illustrate why context may be the most important conceptual category in public address criticism today. Here I claimed that three distinct interpretive communities understood Reconstruction violence in dramatically different ways, precisely because each community created a different context to animate both its perception of that violence and how it defined and described violence to federal investigators. As public address critics we do precisely the same rhetorical/hermeneutic work. At times we highlight the contexts that our historical subjects articulate. At other moments, we employ the contexts established by historians or sociologists. Frequently, we use theories or terminology that stem from our academic discipline. Regardless of the source of the contexts we articulate, we are engaged in the productive labor that has always characterized public address – building narratives of the past to meet the intellectual, social, and even personal demands of the present.

When we recognize context as a product of hermeneutic and rhetorical behavior and not a static historical situation in which the more important work of oratory transpires, we begin to extend the "case study" methods of public address in interesting ways. Critics of public address allege that although the subfield excels at case studies, the case study model has limited intellectual force. According to Roderick Hart, case studies are so particular that only limited significant theoretical or general insight is possible.[85] This critique of public address implies that while an analysis of the personal testimony about Reconstruction violence might inform the reader about social conflict after the Civil War, it contributes little to our knowledge of political rhetoric or rhetorical theory generally. Furthermore, the analysis remains uninteresting to the majority of communication scholars who do not care about the period from 1865 to 1877.

Several persuasive counter-arguments already exist to this critique,[86] but this chapter's conceptual claims suggest yet another. When we explore the dynamic nature of contexts, both in the moments of articulation that we study and in the process of writing our own criticism, we are simultaneously arguing about *how* a past rhetorical event is meaningful beyond the temporal boundaries of that particular case. This claim is founded not on a naïve presumption that history repeats itself, but on the more radical notion that *we repeat history*. That is, human beings discursively constitute contexts that shape the past to make sense of the decisions, actions, and values of the present. In the early twentieth century, the Ku Klux Klan was interpreted as the heroic savior of white culture from the depravations of brutal, rapacious, and criminal African Americans. This use of history helped to justify the continued practice of lynching (physical violence) and the rhetoric of difference and inferiority (symbolic violence) that maintained racial segregation. During the modern civil rights move-ment, white liberals interpreted Southern segregation and white "resistance" as a conspiracy to keep Southern blacks subjugated. This contextual frame, which had a precedent in the Reconstruction era, deflected attention from the racial discrimina-tion experienced by many blacks in urban areas across the country, North and South, East and West. African Americans have frequently, though not exclusively, interpreted the physical and symbolic violence they experience as part of an intimate context of interpersonal struggle over the benefits of citizenship and the American Dream. In each of these instances, the interpretive and rhetorical labor performed during the Reconstruction era was performed yet again at another strategic moment of social conflict. This is the kind of insight and "argued-for knowledge" that public address studies can offer. It is my hope that future public address scholars will embrace their role as *a*, not *the*, producers of critical contexts that facilitate a rich knowledge of the political, cultural, and even racial histories that we all share.

Notes

1   Stephen Howard Browne, "Context in Critical Theory and Practice," *Western Journal of Communication* 65 (2001): 330.

2   See Dilip P. Gaonkar, "Object and Method in Rhetorical Criticism: From Wichelns to Leff and McGee," *Western Speech Communication Journal* 54 (1990): 290–316; Martin J. Medhurst, "The Academic Study of Public Address," in *Landmark Essays on American Public Address*, ed. Martin J. Medhurst (Davis, CA: Hermagoras Press, 1993); Martin J. Medhurst, "The Contemporary Study of Public Address: Renewal, Recovery, and Reconfiguration," *Rhetoric & Public Affairs* 4 (2001): 495–522; Martin J. Medhurst, "The History of Public Address as an Academic Study," Chapter 1, this volume; David Zarefsky, "History of Public Discourse Studies," in *The Sage Handbook of Rhetorical Studies*, ed. Andrea A. Lunsford et al. (Thousand Oaks, CA: Sage, 2009); and Karlyn Kohrs Campbell and Zornitsa D. Keremidchieva, "Race, Sex, and Class in Rhetorical Criticism," in *The Sage Handbook of Rhetorical Studies*, ed. Lunsford et al., 461–476.

3   Ernest Wrage, "Public Address: A Study in Social and Intellectual History," *Quarterly Journal of Speech* 33 (1947): 451–457.

4   Wrage, "Public Address," 452.

5   Wrage, "Public Address," 457.

6   Zarefsky, "History of Public Discourse Studies," 435–436.

7   See Medhurst, "History of Public Address as an Academic Study"; and Thomas Rosteck, "Form and Cultural Context in Rhetorical Criticism: Re-Reading Wrage," *Quarterly Journal of Speech* 84 (1998): 471–490.

8   For discussions of this tension see Barnet Baskerville, "Must We All Be 'Rhetorical Critics'?" *Quarterly Journal of Speech* 63 (1977): 107–116; Bruce E. Gronbeck, "Rhetorical History and Rhetorical Criticism: A Distinction," *Speech Teacher* 24 (1975): 309–320; and Stephen Lucas, "The Schism in Rhetorical Scholarship," *Quarterly Journal of Speech* 67 (1981): 1–20.

9   See C. M. Wise, "Negro Dialect," *Quarterly Journal of Speech* 19 (1933): 522–528; William Pipes, "Old-Time Negro Preaching: An Interpretive Study," *Quarterly Journal*

of Speech 31 (1945): 15–21; William H. Honan, "John Jaspers and the Sermon That Moved the Sun," *Speech Monographs* 23 (1956): 255–261; Vio Mae Powell, "Dramatic Ritual as Observed in the Sun Dance," *Quarterly Journal of Speech* 33 (1947): 167–171; Richard Moody, "Negro Minstrelsy," *Quarterly Journal of Speech* 30 (1944): 321–328; and Marcus H. Boulware, "Speech Training in Negro Colleges," *Quarterly Journal of Speech* 33 (1947): 509–514.

10   David J. Brewer et al., *The World's Best Orations: From the Earliest Period to the Present Time*, 10 vols. (Chicago: F. P. Kaiser, 1899).

11   Wu Ting-Fan, "The Teachings of Confucius" and "China and the United States," in *Modern Eloquence*, ed. Thomas B. Reed et al. (New York: American Law Book Co., 1903), 1225–1235, 1284–1287; and Booker T. Washington, "Progress of the American Negro" and "The American Standard," in *Modern Eloquence*, ed. Reed et al., 1136–1140, 1140–1142.

12   Carter Godwin Woodson, *Negro Orators and Their Orations* (Washington, DC: Associated Publishers, 1925).

13   Russell H. Wagner, "Book Review: *Negro Orators and Their Orations*," *Quarterly Journal of Speech Education* 12 (1926): 381.

14   William Norwood Brigance, ed., *A History and Criticism of American Public Address*, 2 vols. (New York: McGraw-Hill, 1943).

15   Campbell and Keremidchieva, "Race, Sex, and Class in Rhetorical Criticism."

16   Brigance, *A History and Criticism*, 1: vii.

17   Lester Thonssen and Albert Craig Baird, *Speech Criticism: The Development of Standards for Rhetorical Appraisal* (New York: Ronald Press, 1948), 290.

18   Marie Hochmuth Nichols, *Rhetoric and Criticism* (Baton Rouge: Louisiana State University Press, 1963), 57–58.

19   Rhetorical and historical scholarship in recent decades has demonstrated that formal and informal efforts to exclude African Americans and women from the public sphere were unsuccessful; nevertheless, in the 1950s the dominant presumption among scholars of public address seems to be that neither community had played significant roles in America's social or political oratorical history.

20   Gaonkar, "Object and Method in Rhetorical Criticism."

21   Edwin Black, *Rhetorical Criticism: A Study in Method* (Madison: University of Wisconsin Press, 1978), 3.

22   Lloyd F. Bitzer and Edwin Black, eds., *The Prospect of Rhetoric: Report of the National Developmental Project* (Englewood Cliffs, NJ: Prentice Hall, 1971), 214.

23   Lloyd F. Bitzer, "Rhetoric's Prospects: Past and Future," in *Making and Unmaking the Prospects of Rhetoric*, ed. Theresa Enos (Mahwah, NJ: Lawrence Earlbaum, 1997), 19–20.

24   Edward Schiappa, "Second Thoughts on the Critiques of Big Rhetoric," *Philosophy & Rhetoric* 34 (2001): 260–274.

25   Schiappa, "Second Thoughts," 261–262.

26   Malcolm O. Sillars, "Rhetoric as Act," *Quarterly Journal of Speech* 50 (1964): 284.

27   Campbell and Keremidchieva, "Race, Sex, and Class in Rhetorical Criticism," 466.

28   Leland M. Griffin, "The Rhetorical Structure of the 'New Left' Movement: Part I," *Quarterly Journal of Speech* 50 (1964): 113–135; and Franklyn S. Haiman, "The Rhetoric of the Streets: Some Legal and Ethical Considerations," *Quarterly Journal of Speech* 53 (1967): 99–114.

29 Donald Hugh Smith, "Civil Rights: A Problem in Communication," *Spectra* 2 (1966): 1–2, 4, 8. See also Donald Hugh Smith, "Martin Luther King, Jr.: In the Beginning at Montgomery," *Southern Speech Journal* 34 (1968): 8–17.

30 Smith, "Civil Rights," 2.

31 Robert S. Browne, "Dialogue Between the Races – A Top Priority," *Today's Speech* 16 (1968): 7.

32 Donald Hugh Smith, "Martin Luther King, Jr.: Rhetorician of Revolt" (PhD Thesis, University of Wisconsin-Madison, 1964); Donald Hugh Smith, "Social Protest and the Oratory of Human Rights," *Today's Speech* 15 (1967), 2–8; and Smith, "Martin Luther King, Jr.: In the Beginning at Montgomery."

33 Patrick C. Kennicott, "Negro Antislavery Speakers in America" (Florida State University, 1967).

34 Patrick C. Kennicott, "Black Persuaders in the Antislavery Movement," *Speech Monographs* 37 (1970): 15–24; and Patrick C. Kennicott and Wayne E. Page, "H. Rap Brown: The Cambridge Incident," *Quarterly Journal of Speech* 57 (1971): 325–334.

35 Andrew A. King, "The Metaphor in Civil Rights Oratory: The Rhetoric of Accommodation" (PhD Thesis, University of Minnesota, 1968).

36 Andrew A. King, "The Rhetorical Legacy of the Black Church," *Central States Speech Journal* 22 (1971): 179–185; and Andrew A. King, "Booker T. Washington and the Myth of Heroic Materialism," *Quarterly Journal of Speech* 60 (1974): 323–328.

37 Philip Charles Wander, "The Image of the Negro in Three Movements: Abolitionist, Colonizationist, and Pro-Slavery" (PhD Thesis, University of Pittsburgh, 1968).

38 Philip C. Wander, "Salvation Through Separation: The Image of the Negro in the American Colonization Society," *Quarterly Journal of Speech* 57 (1971): 57–67; and Philip C. Wander, "The Savage Child: The Image of the Negro in the Pro-Slavery Movement," *Southern Communication Journal* 37 (1972): 335–360.

39 John C. Hammerback, "George Washington Julian: Hoosier Spokesman for the Slave" (PhD Thesis, Indiana University, 1970); and John C. Hammerback, "The Rhetoric of a Righteous Reform: George Washington Julian's 1852 Campaign Against Slavery," *Central States Speech Journal* 22 (1971): 85–93. See also John C. Hammerback and Richard J. Jensen, *The Rhetorical Career of Cesar Chavez* (College Station: Texas A&M University Press, 1998).

40 Raymond Gerald Fulkerson, "Frederick Douglass and the Anti-Slavery Crusade: His Career and Speeches, 1817–1861" (microform, University of Illinois, 1971); and R. G. Fulkerson, "Frederick Douglass and the Kansas–Nebraska Act: A Case Study in Agitational Versatility," *Central States Speech Journal* 23 (1972): 261–269.

41 Elizabeth Flory Phifer and Dencil R. Taylor, "Carmichael in Tallahassee," *Southern Speech Journal* 33 (1967): 88–92; Parke G. Burgess, "The Rhetoric of Black Power: A Moral Demand?" *Quarterly Journal of Speech* 54 (1968): 122–133; J. A. Hendrix, "Black Power: The Politics of Liberation in America/Report of the National Advisory Commission on Civil Disorders," *Today's Speech* 16 (1968): 54; Howard Schwartz, "The Black Power Revolt," *Today's Speech* 16 (1968): 53; Richard B. Gregg et al., "The Rhetoric of Black Power: A Street-Level Interpretation," *Quarterly Journal of Speech* 55 (1969): 151–160; Finley C. Campbell, "Voices of Thunder, Voices of Rage: A Symbolic Analysis of a Selection from Malcolm X's Speech, 'Message to the Grass Roots,'" *Speech Teacher* 19 (1970): 101–110; Charles Urban Larson, "The Trust-Establishing Function of the Rhetoric of Black Power," *Central States Speech Journal* 21 (1970): 52–56; Robert D. Brooks, "Black

Power: The Dimensions of a Slogan," *Western Speech* 34 (1970): 108–114; Billy W. Reed and Peter E. Kane, "The Black Panther Speaks," *Today's Speech* 19 (1971): 55–56; Larry S. Richardson, "Stokely Carmichael: Jazz Artist," *Western Speech* 34 (1970): 212–218; Kathleen Eggerton Kendall, "The Rhetoric of the Civil-Rights Movement," *Today's Speech* 18 (1970): 49–50; Arthur Pollock, "Stokely Carmichael's New Black Rhetoric," *Southern Speech Communication Journal* 37 (1971): 92–94; Jack L. Daniel, "The Challenge of Blackness/Profiles in Black Power (Book)," *Quarterly Journal of Speech* 59 (1972): 367; and Robert L. Heath, "Dialectical Confrontation: A Strategy of Black Radicalism," *Central States Speech Journal* 24 (1973): 168–177.

42 Parke G. Burgess, "The Racial Crisis: Intolerable Conflict Versus Democratic Tolerance," *Quarterly Journal of Speech* 55 (1969): 318.

43 Burgess, "The Racial Crisis."

44 Robert L. Scott and Wayne Brockriede, "Hubert Humphrey Faces the 'Black Power' Issue," *The Speaker and Gavel* 4 (1966): 11–17; Robert L. Scott, "Justifying Violence: The Rhetoric of Militant Black Power," *Central States Speech Journal* 19 (1968): 96–104; and Robert L. Scott, "Black Power Bends Martin Luther King," *The Speaker and Gavel* 5 (1968): 80–86.

45 Karlyn Kohrs Campbell, "The Rhetoric of Radical Black Nationalism: A Case Study in Self-Conscious Criticism," *Central States Speech Journal* 22 (1971): 151–160.

46 Molefi K. Asante [Arthur L. Smith], *Rhetoric of Black Revolution* (Boston: Allyn and Bacon, 1969); Molefi K. Asante [Arthur L. Smith], "Henry Highland Garnet: Black Revolutionary in Sheep's Vestments," *Central States Speech Journal* 21 (1970): 93–98; Molefi K. Asante [Arthur L. Smith], "Markings of an African Concept of Rhetoric," *Today's Speech* 19 (1971): 13–18; Molefi K. Asante [Arthur L. Smith], "Some Characteristics of the Black Religious Audience," *Speech Monographs* 37 (1970): 207–210; and Molefi K. Asante [Arthur L. Smith] and Stephen Robb, *The Voice of Black Rhetoric: Selections* (Boston: Allyn and Bacon, 1971).

47 Molefi K. Asante [Arthur L. Smith], "Socio-Historical Perspectives of Black Oratory," *Quarterly Journal of Speech* 56 (1970): 264–269.

48 Cal M. Logue, "IV. Teaching Black Rhetoric," *Speech Teacher* 23 (1974): 115–120.

49 For a discussion of this shift see Melbourne S. Cummings, "The Profession and How it Relates to the Black Experience," *Association for Communication Administration Bulletin* 13 (1975): 27–28.

50 Cal M. Logue, "Rhetorical Ridicule of Reconstruction Blacks," *Quarterly Journal of Speech* 62 (1976): 400–409; Cal M. Logue, "The Rhetorical Appeals of Whites to Blacks During Reconstruction," *Communication Monographs* 44 (1977): 241–251; Cal M. Logue, "Transcending Coercion: The Communicative Strategies of Black Slaves on Antebellum Plantations," *Quarterly Journal of Speech* 67 (1981): 31–46; Cal M. Logue and Thurmon Garner, "Shifts in Rhetorical Status of Blacks After Freedom," *Southern Communication Journal* 54 (1988): 1–39; Cal M. Logue, and Eugene F. Miller, "Communicative Interaction and Rhetorical Status in Harriet Ann Jacobs' Slave Narrative," *Southern Communication Journal* 63 (1998): 182–198; and Cal M. Logue and Howard Dorgan, *A New Diversity in Contemporary Southern Rhetoric* (Baton Rouge: Louisiana State University Press, 1987).

51 See Cal M. Logue and Howard Dorgan, eds., *The Oratory of Southern Demagogues* (Baton Rouge: Louisiana State University Press, 1981); and Cal M. Logue, ed., *Eugene Talmadge: Rhetoric and Response* (New York: Greenwood Press, 1989).

52 Robert L. Heath, "A Time for Silence: Booker T. Washington in Atlanta," *Quarterly Journal of Speech* 64 (1978): 385–399; Karlyn Kohrs Campbell, "Style and Content in the Rhetoric of Early Afro-American Feminists," *Quarterly Journal of Speech* 72 (1986): 434–455; Andrew King, "Voice of Deliverance: The Language of Martin Luther King Jr. and Its Sources," *Rhetoric Society Quarterly* 22 (1992): 71–72; Edward C. Appel, "The Rhetoric of Dr. Martin Luther King, Jr.: Comedy and Context in Tragic Collision," *Western Journal of Communication* 61 (1997): 376–402; Shirley Logan, "Black Women on the Speaker's Platform (1832–1899)," in *Listening to Their Voices*, ed. Molly Wertheimer (Columbia: University of South Carolina Press, 1997), 151–173; Brian R. McGee, "Speaking About the Other: W. E. B. Du Bois Responds to the Klan," *Southern Communication Journal* 63 (1998): 208–219; and Angela G. Ray, "'In My Own Hand Writing': Benjamin Banneker Addresses the Slaveholder of Monticello," *Rhetoric & Public Affairs* 1 (1998): 387–405.

53 Michael C. Leff and Andrew Sachs, "Word the Most Like Things: Iconicity and the Rhetorical Text," *Western Journal of Communication* 54 (1990): 252–273; Michael C. Leff, "Interpretation and the Art of the Rhetorical Critic," *Western Journal of Speech Communication* 44 (1980): 237–249; and Michael C. Leff, "Textual Criticism: The Legacy of G. P. Mohrmann," *Quarterly Journal of Speech* 72 (1986): 377–389.

54 Michael Calvin McGee, "The 'Ideograph': A Link Between Rhetoric and Ideology," *Quarterly Journal of Speech* 66 (1980): 1–16; and Michael Calvin McGee, "Text, Context, and the Fragmentation of Contemporary Culture," *Western Journal of Communication* 54 (1990): 274–289.

55 Gaonkar, "Object and Method in Rhetorical Criticism."

56 Rosteck, "Form and Cultural Context in Rhetorical Criticism," 475.

57 Kirt H. Wilson, *The Reconstruction Desegregation Debate: The Politics of Equality and the Rhetoric of Place, 1870–1875* (East Lansing: Michigan State University Press, 2002). See also Kirt H. Wilson, "The Contested Space of Prudence in the 1874–1875 Civil Rights Debate," *Quarterly Journal of Speech* 84 (1998): 131–149; and Kirt H. Wilson, "Emerson, Transcendental Prudence, and the Legacy of Senator Charles Sumner," *Rhetoric & Public Affairs* 2 (1999): 453–479.

58 Kirt H. Wilson, "The Paradox of Lincoln's Rhetorical Leadership," *Rhetoric & Public Affairs* 3 (2000): 15–32.

59 Kirt H. Wilson, "The Problem With Public Memory: President Benjamin Harrison Confronts the 'Southern Question,'" in *Before the Rhetorical Presidency*, ed. Martin J. Medhurst (College Station: Texas A&M University Press, 2008), 265–288; Kirt H. Wilson, "The Politics of Place and Presidential Rhetoric in the United States, 1875–1901," in *Civil Rights Rhetoric and the American Presidency*, ed. James Arnt Aune and Enrique D. Rigsby (College Station: Texas A&M University Press, 2005), 16–40; and Wilson, "Emerson, Transcendental Prudence, and the Legacy of Senator Charles Sumner."

60 Kirt H. Wilson, "Towards a Discursive Theory of Racial Identity: The Souls of Black Folk as a Response to Nineteenth-Century Biological Determinism," *Western Journal of Communication* 63 (1999): 193–215.

61 Kirt H. Wilson, "Interpreting the Discursive Field of the Montgomery Bus Boycott: Martin Luther King Jr.'s Holt Street Address," *Rhetoric & Public Affairs* 8 (2005): 299–326; and Kirt H. Wilson, "Is There Interest in Reconciliation?" *Rhetoric & Public Affairs* 7 (2004): 367–377.

62 Robert J. Branham and W. Barnett Pearce, "Between Text and Context: Toward a Rhetoric of Contextual Reconstruction," *Quarterly Journal of Speech* 71 (1985): 19–36.

63 Branham, and Pearce, "Between Text and Context," 20.

64 I've reconstructed this story from the testimony of Mary and Simon Elder in *Affairs in the Insurrectionary States: Testimony taken by the Joint Select Committee to Inquire into the Condition of the Southern States, Georgia* (hereafter *AIS, Georgia*), vol. 2., pt. 7 (Washington, DC: Government Printing Office, 1872), 731–735. The Elders do not identify a specific date for the narrative.

65 Eric Foner, *Reconstruction: America's Unfinished Revolution, 1863–1877* (New York: Harper and Row, 1988), 430–431; Stewart E. Tolnay and E. M. Beck, *A Festival of Violence: An Analysis of Southern Lynchings, 1882–1903* (Urbana: University of Illinois Press), 4–6; and George C. Rable, *But There Was No Peace: The Role of Violence in the Politics of Reconstruction* (Athens: University of Georgia Press, 1984), 38–39, 53–58.

66 A Federal District Court indicted James von Brunn with first-degree murder, firing a gun in a federal building, and committing a "bias-motivated crime." The hate crime charges stemmed from von Brunn's documented history of racially motivated hate speech, his website HolyWesternEmpire.org, and evidence collected by federal agents. Several newspapers reported that von Brunn left a note in his car that declared: "The Holocaust is a lie. Obama was created by Jews. Obama does what his Jew owners tell him to do." Stephen Tyrone Johns was an African American guard whom von Brunn shot fatally in the upper chest as Johns opened the door to the museum building. See Theo Emery and Liz Robbins, "In Note, More Clues to Killing at Holocaust Museum," *New York Times*, June 12, 2009, A17; Associated Press, "Indictment In Shooting at Holocaust Museum," *New York Times*, July 30, 2009, A16; and Herb Boyd, "White Supremacist Slays Guard at Holocaust Museum," *New Amsterdam News*, June 18, 2009, 15, 28.

67 Mark Potok, "Editorial: Resurgence on the Right," *Intelligence Report*, www.splcenter. org/intel/intelreport/article.jsp?aid=1052 (accessed August 1, 2009).

68 Ambrose R. Wright, *AIS, Georgia*, 1: 265.

69 Wade Hampton, *Affairs in the Insurrectionary States: Testimony taken by the Joint Select Committee to Inquire into the Condition of the Southern States, South Carolina* (hereafter *AIS, South Carolina*), vol. 2 (Washington, DC: Government Printing Office, 1872), 1218–1219. See the speech of B. H. Hill, October 13, 1868, recorded in *AIS, Georgia*, 2: 792.

70 Aldrich, *AIS, South Carolina*, 1: 166.

71 Aldrich, *AIS, South Carolina*, 1: 167.

72 "Public Meetings," *Yorkville Enquirer*, April 6, 1871, in *AIS, South Carolina*, 3: 1542–1543.

73 Allen W. Trelease, *White Terror: The Ku Klux Klan Conspiracy and Southern Reconstruction* (New York: Harper and Row, 1971), 4.

74 Trelease, *White Terror*, 3–27; Rable, *But There Was No Peace*, 69–74; and Salley E. Hadden, *Slave Patrols: Law and Violence in Virginia and the Carolinas* (Cambridge, MA: Harvard University Press, 2001), 207–211.

75 Isham McCary, *AIS, South Carolina*, 1: 539.

76 For additional examples of this activity see Samuel Gaffney, *AIS, South Carolina*, 2: 603; Andrew Cathcart, *AIS, South Carolina*, 3: 1592; and Lucy McMillan, *AIS, South Carolina*, 2: 604–605.

77 Trelease, *White Terror*, 384–398; Rable, *But There Was No Peace*, 106–108; and W. R. Brock, "The Waning of Radicalism," in *Reconstruction: An Anthology of Revisionist Writings*, ed. Kenneth M. Stampp and Leon F. Litwack (Baton Rouge: Louisiana State University Press, 1969), 497.

78   See René Girard, *Violence and the Sacred*, trans. Patrick Gregory (Baltimore: Johns Hopkins University Press, 1972); and René Girard, *Things Hidden Since the Foundation of the World*, trans. Stephen Bann and Michael Metter (Stanford, CA: Stanford University Press, 1987).

79   Leo D. Lefebure, "Victims, Violence and the Sacred: The Thought of René Girard," *The Christian Century*, December 11, 1996, 113, 1226–1230.

80   Kirt H. Wilson, "The Racial Politics of Imitation in the Nineteenth Century," *Quarterly Journal of Speech* 89 (2003): 89–108.

81   These quotations appear in Foner, *Reconstruction*, 78.

82   Note that Stewart wrote these comments in 1831, but they weren't published until the Reconstruction era. Quoted in Carla L. Peterson, *"Doers of the Word": African-American Women Speakers and Writers in the North, 1830–1880* (New York: Oxford University Press, 1995), 13.

83   Thomas Allen, *AIS, Georgia*, 2, pt. 7: 610.

84   Allen, *AIS, Georgia*, 2, pt. 7: 607–608.

85   See Roderick P. Hart, "Contemporary Scholarship in Public Address: A Research Editorial," *Western Journal of Speech Communication* 50 (1986): 283–295; and Roderick P. Hart, "Doing Criticism My Way: A Response to Darsey," *Western Journal of Communication* 58 (1994): 308–312.

86   See David Zarefsky, "Knowledge Claims in Rhetorical Criticism," *Journal of Communication* 58 (2008): 634–637.

9

Lilies and Lavatory Paper
The Public and the Private in British Suffrage Archives

Cheryl R. Jorgensen-Earp

In the spring of 1912, Janie Terrero, a member of the Women's Social and Political Union (WSPU), the violent militants of the British women's suffrage movement, wrote the following letter to her husband (who was, himself, a suffrage activist):

> My dearest husband,
>
> Do not be very upset but I am going on the deputation. I sent up my name last Febry, after due consideration, but I could not tell you this as I know with your usual kindness and consideration for me you would want to go too, and this I could not allow. After what happened on the 10th of last Nov I feel my honour as a woman at stake and I must take up my stand with the rest. If I should get into Prison don't pay my fine, but let me go through with it properly ...
>
> With much love
>
> Yr. Affectt. Wife
> Janie[1]

Janie Terrero's letter to her husband is emblematic of the archival bits and pieces that lend so much meaning to the study of women's rhetoric. Such discourse immediately raises questions for those who prefer easy categorization: Is this, as it appears, simply a private letter? Because both of the Terreros were public activists, is this more properly considered a letter determining public strategy? Does Terrero's need to negotiate with her husband the details of her own public arrest and imprisonment suggest his control over her public actions? Do we see here an egalitarian relationship on a very modern level? Or, are these very concepts of public versus private more of a hindrance in the analysis of this letter and women's rhetoric in general?

The period from the eighteenth century through the opening years of the twentieth century poses particular challenges in the interpretation of women's public rhetoric. Although women's private influence on politics and culture had elements of polite fiction in the eighteenth century, the restrictions on women's public voice would only increase with the rise of the Industrial Revolution and increasing modernity. Under the "separate spheres" ideology increasingly codified at this time, men had dominion over the public sphere of politics and the world at large; women's reign was restricted to the private sphere of home and family.[2] Women speaking at the time of the "Cult of True Womanhood"[3] confronted a culture that hallowed women's public silence and presented such restraint as the necessary "trade-off" for the right of private influence.[4] As Karlyn Kohrs Campbell so succinctly puts it, "no 'true woman' could be a public persuader."[5] Because of the need to negotiate these constraints, women's public rhetoric during this time period cannot necessarily be taken at face value.

Thus, private documents, such as letters and diaries, take on greater importance in understanding the rhetoric of women from the late eighteenth through the early twentieth centuries. In recent scholarship, the private writings of nineteenth-century women, particularly letters between activist women, have been studied as a "transitional space" that "bridged their public and private lives."[6] Such private writings are even more important as interpretive tools, however, for they allow us to read more closely the public texts of women's speaking and writing. Yet, some rhetorical theorists are now calling into question the continued division of rhetoric into public/private dimensions and have examined the impact of that dichotomy on textual analysis.[7] These new theoretical perspectives on the modern public/private distinction are welcome, but they do little to resolve the interpretive problems associated with analyzing women's discourse from the era of separate spheres.

After examining some of the recent challenges and correctives to separate spheres and the public/private distinction, I will argue for the analytical value of both concepts when used in a revised form. Although the separation of men and women into respective public and private realms does not adequately reflect the realities of nineteenth-century life, the concept itself had pervasive influence at the time. It is important to understand the discursive power of separate spheres while avoiding its use as a template for the actual lives of women. So, too, the distinction between public and private retains its usefulness but only when applied in a flexible manner. With that goal of flexibility in mind, I will present three different conceptualizations of the public/private distinction. The first presents the familiar idea that private interactions bolster public rhetoric, uniting both aspects in a two-sided fashion. The active interplay between distinct public and private realms remains a useful concept when analyzing some archival material. The second conceptualization of public and private intertwines the two in a manner more reflective of women's lives. When relational concerns intermingle with political efforts, private and public become not merely indivisible but often indistinguishable. Attempting to pry these aspects apart only gives a false sense of separation and complicates the analysis of archival texts. Such texts must be read *in situ*, with sensitivity to the realities of the lives they describe. Finally, the third conceptualization moves the concept of private to an interior realm and considers those archival materials that reveal the subject's deepest thoughts and emotions. These very private deliberations may also be publicly reflected in a woman's speaking, writing, and actions. Because self-reflection is so complex, it is this third approach that requires the most interpretive flexibility and sensitivity.

This essay uses the private writings of British suffrage activists during the early twentieth century to illustrate these three conceptualizations and how private archival materials might shed light on the public rhetoric of women activists. Although the act of women speaking in public was at that point neither new nor particularly controversial in itself, the dominant images of the New Woman were simple variations on True Womanhood.[8] In their public rhetoric, activist women were dealing with these old images while also determining the extent to which they would participate in new militant forms of protest rhetoric. The decision to court arrest, undergo hunger strikes and forcible feeding, or escalate into the violence of arson and bombings was often discussed privately with friends, family, and fellow activists. The nuance provided by these sometimes surprising private documents lends depth to an interpretation of the suffragist's public words and actions. In terms of critical theory, these private texts, as one element embedded in the larger context, become an important aid in textual analysis.

A Slippery Dichotomy

Although the influence of "True Womanhood," and its constraints on women's rhetoric in the public sphere, has been firmly established in historical and rhetorical studies, a challenge to this understanding recently began on two fronts. The first challenge specifically concerns the separate spheres ideology and whether industrialization actually brought about a substantially new concept of gender roles. The enhancement of gender differences by the nineteenth century into what became known as the separate spheres ideology has been attributed to any number of influences from the Evangelical Revival to the portrayal of women in novels.[9] In an important 1987 study, Leonore Davidoff and Catherine Hall ascribe the emergence of this concept to "a time of exceptional turmoil and threatening economic and political disorder." As industrialization changed the landscape of home and work, "[a] heavily gendered view of the world was utilized to soften, if not disavow, the disruption of a growing class system."[10] Most researchers follow Davidoff and Hall's lead in attributing a more codified sense of gender roles to industrialization, urbanization, and the rise of a distinct middle class. Others, like Thomas Laqueur, argue that additional issues, such as new understandings of female physiology and sexuality, changed gender roles at that time.[11]

Perhaps the most intriguing of all the explanations for the increased reification of separate gender roles comes almost as a side note in Jürgen Habermas's discussion of the rise of the public sphere. Habermas describes the growing popularity in the eighteenth century of coffee houses as sites of public discussion, first about the arts, and then about politics, economics, and a whole host of other public concerns.

At the same time, the coffee houses opened this interchange to "the wider strata of the middle class, including craftsmen and shopkeepers." Then, in what almost seems like a throwaway comment, Habermas mentions "the fact that only men were admitted to coffee-house society ... whereas the style of the *salon* ... was essentially shaped by women. Accordingly the women of London society, abandoned every evening, waged a vigorous but vain struggle against the new institution."[12] Habermas, in acknowledging women's exclusion, frames it as a social loss in terms of being left behind at home, not in terms of their exclusion from the civic conversation. Yet, the rise of public spaces based on gender exclusivity (coffee houses and men's clubs, for example) provided a norm of women's absence that sought its own explanation in the new ideology. Probably all of these influences played a role. Most significantly, however, this hardening ideology promised stability in the private lives of both genders at a time of change and expansion in the public affairs of men.

In 1993, Amanda Vickery mounted a challenge to the idea "that sometime between 1650 and 1850 the public/private distinction was constituted or radically reconstituted in a way that transformed relations between the sexes."[13] Pointing to the idea that there "have always been separate spheres of gender power," Vickery saw more continuity between the nineteenth century and previous eras than she saw differences. What Vickery disputed was *not* that the rhetoric of public and private spheres had "currency" in Victorian society, but that this duality constituted nineteenth-century society in a unique way.[14] Robert Shoemaker, in examining the period from 1650 to 1850, agrees with Vickery that there were "far more continuities in gender roles" than are generally acknowledged by historians. Unlike Vickery, however, Shoemaker maintains that "gender differences *were* more sharply divided" by the end of this 200-year period than at the beginning and these divisions had an impact on the development of public life.[15] As Shoemaker states:

> The public sphere thus expanded in gendered ways, in the sense that older ideas of the respective duties and virtues of men and women were used to determine how new public activities would be gendered. These expectations were not new, but as a result of the growing importance of public life they did become more manifest.[16]

Although it is safe to acknowledge its continuity with gender roles from preceding centuries, the hardening of the "separate spheres" categories had a clear prescriptive weight, influencing gendered expectations wherever they fell in terms of the public and private divide.

Even though the term "sphere" was increasingly used during the nineteenth century, it is clearly wrong to envision a complete separation whereby women were somehow locked away in their homes. The strength of the "cult of domesticity"[17] should never be taken to imply that women and men were banned from each other's presence, for the "spheres were never truly separate, certainly not physically."[18] Nor were men purely political/public/economic masters; they also carried their control (backed by the weight of law) into the private sphere. The concept that women were queens of their private realms (as Ruskin and other nineteenth-century writers would have it) was an artificial, if poetic, sop at a time when women were not even the legal guardians of their own children.[19] The notion of separate spheres was always more metaphor than reality, promising women a theoretical domain of control and power that was denied them politically. Therefore, separate spheres was not so much a spatial distinction as a set of "separate duties" and gendered expectations of different behavior[20] – duties and expectations that reinforced women's exclusion from Habermas's public sphere.

Jennifer Jones, writing from a French historical perspective, claims that only women of a certain class "were objects of male anxiety," and certainly the propriety of middle- and upper-class women was of primary concern.[21] Poor women worked to survive (as they always have and always will), largely ignored by the fads and philosophies of gendered expectations. As Mary Ryan claims, working-class women entered public areas as a matter of course (giving lie to the term "public women" as a designation reserved for prostitutes). Many working-class women spent their lives serving behind the scenes (in kitchens, sculleries, and laundries) in the private domains of the upper class, positions that confound easy designation as public or private work. Thus, Ryan is right to call "the conflation of womanhood and privacy a fiction that is most meaningful to the emergent middle classes of the nineteenth century."[22] Particularly in the United States, race also influenced gender expectations, and concerns for female propriety were generally restricted to white women. Yet, Maria Miller Stewart and other black activist women discovered that when they attempted to adopt a public persona, they also were pressured to remain in the private sphere.[23] Although women were found in a multitude of supposedly public spaces, their exclusion was most clearly enforced in the "magisterial public sphere," which encompassed the state, the law, and the agencies surrounding these key areas.[24] Thus, the assault on the separate spheres dichotomy, when it came in an organized form, was directed at this magisterial public sphere and focused upon the central issue of the vote.

Several researchers have posited the notion of a "social sphere" as a corrective to the hard-and-fast boundaries between the private and the public spheres. Denise Riley, for example, identifies an "arena for domesticated intervention" that she argues "blurred the ground between the public and the private." This space, defined as social rather than public, allowed women to participate in work for the betterment of society without deviating from the expectation that they perform private duties.[25] Although often demeaned during the period as "playing Lady Bountiful," women were expected to reach out to the poor and destitute as part of their moral influence and good works in the private sphere.[26] By assigning charity and social welfare to women, it was easier for men to ignore these concerns as responsibilities of the public and legal sphere. Women's experiences with charity work opened their eyes to problems of the poor, primarily women and children, which convinced them of their own efficacy and provided the entering wedge for their public work in various reform movements.

In a very intriguing study (and one with implications for this current essay), Karen Hansen also describes a social sphere that better reflected the "fluidity of activity" in real women's lives.[27] By using sociability as the descriptor of the way males and females interacted, built communities, and conducted necessary business to maintain those communities, Hansen seeks a way around what she calls the "flawed but tenacious theoretical framework" of the separate spheres.[28] Adding the category of "social" to her historical analysis, Hansen broadens the framework of the private/public dichotomy, so often criticized as inadequate to "address the broad experiences of white and free black working-class and farm women."[29] This concept of sociability – the notion of a social sphere – opens up for analysis the behavior of minority community activism that in some ways cuts across issues of gender. Used carefully, it also could reveal the "backstage" behavior of women of substance, who used their familial ties to leading public men, and their access to those men in social settings, to exert influence over public affairs.[30]

To question the reality in practice of a hard-and-fast separation between the private and public spheres is not to deny the distinction's primacy in the mental universe of the nineteenth century. Its precepts provided the underlying morality portrayed in art and fiction.[31] Talk of spheres and True Womanhood and overt appeals to these concepts pervaded the rhetoric of both men and women of the time – not only of those applauding the ideal but also of those seeking its reform in the political arena. Even though various forms of this ideology were clearly in play until (and even after) World War I, modern analysts need to be wary of its blandishments. The initial challenge for analysts is to avoid falling into the trap of uncritically imposing this artificial template in the study of women's lives and the archival records they left behind.

The second challenge to our understanding of women's rhetoric at this time is closely related and concerns the usefulness of *any* public/private dichotomy (not simply separate spheres) as a tool for analysis. As Jane Lewis points out, the public/private distinction is not synonymous with the concept of separate spheres,[32] even though the separate spheres ideology drew with darker lines a philosophy of gender differences that has been in play across time and culture. Despite common concerns over the "contested category" of public/private,[33] the perceived differences continue to be put forward as an analytical tool in both historical and contemporary studies. Challengers of this dichotomy use remarkably similar language in their critiques. Leonore Davidoff, Mary Ryan, and Alan Wolfe all use the term "slippery" to describe these categories.[34] Joe Bailey follows the same line of attack by describing how "the two terms construct each other and discursively shift and slide in use."[35] To Susan Gal, the boundary between public and private is "labile and 'shifty,'"[36] a description echoed in some ways by Sandra Graham, who considers this boundary "blurred" and these "categories of opposition" as ones that "quickly dissolve into less tidy, more complex, and illuminating zones of action, strategy, or negotiation."[37] As Jean Bethke Elshtain puts it, "Public and private are categories that bleed into one another. Neither is wholly self-contained, neither stable."[38]

Without belaboring a challenge mounted on many fronts, there are clear difficulties in using public and private as hard-and-fast categories or in granting them the type of stability that comes from conceptualizing them spatially. The question then becomes, do we abandon these categories in our analysis of archival materials? My answer is "no," for if we treat them not as static but in a dialectic interplay, as Mary Ryan suggests, the public/private distinction is "analogous to other useful conceptual pairs, such as the individual versus the collective, home versus work, the intimate versus the anonymous, the free market versus the state."[39] As Ryan explains, the public/private distinction, like other such dichotomous categories, is analytically useful only when "carefully and intensively applied," and it may "become especially germane during specific times and places."[40] Thus, if carefully deployed, the distinction can still help shed light on the rhetoric of early women activists.

Susan Gal provides a particularly intriguing recovery of the public and private by viewing them as "indexical signs," replacing a sense of domains or "spheres of activity" with an understanding of this dichotomy "as a discursive phenomenon." Still more usefully, Gal sees the public/private dichotomy as a "fractal distinction" that is capable of being projected on any number of situations or spaces, thus categorizing (and then recategorizing) them into relatively more or less public or private. What seems an initially strange concept is really quite useful when applied as Gal suggests. Gal uses the American home as an example of private space, divided as it is from the public street. Yet within that house are areas considered more public (living room, entry hall) and those considered more private (bedrooms and bathrooms). Gal further notes how even the supposedly public areas within the house, such as a living room, might be made private in parts by a grouping of chairs, or by "[t]he whispered aside, the confidential turn of bodies toward each other."[41] Viewing the nineteenth-century home in this way, the public doorstep that women would take such care to whiten becomes reframed as an indexical sign of private morality, a "visible manifestation of respectability."[42]

Gal's "nested" view of public and private (like Russian matryoshka dolls, where wooden dolls of decreasing size are contained one inside the other) points up the perceptual nature of what is public and what is private. Gal gives numerous examples of fractal reframing that distinguishes the public from the private. One of the best examples concerns women who self-define as "stay at home moms" despite making impressive earnings through Mary Kay or Avon. Gal thus fights the tendency to overlook the "public inside a private or private inside a public," to ignore more subtle distinctions and to further reify the broader public/private dichotomy.[43] This concept of "nesting" provides a valuable framework, particularly when examining rhetoric where the speaker is actively renegotiating cultural expectations arising out of the public/private distinction. For example, British militant suffrage leader Emmeline Pankhurst's early speeches framed voting (clearly a public act) as neo-traditional – as a new means for women to fulfill their private duties. Even the female anti-suffragists were forced onto the public stage to stem the rising tide of public opinion for women's suffrage. Through a dance of self-deprecation, complete with protestations of their reluctance to speak and men to preside over meetings as stage-dressing, anti-suffrage women redefined the public stage.[44] The public podium was reframed as the outer boundary of the private, forming a necessary barricade where women speakers stood only to prevent the encroachment of public affairs into the sphere of home and family. As Gal would put it, such a move

allowed female anti-suffragists, undertaking the very public functions they condemned in others, "to deny that anything really drastic had been done."[45]

So, even as we recognize the limitations of public/private, we end up embracing
the concept in an altered guise, admitting that it still has something to teach us.
In the remainder of this essay, I will examine some of the archival material dealing
with the British suffrage movement and discuss various approaches to that material
from a more flexible and nuanced public/private framework. Women of that time did
not experience their lives with an artificial line separating the public from the private;
nor, as Lisa Gring-Pemble has argued, did they "simply cross from one realm into the
other."[46] The private and public lives of these women flowed together in much the
same way as they do in the lives of modern women. A framework that makes a hard-
and-fast distinction between public and private spheres, when deployed by modern
rhetorical critics, may inhibit textual analysis of women's early rhetoric. This essay will
argue that the actual impact of the private on a woman's public rhetoric was far more
interstitial, occurring in the close spaces where personal life joined public activity.

Public/Private in British Suffrage Activism

There is a value to examining a period where old expectations were being questioned and where the hardened ideology of separate spheres appeared to be crumbling. Despite the sense of new possibilities associated with the advent of the
twentieth century, the gendered public/private distinction continued to form the
basis of much public rhetoric. A surprising variety of archival material from this
period of the British suffrage movement is housed, among other places, in The
Women's Library (formerly the Fawcett Library) of London Metropolitan University
and in the Suffragette Fellowship Collection at the Museum of London. This material was saved not only because it reflected events integral to these activists' personal
lives, but also because these women knew they were making history. Although
World War I interrupted the suffrage work of some organizations, others continued
non-stop until the franchise was won in 1918, for women over the age of 30.

After the vote was achieved and the war had ended, the Suffragette Fellowship,
composed primarily of erstwhile militant suffragettes of the WSPU, became the
group most responsible for preserving archival material and constructing the public memory of the suffrage campaign. The WSPU, founded by Emmeline Pankhurst
in 1903, was noteworthy as the only suffrage organization to institute a policy of
violence against property and to adopt the name "suffragette," a diminutive originally coined as an insult by the *Daily Mail*.[47] Although non-militants also belonged
to the Fellowship, the organization's ardent work in promoting a particular view of
the suffrage campaign was responsible for Pankhurst's statue in the entry to Victoria
Tower Gardens beside Parliament.[48] It also accounts for the primacy of Pankhurst
generally as the symbol of suffrage in British memory, even though Millicent
Garrett Fawcett led the largest suffrage organization, the National Union of
Women's Suffrage Societies (NUWSS).[49] Despite this post-victory attention

lavished on Pankhurst's WSPU, there is quite a remarkable collection of letters and other documents housed in The Women's Library belonging to Fawcett and the other prominent activists and societies involved in the long struggle for the vote.

In discussing the influence of the public/private dichotomy on interpreting archival material, I will examine what is merely a handful of documents from the vast collection housed at The Women's Library and the Museum of London. It is important to state that I am not trying to impose an analytical template upon these materials; in fact, the point of this essay is that there *is* no template when analyzing private lives and their influence on the public rhetoric of women during this period. Instead, I want to discuss three different layers of analysis, beginning with the most apparent use of public and private, in order to shake off any restrictions wrought by this dichotomy while retaining the dialectical interplay of these categories whenever analytically useful.

The familiar dichotomy

The first category of archival materials we might consider consists of those private documents that directly illuminate public rhetoric (whether discursive rhetoric, such as a public speech or public letter, or extra-discursive rhetoric such as a protest march). This type of archival material reveals the private underpinnings to clearly public events. Here, we can truly see public and private as two sides of the same coin, as the private appears as facilitator of the more visible public moment. Michael Calvin McGee provides the fresher public/private metaphor of two sides, invoking the image of a sound recording which is impossible to split in half in order to "hold a 'hit single' in each hand."[50] Many of the letters between colleagues in the Old Feminist and the suffrage movement fall into this category. Gring-Pemble writes about how the act of letter writing served to create a consciousness-raising space that predated the initial activism of female reformers.[51] Letters between suffrage leaders, some friends but many merely compatriots in the same cause, take on the feel of military leaders planning strategy, as they discuss the logistics of the campaign. On May 18, 1903, for example, Susan B. Anthony wrote to Millicent Garrett Fawcett, who had been active in the British suffrage movement since 1867, to entice her to come to the United States on behalf of the cause:

> … Dear Mrs. Fawcett, do you not ever intend coming to this country? …
>
> You need to do this for the sake of American women. Will you not come over? It isn't enough for any of us simply to work at home. We can do a great deal more sometimes, for home, by going away and telling other people about ourselves. So do come over. Dear Mrs. Maclaren can never come and if you do not come pretty soon you will be saying that you are too old to travel. It is nothing to come across the ocean now.
>
> Affectionately your friend and co-worker,
>
> Susan B. Anthony[52]

This is a private letter but only nominally so. Anthony knew Fawcett personally from her earlier trips to London, and she clearly felt entitled to request a return visit. However, any apparent warmth in the letter appears to reflect zeal for the cause more than personal affection. What comes through from studying this letter is the campaign strategy of internationalizing the cause and the tenacious efforts of Anthony in her behind-the-scenes development of that strategy.

There are private letters that, while direct reflections on public rhetoric, are more revealing of private emotions, sometimes ones that surprise the writer as well as the reader. In 1909, a quite famous debate took place in London during which Millicent Fawcett thoroughly trounced the novelist and anti-suffragist Mrs. Humphry Ward (Mary Augusta Ward). Following the debate, American suffragist Carrie Chapman Catt, who had been present for the event, wrote to Millicent Fawcett with her impressions. After giving her sense of the audience seated near her and her belief that even anti-suffragist men were touched by Fawcett's presentation, Catt continued:

> I am a cold old icicle, and do not know how to gush, but I would like to do so, just to let you really know how proud I was of you that night. ... The comparison [with Ward] to all who have sense to see it was infinitely to your advantage. I am so grateful that you have lived and be, and that you still are. Accept my admiration, and if you will my love as well, for it is yours.[53]

This is hardly the Carrie Chapman Catt portrayed as a hide-bound old fogey in the movie *Iron-Jawed Angels* (HBO, 2004). Her energy and enthusiasm at this moment of her writing can scarcely be contained within the constraints of an otherwise formal letter.

The image of private as the flip side of the public coin is bolstered with certain archival materials, particularly when aspects of the private are manipulated for public benefit. In the Suffragette Fellowship Collection there is a brief letter from Ada Flatman to Jane Warton. Dated January 14, 1910, it reads in its entirety:

> Dear Miss Warton,
>
> Just a line to welcome you to Liverpool, thought you would like to know we are holding a demonstration at Walton gaol tonight at 7:45 if you can join us there we shall be glad as we want our protest to be heard by the brave women inside.
>
> Yours very sincerely,
>
> Miss Ada Flatman [54]

This is an unremarkable letter until the reader realizes that it sets up one of the most notable events in the suffrage campaign. Miss Warton did not actually exist. She was the creation of Lady Constance Lytton, a WSPU member of high birth and chronic ill health. These factors of nobility combined with a bad heart had conspired to prevent "Lady Con" from participating fully in the rigors of the militant campaign. When arrested with her colleagues during WSPU demonstrations, she was held separately and released early rather than being allowed to participate in a hunger strike or be forcibly fed. She always suspected that her title had more to do with her special treatment than her "ticky" heart.

To test this belief that class influenced the treatment of suffrage activists, Lady Con invented Jane Warton, a "spinster seamstress" who fulfilled all the stereotypes of the militant suffragette. An unattractive hair style, drooping tweed hat, spectacles, and other props provided an effective disguise for the frail and attractive Lady Lytton. "Jane Warton" wrote to Ada Flatman and arranged a trip to Liverpool to participate with suffrage activists in a demonstration. At this demonstration, Warton symbolically threw a stone, thus forcing her arrest and leading to her imprisonment, hunger strike, and forcible feeding. The fact that working-class Jane Warton was forcibly fed while Lady Constance was not (despite both being tested by doctors and both obviously possessing the same heart) was a great scandal at the time. Lytton wrote of her prison experiences and spoke about them in a public speech at the Queen's Hall.[55] Although her aims were positive and her strategy for uncovering class bias (while garnering attention for the suffrage cause) was quite brilliant, it cannot be glossed over that Lytton was fooling more than the government and prison establishment. Ada Flatman was far from a "nobody" in the suffrage ranks, yet she was privately duped and used for larger public purposes. It is unclear why Lytton opted not to take her own colleagues into her confidence and include them in her plans. For the purposes of this essay, however, the point is that this deception – whatever the motivation behind it – is revealed by a type of archival material rooted in the public/private dichotomy. This letter, with its private discussion of public events, comes closest to realizing Erving Goffman's concept of "backstage" behavior fueling the events "frontstage."[56]

Intertwined realms

This concept of the public/private dichotomy, however, does not begin to meet the analytical/interpretive challenges presented by some of the other materials encountered in these archives. For these Edwardian women, the pressures of family and the sense of what they owed those who loved them could not easily be compartmentalized into a "private" realm. Even the corrective of a social sphere (although opening up a valuable arena of male/female interaction that is often overlooked) does not adequately reflect the lived experience of these women working for a public cause. They did not experience their lives divided into segments. Instead, their experiences were interconnected with others in complex relationships of family, friends, and colleagues. This is where a spatial concept of public and private proves most inadequate as a critical tool. Even if this unseen "boundary" is admitted to be porous – even if this space is accepted as liminal – such a metaphor cannot capture the twisted interweaving of relationships in every area of people's lives.

This complexity is particularly clear in familial exchanges where (in a reversal of the old second-wave feminist phrase) the political is personal. It is in this category that I would place the letter from Janie Terrero quoted at the beginning of this chapter.

Terrero's initial letter telling of her decision to protest and to face almost certain imprisonment was followed by another cheerful letter on March 2, 1912, written after her arrest on March 1 for breaking three large windows on Oxford Street:

> Dearest Husband – Do not worry. I am quite all right & we are to refuse bail, so I suppose I shall be sent to Prison today on remand or on custody ... Do be cheerful & brave or it will make it harder for me –
>
> Fondest love & kisses & take care of yourself –
>
> Yr. devoted wife,
> Janie[57]

These letters, with their expressions of genuine affection and worry for the other's welfare, cannot be adequately analyzed by a formula playing private and public interests against each other. There are layers of personal concern here (poorly hidden under a breezy air) vying with deep respect for the other's autonomy, a situation where decisions to act publicly are tied up in the values of relationship and in the ethics of care.

This entwining of lives is perhaps most clear in a series of letters between Millicent Garrett Fawcett and her sister Elizabeth Garrett Anderson. Anderson was as remarkable as her sister, if not more so. She was the first woman qualified as a doctor in Britain and also the first female mayor of a British city. The letters between these brilliant activist women were very warm, addressed to "Dearest Milly" and "My Dearest Eth," and concluded with "Yr Ever Loving" or "Your ever affec. Sis." However, both women followed these affectionate phrases with initials or formal names ("E G Anderson") as signatures, indications perhaps of a more formal time or simply the number of letters each woman wrote in a day.

The most fascinating aspect of the relationship between Fawcett and Anderson was their membership in suffrage organizations with very different views of activism. As mentioned previously, Fawcett was the head of the NUWSS, the largest suffrage organization and one that was determinedly constitutional and nonmilitant in its approach. Anderson and her daughter, Louisa Garrett Anderson, instead became members of the WSPU, the militant suffrage organization led by Emmeline Pankhurst. These differing affiliations, not surprisingly, reflected differences of opinion on proper strategy in attaining the vote. Their letters nonetheless represented a lively and warm mix of details about their life and work. For example, it is great fun to read Anderson's letter discussing multiple matters with her sister, only to have her stop midstream to insert this frank jab at Mrs. Humphry Ward: "I shd like to wring Mrs. H W's neck."[58] And during "Black Friday," the deputation to Parliament on November 18, 1910, which ended with WSPU members being beaten and sexually mauled by police, Anderson wrote to her sister to allay her fears. On a small postcard addressed to Millicent Fawcett, Anderson scribbled: "All right so far. LGA [Louisa] is staying on to the end but is returning an hour or more later. About 70 arrested. Alan [Garrett Anderson, her son] turned up at the moment he was wanted & steered me thro the crowd. All are rather hungry & cold but nothing worse."[59] Of course, the situation was not as benign as Anderson suggested. During "Black Friday," many women sustained serious injuries, and the veneer of civility and respect was torn away, changing the dynamic of the entire suffrage campaign.[60]

The pair of letters that best illustrate the difficulty of unraveling personal relations from public events was written a year later, following the WSPU's turn to violence against property. In November 1911, the government introduced an unsought bill extending universal suffrage to men, in lieu of a popular bill giving the vote to some women. The action was widely viewed by suffrage activists as a betrayal of trust. The WSPU responded with a window-breaking demonstration on the streets of London, marking the start of an ongoing strategy of violent militancy. On December 3, 1911, Fawcett wrote to her sister. She opened her letter to "My Dearest Eth" by describing the WSPU strategy as "a very big blunder." She then stated that "we shall lose no opportunity of discussing it and making people understand that we condemn it." Of course, such condemnation could have the effect of splitting the suffrage movement into factions, and Fawcett added, "It is horrid to have to do it, but I feel there is no choice." To this point, the letter was business-like and could have been a letter between colleagues rather than sisters. Then, Fawcett eased her way to the heart of the matter and the true impetus for her writing:

> Mr. Brailsford's article in The Englishwoman which I am sending you is a fair state-ment of the political outlook. He cannot be accused of want of sympathy with the militants but he has kept his head and has a first hand knowledge of political condi-tions & prospects. I hope we shant drift apart over this but I believe the chances of this misfortune (which w' be a very great loss to me) are less if we are quite frank and open with one another.[61]

The movement to her final sentence was so seamless that Fawcett almost seemed to be referring to her relationship with Brailsford. But, of course, her fear was that this rift between organizations could easily become a rift between sisters. If Brailsford "kept his head," would her sister do the same? If Brailsford could not be accused of lacking sympathy for the militants, would her own sister level that accu-sation against Fawcett?

The answer would come the very next day from Elizabeth Anderson. That letter, dated December 4, 1911, read:

> Dearest Milly
>
> I am quite with you about WSPU. I think they are quite wrong. I wrote to Mrs. Pankhurst before [scratched out] (no I think it was the day after) the demonstra-tion but she took no notice. I have now told her I can go no more with them. It is dreadfully sad to have to be divided but I cannot help it.
>
> Your loving S
>
> E G Anderson[62]

Yet what united the sisters philosophically came to divide mother and daughter. Louisa Garrett Anderson would remain with the WSPU and participate in the full round of violent actions, imprisonment, hunger strikes, and forcible feedings. This did not sever the ties or strain the deep love between them, but it would cause Elizabeth Anderson great anxiety for her "Louie." In early 1913, as the violence accelerated toward arson and bombings, Anderson's fears for her daughter were clearly evident in a letter to Fawcett: "I thought my poor dear Louie looked very anguished when we parted & I fear they will try to get her to do something horrid, & that she will feel she cannot refuse!"[63] In this exchange of letters, there is no clear distinction between private and public. In interpreting this type of archival material, it is more useful to let go of the image of private (backstage) concerns motivating public (frontstage) action. Private lives, familial ties, political strategizing, group motivations, and public action all flow together, as if linked together by unseen ligaments in a single body. One part affects another, although the lines of influence run in multiple directions and are sometimes manifested in surprising, subtle ways.

A level deeper

Finally, another approach, sometimes needed when analyzing these materials, hints at the deepest thoughts, feelings, dreams, and inspirations of the archival subjects. If considered against the old dichotomy, these archival materials speak of an interior space that transcends the concept of privacy. Often revealed to family members through private letters (or in journal/diary entries addressed to the writer's reflective self), this is the most intimate realm, yet one that is sometimes displayed in public spectacle. It is also a dangerous area for interpretation, for the attempt at analysis often smacks of naïve psychoanalysis, often of a long-dead subject. Yet, in studying a reform movement such as suffrage, and particularly the British militants, it is vital to tap into a deeper level of motivation if one hopes to fully understand the visible deed. This was a movement that relied heavily upon "body rhetoric,"[64] with participants risking their health and even their lives for the sake of the cause. In order to understand their choices, we must look for that elusive "something" in the archives that might help explain such depth of devotion. And the meaning behind certain archival items may only yield to a frankly speculative approach.

Much has been written about the rigors of forcible feeding, a process instituted by the British government in response to the hunger strikes of suffrage activists seeking status as political prisoners. The suffragettes' accounts of being pinned down by wardresses while a tube was forced through nose or mouth (even when nasal passages were swollen and blocked or teeth were clenched) were detailed and quite harrowing. Sometimes the tube went astray into the lungs, and the contents poured into the prisoner's stomach were often vomited back while the process was still ongoing. There were reportedly even attempts to feed by way of tubes inserted into the vagina or rectum, making inescapable the analogy with rape.[65] Forcible feeding was a violation of the physical body, but it also was a violation of the psyche and deepest emotions of the prisoner – a complete loss of control over one's own body. There was no lack of public talk about such controversial treatment of what were, after all, British citizens. Only rarely was the deeper impact on the women examined, however, and that discussion was mainly in the religious, poetic speeches and writings of Lady Constance Lytton. Lytton was surprisingly forthcoming about her thoughts and fears before, during, and after her feeding as "Jane Warton." She even chronicled her efforts to overcome the hatred she felt toward the prison staff and doctors. Her public accounts are paeans to self-actualization and the ability of the higher self to overcome the revulsion and hatred of a baser instinct.[66]

Archival materials reveal Lytton working through her emotions prior to imprisonment. One of the most interesting is a letter written prior to her first arrest in 1909 and addressed to her mother. As she wrote this letter, Lytton could not know that she would be released this time without sharing in the forcible feedings that awaited her colleagues. True, this is a letter to a close relative and could easily be analyzed in terms of either the public/private dichotomy or the intertwined relationships discussed earlier in this chapter. For example, in her letter to "My angel Mother," Lytton negotiated the public nature of her acts with the one most affected privately. This relational consideration is very clear when she wrote, "My darling Muddy, you will never know, I trust, the pain it is to have to do this thing without your sympathy and help – with on the contrary, the certainty that it shocks you and hurts you and makes you suffer in numberless ways." But this is also a letter written on another level, one that functions more intimately. Lytton wrote, "If you ever see this letter it will mean that, after joining the deputation, I have been arrested and shall not see you again until I have been to Holloway." This is, therefore, a "hypothetical" letter, written with a particular audience in mind but only to be read under specific projected circumstances. It most closely resembles in-the-event-of-my-death letters left by parents for their small children to be read at a later date.[67]

In this letter, written to be read (or perhaps never to be read) by her mother, it is sometimes as if Lytton were writing to herself. She reached to articulate beliefs that she was still formulating and strained to put her deepest fears and desires into words. Perhaps freed by the knowledge that she was not writing a letter to send but one that could be put in abeyance indefinitely, portions of Lytton's letter have the texture of an especially frank diary entry. She spoke of her deepening interest in prisons as her "hobby," revealing that, "It's my journeying after the hobby that sucks up my soul like a tide. My Nile-sources, my Thibet, my Ruvenzori."[68] The concern "gradually awakening in me over the fate of prisoners" had grown over time "till now the thought of them, the yearning after them, turns in me and tugs at me as vitally and irrepressibly as ever a physical child can call upon its Mother." This articulation of her deepest passion is matched by her confession of her greatest fear: that the bodily weakness she had grappled with all her life would betray her best efforts. Thus, she combined concern, hope, and longing, allowing them to burst out in a loving appeal:

> I am no hero but the thought of other travellers' much worse privations on that road will, I believe, fizzle up my flimsy body enough for what is necessary, and if only I knew you were helping me in your heart, I <u>know</u> I should not, could not fail, Muddy darling.

Here Lytton seemingly was telling herself (as well as her mother) well-meaning lies. Although apparently glossing her knowledge of prisons with a pleasant fantasy ("In my little warm cupboard nest in Holloway my only thought of the outer world will be of you"[69]), Lytton's presentiment of what was to come still hovered around her words. In fact, she was knowingly venturing down a path that could and did lead to physical pain, the collapse of her health, and ultimately an early death. This document is not merely a rhetorical letter functioning in the private sphere, but a window into the thoughts and motivations of a very brave woman weighing personal risk against the public gain she sought for others.

And what are we, as rhetorical analysts, to make of one particular movement relic turned over to the Suffragette Fellowship many years ago by suffragist Teresa Billington-Grieg? It is a bit of folded brown paper, originally coarse but softened by age, with a faded message written in pencil. This was a letter surreptitiously written in 1910 on a piece of lavatory paper by the actress Sime Seruya and smuggled out in the shoe of an ordinary prisoner who was being released. Its very substance speaks of the most intimate and personal bodily functions and of the routine denial of privacy, autonomy, and dignity. Yet it became a communicative link – a message in a bottle to the outer world – which gave outsiders some sense of life inside Holloway and made the prisoners more visible. Much of the letter concerned plans for the green, white, and gold fair (a fundraiser by the nonviolent militants of the Women's Freedom League) to be held for the suffrage cause and addressed such mundane concerns as the design for scarves and the plans for a mock cell as an exhibit. Yet the letter ended on a personal note: "Beastly being cooped in a cell – oh so vilely cold – no fear of breaking any windows whilst I am here. The earliest that I can get out of this hell ... is March 26th that is if I am very good and don't get found out."[70] Few things could tell us more clearly of Seruya's desire for contact than her willingness to risk longer imprisonment simply to challenge prison authority and reach out beyond the prison walls to her colleagues.

Nor is Seruya's the only writing on prison lavatory paper to have survived the years, fragile yet intact. In the Suffragette Fellowship Collection there are several anonymous examples, one of which resembles free verse:

> Cruelty
> Dr. Gordon on <u>silence</u>
> I said if we did not transgress
> we should go mad. That it was
> enforced here to the extent of cruelty.
> She advised just to go on as we
> were doing & whisper when you think
> officer is not looking.
> Silence she said was enforced
> in prisons to prevent quarreling
> & bad language–
> I think how much more sensible
> it would be to use silence as a

> punishment days or week for
> use of bad language or quarreling
> They tell me the language in prisons
> would be so awful.[71]

Such an archival object confounds easy categorization and interpretation. It reports a private conversation over a public policy, but more importantly, it reflects the personality, concerns, and mindset of the anonymous author. As with all archival material hinting of the intimate thoughts of the writer, it is best analyzed unconstrained, free of templates and open to the author's potentially deeper meanings.

Conclusion

In the archives of The Women's Library there is a lily that has been carefully preserved since 1913.[72] Originally, it was held by a member of the WSPU honor guard who marched in the funeral procession of Emily Wilding Davison. Davison was the WSPU militant who darted onto the racetrack at Epsom Downs during the 1913 Derby and died in her attempt to stop the king's horse. This lily (and what it represents) speaks to all levels of analysis discussed in this essay. Davison's private act was taken by the WSPU and transformed into the public spectacle of her funeral procession through the streets of London. Davison became a martyr for the suffrage cause, more particularly for the violent wing of the British movement. However, this play of the private against the public cannot capture the complexity of Davison's life, the pressures and inspiration of group action, the impact of her political actions on her family, and the grief they felt at her loss. In the same archive is a black-bordered card from Davison's family addressed to the "Editress of 'The Suffragette,'" expressing the "profound gratitude" of the family to those who took part in the funeral cortege.[73] It is not possible to neatly compartmentalize Davison's life; it requires a more free-flowing frame, where we recognize that the many aspects of her life intersected closely with each other. Yet, Davison's act is also a mystery. Was it suicide – intentional martyrdom – or just a terrible accident? She carried a return ticket for Victoria Station, and her appointment diary revealed her plans for suffrage work during the coming week. Close analysis of the film of her death reveals her effort to grab the bridle of the king's horse rather than any attempt to throw herself in his path.[74] Davison's writings and testimony from her colleagues have all been mined for some indication of her psychological state prior to this final protest. Still, it is important to approach the archival evidence free of preconceptions – and free to speculate (based on good evidence) about Davison's deeper motivations.

   This essay is not intended to echo those who call for abandoning the concept of separate spheres or the public/private dichotomy. The idea that there are proper realms of action based on gender boundaries has always existed in various forms. And it is safe to say that the nineteenth and early twentieth centuries saw a hardening of those categories into a clear and pervasive ideology. Political women would shadow-box that ideology not only in the Old Feminist and suffrage movements, but also in the crusades for abolitionism and temperance. Nor would this concept die after the Progressive era. In post-World War II America, the ideology of separate spheres would be reborn and battled anew by a second wave of feminists. Thus, despite the ideology's understandable hold on our analytical imaginations, its grip should be loosened and the concept employed only where appropriate. The detritus found in archives comes from the lives of real people – contradictory, maddening, and fasci-nating. In the freedom to understand women's lives as they actually lived them, we may find new discernment of all that the archives have to offer.

Notes

1   Janie Terrero to Manuel Terrero, 50.82/1116, Suffragette Fellowship Collection, Museum of London.

2   Aileen S. Kraditor, ed., *Up From the Pedestal: Selected Writings in the History of American Feminism* (Chicago: Quadrangle Books, 1968), 8–10.

3   Barbara Welter, "The Cult of True Womanhood, 1820–1860," *American Quarterly* 18 (1966): 151–174.

4   Nan Johnson, "Reigning in the Court of Silence: Women and Rhetorical Space in Postbellum America," *Philosophy & Rhetoric* 33 (2000): 237.

5   Karlyn Kohrs Campbell, *Man Cannot Speak for Her: A Critical Study of Early Feminist Rhetoric*, vol. 1 (New York: Praeger, 1989), 9–10.

6   Lisa Gring-Pemble, "Writing Themselves into Consciousness: Creating a Rhetorical Bridge Between the Public and Private Spheres," *Quarterly Journal of Speech* 84 (1998): 42–43.

7   Cindy L. Griffin, "The Essentialist Roots of the Public Sphere: A Feminist Critique," *Western Journal of Communication* 60 (1996): 21–39.

8   Cheryl R. Jorgensen-Earp, "The Lady, The Whore, and The Spinster: The Rhetorical Use of Victorian Images of Women," *Western Journal of Speech Communication* 54 (1990): 82–98.

9   Robert B. Shoemaker, *Gender in English Society, 1650–1850: The Emergence of Separate Spheres?* (London: Longman, 1998), 313.

10 Leonore Davidoff and Catherine Hall, *Family Fortunes: Men and Women of the English Middle Class, 1780–1850* (Chicago: University of Chicago Press, 1987), 30.

11 Shoemaker, *Gender*, 8.

12 Jürgen Habermas, *The Structural Transformation of the Public Sphere: An Inquiry into a Category of Bourgeois Society*, trans. Thomas Burger (Cambridge, MA: MIT Press, 1989), 32–33.

13 Amanda Vickery, "Golden Age to Separate Spheres? A Review of the Categories and Chronology of English Women's History," *Historical Journal* 36 (1993): 411–412.

14 Vickery, "Golden Age," 401.

15 Shoemaker, *Gender*, 10.

16 Shoemaker, *Gender*, 317.

17 Welter, "The Cult."

18 Shoemaker, *Gender*, 318.

19 John Ruskin, "The Nature of Woman," from "Of Queen's Gardens," *The Norton Anthology of English Literature: Norton Topics Online*, www.wwnorton.com/college/english/nael/victorian/topic_2/ruskin.htm.

20 Shoemaker, *Gender*, 31.

21 Joan B. Landes, "Further Thoughts on the Public/Private Distinction," *Journal of Women's History* 15 (2003): 38n.9.

22 Mary P. Ryan, "The Public and the Private Good: Across the Great Divide in Women's History," *Journal of Women's History* 15 (2003): 24.

23 Jacqueline Jones Royster, *Traces of a Stream: Literacy and Social Change Among African American Women* (Pittsburgh, PA: University of Pittsburgh Press, 2000), 166.

24 Lawrence E. Klein, "Gender and the Public/Private Distinction in the Eighteenth Century: Some Questions About Evidence and Analytic Procedure," *Eighteenth-Century Studies* 29 (1996): 103.

25 Shoemaker, *Gender*, 307.

26 Joan Perkin, *Victorian Women* (New York: New York University Press, 1993), 202.

27 Karen V. Hansen, "Rediscovering the Social: Visiting Practices in Antebellum New England and the Limits of the Public/Private Dichotomy," in *Public and Private in Thought and Practice: Perspectives on a Grand Dichotomy*, ed. Jeff Weintraub and Krishan Kumar (Chicago: University of Chicago Press, 1997), 270.

28 Hansen, "Rediscovering," 291.

29 Hansen, "Rediscovering," 273.

30 Catherine Allgor, *Parlor Politics: In Which the Ladies of Washington Help Build a City and a Government* (Charlottesville: University Press of Virginia, 2000), 138–146.

31 Helene E. Roberts, "Marriage, Redundancy or Sin: The Painter's View of Women in the First Twenty-Five Years of Victoria's Reign," in *Suffer and Be Still: Women in the Victorian Age*, ed. Martha Vicinus (Bloomington: Indiana University Press, 1972), 45–76.

32 Jane Lewis, "Reconstructing Women's Experience," in *Labour and Love: Women's Experience of Home and Family, 1850–1940*, ed. Jane Lewis (Oxford: Blackwell, 1986), 20n.1.

33 Landes, "Further Thoughts," 28.

34 Leonore Davidoff, "Gender and the 'Great Divide': Public and Private in British Gender History," *Journal of Women's History* 15 (2003): 11; Ryan, "The Public and the Private Good," 11; and Alan Wolfe, "Public and Private in Theory and Practice: Some Implications of an Uncertain Boundary," in *Public and Private in Thought and Practice*, ed. Weintraub and Kumar, 182.

35 Joe Bailey, "From Public to Private: the Development of the Concept of the 'Private,'" *Social Research* 69 (2002): 15–16.

36 Susan Gal, "A Semiotics of the Public/Private Distinction," *Differences: A Journal of Feminist Cultural Studies* 13 (2002): 82.

37 Sandra Lauderdale Graham, "Making the Private Public: A Brazilian Perspective," *Journal of Women's History* 15 (2003): 29.

38 Jean Bethke Elshtain, "The Displacement of Politics," in *Public and Private in Thought and Practice*, ed. Weintraub and Kumar, 167.

39 Ryan, "The Public and the Private Good," 14.

40 Ryan, "The Public and the Private Good," 14.

41 Gal, "A Semiotics," 82.

42 Lewis, "Reconstructing," 11.

43 Gal, "A Semiotics," 85.

44 Martha Hagan, "The Antisuffragists' Rhetorical Dilemma: Reconciling the Private and Public Spheres," *Communication Reports* 5 (1992): 73–81.

45 Gal, "A Semiotics," 90.

46 Gring-Pemble, "Writing Themselves," 44.

47 Roger Fulford, *Votes for Women: The Story of a Struggle* (London: Faber and Faber, 1957), 139.

48 The British suffrage movement can be divided into the violent militants (WSPU) that utilized violence against property, the nonviolent militants (such as the Women's Freedom League) that limited militancy to civil disobedience, and the constitutionalists (NUWSS) that followed traditional methods of legal reform.

49 Laura E. Nym Mayhall, "Domesticating Emmeline: Representing the Suffragette, 1930–1993," *NWSA Journal* 11 (1999): 1–24.

50 Michael Calvin McGee, "An Essay on the Flip Side of Privacy," in *Proceedings of the 1983 NCA/AFA Summer Conference on Argumentation*, ed. Malcolm O. Sillars, David Zarefsky, and Jack Rhodes (Annandale, VA: National Communication Association, 1983), 105.

51 Gring-Pemble, "Writing Themselves," 42.

52 Susan B. Anthony to Millicent Garrett Fawcett, 18 May 1903, 7MGF/1/024, The Women's Library, London Metropolitan University.

53 Carrie Chapman Catt to Millicent Garrett Fawcett, 7MGF/1/036, The Women's Library, London Metropolitan University.

54 Miss Ada Flatman to Miss Warton, 14 January 1910, 10/82/1119, no. 18, Suffragette Fellowship Collection, Museum of London. Gaol was the common British spelling of "jail" at the time of this letter.

55 "A Speech by Lady Constance Lytton: Delivered at the Queen's Hall, January 31, 1910," in *Speeches and Trials of the Militant Suffragettes*, ed. Cheryl R. Jorgensen-Earp (Cranbury, NJ: Fairleigh Dickinson University Press, 1999), 107–113.

56 Erving Goffman, *The Presentation of Self in Everyday Life* (New York: Doubleday, 1959), 107–137.

57 Janie Terrero to Manuel Terrero, 2 March 1912, Prison Experiences of Janie Terrero, 50.82/1116, Suffragette Fellowship Collection, Museum of London.

58 Elizabeth Garrett Anderson to Millicent Garrett Fawcett, 11 Jun 1910, 7MGF/A/1/045, The Women's Library, London Metropolitan University.

59 Elizabeth Garrett Anderson to Millicent Garrett Fawcett, 18 Nov 1910, 7MGF/A/1/049, The Women's Library, London Metropolitan University.

60 See Caroline Morrell, *"Black Friday": Violence Against Women in the Suffragette Movement* (London: Women's Research and Resources Centre, 1990).

61 Millicent Garrett Fawcett to Elizabeth Garrett Anderson, 3 Dec 1911, 7MGF/A/1/055, The Women's Library, London Metropolitan University.

62 Elizabeth Garrett Anderson to Millicent Garrett Fawcett, 4 Dec 1911, 7MGF/A/1/056, The Women's Library, London Metropolitan University.

63 Elizabeth Garrett Anderson to Millicent Garrett Fawcett, 25 Jan 1913, 7MGF/1/075, The Women's Library, London Metropolitan University.

64 Leland M. Griffin, "The Rhetorical Structure of the 'New Left' Movement: Part I," *Quarterly Journal of Speech* 50 (1964): 127.

65 June Purvis, "The Prison Experiences of the Suffragettes in Edwardian Britain," *Women's History Review* 4 (1995): 103–132.

66 Cheryl R. Jorgensen-Earp, "The Waning of the Light: The Forcible Feeding of Jane Warton, Spinster," *Women's Studies in Communication* 22 (1999): 125–151.

67 Lady Constance Lytton to Lady Lytton, 24 February 1909, Autograph Letter Collection: Letters of Constance Lytton, GB 0106 9/21, The Women's Library, London Metropolitan University.

68 Lytton was probably thinking of the successful climb made by the Duke of the Abruzzi (a cousin of the king) of Mount Rubenzori on June 18, 1906. See "Abruzzi's Latest Feat," *New York Times*, July 6, 1906, New York Times Archive.

69 Lytton to Lady Lytton, 24 February 1909.

70 Letter from Holloway Prison from Sime Seruya to Edith Craig, 1910, 7EWD/F/1, The Women's Library, London Metropolitan University.

71 Letter on Holloway lavatory paper, 96.103/19, Suffragette Fellowship Collection, Museum of London.

72 Lily Flower, 4NVA/6/3/06/4, closed access until 01/01/2031, Box FL119, The Women's Library, London Metropolitan Museum.

73 Captain Henry Davison to the Editress of *The Suffragette*, 16 June 1913, GB/106/EWD/K1, The Women's Library, London Metropolitan University.

74 See Liz Stanley and Ann Morley, *The Life and Death of Emily Wilding Davison: A Biographical Detective Story* (London: Women's Press, 1988); and John Sleight, *One Way Ticket to Epsom* (Morpeth: Bridge Studios, 1988).

10

Studying Visual Modes of Public Address
Lewis Hine's Progressive-Era Child Labor Rhetoric

Cara A. Finnegan

The movement to regulate child labor in the United States was one of the most successful social movements of the early twentieth century.[1] From 1870, when the census first recorded the number of child workers in the United States, to 1941, when the Supreme Court upheld the legality of the Fair Labor Standards Act and its child labor provisions, the issue of child labor was a staple of the national political agenda.[2] During the Progressive era child labor reform drew the attention, involvement, and activism of a range of well-known and powerful figures, including Theodore Roosevelt, Jane Addams, Albert Beveridge, and Woodrow Wilson. Yet few studies in public address have examined the rhetoric of child labor reform.[3] Furthermore, child labor texts are rarely anthologized for easy access and study.[4]

One possible explanation for these absences is that some of the most eloquent and enduring child labor rhetoric was visual rather than oratorical. While public address studies have tended to favor the oratorical, the child labor debate is best remembered today for the eloquent visual rhetoric of Lewis Wickes Hine. In 1908, Lewis Hine was hired as a photographic investigator for the National Child Labor Committee (NCLC), a privately funded group of activists and social work professionals who had been working to change child labor laws and practices in the United States.[5] Between 1908 and 1918, Hine made thousands of photographs under the auspices of the NCLC. The images were displayed as slide shows, shown at exhibits on child labor, and appeared in NCLC reports and journals; Hine frequently wrote articles to accompany them.[6] Thanks to Hine, reformers recognized the power of documenting social conditions via photography. The man who hired Hine at the NCLC, Owen Lovejoy, remarked years later in a letter to the photographer, "In my judgment the work you did under my direction for the National Child Labor Committee was more responsible than any or all other efforts to bring the facts and conditions of child employment to public attention."

Scholars in other fields frequently describe Hine's work in terms of communication and persuasion, while those of us who regularly employ tools for analyzing communication and persuasion have largely ignored him.[7] Why the paradox?

Perhaps part of the answer is that our changing understandings of public address have not kept up with our methods for studying it. More than 20 years ago Stephen Lucas asked of the field,

> What if we move beyond the traditional paradigm? What if we think of public address not just as the study of historical speakers and speeches, but as the study of the full range of public, discursive rhetorical acts – historical and contemporary, oral and written, considered individually or as part of a broader campaign or movement?[8]

Lucas contended that public address scholarship in the 1960s and 1970s did not "die," but "underwent a dramatic metamorphosis" fueled by what appeared to be an increasingly complex rhetorical-political world.[9] Similarly, in a 1989 essay, David Zarefsky observed that one sign of "vitality" in public address was a shift in the field's understanding of what constitutes the "address" of public address. Zarefsky declared that public address scholarship was undergoing a shift from attention to the *modes* of public address (e.g., oratory) to its *functions*: "By embracing a broader conception of public address and not reducing the term to formal oratory, our studies have enhanced the potential for understanding historical or rhetorical situations and for formulating theoretical generalizations."[10] Zarefsky's point – that we should be more focused on what public address *does* than on any particular *mode* of that doing – was liberating, especially for scholars interested in nonoratorical modes of public address. Yet that liberation arguably came at the cost of methodological clarity. When public address was opened up to a range of previously unexplored discourses, new questions arose about methodology: How should one proceed when examining nonoratorical modes? To be more specific, what precisely would we do if we wanted to study Lewis Hine's photographic rhetoric?

In this chapter I present a critical perspective on the study of visual modes of public address. Although the case study I develop focuses on the photography of Lewis Hine, the perspective presented here fits a range of other visual images and artifacts as well. This chapter is not a complete guide to visual methodologies, but it does offer starting points for those who wish their explorations of public address to include visual discourses.[11] In what follows I present five approaches to analyzing visual images in terms of their production, composition, reproduction, circulation, and reception. Taken together, these constitute a critical perspective on the study of visual modes of public address. By "perspective," I mean something quite literal: *a way of seeing* the role of visual images in public culture. This perspective assumes that visual modes of public address shape and frame our experience of public life. In embracing the constitutive role of images, it sets aside the erroneous presumption that the "best" deliberation takes place solely in the modes of talk and text.[12]

Furthermore, this perspective recognizes not only that public address is frequently visual, but that it always has been. Despite claims that visual modes of rhetoric are more dominant now than they were in the past, the history of American public address is very much a visual as well as a textual/oratorical history.[13] Finally, the perspective I develop here assumes that to study visual modes of public address is to do interdisciplinary work; this chapter taps into more than three decades of scholarship in the field of communication and is informed by work in related fields such as art history, American studies, and literary cultural studies.[14] Overall, I treat the visual as a potent mode of public address which should be studied in ways that recognize images' political, cultural, and historical specificity, as well as their fluidity as circulating objects in public culture. After I present each of the five approaches, I illustrate the historical power of visual public address through a case study of a Lewis Hine child labor poster published in *Child Labor Bulletin* in 1915. In this context of reproduction, Hine's photograph-text assemblage, titled "Making Human Junk," served not as a stand-alone visual argument but as a summary statement punctuating broader arguments about child labor, national health, and the value of children and childhood. My analysis not only models the perspective I describe below, it also illustrates the important role of visual rhetorics of child labor reform during the Progressive era.

Critical Approaches to Visualizing Public Address

Students of public address typically come to the study of visual rhetoric through a more general interest in rhetoric; engaged by visual artifacts, they wonder precisely how to proceed. As with all research, one's approach should follow from one's critical questions. Depending on those questions, one or more of the following approaches may be most appropriate. In studying *production* the critic examines not only the technical aspects of image-making but also the generic, institutional, and authorial factors that influence the creation of images. In studying *composition*, the critic attends to the visual features of the image itself, as well as any historical referents or commonplaces they activate. The study of *reproduction* invites the critic to examine the specific "textual events" in which images appear. The study of *circulation* asks the critic to study how the image moves in and through various contexts of public culture. Finally, the critic studying *reception* attempts to gauge audiences' responses to images. The five approaches are not mutually exclusive, nor must a single case study include all approaches or work in a linear fashion through them. Instead, they are presented here to offer the critic a variety of approaches for answering particular questions about the roles images play in public culture.

Production

When we attend to production we examine "where images come from and why they appear in the spaces where we find them."[15] Four elements of production are important starting points for examining visual images: the technical, the generic, the authorial/creative, and the institutional. While few would argue that technology alone should determine any potential reading of an image, Gillian Rose suggests it may be useful to know some technical information: "visual technologies do matter to how an image looks and therefore to what it might do and what might be done to it."[16] For example, whether an image is a photograph or an oil painting matters to our interpretation of it, though to what degree it matters may be debatable in any given case. In the case of historical photography, we would want to know how photographs were typically produced in a given period, what kind of camera was used, or what affiliated technologies were or were not available (e.g., flash photography, color film). Knowing this information may help the critic mount a more informed interpretation of the image's history, composition, or reception.

Just as public address scholars turn to genre to understand oratorical texts, the visual critic may also find it useful to consider genre. Is the image an example of documentary? Editorial cartoon? Advertising? Religious iconography? Understanding something about the genre in which an image participates not only gives the critic access to norms of its production, but may also provide additional insight into the norms of its composition. For example, Barbie Zelizer's studies of historical and contemporary news photography rely heavily on Zelizer's knowledge of the norms of the photojournalism genre.[17]

Public address scholars frequently are interested in the creator of public discourse; we want to know how speakers come to make their speeches, what constraints they faced, what their purposes might have been. We may be interested in their rhetorical training, how they drafted and revised their work, or with whom they collaborated. Similarly, attention to the creator of images may reveal important contextual information as well as potential motives of the creator.[18] Knowing that 1930s documentary photographer Dorothea Lange was trained as a portrait photographer, for example, helps critics of her images better understand how her portraits pay visual witness to individual experience.[19]

Institutions affect image production as well. Studies of image production frequently involve "detailed analyses of particular industries which produce visual images."[20] How one analyzes institutions will vary by case, but attention to institutions typically involves studying the economics of production, the ideological aspects of an institution's goals or ideals, and institutional forces that enable or constrain the production of particular kinds of images. For example, both Diane S. Hope and Nancy Martha West have explored how the Eastman Kodak company sold the family romance of photography to Americans in order to sell their products.[21] Information about production frequently is found in archives, where the researcher may locate materials related to the individuals or institutions that produced the images. The critic may wish to access these to locate information about the elements of production outlined above, particularly those of institutions and creators.[22]

Composition

Compositional analysis involves the description and interpretation of the visual grammar of images. Just as the close reader of texts benefits from having at her command a lexicon for interpretation (e.g., familiarity with tropes, figures, and argument strategies mobilized in the text or recognition of allusions and references therein), so too the visual critic needs specific analytical tools. Such tools enable the critic to get at both content and form, which work together to construct potential meanings in a work.[23] The compositional approach invites the critic to focus on a number of features of a visual image, including its content, color, light, and spatial organization.[24]

The content of an image is what the image shows or depicts. Even if the image is representational (that is, it offers realistic-looking figures), the image's content may not always be obvious. Social, cultural, and historical knowledge often comes into play: "some images picture particular religious, historical, mythological, moral or literary themes or events" which will require additional research in order to be fully understood.[25] Critics may recognize in the content of an image particular topoi, or commonplace themes.[26] Richard Lanham defines visual commonplaces as "large libraries of images and icons."[27] They are the stock images of public culture: familiar to audiences, culturally ubiquitous, readily available, and recurrent across space and time. Some visual topoi become so culturally powerful that they consolidate into more dominant rhetorical forms; we term these icons or visual ideographs.[28] But other visual topoi may not be so easily recognizable to us today. For example, in his visual history of the American ideals of freedom and liberty, David Hackett Fischer describes the "liberty pole"; literally a tall pole with a cap on top, the liberty pole came to symbolize freedom and liberty for many American colonists. Although we might not know of the liberty pole today, representations of it circulated widely during the Revolutionary period and would have had symbolic resonance for audiences.[29] Because visual topoi are culture-bound and tied to the *doxa* of communities, they are sometimes difficult to recognize, especially for those unfamiliar with visual history. Fortunately, there are numerous reference works that researchers may use to familiarize themselves with such visual topoi. In the Western context, the *Encyclopedia of Comparative Iconography* is a useful two-volume work that indexes common mythological, literary, and religious themes in the history of Western art.[30] Scholars working in the US context may wish to keep handy one or two introductory texts on American art.[31]

Analyzing image content may involve exploring how the gaze is activated. All images activate a field of looking, whether between the image and the viewer or within the image itself. Sylvan Barnet suggests that critics should ask, "What is the relation of the viewer's (and artist's) gaze to the gaze of the figure(s)? … Does this Other return the viewer's gaze, thereby asserting his or her identity and power, or does the subject look elsewhere, unaware of the voyeur viewer-painter?"[32] Gunther Kress and Theo van Leeuwen note that images in which the gaze is directed at the viewer of the image create "a visual form of direct address. It acknowledges the viewers explicitly, addressing them with a visual 'you.'" Kress and van Leeuwen call these images "demand" images because they demand "that the viewer enter into some kind of imaginary relation with him or her."[33] A classic example of the "demand" image is the Uncle Sam recruiting poster, "I Want YOU." Critics may also examine the "organization of looks" in an image: Who looks at whom, and how does that direct the viewer's attention? Who avoids the gaze or looks away? How does the grammar of the gaze construct a relationship between the image and the viewer?[34]

Attention to composition involves studying formal characteristics of images as well as their content. One should attend to color, light, and spatial organization. Color differentiates elements in an image, stresses certain elements over others, creates a sense of harmony or discord, and expands or contracts the impression of space, among other functions.[35] Color is also culturally expressive, such as the traditional blue "conventionally used for the cloak of the Virgin Mary" or gold frequently used to signify wealth.[36] Color itself may be broken down into three components: *hue* (the actual color, i.e., whether something is yellow or red); *saturation* (the purity of a given color); and *value* (the color's relative lightness or darkness).[37] Kress and van Leeuwen suggest that color influences our sense of the realism of images; for example, an image of a beach scene with bright, highly saturated blue water may create the impression of a rich fantasy world or dreamy paradise.[38]

Critics will also want to account for light in an image. Light may be used to emphasize certain parts of the image, deemphasize others, construct an emotional atmosphere, imply relationships, produce shadows, and the like. In short, light can bring elements of a picture together or produce marked contrasts. The source of light is also relevant; for example, photographs made indoors with a flash might have harsh, artificial-looking light that creates distinct areas of visual contrast within the frame.[39]

The critic engaging spatial organization explores how objects are positioned in relation to one another, how lines and shapes interact to suggest what is more or less salient within the frame, and how the image activates the geometry of perspective to create a sense of distance/closeness, logic/distortion, or balance/imbalance.[40] Spatial analysis should consider not only how objects in the image relate to one another in the bounded space of the image, but also how the image is positioned to be experienced by a viewer.[41] Viewers participate in what art historian Michael Ann Holly calls an image's "logic of figuration," the way the picture presents itself to be viewed: "We stand where the works tell us to stand and we see what they choose to reveal."[42] In examining the image's logic of figuration, the critic should consider not only the ways that gazes or glances are activated in the image (described above), but also the angles at which the viewer encounters the image.[43] Kress and van Leeuwen contend that horizontal angles activate various senses of involvement between the viewer and the subject of the image, while vertical angles suggest power differences.[44] Finally, the critic may wish to consider the size or scale of the image: How large or small is it? What might its relative magnitude convey about its subject?[45]

Compositional analysis initially functions descriptively as the critic catalogues elements of form and content. But description should give way to a more sophisticated interpretation which emerges from the critic's understanding of how form and content work together to construct particular visual logics. An excellent example of compositional analysis that makes such interpretive moves is Davi Johnson's analysis of news photographs made in Birmingham, Alabama, during Martin Luther King, Jr.'s 1963 civil rights campaign. Johnson shows how space, line, light, and perspective work together in photographs by Charles Moore to "visually identif[y] the state with uncivilized violence."[46]

Reproduction

While attention to production helps the critic understand technical, generic, authorial, and institutional origins of images, and attention to composition gives a critic access to images' form and content, reproduction is interested in what images do in the specific contexts in which they appear. David Zarefsky observes that the rhetorical historian views human conduct from the "perspective of how messages are created and used by people to influence and relate to one another." Such a perspective entails viewing "history as a series of rhetorical problems, situations that call for public persuasion to advance a cause or overcome an impasse. The focus of the study would be on how, and how well, people invented and deployed messages in response to the situation."[47] Following Zarefsky, we might say that critics investigating reproduction are interested in how visual images participate in messages created to address rhetorical problems. Traditional approaches to criticism encourage attention to the contexts that frame and are framed by rhetorical discourse.[48] Similarly, a study of image reproduction should account for images in the context of their participation in a "textual event"; it should study the local context of that textual event; and it should attend to the visual culture in which the image participates.

The notion of "textual event" emphasizes two aspects of the public appearance of images: their participation in contexts that include other images as well as written texts, headlines, or captions, and their eventfulness as particular moments of discourse occurring in space and time. A textual event might be a gallery or museum exhibit, a parade, a magazine article, or even (as I note below) a factory floor. Using photography as her example, M. K. Johnson explains, "a photograph as it appears in a gallery would be one textual event; the same photograph appearing in conjunction with a newspaper review of the gallery show would be another textual event."[49] The critic examining the image as part of a specific textual event thus asks questions such as: How does the image work within this particular piece of rhetoric? How does it interact with other features of that rhetoric, e.g., other images, texts, or spaces? In analyzing the Farm Security Administration (FSA) photographs produced by the US government in the 1930s, I examined how the photographs were used in magazine stories about rural poverty. In my study of specific textual events, I not only engaged the images themselves, but also explored their placement on the page, their relationship to the articles they were used to illustrate, their relationship to other images in the articles, and their relationship to captions and headlines.[50]

In addition to studying the textual event of reproduction, the critic will also want to look at the local context in which the textual event appears. With the FSA photographs, I studied non-FSA content in the magazines and considered its relationship to the FSA photographs and stories. In addition, studying local context sometimes entails introducing questions of production such as: Why did this magazine publish this story? What were the institutional goals of this outlet? How were stories selected or rejected? Who selected the photographs and decided on the final product? A critic engaging other contexts of reproduction would ask related questions. A study of images displayed in a museum exhibit, for example, might investigate the history of the museum, discover who made decisions about exhibits, and locate archival materials related to how the exhibit was assembled.

Finally, the critic studying reproduction will want to understand the social, historical, political, and institutional forces involved in the case being analyzed. In addition to the typical things one would consider – the rhetorical situation that produced the need for the discourse, the competing persuasive forces at play, and the rhetor's position in the context of the rhetorical situation and problem – the critic of visual discourse will also want to explore the visual culture of the period being studied. If culture may be defined as what Marita Sturken and Lisa Cartwright term "the shared practices of a group, community, or society, through which meaning is made out of the visual, aural, and textual world of representations" – that is, as a contingent "social practice" – then visual culture involves "those aspects of culture that are manifested in visual form."[51] However, there is no monolithic, empirically identifiable visual culture "out there" waiting to be discovered. Our knowledge of visual culture must be pieced together intertextually from fragments we discover and engage. In investigating visual culture, the critic will want to ask questions such as: Is the image in question unusual for its time, or ubiquitous? Where would audiences likely have encountered such an image? What other kinds of images circulated during this era? What visual practices or ways of seeing were available to viewers during the period? As we shall see below, attention to visual culture also directs us outward from the image and its local context toward broader issues of circulation and reception.

Attention to reproduction may allow the critic to situate the image within a highly specific context. An excellent analysis of this kind is James Kimble and Lester Olson's examination of J. Howard Miller's famous "Rosie the Riveter" print. Kimble and Olson mobilize numerous archival sources to show that Miller's iconic image is widely misunderstood to have been created to recruit women into the war effort. However, it first appeared as a "shop poster" hung on the factory floor to communicate to women workers in Westinghouse plants. Using archival research to uncover "the poster's time- and place-bound meanings within Westinghouse's organizational culture" – that is, the relationship of its production to its reproduction – Kimble and Olson skillfully read the poster in the context of worker practices and alongside other posters produced in a series designed to bolster worker motivation to produce.[52]

Circulation

If the study of composition and reproduction helps us discover the specificity of images' rhetorical work, the study of circulation helps us discover their fluidity. Scholars theorizing circulation reject definitions that characterize circulation as simply the passive transmission of ideas, information, or images. Rather, circulation does important cultural work, including creating interpretive communities and constituting publics.[53] Michael Warner argues that circulation is in fact what constructs publics: "a public is the social space created by the reflexive circulation of discourse."[54]

Robert Hariman and John Lucaites concur that "images and their circulation are important means for the formation of public opinion and public agency."[55] Because circulation is a key feature of visual culture, the critic of visual modes of public address may be interested in examining how and where images move.

Circulation is difficult to study because it involves movement of discourse. Thus it may be most useful for the critic to begin by tracking multiple instances of reproduction. By accumulating a collection of these, the critic may develop a sense of the image's circulation. Depending upon the critic's interests, it may be enough simply to note the fact of circulation; for example, an account of circulation may be made in order to enable the critic to say something about audiences' potential exposure to an image. Yet merely accounting for the fact of circulation may not be enough; the critic may wish to make circulation itself a subject of study. For example, Lester Olson tracked the circulation of a popular Revolutionary-era image of a segmented snake known as "JOIN, or DIE," originally produced by Benjamin Franklin. By examining contexts of print culture through which the image circulated in the American colonies and Europe, Olson showed how the available meanings of this iconic image changed as it circulated. The segmented snake that initially connoted the British colonists' solidarity in face of threats from France later came to stand for colonial unity against the British.[56] Olson was able to track circulation so closely because he spent considerable time and energy doing archival research. In the case of well-known bodies of images, secondary source material in the form of encyclopedia articles, annotated bibliographies, or other reference works may also help the critic track circulation.

Scholars who explore circulation frequently encounter appropriations of the image they are tracking. Sturken and Cartwright define appropriation as "the act of borrowing, stealing, or taking over others' meanings to one's own ends." Often, though not always, appropriation is "one of the primary forms of oppositional production and reading."[57] The study of appropriation not only involves attention to circulation but may also provide access to response and reception. Hariman and Lucaites demonstrate the utility of attention to appropriation in their book, *No Caption Needed*, which examines eight iconic photographs and dozens of related appropriations.[58]

The study of circulation cautions us against reifying any one interpretation of an image or its accompanying textual event. While the critic may activate an interpretation of an image in one context, it is not necessarily the case that all elements of that interpretation will make sense when the image circulates in other contexts. By combining attention to circulation with the study of reproduction, the critic is able to explore both the specificity and fluidity of visual images.

Reception

Finally, the rhetorical critic may be interested in exploring avenues for assessing audiences' responses to a work. Like all forms of rhetorical discourse, visual images have effects on audiences. Yet just because an image has the potential to produce certain effects does not mean that it did, in fact, produce such effects. If we want to be able to say something substantive about actual audience responses, we need to construct a robust study of reception.

Why might a critic study response? First, the critic may want concrete evidence for claims about the impact of a work. In addition, the critic may wish to "check" his or her interpretation of the work against how audiences may have received it; Leah Ceccarelli explains that the critic might follow up "a close reading of the primary text" with "a close intertextual reading of responses ... to see whether the rhetorical strategies worked in the way" the critic believes.[59] In addition, studying reception enables the critic to locate other potential interpretations that might have been missed, because one working at a distance from the time period will never have full access to the historical contingencies of any given moment. Finally, the critic may be as interested in the reception of a work as in the work itself. That is, a critic may study reception to increase our understanding of available or prevalent viewing practices in a particular time and place.

Rhetorical scholars typically study response empirically, intertextually, or using some combination of these. In empirical studies of reception, the critic uses secondary or primary source material to assemble evidence as to audiences' reception of a work. Such evidence might include texts that comment on the work such as histories, personal narratives, newspaper or magazine articles, letters to the editor, critical reviews, or material located in letters or diaries. The study of an image's circulation and/or appropriation, as noted above, may also suggest something about how audiences received a work. Those studying contemporary discourse may even ask viewers what they think. For example, in their study of *National Geographic*, Catherine Lutz and Jane Collins interviewed a sample of readers about their experiences with the magazine and asked them to interpret individual photographs. Obviously such an approach is not available when examining visual rhetoric of past periods, but it may be helpful in the analysis of contemporary texts.[60]

In addition to collecting empirical evidence of response, the critic may also wish to analyze what Ceccarelli calls "intertextual material produced in response to a primary text."[61] Here the critic examines the residue of audience response to discover how audiences interpret or remake the work for their own rhetorical purposes. A good example of how one might use intertextual analysis is my study of how readers of *McClure's* magazine responded to a photograph of Abraham Lincoln published for the first time in 1895, 30 years after his assassination. By analyzing a group of letters to the editor, I discovered that late nineteenth-century viewers read the photograph as proof that Lincoln was the first "true" American. For elites anxious about the shifting nature of American identity at the turn of the twentieth century, framing Lincoln in this way was rhetorically useful.[62]

The five approaches discussed above offer tools that enable critics to answer a range of questions about visual modes of public address. Below I offer a case study that mobilizes some of these tools to study a Lewis Hine poster called "Making

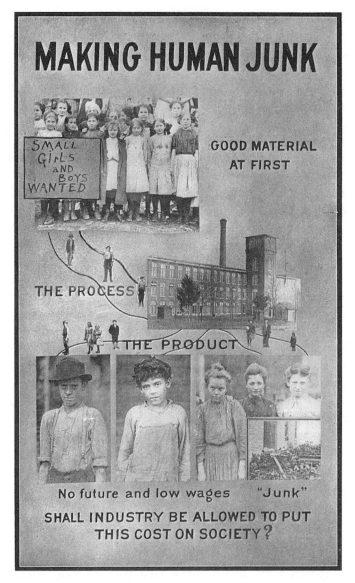

Figure 10.1 Lewis Hine, "Making Human Junk," *Child Labor Bulletin* 3.4 (1915): 35.

Human Junk" (Fig. 10.1).[63] While I will not explore this child labor image utilizing all five approaches, I will illustrate how some of the approaches may be combined in a single case study. Attending to elements of composition, production, and a single reproduction of the Hine image, I show that although "Making Human Junk" appears initially to be a self-contained argument about the evils of child labor, it really functions more expansively as a summative statement on the relationship between child labor and the health of the nation.[64]

"Making Human Junk": Visualizing Child Labor and National Health

Let us begin with composition. The poster, reproduced in the pages of the journal *Child Labor Bulletin*, is longer than it is wide, its light-colored background contrasting with the title at the top in strong, black, capital letters: "MAKING HUMAN JUNK." A series of large photographs and small photographic cutouts of children fill the rest of the space. The verticality of the poster encourages the viewer to read the images and text (both hand-lettered and typographic) from top to bottom; they work together to create a narrative emphasizing three stages in the making of "human junk." In the first stage, children are "good material," smiling in a photograph reminiscent of a class picture. But, as Hine's hand-lettered sign announces, "small boys and girls" are "wanted." Children who start out as "good material" are then subjected to what Hine calls "THE PROCESS."

Hine visualizes what happens to the children by positioning photographic cutouts as if they are entering and departing a photographic image of a factory; curvy, hand-drawn lines suggest their movement into and out of the building. Like the raw material the factory transforms into products, the children are also subjected to the factory process. What exactly happens to them inside is unclear (Hine does not give us visual access to the interior), but the outcome of the process is visualized in the third and final element of the story, "THE PRODUCT." Here, we see what the factory turns out: unsmiling, worn children whose gazes make a demand on the viewer. Gone are the smiles from the group of girls above; gone too are the "HIGH WAGES" that used to characterize factory work. These have given way to the stooped shoulders, blank stares, "NO FUTURE" and "LOW WAGES" that are the result of the child's participation in industrial labor. Combining large photographs, smaller photographic cutouts, directional lines, and short bursts of text, Hine suggests that the children themselves are products of industrialization. The rhetorical question posed on the bottom of the poster, "Shall industry be allowed to put this cost on society?," punctuates the direct visual address of the children in the photographs.

Hine's image appears to communicate a relatively straightforward claim: Child labor turns out "junk" in the form of damaged children. As a result, it suggests, industry should be pressured to change its ways or society will suffer. But specific evidence for the claim of damage is lacking. What, for example, constitutes the poster's evidence that the children depicted have been turned into "junk"? Are we to read it in their faces, body language, clothing? How are we to tell visually what makes the children at the top of the poster "good material" and those at the bottom of the poster "junk"? What happens to the children inside the factory? What exactly is the "process" by which "good material" is turned into "junk"? The poster does not visualize these things.

In order to situate Hine's visual text in ways that help us understand how its claims about child labor function, we may want to ask questions that connect Hine's image to other images, to his photographic practices, and to Progressive-era rhetorics of child labor more generally. When it was reproduced, did the image appear alone or did it appear alongside other images about child labor? Is this image representative of Hine's work, or distinct? Does the claim that child labor turns children into "junk" constitute an original contribution to the child labor debate, or does it echo or reflect prevailing public sentiment? And so on. Exploring these questions below, I argue that when we study "Making Human Junk" in at least one of its contexts of reproduction, we see that the poster's lack of specificity is precisely what gives it its particular rhetorical force. "Making Human Junk" functions not as an isolated visual argument, but as a summative statement for broader arguments about child labor. It summarized the anti-child labor position in ways that connected it to broader arguments linking the health of the child to the health of the nation.

"Making Human Junk" was produced sometime in 1914 or early 1915. It was one of several posters Hine created during this period, images he idiosyncratically called "time exposures," which have been described as "a series of picture-text assemblages about child labor issues, presented in diptych and triptych form."[65] A diptych is a work that consists of two same-sized, separate panels or images hinged or hung together to be viewed as a single message or work of art; a triptych would be three of these.[66] While some who have studied the time exposures suggest they were meant to function as "stand-alone texts," evidence of their reproduction in multiple contexts suggests otherwise.[67] Hine frequently presented them in twos and threes alongside other time exposures, which suggests they were designed to work with other materials.[68]

Hine's corpus of child labor photographs served as raw material for the time exposures. The posters thus recycled images Hine made years earlier; many of these same images had been widely reproduced and circulated in other contexts, such as NCLC reports and social welfare magazines.[69] The time exposures departed from the work that Hine had created in the past. In his initial child labor images, Hine worked like a visual sociologist, meticulously documenting his photographs with the names of his subjects, detailed captions, and extensive notes – information which frequently found its way into stories he produced for magazines. Noting that Hine wrote captions "like an investigative reporter," Daile Kaplan observes that Hine "was not simply an 'illustration' photographer who provided photographs to editors and writers to be used as they wished; he was an active participant in shaping the format in which his photographs were reproduced."[70] But "Making Human Junk" does not offer this kind of specificity. The charges Hine activates in the poster are general ones; he does not identify specific children, nor does he name a specific factory. Instead, he comments on a broad level about the impact of child labor practices on society. This lack of specificity, combined with the time exposures' display in pairs or groups, suggests that they served a rhetorical function different from Hine's other child labor work.

If the time exposures were not created to function as single, isolated instances of visual argument, then it makes sense to perform a critical reading of "Making Human Junk" in the contexts of its reproduction. Below I explore the reproduction of "Making Human Junk" in the February 1915 issue of *Child Labor Bulletin*, the journal of the National Child Labor Committee. When Hine's poster is examined in this context, we can see how it fit into a series of images and texts designed to educate the public about the multiple dangers of child labor.

The February 1915 issue of *Child Labor Bulletin* contained a reproduction of an exhibit handbook made by Lewis Hine called "The High Cost of Child Labor."[71] The handbook was produced as a companion to a "new twenty-five panel exhibit" set to open at the Panama-Pacific International Exposition (World's Fair) of San Francisco in late February. The handbook, according to the editor's note in *Child Labor Bulletin*, was designed to "[amplify] the statements of the panels" and would not only be available for purchase at the World's Fair, but also available to the journal's readers at ten cents a copy.[72]

The reprint of the exhibit handbook consists of 25 pages inserted into the end of the issue. It is divided into four sections presented in a problem–solution structure: "The Cost to the Child"; "The Cost to Industry"; "The Cost to Society"; and "What Are We Going To Do About It?" Each section utilizes both pictures and text. Nine of Hine's time exposures are reproduced, along with one additional photograph and a chart. In each of the handbook's sections, Hine offers statistical evidence to support his claims and cites sources extensively. For example, part one, which examines the cost of child labor to children, is divided into four separate sections: physical effects; accidents; juvenile crime; and loss of education.[73] Throughout the handbook, Hine includes references to sources such as the Federal Bureau of Labor, state legislative initiatives, the NCLC itself, and newspapers from around the country. Part two is similarly structured.

"Making Human Junk" appears in a section called "The Cost to Society," immediately following ten pages of visual and textual evidence offering much more specificity about the ills of child labor than we found in the poster itself. Estimating that child labor places a cost on society upwards of 20 to 25 million dollars a year, Hine reproduces "Making Human Junk" and writes,

> Not only the child, but the parent, the humane employer, and society in general pay tribute to the child employer. He injures all of us because by forcing down wages he ruins the health and souls of future generations, and thus he weakens the nation. The cost to the child and the cost to industry become a cost to society.[74]

Encountering "Making Human Junk" in the context of Hine's discussion of the relationship between the health of the child and the health of the nation, the viewer is given the ultimate reason to care about child labor: Healthy children equal a healthy society. Having encountered the handbook's earlier discussion of costs to children and industry, the viewer of "Making Human Junk" in this context would know what happens inside the factory to turn children into human junk; the reader would be able to fill in the evidence missing from the poster itself. Furthermore, because "Making Human Junk" and the text that accompanies it broaden the discussion to include not just children and industry but all of society, the audience for the handbook is prepared for the long list of solutions offered in the final section of the handbook, "What Are We Going To Do About It?"[75] When read in the context of claims about the social costs of child labor, "Making Human Junk" serves a summative function, punctuating the earlier discussion of the problem and preparing the way for the call to action.[76]

My compositional analysis revealed a tension – the poster's lack of specificity – that was further explored by examining elements of production and reproduction. Situating Hine's time exposure in the contexts of Hine's photographic practices and the image's reproduction as part of a particular textual event – the exhibit handbook published in *Child Labor Bulletin* – helped me to link Hine's poster to the period's discourses about child labor. But broader elements of context are worth considering here as well: How was Hine's rhetoric similar to or different from other rhetoric in the child labor debate? How did Hine's work fit in with other visual discourse about child labor? About childhood in general? There is much that could be said on these points, but at minimum, I note that Hine's arguments about the costs of child labor to society were deeply intertwined with other discourses about the same topic. Child labor discourse – even arguments in support of child labor – heavily utilized rhetorics of health.[77] Furthermore, all sides of the child labor debate emphasized that children were precious products that needed to "turn out" well or risk the physical and moral degeneracy of the nation. In a 1911 speech called "The Conservation of Childhood," for example, Theodore Roosevelt offered what might be considered a verbal analogue to Hine's "Making Human Junk":

> Remember, that the human being is the most important of all products to turn out. …
> If you do not have the right kind of citizens in the future, you cannot make any use
> of the natural resources … the greatest duty of this generation is to see to it that the
> next generation is of the proper kind to continue the work of this nation.[78]

For Roosevelt, as for Hine, children were products, natural resources that needed to be protected and kept healthy. The trope of child health, upon which Hine, Roosevelt, and others drew, emerged after a profound shift in cultural understandings of children and childhood in the late nineteenth century. Viviana Zelizer has chronicled this shift, terming it the "sacralization of childhood." She notes that during this period an image of the ideal child emerged which held children to be precious and priceless products, valuable more for sentimental reasons than for economic ones.[79] Visual culture of the period also emphasized the "sacred child" as a prominent visual topos.[80] In mobilizing arguments against child labor, "Making Human Junk" visualized the widely circulated belief that children were precious commodities who could be corrupted by a system that did not protect their moral and physical health.

When child labor reformers such as Owen Lovejoy praised Lewis Hine for his "efforts to bring the facts and conditions of child employment to public attention," they were doing so for a variety of reasons. Hine not only chronicled visually the conditions facing child workers in the United States, he also mobilized his photographs into multimodal texts that creatively summarized the problems of child labor and articulated the national values that should guide the debate. No single case study can hope to express the diversity and significance of Hine's work, of course.

But this brief study of Hine has served as an illustration of the rhetorical significance of visual modes of public address during Progressive-era child labor debates.

Conclusion

At the outset of this chapter, I set forth a perspective on the study of visual modes of public address grounded in several assumptions: that visual modes of public address shape our experience of public life, that they have just as much capacity to be deliberative as talk and text, and that they are just as much a part of our rhetorical histories as oral and written modes. Decades of increased study of visual culture, combined with increased openness to nonoratorical modes, have put public address scholars in a place where we may begin with such assumptions rather than spend time proving them. This is a very good thing. However, a few tasks remain if the study of visual modes of public address is to mature as it should. One of those tasks, which I have performed in this chapter, is to clarify the variety of potential approaches to the study of visual modes. While no single study needs to employ all of them, taken together the approaches I have outlined here encourage us to take up images in ways that recognize both their specificity as rhetorical documents and their fluidity as circulating artifacts in public culture.

Another important task, one I have modeled here by exploring Lewis Hine's work, is that of recovering visual histories of American public address. Rhetorics of our past were not just read and heard, they were also seen; they deserve to be recovered and seen again. While a few public address scholars have concentrated their work on visual history, countless artifacts are yet to be explored and countless dissertations, articles, and books are yet to be written. We miss much if we neglect the vital work of recovery.

Finally, when we "visualize" public address we come to understand rhetorical history itself differently. Regardless of whether they study images or not, scholars of public address should be as interested in what people view and depict as they are in what they read, write, and speak. Why? Because visual culture participates in rhetorical culture. For example, knowing how ideas such as liberty and freedom were communicated visually throughout American history may enliven and enrich our readings of how oratorical texts mobilized these same ideas.[81] Thus, when we embrace visual modes of public address, we not only validate the role of visuality in public culture, we also open up new avenues for understanding how all modes of rhetoric frame, shape, and frequently challenge our ways of seeing.

Notes

1 On the history of the early twentieth-century child labor reform movement, see Walter I. Trattner, *Crusade for the Children: A History of the National Child Labor Committee and Child Labor Reform in America* (Chicago: Quadrangle Books, 1970).

2   Trattner, *Crusade*, 32, 208.

3   The single exception in our field's journals is J. Robert Cox, "The Rhetoric of Child Labor Reform: An Efficacy-Utility Analysis," *Quarterly Journal of Speech* 60 (1974): 359–370.

4   For example, no speech devoted specifically to child labor appears in Stephen E. Lucas and Martin J. Medhurst, eds., *Words of a Century: The Top 100 Speeches, 1900–1999* (New York: Oxford University Press, 2008).

5   On the history of the NCLC see Trattner, *Crusade*.

6   On Hine's photography, see Alan Trachtenberg, *Reading American Photographs: Images as History from Mathew Brady to Walker Evans* (New York: Noonday Press, 1989), 164–230; Maren Stange, *Symbols of Ideal Life: Social Documentary Photography in America, 1890–1950* (Oxford: Cambridge University Press, 1989), 47–87; and Judith Mara Gutman, *Lewis W. Hine and the American Social Conscience* (New York: Walker and Company, 1967).

7   On Hine as a communicator, see Vicki Goldberg, "Lewis W. Hine, Child Labor, and the Camera," in *Lewis W. Hine: Children at Work*, ed. Vicki Goldberg (New York: Prestel, 1999), 18; George Dimock, "Children of the Mills: Re-Reading Lewis Hine's Child Labor Photographs," *Oxford Art Journal* 16 (1993): 37–54; and Patricia Pace, "Staging Childhood: Lewis Hine's Photographs of Child Labor," *The Lion and the Unicorn* 26 (2002): 324–352. The lone study of Hine in rhetorical studies is Stephen Dane Iseman, "Showing as a Way of Saying, The Photograph and Word Combinations of Lewis Hine in Support of Child Labor Reform" (PhD Diss., Ohio State University, 1993).

8   Stephen E. Lucas, "The Renaissance of American Public Address," in *Landmark Essays on American Public Address*, ed. Martin J. Medhurst (Davis, CA: Hermagoras Press, 1993), 181.

9   Lucas, "Renaissance," 181.

10 David Zarefsky, "The State of the Art in Public Address Scholarship," in *Landmark Essays*, ed. Medhurst, 205.

11 Two useful resources for thinking through visual methodologies are Gillian Rose, *Visual Methodologies: An Introduction to the Interpretation of Visual Materials* (Thousand Oaks, CA: Sage, 2001); and Gunther Kress and Theo van Leeuwen, *Reading Images: The Grammar of Visual Design* (London: Routledge, 1996).

12 For challenges to the dominance of the talk-and-text metaphor, see John Durham Peters, *Speaking Into the Air: A History of the Idea of Communication* (Chicago: University of Chicago Press, 1999), 62; Michael Warner, "Publics and Counterpublics," *Public Culture* 14 (2002): 49–90; and Cara A. Finnegan and Jiyeon Kang, "'Sighting' the Public: Iconoclasm and Public Sphere Theory," *Quarterly Journal of Speech* 90 (2004): 377–402.

13 For examples of the claim that the visual is more "primary" today than in the past, see Martin J. Medhurst and Thomas W. Benson, eds., *Rhetorical Dimensions in Media: A Critical Casebook* (Dubuque, IA: Kendall/Hunt, 1984), vii; and Sonja K. Foss, "A Rhetorical Schema for the Evaluation of Visual Imagery," *Communication Studies* 45 (1994): 213.

14 For an exploration of the history of visual rhetoric in the discipline of communication, see Lester C. Olson, Cara A. Finnegan, and Diane S. Hope, "Visual Rhetoric in Communication: Continuing Questions and Contemporary Issues," in *Visual Rhetoric:*

A Reader in Communication and American Culture, ed. Lester C. Olson, Cara A. Finnegan, and Diane S. Hope (Thousand Oaks, CA: Sage, 2008), 1–14.

15 Cara A. Finnegan, "Doing Rhetorical History of the Visual: The Photograph and the Archive," in *Defining Visual Rhetorics*, ed. Charles Hill and Marguerite Helmers (Mahwah, NJ: Lawrence Erlbaum, 2004), 200.

16 Rose, *Visual Methodologies*, 17.

17 Barbie Zelizer, *Remembering to Forget: Holocaust Memory through the Camera's Eye* (Chicago: University of Chicago Press, 1998).

18 A good source for preliminary information on an artist is Oxford Art Online, a database that gathers together full-text reference works, including *The Oxford Companion to Western Art, The Concise Oxford Dictionary of Art Terms*, and *The Encyclopedia of Aesthetics*.

19 On Lange see Milton Meltzer, *Dorothea Lange: A Photographer's Life* (New York: Farrar, Straus, and Giroux, 1978).

20 Rose, *Visual Methodologies*, 21.

21 Diane S. Hope, "Memorializing Affluence in the Postwar Family: Kodak's Colorama in Grand Central Terminal (1950–1990)," in *Visual Communication: Perception, Rhetoric, and Technology*, ed. Diane S. Hope (Cresskill, NJ: Hampton Press/Rochester Institute of Technology Cary Graphic Arts Press, 2006), 91–110; and Nancy Martha West, *Kodak and the Lens of Nostalgia* (Charlottesville: University Press of Virginia, 2000).

22 On the role of the archive in public address studies, see Charles E. Morris III, ed., "The Politics of Archival Research," *Rhetoric & Public Address* 9 (2006): 113–152.

23 Sylvan Barnet, *A Short Guide to Writing About Art*, 9th ed. (Upper Saddle River, NJ: Pearson/Prentice Hall, 2007), 52–53.

24 Rose, *Visual Methodologies*, 46. See also Barnet, *Short Guide,* chs. 3–4.

25 Rose, *Visual Methodologies*, 39.

26 Richard Lanham defines commonplace as "a general argument, observation or description a speaker could memorize for use on any number of possible occasions." See Lanham, *A Handlist of Rhetorical Terms*, 2nd ed. (Chicago: University of Chicago Press, 1991), 169.

27 Lanham, *Handlist*, 170.

28 On the icon as it applies to photojournalism, see Robert Hariman and John Louis Lucaites, *No Caption Needed: Iconic Photographs, Public Culture, and Liberal Democracy* (Chicago: University of Chicago Press, 2007). Rhetorical scholar Michael McGee's notion of the ideograph frequently has been applied to visual images; see Janis Edwards and Carol K. Winkler, "Representative Form and the Visual Ideograph: The Two Iwo Jima Images in Editorial Cartoons," *Quarterly Journal of Speech* 83 (1997): 289–310; Dana L. Cloud, "'To Veil the Threat of Terror': Afghan Women and the 'Clash of Civilizations' in the Imagery of the US War on Terrorism," *Quarterly Journal of Speech* 90 (2004): 285–306; and Catherine H. Palczewski, "The Male Madonna and the Feminine Uncle Sam: Visual Argument, Icons, and Ideographs in 1909 Anti-Woman Suffrage Postcards," *Quarterly Journal of Speech* 91 (2005): 365–394.

29 David Hackett Fischer, *Liberty and Freedom: A Visual History of America's Founding Ideas* (New York: Oxford University Press, 2005), 37–49.

30 Hélène E. Roberts, ed., *Encyclopedia of Comparative Iconography: Themes Depicted in Works of Art*, 2 vols. (Chicago: Fitzroy Dearborn, 1998).

31 Two popular and well-illustrated histories are Wayne Craven, *American Art: History and Culture*, rev. ed. (Boston: McGraw-Hill, 2003); and Frances K. Pohl, *Framing America: A Social History of American Art* (New York: Thames and Hudson, 2002).

32 Barnet, *Short Guide*, 58. The classic treatment of the gaze is Laura Mulvey, *Visual and Other Pleasures* (Bloomington: Indiana University Press, 1989). See also Marita Sturken and Lisa Cartwright, *Practices of Looking: An Introduction to Visual Culture* (New York: Oxford University Press, 2001), 76–108.

33 Kress and van Leeuwen, *Reading Images*, 122.

34 Rose, *Visual Methodologies*, 24.

35 Rose, *Visual Methodologies*, 38–39.

36 Barnet, *Short Guide*, 66.

37 Rose, *Visual Methodologies*, 39. Value is typically expressed on a continuum from "low" to "high," "low" being the color's form closest to black, "high" being its form closest to white; see also Barnet, *Short Guide*, 67.

38 Kress and van Leeuwen, *Reading Images*, 163–165.

39 Barnet, *Short Guide*, 68, 108.

40 Kress and van Leeuwen, *Reading Images*, 135–140, 182–183.

41 Rose, *Visual Methodologies*, 40.

42 Michael Ann Holly, *Past Looking: Historical Imagination and the Rhetoric of the Image* (Ithaca, NY: Cornell University Press, 1996), 9. See also Rose, *Visual Methodologies*, 44.

43 Kress and van Leeuwen, *Reading Images*, 135–148.

44 Kress and van Leeuwen, *Reading Images*, 140–146.

45 Barnet, *Short Guide*, 71–72.

46 Davi Johnson, "Martin Luther King Jr.'s 1963 Birmingham Campaign as Image Event," *Rhetoric & Public Affairs* 10 (2007): 8.

47 David Zarefsky, "Four Senses of Rhetorical History," in *Doing Rhetorical History: Concepts and Cases*, ed. Kathleen J. Turner (Tuscaloosa: University of Alabama Press, 1998), 30.

48 On historical-contextual analysis, see for example Karlyn Kohrs Campbell and Thomas R. Burkholder, *Critiques of Contemporary Rhetoric*, 2nd ed. (Belmont, CA: Wadsworth, 1997), 49–56.

49 M. K. Johnson, "(Re)Framing the Photograph," *World and Image* 9 (July–September 1993): 247.

50 Cara A. Finnegan, *Picturing Poverty: Print Culture and FSA Photographs* (Washington, DC: Smithsonian Institution Press, 2003).

51 Sturken and Cartwright, *Practices of Looking*, 3–4.

52 James J. Kimble and Lester C. Olson, "Visual Rhetoric Representing Rosie the Riveter: Myth and Misconception in J. Howard Miller's 'We Can Do It!' Poster," *Rhetoric & Public Affairs* 9 (2006): 548.

53 On the constitutive nature of circulation and "cultures of circulation," see Benjamin Lee and Edward LiPuma, "Culture of Circulation: The Imaginations of Modernity," *Public Culture* 14 (2002): 191–213.

54 Warner, "Publics and Counterpublics," 62.

55 Hariman and Lucaites, *No Caption Needed*, 295.

56 Lester C. Olson, *Benjamin Franklin's Vision of American Community: A Study in Rhetorical Iconology* (Columbia: University of South Carolina Press, 2004), 27–76.

57 Sturken and Cartwright, *Practices of Looking*, 350.

58 Hariman and Lucaites, *No Caption Needed*, 37. On appropriation, see also Robert Hariman and John Louis Lucaites, "Problems and Prospects in the Study of Visual Culture," *Review of Communication* 8 (2008): 16–20.

59 Leah Ceccarelli, *Shaping Science With Rhetoric* (Chicago: University of Chicago Press, 2001), 171.

60 Catherine A. Lutz and Jane L. Collins, *Reading National Geographic* (Chicago: University of Chicago Press, 1993).

61 Ceccarelli, *Shaping Science*, 8.

62 Cara A. Finnegan, "Recognizing Lincoln: Image Vernaculars in Nineteenth-Century Visual Culture," *Rhetoric & Public Affairs* 8 (2005): 31–58.

63 "Making Human Junk," time exposure by Lewis Hine, *Child Labor Bulletin* 3.4 (1915): 35. Iseman briefly describes the composition of this image in his discussion of Hine's work on child labor exhibits. See Iseman, "Showing," 207–210.

64 Some scholars have explored parts of this image in terms of circulation and reception. George Dimock has examined the circulation of specific photographs from "Making Human Junk" and showed not only how Hine himself mobilized those images in other contexts, but also how opponents of child labor reform mobilized them. See Dimock, "Children of the Mills."

65 The term "time exposure" is unique to Hine, and seems to suggest his interest in visualizing a process as opposed to the typical frozen moment in time usually captured by a photograph. See Daile Kaplan, ed., *Photo Story: Selected Letters and Photographs of Lewis W. Hine* (Washington, DC: Smithsonian Institution Press, 1992), xxviii.

66 "Diptych," *The Oxford Dictionary of Art*, ed. Ian Chilvers (New York: Oxford University Press, 2004), Oxford Art Online, www.oxfordartonline.com (accessed July 20, 2009).

67 Though he acknowledges that Hine's time exposures frequently appeared alongside magazine articles or with exhibit materials, Iseman describes them as "stand-alone units" and "complete self-contained communication" ("Showing," 190).

68 For evidence that time exposures were displayed as diptychs or triptychs, Kaplan reproduces an image made at the child labor exhibit at the San Francisco World's Fair in 1915; it appears between pages 26 and 27 in Kaplan, *Photo Story*.

69 Peter Seixas, "Lewis Hine: From 'Social' to 'Interpretive' Photographer," *American Quarterly* 39 (1987): 381–409; and Dimock, "Children of the Mills."

70 Kaplan, *Photo Story*, xx–xxi. On the specificity of Hine's documentation in his early child labor work, see also Dimock, "Children of the Mills," 39.

71 Lewis Hine, "The High Cost of Child Labor," *Child Labor Bulletin* 3.4 (1915): 25–45.

72 "Notes: San Francisco Exhibit," *Child Labor Bulletin* 3.4 (1915): 7. The price of the exhibit handbook is advertised at the back of the issue, on 47.

73 Hine, "The High Cost," 26–30.

74 Hine, "The High Cost," 34.

75 Hine, "The High Cost," 39.

76 One could also begin to track the circulation of "Making Human Junk" during this period by exploring its reproduction in the San Francisco World's Fair exhibit from which the handbook text and images are drawn. In doing so, the critic could explore the time exposure's role in the complete exhibit on child labor, as well as the context of its reproduction and staging amid the spectacles and entertainments of the fair itself.

77 On arguments that used the trope of child health, see Cara A. Finnegan, "'Liars May Photograph': Image Vernaculars and Progressive Era Child Labor Rhetoric," *Poroi* 5.2 (2008): 93–139; *Poroi: An Interdisciplinary Journal of Rhetorical Analysis and Invention*, ir.uiowa.edu/poroi/vol5/iss2/3/ (accessed July 20, 2009).

78 Colonel Theodore Roosevelt, "The Conservation of Childhood," *Annals of the American Academy of Political and Social Science* (New York: National Child Labor Committee, 1911), 8.

79 Viviana Zelizer, *Pricing the Priceless Child: The Changing Social Value of Children* (Princeton, NJ: Princeton University Press, 1994).

80 Anne Higonnet, *Pictures of Innocence: The History and Crisis of Ideal Childhood* (London: Thames and Hudson, 1998); and West, *Kodak and the Lens of Nostalgia*.

81 Fischer, *Liberty and Freedom*.

11

Theory and Public Address
The Allusive Mr. Bush

John M. Murphy

In 1965, Edwin Black published *Rhetorical Criticism: A Study in Method*.[1] Disciplinary histories agree that Black changed the terrain of public address studies and the book "is widely credited with ushering in the final demise of neo-Aristotelian criticism."[2] James Jasinski calls it "perhaps the most notable piece of metacriticism in the field." Dilip P. Gaonkar argues that Black "set the stage for the ensuing pluralist hiatus that persists to this day." Although David Zarefsky disagrees with the claim that public address studies disappeared after Black's book, he, too, tells the accepted tale: "But, the story continues, all that was changed in the mid-1960s when Edwin Black exposed the pitfalls of neo-Aristotelianism. In response to his clarion call, scholars abandoned public address, rushing instead to call themselves rhetorical critics or theorists."[3]

Of course, these scholars and others complicate Black's work in useful ways. So far as I know, however, only Stephen Lucas recovers this aspect of Black's legacy: "In addition to being attuned to growing discontent among scholars of rhetoric, *Rhetorical Criticism* coincided with the emancipatory impulse of much social, political, and academic discourse in the 1960s." Lucas does not wish to "trivialize" political activists. But, he notes, "what Black identified as a central defect of neo-Aristotelianism – its equivocation on the moral dimensions of rhetorical discourse – could not help but resonate with the moral underpinnings of the major protest movements of the day, especially the quest for civil rights."[4]

For the most part, the anxiety produced by that emancipatory impulse has escaped the notice of those concerned with the relationship between rhetorical theory and public address. For instance, the most widely cited quotation from the 1970 Wingspread Conference report is probably this one: "Whether rhetorical criticism *ought* to contribute to theory seems to us beyond question."[5] This statement has become part of a common narrative that decries the subordination of public address to rhetorical theory, a story that suggests that critics of the time pursued the false god of science.[6] Yet, *The Prospect of Rhetoric* reveals another reason for the emphasis on theory: Fear. The book throbs with concern for the field's ability to manage moral and political upheavals; its contributors hope that theory will allay their difficulties. Wayne Booth draws on his experiences at the University of Chicago to plead: "What I would like someone to provide for me ... is an 'art of invention' that would help me deal with ... the fact that two of my former students, students with whom I have worked closely for a full year, are now members of the Weatherman crowd."[7] Wayne Brockriede notes in that volume: "If contemporary rhetorical practice is experiencing a revolution, conceptual models for that practice must also be revolutionized."[8] I recognize the intellectual impulse to transform criticism, but the examples suggest another motivation: In the face of political activism, these scholars grappled with the practical and moral force of rhetorical theory and its relationship to the public address they experienced every day.

Since then, concern for the "moral dimensions" of public address has periodically erupted into scholarly work, from Black's 1970 "Second Persona" to the 1972 Hill/Campbell debate through Philip Wander's 1983 call for ideological criticism.[9] Yet, I am not sure that we have fully grasped the effect of such debates on the relationship between public address and rhetorical theory. If the "pluralist hiatus" disrupted our intellectual foundations, it also undermined the moral consensus sustaining public address scholarship. Martin J. Medhurst has summarized the traditional normative goals of such work: "To be able to articulate a point of view, defend a proposition, attack an evil, or celebrate a set of common values was seen as one of the central ways in which the people retained their freedoms and shaped their society. Training in public address was thus understood to be preparation for citizenship in a democratic Republic."[10] The subsequent destabilization can be measured by the ways in which these words now wobble; for instance, the "people," as Michael McGee defined them, is no longer a univocal term that warrants public address study.[11] To trace the relationships between theory and text demands concomitant attention to our moral commitments. I argue this generally unexplored connection has played a major role in crafting the public address scholar's view of theory.

Essays such as this one often adopt the form of a progress narrative; they point out past deficiencies and suggest a new relationship between theory and text that should shape future work. I resist that impulse (imperfectly, I know) because I suspect the old ways of integrating theory and text remain even as we chart new departures. More radically, some wish to excise theory from public address study. I do not think that would be a useful choice.[12] I cannot put it better than Thomas Farrell: "Theory in the area of study called *rhetoric* can be divorced from practice only at great cost to both. For the very aim of rhetorical theory has always been to define and articulate a vision of what the highest potential of rhetorical practice might be ... theorists of rhetoric are absorbed in an enterprise that is unmistakably of ethical, aesthetic, and normative significance. They are concerned with the modes of realizing the highest possibilities of the practice known as rhetoric."[13]

In this essay, I explore four modes of theoretical reflection that public address scholars use in order to realize the possibilities of rhetoric: classification, generalization, subversion, and abduction. Although the order follows roughly the historical development of these modes, each continues to influence public address studies. I follow these discussions with a brief analysis that illustrates how the modes craft critical practice. Specifically, I focus on the allusions, the shadow text, that haunt the explicit argument of President George W. Bush's Second Inaugural Address.

Modes of Reflection

The term "modes of reflection" indicates my interest in how we ponder the relationships between rhetorical theory and public address. Like Farrell, I see these as "modalities" rather than "ahistorical universals." They are unfinished efforts, affected by time and circumstance, liable to revision.[14] Each carries with it a vocabulary with characteristic concerns for power, aesthetics, and norms. Each offers the danger that critics will get carried away as we pursue its implications, but each also assists critics in specifying the "highest possibilities" of rhetoric. Neither are they mutually exclusive; a particular work may favor one, but all likely entangle themselves in the final result. I turn now to these modes.

Classification

Since Black's demolition of neo-Aristotelianism and Brockriede's attack on criticism that merely categorizes, classification has fallen into bad odor.[15] Particularly for the generation of critics who grew up reading Brockriede (mine), there is no greater critical sin than classification. Yet this generation has also spent time in the classroom trying to teach criticism and learned anew old truths. Students need names to "see" rhetorical action. Names flow from efforts to make a disorderly world orderly. That means we classify. Karlyn Kohrs Campbell and Kathleen Hall Jamieson assert, "To deal with anything at all without classifying or typing it, without remarking on similarities or dissimilarities to other like or unlike things, is simply not possible."[16]

This realization has led to the popularity of Jasinski's *Sourcebook on Rhetoric*, Richard Lanham's *A Handlist of Rhetorical Terms*, Thomas Sloane's *Encyclopedia of Rhetoric*, and even to a renewed appreciation for Chaim Perelman and Lucie Olbrechts-Tyteca's *The New Rhetoric*.[17] These books, like my essay, harness the impulse to name and classify the rhetorical phenomena we observe on a regular basis. Despite their varying views, I believe the authors share a common desire to name the rhetorical world and, by doing so, exert control over it. The metaphors of "sight" and "light," our Enlightenment intellectual legacy, pop up here. If we can name it, we can see it. If we can see it, we can understand it. If we can understand it, we can control it. This mode of engagement hews most closely to the traditional civic justification for public address study. By knowing how the civic world works and by teaching that to our student-citizens, we improve the state of the Republic.

It is no accident, I think, that this impulse has resurfaced in an era when citizens feel ever more helpless to control the institutions supposedly subject to their authority as a sovereign people. In that sense, the study of presidential rhetoric provides an instructive example. Particularly since the concept of the "rhetorical presidency" entered our critical lexicon, scholars have sought to trace and understand the lineaments of presidential talk.[18] Projects focus on individual speeches, persuasive campaigns, or political controversies. What they have in common is an apparent desire to name and understand the rhetorical resources available to the president and the ways in which those resources interact with or constitute the institution.

Campbell and Jamieson provide an explicit justification for this effort. They argue first that generic criticism is a useful way to approach public rhetoric.[19] Genre means type or sort. As I note above, we understand discursive events through comparison to other like or unlike events. Clearly, the inductive categories one uses do not provide a fail-safe means of knowledge, but then no system does. What a generic perspective offers is a longitudinal view of acts; over time, it allows us to observe the features that emerge consistently from, in this case, presidential rhetoric and to ask why those features matter. Campbell and Jamieson argue next that most people tend to talk about presidential rhetoric in terms of genres, from inaugurals to states of the union to war speeches to veto addresses. This fact suggests "that symbolic institutional needs are at least as powerful as the force of events in shaping the rhetoric of any historical period."[20] This is a claim that can be tested. The creation of a "people" to witness the investiture of a new president, for instance, charges inaugurals through the centuries. Thus, Campbell and Jamieson contend, we interpret the institution, in part, through its genres. Material and political forces help constitute the presidency, but the institution also defines and renews itself through recourse to its characteristic ways of talking.[21] We appreciate the aesthetic or ethical qualities of a specific presidential address through comparison to others in its genre. We understand the genres of governance, in turn, with reference to specific exemplars; they show us what the presidency can be at its best and at its worst. Whether critics focus on the specific or the general, they grasp the workings of the presidency as an institution from a generic perspective.

As this example demonstrates, generic criticism, perhaps the exemplar of our classificatory impulse, illuminates most nicely discourses connected to institutions. When critics go in search of "The Rhetoric of…" without any purpose, they categorize for no reason and fulfill the stereotypes we have about this mode. Yet the institutional focus for genre study gives it critical purchase. Criticism not explicitly concerned with genre often accounts for it as scholars seek to understand the ways that institutions affect rhetoric, and vice versa. Bonnie J. Dow cares more about feminism than genre, but when she examines the mediation of feminism by entertainment television, she explores the norms of situation comedy. Similarly, Trevor Parry-Giles recognizes the recurrent features of Supreme Court nomination fights even as he focuses on the communal definitions of judicial character that emerge from these debates.[22]

Within this mode of theoretical engagement, there is a Deweyan impulse. The problem with the public is clear; they do not know enough about the discourses that shape communal life in the United States. If critical work provides that knowledge, then education can improve public rhetoric and prepare student and teacher for citizenship in a republic. The best exemplars, such as Lincoln's Second Inaugural, become standards by which succeeding instances are judged. Whether at the level of textual strategy (amplification) or institutional genre (inaugural), classification gives us the means to make comprehensible rhetorical worlds. If we know them, we can improve them.

Generalization

At the least, classification implies the next mode of theoretical engagement – generalization. Categories that do not endure are not particularly useful. Yet public address scholars generalize not only across time, but also across discursive strategies, spaces, and activities. The call to generalize suggests critics bear the same burden as students of psychology, genetics, or leisure studies; all must account for a coherent body of plausible knowledge that people can use. Much like scientists, then, public address scholars need to create a powerful conceptual record that encourages generalization from the specific case study to a larger theory of public rhetoric. Edwin Black, again, is most often praised or blamed for this impulse.

Black's 1965 comparison of the critic and the scientist is an early effort to see public address research as a sort of science. The analogy posits that scientists produce generalizable knowledge, an epistemological achievement to which critics should aspire. The logic of this call for generalization takes specific shape in Kenneth Burke's justification for studying *Mein Kampf*: "let us try also to discover what kind of 'medicine' this medicine-man has concocted, that we may know, with greater accuracy, exactly what to guard against, if we are to forestall the concocting of a similar medicine in America."[23] Burke assumes that the symbolic action of *Mein Kampf* flows across time and space. We must understand it, and beware of it. Scapegoating Germany's Jews may be key to Adolf Hitler's rhetoric, but this sort of scapegoat concoction could spread to the United States and so we must be prepared for its appearance.

Sadly, that horse left the barn long ago. As Michael Pfau notes, for instance, Americans have demonized scapegoats in a long history of conspiracy discourse.[24] Since the settlement of the continent, orators have posited conspiracies, the secret cooperation of powerful cabals for some base purpose. From King George III's ministers to CIA assassins, patriots and film directors have "revealed" the evildoers lurking behind the arc of US history. Yet Pfau also notes that conspiracy discourse has regularly moved into the American mainstream. Drawing on the work of Richard Hofstadter, David Zarefsky, and others, Pfau explores "the political style of conspiracy" through critique of early Republicans (Salmon P. Chase, Charles Sumner, and Abraham Lincoln) who feared the "slave power."[25] Much like a social scientist, Pfau defines his terms, reviews the literature, and generalizes the rhetorical elements of a conspiracy – a perfect scapegoat, a plausible plot, a surfeit of proof – to cabals past and present. He concludes that a "critical and hermeneutic approach is essential" to equipping "citizens with the means to make sense of and evaluate the barrage of conspiratorial interpretations increasingly characterizing early twenty-first-century discourse."[26] In this view, theoretical and practical goods flow from basic research into rhetoric, as they do from basic research into psyches, genes, or leisure choices. A reader learns about the ubiquitous content and form of conspiracy rhetoric from Pfau's study of the slave power, but one learns also to generalize antebellum rhetorical patterns to "early twenty-first-century discourse."

In accounting for the "scientizing" of criticism, however, William Nothstine, Carole Blair, and Gary Copeland take the opposite tack. They begin with Black as they trace the genealogy of generalization in public address.[27] They see the analogy as an impossible dream. Scientists produce valid and reliable knowledge, qualities that make generalization possible. Perhaps that can be done in other arenas, but they doubt rhetoric can do it. Rhetorical practice is too messy for generalization. We warp rhetoric when it becomes an "object" of scientific study. The analogy promotes an ideology that disengages critics from political and moral responsibilities inherent to the activity. In effect, it is a deal struck with the Establishment. Critics are professionals. They speak to each other, add to the conceptual record, and annoy no one. They should be granted academic freedom because they are harmless.[28] Nothstine, Blair, and Copeland trace the trend from Black to Wingspread to Campbell to Brockriede to Hart to others; it seems a damning account.

Too damning, perhaps. It also ironically reveals a trace of the conspiracy discourse (a surfeit of proof) that Pfau delineates. There is little doubt that public address scholars generalize as Pfau does, despite these objections. Drawing inspiration from Burke, Northrop Frye, and others, critics believe, as Frye writes, "that just as there is an order of nature behind natural sciences, so literature is not a piled aggregate of 'works,' but an order of words."[29] This is the conceptual record of which Roderick Hart so polemically wrote.[30] There is a rhetorical order of words to which we return, an imbrication of content and form, such as conspiracy rhetoric (or jeremiads or romances) that provide inventional resources for orators across time and space. Given the assumption of a "natural" order of words, we generalize from context to context. Science's language is part and parcel of what even the most radical or particularist of critics do, as Bonnie Dow argues.[31]

It is important to note, however, that few critics see generalization as the sole end of public address study. James Darsey's critique of Hart's perspective thrills most hearts.[32] As Darsey argues, we risk losing the texture of specific rhetorical acts in the elucidation of a broad discursive order. So, Nothstine, Blair, and Copeland are not entirely wrong, either. It is significant that the two critics who most inspire generalization, Kenneth Burke and Northrop Frye, wrote prolifically in the 1950s, the height of the American century. Generalization as a legitimation device for academic disciplines works most efficiently in a technocratic society, one defined by the end of ideology, in that famous phrase. There is truth in such a social order. We can see it, measure it, and define it. Those who do so legitimate their work.

That ideological and scientific consensus, however, almost invariably leaves someone out. Taken to the end of the line, generalization operates not through induction but through definition; rather than modifying assumptions in light of new, different, or recalcitrant cases, theorists exclude particulars that do not meet generalized norms.[33] Armed with definitions, rhetorical theorists are never wrong. Cases that fail to fit are dropped from the legitimate domain of discourse so that the theory is always true. Speeches that disrupt the theory are "obviously" flawed, imperfect copies of "correct" rhetorical strategies or cultural norms. As such, no one need account for them. To save the general, the particular is sacrificed – or forced to conform. The moral implications are obvious, at least to those who do not fit the appropriate mold.

Subversion

Thus, we reach the third mode of engagement, subversion. The impulse to subvert the order of words in public address arose primarily from studies of war and antiwar rhetoric, civil rights, feminism, student activism – the social movements that seemingly led to the end of the American century's liberal consensus.[34] In the eyes of feminist, neo-Marxist, and poststructuralist critics, the order of words shapes not a heuristic generalization of theoretical terms but a continuing domination of people's lives. A critic's task in such circumstances is to subvert, undermine, or deconstruct the social order and reveal its arbitrary nature. Recently, the most resonant version of this impulse takes the form of critical rhetoric and the most coherent account of that for working critics of public address comes from John Sloop.

In *Disciplining Gender*, Sloop lists three qualities that characterize critical rhetoric.[35] First, he emphasizes "*doxastic* rather than *epistemic* knowledge."[36] Instead of proving "the truth" about rhetorical phenomena (gender, in this case), critical rhetoricians explore their cultural construction. Second, following Judith Butler, critical rhetoric sees rhetorical acts, like its own writing, as political performances. The order of words, including criticism, rests on no sure foundation. Instead, that order relies on mutable discourses; they are performances, iterations of norms, not undeniable truths. Finally, theoretically pliable discursive formations are, paradoxically, material. Through repetition, words thicken. A particular "way of life becomes a rigid object of discourse." That rhetoric merges "with a vast array of mass mediated, educational, and governmental discourses that ultimately work in the interests of the governing (and economically powerful)."[37]

Practically, two other critical choices emerge from this perspective. If the order of words is of interest, then single texts are not. Sloop and others operating from this perspective survey an array of rhetoric – "fragments" in Michael McGee's terms – for discursive patterns that shape ways of life or (to use another term) the common sense of a culture. The sense of the community that results from this mass of discourse, its *doxa*, disciplines citizens. Sloop, following Celeste Condit, conceptualizes the consensus not as pure domination by the powerful, but rather as "concordance," partially agreed to by all subjects, although the powerful wield undue influence in the process.[38]

Critical rhetoric is only one manifestation of this impulse in public address studies.[39] Yet, it incarnates qualities that characterize the subversive mode of engagement. From Wander to Kent Ono to Ron Greene, critics oppose important elements of contemporary culture and politics; they deny the intrinsic "truth" of its aesthetics, ethics, and discourses; they rearrange the narratives, keywords, ideologies, audiences, and structures that constitute the social order; and they undermine the efficacy of such discourses by revealing their arbitrary construction and deleterious effects. Theory becomes a means with which one subverts addresses to publics constituted by discourses. Deconstruct the discursive orders and you deconstruct the publics that warrant oppressive policies.

As Sloop's critiques demonstrate, the perspectives percolating within this mode offer a rich theoretical vocabulary to reach that end. These languages establish legitimacy in a contentious time through identification with political activists. Yet that alignment does not necessarily extend to the reforms forwarded by those advocates. A new order, it is feared, creates new relations of dominance that must again be subverted. Sloop writes: "Significantly, in highlighting the discursive elements of ideological discipline, I would argue that we are simultaneously deconstructing it."[40] That may be true, but it fails to provide us with a place called home. What replaces a corrupt order? How might that be accomplished? At best, critical rhetoricians posit a constant complication, an unceasing effort to undermine the norms of an oppressive community.[41]

Abduction

When taken to their extremes, generalization and subversion emphasize the extent and power of discursive order, although they offer different evaluations of it. Those practicing generalization rejoice at their theoretical reach while those practicing subversion decry the oppressive power of discursive structures. The fourth mode, abduction, flows from an alternative perspective on discourse and community, nicely expressed by the slogan, "Think globally, act locally." Consistent with scholars across the academy, some critics now posit theory without modernity.[42] They have haphazardly developed what Jasinski defines as "conceptually oriented criticism" or "*abduction*, which might be thought of as a back and forth tacking movement between text and the concept or concepts that are being investigated simultaneously."[43]

This mode grows out of the close reading school of criticism. For some time, Michael Leff and others have argued that critical pluralism draws scholars farther away from, not deeper into, a key critical object: the text or, more specifically, a "paradigm of rhetorical excellence – a touchstone which concretely embodies the potential of the art and exploits resources common to the art in an exemplary fashion."[44] Leff and Andrew Sachs view a text "not as a mirror of reality, but as a field of action unified into a functional and locally stable product."[45] Locally stable products, in turn, compose style and content, form and argument into a discursive whole. Such speeches craft a coherent meaning out of the disparate scraps of public life and call upon audiences to accept that interpretation of their experience. In the eyes of critics such as Leff, Stephen Lucas, and Stephen Browne, orators invite audiences to understand and act in the world as the orator understands and acts – to have representation as Edmund Burke represented it or to mark slavery as Abraham Lincoln would have it marked.[46]

The focus on touchstones seems to imply an anti-theoretical stance, as do occasional comments such as "understanding locates itself in the full complexity of a particular transaction rather than in the discovery of abstract regularities or disembodied theoretical principles."[47] That is not the case, however. Rather, the angle of vision differs from modernist theory. Leff's readings, for instance, are nearly always guided by rich theoretical concepts such as *kairos*. As Jasinski explains, rather than creating a "method" to be used deductively, abduction thickens text and concept; understanding of the text's action grows as the text, in turn, illuminates concepts such as prudence, disposition, charisma, style, decorum, circulation, or other "intermediate" terms guiding analysis. The goal is not generalization. Instead, abduction deepens understanding of a region of shared public experience and the rhetorical moves that make it so. In a sense, as Browne and Leff contend, this mode asks critics to "exercise the same kind of situated judgment that argumentative performance exhibits."[48] Much as orators move between the general and the particular, judging in light of both, so, too, should critics.

In fact, judgment, prudence, *phronesis*, or other aligned terms inspired this mode.[49] In his study of Henry Clay's defense of the 1850 compromise on slavery, for instance, Jasinski contrasts abduction to critiques focusing either on "substantive historical doctrine" or "formal, timeless technique." Instead, he argues, concepts such as prudence "endure through time in an abstract, inchoate form and achieve concrete existence in particular discursive performances." In this case, he focuses on Clay as he negotiates the public controversy over the compromise measures. Specifically, Jasinski posits that the "strategies and gestures" in Clay's famous oration constitute "a particular form of prudence" he terms "prudential accommodation."[50] The critique deepens and thickens our understanding of this form of judgment by revealing the specific strategies embodied in it (such as dissociation and locus of the existent) as well as by contrasting it to its close relation, prudential audacity. Clay's judgment and the shared region of public experience he posits come alive in the critique even as the concept of prudence itself takes on additional weight and meaning.

Yet Jasinski's sailing metaphor suggests resistance to this theoretical move; to "tack" means to turn "a boat's head into and through the wind." It is difficult, as novelists from C. S. Forester to Patrick O'Brian have taught us. I suspect that difficulty rests partly in the fact that concepts never look quite the same in different performances; Edmund Burke and Henry Clay share conservative views, but prudence, whatever its core attributes, will feel different in their respective orations. In addition, key rhetorical concepts present different shadings as they take shape

within what scholars have variously termed performative traditions, language paradigms, or political idioms.[51] The civic republican and liberal traditions, for instance,
invoke different senses of judgment. In short, this mode does "not take the form
of a ladder leading up to and down from high order abstractions." Instead, as
Leff's rather purple but still instructive metaphor suggests, the development of a
concept "moves across a discipline as a fire burns through a forest, growing, shifting, and receding in irregular patterns, gathering intensity from the matter it con-
sumes, but having no existence apart from that matter."[52]

Taken to the end of the line, however, such work threatens to focus scholarly
attention solely on the fire, as it were, to the neglect of concrete political decisions.
It threatens, in other words, to become a kind of intellectual or aesthetic history.
Critics lose the concrete realities of the struggle for social and political justice and,
instead, content themselves with the ebb and flow of orations and concepts. Farrell
reminds us: "in the ongoing story line of rhetoric, audience and advocate together
engage urgent, unsettled matters through recurrent but reflective conflict. What
may or may not be good or noble or just in the particular case is settled (for *now*)
through the engaged decision of competent others." As we settle matters for *now*,
rhetoric works "to establish a mode of reflection involving something more general, emergent, and unfolding – the virtues and convictions of culture and an interested audience necessarily involved in unfinished episodes of public life."[53] I would
only add that there are multiple modes of reflection, ways of organizing public
thought to cope with the need to decide. In American politics, one occasion that
invites such reflection is the inauguration of an American president.

Allusive Shadows

Campbell and Jamieson acknowledge the pedestrian reputation of most inaugural
addresses, but argue that "inaugurals are maligned because their symbolic function
is misunderstood ... they are an essential element in a ritual of transition in which
the covenant between the citizenry and their leaders is renewed."[54] That covenant
constrains and inspires. Its terms cannot alter dramatically from president to president, yet each president puts his mark on the relationship between leader and led.
In making that mark, presidents face an inventional obstacle; on this sort of occasion, epideictic speech offers no immediate exigence to which an orator must
respond. As a result, Campbell and Jamieson note, *memoria*, "or recollection of a
shared past becomes an exceptionally important resource."[55]

One way into *memoria*, they note in passing, is through previous presidents.
Inaugural addresses display a powerful proclivity toward intertextuality or "the way
in which utterances and texts intermingle with each other as well as the way in
which one text is frequently derived from another."[56] Campbell and Jamieson
write, "In other words, presidents recognize, capitalize on, and are constrained by
the inaugurals of their predecessors, which, taken together, form a tradition."[57] I
want to suggest briefly that such intertextuality crafts a kind of shadow text, one

that can infuse and unify, but one that can also haunt and divide the rhetorical performance. Such is the case with George W. Bush's Second Inaugural.

On this occasion, Bush dealt less with the need to enact his leadership and more with the desire to justify his foreign policy, specifically the invasion of Iraq and the idea of preemptive war. Those acts emphasized his role as commander-in-chief, but brought into question the role of the people in public deliberation. If he could take the nation into war on a false premise (the fabled "weapons of mass destruction"), then what was left of the covenant between leader and led? Were we supposed simply to trust him? What sort of people did he think he led? Identity also bedeviled his key constituency, the conservative movement. On the one hand, they believed in the "self-made" man, the liberal actor who thrived absent the heavy hand of government.[58] On the other hand, they believed in what Andrew Sullivan called "the Theoconservative Project": "the elevation of a set of religious doctrines as the primary means to understand and govern a disillusioned, chaotic world."[59] Needless to say, one of these people was not the other. One freed itself through action in the arena; the other freed itself through obedience to God's will. In his First Inaugural, Bush leaned heavily toward the latter.[60] As he again took the oath, the tension between them took center stage.

The tension appears early and develops throughout the speech. After the normal salutations, Bush defines the day as many have done. Specifically, he echoes John Kennedy's rhythmic language of celebration: "On this day, prescribed by law and marked by ceremony, we celebrate the durable wisdom of our Constitution, and recall the deep commitments that unite our country. I am grateful for the honor of this hour, mindful of the consequential times in which we live, and determined to fulfill the oath that I have sworn and you have witnessed."[61] The imagery emphasizes traditional ideals: durable wisdom, deep commitments. The "rolling triad" echoes Kennedy's rhetoric as well as one of JFK's favorites, Winston Churchill.[62] However, the words sunder what Kennedy's Inaugural held together. Kennedy, Campbell and Jamieson argue, redefined the oath of office as a pledge for all: "This much we pledge – and more."[63] In his text, the president and the people took the oath of office. Bush, in the first person, is the only one to take his oath; the "people," "you," in his awkward construction, merely witness. The shadow of Kennedy's language highlights the contrast.

Of course, presidents always seek to constitute the audience as witnesses to the ceremony; great inaugurals, however, "reenact the original process by which the people and their leaders 'form a more perfect union.'"[64] That does not happen here. In fact, the audience's passivity widens and deepens in the next section. Typical of second inaugurals, Bush turns to the past and shapes history: "At this second gathering, our duties are defined not by the words I use, but by the history we have seen together."[65] Note the causal logic: History necessitates duty and words fail in the face of the visual directive. Bush also repeats a metaphor dear to his heart; we have "seen" this history together. The people are positioned as passive witnesses to history. As Bush did in his address to Congress on September 20, 2001, he defines the visual as self-evident truth; we see and therefore we know.[66] No interpretation required.

In a dumbfounding passage, Bush extends that role to the Cold War: "For a half century, America defended our own freedom by standing watch on distant borders. After the shipwreck of communism came years of relative quiet, years of repose, years of sabbatical – and then there came a day of fire."[67] Veterans of Korea and Vietnam, as well as of other hot moments in a Cold War, might be surprised that they merely stood watch. They likely assumed that they took a more active role. As metaphor, "shipwreck" also implies that communism came to grief of its own accord; the captain steered the ship onto the rocks. Again, veterans and presidents might think the United States did something more; they might think that they had "been granted the role of defending freedom in its hour of maximum danger," as President Kennedy said.[68] Also, President George H. W. Bush, President Bill Clinton, and thousands of veterans probably believe that the first Iraq War, Panama, Somalia, Bosnia, and Kosovo constitute something more than a sabbatical.

In my view, President Bush reconfigures history for three reasons. First, the ease of the recent past emphasizes his Churchillian stature; only World War II, he and his colleagues have said, compares to the present.[69] Yet, his references to Kennedy's Inaugural create tension. If the only true precedent is World War II, then why allude to 1961? Second, Bush implies a deterministic view of history. Opposition to his course, then, is not only undesirable but irrational. One cannot oppose the predetermined arc of history. Again, however, his favorite presidential forebears, from Kennedy to Reagan, would deny this claim. In their view, the American people and their president make history. Finally, Bush exploits the capacity of epideictic address to craft a new world of the old. As I argue elsewhere, that transformation is a consistent strategy in his rhetoric.[70] The "day of fire" marks a new time and justifies unprecedented actions, such as officially sanctioned torture.[71] Again, however, intertextuality combats this impulse. A text infused with the past cannot deny its own relevance in a new day while claiming all the while that history rules us all. The contradictions multiply in the next section.

In Bush's new world, we can turn only to our old ideals. He defines "the deepest source" of our "vulnerability" through cooking metaphors: "whole regions of the world simmer in resentment and tyranny – prone to ideologies that feed hatred and excuse murder."[72] Such language cannot help but suggest the president's Platonic view of rhetoric as "mere cookery" and, perhaps, his view of the sort of "republic" he governs. Only "one force of history," he asserts, can take the simmering pot off of the stove: "human freedom. We are led, by events and common sense, to one conclusion: The survival of liberty in our land increasingly depends on the success of liberty in other lands."[73] This again references President Kennedy, but the most remarkable presence in this passage is an absence: the American people. Recall the beautifully crafted original: "Let every nation know, whether it wishes us well or ill, that we shall pay any price, bear any burden, meet any hardship, support any friend, oppose any foe to assure the survival and success of liberty."[74] Moya Ball and others have taken issue with this passage, seeing in it the seeds of Vietnam, but all must agree that the agency of the American people could not be more apparent.[75] We oppose any foe and we support any friend. We make the survival and success of liberty possible. By contrast, Bush speaks in the passive voice ("We are led"), defers to events and common sense, and attributes agency only to what he appears to see as Platonic ideals: freedom and liberty. "Freedom, free, and liberty" appear roughly 50 times in this short speech. He marks these ideals again later in the address when he chooses to "speak anew to my fellow citizens."[76]

At this point, he asks for the "patience" of Americans as we "act" in the "great liberating tradition of this nation." We can act. But in the metaphorical mess that follows, a limited human agency is overwhelmed by natural imagery: "By our efforts, we have lit a fire as well – a fire in the minds of men. It warms those who feel its power, it burns those who fight its progress. And one day this untamed fire of freedom will reach the darkest corners of the world."[77] Not even you can prevent freedom fires. The passage mangles Kennedy's original: "The energy, the faith, the devotion which we bring to this endeavor will light our country and all who serve it – and the glow from that fire can truly light the world."[78] Again, note the deflation of agency. In Kennedy's version, our character, energy, and devotion take center stage. In Bush's version, the "untamed" fire assumes the leading role. We light it but, once lit, as Smokey Bear would warn us, it spreads beyond human control. As subject, the fire warms, burns, and reaches. We are but the objects of its natural action.

At this point in the speech, the people have acted only as vessels for ahistorical ideals, strongly suggesting Bush's theoconservative project. That shifts, however, when Bush turns to the economy. He links foreign policy and economic concerns through the ideal of liberty: "In a world moving toward liberty, we are determined to show the meaning and promise of liberty." As Ronald Reagan might say, America shall become as a shining city on a hill, showing the promise of liberty to the world. Consistent with classic liberalism, Bush says that in America, "citizens find the dignity and security of economic independence, instead of laboring on the edge of subsistence."[79] Bush implicitly deploys a key topic of American liberalism. In the new world, citizens craft themselves; in the old, they labor at the edge of subsistence for others. Isaac Kramnick explains the role at the heart of the liberal idiom: "Individuals increasingly came to define themselves as active subjects. They no longer tended to see their place in life as part of some natural, inevitable, and eternal plan. Their own enterprise and ability mattered; they possessed the opportunity (a key word) to determine their place through their own voluntary actions in this life and in this world."[80] Government, religion, tradition, and Edmund Burke stood in the way of such dreams; in later versions, only government seemed to remain, as Ronald Reagan memorably declared, "In this present crisis, government is not the solution to our problem; government is the problem."[81]

One expects Bush to embrace Reagan; we instead see the shipwreck of neoliberalism. Bush notes how his "broader definition of liberty ... motivated the Homestead Act, the Social Security Act, and the G.I. Bill of Rights." Admirable as they are, one wonders why a neoliberal would make legislative acts examples of liberty. "We," he says, "will extend this vision by reforming great institutions to serve the needs of our time."[82] He foreshadows here his attempt to privatize Social Security, but "we" must mean government, an interpretation he quickly reinforces:

> To give every American a stake in the promise and future of our country, we will bring
> the highest standards to our schools, and build an ownership society. We will widen the
> ownership of homes and businesses, retirement savings and health insurance – prepar-
> ing our people for the challenges of life in a free society. By making every citizen an
> agent of his or her own destiny, we will give our fellow Americans greater freedom
> from want and fear, and make our society more prosperous and just and equal.[83]

"We," the subject, make the object – the people. The "we" must be government.
Such a relationship is antithetical to, say, Ronald Reagan's vision. American heroes,
Reagan consistently said, do not need government to give us a stake in our nation;
we *are* the nation. American heroes do not need a "we" to "prepare" us for life in a
free society; we *are* a free society. American heroes do not need a "we" to make us
agents; we *are* agents. "We," Reagan said in his First Inaugural, "have every right
to dream heroic dreams," after all, "why shouldn't we believe that? We are
Americans."[84]

Choice appears, but each time, Bush reins in the limited agency he grants. We
witness, but do not make history. We light, but do not control the fire. We seek
individual dignity, but only through government programs. The contradictions culminate in the penultimate paragraph. In a sense, it represents the whole of the
speech and the first line represents the whole of the paragraph: "We go forward
with complete confidence in the eventual triumph of freedom – not because history
runs on the wheels of inevitability; it is human choices that move events; not because
we consider ourselves a chosen people; God moves and chooses as He wills."[85] This
is incoherent. If the latter assertions are true, the former cannot be true. We cannot
have complete confidence in a contingent world. The tension between classic liberalism and the theoconservative project disrupts completely the logic of the text.
Both cannot be true in the same sentence. Explanation is required:

> We have confidence because freedom is the permanent hope of mankind, the hunger
> in dark places, the longing of the soul. When our Founders declared a new order of the
> ages, when soldiers died in wave upon wave for a union based on liberty, when citizens
> marched in peaceful outrage under the banner "Freedom Now," they were acting on
> an ancient hope that is meant to be fulfilled. History has an ebb and flow of justice, but
> history also has a visible direction, set by liberty, and the Author of Liberty.[86]

The Reverend King was wrong; the arc of history may bend toward justice but
liberty controls both and all three, in turn, are set by God. God moves and chooses,
but he *always* ends up endorsing an American hope of liberty that is "meant to be
fulfilled." As the president does in the speech as a whole, he declares and then cor-
rals the agency of the audience. Ideal trumps choice. The philosopher president
knows the truth.

Lest I be accused of unfairly distinguishing Bush from a parade of presidents who
have declared that God is American, recall Kennedy's invocation of God: "With a
good conscience our only sure reward, with history the final judge of our deeds, let
us go forth to lead the land we love, asking His blessing and His help, but knowing

that here on Earth God's work must truly be our own."[87] Contingency saturates his words. We ask for God's help, but we do not know his will. We go forth, but a good conscience is our only reward. From Kennedy's perspective, those dying soldiers and marching citizens made liberty possible. They did not follow a visible direction. Instead, they chose to go up the hills and face the clubs. They understood the paradox at the heart of the American experiment: Liberty only lives when we choose. By definition, freedom cannot be inevitable. That is the legacy of our liberal tradition.

President Bush has a difficult time with this legacy and the tension haunts him. As this Inaugural demonstrates, Bush is a theoconservative. He knows the truth and obedience to his truth will set you free. But the active subject of the liberal tradition cannot easily be tamed, in the text or in the world. Its capacity to choose disrupts Bush's logic. His Second Inaugural Address sweats and strains to bind the self-made man to the great chain that stretches from God through a sanitized ideal of freedom to the president. I have argued that a spectre haunts the speech; the text reveals that ghost to be John Fitzgerald Kennedy. Amid the allusions, Bush notably ignores the following passage: "In your hands, my fellow citizens, more than mine, will rest the final success or failure of our course."[88] In this analysis, then, I argue that Kennedy's text infuses Bush's speech, disrupting its logic and offering an alternative democratic covenant. That claim derives from my focus on the concept of allusion, but also from the speech's generic status, from an understanding of allusion as a strategy that spreads across historical and critical contexts, and from a desire to subvert President Bush's theocratic order. In the practical act of criticism, all four modes likely enter into any one reading.

Edwin Black would not be surprised. Like Kenneth Burke, Black's work reveals a desire to "use all that there is to use" and most critics find themselves working within and between the modes I have identified. More important should be the recognition that rhetorical theories organically grow from our discursive times. This essay has, in a sense, rediscovered the truism that theory is rhetoric. At its best, it seeks to explain the world around us and account for the advocacy we face on a daily basis. In short, we develop relationships between rhetorical theory and public address in the context of political and moral challenges, from the war in Vietnam to the war on terror, from the advocacy of integration to the endorsement of torture. The public address we hear and see, like the discourse that disturbed the scholars meeting at Wingspread, shapes the theory that we often believe derives purely from our intellectual efforts. That is seldom the case. Rather, rhetorical theory and the art of oratory are creatures of public controversy. At our best, we make and remake our theory to explain that annoying case. I would not have it any other way.

Notes

1   Edwin Black, *Rhetorical Criticism: A Study in Method* (New York: Macmillan, 1965).
2   James Jasinski, "The Status of Theory and Method in Rhetorical Criticism," *Western Journal of Communication* 65 (2001): 250.

3   Jasinski, "The Status of Theory," 250; Dilip P. Gaonkar, "Object and Method in Rhetorical Criticism: From Wichelns to Leff and McGee," *Western Journal of Speech Communication* 54 (1990): 303; and David Zarefsky, "The State of the Art in Public Address Scholarship," in *Texts in Context: Critical Dialogues on Significant Episodes in American Political Rhetoric*, ed. Michael C. Leff and Fred J. Kauffeld (Davis, CA: Hermagoras Press, 1989), 13.

4   Stephen E. Lucas, "The Legacy of Edwin Black," *Rhetoric & Public Affairs* 10 (2007): 515.

5   Thomas O. Sloane et al., "Report of the Committee on the Advancement and Refinement of Rhetorical Criticism," in *The Prospect of Rhetoric: Report of the National Developmental Project*, ed. Lloyd F. Bitzer and Edwin Black (Englewood Cliffs, NJ: Prentice Hall, 1971), 222.

6   See William L. Nothstine, Carole Blair, and Gary A. Copeland, *Critical Questions: Invention, Creativity, and the Criticism of Discourse and Media* (New York: St. Martin's Press, 1994), 31–42.

7   Wayne C. Booth, "The Scope of Rhetoric Today," in *The Prospect of Rhetoric*, ed. Bitzer and Black, 98–99.

8   Wayne Brockriede, "Trends in Rhetoric: Blending Criticism and Science," in *The Prospect of Rhetoric*, ed. Bitzer and Black, 124.

9   Edwin Black, "The Second Persona," *Quarterly Journal of Speech* 56 (1970): 109–119; the various Campbell and Hill essays, as well as others on the address, are collected in James R. Andrews, *The Practice of Rhetorical Criticism*, 2nd ed. (New York: Longman, 1990), 91–150; and Philip Wander, "The Ideological Turn in Modern Criticism," *Central States Speech Journal* 34 (1983): 1–18.

10 Martin J. Medhurst, "The Academic Study of Public Address: A Tradition in Transition," in *Landmark Essays in Public Address*, ed. Martin J. Medhurst (Davis, CA: Hermagoras Press, 1993), xi.

11 Michael C. McGee, "In Search of the 'People': A Rhetorical Alternative," *Quarterly Journal of Speech* 61 (1975): 235–249.

12 For both sides of the "theory debate," see Martin J. Medhurst, "Public Address and Significant Scholarship: Four Challenges to the Rhetorical Renaissance," in *Texts in Context*, ed. Leff and Kauffeld, 29–42; and James Arnt Aune, "Public Address and Rhetorical Theory," in *Texts in Context*, ed. Leff and Kauffeld, 43–52.

13 Thomas B. Farrell, *Norms of Rhetorical Culture* (New Haven, CT: Yale University Press, 1993), 3.

14 Farrell, *Norms*, 211, 154.

15 Wayne Brockriede, "Rhetorical Criticism as Argument," in Andrews, *The Practice of Rhetorical Criticism*, 294–303.

16 Karlyn Kohrs Campbell and Kathleen Hall Jamieson, *Deeds Done in Words: Presidential Rhetoric and the Genres of Governance* (Chicago: University of Chicago Press, 1990), 7.

17 James Jasinski, *Sourcebook on Rhetoric: Key Concepts in Contemporary Rhetorical Studies* (Thousand Oaks, CA: Sage, 2001); Richard A. Lanham, *A Handlist of Rhetorical Terms*, 2nd ed. (Berkeley: University of California Press, 1991); Thomas O. Sloane, Editor in Chief, *Encyclopedia of Rhetoric* (Oxford: Oxford University Press, 2001); and Chaim Perelman and Lucie Olbrechts-Tyteca, *The New Rhetoric: A Treatise on Argumentation* (Notre Dame, IN: University of Notre Dame Press, 1969).

18   See, for instance, Jeffrey Tulis, *The Rhetorical Presidency* (Princeton, NJ: Princeton University Press, 1987); Roderick P. Hart, *The Sound of Leadership: Presidential Communication in the Modern Age* (Chicago: University of Chicago Press, 1987); Mary E. Stuckey and Frederick J. Antczak, "The Rhetorical Presidency: Deepening Vision, Widening Exchange," in *Communication Yearbook 21*, ed. Michael E. Roloff (Thousand Oaks, CA: Sage, 1998), 405–441; Martin J. Medhurst, ed., *Beyond the Rhetorical Presidency* (College Station: Texas A&M University Press, 1996); Campbell and Jamieson, *Deeds Done in Words*. For a lovely review of presidential rhetoric scholarship, see Martin J. Medhurst, "From Retrospect to Prospect: The Study of Presidential Rhetoric, 1915–2005," in *The Prospect of Presidential Rhetoric*, ed. James Arnt Aune and Martin J. Medhurst (College Station: Texas A&M University Press, 2008), 3–27.

19   I am drawing generally from the argument of the book and more specifically from Campbell and Jamieson, *Deeds Done in Words*, 6–9.

20   Campbell and Jamieson, *Deeds Done in Words*, 8.

21   Implicit within this approach is structuration theory's concern with an institution's chronic rhetorical reproduction of itself. For this argument in a different context, see John M. Murphy and Thomas R. Burkholder, "The Life of the Party: The Contemporary Keynote Address," in *New Approaches to Rhetoric*, ed. Patricia A. Sullivan and Steven R. Goldzwig (Thousand Oaks, CA: Sage, 2004), 129–148.

22   Bonnie J. Dow, *Prime-Time Feminism: Television, Media Culture, and the Women's Movement Since 1970* (Philadelphia: University of Pennsylvania Press, 1996); and Trevor Parry-Giles, *The Character of Justice: Rhetoric, Law, and Politics in the Supreme Court Confirmation Process* (East Lansing: Michigan State University Press, 2006).

23   Kenneth Burke, *The Philosophy of Literary Form*, 3rd ed. (Berkeley: University of California Press, 1973), 191.

24   Michael William Pfau, *The Political Style of Conspiracy: Chase, Sumner, and Lincoln* (East Lansing: Michigan State University Press, 2005).

25   Richard Hofstadter, *The Paranoid Style in American Politics and Other Essays* (Cambridge, MA: Harvard University Press, 1964); David Zarefsky, *Lincoln, Douglas and Slavery: In the Crucible of Public Debate* (Chicago: University of Chicago Press, 1990). The "slave power" was a term that designated a conspiracy on the part of the wealthy, Southern planter class in the United States to strengthen and extend slavery across the continent, while also dominating American political life. For a contemporary account, see Garry Wills, *"Negro President": Jefferson and the Slave Power* (Boston: Houghton Mifflin, 2003).

26   Pfau, *The Political Style of Conspiracy*, 180.

27   Nothstine, Blair, and Copeland, *Critical Questions*, 30–50.

28   See, in particular, Nothstine, Blair, and Copeland, *Critical Questions*, 30, 42–50. For those interested in such questions, their account partakes of the modernist impulse to separate appearance and reality; under the influence of scientism, we only appear to engage in critique. "Recovering Critical Invention from the Void" makes *real* criticism possible. For further analysis of this modernist trace in postmodern critique, see Bonnie J. Dow, "Criticism and Authority in the Artistic Mode," *Western Journal of Communication* 65 (2001): 336–348; and John M. Murphy, "Critical Rhetoric as Political Discourse," *Argumentation and Advocacy* 32 (1995): 1–15.

29   Northrop Frye, *Anatomy of Criticism: Four Essays* (Princeton, NJ: Princeton University Press, 1957; 1973), 12, 17.

30 Roderick Hart, "Contemporary Scholarship in Public Address: A Research Editorial," _Western Journal of Speech Communication_ 50 (1986): 283–295.

31 Dow, "Criticism and Authority," 337, 342–343. Her entire essay makes this point, but these pages focus specifically on Carole Blair's essay in the same volume.

32 James Darsey, "Must We All Be Rhetorical Theorists? An Anti-Democratic Inquiry," _Western Journal of Communication_ 58 (1994): 164–181.

33 This argument, indeed the paragraph, is drawn from: Edwin Black, "A Note on Theory and Practice in Rhetorical Criticism," _Western Journal of Speech Communication_ 44 (1980): 331–336.

34 For examples of much of this sort of work, see Charles E. Morris III and Stephen H. Browne, eds., _Readings on the Rhetoric of Social Protest_, 2nd ed. (State College, PA: Strata, 2006).

35 John M. Sloop, _Disciplining Gender: Rhetorics of Sex Identity in Contemporary US Culture_ (Boston: University of Massachusetts Press, 2004), 17–24. Raymie McKerrow coined the term "critical rhetoric," although his work has generally remained resolutely theoretical while Sloop offers clear guidance to the student of public address. See Raymie McKerrow, "Critical Rhetoric: Theory and Praxis," _Communication Monographs_ 56 (1989): 91–111. An additional point of origin is: Michael C. McGee, "Text, Context, and the Fragmentation of Contemporary Culture," _Western Journal of Speech Communication_ 54 (1990): 274–289.

36 Sloop, _Disciplining Gender_, 18.

37 Sloop, _Disciplining Gender_, 21.

38 Sloop, _Disciplining Gender_, 22.

39 I understand completely that these perspectives differ significantly on a variety of issues. Yet what they hold in common is the determination to subvert the existing social order and its discourses. For discussions of feminism in rhetorical and communicative studies, see Bonnie J. Dow and Julia T. Woods, eds., _The Sage Handbook of Gender and Communication_ (Thousand Oaks, CA: Sage, 2006); for discussions of neo-Marxist approaches, two excellent sources are: James Arnt Aune, _Rhetoric and Marxism_ (Boulder, CO: Westview Press, 1994); and Dana L. Cloud, "_The Matrix_ and Critical Theory's Desertion of the Real," _Communication and Critical/Cultural Studies_ 3 (2006): 328–354.

40 Sloop, _Disciplining Gender_, 24.

41 For a longer version of this argument, see Murphy, "Critical Rhetoric as Political Discourse."

42 For a discussion of this idea, see Robert Hariman, "Theory Without Modernity," in _Prudence: Classical Virtue, Postmodern Practice_, ed. Robert Hariman (University Park, PA: Pennsylvania State University Press, 2003), 1–34. For a perspective from another discipline, see Terry Eagleton, _After Theory_ (Cambridge, MA: Perseus Books, 2003).

43 Jasinski, "The Status of Theory," 256.

44 Michael Leff and Andrew Sachs, "Words Most Like Things: Iconicity and the Rhetorical Text," _Western Journal of Speech Communication_ 54 (1990): 269.

45 Leff and Sachs, "Words Most Like Things," 255.

46 On Burke, see Leff and Sachs, "Words Most Like Things"; Stephen H. Browne and Michael C. Leff, "Political Judgment and Rhetorical Argument: Edmund Burke's Paradigm," in _Argument and Social Practice: Proceedings of the Fourth SCA/AFA Conference on Argumentation_, ed. J. Robert Cox, Malcolm O. Sillars, and Gregg

B. Walker (Annandale, VA: Speech Communication Association, 1985), 193–210; on Lincoln, see James Jasinski, "Instrumentalism, Contextualism, and Interpretation in Rhetorical Criticism," in *Rhetorical Hermeneutics: Invention and Interpretation in the Age of Science*, ed. Alan G. Gross and William M. Keith (Albany: State University Press of New York, 1997), 195–224; and Michael C. Leff, "Lincoln at Cooper Union: Neo-Classical Criticism Revisited," *Western Journal of Communication* 65 (2001): 232–248.

47 Leff and Sachs, "Words Most Like Things," 256.

48 Browne and Leff, "Political Judgment," 199.

49 See the studies in Hariman, *Prudence*.

50 James Jasinski, "The Forms and Limits of Prudence in Henry Clay's (1850) Defense of the Compromise Measures," *Quarterly Journal of Speech* 81 (1995): 455.

51 On these constructions, see Jasinski, "Instrumentalism"; and Isaac Kramnick, *Republicanism and Bourgeois Radicalism: Political Ideology in Late Eighteenth-Century England and America* (Ithaca, NY: Cornell University Press, 1990).

52 Michael C. Leff, "Interpretation and the Art of the Rhetorical Critic," *Western Journal of Speech Communication* 44 (1980): 347–348.

53 Farrell, *Norms*, 80–81.

54 Campbell and Jamieson, *Deeds Done in Words*, 14.

55 Campbell and Jamieson, *Deeds Done in Words*, 15.

56 Jasinski, *Sourcebook on Rhetoric*, 322.

57 Campbell and Jamieson, *Deeds Done in Words*, 21.

58 For more on that concept, see John G. Cawelti, *Apostles of the Self-Made Man: Changing Concepts of Success in America* (Chicago: University of Chicago Press, 1965).

59 Andrew Sullivan, *The Conservative Soul: How We Lost It/How To Get It Back* (New York: HarperCollins, 2006), 6.

60 John M. Murphy, "Power and Authority in a Postmodern Presidency," in *The Prospect of Presidential Rhetoric*, ed. Aune and Medhurst.

61 George W. Bush, "President Sworn-In to Second Term," www.whitehouse.gov/news/releases/2005/01 (accessed July 1, 2008), 1.

62 For discussion of Churchill and Bush, see John M. Murphy, " 'Our Mission and Our Moment': George W. Bush and September 11th," *Rhetoric & Public Affairs* 6 (2003): 607–632.

63 Campbell and Jamieson, *Deeds Done in Words*, 18.

64 Campbell and Jamieson, *Deeds Done in Words*, 17.

65 George W. Bush, "President Sworn-In to Second Term."

66 Murphy, " 'Our Mission and Our Moment.' "

67 George W. Bush, "President Sworn-In to Second Term."

68 John F. Kennedy, "Inaugural Address," in *American Speeches: Political Oratory from Abraham Lincoln to Bill Clinton*, ed. Ted Widmer (New York: Library of America, 2006), 535.

69 David Hoogland Noon, "Operation Enduring Analogy: World War II, The War on Terror, and the Uses of Historical Memory," *Rhetoric & Public Affairs* 7 (2004): 339–366.

70 Murphy, " 'Our Mission and Our Moment,' " 610.

71 Jane Mayer, *The Dark Side: The Inside Story of How the War on Terror Turned into a War on American Ideals* (New York: Doubleday, 2008).

72 George W. Bush, "President Sworn-In to Second Term."

73 George W. Bush, "President Sworn-In to Second Term."

74 Kennedy, "Inaugural Address," 535.

75 Moya Ann Ball, *Vietnam-on-the-Potomac* (New York: Praeger, 1992).

76 Like Kennedy, Bush sometimes separates sections of the speech by audience: "Today, America speaks anew to the peoples of the world" and "Today, I also speak anew to my fellow citizens." The words awkwardly rewrite Kennedy's crisp introductions to his famous antitheses: "And so, my fellow Americans" and "My fellow citizens of the world." See Kennedy, "Inaugural Address," 538. Note also that Kennedy is one with his "fellow citizens of the world" while Bush offers only an ideal as the subject ("America") and it speaks to "people," not "citizens." Bush's phrasing also suggests Kennedy's earlier addresses to various audiences in the midst of the pledge: "To those old allies," "To those new states," etc. See, Kennedy, "Inaugural Address," 535–536.

77 George W. Bush, "President Sworn-In to Second Term."

78 Kennedy, "Inaugural Address," 538.

79 George W. Bush, "President Sworn-In to Second Term."

80 Kramnick, *Republicanism and Bourgeois Radicalism*, 8.

81 Ronald Reagan, "First Inaugural Address," in *American Rhetorical Discourse*, ed. Ronald F. Reid and James F. Klumpp, 3rd ed. (Long Grove, IL: Waveland Press, 2005), 768.

82 George W. Bush, "President Sworn-In to Second Term."

83 George W. Bush, "President Sworn-In to Second Term."

84 Ronald Reagan, "First Inaugural Address," 769, 771.

85 George W. Bush, "President Sworn-In to Second Term."

86 George W. Bush, "President Sworn-In to Second Term."

87 Kennedy, "Inaugural Address," 538.

88 Kennedy, "Inaugural Address," 537.

Part IV

Questions of Effect in Rhetoric and Public Address

12

Jimmy Carter, Human Rights, and Instrumental Effects of Presidential Rhetoric

Mary E. Stuckey

Presidents use rhetoric for instrumental purposes. They speak because they think speaking will accomplish something that silence would not. They believe speech will help them motivate voters to support them, donors to finance their campaigns, or policymakers to approve their programs. Presidents wouldn't speak at all if they didn't believe – wisely or not – that their speech mattered in specific, material ways. They are not alone in this belief. When disaster strikes, when there is good news to report, whenever important events of any kind occur, we expect to hear from our presidents. We listen to them talk about fires, riots and tsunamis, moon landings, literary achievements, and Super Bowl championships. The president's words are the fodder of news and talk shows, blogs, and casual conversations. We listen to, report on, and analyze a president's words because we believe they matter. Surely so many people cannot be wrong.

Yet there is an important body of research declaring that we are, in fact, quite wrong. According to these scholars, presidential talk does not matter much and it does not have the consequences both presidents and the public assume it has. While presidents speak increasingly often, these scholars argue that they speak with less and less impact; presidential influence over the public agenda, public opinion, and national policy is actually decreasing, they suggest, with every word they speak. Presidents would thus be better served if they devoted their persuasive efforts to private bargaining and negotiation with other elites. "Going public," these skeptics conclude, is a waste of valuable presidential time.[1]

No one argues that presidents talk only to hear themselves talk. But there is a divergence of opinion on what it may mean for presidential speech to "matter" and how we might measure the consequences of such speech. On one side of the debate are those who look at presidential rhetoric as having significance only so long as it can be demonstrated that a specific speech act had a decisive and measurable effect on public opinion – as measured by the polls – on a particular issue.[2] The argument here is that absent such demonstrable effects, presidential rhetoric is often mean-ingless. Other scholars concede that presidential rhetoric has instrumental effects but suggest that those effects are actually destructive to the health of the polity.[3] If these scholars are correct, it is clear that scholarly efforts would be better expended on finding ways to reform presidential rhetorical practices rather than trying to understand the forms and content of presidential speech as currently practiced.

There is yet another side to this debate, however – a side that holds that all of these skeptics and critics have an overly narrow view of the functions and power of presidential speech.[4] These scholars variously argue for several alternative ways of understanding the instrumental effects of presidential speech: Such effects might be more long rather than short term; they might involve reinforcement rather than changes in opinion; they might involve determining which issues get on the national agenda; or they might concern how those issues are defined, understood, and debated. In this understanding of presidential rhetoric, measuring effects is quite complicated. Scholarly efforts to understand the potential of such speech is concentrated on its influence over social constructions of reality – how Americans define and interpret not only issues but the nation's identity and character as well – rather than the effectiveness of a particular speech in swaying the public for or against a specific policy.

This essay responds to these critiques of presidential rhetoric by arguing that presidential words do have instrumental effects, although they are not necessarily the simple, direct, and easily measurable effects that some scholars have hoped to find. They are, instead, a combination of more subtle, indirect, and long-term effects, such as putting an issue on the national agenda, framing an issue in specific ways, or influencing the national understanding of an issue over time. I agree that one important test of a president's persuasive ability is the capacity to influence a specific audience on a specific issue. I also argue, however, that this is not the *only* test of the instrumental effects of presidential speech, and that presidential rhetoric also has more subtle, more indirect instrumental effects on the ways in which issues are defined, prioritized, and subsequently discussed and debated. To make this argument, I examine, in turn, each of the various ways we might understand instrumental effects, with specific reference to the case of Jimmy Carter and the issue of human rights. In the case of Carter's human rights rhetoric, there may be little evidence of immediate or short-term effects on public opinion, at least as measured by the polls. But Carter did help put human rights on the national agenda, and over time he helped make the issue a persistent theme in debates over US foreign policy.

Putting Human Rights on the National Agenda

The most obvious way to approach the question of whether presidential speech has instrumental consequences is to examine the issues that are featured on the national agenda, and many political scientists have done just that. These scholars take as their data presidential words – usually in State of the Union Addresses – and public opinion polls. When polls reflect the substance of presidential speech, that speech is understood as influential. Significant attention has been paid to the question of whether that influence exists, what factors determine its nature and extent, and how it might be best understood; there also has been some difference of opinion as to whether presidents exert significant influence over public opinion.

There are two possible ways to understand a president's speech as having power over the national agenda: whether he (and eventually she) is able to get the public and/or other elites to think about a specific issue that had not been previously considered, and whether he influences attitudes on a specific issue, evidencing in some way that persuasion has occurred.

In the first case, there is some evidence that presidents do indeed exercise influence over the national agenda. Jeffrey Cohen, for instance, has found that the more attention the president gives to an issue in his State of the Union Address, the more concerned the public becomes with that issue.[5] Presidents, of course, are also likely to talk about issues that they believe are of concern to the media and to the mass public, so there is a reciprocal relationship among polls, the media, and presidential speech, making it hard to know exactly how much influence one exerts over the others.[6] But it is clear that a president's ability to influence the agenda is greatest in the absence of controversy among elites – that when other policymakers agree that an issue is important, the president will have an easier time putting that issue on the agenda and persuading the public that it is important.[7]

This was the case with Carter and human rights. Jimmy Carter's presidency coincided with an increase of interest in and attention to human rights by the media, politicians, and the general public.[8] Both Congress and the American public as a whole were increasingly disturbed by Vietnam, Watergate, and what those events meant for America's image as the world's moral leader. For Carter, the issue of human rights was also a way to restore America's faith in itself and to reunite an increasingly fractured nation. In other words, it was not just about policies or programs; for Carter, the rhetoric of human rights was about America's identity, ideals, and reputation.

In talking about the moral foundations of American leadership in the international political arena, Carter said, "As you know, 204 years ago today America declared its independence with a truth that still sets people free throughout a troubled world, that all people are endowed with rights that cannot be bought or sold, rights that no power on Earth can justly deny."[9] For Carter, a rhetoric of human rights was thus a natural outgrowth of America's ideological tradition. As an expressed concern with human rights helped to restore national confidence in America's political leadership, Carter expected it to work in similar ways around the world, inspiring American allies and restoring America's credibility on the world stage.

But stressing the moral value of human rights led to charges that Carter was overly preachy, perhaps weak, and certainly naïve. To counter those charges, he was careful to argue that, given the prevailing international context, a rhetoric of human rights had practical as well as moral value. Discussing the concrete reasons for American leadership on human rights, Carter said:

> The world is still divided by ideological disputes, dominated by regional conflicts, and threatened by danger that we will not resolve the differences of race and wealth without violence or without drawing into combat the major military powers. We can no

longer separate the traditional issues of war and peace from the new global questions
of justice, equity, and human rights. It is a new world, but America should not fear it.
It is a new world, and we should help to shape it. It is a new world that calls for a new
American foreign policy – a policy based on constant decency in its values and on
optimism in our historical vision.[10]

The world had changed, Carter argued; the imperatives of foreign affairs were now
different, and the nation's policy needed to reflect those differences and changes.
In addition to its moral value, he concluded, the protection of human rights would
lead to a more peaceful and thus more stable world.[11]

Indeed, Carter argued, the growing interdependence of the world made a rhetoric of human rights a practical necessity. As Americans, he argued, "we cannot
overlook the way that our fate is bound to that of other nations. This interdependence stretches from the health of our economy through war and peace, to the
security of our own energy supplies." According to Carter, this interdependence
had changed everything: "It's a new world in which we cannot afford to be narrow
in our vision, limited in our foresight, or selfish in our purpose."[12] For Carter, the
crucial fact of the new international context was global interdependence. He
stressed how human rights would help the United States successfully navigate this
interdependent world in ways that previous policy paradigms could not – an argument that helped give human rights a permanent place on the national agenda.

Finally, Carter argued that emphasizing human rights would put the United
States in the forefront of an international movement that was both important and
inevitable. "The passion for freedom," he said in his Inaugural Address, "is on the
rise." Tapping into this "new spirit," he argued, could restore America's moral
leadership in world affairs, for there could be "no nobler nor more ambitious task
for America to undertake on this day of a new beginning than to help shape a just
and peaceful world that is truly humane."[13] For Carter, a more just world was a
more humane world; a more humane world was a more peaceful one; and a more
peaceful world was a more stable world. Stressing human rights was thus not only
the right thing to do; it was both a moral *and* a practical necessity.

For Carter, the issue of human rights encompassed a set of policies that responded
to the political exigencies of both the national and international contexts. The
policies connected to his advocacy of human rights allowed Americans to reunite
at home and to reclaim America's stature internationally following the Vietnam
conflict. In the short term, human rights was a way for him to communicate the
moral ideals of his administration, to unite the nation around the idea of restoring
America's moral authority, and to distinguish his policies – both foreign and
domestic – from those of his immediate predecessors. Whether or not these policies were understood as successful is less important to my argument than the fact
that this understanding of his presidency was indeed widely shared. Jimmy Carter
wanted his administration to be identified with the cause of human rights, and in
the short term he succeeded. The evidence shows that political elites, the media,
and the American public understood his presidency in precisely those terms.[14]

Of course, it is easier to put an issue on the agenda – to influence what issues people think *about* – than it is to influence their specific attitudes or opinions on those issues.[15] And while presidents dedicate an increasing amount of time and energy to trying to influence public opinion on specific issues – and through public opinion, the actions of Congress[16] – there is widespread skepticism among scholars that such efforts make a difference. In the field of presidential studies, no one has been more skeptical about the president's ability to influence congressional action by molding public opinion than George C. Edwards III. In numerous venues, over a long period of time, Edwards has argued that if presidential rhetoric has any impact at all, it is merely "at the margins" of the policymaking process and that, as a general rule, presidential speech falls "on deaf ears."[17] For Edwards, "going public" is best understood as a waste of valuable presidential time. He argues that even the most able presidential speakers generally fail to influence policy either by changing public opinion on specific issues or by enhancing their own approval ratings. And if these indices were the only measures of success, Edwards undoubtedly would be right. But there are several problems with Edwards's understanding of the instrumental effects of presidential rhetoric.

First, the effects of presidential rhetoric may be subtle and delayed rather than dramatic and immediate. When the efficacy of presidential rhetoric is measured by public opinion polls taken immediately after a single speech, the assumption is that the change must be both instantaneous and significant – or there has not been any change at all. Yet it is certainly possible that small changes may occur over time, or that the public may be led incrementally to very different positions than they initially held.

Second, the effects of presidential rhetoric may be manifested in ways other than opinion *change*. When public opinion is measured, especially in efforts to locate the influence of presidential rhetoric, there is a tendency to look only for evidence that the public has changed its mind. Yet the influence of presidential rhetoric also might be seen in the crystallization of new opinions or in the reinforcement of existing opinions. There is evidence that presidents may not be able to *create* public opinion out of whole cloth and make it coincide perfectly with their preferred policy position. But that may not be the best way to understand the relationship between the public and presidential rhetoric, and it certainly is not the best way to understand the role Jimmy Carter played in advancing his human rights agenda. In Carter's case, the public was neither ignorant nor disinterested in human rights prior to his time in office, yet that interest in human rights lacked focus and salience. It remained for Carter to give it form and direction.

Carter did just that by rhetorically connecting human rights to specific issues and events. The principal effect of his rhetoric seems to have been reinforcement, as he reminded Americans of their commitment to human rights and explained how it related to various policy issues. Generally, the mass public was not interested enough in human rights to mention it on surveys without prompting, but it became a powerful warrant for action when people were prompted to think about it in relation to specific foreign policy questions.[18] Put another way, the attitudes on human rights were "out there," as potential warrants for presidential action; all that was needed was a nationally prominent leader ready to make the case. That is precisely what Jimmy Carter did after he was elected to the presidency, and both public opinion polls and media coverage reflect that rhetorical process.

Throughout US history, as Anne Geyer and Robert Shapiro have argued in a review of polling data, "the defense of human rights in other countries has been a strikingly unimportant issue for the American public." Yet the "human rights stand of President Jimmy Carter and public opposition to [earlier] US support for repressive Third World governments added to public concern for human rights" in the 1970s. In other words, Americans responded to the call, as Geyer and Shapiro have suggested: "When the issue has been raised, there has been little public opposition to defending, in principle, international human rights: Americans oppose the murder or arbitrary imprisonment of political dissenters in all countries, and torture is opposed without reservation."[19] Absent such leadership, Americans might have focused on other, more personally pressing matters. But when the president raised the issue, the public apparently did respond.

Noticing the enhanced interest in human rights, journalists and pundits at the time generally credited Jimmy Carter for elevating the salience of such issues. Catherine Cassara, for instance, tells us that, "Foreign correspondents active during the period report that the Carter policy fundamentally altered how the US press covered Latin America."[20] *Newsweek* noted that, "In the last half year, human rights have suddenly become a major theme in world diplomacy,"[21] while the *New Republic* said that Carter had "made the world more aware of human rights."[22] A few observers noted that Carter's emphasis on human rights was not without risk, yet most still found much to praise in the president's efforts. Reporting in March of 1977, for example, the *ABC Evening News* observed that the American people were solidly behind Carter, even those who believed his human rights policy was a "risky venture":

> It is possible that the most important development anywhere in the world at present is President Carter's personal crusade for human rights. No President or other world leader has ever tried such a risky venture before. It could end up a calamity for US influence as offended governments withdraw cooperation, as some South American countries and Mr. Brezhnev threatens to do. It could, if it catches on, change the human tone of the world vastly for the better. It's far too early to guess which way things will go. But one thing we may not have suspected is clear: Among people there is a hungry market for his stand. ... It feels rather good to be on the side of the angels again, the way Jefferson prescribed, 200 years ago.[23]

In its report, ABC credited the president with increased talk about human rights and embraced his framing of the issue. The rhetoric of human rights, the report suggested, was both consistent with America's traditions and a radically new departure. Moreover, the public was "hungry" for such a change and felt "good" about the policy. When the news media pick up not only the issue but also the way in which the president has framed the issue (treating both as obvious or inevitable), that amounts to a pretty good case for presidential influence over the news media's agenda. That news media attention may or may not translate into changes in public opinion, but it is significant nevertheless.

Based on the Carter example, then, it seems plausible to argue that presidents can indeed have some influence over the national agenda, but that this influence is likely to be strengthened when the topic of concern has (1) already been present to some degree in the national mind, (2) when it seems to make sense within the broader political context, and (3) when it is reinforced by other political actors and events. Rhetoric – even when spoken by as powerful a political actor as the US president – occurs within a wider context. It is not, in and of itself, determinative of political reality; exigence matters. This fact points to the importance of taking a long-term perspective on the instrumental effects of presidential rhetoric.

The Long-Term Effects of Presidential Rhetoric

There are surely moments when issues of concern to a particular president are ignored by other elites as well as by the mass public. There are also moments when issues that dominated one presidency fade into irrelevancy under another. Presidents are constrained by the times in which they govern. But forceful and persistent presidential speech on a given topic can give a topic lasting resonance, and this points to the potential long-range consequences of presidential speech.

There are at least three distinct ways we might understand these long-term effects. First, the way a president frames a specific issue can affect the nature of subsequent discourse on that topic. Second, the president can help transform ordinary words or phrases into "ideographs," or abstract terms that summarize a particular culture's political and moral commitments. Finally, presidential rhetoric can serve a long-term educative function, raising public consciousness about particular issues or starting conversations that, over the long term, affect a variety of specific policies.

Presidential framing

As we have seen, presidential speech can be an important factor in determining the level of attention a given issue receives. But it is also true that the *way* in which a president talks about an issue makes a difference. In the case of Jimmy Carter and human rights, for instance, how the president framed the issue was of considerable significance. He tied human rights not only to his personal ethos, but also to that of the whole nation. By so closely connecting human rights to his own beliefs and to those of the nation, he committed both his own administration and the country as a whole to the cause of human rights in a way that would help the issue eventually to transcend his presidency.

Carter's own personal ethos was closely connected to his stance on human rights. Even though he came to human rights rather late in his political career – even rather late in his first presidential campaign – he nonetheless had the proper credentials to make human rights his own. He was thus able both to help maintain human rights as a national agenda item, and to use it effectively as a rhetorical weapon against his opponents. As one of his top aides put it,

> Carter's personal philosophy was the point of departure for the foreign policy priorities of the new Administration. He came to the Presidency with a determination to make US foreign policy more humane and moral. In part because of his religious feelings, in part because it was useful in the campaign, he went on record not only in rejecting the "Lone Ranger" style of the preceding Administration but in criticizing it for an excessive preoccupation with practicing balance-of-power politics. I know that he genuinely believed that as President he could shape a more decent world.[24]

Human rights were thus both a natural extension of Carter's own personality and an important source of rhetorical power for him.

Carter used his personal history and his regional identity to establish his ethos on human rights.[25] As he told an Alabama audience in 1980, "As the first man from the Deep South in 140 years to be President of this Nation, I say that these people in white sheets do not understand our region and what it's been through, they do not understand what our country stands for, they do not understand that the South and all of America must move forward. Our past is a rich source of inspiration. We've had lessons that we've learned with a great deal of pain. But the past is not a place to live."[26] By both lauding the South and distancing himself from the more despicable aspects of its history, Carter could play both on regional pride and his own regional identity to make claims that would be less acceptable to Southern audiences had they come from someone from outside that region. The South here served the same role that the nation's checkered history would in other contexts. It allowed him to admit to mistakes and to argue that such admissions made reconciliation and progress possible.

This is clearly a Christian view of politics, with an admission of error paving the way for redemption. Indeed, his Christian faith played an important role in Carter's ethos, and his reputation as a religious man in turn did a great deal to enhance his credibility on human rights.[27] For Carter, human rights also had political roots in the foundational documents of the American republic, but it was first and foremost a religious mandate, authorized by God. He was not shy about discussing his religion – and its connection to his advocacy of human rights – in public: "My own religious convictions are deep and personal. I seek divine guidance when I make a difficult decision as President and also am supported, of course, by a common purpose which binds Christians together in a belief in the human dignity of mankind and in the search for worldwide peace – recognizing, of course, that those who don't share my faith quite often have the same desires and hopes."[28] Acknowledging that those who did not share his religion could still share his values,

Carter enacted the tolerance he advocated in political affairs. In the process, he further strengthened his own ethos and his argument. Carter claimed to "worship daily," and he argued that religion represented a "stabilizing factor in my life."[29] Yet he also insisted that "I have never detected nor experienced any conflict between God's will and my political duty."[30] For Carter, enacting human rights as a national policy was the best example of the confluence between God's will and his political duties as a Christian.[31]

Carter argued that the cause of human rights transcended his leadership, setting the stage for its continuance after his departure from office. According to Carter, human rights was not only a mandate from God, but a "movement" sweeping the world: "Some claim ... that Jimmy Carter elevated human rights and democracy on the international agenda and that the agenda will change when I leave my office. They are wrong. Hemispheric support for human rights is a historic movement."[32] In this way, Carter connected his personal ethos to a wider cause, giving both added credibility.[33] Throughout his administration, Carter tied his personal life, values, experiences, and political commitments to human rights. It became his signature issue because of the effort he made to claim human rights as his own. That effort extended from his personal ethos to that of the nation as a whole.

Carter consistently maintained the importance of human rights to the nation's self-identity, connecting the issue to the foundational principles of the American republic: "In ancestry, religion, color, place of origin, and cultural background, we Americans are as diverse a nation as the world has ever seen. No common mystique of blood or soil unites us. What draws us together, perhaps more than anything else, is our belief in human freedom. We want the world to know that our Nation stands for more than financial prosperity."[34] Suggesting that the United States was less of a place than an idea, Carter identified that defining idea as an unwavering respect for "human rights."

For Carter, American policy was not to be grounded in material interests (although he never denied their importance) but instead was associated with time-less issues of ethics: "Our policy is based on an historical vision of America's role. Our policy is derived from a larger view of global change. Our policy is rooted in our moral values, which never change. Our policy is reinforced by our material wealth and by our military power. Our policy is designed to serve mankind."[35] For Carter, such a policy was more consistent with both American history and American ideals than were the policies of his immediate predecessors, and his stance on human rights was a powerful warrant in support of that argument.

Carter also grounded his commitment to human rights in the revolutionary heritage of the United States. In his 1979 State of the Union Address, for example, Carter stated:

> To establish those values, two centuries ago a bold generation of Americans risked their property, their position, and life itself. We are their heirs, and they are sending us a message across the centuries. The words they made so vivid are now growing faintly indistinct, because they are not heard often enough. They are words like "justice,"

"equality," "unity," "truth," "sacrifice," "liberty," "faith," and "love." These words remind us that the duty of our generation of Americans is to renew our Nation's faith – not focused just against foreign threats but against the threats of selfishness, cynicism, and apathy.[36]

Here Carter invoked a rhetoric of purification, suggesting that the problem with American foreign policy was that America itself had lost touch with its fundamental values. Carter's rhetoric of human rights thus called upon the American republic itself to change its ways. By renewing the founders' commitment to justice, equality, faith, and even love, America could be morally and politically reborn.

Carter's dedication to changing the direction of American foreign policy was clear. "For too many years," he argued, "we've been willing to adopt the flawed and erroneous principles and tactics of our adversaries, sometimes abandoning our own values for theirs. We've fought fire with fire, never thinking that fire is better quenched with water." That old approach had "failed," according to Carter, "with Vietnam the best example of its intellectual and moral poverty." But through this failure Americans had "found our way back to our own principles and values" and "regained our lost confidence."[37] Carter may have been overly optimistic in his assessment of the lessons learned from Vietnam, but given the nature of his political times and the fragility of his political coalition, the political utility (if not the political necessity) of claiming unity was obvious. Equally obvious was the centrality of human rights to the creation and protection of that unity – and to Carter's own political success in making human rights a central tenet of American foreign policy.

Carter understood that many in his international audience might construe his new human rights policy as just another rhetorical cover for American ideological dominance. He consistently denied any such intent: "We must recognize that basing our own behavior on American values does not mean that we should insist on identical standards from every other country. We must realize that ours is not the only system of government that is acceptable to people; ours is not the only set of values by which men and women can live happily." In issuing these reassurances, Carter displayed his familiarity with history, not as taught in US history books, but as perceived by many outside of the United States: "I do not want to see us abandon the cynical manipulation of nations and peoples only to see a return to the excessive moralistic zeal of an earlier era – a moralism which often cloaked other motives and helped lead us into the tragedy of Vietnam."[38] Carter thus defined his human rights policy in contrast to the "bad old days" of American imperialism and reinforced its associations with more positive expressions of American beliefs and values. As Carter presented the new policy, it entailed respect for others, not a new rhetorical cover for American domination.

Like most US presidents, Carter spoke of the United States as "a strong nation." Yet he insisted that "we don't have to be a bully to show it," and he suggested that the United States could win friends and allies by remaining true to its ideals: "We want to be the kind of nation that arouses the understanding and the admiration and the friendship of smaller countries, those that are poor, those that are uncertain, those that are new, those whose citizens might be black or brown or yellow. We're trying to extend the influence of our Nation and its principles throughout the world in a good, decent way, to make Americans proud."[39] In Carter's vision, American influence would be extended through the example it set, not through military power. Yet if the United States hoped to serve as an example to the world, it had to remain faithful to the values it espoused. Carter made that point clear in his Inaugural Address: "The best way to enhance freedom in other lands is to demonstrate here that our democratic system is worthy of emulation. To be true to ourselves, we must be true to others. We will not behave in foreign places so as to violate our rules and standards here at home, for we know that the trust which our Nation earns is essential to our strength."[40]

Presidents can hope to get more attention for their favorite issues simply by talking about them. But *how* presidents talk about their issues also influences the nature and amount of attention an issue may receive. In this case, Carter tied human rights so closely to his own political persona and to the values of the nation that – for better or for worse – it became almost impossible to discuss the Carter administration without also discussing human rights. In short, Carter *framed* the issue effectively. He not only guaranteed that "human rights" would forever be associated with his administration, but also that the term would be identified with the principles and ideals of America itself.

The ideographic functions of "human rights"

The fact that Carter rhetorically linked both his own political identity and the nation's ideals to "human rights" gave that term itself a new level of prominence in American public discourse. In other words, it helped transform the term "human rights" into what rhetorical scholars have called an "ideograph," or a high-level abstraction that encapsulates or summarizes the definitive principles or ideals of a political culture. Of course, Carter's human rights policies were sometimes controversial; the term "human rights" itself also remained vague, so his preferred understanding of the term did not always prevail in later administrations. Nevertheless, the *term* remained central to the rhetoric of American foreign policy for decades to come. In the long run, the very controversy attending Carter's policies, coupled with the ambiguity of the term "human rights," may well have contributed to the issue's longevity on the national political agenda.

Much of the power of rhetoric comes from the interactions among speakers, audiences, and the language that unites them. Meaning is always negotiated. One of the vehicles of this negotiation is what rhetorical scholar Michael McGee labeled the "ideograph." Ideographs are culturally bound summary terms that capture important ideological associations. As high-order abstractions, they have the potential to unify diverse audiences around vaguely shared sets of meanings. Their very vagueness allows for those meaning to be adapted to fit time, circumstance, and rhetorical exigency, although they are not entirely flexible and do require the creation and maintenance of a certain level of cultural consensus.[41] Ideographs are words or phrases, like "equality," "freedom," and "the rule of law," that serve as powerful warrants for political action and can be used to justify and defend a variety of different policies across a variety of contexts.[42] For decades after Carter left office, presidents would invoke "human rights" to warrant political action, even if they did not embrace the specific policies of the Carter administration.

Ronald Reagan, Bill Clinton, and George W. Bush all used the term "human rights" to advance their foreign policy agendas, even though their policies differed significantly from those espoused by the Carter administration.[43] As John Kane notes, "The beauty of human rights was that they seemed simply moral, unideo-logical, almost apolitical."[44] This is an apt description of the invisible nature of the work ideographs do. They go by unnoticed, providing warrants for action and con-necting actions to deeply held beliefs and the *narratives* we have constructed around those beliefs. It is the nature of the language used – language made prom-inent and popular by Jimmy Carter – that has given presidential appeals to "human rights" their political force.

Kane argues that Carter relied heavily upon notions of American exceptionalism and sought to salvage that myth, which had been damaged by the policies of the Johnson and Nixon administrations. Carter explicitly argued that through a policy grounded in human rights, American power could once again be put in the service of America's moral ideals. For Carter, Kane notes, a human rights policy would redeem America from its sins; it would purge the nation of the "enemy" within.[45]

Carter's successor, Ronald Reagan, chose to deny American sin and simply assert the superiority of American values. For Reagan, "human rights" became a weapon to wield against the Soviet Union and other communist states – a neocon-servative response to the "enemy" without. For Reagan, "human rights" did not imply American guilt, as it did for Carter, but rather was the wellspring of American wealth and power. As Kane notes, where Carter used "human rights" to conjure up an idealized image of the global community, Reagan used the term almost exclusively to bludgeon the Soviet Union.[46] Carter emphasized expunging American sin as a way of restoring the nation's belief in the exceptionalist myth; Reagan simply reasserted that myth with his more muscular talk of America and its global mission.[47]

Bill Clinton, relieved of the burdens of the Cold War, lacked Reagan's warrants for action. Nevertheless, he too invoked "human rights" as a warrant for policy, but with an emphasis on how the world had changed and the need for new proce-dures and policies. As head of the world's only remaining superpower, Clinton faced the challenge of asserting American leadership in the absence of a commonly accepted foil against which to proclaim America's moral superiority. So Clinton focused on context: The world had changed, America faced new challenges, and there were new opportunities on the horizon. Like the presidents who had gone before him, Clinton's "human rights" policy emphasized the virtues of democratic capitalism. Like Reagan, he also talked about the importance of individualism, and like Carter, he saw the world as increasingly interdependent. Above all, however,

Clinton stressed the importance of process; for Clinton, "human rights" raised procedural questions. This allowed him to gloss over some important questions of the exact nature and content of these rights, while stressing the importance of free markets, individual liberty, and democratically elected governments in the protection of human rights. Clinton thus adopted a little from both Carter and Reagan, seeking the flexibility characteristic of his so-called "third way" of governing.[48] In addition, he called on Carter more directly, asking his advice on matters concerning human rights and encouraging his trips abroad on behalf of the issue. Carter remained a rhetorical leader on human rights long after he left office.

Finally, George W. Bush adopted the language of "human rights" as a war-time president, invoking the term in ways clearly inconsistent with the ideals of the broader human rights movement. He too relied upon the myth of American exceptionalism in making his case, and he most clearly connected rhetorically to Reagan's rendering of that myth. He also has been the most fully developed neoliberal of the presidents; for him, the global marketplace is of singular significance, and the connections between democratic forms of government, capitalistic modes of economic organization, and the protection of "human rights" are clear. Yet by waging a preemptive war and condoning human rights violations at Guantánamo Bay and elsewhere, Bush has also gone farther than any of his predecessors in contravening Carter's conception of human rights. In doing so, Bush may have finally destroyed the rhetorical power of the ideograph, making it more difficult for future American presidents to invoke "human rights" as a warrant for political action.[49]

"Human rights" has been a powerful ideograph because presidents since Carter have found the term politically useful. That utility stems from the label's ideological power and its interpretive flexibility. By wielding ideographs in relation to national policy choices, more recent presidents have demonstrated the long-term influence of Carter's rhetoric of human rights. These presidents may not have understood or deployed the rhetoric of "human rights" exactly as Carter did, but the fact that they invoked the ideograph points to the lasting impact of Carter's rhetoric.

By adopting the term "human rights," the presidents who followed Carter also had to adopt some of its meanings; we became a nation that was constituted by its adherence to values like human rights and a nation whose policies were determined, to at least some extent, by those values. That is, we did not just believe in human rights, we were also expected to act consistently with them and to defend them both at home and abroad.

The educative functions of presidential rhetoric

There seems to be at least some evidence that when a president talks about an issue, that issue achieves more prominence, both in the news media and in the public's mind. It is obvious that getting an issue on the national agenda is not the same as winning agreement on that issue, but without the first, the second is certainly unlikely. Generally, presidential scholars have argued that a president's best strategy for gaining agreement with his specific positions is to talk loudly, consistently, and exclusively about one subject and to instruct the administration's surrogates to do the same.[50] There may be another model of presidential leadership, however, which has more to do with long-term education than with short-term policy changes.

The presidency is at its most rhetorically powerful when the president's ethos and his message mesh – and when both are backed by the power of the institution. For presidential rhetoric to have a significant impact on the public agenda, it needs to be understood as "presidential" in the institutional sense. Presidential rhetoric is most persuasive when it resonates with prevailing public opinion, promotes incremental rather than radical change (it is easier to make small changes than large ones), and comes across as consistent with the president's existing ethos so that it seems both sincere and ethically motivated. The president can also enhance the power of his rhetoric by mobilizing the communicative resources of the institution of the presidency behind the issue. All of these factors contributed to the long-term influence of Jimmy Carter's rhetoric on human rights.

"Human rights" is, at the least, a vague term, which allowed members of various constituencies to pour their own meanings onto it. For some, it meant social and economic rights; for others, it suggested the integrity of the individual; and for still others, its meaning was restricted to political and civil rights. Some saw it as a weapon in the ideological war against the Soviet Union; for others, it was a way to redeem American claims to moral superiority, damaged by years of support for right-wing regimes in Latin America, neglect of emerging nations in Africa, and ignorance of politics in Asia and the Middle East. That vagueness – and the inconsistencies it seemed to produce – created a host of problems for the Carter administration. At times, the Carter administration seemed to have difficulty developing a coherent and consistent policy on human rights. Yet the very vagueness and inconsistencies that created obstacles to the formation of policy may have contributed to the long-term, educational effects of Carter's human rights rhetoric. Put another way, Carter's rhetoric of human rights may not have produced many immediate policy victories, but it did have long-term impacts on the way Americans talked about foreign policy.

Clear, consistent, and focused communication can sometimes actually work against a president's long-term goals. If Carter hoped to start a conversation about human rights, raise consciousness about how American foreign policy had abandoned its foundational principles, and begin a long-term process of policy reform, it may have been to his advantage to be vague about "human rights" and its implications for specific policies. To the extent that a president allows an issue to be understood in only one way, its utility to other political actors may be limited. Carter had one understanding of "human rights." It was not shared by Ronald Reagan, who nevertheless invoked "human rights" for his own purposes, and thus perpetuated the conversation. The same can be said for presidents who followed Reagan. Carter clearly did not agree with George W. Bush's use of "human rights" as a justification for the war in Iraq. But the fact that "human rights" remains central to the debate over American foreign policy today is in no small way a tribute to

Carter. It is all but impossible to talk about human rights without also talking about Jimmy Carter.[51] In that sense, Carter's rhetorical legacy is secure.

There are, of course, different ways of talking about the influence of presidential rhetoric. One model is common to the literature of political science: A president should speak clearly and consistently on a particular issue; the president and administrative members should train their rhetorical, administrative, and political efforts on that issue; and when legislative or policy victory has been gained, they should loudly proclaim victory before moving on to the next issue. Carter's rhetoric of human rights seemed to reflect another model, one less focused on immediate legislative goals and more attuned to gradual change and the long-term education of the American public. In this model, the president may hope merely to place an issue on the national agenda, to start a national conversation about the broader philosophical or moral underpinnings of certain policies, and to raise public awareness of the principles and ideals at stake in the debate. In other words, the president serves more as an educator in this model, exploring with the public the implications and importance of various courses of action in different contexts over a longer period of time.[52] Debates over issues like space exploration, which have been tied to ideographs like "progress" and the myth of the frontier, and welfare reform, which has been tied to the ideograph "equality" and the myth of the American Dream, are perhaps best understood in terms of this model of presidential rhetoric. In these cases, the influence of presidential rhetoric may be hard to measure empirically and may be considered more constitutive than instrumental. But to the extent that such language influences public opinion on a policy, it has clear instrumental effects as well.[53]

Conclusion

One model of presidential rhetoric relies on short-term measures that equate rhetorical influence with legislative victories or movement in the public opinion polls. That may be one way to assess the influence of presidential rhetoric. But it is not the only way, nor is it necessarily the best way to think about the instrumental effects of a president's words.

As the case of Jimmy Carter's rhetoric on human rights illustrates, presidential rhetoric may have both short- and long-term effects that the prevailing model of rhetorical influence neglects to take into account. Among these effects is the short-term effect of uniting and mobilizing either electoral or governing coalitions, as Carter did by arguing that the nation had a shared commitment to human rights. Another short-term effect is to reinforce public concern over an issue – as when Carter took human rights, already a matter of interest on Capitol Hill, and gave it increased prominence. By the end of his term, no one could talk about human rights without mentioning Jimmy Carter – or about Jimmy Carter without mentioning human rights. Presidential rhetoric also has important long-term instrumental effects. Political speech has the capacity to focus attention on an issue, to reinforce or to change the terms with which we debate an issue, or to give an issue a particular valence that affects how we interpret it. There is a huge difference between fighting a "war for oil" and a "War against Terror." Presidents cannot control completely how we talk about an issue; in that sense, those who emphasize the limits of presidential rhetoric are correct. But they are wrong to exclude the possibility that presidential rhetoric nevertheless has significant influence over the transmission of meaning and the interpretation of issues in American political culture. Presidential rhetoric *matters*, in a variety of ways.

Having influence, of course, does not mean that Carter's preferences were necessarily enacted into policy. Many Republicans remained unswayed by Carter's human rights appeals; others actually may have been influenced in a negative way. But Carter continues to speak with authority on human rights issues to this day, and his influence must be taken into account whenever human rights issues are under discussion. In short, Carter had – and continues to have – influence on these issues, even if that influence has not had dramatic effects on policy.

Scholars need to be careful when talking about the effects of any particular statement or speech by the president. We also need to be clear what we mean when we talk about effects, and we need to provide the best evidence possible – garnered from the texts themselves, from public opinion polls, from news accounts, and from other sources – to support our claims about the instrumental effects of rhetoric. We also need to be careful, however, not to jump too quickly to the conclusion that presidential rhetoric has *no* effects. The case for or against instrumental effects needs to be made carefully, based on the evidence for any particular example of presidential speech. Presidential speech matters, but it matters in many different ways depending on the president, his language choices, the issue, and the political context.

Notes

1   See, most prominently, George C. Edwards III, *On Deaf Ears* (New Haven, CT: Yale University Press, 2003); and Samuel Kernell, *Going Public: New Strategies of Presidential Leadership* (Washington, DC: CQ Press, 1997).

2   Edwards, *On Deaf Ears*.

3   Some of these scholars argue that presidential rhetoric is influential, but that it is also deleterious. The issue of whether presidential speech is normatively good or bad in terms of the health of our democracy is well beyond the scope of this essay, but good examples of this argument can be found in Roderick P. Hart, *The Sound of Leadership: Presidential Communication in the Modern Age* (Chicago: University of Chicago Press, 1987); Kathleen Hall Jamieson, *Eloquence in an Electronic Age: The Transformation of Political Speechmaking* (New York: Oxford University Press, 1988); Jeffrey Tulis, *The Rhetorical Presidency* (Princeton, NJ: Princeton University Press, 1987); and most recently, Elvin T. Lim, *The Anti-Intellectual Presidency: The Decline of Presidential Rhetoric from George Washington to George W. Bush* (New York: Oxford University Press, 2008).

4   See, for example, Martin J. Medhurst, "Introduction," in *Beyond the Rhetorical Presidency,* ed. Martin J. Medhurst (College Station: Texas A&M University Press, 1996), xi–xxv; and David Zarefsky, "Presidential Rhetoric and the Power of Definition," *Presidential Studies Quarterly* 34 (September 2004): 607–620.

5   Jeffrey E. Cohen, "Presidential Rhetoric and the Public Agenda," *American Journal of Political Science* 39 (February 1995): 87–107.

6   Todd M. Schaefer, "Persuading the Persuaders: Presidential Speeches and Editorial Opinion," *Political Communication* 14 (January–March 1997): 97–111.

7   Shanto Iyengar and Adam Simon, "News Coverage of the Gulf Crisis and Public Opinion: A Study of Agenda-Setting, Priming, and Framing," *Communication Research* 20 (June 1993): 365–383.

8   Catherine Cassara, "US Newspaper Coverage of Human Rights in Latin America, 1975–1982: Exploring President Carter's Agenda-Building Influence," *Journalism and Mass Communication Quarterly* 75 (Autumn 1998): 478–486; Dan F. Hahn and Justin J. Custainis, "Anatomy of an Enigma: Jimmy Carter's State of the Union Address," *Communication Quarterly* 33 (Winter 1985): 43–49; and Ernst B. Haas, "Human Rights: To Act or Not to Act?" in *Eagle Entangled: US Foreign Policy in a Complex World*, ed. Kenneth A. Oye, Donald Rothchild, and Robert J. Leiber (New York: Longman, 1979), 1671–1698.

9   Jimmy Carter, "Remarks to the National Association for the Advancement of Colored People," *Public Papers of the Presidents of the United States: Jimmy Carter, 1980–81*, bk. 2 (Washington, DC: Government Printing Office, 1982), 1322.

10 Jimmy Carter, "Address at Commencement Exercises at the University of Notre Dame," *Public Papers of the Presidents of the United States: Jimmy Carter, 1977*, bk. 1 (Washington, DC: Government Printing Office, 1977), 957.

11 See, for example, Jimmy Carter, "Remarks at the Annual Convention of the American Legion," *Public Papers of the Presidents of the United States: Jimmy Carter, 1980–81*, bk. 2, 1551.

12 Jimmy Carter, "Remarks at the 31st Annual Meeting of the Southern Legislative Conference," *Public Papers of the Presidents of the United States: Jimmy Carter, 1977*, bk. 2 (Washington, DC: Government Printing Office, 1978), 1310. He maintained this claim to morality and unselfishness even in his responses to the Iranian hostage crisis. See Jimmy Carter, "Remarks at the 13th Constitutional Convention of the American Federation of Labor and the Congress of Industrial Organizations," *Public Papers of the Presidents of the United States: Jimmy Carter, 1979*, bk. 2 (Washington, DC: Government Printing Office, 1981), 2126.

13 Jimmy Carter, "Inaugural Address," *Public Papers of the Presidents of the United States: Jimmy Carter, 1977*, bk. 1, 3.

14 Judging from the extant research on his presidency, this view is indeed generally accepted, regardless of how his presidency is judged. See Peter C. Bourne, *Jimmy Carter: A Comprehensive Biography from Plains to Presidency* (New York: Scribner, 1997); Kenneth Cmiel, "The Emergence of Human Rights Politics in the United States," *Journal of American History* 86 (December 1999): 1231–1250; John Dumbrell, *The Carter Presidency: A Re-Evaluation* (Manchester: Manchester University Press, 1993); Gary M. Fink and Hugh Davis Graham, eds., *The Carter Presidency: Policy Choices in the Post-New Deal Era* (Lawrence: University Press of Kansas, 1988); Leslie H. Gelb and Justine A. Rosenthal, "The Rise of Ethics in Foreign Policy: Reaching

a Values Consensus," *Foreign Affairs* 82 (May/June 2003): 2–7; Erwin Hargrove, *Jimmy Carter as President: Leadership and the Politics of the Public Good* (Baton Rouge: Louisiana State University Press, 1988); Burton I. Kaufman, *The Presidency of James Earl Carter, Jr.* (Lawrence: University Press of Kansas, 1993); Mark Rozell, *The Press and the Carter Presidency* (Boulder, CO: Westview Press, 1989); Donald S. Spencer, *The Carter Implosion: Jimmy Carter and the Amateur Style of Diplomacy* (New York: Praeger, 1988); and Robert A. Strong, *Working in the World: Jimmy Carter and the Making of American Foreign Policy* (Baton Rouge: Louisiana State University Press, 2000).

15 Among the other difficulties with influencing attitudes is the persistent question of whether the mass public can be said to have attitudes, and if they do, whether those attitude are either rational or constrained. There is an extensive literature on this point. See, among many others, Angus Campbell, Philip E. Converse, Warren E. Miller, and Donald E. Stokes, *The American Voter* (New York: Wiley, 1960); Philip E. Converse, "The Nature of Belief Systems in Mass Publics," in *Ideology and Discontent*, ed. David E. Apter (New York: Free Press of Glencoe, 1964), 206–261; Benjamin I. Page and Robert Y. Shapiro, *The Rational Public: Fifty Years of Trends in Americans' Policy Preferences* (Chicago: University of Chicago Press, 1992); and John R. Zaller, *The Nature and Origins of Mass Opinion* (Cambridge: Cambridge University Press, 1992).

16 See, again among many others, Matthew A. Bodnick, " 'Going Public' Reconsidered: Reagan's 1981 Tax and Budget Cuts and Revisionist Theories of Presidential Power," *Congress and the Presidency* 17 (Spring 1990): 13–29; Matthew Corrigan, "The Transformation of Going Public: President Clinton, the First Lady, and Health Care Reform," *Political Communication* 17 (Apr–Jun 2000): 149–169; Matthew Eshbaugh-Soha, *The President's Speeches: Beyond "Going Public"* (Boulder, CO: Lynne Reiner, 2006); and Tulis, *The Rhetorical Presidency*.

17 George C. Edwards III, *At the Margins: Presidential Leadership of Congress* (New Haven, CT: Yale University Press, 1989); and Edwards, *On Deaf Ears*.

18 The Gallup Organization, *Attitudes of the American People Related to Foreign Policy*, Submitted to the Chicago Council on Foreign Relations, December 1998, 10. See also Ole R. Holsti, *Public Opinion and American Foreign Policy*, rev. ed. (Ann Arbor: University of Michigan Press, 2004), 92; John E. Reilly, ed., *American Public Opinion and Foreign Policy* (Chicago: Chicago Council on Foreign Relations, 1975); and John E. Reilly, ed., *American Public Opinion and Foreign Policy* (Chicago: Chicago Council on Foreign Relations, 1979).

19 Anne E. Geyer and Robert Y. Shapiro, "The Polls – A Report: Human Rights," *Public Opinion Quarterly* 52 (Fall 1988): 386.

20 See, for example, Catherine Cassara, "US Newspaper Coverage of Human Rights in Latin America, 1975–1982: Exploring President Carter's Agenda-Building Influence," *Journalism and Mass Communication Quarterly* 75 (Autumn 1998): 478.

21 *Newsweek*, June 22, 1977, "The Push for Human Rights," folder: Human Rights 1977 [1], Box 2: Hendrik Hertzberg Speech Files Jefferson-Jackson. ENERGY, Des Moines, Iowa, October 21, 1977 through Human Rights, 1977 [2], Carter Library.

22 David Hawk, "Human Rights at Half-Time," *The New Republic*, April 7, 1979, no discernible page numbers, folder Human Rights [2], Box 2: Hendrik Hertzberg Speech Files, Jefferson-Jackson. ENERGY, Des Moines, Iowa, October 21, 1977 through Human Rights, 1977 [2], Carter Library.

23 *ABC News*, "Commentary," Tuesday, March 22, 1977, Folder: Human Rights February–March 1977, Box 1: First Lady's Staff Files, First Lady's Press Office, Speech Notes of Campaign 1976 through Governor's Dinner March 1, 1977, Carter Library.

24 Zbigniew Brzezinski, *Power and Principle: Memoirs of the National Security Advisor, 1977–1981* (New York: Farrar, Straus, and Giroux, 1983), 48.

25 He continues to do so. See Jimmy Carter, *Our Endangered Values: America's Moral Crisis* (New York: Simon and Schuster, 2005), 8.

26 Jimmy Carter, "Remarks at a Campaign Rally at Spring Park," *Public Papers of the Presidents of the United States: Jimmy Carter, 1980–81*, bk. 2, 1602.

27 See Niels C. Neilson, Jr., *The Religion of President Carter* (Nashville, TN: Thomas Nelson, 1977), 91.

28 Jimmy Carter, "The President's Press Conference," *Public Papers of the Presidents of the United States: Jimmy Carter, 1977*, bk. 2, 2207.

29 Jimmy Carter, "Remarks and a Question-and-Answer Session with New Hampshire High School Students," *Public Papers of the Presidents of the United States: Jimmy Carter, 1978*, bk. 1 (Washington, DC: Government Printing Office, 1979), 370.

30 Jimmy Carter, "Remarks to Members of the Southern Baptist Brotherhood Commission," *Public Papers of the Presidents of the United States: Jimmy Carter, 1978*, bk. 1, 1115.

31 Jimmy Carter, "Remarks to Members of the Southern Baptist Brotherhood Commission," 1115.

32 Jimmy Carter, "Remarks at the 10th Regular Session of the General Assembly of the Organization of American States," *Public Papers of the Presidents of the United States: Jimmy Carter, 1980–81*, bk. 3 (Washington, DC: Government Printing Office, 1982), 2735.

33 He made a similar argument after leaving office, arguing in his presidential memoirs that, "As President, I hoped and believed that the expansion of human rights might be the wave of the future throughout the world, and I wanted the United States to be at the crest of this movement." See Jimmy Carter, *Keeping Faith: The Memoirs of a President* (New York: Bantam, 1982), 144.

34 Jimmy Carter, "Address at the Commencement Exercises at the University of Notre Dame," *Public Papers of the Presidents of the United States: Jimmy Carter, 1977*, bk. 1, 958. For other examples of arguments that human rights were crucial to the American founding, see Jimmy Carter, "The President's News Conference," *Public Papers of the Presidents of the United States: Jimmy Carter, 1977*, bk. 2, 2115.

35 Carter, "Notre Dame," 961–962.

36 Jimmy Carter, "Address Before a Joint Session of Congress on the State of the Union," *Public Papers of the Presidents of the United States: Jimmy Carter, 1979*, bk.1 (Washington, DC: Government Printing Office, 1980), 108.

37 Carter, "Notre Dame," 956.

38 Jimmy Carter, B'nai Brith speech draft; draft dated September 1–2; speech file dated 9/1/76, Jimmy Carter Papers-Pre-Presidential, 10, folder: B'nai Brith Speech, Box 2: 1976 Presidential Campaign Issues Office–Stuart Eizenstat, Arms Control, 2/76–9/76 through Campaign Planning and Strategy, 6/76–11/76, Carter Library.

39 Jimmy Carter, "Remarks at a Democratic Party Rally for John Ingram," *Public Papers of the Presidents of the United States: Jimmy Carter, 1978*, bk. 2, 1389. See also Jimmy Carter, "Remarks at a State Democratic Party Reception," *Public Papers of the Presidents of the United States: Jimmy Carter, 1978*, bk. 2, 1623; Jimmy Carter, "Remarks at a

Fundraising Dinner," *Public Papers of the Presidents of the United States: Jimmy Carter, 1978*, bk. 2, 1648; Jimmy Carter, "Remarks at the Greater Buffalo International Airport," *Public Papers of the Presidents of the United States: Jimmy Carter, 1978*, bk. 2, 1887.

40   Jimmy Carter, "Inaugural Address," 2.

41   Michael Calvin McGee, "In Search of 'the People': A Rhetorical Alternative," *Quarterly Journal of Speech* 61 (October 1975): 235–249; Michael Calvin McGee, " 'Not Men, But Measures': The Origins and Import of an Ideological Principle," *Quarterly Journal of Speech* 64 (April 1978): 141–155; Michael Calvin McGee, "The 'Ideograph': A Link Between Rhetoric and Ideology," *Quarterly Journal of Speech* 66 (February 1980): 1–17; and Michael Calvin McGee, "Ideograph," in *Encyclopedia of Rhetoric*, ed. Thomas O. Sloane (New York: Oxford University Press, 2001), 378–381.

42   Celeste M. Condit and John L. Lucaites, *Crafting Equality: America's Anglo-African Word* (Chicago: University of Chicago Press, 1993).

43   John Kane, "American Values or Human Rights? US Foreign Policy and the Fractured Myth of Virtuous Power," *Presidential Studies Quarterly* 33 (December 2003): 772–800.

44   Kane, "American Values," 784.

45   Kane, "American Values," 775.

46   Kane, "American Values," 787.

47   John Orman, *Comparing Presidential Behavior: Carter, Reagan, and the Macho Presidential Style* (New York: Greenwood Press, 1987).

48   See Democratic Leadership Committee, "About the Third Way," June 1, 1998, www.ndol.org/ndol_ci.cfm?kaid=1288&subid=187&contentid=895 (accessed June 20, 2007).

49   For an extended discussion of this point, see Mary E. Stuckey and Joshua R. Ritter, "George Bush, 'Human Rights' and American Democracy," *Presidential Studies Quarterly* 37 (December 2007): 646–666.

50   Scholars generally assume that focused communication is always more effective communication. See, most recently, David Domke, Erica Graham, Kevin Coe, Sue Lockett John, and Ted Coopman, "Going Public as a Political Strategy: The Bush Administration, an Echoing Press, and the Passage of the Patriot Act," *Political Communication* 23 (July/September 2006): 291–312.

51   This did not always work to a president's advantage. Bill Clinton, for example, had to deal with questions from the press regarding Carter's positions on sanctions concerning North Korea; see William J. Clinton, "Remarks at the Signing Ceremony for the Supplemental Agreements to the North American Free Trade Agreement," September 14, 1993, www.presidency.ucsb.edu/ws/index.php?pid=47070 (accessed July 20, 2009). Carter's opinions on world leaders vis-à-vis human rights concerns were still being referenced during the George W. Bush administration. See, for example, "Press Briefing by Tony Snow," September 12, 2007, www.presidency.ucsb.edu/ws/index.php?pid=75749 (accessed July 20, 2009).

52   See Fred I. Greenstein, *The Presidential Difference*, 2nd ed. (New York: Free Press, 2004).

53   I am thinking here of an example like declaring war on poverty, or understanding affirmative action as a policy intended to provide equality of opportunity when that is seen through the metaphor of a foot race. See, for example, David Zarefsky, *President Johnson's War on Poverty: Rhetoric and History* (Tuscaloosa: University of Alabama Press, 2005).

13

Analyzing Constitutive Rhetorics
The Virginia and Kentucky Resolutions and the "Principles of '98"

James Jasinski and Jennifer R. Mercieca

In his seminal 1925 essay "The Literary Criticism of Oratory," Herbert Wichelns contrasted the avocations of literary and rhetorical criticism. He concluded that rhetorical criticism's "point of view is patently single. It is not concerned with permanence, nor yet with beauty. It is concerned with effect." Wichelns's next sentence indirectly inserted an adjectival modifier before the word effect which narrowed its semantic potential. He wrote: Rhetorical criticism "regards a speech as a communication to a specific audience." By emphasizing that public discourse always addresses specific audiences, and suggesting that the rhetorical critic should focus his or her analytic attention on "the orator's method of imparting his [*sic*] ideas" to the specific audience, Wichelns circumscribed the range of discursive effects which the critic might examine. For example, focusing on how a message affects the specific or extant audience diminishes the temporal reach of discursive action. Wichelns appears to have assumed that discourse exhausts its rhetorical potential, its ability to exert influence, in the moment of immediate audience reception.[1]

Surveying the metacritical literature in rhetorical studies in the mid-twentieth century, we find a handful of essays questioning the restricted approach to discursive effect that Wichelns's essay helped instigate.[2] We also discover essays such as Lloyd Bitzer's influential "The Rhetorical Situation" that provided conceptual reinforcement for an emerging "instrumental" critical paradigm organized around a circumscribed view of effect. Through concepts such as "exigence" and "constraint," Bitzer's reconstruction of rhetorical situations included more factors than immediate audience; he nevertheless buttressed an instrumental approach to discursive effect. According to Bitzer's formulation, discourse engaged or resolved urgent, objective problems (exigencies) while managing or negotiating various obstacles (constraints). Public discourse, Bitzer insisted in 1968, functioned instrumentally, enabling individuals and groups to respond to preexisting situations.[3]

While Bitzer's account of rhetorical situations advanced an instrumentalist critical orientation, other scholars began developing concepts such as "rhetoric is epistemic," the "ego-function" of rhetoric, and "fantasy-theme analysis," which indirectly challenged a narrow account of discursive effect.[4] Indebted to these internal conceptual developments as well as to developments in other disciplines, rhetoricians began urging the discipline to rethink the concept of effect in the early 1980s.[5] In his review of the 1984 University of Iowa conference on "The Rhetoric of the Human Sciences," John Lyne suggested that the "constitutive function of rhetoric ... should probably get more attention in our literature than it does, since it helps explain why the study of discourse is important independent of whether it can be demonstrated to have 'caused' events."[6] In his review, Lyne contrasted a narrow, "causal" model of effect with one that is more capacious, and like others, he urged scholars to embrace a more expansive understanding of discursive effect. Lyne's contrastive terminology – the idea of rhetoric's "constitutive function" – has become an important part of the contemporary rhetorical lexicon.[7]

Two scholars in particular helped popularize what we might call a constitutive framework for rhetorical criticism and public address scholarship. Maurice Charland and James Boyd White developed their conceptualizations of "constitutive rhetoric" independently, drawing largely on different theoretical traditions. Charland was heavily influenced by Kenneth Burke as well as by various strands of continental philosophy and social theory (especially Louis Althusser);[8] in one of his early books White identified a number of writers who influenced his approach to language and rhetoric, including so-called "New" Critics and reader-response scholars in American literary studies, language philosophers such as Wittgenstein, Austin, and Searle, and of course Kenneth Burke.[9] While the different intellectual traditions from which they draw will allow us to contrast Charland and White's perspectives, at this point we would like to highlight their shared assumptions. Reflecting on a variety of contemporary theoretical traditions, including language philosophy, literary and philosophical deconstruction, and poststructuralism, we contend that Charland and White's versions of "constitutive rhetoric," as well as the various critical studies which have tried to develop and expand on their perspectives, share basic social constructionist assumptions about the contingency of human beliefs and institutions and the generative potential of discursive action.[10]

Jasinski suggests that the constitutive "turn" in contemporary rhetoric is "both a return to a neglected aspect of the rhetorical tradition and an encounter with a broader 'constructivist' or structurational agenda in the humanities and social sciences." He identifies the rejection of "the once traditional view that language is principally a medium of representation" as a crucial assumption shared by social constructionists. Constructivism and constitutive rhetoric, he continues, advance the somewhat paradoxical position that "linguistic or discursive practices create what they describe as they simultaneously describe what they create." As a brief summary description of the constitutive potential inherent in discursive practice, Jasinski endorses Louis Montrose's statement that "representations of the world in ... discourse are engaged in constructing the world, in shaping the modalities of social reality, and in accommodating their writers, performers, readers, and audiences to multiple and shifting subject positions within the world they both constitute and inhabit."[11]

In his 1998 essay in *Doing Rhetorical History*, Jasinski modifies Michael Leff's distinction between two senses of persuasion – intentional and extensional – in order to locate two distinct trajectories of constitutive influence or effect.[12] Jasinski's effort, we believe, is consistent with recent attempts to distinguish between a "rhetoric of interiors" and a "rhetoric of exteriors."[13] In the next section of the chapter, we draw on Charland, White, and other examples of constitutive critical analysis to outline important themes and questions that might guide interior and exterior modes of constitutive critical inquiry. In the third section of the chapter, we illustrate each analytic trajectory in an extended discussion of the Virginia and Kentucky *Resolutions* drafted in 1798 by, respectively, James Madison and Thomas Jefferson. Examining their constitutive legacy is appropriate since the *Resolutions* were an instrumental failure in their immediate historical context, yet they rather quickly became canonized as the "principles of '98."

Interior and Exterior Trajectories of Constitutive Analysis

Jasinski initially adumbrates the two trajectories in the following terms: "Intentionally, texts exhibit constitutive potential through the invitations inscribed in various discursive forms (tropes, arguments, etc.). Extensionally, texts exhibit constitutive force through the cultural circulation and discursive articulation of its textual forms in ways that enable and constrain subsequent practice."[14] While we find this initial formulation useful, we will organize our discussion in terms of interior and exterior constitutive rhetorics because the term "intention" often connotes an instrumental critical logic. Beginning with Charland and White and continuing through more recent studies by Vanessa Beasley, Nathaniel Cordova, and Dexter Gordon,[15] critics have examined textual interiors – the various discursive forms which inhabit or reside in the text – in various ways, thereby uncovering a text's constitutive capacity (or capacities) and its potential to shape audience identity, communal values, and social reality.[16]

Charland's 1987 study of Quebec nationalism concentrates on the Parti Québécois White Paper "Quebec-Canada: A New Deal," released in November 1979. He focuses on the White Paper's historical narrative of oppression combined with "a teleological movement towards emancipation," arguing that "within the formal structure of a narrative history ... it is possible to conceive of a set of individuals as if they were but one." He continues a paragraph later: "Form renders the 'Québécois' a real subject within the historical narrative." Charland qualifies this claim a few paragraphs later, remarking: "The ideological effects of constitutive rhetoric that I have outlined are not merely formal effects inscribed within the bracketed experience of interpreting a text. In other words, these do not only permit a disinterested understanding of a fictive world." In our reading, Charland attempts to transcend an analysis of textual interiors – reconstructing the White Paper's historical narrative of oppression – by suggesting that such an analysis of interior form only provides access to "a fictive world." He insists that his analysis of "[t]he White paper's constitutive rhetoric, as it articulates the meaning of being 'Québécois,' is not a mere fiction. It inscribes real social actors within its textualized structure of motives, and then inserts them into the world of practice." From our perspective, Charland's effort to link interior form with fiction, thereby exceeding an interior mode of analysis, represents a canard. Despite claims to the contrary, Charland's analysis concentrates on narrative form, making no effort to trace the White Paper's circulation or to disclose the way Quebec citizens used it to shape their "practices" or their understanding of social reality. It remains a conceptually sophisticated, but nevertheless interior, mode of constitutive analysis.[17]

Charland's conceptual sophistication stems from the way he employs the work of Louis Althusser to describe a "rhetoric of interpellation." By following "the radical edge of Burke's identificatory principle," Charland attempts to surmount the model of instrumental persuasion, and in so doing, he discovers Althusser's concept.[18] According to Charland, interpellation is not the result of rhetorical appeal; it emerges in "the very act of *addressing*," and "occurs at the very moment one enters into a rhetorical situation ... as soon as an individual recognizes and acknowledges being addressed." By "participat[ing] in the discourse that address[es]" them, people are "inscrib[ed] ... into ideology," inserted into specific "discursive position[s]." Rhetorical interpellation, Charland concludes, is the principal apparatus of constitutive rhetoric, and "collective identities" are the primary "ideological effect" of rhetorical interpellation.[19]

A number of rhetorical scholars have followed Charland's lead in probing the way various discursive forms – narrative in particular – function to constitute identities. For example, Beasley draws upon Charland's discussion of Burke and Althusser, arguing that "to find evidence of how presidents have promoted certain forms of American national identity within their discourse, we need not look for overt appeals in which chief executives have told their listeners what to think or which policy to support. Instead, critics can look at ways that presidential discourse subtly reinforces the audience's presumed collective identity as national subjects." While locating a variety of "constitutive themes of American nationalism," she concludes that presidents have "most commonly associate[d] American national identity with Puritan notions of an American civil religion." Americans are linked by a providential narrative that has positioned them "as God's chosen people."[20] Similarly, Cordova examines the way the *Catecismo del Pueblo*, produced by Puerto Rico's Popular Democratic Party in the late 1930s, relied on "an historical Christian narrative of oppression" as well as "the traditional catechism form of question and answer" to "interpellate a subject." According to Cordova, the *Catecismo* provided Puerto Ricans with a collective identity; it "summon[ed] a people to take up their appointed role in history [which included] upholding a Christian duty to advance social justice by voting for the PPD."[21] In his study of nineteenth-century black nationalist discourse, Gordon traces the interpellative process, "rhetoric's construction of individuals into a collective subject," from David Walker's *Appeal* and Robert Young's *Ethiopian Manifesto* published in 1829 through key performances in the 1840s and 1850s by Martin Delany, Frederick Douglass, and Henry Highland

Garnet. In a chapter devoted to Walker and Young, Gordon describes the way "black nationalism's narrative structure … interpellated blacks into a collective identity by articulating nineteenth-century blacks in [a] rich, militant black history."[22] The analytic trajectory from Charland through Beasley, Cordova, and Gordon[23] reveals two principal features: (1) analyses of textual interiors (particularly narrative structures) which warrant interpretive claims regarding presumed discursive effect that (2) emphasize identity constitution.

James Boyd White elaborates his framework for analyzing the constitutive potential of textual interiors in two collections of essays: *When Words Lose Their Meanings* and *Heracles' Bow*. White begins with the assumption that "text-making" is a "kind of 'action with words.'" He continues by maintaining that texts come into existence "whenever any of us acts with words in our own lives to claim meaning for experience or to establish a relation with another."[24] We'll begin with White's conceptualization of the way texts establish or create relationships with readers since this analytic path most closely parallels Charland's sense of constitutive rhetoric.

White invites his readers to consider that the "interaction between mind and text … works like an interaction between people." A text, White continues, "asks its reader to become someone and … by doing so it establishes a relationship with him [*sic*]." He offers this example:

> Think … of what happens when a person opposed to racism is told a successful racist joke: he laughs and hates himself [*sic*] for laughing; he feels degraded, and properly so, because the object of the joke is to degrade. … Nor should he be ashamed that these possibilities are realized in him against his will, for a great work of literature might evoke such possibilities against the will of the reader in order to help him understand and correct them, and this would be an act of the deepest friendship. But the one who responds to the joke is ashamed of having this happen at the instigation of one who wishes to use those possibilities as the basis for ridicule or contempt; he is ashamed at who he has become in this relationship with this speaker.[25]

We think it useful to consider how Charland's sense of constitutive rhetoric might be used to explain White's example. Charland's framework emphasizes a cluster of verbs – inscribe, insert, interpellate – that might elucidate how the joke positions the person to whom it is told. These verbs invoke a world where agency resides primarily in texts (or, perhaps more precisely, in the moment someone recognizes that they are being addressed), and effects are presented as a *fait accompli*. In contrast, White's typical verbs – ask, invite, offer[26] – envision a world of shared agency and self-conscious readers (and speakers/writers) capable of considering – perhaps accepting, but also potentially rejecting – textual solicitations. In short, White's understanding of discursive action is more dialogic than Charland's.

Charland and White both concentrate on textual interiors as they seek to disclose the way discourse shapes individual and communal identities. Their respective versions of constitutive rhetoric differ in that each approach has been formulated in a different conceptual register. In the present context, we do not believe it necessary to engage the broader conversations concerning agency, identity, and subjectivity which these different registers facilitate; we do, however, think it important to note that because of its conceptualization of agency, White's version of constitutive rhetoric encourages critics to move beyond textual interiors to examine exterior trajectories of reception and circulation – a position that is reinforced by a second mode of textual action that White highlights.

White argues that when people "claim meaning for experience," they "must speak a language that has its existence outside" of their individual selves. "This language," he continues, provides a person with "his [*sic*] terms of social and natural description, his words of value, and his materials for reasoning; it establishes the moves by which he can persuade another, or threaten or placate or inform or tease him, or establish terms of cooperation or intimacy; it defines his starting places and stopping places and the ways he may intelligibly proceed from one to the other." The linguistic resources that "establish the possibilities of expression" both enable and constrain discursive performance. But this realization, White insists, does not lead to a deterministic conceptualization of language for as people claim meaning for experience, they "both act with and upon the language ... at once employing and reconstituting its resources."[27] Extending White's observations, Jasinski suggests that "[t]he idioms of public life (for example, liberalism, conservatism, free market capitalism, pro-choice or pro-life, etc.) and the specific concepts that organize, link, and separate these idioms are continually reconstituted through quotidian interaction as well as more nuanced textual practices. Charting such alterations in 'usages' is a central aspect of a constitutive rhetorical history."[28]

Drawing on White's more expansive understanding of discursive constitution as well as other strands of contemporary language and social theory, Jasinski has proffered additional loci for constitutive analysis. For example, he argues that J. Robert Cox and Robert Hariman's respective studies of King's "I Have a Dream" speech illustrate "the constitution of [a community's] temporal experience." Cox reveals the ways King's "metaphoric critique of gradualism" sought to constitute time as urgent, while Hariman more fully describes King's complicated persuasive field in order to uncover King's "subtle reconstitution of gradualism."[29] In addition to the discursive constitution of temporal experience, Jasinski suggests that "the ongoing discursive negotiation of the spatial categories 'public' and 'private'" merited the attention of rhetorical scholars. He encourages scholars to examine how "a plethora of discursive forces (e.g., legal, feminist, children's advocates, bureaucratic)" reconfigure our experience of the categories public and private. Jasinski's final analytic locus is communal reconstitution. He observes:

> Communal reconstitution can take a variety of discursive forms and rely on different textual practices as specific questions of social and political authority, power, bonds of affiliation, meaning, value, and institutional practice are confronted and negotiated. A history of American public discourse is, in part, the reconstruction and analysis of specific moments wherein an American community, and its constituent sub-communities, confronted threats to its existence (internal as well as external) and engaged in its own reconstitution.[30]

Charland, White, and the many scholars who have drawn upon and extended their respective versions of constitutive rhetoric demonstrate the myriad strategies for examining rhetorical interiors. In our judgment, analytic explorations of the constitutive nature of rhetorical exteriors are not as robust, but nevertheless point in some extremely promising directions.[31] Three concepts are, we believe, central in any effort to track rhetorical exteriors: reception, circulation, and articulation.

At first glance, Leah Ceccarelli's effort to unpack various senses of polysemy and Davis Houck and Mihaela Nocasian's discussion of Franklin Roosevelt's "First Inaugural" appear to have little in common, but in our judgment each of these essays illustrates how the examination of rhetorical exteriors – in each case how listeners and readers respond to a message – can help critics document a text's constitutive potential as well as its instrumental situational impact.[32] Ceccarelli observes that "[m]ost critics do not currently focus on how texts were received by their contemporary audiences, choosing instead to imagine how an audience in a particular rhetorical situation *might* have responded to the text's invitation" (emphasis in original). She continues: "By engaging a close analysis of both the primary text and the texts that are produced in response to it, the critic can recognize both polysemic potential and the actualization of that potential by audiences."[33] In addition to providing evidence of the way readers and listeners actualize semantic possibilities, we suggest extending Ceccarelli's insight to examine how actual audiences engage a text's constitutive invitations to, for example, inhabit a particular subject position, embrace a certain memory of the past, or employ the culture's vocabulary of key terms in a certain way. Houck and Nocasian specifically draw on Ceccarelli's insight and, in so doing, indirectly demonstrate this analytic possibility. For example, based on a careful reading of newspaper accounts of Roosevelt's First Inaugural, as well as letters written to the new president, they observed that "[o]ne dominant interpretive pattern by which the public (and the press) reacted to the speech involved confidence."[34] The reception evidence they uncovered helps reveal, we would argue, the way many Americans in 1933 accepted Roosevelt's invitation to reconstitute and re-embrace this communal attitude.

While Ceccarelli and Houck and Nocasian urge scholars to examine text reception, scholars of visual rhetorics encourage rhetoricians to broaden their analytic vision by tracing processes of image and "text" (e.g., specific arguments, tropes, ideographs) circulation. Extending on the work of Benjamin Lee and Edward LiPuma, Michael Warner, and Bruno Latour, Cara Finnegan and Jiyeon Kang argue that conceptual reflection has moved beyond a "passive transmission" model of circulation and has been replaced by a sense of "circulation as a constitutive process." Following Finnegan and Kang's recommendation to make "circulation a theme [in] our study of discourse" will force critics to recognize that, however powerful a particular rhetorical performance (and resulting text) may be, constitutive rhetorics do not enter the public sphere fixed and fully developed.[35] Public utterances issue constitutive invitations that are, in Ceccarelli's terms, realized in acts of reception and subsequent circulation; those acts, in turn, define, shape, and even transform the utterance's initially inchoate constitutive potential.[36] Over time, circulation practices produce a constitutive legacy that critical analysis can reconstruct. Existing studies that trace the career of a specific trope or pattern of argument exhibit a proto-circulatory critical logic and, as such, illustrate some ways critics might analyze the process of constitutive circulation and the production of constitutive legacies.[37]

While the concept of circulation foregrounds the collaborative production of constitutive rhetoric, it does not provide an adequate framework for analyzing the way rhetorical exteriors actualize constitutive potential. When advocates shift a trope, an argument, or a visual image from one historically particular rhetorical situation into a new context or connect it to a new controversy, circulation occurs via specific articulatory practices.[38] In some cases these articulatory practices will highlight a diachronic dimension (the case in 1848 when the women at Seneca Falls appropriated the language of America's Declaration of Independence and inserted it into their Declaration of Sentiments) while in other cases articulation moves synchronically (the case in 1967 when Martin Luther King, Jr. defended his decision to speak out against the war in Vietnam by identifying the ideological threads that connected his civil rights and antiwar positions). We also believe it worth noting that accepted articulations can be resisted, and efforts to disarticulate sutured concepts are part of the concepts' ongoing circulation (e.g., Emma Goldman's efforts in the early twentieth century to sever the link between the concept of "love" and the institution of heterosexual marriage).

In tracing the two trajectories of constitutive criticism, we have shown how the interior trajectory, marked by a predominant interest in identity formation, is well established. We believe it appropriate to expand interior analysis to include examinations of how texts invite listeners and readers to modify the meaning of a culture's key terms, to reconceptualize a culture's experience of public time (including the past), to reaffirm or reconfigure accepted demarcations of social space, and to affirm as well as challenge established sources of cultural authority, bonds of affiliation, and institutional relationships. The exterior trajectory is, as our discussion suggests, much less fully realized at present. By drawing on extant scholarship, we have tried to convey a sense of how critics might extend that mode of analysis. The case study that follows illustrates both analytic trajectories.

Before proceeding to the case study, one final observation is in order. As some scholars have already observed and as our case study will further illustrate, a constitutive rhetoric does not exist in a vacuum. Its textual vehicles emerge and circulate within a world of alternative, frequently competing, constitutive rhetorics. For pragmatic reasons critics will typically need to limit the scope of inquiry. Nevertheless, critics must recognize the multiplicity of constitutive rhetorics and the impact that they might have on each other. As we discuss more fully in the next section, the constitutive potential of the "principles of '98" would be embraced by many Americans, but the *Resolutions* were never able to circulate with sufficient force to displace completely an alternative "nationalistic" constitutive rhetoric. Tracing the subsequent circulation of the "principles" also reveals how divisions and disagreements emerged within the political collectivity that the "principles" helped constitute.

The "Principles of '98": Interior Constitutive Invitations and Exterior Constitutive Legacy

Historians employ a variety of terms to describe the ideological conflicts that shaped American political discourse in the late eighteenth and early nineteenth centuries: cosmopolitan versus localist, federalist versus anti-federalist, nationalist versus states' rights, consolidation versus anticonsolidation, and liberal versus strict construction are some of the more common. While the terminology varies, the scholarly consensus is clear: During the nation's formative period, the Constitution came to occupy a central place in the nation's political imagination. But many Americans nevertheless imagined fundamentally different political regimes, with different visions of citizenship, different terms of value, and different accounts of the nation's development.[39] In his study of slavery and the US Constitution, Mark Brandon observes: "[A]t the level of ... constitutive narrative, from the very start of the constitutional order there were two prominent competing accounts of the Constitution – what it *meant* and what it *was*."[40]

These two competing narratives – or constitutive rhetorics – began to take shape during the 1787–1788 ratification debates as advocates committed to a more localist political regime challenged the centralizing thrust that they perceived in the proposed Constitution. Their development continued in the 1790s as a congressional coalition emerged to oppose Alexander Hamilton's aggressive program for economic expansion. According to Larry Kramer, by 1800 "lines [were] clearly drawn between a Republican Constitution and a Federalist one."[41] Countless public advocates and a considerable body of discourse brought these competing constitutive rhetorics into existence and were responsible for their continuing circulation and transformation. Resolutions adopted by the Virginia and Kentucky state legislatures in 1798 and 1799 along with a report issued by the Virginia legislature in 1800 whose content is often referred to collectively as "the principles of '98" imagined the most significant alternative to the nationalist vision. Uncovering the constitutive invitations (or constitutive vision) and reconstructing the constitutive legacy of these four pivotal documents helps reveal the way discursive performances shaped the development of the nation's constitutional order and allows us to demonstrate how discourse continues to constitute political thought and action long after its immediate instrumental situation.[42]

Thomas Jefferson's Kentucky *Resolutions* and James Madison's Virginia *Resolutions* were prepared to protest the 1798 Alien and Sedition Acts which Federalist President John Adams and his congressional supporters promoted. According to William Watkins, "[o]stensibly aimed at securing the home front as the [nation] braced for French invasion, the acts served the much broader purpose of Federalist political hegemony. Through this legislation, the Federalists sought to restrain democratic-minded foreigners and silence all criticism of the national government."[43] The Alien and Sedition Acts consisted of four laws: The Naturalization Act drastically limited citizenship and suffrage rights; the Alien Act gave the president the power to evict any alien "he shall judge dangerous to the peace and safety of the United States"; the Alien Enemies Act allowed the president to arrest, imprison, and deport any alien subject to an enemy power during wartime; and the Sedition Act defined sedition in such narrow terms that the law could be used to prosecute anyone who published anything negative about the federal government. According to Hartnett and Mercieca, congressional opponents attacked the acts on the grounds that they would augment executive power and endanger the Constitution's balance of powers, were vague and invited abuse of the newly granted powers, and were potentially unconstitutional.[44]

President Adams's congressional supporters discounted these concerns, and Congress adopted the acts during June and July 1798. Once enacted, the opponents' situational exigencies changed: They now had to decide whether and how to continue their opposition. Watkins observes that "[t]hough the details of the planning phase of the Kentucky and Virginia *Resolutions* elude us, the choice of state legislatures as the vehicles of protest is not shrouded in mystery." "A custom of turning to state legislatures to rally opposition to an overreaching central government was," Kramer avers, "well established" by the late eighteenth century, having been endorsed by both of the *Federalist Papers'* principal authors: Hamilton and Madison.[45] Jefferson's Kentucky *Resolutions* were introduced in the state legislature by John Breckinridge and adopted in November 1798; Madison's Virginia *Resolutions* were introduced by John Taylor of Caroline and adopted the following month.[46] The *Resolutions* denounced the acts as inexpedient and unconstitutional, and they invited Kentucky and Virginia's sister states to endorse their vision of the nation's constitutional order.

Analyzing textual interiors/reconstructing constitutive invitations

We want to identify four ways that the *Resolutions* invited readers to imagine the nation's situation and emerging constitutional order. First, the texts located the Alien and Sedition Acts within an ominous narrative structure. Virginia's *Resolutions* asked readers to accept the claim that "a spirit has in sundry instances been manifested by the Federal Government to enlarge its powers by forced constructions of the constitutional charter." The acts, Virginia legislators intimated, were part of "a design to expound certain general phrases ... so as to destroy the [Constitution's] meaning and effect"; they represented a "spirit" whose "obvious tendency and inevitable consequence ... would be to transform the present republican system of the United States into an absolute, or, at best, a mixed monarchy." The *Resolutions* established a narrative trajectory in which the "states by degrees" will be "consolidate[d] ... into one sovereignty."[47] Kentucky's 1799 *Resolutions* predicted that "if the general government be permitted to transgress the limits fixed by" the Constitution, "an annihilation of the state governments, and the creation upon

their ruins of a general consolidated government, will be the inevitable consequence." The shared fear of inevitable consolidation led Kentucky to conclude in
its 1798 *Resolutions* that the assumption of "unlimited powers" by the federal government must be "arrested on the threshold."[48] The "threshold" image, a manifestation of the commonplace locus of the irreparable, constituted the situation as
precarious and urgent and invited readers, especially legislators in the other states,
to ratify that definition of the situation through decisive action.

Second, the resolutions offered readers a narrative account of the constitutional
order's emergence. Kentucky's 1798 *Resolutions* began by foregrounding the states
syntactically as the sentence's subject and as the primary narrative agent: "[T]he
several States composing the United States of America ... constituted a general
government for special purposes [and] delegated to that government certain definite powers, reserving each State to itself, the residuary mass."[49] A decade earlier,
many of Jefferson and Madison's republican allies had attacked the proposed
Constitution because they perceived it as a threat to state sovereignty. Thanks to
the Tenth Amendment, prominently featured in Kentucky's first five Articles,
Jefferson repositioned the states and reimagined their role in the Constitution's
development. Rather than victims of a nationalist coup, Jefferson imagined the
states as primary players in the new constitutional order. They constituted, they
delegated, they reserved, and now – Jefferson and Madison suggested – they were
authorized "to oppose in a constitutional manner, every attempt ... to violate that
compact."[50] As Virginia explained in 1798: "[T]he states ... have the right and are
in duty bound to interpose for arresting the progress of the evil, and for maintaining within their respective limits the[ir] authorities, rights, and liberties."[51]

Perhaps even more important than reimagining the states' role in the constitutional narrative, Jefferson and Madison reimagined the new constitutional order
contractually as a compact.[52] In so doing they adjusted old concepts to the new
order: As Powell suggests, the traditional compact between "the governed and the
governors ... by which freedom was maintained" was "converted" into a new
"political ontology" in which the states constituted and controlled national power.[53]
In the 1790s the states attempted, not always successfully, to exert control over
national power via their representatives and a variety of expedience arguments. As
early as the 1791 debate over Hamilton's proposed national bank, the emerging
Jeffersonian opposition invented a new argument practice – constitutional interpretation – in their effort to frustrate Hamilton's agenda and control national
power. As Powell observes, "Americans have become so accustomed to associating
constitutional debate with discussions about the meaning of texts that it is easy to
overlook the significance of Madison's [and Jefferson's] textualism. English constitutional argument, with which the founding generation grew up, was not fundamentally textual."[54] In short, the republican opposition imagined "constitutional
debate" to be "essentially a legal discussion of the proper interpretation of a written instrument."[55]

Beginning in the early 1790s, Madison and Jefferson began inviting their fellow
citizens to embrace a "radically textual understanding of the constitutional

enterprise."[56] This "rigorous textualism" was, Powell argues, "a central feature of the principles of '98" and is, we suggest, a third constitutive feature of the *Resolutions*' rhetorical interior.[57] As Powell observes, the *Resolutions* "supported their claim that the Alien and Sedition Acts were unconstitutional with specific textual arguments."[58] For example, in its fifth resolution, the Kentucky legislature sought to subvert both the Alien and Alien Enemies Acts by citing Article One, Section Nine, which stated: "the migration or importation of such persons as any of the States now existing shall think proper to admit, shall not be prohibited by the Congress prior to the year 1808." The resolution then argued that since "a provision against prohibiting their migration is a provision against all acts equivalent thereto," giving the president the power "to remove them when migrated is equivalent to a prohibition of their migration, and is therefore contrary to the said provision of the Constitution, and void."[59]

Republican textualism was, as Powell notes, decidedly "protestant."[60] While Jefferson and Madison understood the interpretive potential of precedents (and that understanding helps explain their determination to "arrest ... on the threshold" the unconstitutional expansion of federal power), they typically adopted a Protestant fixation with the text and only the text.[61] Precedents were pernicious precisely because they led interpreters away from the authoritative text. The *Resolutions* also manifested the common Protestant commitment to "the legitimacy of individualized (or at least nonhierarchical communal) interpretation."[62] In its 1799 response to its sister states, the Kentucky legislature maintained that allowing "the general government [to be] the exclusive judge of the extent of the powers delegated to it" was "despotism." In good Protestant fashion, the legislature invited its sister states to embrace the proposition "that the several states who formed that instrument ... have the unquestionable right to judge of the infraction."[63] The states, and ultimately the people – not the federal courts – were the Constitution's authorized interpreters.[64]

While Kentucky and Virginia summoned their sister states and the citizenry at large to constitute a Protestant community devoted to upholding "the plain intent and meaning" of the "federal Compact," their resolutions invited readers to assume a rather uncharitable attitude towards those citizens entrusted with the reigns of federal power. The *Resolutions*' fourth significant constitutive invitation focused on the relationship between the practices (and texts) of those entrusted with power and the citizenry at large. Kentucky's *Resolutions* insisted that "free government is founded in jealousy and not in confidence." Confidence, the Kentucky legislature suggested, invites consolidation and "the destruction of all ... limits" on power. Kentucky's *Resolutions* continued: "[I]t is jealousy and not confidence which prescribes limited Constitutions to bind down those whom we are obliged to trust with power. ... In questions of power then let no more be heard of confidence in man, but bind him down from mischief by the claims of the Constitution."[65] Jealousy, suspicion, or – in Powell's terms – "ceaseless vigilance" were revealed as the hermeneutic norms appropriate for a republican regime.[66] Virginia and Kentucky invited their sister states, and ultimately all Americans, to emulate their hermeneutic posture and constitute a national community that distrusted those selected to govern.

When Virginia and Kentucky requested other states to ratify their vision of the nation's constitutional order, they were rebuked. The legislatures of New Hampshire, Vermont, Massachusetts, Rhode Island, Connecticut, New York, Pennsylvania, Delaware, and Maryland each sent replies to Kentucky and Virginia rejecting their resolutions. No state legislature sent a reply concurring with Kentucky and Virginia. In short, the states that chose to reply to Virginia and Kentucky's *Resolutions* abjectly rejected them as erroneous, dangerous, and hostile to the Constitution and nation. In their immediate context, the *Resolutions* were instrumental failures.

Analyzing rhetorical exteriors/uncovering constitutive legacies

For pragmatic reasons, our case study focuses on how the *Resolutions* circulated in the period from the end of the War of 1812 (the beginning of the "era of good feelings") to the end of the "nullification crisis" in the early 1830s. Our analysis is thus illustrative and not exhaustive. While our discussion concludes with the nullification crisis, the "principles of '98" continued circulating in antebellum America (culminating in southern secession). The "principles" were also appropriated by Northerners opposed to the war of 1812 (during the Hartford Convention) and federal government policies regarding fugitive slaves (through the efforts of state courts in Ohio and Wisconsin). They reemerged during the twentieth century in various contexts, perhaps most notably in Southern resistance to *Brown* and federal court-mandated desegregation.[67] Efforts to rearticulate the "principles" in the early twenty-first century continue. William Watkins concludes his study of the *Resolutions* by observing: "If Americans embrace the Resolves' lessons about ultimate sovereignty and divided legislative sovereignty, then a renewal of federalism and a restoration of our Constitution is possible."[68] A comprehensive circulation study would need to examine the efforts of myriad advocates from antebellum America to the present day who have sought to rearticulate the "principles" into new contexts.[69]

The 1815 Treaty of Ghent concluded the War of 1812 and allowed Americans to refocus their energies on economic development. Congressmen such as John Calhoun and Henry Clay began to encourage the federal government to adopt various national economic development policies. At President Madison's urging, the Fourteenth Congress quickly approved legislation enacting a protective tariff and creating a second Bank of the United States. But opposition to nationalist "consolidation" emerged among Virginia's "old republicans" who claimed to remain committed to the unadulterated "principles of '98." These Jeffersonian purists led the opposition to Calhoun's plan to commit the 1.5 million dollar bonus due the federal government from the new national bank to a permanent fund for building roads and canals throughout the nation (the "Bonus bill"). Rediscovering his own constitutional scruples, Madison surprised Calhoun and Clay by vetoing the "Bonus bill" the day before he left office. Echoing sentiments he expressed nearly 20 years earlier, Madison's "Veto Message" insisted that (1) Congress could not exercise powers not specifically enumerated in the Constitution, (2) no "just interpretation" of relevant constitutional provisions (the "necessary and proper" clause, the "commerce" clause) could authorize the "Bonus bill's" provisions, and (3) the "Bonus bill" threatened "the permanent success of the Constitution [which] depends on a definite partition of powers between the General and the State Governments." While it reanimated important aspects of the earlier "principles," Madison's veto could not eradicate the reemerging nationalist (or consolidationist) constitutional heresy.[70]

In his first message to Congress, new President James Monroe endorsed Madison's recommendation that Congress adopt and send to the states a constitutional amendment explicitly granting the federal government the power to institute a range of internal improvements. In response Henry St. George Tucker, a Virginian opposed to the "old republicans," helped to draft and then presented an ad hoc House committee report which argued that no amendment was needed because Congress already possessed adequate power to fund a system of internal improvements. In the subsequent debate, Speaker Henry Clay defended Tucker's report after it had been criticized by Virginia "old republican" Philip Barbour. Clay began by insisting that "he had imbibed his political principles from the same source" as Barbour: "[f]rom the celebrated production of Mr. Madison, when a member of the Virginia Legislature, of the period 1799." According to Clay, he and "old republicans" like Barbour "professed to acknowledge the same authority"; their differences were "not as to principles, but as to the application of them." He explained: "At the period which gave birth to those papers ... [Virginia] bore a conspicuous part in arresting the career of a mad administration. The attempt then was to destroy the Constitution. ... [Clay] begged the gentleman from Virginia to reflect, that that was not the only malady by which the Constitution could be afflicted; another complaint, equally dangerous to that Constitution, was an atrophy. ... I do not go along with them in the water-gruel regimen they would administer to the Constitution, in constructing it to a dead letter, and reducing it to an inanimate skeleton." But, Clay insisted, just because he sought to protect the Constitution from a different kind of danger, "let me not be charged with abandoning principle."[71]

Clay's 1818 performance, we suggest, merits attention for the way he both articulated the "principles of '98" into a new context and reaccentuated their meaning. Old republicans drew upon the "principles" to accuse Clay and other nationalists of abandoning "true" republican constitutionalism (America's unique "federal" system which privileged states' rights) by trying to erect a consolidated national government via constitutional interpretation. Public suspicion and vigilance, Barbour and his "old republican" colleagues agreed, was necessary to thwart the nationalists' consolidationist plot. On behalf of republican nationalists, Clay accused "old republicans" of abandoning "true" republican constitutionalism by trying to reintroduce the "water-gruel regimen" of the Articles of Confederation via constitutional interpretation. When republican nationalists and old republican states' rights advocates debated Joseph Hemphill's General Survey Bill in 1824, Clay would more explicitly reject a narrow reading of the "principles of '98" by articulating them to the failed Articles and, in so doing, reaccentuate the "principles," rendering them compatible with the nationalists' policy objectives.

Again responding to Barbour, Clay endorsed, as he had in 1818, "the old, 1798, republican principles (now become federal, also), by which the Constitution is to be interpreted." Employing the rigorous textualism that characterized the 1798 *Resolutions*, Clay appropriated a textual strategy Madison employed in the 1800 *Report*, suggesting that "a better rule than that which [Barbour] furnished for interpreting the Constitution might be deduced from an attentive consideration of the peculiar character of the Articles of Confederation, as contrasted with ... the present Constitution." Juxtaposing the respective texts, Clay observed:

> It ought to be borne in mind that this power over roads was not contained in the Articles of Confederation, which limited Congress to the establishment of post offices; and that the general character of the present Constitution, as contrasted with those articles, is that of an enlargement of power. But, if the construction of the opposite side be correct, we are left precisely where the Articles ... left us, notwithstanding the additional words contained in the present Constitution.[72]

While the clash between states' rights and nationalist republicans over internal improvements and constitutional construction was significant in its own right, in retrospect it served as a prelude to the massive struggle over federal tariff policies and state resistance to those policies. In 1816 Georgia Representative Thomas Telfair refined republican textualism when he challenged the tariff's constitutionality by distinguishing between tariffs designed to raise revenue and those designed explicitly to protect domestic manufactures.[73] Virginian Barbour extended Telfair's distinction in 1824, arguing that while the Constitution granted Congress "the power to impose taxes and duties ... [that power] was given to us for the purpose of raising revenue, which revenue is to be applied to the ends pointed out in the Constitution." Given the Constitution's explicit language, Barbour conceded that a federal tariff was not "a violation of the letter of the Constitution," but he nevertheless insisted that a protective tariff "violate[d] the spirit of the Constitution." "[A]pplying a power for a different purpose from that for which it was given" might, Barbour feared, cause "the whole Constitution ... to swing from its moorings."[74] As Jefferson and Madison had suggested in 1798, Barbour believed that the nation's constitutional experiment depended on vigilant opposition to unauthorized federal power.

In the decade following Barbour's speech, the tariff's constitutional status – and individual states' ability to resist purported unconstitutional federal policies – would generate one of the early republic's most significant crises. Throughout the crisis, the "principles of '98" continued to circulate as anti-tariff advocates described the growing threat of nationalist consolidation and urged state legislatures to attack the tariff's constitutionality.[75] In South Carolina, proponents of nullification sought to declare it unconstitutional and void within the state's borders. At the same time, nullification opponents sought to deny that doctrine's constitutional foundation and disarticulate such extreme modes of state resistance from Jefferson and Madison's resistance to the Alien and Sedition Acts.

Responding to the pro-tariff, protectionist movement which culminated in the July 1827 Harrisburg convention, President John Quincy Adams and Secretary of State Henry Clay supported tariff revisions during Congress's spring 1828 session. But since it was an election year, the political machinations of Clay and Adams's rivals – Martin Van Buren and those allied with Andrew Jackson – helped to produce what would become known as the "Tariff of Abominations." Remonstrances against protectionism, the American System, and the Tariff of 1828 poured in from numerous states. When South Carolina's congressional delegation and state legislature requested that he help develop a formal statement of grievances, Vice President John Calhoun agreed, and in the summer and early fall of 1828 he drafted what would become the South Carolina *Exposition and Protest*. Calhoun was concerned that extremists might urge rash action, so he sought, in the words of biographer John Niven, "to present [South Carolina's] case in a cool, considered manner that would dampen any drastic moves yet would set in motion the machinery for repeal of the tariff act." Calhoun borrowed his machinery from the Virginia and Kentucky *Resolutions*: interposition and nullification.[76]

With Calhoun as his running mate, Andrew Jackson's election in 1828 led many Americans to believe that authentic republican, states' rights constitutionalism had been restored. But Jackson's decisions did not always please republican purists, especially in South Carolina. When, in the face of known opposition from many Southern states, Jackson signed the Tariff of 1832, South Carolina responded. Drawing on his *Exposition and Protest* as well as his 1831 "Fort Hill Address," Calhoun sent a lengthy and often reprinted letter to South Carolina Governor James Hamilton in August which rehearsed South Carolina's emerging position on the constitutionality of the tariff and of a state's right to nullify federal law. On November 19, 1832, South Carolinians convened a convention and, after five days in closed session, emerged with a Nullification Ordinance that echoed Calhoun's 1828 interpretation of the "principles of '98." Responding to what they perceived was an effort to subvert the Constitution and violate states' rights, South Carolina declared the tariffs of 1828 and 1832 unconstitutional and unenforceable within its borders after February 1, 1833. On December 10, 1832, President Jackson issued a special *Proclamation* which addressed South Carolina's threat of nullification. In his *Proclamation*, Jackson unequivocally insisted that South Carolina had no right to nullify a federal law and that any state officials who attempted nullification would be considered traitors and treated as such by the federal government. Undeterred by the tepid response from her sister states, South Carolina began enforcing its Nullification Ordinance on February 1, 1833, and made preparations to defend its right to do so with military force. On March 2, 1833, Congress authorized Jackson to employ military force against South Carolina if necessary while also adopting a new tariff that it hoped would appease South Carolinian nullifiers. Responding to these moves by the federal government, the South Carolina convention reconvened on March 11, 1833, and repealed its Nullification Ordinance.[77]

Virtually all of the significant rhetorical performances during the nullification crisis – from Calhoun's various statements, to the public documents issued by South Carolina's Convention, to Jackson's *Proclamation* and the various state responses to South Carolina – were vehicles through which the "principles of '98" circulated. Each of the participants in the constitutional drama defended his or their position as sound Jeffersonian republicanism. Advocates rearticulated a story of the nation's founding, considered what role – if any – states could or should play in determining the constitutionality of federal legislation, and explicitly considered whether and how the "principles" applied to the issues which produced the crisis. Our examination of the way the "principles" circulated during the nullification crisis demonstrates precisely how complicated the question of tracing and assessing constitutive legacy can be – both for historical actors and for scholars of public address.

In his letter to Governor Hamilton, Calhoun positioned nullification upon the "plain historical facts connected with the origin and formation of the Government." Calhoun believed that the "formation and adoption of the Constitution" were events "so recent … that it would seem impossible that there should be the least uncertainty in relation to them." But when he surveyed what had been "constantly heard and seen," it became clear that "there are few subjects on which the public opinion is more confused."[78] This confusion prevented Americans from recognizing that "the Constitution is the work of the people of the States, considered as separate and independent political communities; that they are its authors – their power created it, their voice clothed it with authority; that the government formed is, in reality, their agent; and that the Union, of which the Constitution is the bond, is a union of States, and not of individuals."[79] Drawing on the "journals and proceedings of the Convention which formed the Constitution," Calhoun reanimated Jefferson's earlier origin narrative. He pointed to comments made by Edmund Randolph, James Madison, and others during the Constitutional Convention to support his account that states were the primary agents in the Constitution's development and, as such, enjoyed primacy in their relationship with the federal government. Calhoun maintained that his narrative demonstrated "in a manner never to be reversed, that the Convention which framed the Constitution, was opposed to granting the power to the General Government in any form, through any of its departments … to coerce or control a State."[80] Calhoun insisted that the convention debates "ought to settle for ever the question of the surrender or transfer of the power under consideration; and such, in fact, would be the case, were the opinion of a large portion of the community not biased, as, in fact, it is, by interest."[81] In his rendering of the Constitution's development, Calhoun rearticulated the "principles of 1798" to constitute the people of South Carolina as the dominion of South Carolina alone, the states as perpetually sovereign governments, the people of the

United States as a fiction because "no such political body either now or ever did exist," the United States Constitution as a "treaty," and the federal government as a confederation of equal, sovereign states.[82]

Calhoun's narrative shaped four public statements crafted by South Carolina's convention: its *Report, Nullification Ordinance, Address to the People of the United States,* and *Address to the People of South Carolina.* Each of these documents further circulated Calhoun's description of the nation's founding and the relationship between the states and the federal government and invited Americans to emulate South Carolina's vigilant defense of the Constitution and states' rights.[83] In his *Nullification Proclamation,* President Jackson explicitly rejected this narrative.[84] Jackson argued that Calhoun's position constituted a "new doctrine" that transformed the Constitution into no more than an "airy nothing," a "wretched, inefficient, clumsy contrivance." Jackson insisted that no matter how much Calhoun and South Carolina wanted to believe otherwise, "our Constitution does not contain the absurdity of giving power to make laws, and another power to resist them."[85] Not satisfied with simply subverting Calhoun's narrative, Jackson constructed his own. If Americans "search[ed] the debates in all [the states'] Conventions," Jackson maintained, if they "examine[d] the speeches of the most zealous opposers of Federal authority," and "look[ed] at the amendments that were proposed," they would discover that these documents "are all silent – not a syllable uttered, not a vote given, not a motion made to correct the explicit supremacy given to the laws of the Union over those of the States – or to show that implication, as is now contended, could defeat it."[86] According to Jackson, "the people of the United States formed the Constitution, acting through the State Legislatures [and] in making the compact ... we [became] one people."[87] Although Jackson's origin narrative echoed the Preamble's "We the People," he nevertheless maintained that his account remained consistent with the states' rights position of Jeffersonian constitutionalism.

"I do not claim for a State the right to abrogate an act of the General Government," Calhoun wrote to Hamilton,

> [i]t is the Constitution that annuls an unconstitutional act. Such an act is of itself void and of no effect. What I claim is the right of the State, as far as its citizens are concerned, to declare the extent of the obligation, and that such declaration is binding on them – a right, when limited to its citizens, flowing directly from the relation of the State to the General Government on the one side, and its citizens on the other.

Consistent with the "principles," Calhoun imagined a political world in which states were supreme; they controlled the actions of their common agent and reserved the right to reject the agent's reading of the founding compact. In short, each state, "has a right, in her sovereign capacity, in convention, to declare an unconstitutional act of Congress to be null and void."[88] Calhoun described the states' right to judge an act of the federal government as "the great conservative principle of our system." That principle, he explained, was "known under the various names of nullification, interposition, and State Veto."[89] According to Calhoun, every state had the right, power, and obligation to be vigilant in its self-defense.

President Jackson responded that Calhoun's argument was a "strange position": strange in that it was new, unfamiliar, and odd. Jackson positioned Calhoun's doctrine as novel while claiming the mantle of tradition for his version of Jeffersonian constitutionalism. He noted that "our social compact in express terms declares, that the laws of the United States, its Constitution, and treaties made under it, are the supreme law of the land."[90] Jackson argued that "the doctrine of a State veto, upon the laws of the Union, carries with it internal evidence of its impracticable absurdity" and that the nation's "constitutional history" provided "abundant proof that it would have been repudiated with indignation, had it been proposed to form a feature in our Government."[91] He insisted that nullification was an "absurd and dangerous doctrine," and he denied that it represented the nation's constitutional tradition.[92]

While Calhoun's *Exposition and Protest* and "Fort Hill Address" frequently referred to the Virginia and Kentucky *Resolutions* and Madison's Virginia *Report*,[93] his 1832 letter to Hamilton did not mention them by name. Whatever Calhoun's reason for omitting explicit reference to the "principles of '98," the South Carolina Convention's *Report, Ordinance*, and its *Addresses to the Citizens of the United States* and the *Citizens of South Carolina* explicitly articulated the Virginia and Kentucky *Resolutions* to South Carolina's nullification doctrine. For example, its *Report* justified nullification by calling upon "the clear and emphatic language of Mr. Jefferson" and quoted at length from the Kentucky *Resolutions* to argue that Jefferson understood "the true nature of the Federal Compact."[94] The *Report* claimed the authority and borrowed the narrative structure of both the Virginia and Kentucky *Resolutions* to imagine a plot to subvert states' rights and argue that "when the rights reserved to the several States are deliberately invaded, it is their right and their duty" to defend them.[95] Furthermore, South Carolina maintained that "in asserting the principles, and adopting the course, which they are about to recommend, South Carolina will be carrying out the doctrines which were asserted by Virginia and Kentucky in 1798, and which have been sanctified by the high authority of Thomas Jefferson" – from "the pen of the great apostle of liberty."[96] Likewise, South Carolina's *Address to the People of South Carolina* liberally invoked Jefferson and the Virginia and Kentucky *Resolutions* to support its arguments.[97] South Carolinians insisted that nullification was consistent with the "principles of '98."

Among the formal state responses to the *Report* and *Ordinance*, Virginia most explicitly rejected South Carolina's effort to rearticulate the "principles of '98." In its *Resolves* the Virginia legislature affirmed that:

> they continue to regard the doctrines of State Sovereignty and States Rights, as set forth in the Resolutions of 1798, and sustained by the Report thereon of 1799, as a true interpretation of the Constitution of the United States, and of the powers therein given to the General Government; but that they do not consider them as sanctioning the proceedings of South Carolina, indicated in her said Ordinance.[98]

Virginia urged South Carolina to reconvene its Convention and reconsider its *Ordinance* and dispatched the Honorable Benjamin Watkins Leigh to South Carolina to help its citizens discover the real meaning of the "principles of '98."[99]

While South Carolina's Convention rescinded its nullification *Ordinance*, it nevertheless crafted a *Report* responding to Virginia's *Resolves*. While denying that it desired to promote the "invidious spirit of controversy," South Carolina's Convention continued to insist that it had read Virginia's 1798 *Resolution* as announcing "nothing more or less" than "the remedy which South Carolina has resorted to, through her State interposition." Yet Virginia's "recent Resolutions" declared "that she does not regard the *Resolutions* of 1798 and '99, as sanctioning the proceedings of South Carolina, as indicated in the Ordinance of her Convention." "[W]ith all proper deference" to Virginia, in good Protestant fashion, the Convention announced that South Carolina would adhere "to her own construction" of the "principles of '98." The Convention's *Report* insisted that "it is within the providence of God that great truths should be independent of the human agents that promulgate them. Once announced, they become the subjects and property of reason, to all men and in all time to come."[100]

The Convention's acknowledgment of "human agents that promulgate" great truths was most likely a reference to James Madison. Both sides in the nullification crisis actively solicited his support. Shortly after his debate with Daniel Webster in early 1830, South Carolina Senator Robert Hayne sent the former president a copy of his speeches. To Hayne's surprise, Madison responded by attempting to separate the circumstances which provoked the 1798 protests from those which generated South Carolina's theory of nullification. He also distinguished between the principles involved in each protest. During the summer of 1830, Madison revised his response to Hayne, which he sent to Edward Everett who, with Madison's blessing, had it published in the *North American Review*. In the letter Madison acknowledged that "the nullifying claim for states" might rest upon the "proceedings of the Legislature of Virginia, in '98 and '99, against the alien and sedition-acts." But such a claim, he continued, was a result of "erroneous constructions, not anticipated, [and] not ... sufficiently guarded against, in the language used." "[D]istinguished individuals," Madison insisted, "have misconceived the intention of those proceedings."

While Madison sought to disarticulate nullification from the "principles of '98" by appealing to intentionalist hermeneutics, other advocates reanimated Madison and Jefferson's Protestant textualism to reaffirm the link. During an 1833 debate in the Virginia legislature on whether Madison's 1830 letter to Everett should be circulated in conjunction with a reprinting of Virginia's 1800 *Report*, William Brodnax maintained: "Nothing can be more improper, instead of looking at the document itself ... to be enquiring, thirty years after, on one of the body who adopted it." As we noted above, the Virginia legislature refused to sanction South Carolina's effort to articulate nullification to the "principles of '98." Yet the delegates reaffirmed their commitment to republican textualism by recirculating the 1800 *Report* without Madison's explanatory letter.[101]

Conclusion

In this chapter's first two sections, we described how rhetoricians initially conceptualized constitutive analysis as a way of broadening the idea of rhetorical effect. Drawing on a variety of examples, we noted that critics have been concerned primarily with the way discourse constitutes individual and group identities. We suggested that critics consider expanding constitutive inquiry in two ways. First, in addition to exploring discourse's capacity to constitute identity, we urged critics to consider how texts invite listeners and readers to modify the meaning of a culture's key terms, to reconceptualize a culture's experience of public time (including the past), to reaffirm or reconfigure accepted demarcations of social space, and to affirm as well as challenge established sources of cultural authority, bonds of affiliation, and institutional relationships. Second, in addition to examining constitutive invitations that appear in the text (that inhabit textual interiors), we urged critics to examine textual exteriors by tracing the text's reception, circulation, and articulation. Doing so enables critics to sketch the way constitutive invitations become realized, and constitutive legacies established.

We sought to illustrate many of our analytic recommendations through our case study of the Virginia and Kentucky *Resolutions* and the "principles of '98." Because public advocates can always engage in the practices of accentuation and articulation, the "principles of '98" and the specific constitutive invitations we identified – American citizens constituted as suspicious of and vigilant with regard to national power, the dangers of consolidationism, and the economic and political factions which promoted this brand of constitutional heresy; the states depicted as sites for organizing political resistance to national policy, for critiquing federal law, and for adjudicating constitutional controversies; constitutional argument represented as a form of Protestant textualism; and the founding remembered as a compact between independent and sovereign states – continued to circulate and shape the nation's political imagination well into the twentieth century and have remained resources for (re)constituting our political imagination.[102]

While the Virginia and Kentucky *Resolutions'* ultimate constitutive legacy has not (and given our argument cannot be) produced, our account of the *Resolutions'* circulation in the nineteenth century supports some provisional observations. When advocates accentuated the "principles" as a form of extreme state sovereignty and articulated them to demands for robust resistance to federal power, they failed to energize a national constituency or constitute the nation's understanding of constitutional government. But despite the apparent rejection of this mode of accentuation and articulation, a vibrant tradition of states' rights and state sovereignty persisted. And despite the best efforts of eloquent advocates such as John Marshall and Daniel Webster, Americans remained suspicious of national power and worried about consolidationist tendencies.[103] If Americans rejected the constitutive invitations offered by *über* nationalists and the advocates of nullification, the constitutive invitations that Americans did embrace are much less clear. Professing their adherence to the "principles of '98," some political leaders tried to imagine a middle course between Robert Hayne and Daniel Webster.[104] In so doing, Edward Livingston, James Madison, and others sought to imagine a federal constitutional system that represented a *tertium quid* between extreme nationalism and nullification. The constitutive legacy of the Virginia and Kentucky *Resolutions* and the "principles of '98" consists, at least in part, in our continued efforts to stabilize and inhabit this constitutional tradition.

Notes

1   Herbert A. Wichelns, "The Literary Criticism of Oratory," in *Studies in Rhetoric and Public Speaking in Honor of James Albert Winans*, ed. A. M. Drummond (1925; rpt. New York: Russell and Russell, 1962), 209. For a more extensive analysis of Wichelns's essay and the instrumentalist tradition it helped inaugurate, see James Jasinski, "Instrumentalism, Contextualism, and Interpretation in Rhetorical Criticism," in *Rhetorical Hermeneutics*, ed. William Keith and Alan G. Gross (Albany: State University of New York Press, 1997).

2   For example, see Wayland Maxfield Parrish, "The Study of Speeches," in *American Speeches*, ed. Wayland Maxfield Parrish and Marie Hochmuth (New York: Greenwood Press, 1954); and Thomas R. Nilsen, "Criticism and Social Consequences," *Quarterly Journal of Speech* 42 (1956): 173–178.

3   Lloyd Bitzer, "The Rhetorical Situation," *Philosophy & Rhetoric* 1 (1968): 1–14.

4   In his essay "Cicero's *Pro Murena* and the Strong Case for Rhetoric," Michael Leff observed that many of the disparate concepts and research programs in contemporary rhetorical studies are linked in an at least implicit conceptualization of public discourse as a constitutive or generative medium. See Leff, "Cicero's *Pro Murena*," *Rhetoric & Public Affairs* 1 (1998): 61–88. For a review of these and other relevant concepts and associated literatures, see James Jasinski, *Sourcebook on Rhetoric: Key Concepts in Contemporary Rhetorical Studies* (Thousand Oaks, CA: Sage, 2001).

5   For example see Stephen E. Lucas, "The Schism in Rhetorical Scholarship," *Quarterly Journal of Speech* 67 (1981): 1–20; and Richard A. Cherwitz and John Theobald-Osborne, "Contemporary Developments in Rhetorical Criticism: A Consideration of the Effects of Rhetoric," in *Speech Communication: Essays to Commemorate the Seventy-Fifth Anniversary of the Speech Communication Association*, ed. G. M. Phillips and J. T. Wood (Carbondale: Southern Illinois University Press, 1990).

6   John Lyne, "Rhetorics of Inquiry," *Quarterly Journal of Speech* 71 (1985): 68.

7   While contrasting these different "models of rhetorical effectivity" has, we believe, become common (e.g., see Ronald Greene, "Another Materialist Rhetoric," *Critical Studies in Mass Communication* 15 [1998]: 21–41), we do not want to suggest the existence of a rigid binary opposition between instrumental and constitutive effects. We maintain that discourse functions instrumentally when designed to address situational exigencies. In these cases, potential constitutive effects are epiphenomenal to the discursive resolution of exigencies. For example, in an effort to secure votes and win elections, conservative politicians might invite audiences to consider themselves "real Americans." Typically, rhetoricians hold identity construction to be a form of constitutive rhetoric,

but in this case we would argue that conservative efforts to constitute audiences as "real Americans" functions instrumentally to resolve the primary exigence of their electoral situation. But as a number of critics have illustrated, the relationship between the two forms of effect can be fluid. For example, in his study of Theodore Roosevelt, Leroy Dorsey demonstrates that in the late nineteenth and early twentieth centuries the issue of American national identity was a significant public "crisis" or exigence. Roosevelt's discursive efforts, as Dorsey suggests, responded instrumentally to a perceived exigence by deploying a constitutive rhetoric encouraging adherence to a particular vision of "Americanism" (Leroy G. Dorsey, *We Are All Americans, Pure and Simple: Theodore Roosevelt and the Myth of Americanism* [Tuscaloosa: University of Alabama Press, 2007]). On the fluid relationship between instrumental and constitutive effects, see also Michael Leff and Ebony Utley, "Instrumental and Constitutive Rhetoric in Martin Luther King Jr.'s 'Letter from Birmingham Jail,'" *Rhetoric & Public Affairs* 7 (2004): 37–51.

8   Maurice Charland, "Constitutive Rhetoric: The Case of the *Peuple Québécois*," *Quarterly Journal of Speech* 73 (1987): 133–150.

9   James Boyd White, *When Words Lose Their Meaning: Constitutions and Reconstitutions of Language, Character, and Community* (Chicago: University of Chicago Press, 1984), 286–291.

10   "Social constructionism can be thought of as a theoretical orientation which to a greater or lesser degree underpins all of these newer approaches" (Vivien Burr, *An Introduction to Social Constructionism* [London: Routledge, 1995], 1).

11   Louis A. Montrose, "Professing the Renaissance: The Poetics and Politics of Culture," in *The New Historicism*, ed. H. Aram Veeser (New York: Routledge, 1989), 16. See James Jasinski, "A Constitutive Framework for Rhetorical Historiography: Toward an Understanding of the Discursive (Re)constitution of 'Constitution' in *The Federalist Papers*," in *Doing Rhetorical History: Concepts and Cases*, ed. Kathleen J. Turner (Tuscaloosa: University of Alabama Press, 1998), 74.

12   Michael Leff, "Things Made By Words: Reflections on Textual Criticism," *Quarterly Journal of Speech* 78 (1992): 223–231.

13   See Joshua Gunn, "Refiguring Fantasy: Imagination and Its Decline in US Rhetorical Studies," *Quarterly Journal of Speech* 89 (2003): 41–59.

14   Jasinski, "Constitutive Framework," 74.

15   Vanessa B. Beasley, *You, the People: American National Identity in Presidential Rhetoric* (College Station: Texas A&M University Press, 2004); Nathaniel I. Cordova, "The Constitutive Force of the *Catecismo del Pueblo* in Puerto Rico's Popular Democratic Party Campaign of 1938–1940," *Quarterly Journal of Speech* 90 (2004): 212–233; and Dexter B. Gordon, *Black Identity: Rhetoric, Ideology, and Nineteenth-Century Black Nationalism* (Carbondale: Southern Illinois University Press, 2003).

16   Our focus on textual interiors, the arguments, narratives, and/or tropes which inhabit or reside in texts, should be distinguished from efforts to elaborate a "rhetoric of the interior" in which interior is roughly synonymous with psychological. See Thomas S. Frentz, "Reconstructing a Rhetoric of the Interior," *Communication Monographs* 60 (1993): 83–89.

17   Charland, "Constitutive Rhetoric," 144, 140–142.

18   But as we have just argued, we are skeptical that Charland has effectively transcended interior analysis of rhetorical form.

19 Charland, "Constitutive Rhetoric," 137–139.

20 Beasley, *You, the People*, 9, 44, 47.

21 Cordova, "Constitutive Force," 221, 225, 215.

22 Gordon, *Black Identity*, 33, 98.

23 See also Jacqueline Bacon, "'Acting as Freemen': Rhetoric, Race, and Reform in the Debate over Colonization in *Freedom's Journal*, 1827–1828," *Quarterly Journal of Speech* 93 (2007): 58–83; Mary E. Stuckey, *Defining Americans: The Presidency and National Identity* (Lawrence: University Press of Kansas, 2004); and Kenneth S. Zagacki, "Constitutive Rhetoric Reconsidered: Constitutive Paradoxes in G. W. Bush's Iraq War Speeches," *Western Journal of Communication* 71 (2007): 272–293.

24 White, *When Words*, 5. White's use of the coordinate conjunction "or" in this passage is, we believe, misleading because it seems to suggest that one *or* the other type of action will take place. But as White's readings of various texts demonstrate, both forms of action frequently emanate from a single text.

25 White, *When Words*, 18, 15.

26 Wayne Booth, in *The Company We Keep: An Ethics of Fiction* (Berkeley: University of California Press, 1988), relies on a similar cluster of verbs to unpack the "text as friend" metaphor.

27 White, *When Words*, 6–8.

28 Jasinski, "Constitutive Framework," 78. Jasinski argued that Condit and Lucaites's ideographic study of the reconstitution of "equality" represented one way rhetorical scholars might analyze linguistic reconstitution. See Celeste Michelle Condit and John Louis Lucaites, *Crafting Equality: America's Anglo-African Word* (Chicago: University of Chicago Press, 1993). Drawing on White's work, Trevor Parry-Giles makes a similar point, arguing that the "public debates about Supreme Court nominees … are moments of constitutive formation for American conceptions of law, justice, and democracy." See Trevor Parry-Giles, *The Character of Justice: Rhetoric, Law, and Politics in the Supreme Court Confirmation Process* (East Lansing: Michigan State University Press, 2006), 3.

29 The discursive (re)constitution of memory is an aspect of a community's temporal experience that Jasinski neglected in his "Constitutive Framework" essay. On this topic, see the discussion and sources cited in Jasinski, *Sourcebook*, 193, 355–363. See also M. Lane Bruner, *Strategies of Remembrance: The Rhetorical Dimensions of National Identity Construction* (Columbia: University of South Carolina Press, 2002). In this series of case studies Bruner links memory construction and identity formation. On the relationship between rhetoric and memory, see Kendall R. Phillips, ed., *Framing Public Memory* (Tuscaloosa: University of Alabama Press, 2004).

30 Jasinski, "Constitutive Framework," 76–77. For a recent case study of such a reconstitution, see Mary E. Stuckey, *Slipping the Surly Bonds: Reagan's Challenger Address* (College Station: Texas A&M University Press, 2006). Both Bruner (in *Strategies of Remembrance*) and Stuckey demonstrate the way eulogies function to reconstitute communities.

31 We are not suggesting that rhetorical scholars have not engaged a range of critical objects (e.g., congressional debates, public controversies, social movements) longitudinally. Our point is that charting the temporal evolution of a controversy or debate need not involve, and typically has not involved, careful attention to the reception and circulation of specific texts, arguments, or other rhetorical strategies.

32 Leah Ceccarelli, "Polysemy: Multiple Meanings in Rhetorical Criticism," *Quarterly Journal of Speech* 84 (1998): 395–415; and Davis W. Houck and Mihaela Nocasian,

"FDR's First Inaugural Address: Text, Context, and Reception," *Rhetoric & Public Affairs* 5 (2002): 649–678.

33　Ceccarelli "Polysemy," 407.

34　Houck and Nocasian, "FDR's First Inaugural Address," 655.

35　Cara A. Finnegan and Jiyeon Kang, "'Sighting' the Public: Iconoclasm and Public Sphere Theory," *Quarterly Journal of Speech* 90 (2004): 393, 396. See also Cara A. Finnegan, *Picturing Poverty: Print Culture and FSA Photographs* (Washington, DC: Smithsonian Institution Press, 2003).

36　We think it worth noting that the "chaining process" described by fantasy-theme critics anticipates the emergence of a collaborative and constitutive understanding of circulation. See Jasinski, *Sourcebook*, esp. 252.

37　For example, see Ronald H. Carpenter, "America's Tragic Metaphor: Our Twentieth-Century Combatants as Frontiersmen," *Quarterly Journal of Speech* 76 (1990): 1–22; Robert L. Ivie, "The Ideology of Freedom's 'Fragility' in American Foreign Policy Argument," *Journal of the American Forensics Association* 24 (1987): 27–36; and Kathryn M. Olson, "The Role of Dissociation in Redeeming Knowledge Claims: Nineteenth-Century Shakers' Epistemological Resistance to Decline," *Philosophy & Rhetoric* 28 (1995): 45–68.

38　We draw here on Jasinski, *Sourcebook*, esp. 65–67.

39　Our use of the term "imagine" here and elsewhere in this section extends L. H. LaRue's interest in examining "what sort of world does [a text] imagine?" LaRue's perspective is, as he acknowledges, informed by James Boyd White's version of "constitutive rhetoric." See LaRue, *Constitutional Law as Fiction: Narrative in the Rhetoric of Authority* (University Park: Pennsylvania State University Press, 1995), 21.

40　Mark E. Brandon, *Free in the World: American Slavery and Constitutional Failure* (Princeton, NJ: Princeton University Press, 1998), 37 (emphasis in original).

41　Larry D. Kramer, *The People Themselves: Popular Constitutionalism and Judicial Review* (New York: Oxford University Press, 2004), 137.

42　While our analysis focuses on the tension between nationalists and localists, we do not want to suggest that these were the only constitutive rhetorics circulating in antebellum America. In addition to the black nationalist vision that Dexter Gordon has analyzed, various religious sects, moral reform organizations, labor groups, and women's organizations developed constitutive rhetorics as they negotiated various situational exigencies. On the constitutive rhetoric of antebellum women, see Alisse Portnoy, *Their Right to Speak: Women's Activism in the Indian and Slave Debate*s (Cambridge, MA: Harvard University Press, 2005).

43　William J. Watkins, Jr., *Reclaiming the American Revolution: The Kentucky and Virginia Resolutions and Their Legacy* (New York: Palgrave Macmillan, 2004), 27.

44　Stephen John Hartnett and Jennifer Rose Mercieca, "'Has Your Courage Rusted?': National Security and the Contested Norms of Republicanism in Post-Revolutionary America, 1798–1801," *Rhetoric & Public Affairs* 9 (2006): 79–112.

45　Watkins, *Reclaiming*, 56; and Kramer, *People Themselves*, 136. *The Federalist Papers* #26 (Hamilton), #51 (Madison), rpt. in *The Federalist Papers* (New York: New American Library, 1961), esp. 172, 323–325.

46　Watkins, *Reclaiming*, 55.

47　Virginia *Resolutions*, December 24, 1798, rpt. in *Documents of American History*, ed. Henry Steele Commager, 7th ed. (New York: Appleton-Century-Crofts, 1963), 182.

48   Kentucky *Resolutions*, February 22, 1799, in *Documents*, 183; and Kentucky *Resolutions*, November 16, 1798, in *Documents*, 181.

49   Kentucky *Resolutions*, November 16, 1798, in *Documents*, 178.

50   Kentucky *Resolutions*, February 22, 1799, in *Documents*, 184.

51   Virginia *Resolutions*, December 24, 1798, in *Documents*, 182.

52   See especially H. Jefferson Powell, "The Principles of '98: An Essay in Historical Retrieval," *Virginia Law Review* 80 (1994): esp. 715–722. Powell notes that "[l]ate eighteenth-century usage did not distinguish 'compact' and contract'" (716n.107). Our discussion here and the next few paragraphs draws on and extends Powell's analysis of the "principles of '98."

53   Powell, "The Principles of '98," 716–717.

54   Powell, "The Principles of '98," 707.

55   Powell, "The Principles of '98," 722.

56   Powell, "The Principles of '98," 707.

57   Powell, "The Principles of '98," 714.

58   Powell, "The Principles of '98," 713.

59   Kentucky *Resolutions*, November 16, 1798, in *Documents*, 179–180.

60   Powell, "The Principles of '98," 739. See Sanford Levinson, *Constitutional Faith* (Princeton, NJ: Princeton University Press, 1988), esp. 27–53.

61   In its 1799 *Resolutions*, the Kentucky legislature voiced its concern that "a supposed acquiescence on the part of this commonwealth in the unconstitutionality of those laws ... [might] be thereby used as precedents for similar future violations of the federal compact." In *Documents*, 184.

62   Levinson, *Constitutional Faith*, 29.

63   Kentucky *Resolutions*, February 22, 1799, in *Documents*, 184.

64   As Powell and other scholars have observed, the resolutions of '98 and '99 and Virginia's 1800 *Report* "did *not* underwrite a clear theory of state autonomy or supremacy" because "Jefferson and Madison ... presented significantly different accounts of what sort of contract the Constitution was" ("The Principles of '98," 736).

65   Kentucky *Resolutions*, November 16, 1798. in *Documents*, 181.

66   Powell, "The Principles of '98," 727.

67   For one example, see James Jackson Kilpatrick, *The Sovereign States: Notes of a Citizen of Virginia* (Chicago: Henry Regnery, 1957).

68   Watkins, *Reclaiming*, 163.

69   On April 1, 2009, by a 43:1 vote, the Georgia State Senate adopted resolution 632 reaffirming "states' rights based on Jeffersonian principles" (S.R. 632). In early May a blogger at *Washington Monthly* noted that most of the resolution plagiarized Jefferson's draft for the 1798 Kentucky *Resolutions* (see www.washingtonmonthly.com/archives/individual/2009_05/018093.php). The circulation and attempted rearticulation of the "principles of '98" continues. We thank John Murphy for drawing this episode to our attention.

70   Madison, "Veto Message," March 3, 1817, in *A Compilation of the Messages and Papers of the Presidents, 1789–1897*, ed. James Richardson (Washington, DC: N.P., 1897), 1: 584–585. Numerous historians have recounted the nation's postwar constitutional politics. We have relied on John Lauritz Larson, *Internal Improvements: National Public Works and the Promise of Popular Government in the Early United States* (Chapel Hill: University of North Carolina Press, 2001), esp. 63–69, 109–148; Charles Sellers,

The Market Revolution: Jacksonian America, 1815–1846 (New York: Oxford University Press, 1991), esp. 70–102.

71 Henry Clay, Speech in House of Representatives, March 7, 1818, in *Annals of Congress*, 15th Congress, 1st Session, 1165.

72 Henry Clay, Speech in House of Representatives, January 14, 1824, in *Annals of Congress*, 18th Congress, 1st Session, 1026, 1030, 1034. Both Madison and Clay relied on the Blackstonian distinction between declaratory and remedial statutes (and the strategies for interpreting these different types of statutes). As James Stormer explains, "regarding the remedial character of the Constitution … suggests that we read the document in comparison to the Articles of Confederation." See Stormer, *Common Law and Liberal Theory: Coke, Hobbes, and the Origins of American Constitutionalism* (Lawrence: University Press of Kansas, 1992), 216.

73 Thomas Telfair, Speech in House of Representatives, April 3, 1816, in *Annals of Congress*, 14th Congress, 1st Session, 1316–1317. The type of distinction which Telfair proposed was common during the colonists' struggle with Great Britain over the Stamp Act and other British efforts to raise revenues via colonial taxation.

74 Philip Barbour, Speech in House of Representatives, March 26, 1824, in *Annals of Congress*, 18th Congress, 1st Session, 1918–1919. As Powell suggests, dissociative appeals to the Constitution's "spirit," and eventually appeals to the framers' intentions, helped reshape nineteenth-century constitutional argument. See H. Jefferson Powell, "The Original Understanding of Original Intent," *Harvard Law Review* 98 (1985): 885–948.

75 For example, on March 4, 1826, the Virginia General Assembly adopted resolutions that, after quoting extensively from Madison's earlier Report, concluded that "the imposition of taxes and duties … for the purpose of protecting and encouraging domestic manufactures, is an unconstitutional exercise of power." The following year the Assembly again went on record arguing that because "the protection of manufactures [was] not … amongst the grants of power to [the federal] Government, specified in the Constitution … [it was] unconstitutional, unwise, unjust, unequal, and oppressive." The 1826 and 1827 Resolutions are reprinted in *State Documents on Federal Relations: The States and the United States*, ed. Herman V. Ames (Philadelphia: University of Pennsylvania, 1906), 140–144. Ames's volume reprints a number of state legislative protests against the 1824 tariff.

76 John Niven, *John C. Calhoun and the Price of Union* (Baton Rouge: Louisiana State University Press, 1988), 161. Similarly, Keith Whittington maintains that Calhoun "was actually concerned to defend his version of federalism against both more nationalist sentiment from the North and West and extreme disunionist sentiment from the South." See Whittington, *Constitutional Construction: Divided Powers and Constitutional Meaning* (Cambridge, MA: Harvard University Press, 1999), 79.

77 In what historians typically regard as a face-saving gesture, the South Carolina convention refused to abandon its understanding of the "principles of '98" and therefore nullified Congress's "Force Bill."

78 John C. Calhoun to James Hamilton, August 28, 1832, in *The Works of John C. Calhoun*, vol. 6, ed. Richard K. Crallé (New York: D. Appleton and Company, 1854), 144–193, 145.

79 John C. Calhoun to James Hamilton, August 28, 1832, in *Works*, 148.

80 John C. Calhoun to James Hamilton, August 28, 1832, in *Works*, 155.

81 John C. Calhoun to James Hamilton, August 28, 1832, in *Works*, 156.

82 John C. Calhoun to James Hamilton, August 28, 1832, in *Works*, 147.

83 For example, see South Carolina's *Report*, 8, 11–12; *Address to the People of South Carolina*, 38–41, 47–48, 51–52; *Address to the People of the United States*, 60, all collected by the General Court of Massachusetts, *State Papers on Nullification: Including the Public Acts of the Convention of the People of South Carolina, Assembled at Columbia, November 19, 1832 and March 11, 1833; the Proclamation of the President of the United States, and the Proceedings of the Several State Legislatures Which Have Acted on the Subject* (Boston: Dutton and Wentworth, 1834). Although many of these documents are available elsewhere, we have used the versions in this collection because it provides an excellent and convenient repository for the various state and federal documents.

84 Andrew Jackson, *Nullification Proclamation*, December 10, 1832, in *State Papers* on NULLIFICATION: *Including the Public Acts of the* CONVENTION OF THE PEOPLE *of South Carolina, Assembled at Columbia, November 19, 1832 and March 11, 1833; the Proclamation of the President of the United States, and the Proceedings of the Several State Legislatures Which Have Acted on the Subject* (Boston: Dutton and Wentworth, 1834), 75–97.

85 Andrew Jackson, *Nullification Proclamation*, December 10, 1832, in *State Papers*, 81.

86 Andrew Jackson, *Nullification Proclamation*, December 10, 1832, in *State Papers*, 82.

87 Andrew Jackson, *Nullification Proclamation*, December 10, 1832, in *State Papers*, 85–86.

88 John C. Calhoun to James Hamilton, August 28, 1832, in *Works*, 144–193, 149–150.

89 John C. Calhoun, in *Works*, 159–160.

90 Andrew Jackson, *Nullification Proclamation*, December 10, 1832, in *State Papers*, 77–78.

91 Andrew Jackson, *Nullification Proclamation*, December 10, 1832, in *State Papers*, 78–79.

92 Andrew Jackson, *Nullification Proclamation*, December 10, 1832, in *State Papers*, 81.

93 As Keith Whittington notes, "Repeatedly invoking the memory of Jefferson and the 'spirit of '98,' Calhoun portrayed nullification as the logical extension of the state interposition that lay at the base of Republican politics" (*Constitutional Construction*, 80).

94 South Carolina Convention's *Report, Ordinance, Address to the Citizens of the United States, Address to the Citizens of South Carolina*, in *State Papers*, 9.

95 South Carolina Convention's *Report*, in *State Papers*, 24.

96 South Carolina Convention's *Report*, in *State Papers*, 25.

97 South Carolina Convention's *Address to the People of South Carolina*, November 24, 1832, in *State Papers*, 1–71.

98 Virginia *Resolves*, January 26, 1833, in *State Papers*, 195–197.

99 See the correspondence between Virginia and South Carolina, in *State Papers*, 322–358.

100 South Carolina Convention's *Report on the Mediation of Virginia*, March 16, 1833, in *State Papers*, 355–358.

101 James Madison to Edward Everett, August 1830, *The Virginia Report of 1799–1800, Touching the Alien and Sedition Laws; Together with the Virginia Resolutions of December 21, 1798, the Debate and Proceedings Thereon in the House of Delegates of Virginia, and Several Other Documents Illustrative of the Report and Resolutions* (Richmond: J. W. Randolph, 1850), 249–256. Among the many excellent discussions of Madison's rhetorical efforts during the nullification crisis, see Drew McCoy, *The Last of the Fathers: James Madison and the Republican Legacy* (Cambridge: Cambridge University Press, 1989), esp. 119–170. McCoy quotes Brodnax's comments on 154.

102 Efforts to rearticulate the "principles" in early twenty-first-century American politics are growing. "Tenthers," proponents of "state sovereignty resolutions" and members of what many identify as the "Tenth Amendment Movement," frequently refer to Jeffersonian constitutionalism and the Virginia and Kentucky *Resolutions*. For example, visit: www.thetenthamendmentcenter.com.

103 We would need an essay at least as long as this one to sketch the nationalists' constitutive vision and trace its circulation. But as we have suggested, constitutive rhetorics cannot be examined in isolation.

104 Our discussion here draws from and seeks to extend observations by Richard Ellis and Drew McCoy. See Ellis, *The Union at Risk: Jacksonian Democracy, States' Rights and the Nullification Controversy* (New York: Oxford University Press, 1987); and McCoy, *The Last of the Fathers*.

Part V

The Politics of Rhetoric and Public Address

14

Feminism and Public Address Research
Television News and the Constitution of Women's Liberation

Bonnie J. Dow

"Feminism" is a polysemous term in the context of public address research. For example, one may speak of feminism as a *topic* for the rhetors that public address scholars study; in fact, the study of feminist orators is the earliest and most obvious way that feminism and public address research are linked. One may also speak of feminism as a *theory*, *methodology*, or *critical perspective* that informs the work of public address scholars. This sense of feminism developed later in US public address scholarship, and its presence sometimes is implicit. Finally, and most foundationally, one may use "feminism" to refer to a series of social and political *movements* that have spanned centuries and that have had, at different moments, a variety of goals but a consistent commitment to "gender justice." As Celeste Condit and I have defined it, "'gender justice' may include but can also go beyond the seeking of equality between men and women, to include understanding of the concept of gender itself as politically constructed."[1] This definition acknowledges that "feminist work always understands gender as a political concept – that is, as a concept that functions within, as well as functions to create, maintain, and challenge, power relations."[2]

Feminist public address scholarship has long been influenced by the interplay of these multiple meanings of feminism: It has involved the study of discourse produced by feminist movements, has employed feminist theories and methods, and has pursued feminist goals. In this chapter I discuss several overlapping threads in feminist public address scholarship that have emerged from these concerns, including the recovery of women's and feminist public address, feminist critique of contemporary (increasingly mass-mediated) political discourse, and public address scholars' engagement with feminist and critical theories. Developments on these fronts have at times created productive tensions, resulting in recent scholarship that complicates traditional notions of text and context as well as subjectivity and agency. I conclude that feminist research in public address is thriving in a variety of directions, and I point toward two areas deserving further development: the feminist study of masculinity in traditional public address texts and the need for feminist study of visual rhetorics. Bringing together three foci that have been important to the growth of feminist work in public address – the study of feminist movements, analysis of mass-mediated discourse, and attention to visual rhetorical strategies – I conclude with a case study involving news coverage of the second wave of US feminism. My analysis illustrates the ways that the study of late twentieth-century feminism (and beyond) encourages public address scholars to expand their focus – by including not just oratory but also mass media and not just words but also images – in order to fully understand how feminism's meaning has been constituted for US audiences. Ultimately, scholars of feminist public address are united by the goal of understanding the many ways that gender functions as a mode of meaning, identity, and power in the public sphere.

The Recovery Project

I suggest a starting point for the history of feminism and public address research that begins over 80 years ago, with the 1937 publication of Doris Yoakam's essay, "Pioneer Women Orators of America," in the *Quarterly Journal of Speech*.[3] Six years later, Yoakam's chapter, "Women's Introduction to the American Platform," would be included in the first volume of William Norwood Brigance's *A History and Criticism of American Public Address*. Yoakam also penned the chapter on Susan B. Anthony – the only woman to get a chapter of her own – in the third volume of that series.[4] In 1954, the first book-length treatment of women's rhetoric appeared with the publication of Lillian O'Connor's *Pioneer Women Orators: Rhetoric in the Ante-Bellum Reform Movement*.[5]

These early publications may be seen as the initial phase of what feminist scholars have termed the "recovery project" in feminist rhetoric and public address.[6] We can understand these recovery efforts as feminist because, as I have argued elsewhere, by focusing on women's discourse these early scholars "were clearly guided by a motivation to correct a gendered bias toward certain objects of study, primarily the political discourses of white, male, national leaders."[7] Most of the orators studied in this scholarship took to the platform in order to argue for women's rights, particularly the right to vote, during the "first wave" of US feminism (generally dated from 1848 to 1920).

The recovery project is not only the first phase of feminism's encounter with the public address tradition, it also is the longest lived. The spate of attention to women's discourse in the mid-twentieth century was followed by a long gap, but the development of the second wave of feminism in the late 1960s and early 1970s created an appetite for discovering and analyzing historical as well as contemporaneous feminist discourse. By the 1980s, the recovery project had entered a new and active phase: Scholars were arguing that public address anthologies were incomplete without the voices of women, anthologies of women's oratory were being published, and a wave of analyses of first-wave feminist discourse began to appear in scholarly publications.[8]

In 1989, Karlyn Kohrs Campbell published *Man Cannot Speak for Her: A Critical Study of Early Feminist Rhetoric*, which was accompanied by *Man Cannot Speak for Her: Key Texts of the Early Feminists*. In these two volumes, Campbell set the standard for the recovery project in feminist public address. Not only did she provide well-researched and critically insightful analyses of the rhetorical power and historical significance of examples of feminist public address between 1832 and 1920, she also dramatically increased the accessibility of rhetorical texts that other scholars might use as the basis for further work. In the early 1990s, Campbell followed up with two edited collections of essays treating women rhetors between 1800 and 1993.[9] Since then, feminist scholars have continued to produce a variety of publications linked to the recovery project.[10]

If characterized as a specific brand of feminism, the political motives behind the recovery project would have most in common with liberal feminism, in the sense that this type of scholarship is generally reformist in tone and purpose and seeks equality between men and women within existing structures. Thus, it shares the assumptions of traditional public address studies that rhetorical excellence should be recognized but expands that tradition to include women rhetors. Until fairly recently, much of this work has taken an agent-centered and instrumental approach, focusing primarily on analysis of the achievements of individual rhetors in response to particular rhetorical contexts, another characteristic it shares with traditional public address scholarship.[11]

Despite such similarities to traditional public address scholarship, feminist scholars working within the recovery project also have argued that understanding women as public address rhetors and audiences requires rethinking traditional assumptions about what constitutes rhetorical excellence. For example, some have argued that the immediate effects criterion is generally unsuitable for judging women's rhetoric because of the formidable obstacles that women rhetors faced. Moreover, they also have advocated the rethinking of traditional binaries between the public (male) and private (female) spheres and the ways that this traditional division shapes our understanding of women's rhetorical activities.[12] Scholars working within the recovery project generally agree that fully understanding women's public address requires recognition that women rhetors faced tremendous challenges, not least among them the assumption that it was improper for them to speak in public at all.[13]

Campbell has argued that some early woman rhetors adopted a mode of speaking that she termed "feminine style" as a way of managing their difficult rhetorical situations. She argues that these orators adapted to their disempowered female audiences by using inductive structure and a personal tone as well as by relying on personal experience, examples, and other techniques that functioned to encourage audience identification and participation. Although Campbell does not claim that such a style is only used by women, she does root its origins in the craft traditions, dependent on experiential knowledge, that were developed by women in the domestic sphere. She concludes that, because its goal is empowerment and the development of a sense of agency in audience members, feminine style holds the potential to be especially effective for rhetors and audiences that are members of marginalized groups.[14]

The varied reactions to Campbell's formulation of a feminine style signaled feminist rhetorical scholars' engagement with the debate over gender essentialism that developed across the academy in the 1980s and 1990s. In 1995, the publication of Sonja K. Foss and Cindy L. Griffin's essay, "Beyond Persuasion: A Proposal for an Invitational Rhetoric," further fueled the controversy.[15] In short, Foss and Griffin characterized traditional persuasion as patriarchal and coercive in its attempt to change others, thus dominating and devaluing their perspectives. In its stead, they offered a theory of invitational rhetoric, which they explained as "an invitation to understanding as a means to create a relationship rooted in equality, immanent value, and self-determination. Invitational rhetoric constitutes an invitation to the audience to enter the rhetor's world and to see it as the rhetor does."[16] Claiming that the values undergirding this approach were not just feminist but female, rooted in women's biological and relational roles, Foss and Griffin sought to replace what they perceived as persuasion's emphasis on change and domination with an emphasis on understanding.[17]

More than one scholar has treated both feminine style and invitational rhetoric as instantiations of cultural feminism, which holds that, rather than seeking access to traditionally masculine forms of power, feminism should encourage the valuing of women's distinctive attributes and values ("women's culture") that are biologically and/or culturally derived. Feminist scholars who critiqued invitational rhetoric or feminine style (or both) took issue with these perspectives' implication that all women have some common essence that is deployed rhetorically in predictable ways. They argued that diversity across and within genders is considerable (and affected by factors such as race, class, sexuality, ethnicity, and nationality) and that essentialism works to reify gender stereotypes that affect women in negative ways. They also contended that male rhetors have access to feminine style as well, and, as I further discuss below, that poststructuralist theories of gender should caution scholars against assuming gender's stability in any case.[18]

As has been the case in feminist studies across the academy, the case against gender essentialism has been persuasive in feminist rhetorical studies. Foss and Griffin's proposal for invitational rhetoric did not generate a stream of scholarship dedicated to applying its precepts to public address. However, in the two decades since Campbell's initial formulation, several scholars have utilized the concept of feminine style to elucidate the discourse of a variety of historical and contemporary rhetors. These scholars generally make a point of distancing feminine style from essentialism, making specific claims about its usage in discrete contexts.[19]

Generally, we may consider the recovery project successful if the central criterion for that success is the inclusion of women's discourse in teaching and scholarship about public address. Women's texts have entered what Campbell has termed the "loose canon" of public address, and a few – such as Angelina Grimké's 1838 speech at Pennsylvania Hall and Elizabeth Cady Stanton's 1892 "Solitude of Self" speech – have become required reading in many public address courses.[20] Analyses of women's public address have regularly appeared in major journals in rhetorical studies since the early 1990s, and the number of book-length studies of women's public address has been steadily increasing as well. These studies have focused on a wide variety of issues under the rubric of the recovery project, including the rhetorical personae, styles, and strategies of feminist rhetors, as well as the various genres women rhetors have used, including letters, petitions, and lyceum lectures. They also have examined the interaction of woman's rights/woman suffrage and other US movements such as abolition, temperance, anti-suffrage, dress reform, anti-lynching, and birth control.[21]

Determining the limits of the recovery project is difficult. Thus far, for instance, I have discussed scholarship that treats the intersections of feminism and public address from America's beginnings through the early twentieth century, a span easily understood as "historical," generally focusing on activism with a relationship to US feminism's first wave. Yet, research on the rhetoric of women's activism in the second wave of US feminism – now 30-plus years in the past – is also an important strain in the study of feminism and public address. The active phase of the second wave can be loosely dated from the late 1960s through the mid-1970s, although its ending point is sometimes dated to 1982, the year that the Equal Rights Amendment ratification campaign failed. Less coherent than the first wave, with its eventual central focus on gaining the vote for women, the second wave encompassed both liberal and radical groups and ideologies with contrasting goals of, respectively, changing discriminatory laws and challenging cultural sex-role stereotypes and expectations.[22] Campbell's 1973 essay, "The Rhetoric of Women's Liberation: An Oxymoron," was the first influential treatment of radical second-wave rhetoric among communication scholars, and it is often credited with sparking the interest in women's rhetoric that led to the resurgence of the recovery project in US public address during the 1980s.[23] Campbell's argument that women's liberation discourse was characterized by the strategy of consciousness-raising has been profoundly influential in scholarship about a wide range of feminist rhetoric. Indeed, Campbell recently elevated consciousness-raising to the level of an overarching perspective on women's discourse, arguing that "it is the thread that links the recovery of texts, their recuperation through criticism, and the extraction of theoretical principles that underlie women's ways of persuading" across historical and contemporary contexts.[24]

In the decade or so that followed the publication of Campbell's 1973 essay, scholars produced several analyses of discourses emanating from second-wave activism. Nevertheless, the amount of published work on the second wave by feminist scholars of rhetoric and public address has never approached the volume of work on the first wave.[25] As I have argued elsewhere, the second wave is a movement much less amenable to traditional public address perspectives.[26] For example, public address scholars tend to study the public speeches and essays of social movement leaders, who tend to be rhetorically skilled (e.g., Elizabeth Cady Stanton, Martin Luther King, Jr.). Yet the second wave's radical branch was resolutely anti-hierarchical, and those women who did emerge as "leaders" were more likely to have been appointed as such by mass media than by movement members. Oratory was not a central form of public influence for radical second-wave feminist rhetors; much of their discourse appeared in (often ephemeral) pamphlets, newspapers, newsletters, and books. The emphasis of the movement's radical contingent on consciousness-raising in small groups and through direct action also does not leave scholars with readily available textual artifacts, although additional recovery work may still yield important discoveries. Members of the movement's liberal branch, who focused many of their efforts on influencing legislative and judicial reform, were more likely to produce traditional oratory accessible to scholars (e.g., testimony at Equal Rights Amendment hearings). Although it is historically important, this discourse is rarely distinguished by rhetorical creativity, which perhaps explains the limited attention it has received. In spite of these challenges, contemporary feminist scholars have increasingly scrutinized the rhetorical strategies of second-wave activism, focusing on newspapers, manifestoes, books, and media coverage, as well as oral discourse.[27]

In the last decade, feminist rhetorical scholars also have turned their attention to the rhetoric of what has been termed the "third wave" of US feminism, which is generally dated from the early 1990s. Third-wave feminism is distinguished by its rejection of gender essentialism and its embrace of gender fluidity, as well as by a strong emphasis on gender's interaction with race, class, ethnicity, nationality, and sexuality. Deeply influenced by poststructuralist and postmodernist thought, third-wave feminism is a body of ideas and a way of thinking more than a coherent ideology or activist agenda. Several popular press books have attempted to outline the tenets of third-wave thinking, often through collections of personal narratives by young women who identify as third-wavers. Rhetorical scholars have produced several analyses of this literature, as well as of mass media discourses that they argue manifest third-wave thought.[28]

In comparison to the first wave of US feminism, second- and third-wave feminisms are more diffuse in every way – historically, rhetorically, and ideologically – and thus present a different set of challenges to public address scholars. For example, my own recent work, as I will discuss later in this chapter, deals with mainstream media framing of the activities of the second wave, based on the conviction that most contemporary Americans have come to their understanding of feminism through its treatment by mass media. Thus, understanding the second wave's influence on public consciousness requires analysis of its mediated representation, which I characterize as the most influential mode of public address about the movement.

Challenges to and for the Recovery Project

Some feminist rhetorical scholars have found the recovery project's liberal foundations troubling. In a 1992 essay, Barbara Biesecker praised Campbell's efforts at "destabilizing the subject of rhetorical history that up to this point has been exclusively male." However, she also suggested that Campbell's approach encouraged a kind of tokenism and elitism with its emphasis on individual rhetorical achievement (rather than collective rhetorics) and its implication that "most women simply do not have what it takes to play the public, rhetorical game."[29] In doing so, Biesecker called attention to some of the problems of the liberal framework within which the recovery project has operated (in this sense, her critique resembles Foss and Griffin's). As she notes, "while we may have managed to insert some women into the canon (and, again, this is no small thing), we will have not yet begun to challenge the underlying logic of canon formation and the uses to which it has been put that have written the rhetorical contributions of collective women into oblivion."[30] Alternatively, she suggests that the feminist study of rhetoric should discard its commitment to the stable and transcendent subject and, following the poststructuralist thought of Michel Foucault and Jaques Derrida, replace the question "who is speaking" with "what play of forces made it possible for a particular speaking subject to emerge?"[31] In short, such a perspective recommends that our feminist critique target not the techniques of individual exemplary orators, but, rather, the entire constellation of traditions (the "conditions of possibility") that have led us to recognize certain rhetorical practices (and practitioners) as worthy of attention while rendering others invisible.

Campbell defended the intentions and integrity of the recovery project in a response to Biesecker, noting that the inclusion of women's voices balances a rhetorical history dominated by men.[32] In retrospect, the Biesecker/Campbell exchange makes clear that their perspectives represented the clash of two quite distinct theoretical positions: the liberal humanism of the recovery project versus poststructuralism's insistence that rhetors are effects rather than agents of discourse. Although Biesecker targeted the study of women's public address in particular, her critique was, in effect, an indictment of the agent-centered, instrumentalist public address tradition as a whole. Yet, as Kathleen Ryan has argued, the majority of the work in women's rhetoric and public address that has followed the Campbell/Biesecker debate has not split neatly into either the "recovery" or the "gender critique" camp, to use Ryan's labels. Instead, Ryan argues that a survey of anthologies, special journal issues, and books between 1989 and 2002 reveals that feminist scholars have made distinct efforts to mediate between the poles that Campbell and Biesecker represented, presenting recovery and gender critique as operating in a causal and complementary relationship. Ryan described this emerging perspective in the following way: "Adding women's voices leads to analysis, rhetorical criticism, and theorizing."[33]

Indeed, as the recovery project continued to progress throughout the 1990s, feminist scholars expanded on Biesecker's call for the integration of poststructuralist insights into public address study in a variety of ways.[34] Most prominently, Judith Butler's work on gender performativity has encouraged feminist rhetorical scholars to rethink our implicit commitment to the stability of gender – to the idea that gender is something possessed by rhetors and reflected in rhetorical practice rather than something that is constituted *by* rhetorical practice.[35] The result is a broadened recovery project that has shifted from an instrumental to a constitutive focus, from measuring the efficacy of rhetoric as a response to specific situations to elucidating how various discourses have enabled the creation of diverse subject positions for women involved in feminist activism.

For example, Susan Zaeske's 2003 book on the antislavery petitioning of white women before the Civil War focuses on collective rhetorical efforts in an attempt to understand how "petitioning provided a conduit for women to assert a modified form of citizenship" as well as contributed to the development of "collective female subjectivities." Zaeske concludes that activist white women gained access to public power by emphasizing their role as representatives of the silent and helpless female slave, an "act of identification [that] ... amounted not only to appropriation but to exploitation."[36] As this example illustrates, scholars concerned with the development of gendered subjectivities through women's public rhetorical activities have been careful to attend to the ways that gendered identities are always simultaneously constituted through discourses of race, class, and sexuality.[37] Not surprisingly, this work has tended to focus on gender's constitutive function vis-à-vis women's identities as public actors, activists, and citizens. The gendered distinction between the public and private spheres has been a central concern for the recovery project since its beginnings, yet recent work influenced by poststructuralism has usefully turned from taking this split as a given to examining the ways that it is constituted through public discourse. Generally, this recent work has moved away from what Nathan Stormer has called an "an implicit theoretical paradigm [that] operationalized 'gender' as women's [preexisting] 'difference.'"[38] Instead, it recognizes gender as a rhetorical process that is always ongoing and that cannot be limited to one side of a culturally maintained female/male or masculine/feminine binary or understood in isolation from other identity categories.

Movement away from an agent-centered conception of women's public address and toward a poststructuralist understanding of the constitution of gender through public discourse has been accompanied by a shift toward nonoratorical and often collective forms of discourse, creatively expanding scholars' notion of what "counts" as public address.[39] While still centering on discourses surrounding women's historical efforts at social reform, recent scholarship has explored the rhetorical dimensions of such visual forms as cartoons, advertising, posters, and parades.[40]

Despite these innovations, feminist research in historical public address primarily has been limited to the study of the constitution and functions of gender in discourses related to women's activism. These discourses were, more often than not, produced by women themselves. Feminist scholars of public address have yet to mount a sustained effort to examine the role of gender in canonical rhetorical texts produced by men. One result is that we have inadvertently fostered a definition of feminist work in public address as meaning "the study of women's texts." Similarly, when we claim to study gender, we usually mean "women" or "femininity."[41] Both men's public address texts and the role of masculinity within them remain largely unexamined by feminist public address critics.[42] As Judith Butler notes in an observation that usefully describes the traditional norms of public address scholarship, "only the feminine gender is marked ... the universal person and the masculine gender are conflated, thereby defining women in terms of their sex and extolling men as the bearers of a body-transcendent universal personhood."[43] Although feminist public address scholars have treated women's rhetorical activities in terms of their relationship to gendered identities, they have done very little similar work on men's rhetorical activities, particularly historical oratory.[44] Such a focus is necessary to truly mine the insights of the poststructuralist project, as well as to more fully understand the workings of gender in rhetorical texts.

For example, a central assumption of the recovery project has been that gender is central to understanding the situations and rhetorical practices of women rhetors because the performance of femininity was assumed to function at cross purposes with the exercise of rhetorical power. Yet gender is equally as central to understanding the situations and rhetorical practices of male rhetors, precisely because the performance of masculinity often is synonymous with the exercise of rhetorical power. A poststructuralist perspective encourages us to recognize that these understandings of gender and their relationship to rhetorical power are interactive, mutually constitutive, and simultaneously enabling and constraining. Feminist public address scholars' failure thus far to interrogate the rhetorical constitution and function of masculinity is to leave ourselves with an incompletely realized critique of gender politics in public address, particularly in pre-twentieth-century discourse produced by men. Although, as I discuss below, feminist public address scholars have recently begun to attend to the function of masculinity in contemporary mediated texts, we seem loathe to turn that same lens toward canonical texts that otherwise receive sustained attention in public address study and pedagogy.

Beyond the Recovery Project: Mass Media, Politics, and Feminist Critique

Studies of public address that are not specifically related to feminist movements but that approach their objects of study from an implicit or explicit feminist perspective are another important area in public address research. These sorts of studies exemplify the second definition of feminism I set out in the introduction to this chapter: feminism as a *theory*, *methodology*, or *critical perspective* that informs the work of public address scholars. Feminist public address research in this category varies widely in the artifacts it studies as well as in the questions it asks of those artifacts. Generally, however, the research I discuss below asks some variation of this implicit question: How does gender ideology function in this discourse and whose interests does it serve? In some cases that focus is prompted by the gender of the rhetor, while in others it is linked to the ideological constitution of gender in rhetorical texts, particularly mass-mediated texts.

For example, both of these foci are evident in feminist research related to the US presidency, long a central area of study in traditional public address. Although feminist public address scholars have not turned their talents to feminist analysis of presidential oratory per se, they have produced important work in two related areas: the study of the rhetoric of US first ladies, and the analysis of the function of gender ideologies in mass-mediated discourse about presidential politics.

Study of the rhetoric of first ladies is a natural corollary to public address scholars' longtime focus on presidential rhetoric. Indeed, Karlyn Kohrs Campbell has argued that the presidency should be seen as a "two person career" in which the first lady also represents the nation, thus making study of first ladies an integral part of the study of the presidency.[45] Studies of the public address of first ladies can be divided into two broad categories, although there is overlap between the two. The first strain of research has much in common with the traditional instrumentalist paradigm of public address that characterizes the early stages of the recovery project; it includes studies of prominent first ladies and their rhetorical action on behalf of public issues.[46] An excellent example of this type of scholarship is Shawn J. Parry-Giles's and Diane M. Blair's essay treating the "rise of the rhetorical first lady," in which they trace the "gradual rise of public persuasion's importance to the first lady position" by examining the political activities of first ladies from Martha Washington to Laura Bush. They conclude that "the first lady pulpit can act as a site for the performance of archetypal femininity; it can also function as a location of feminist advancement that challenges gender stereotypes, expanding women's political space."[47]

More explicitly constitutive in its orientation, the second strain of research examines the ways that the discourse of and about contemporary first ladies (notably Hillary Rodham Clinton) constructs gendered identities for these women. As Karrin Vasby Anderson has noted, more than simply functioning as symbols, "first ladies become 'sites' for the symbolic negotiation of female identity."[48] Campbell, for example, has examined the virulent reactions to Hillary Rodham Clinton, arguing that Clinton's difficulties with her public image are linked to "the problems of public women writ large, the continuing demand that women who play public roles or function in the public sphere discursively enact their femininity, and that women who do not or who do so only to a limited degree … will arouse the intensely hostile responses that seem so baffling."[49]

The other area of feminist research related to the US presidency focuses on the centrality of gender ideologies to cultural conceptions of the presidency, generally focusing on the mobilization of those ideologies by mass media discourse rather than in presidential rhetoric itself. For example, Anna Cornelia Fahey, in a 2007 essay, analyzes national mass media coverage of Democratic presidential candidate John Kerry during the 2004 campaign and argues that media depictions emasculated Kerry by portraying him as "French and feminine."[50] Karrin Vasby Anderson's comparative study of female candidates for the Senate and for the presidency in 2000 is noteworthy for its claim that "gender is a significant but complicated variable in US politics." Rejecting the assumption that gender always disadvantages female candidates, she argues that Hillary Clinton's campaign for the Senate in New York did not generate the kind of gender-linked attacks that had characterized her time as first lady. Rather, Clinton's status as a non-native New Yorker was at issue, and "the 'carpetbagger' question overshadowed the 'bitch' charge."[51] Moreover, it was Clinton's male opponents who faced gender-related charges of acting too aggressively, charges from which Clinton benefited. Yet Anderson argues that Elizabeth Dole, as a Republican candidate for president in the same campaign season, encountered gender-related obstacles repeatedly and could not escape her status as a "woman candidate." Anderson concludes that it was the office that each woman sought that made the difference. More so than any other political office, she argues, the "ceremonial and symbolic role of the US president is tied up with traditional masculinity."[52] This creates a double bind for women candidates who must perform femininity while also proving their qualifications to enter into the masculine tradition of the US presidency.[53]

Feminist study of political discourse also has developed in directions other than those focused on the instrumental pursuit of political office. Some of the most sophisticated recent work by feminist rhetorical scholars analyzes the constitutive role of feminist and gender ideologies in the rhetorical construction of political issues.[54] For example, in her 2006 essay analyzing the discourse around the 2003 capture and rescue in Iraq of Private First Class Jessica Lynch, Shannon L. Holland employs feminist theories of gender performativity to elucidate how gender ideologies infuse public controversy. Exploring a variety of texts, including Lynch's autobiography, media coverage, and a made-for-television movie about the events, Holland argues that the depiction of Lynch as the naïve and victimized Woman/Child reaffirmed the masculine culture of the military while it facilitated new attacks against proponents of gender integration in the military (as well as against feminism generally). She concludes that "representations of Lynch in popular culture obfuscate the political debates over women in combat by metonymically framing Lynch as a representative of all military women, thus deflecting attention away from the thousands of women who perform effectively in the military (and the thousands of men who do not)."[55] Anderson and Holland's studies have in common a welcome emphasis on the interactive nature of gender ideologies; they implicitly reject an all-too-common assumption in feminist research that gender applies only to women. Rather, they focus on the ways that masculinity and femininity mutually constitute each other in specific situations while also pointing out the ways that popular discourses function to reify them as essential, binary, and static.

The influence of poststructuralist approaches has led to welcome developments in both the conceptual frameworks and the objects of study for feminist work in public address. Yet the trajectory of feminist work in public address is not a linear or evolutionary one; it is, rather, eclectic and incremental. The recovery project is by no means complete, and scholars continue to produce both traditional agent-centered, instrumental rhetorical analyses as well as studies of rhetoric's constitutive function with regard to gender. Feminist public address scholars also have increasingly turned their attention to mass-mediated discourses in order to address contemporary public issues. This is all to the good, as a robust feminist public address tradition develops best through an organic process in which our perspectives and assumptions develop and change through grounded critical practice.

The narrative of the development of feminist public address research that I have constructed here also is not one that has occurred in isolation from a larger public address community. Rather, feminist work in public address has constituted and participated in trends in public address scholarship as a whole, where the incorporation of poststructuralist theory and attention to mass-mediated discourse also have been important developments. For example, public address scholars' recent interest in visual rhetoric (generally photographs) as an overlooked form of public address is one to which feminist scholars have much to contribute.[56] Feminist scholars are particularly well positioned as critics of visual public discourse, given the primacy of visual rhetorics in the constitution of gender identity. Marita Gronnvoll offers an instructive case study in her 2007 analysis of the controversy over the photographs of prisoners held at the US military prison at Abu Ghraib, Iraq. Gronnvoll argues that mediated reactions to the Abu Ghraib revelations consistently stressed the role of gender in representations of the identity and behaviors of female US military guards, while consistently eliding the role of gender in representations of their male counterparts. In short, "rather than … being held up as examples of bad soldiers, they [the female soldiers] are classified as bad girls." In contrast, in the same media discourse, the male guards "did not fail to meet some unspecified standard as men; they are not symbols of failed masculinity. They failed as soldiers."[57] Gronnvoll maintains that the reactions to Abu Ghraib constituted the abuses committed by US soldiers there as a crisis of gender transgression – represented by the specific behavior of female soldiers – rather than as a crisis in military culture represented by the behaviors of both male and female soldiers.

Mediated, visual discourses should continue to be a rich area of study for feminist scholars of public address, particularly because mass media are such powerful carriers of gender ideologies. In the remainder of this chapter, I offer a case study of television news discourse about the second wave of feminism in order to illustrate the intersections of three ongoing and important threads in feminist research in public address. The first is the study of feminism itself. Although, as I have noted, the first wave of feminism has received a great deal of attention within the recovery project, study of the second wave has lagged. Second, study of the second wave makes clear the importance of mass media as a form of public address. Oratory was not as central across the second wave compared to other equality movements; print and broadcast news coverage, however, was crucial to constituting feminism's meaning in US public consciousness. Third, I focus on television news coverage to illustrate the importance of attention to both visual and verbal rhetorics in analysis of the constitution and function of gendered identities and ideologies.

Second-Wave Feminism, Mass Media, and Visual Rhetorics of Gender

Although historians differ in their dates of origin for second-wave feminism, they generally concur that 1970 is the year that the movement began to receive extensive media attention. In March of 1970, CBS News became the first television network to take a sustained look at the movement. When CBS offered its three-part series of stories on March 9, 11, and 13, it was in the position of offering an initial interpretation of feminism's meaning and import to millions of Americans across the country.[58] One of the crucial differences between print and broadcast treatment of a topic is television's larger capacity for visuality. Visual analysis is especially important to understanding television's treatment of feminism because the display of women's bodies, through sexist images or images of feminist protest, was central to television news' framing of the second wave. Across print and broadcast, journalists at the time were obsessed with the physical appearance and attractiveness of feminists, and this tendency correlated with the persistent attention they gave to the feminist critique of beauty politics and sexual objectification (the focus of one of the CBS stories, as I discuss below). In news coverage of women's liberation, feminism was an assault on gender difference and thus on traditional femininity, and reporters usually seized the opportunity both to show the images that feminists were critiquing as well as to use their cameras to depict feminists' own violation of gender norms.

In what follows, I focus on the first two stories in the CBS series from 1970, paying close attention to the interaction of verbal and visual discourses in the reports' attempt to explain the feminist movement to its audience. I conclude that this coverage illustrates important tendencies in the constituted meanings of second-wave feminism as expressed in television news. These include the creation of an implicit contrast between liberal feminist equality-based demands (presented as reasonable and pragmatic) and radical feminist behavior (presented as confrontational and extremist), the construction of the movement as a battle among women rather than as a challenge to sexism and patriarchy, and the replacement of political analysis with visual spectacle. Importantly, much of this rhetorical work was accomplished nonverbally; that is, the choice of images in CBS' coverage was central to its point of view.

On March 9, 1970, the first story in the CBS series began with archival footage of suffragists marching in New York City in 1920 as the viewer heard background strains of the "Battle Hymn of the Republic." Reporter David Culhane's voiceover then entered with the following commentary: "The 'Battle Hymn of the Republic,' a Civil War song that was taken over by suffragettes in the early part of this century in *their* civil war to get the vote. They won the franchise fifty years ago, and now in the minds of many people, women are better off than ever before in history." As Culhane spoke, the suffrage footage faded into an image of a group of four second-wave feminists on a stage singing an updated version of "The Battle Hymn of the Republic" with the following lyrics: "Our eyes have seen the future and rejoice in what's to be / Every woman in position to achieve felicity / We will vote ourselves in power with our own majority / For the time for NOW [National Organization for Women] is now."

Images of suffragists marching, followed by images of contemporary feminists singing about voting, created a clever connection between the first and second waves, but these images functioned as entertaining spectacle and told the viewer little about what feminists wanted. Moreover, by noting that women have had the vote for 50 years – and by stating that "many" considered women better off than at any time in history – Culhane implicitly placed the burden on feminists to prove that women actually had any problems worth complaining about.

Yet, as the segment continued, Culhane appeared before a huge room full of women typing at row after row of desks, and he recounted statistics that legitimized feminist complaints. He pointed out that there were 30 million working women, yet "very few are in executive positions," and that the average man made almost twice as much as the average woman. As his voice was heard over images of women nurses and women teachers going about their jobs, he also offered figures on sex-segregated employment, mentioning the dearth of women doctors and college professors. A brief snippet of Betty Friedan, identified as the founder and president of the National Organization for Women, further underscored the approving tone of Culhane's review of liberal feminist grievances. Seated, framed by a medium shot in a typical interview set-up, Friedan pointed out women's under-representation in leadership positions of all kinds, from business to politics. She concluded that, "In the big decisions – of war and peace, of crisis in the cities, even the decisions as to what happens to women's own lives and own bodies, and the self-determination of their own lives … women's voice has not been heard."

Culhane then showed some footage of a meeting of feminists in Northridge, California, focusing on about a dozen women, seated in a middle-class living room, conservatively dressed and coiffed, mostly middle-aged and seemingly middle-class. One of the women offered the following analysis: "Most women are at some time in their life going to have to work as head of household to support an entire household and taxed the same as the man and paid a third as much for identical work. How do we make the public understand that this woman can't compete, even if she has no man at all? She can't compete in the labor market enough to feed her children."

At this point, the story seemed fairly sympathetic: Culhane had offered statistics that support claims of discrimination, he had interviewed the nation's most famous feminist and a leader of its largest feminist organization, and he had shown one of the movement's ubiquitous small groups and allowed them to speak for themselves. Indeed, because Culhane opened the story with footage of suffragists, one can read these early segments in the story as pro-feminist: Just as first-wave feminists had made a reasonable and ultimately successful demand for the vote, second-wave feminists were making reasonable demands for equal pay and equal opportunity.

Culhane's story then moved on to what he termed the "more militant" portion of the movement. At the close of the segment on the feminist group in California, Culhane segued to the next segment – about feminists' disruption of the Senate hearings on the birth control pill in January of 1970 – by saying, "And it's no longer a question of just talking about it." The viewer then saw footage of several young, casually dressed, long-haired women standing up and interrupting testimony at the Senate hearings on the birth control pill. One shouted at the Senators: "Women are not going to sit quietly any longer. You are murdering us for your profit and convenience." As though drawing a conclusion from evidence just presented, Culhane then said: "Some women, especially among the young, are becoming more militant ... On several occasions they disrupted hearings on birth control pills. They left no doubt they think the pill is unsafe and should be taken off the market." The viewer received no further information on the reasoning behind feminist demands regarding the birth control pill, and the images in this segment of the story functioned as what Patricia Bradley has termed "symbolic-only representations of angry women."[59] The segment closed with an image of an exasperated Senator asking the women to sit down or be removed from the hearings, underscoring the feminists' disorderliness and disrespect as the central point of the story.

Continuing his focus on disruptive behavior, Culhane's voiceover then introduced a segment on a feminist protest at a "men-only" bar in Chicago. Although Culhane included the account of this protest in his featuring of "militant" activity, which he was implicitly contrasting with the "moderate" activities of groups like NOW, he failed to note that this particular protest was actually spearheaded by NOW, which focused many of its efforts on public discrimination. Indeed, the women demonstrators seen in the footage were middle-aged and more conservative in appearance than the women at the Senate hearings. Culhane noted that the majority of the restaurant was gender-integrated, but "a small part of it is set aside for men who want to have a quick lunch by themselves" (implying, somehow, that having little space and using it for little time – and only at lunch – made the discrimination unremarkable). The bar's male owner blocked the door as feminists confronted him with accusations of discrimination using a sex/race analogy, a common tactic for an organization that saw itself as the National Association for the Advancement of Colored People (NAACP) for women: "Now we fought the public accommodations fight ten years ago with the Blacks. Are we going to have to start all over again with women? How would you like a sign up there that said 'Blacks only' or 'Whites only?' It's the same principle." Culhane narrated that, after the CBS cameras left, "a scuffle at the bar between a man and a woman demonstrator" ensued, although no one was injured or arrested. After showing the protesters' subsequent discussion about the need for self-defense in such instances, Culhane proceeded to a discussion of feminists' interest in karate, a staple in previous print reporting on the movement.

This segment, the final one in the March 9 story, began with a focus on a woman and a man in martial arts garb on a mat. As the man used a judo throw on the woman, Culhane's voice was heard: "The woman being thrown by a fellow student at the University of Chicago is a militant feminist. Many of them are learning judo and karate and they say it's a splendid equalizer." The viewer then saw the same woman circle the man, shout aggressively, throw him over her shoulder, and pin him to the mat. A group of women watched from the sidelines and cheered as Culhane spoke: "A match between a young man and a young woman. Many feminists think this is an apt symbol of equal rights, [and] that as more women come to know their oppression, the symbol could become a reality." The implication was hard to miss: Martial arts represented an outlet for women's wrath. In their quest for equality, women were willing to use violence. Culhane closed the story with a teaser for the next installment in the series: "In our next report, we will show two traditional roles for women that really make the feminists angry." As Culhane spoke, the last image the viewer saw presumably illustrated such anger: The young woman threw the man to the ground yet again and brought her leg down on his neck as he shouted in pain.

This first story in Culhane's series – the first feature story attempting to explain the movement that appeared on a US nightly newscast – illustrated a central theme that would come to distinguish reporting on second-wave feminism: the drawing of clear distinctions between liberal and radical feminist demands and behavior. The former was constituted as reasonable and credible and the latter as disorderly and extremist, and both verbal and visual means were important to this process. Culhane was respectful of the equality demands made by liberal feminists, linking those demands to women's roles as breadwinners for their families and thus depicting them as pragmatic rather than ideological. Crucially, the visuals were not particularly compelling in these early segments, increasing the salience of the verbal content. For liberal feminism, then, the first story offered a fairly coherent rationale: Women were underpaid and under-represented in many arenas – importantly, Culhane provided those statistics himself – and this discrimination had a negative impact, as he allowed feminists to explain.

As the story moved on to the movement's "militant" factions, however, the visual became ascendant, and the viewer was given a much less coherent verbal explanation for what s/he saw, making it clear that Culhane drew the distinction between moderates and militants on behavioral rather than ideological grounds. That is, because he gave so little information about ideology or political principles that motivated the protesters, the most evident difference between the liberals and the militants in his story had to do with their demeanor: those who rationally discussed their issues were contrasted to those who acted out, who were offered as spectacle with little explanation of their concerns. Culhane's usage of "militant" was interesting in itself. The activities depicted are certainly disruptive, even confrontational. But the women involved were never physically violent, nor did they ever advocate violence. Yet, given gender norms for women, for the feminists to act other than passively and to practice aggression even verbally was a shocking violation of expectations. As Susan Douglas has noted, "militant" was the term used by reporters to demonize any female behavior that violated the norms that women always should be "friendly, accommodating, compliant, docile, and obsequious."[60]

Culhane's lumping of feminist protesters under the "militant" label based on their behavior rather than their beliefs is most evident in the way he equated what *was* a radical feminist action – disruption of the birth control hearings – with a sit-in attempted by NOW members to dramatize public discrimination at a bar. Despite their explicit invocation, on camera, of the parallel to the nonviolent civil rights movement – as well as their emulation of its tactics – he classified the NOW members as militants, arguably more than once. Recall that he used their reaction to being physically attacked by a bar patron as his segue to a discussion of feminists' interest in karate, a segment that he began by reminding viewers that the young woman on the mat was "a militant feminist." By the end of this story, then, militancy had been explicitly connected to women's physical aggression, accompanied by visual images of a woman attacking a man.

Television news' fondness for "good pictures" meant that those feminist activities that presented the opportunity to show engaging, entertaining, or disturbing visuals were much more likely to get airtime. Liberal feminists, who pursued their goals primarily through legislation and the courts, were much less likely to produce powerful visual images. In the first CBS story, for instance, Culhane relied on stock footage of women typing, teaching, and nursing to illustrate his verbal narration of liberal feminist grievances concerning wage and employment discrimination. Feminists who engaged in public confrontation, on the other hand, received less thorough verbal explanation of their positions but more thorough and specific visual representation of their actions. Yet those visuals – which focused on the spectacle of protest, confrontation, and physical aggression – both trivialized radical feminist concerns and cast them as extremist or even threatening.

This imbalance between verbal and visual discourses, and its implications for the mediated image of the movement, was made even clearer in the second story in the CBS series, broadcast on March 11, 1970. Culhane had previewed the second story as an exploration of "two traditional roles that really make the feminists angry," and those two roles turned out to be Miss America and the Playboy Bunny. Narrating over footage of Miss America contestants walking down the runway in Atlantic City, Culhane noted that many Americans considered Miss America "the standard for an ideal woman." Feminists, on the other hand, considered her a "reduction of woman to a kind of domesticated sex object." After footage of the pageant, the story featured film of feminist protesters outside the pageant in 1969. Juxtaposed as they were with images of the pageant itself, the contrast was clear: Calm, smiling, *silent*, conventionally attractive women walked down a runway to applause, while seemingly angry, unglamorous feminists shouted, marched, and made a spectacle of themselves in front of a jeering crowd of onlookers. Miss America may have been a dangerous symbol of misguided ideals of femininity, as feminists charged, but the opening images of this story suggested that the feminists were the truly dangerous ones. And, according to Culhane, the targets of their wrath were other women: the smiling, pretty, traditionally feminine Miss America contestants themselves.

To underscore this point, Culhane's report then segued to a Playboy Club, where the reporter stood with his microphone in front of a room of professionally dressed men being served drinks by Playboy Bunnies. Although Culhane was a faceless narrator earlier in the story, he planted himself squarely in the camera's frame at the Playboy Club and offered the following analysis:

> Another place, and, the new feminists say, another symbol of the oppression of women. One of the Playboy Clubs, where men come to eat, to drink, and, incidentally, to observe some remarkable displays of feminine pulchritude. The woman's

liberation movement despises the "Playboy" concept of women, who they say may have been liberated from a good deal of clothing but little else. So Miss America and the Playboy Bunny – nothing but sex objects – have got to go.

Most important about this segment, however, was not what Culhane said, but what became visible as the camera moved away from him. The camera functioned, in the most conventional sense, as an extension of the masculine gaze, implicitly Culhane's gaze.[61] As he spoke, it traveled up and down a Bunny's body, then followed another Bunny's derrière as she traveled across the room holding a tray of drinks, and finally shifted to a higher angle that allowed the viewer to see down the front of another Bunny's décolleté from above. The footage then ended with the image of a smiling Bunny walking toward the camera.

Read by a feminist critic, these images are ironic confirmation of feminists' charges. Even while noting the feminists' objections to the positioning of women as sex objects, all of the camerawork reified that positioning as it focused on the Bunnies' bodies. For the viewer watching these images in 1970, however, the irony is of a different sort. Like the Miss America contestants in the earlier footage, these women were beautiful, well built, and smiling; they hardly seemed oppressed or objectionable. At the same moment that Culhane verbally recounted feminist objections, the camerawork offered a different message: "Look at these gorgeous, happy women. No problem here." Indeed, all Culhane told the viewer is that feminists did not like Playboy Bunnies; there was so little content to the verbal report that it was easily overwhelmed by the visual, and the rhetorical effect of the segment was the trivialization of feminists' concerns.

By this point in Culhane's second story on the movement, several tendencies that would characterize later reporting were already evident. The tacit approval given to liberal feminist goals in the first story was given even more weight by the second story's focus on sexual objectification. Radical feminists' concern with sex-role stereotypes was presented as trivial in contrast to liberal equality demands, particularly given that women were visually presented as freely participating in those stereotypes. The second story also introduced a strategy that would become standard for news coverage of the second wave: the near invisibility of men's opposition to feminism accompanied by the foregrounding of women's opposition (or sometimes their simple disinterest). Although news coverage often invoked this tactic through explicit, verbal means – by asking "ordinary" women what they thought of the movement[62] – it was skillfully accomplished through the visual discourse of the CBS stories. The images of smiling and happy Miss America contestants and Playboy Bunnies constituted an implicit refutation of the feminists' claims that these women were oppressed by beauty standards or sexual objectification. The only men featured during the segment on Playboy Bunnies simply aspired to "eat, drink, and observe" (according to Culhane's narration), which hardly seemed oppressive. Indeed, no men articulated opposition to the movement throughout the entire series of CBS stories, making it even more likely that feminists would be seen as troublemakers who were only trying to sow discontent where none existed and who were fighting an enemy that only they recognized. Finally, as was evident in both stories, television coverage of the second wave – particularly the activity of its radical contingent – was characterized by the substitution of visual spectacle for political analysis.

Conclusion

Feminist scholarship has contributed to and challenged the larger field of public address for almost a century. Motivated initially by the goal of rescuing women orators from invisibility, feminist scholars have proceeded not only to elevate women rhetors into the canon of rhetorical excellence but also to expand our understanding of how excellence should be understood. Following developments in the academy at large, our formerly singular focus on the rhetorical activities of women has expanded to include a focus on the rhetorical constitution of gender. While moving from a view of gender as a stable entity represented by rhetors or reflected in texts to an understanding of gender as a contingent, rhetorically constituted phenomenon, they also have expanded the category of public address itself. Recent feminist work focused on the deployment of gender as a mode of meaning in public discourse has examined artifacts from oratory to parades to petitions to photographs to media coverage, yet study of these artifacts is driven by many of the same concerns that have animated feminist research in public address for decades. Central among those concerns is elucidating the myriad ways that gender functions as an index of power in public discourse and public life. For instrumentalist analyses of public address, this interest drives scholars' attention to the ways in which women rhetors responded to the rhetorical obstacles presented by cultural ideologies that restricted them to the private sphere. In work from a constitutive perspective, scholars have investigated the diverse ways that gendered identities are constructed and deployed in a variety of verbal, visual, and performative discourses. In each case, feminist scholars have kept sight of the political implications of their work, understanding that their concern with the "difference" that women, or sex, or gender are perceived to represent – in rhetorical situations, in rhetorical discourse, in rhetorical theories, and in disciplinary conversation – is a focus that brings issues of power to the foreground.

I hope this chapter has demonstrated that the feminist project in public address is robust and wide-ranging, yet it is also somewhat unbalanced in its primary focus on the function of gender in rhetorical texts by and about women. As Celeste Condit and I have noted, "a relentless focus on women leads us to the conclusion, however erroneous, that women are the problem and that the feminist project can be accomplished through change on only one side of the (constructed) gender divide."[63] Feminist scholars have turned their attention to masculinity in contemporary mediated texts, but much work remains to be done to develop a fully realized critique of the constitution of gender in historical (and often canonical) public address texts produced by men.

Another arena for development that I have highlighted in this chapter is the feminist analysis of visual forms of public address. As my case study of television coverage of second-wave feminist activities demonstrates, visual public discourses function as significant carriers of gender ideologies. In the case of the second wave (and beyond), scholars cannot fully understand the rhetorical challenges and opportunities that faced (and face) the movement without close attention to both the verbal and visual strategies of mass media. Indeed, such strategies are centrally important to the constitution of a public identity for feminist movements.

The future of feminist study in public address promises to be a vibrant one. While building on the strengths of the recovery project, feminist scholars have expanded the purview of their work in multiple, overlapping directions. Most importantly, a focus on the constitution of gender in all its manifestations should continue to inspire future generations of feminist scholars dedicated to examining the powerful workings of gendered identities and ideologies in public discourse.

Notes

1 Bonnie J. Dow and Celeste M. Condit, "The State of the Art in Feminist Scholarship in Communication," *Journal of Communication* 55 (2005): 448.

2 Bonnie J. Dow, "Feminist Approaches to Communication," in *21st-Century Communication: A Reference Handbook*, vol. 1, ed. William F. Eadie (Thousand Oaks, CA: Sage, 2009), 83.

3 Doris Yoakam, "Pioneer Women Orators in America," *Quarterly Journal of Speech* 23 (1937): 251–259.

4 Doris Yoakam, "Women's Introduction to the American Platform," in *A History and Criticism of American Public Address*, vol. 1, ed. William Norwood Brigance (New York: McGraw-Hill, 1943), 153–192; and Doris Yoakam Twitchell, "Susan B. Anthony," in *A History and Criticism of American Public Address*, vol. 3, ed. Marie Kathryn Hochmuth (New York: Longmans, Green, 1955), 97–132.

5 Lillian O'Connor, *Pioneer Women Orators: Rhetoric in the Ante-Bellum Reform Movement* (New York: Columbia University Press, 1954). For a more extensive version of the historical narrative of the emergence of feminist public address research, see Karlyn Kohrs Campbell, "Consciousness-Raising: Linking Theory, Criticism, and Practice," *Rhetoric Society Quarterly* 32 (2002): 45–64. For a treatment that focuses on gender and public address research, rather than feminism specifically, see Karlyn Kohrs Campbell and Zornitsa Keremidchieva, "Gender and Public Address," in *The Sage Handbook of Gender and Communication*, ed. Bonnie J. Dow and Julia T. Wood (Thousand Oaks, CA: Sage, 2006), 185–199.

6 For a useful discussion of recovery as a feminist scholarly practice, see Kathleen J. Ryan, "Recasting Recovery and Gender Critique as Inventive Arts: Constructing Edited Collections in Feminist Rhetorical Studies," *Rhetoric Review* 25 (2006): 22–40.

7 Dow and Condit, "The State of the Art," 450.

8 See Karlyn Kohrs Campbell, "The Communication Classroom: A Chilly Climate for Women?" *ACA Bulletin* 51 (1985): 68–72 for a critical appraisal of the absence of women's voices from public address textbooks. Anthologies of women's discourse produced

in the 1980s include Judith Anderson, *Outspoken Women: Speeches by American Women Reformers, 1635–1935* (Dubuque, IA: Kendall/Hunt, 1984); and Patricia S. Kennedy and Gloria H. O'Shields, eds., *We Shall be Heard: Women Speakers in America, 1828–Present* (Dubuque, IA: Kendall/Hunt, 1983). For examples of the first wave of critical analyses of feminist rhetoric produced in the 1980s, see Karlyn Kohrs Campbell, "Stanton's 'Solitude of Self': A Rationale for Feminism," *Quarterly Journal of Speech* 66 (1980): 304–312; Karlyn Kohrs Campbell, "Style and Content in the Rhetoric of Early Afro-American Feminists," *Quarterly Journal of Speech* 72 (1986): 434–445; Charles Conrad, "The Transformation of the 'Old Feminist' Movement," *Quarterly Journal of Speech* 67 (1981): 284–297; and Phyllis M. Japp, "Esther or Isaiah? The Abolitionist-Feminist Rhetoric of Angelina Grimké," *Quarterly Journal of Speech* 71 (1985): 335–348.

9   Karlyn Kohrs Campbell, ed., *Women Public Speakers in the United States, 1800–1925: A Bio-Critical Sourcebook* (Westport, CT: Greenwood Press, 1993); and Karlyn Kohrs Campbell, ed., *Women Public Speakers in the United States, 1925–1993: A Bio-Critical Sourcebook* (Westport, CT: Greenwood Press, 1994).

10 See, for example, Marsha Houston and Olga Idriss Davis, eds., *Centering Ourselves: African American Feminist and Womanist Studies of Discourse* (Cresskill, NJ: Hampton Press, 2002); Shirley W. Logan, *"We Are Coming": The Persuasive Discourse of Nineteenth-Century Black Women* (Carbondale: Southern Illinois University Press, 1999); Andrea A. Lunsford, ed., *Reclaiming Rhetorica: Women in the Rhetorical Tradition* (Pittsburgh, PA: University of Pittsburgh Press, 1995); Carla L. Peterson, *Doers of the Word: African-American Women Speakers and Writers in the North, 1830–1880* (New York: Oxford University Press, 1995); Joy Ritchie and Kate Ronald, eds., *Available Means: An Anthology of Women's Rhetoric(s)* (Pittsburgh, PA: University of Pittsburgh Press, 2001); and Molly M. Wertheimer, ed., *Listening to Their Voices: The Rhetorical Activities of Historical Women* (Columbia: University of South Carolina Press, 1997).

11 For a discussion of the instrumental versus constitutive distinction in rhetorical studies, see James Jasinski, "Instrumentalism, Contextualism, and Interpretation in Rhetorical Criticism," in *Rhetorical Hermeneutics: Invention and Interpretation in the Age of Science*, ed. Alan G. Gross and William M. Keith (Albany: State University of New York Press, 1997), 195–224.

12 See Karlyn Kohrs Campbell, *Man Cannot Speak for Her*, 2 vols. (Westport, CT: Praeger, 1989), 1: 3. For a useful discussion of the ways that the public/private binary has operated within rhetorical and public address studies, see Campbell and Keremidchieva, "Gender and Public Address," and Cindy Griffin, "The Essentialist Roots of the Public Sphere: A Feminist Critique," *Western Journal of Communication* 60 (1996): 21–39.

13 Susan Zaeske, "The 'Promiscuous Audience' Controversy and the Emergence of the Early Woman's Rights Movement," *Quarterly Journal of Speech* 81 (1995): 191–207.

14 Campbell, *Man Cannot Speak for Her*, 1: 12–13.

15 Sonja K. Foss and Cindy L. Griffin, "Beyond Persuasion: A Proposal for an Invitational Rhetoric," *Communication Monographs* 62 (1995): 1–18.

16 Foss and Griffin, "Beyond Persuasion," 5.

17 For an excellent discussion of Foss and Griffin's perspective, as well as of the debate over essentialism generally, see Nathan Stormer, "A Vexing Relationship: Gender and Contemporary Rhetorical Theory," in *The Sage Handbook of Gender and Communication*, ed. Dow and Wood, 247–262.

18 See, e.g., M. Lane Bruner, "Producing Identities: Gender Problematization and Feminist Argumentation," *Argumentation and Advocacy* 32 (1996): 185–198; Celeste M. Condit, "In Praise of Eloquent Diversity: Gender and Rhetoric as Public Persuasion," *Women's Studies in Communication* 20 (1997): 91–116; and Bonnie J. Dow, "Feminism, Difference(s), and Rhetorical Studies," *Communication Studies* 46 (1995): 106–117. For responses to critiques of invitational rhetoric, see Sonja K. Foss, Cindy L. Griffin, and Karen A. Foss, "Transforming Rhetoric through Feminist Reconstruction: A Response to the Gender Diversity Perspective," *Women's Studies in Communication* 20 (1997): 117–135; and Jennifer Emerling Bone, Cindy L. Griffin, and T. M. Linda Scholz, "Beyond Traditional Conceptualizations of Rhetoric: Invitational Rhetoric and a Move Toward Civility," *Western Journal of Communication* 72 (2008): 434–462.

19 See, e.g., Bonnie J. Dow and Mari Boor Tonn, "Feminine Style and Political Judgment in the Rhetoric of Ann Richards," *Quarterly Journal of Speech* 79 (1993): 286–303; Sara Hayden, "Re-Claiming Bodies of Knowledge: An Exploration of the Relationship Between Feminist Theorizing and Feminine Style in the Rhetoric of the Boston Women's Health Group Collective," *Western Journal of Communication* 61 (1997): 161–173; Sara Hayden, "Negotiating Femininity and Power in the Early Twentieth-Century West: Domestic Ideology and Feminine Style in Jeannette Rankin's Suffrage Rhetoric," *Communication Studies* 50 (1999): 83–102; and Shawn J. Parry-Giles and Trevor Parry-Giles, "Collective Memory, Political Nostalgia, and the Rhetorical Presidency: Bill Clinton's Commemoration of the March on Washington, August 28, 1998," *Quarterly Journal of Speech* 86 (2000): 417–437.

20 Campbell, "Consciousness-Raising," 54. From my recent experience, the public address anthology that is most available and widely used in undergraduate courses is Ronald F. Reid and James F. Klumpp, *American Rhetorical Discourse*, 3rd ed. (Prospect Heights, IL: Waveland Press, 2005). Reid and Klumpp represent women's early public address (before 1920) with complete oratorical texts by Elizabeth Cady Stanton and Sojourner Truth as well as excerpts from the discourse of Susan B. Anthony and Carrie Chapman Catt. They also include the 1848 Declaration of Sentiments from the Seneca Falls Woman's Rights Convention and Sarah and Angelina Grimké's response to the 1837 Pastoral Letter against women speaking in public.

21 For recent examples, see Patricia Bizzell, "Frances Willard, Phoebe Palmer, and the Ethos of the Methodist Woman Preacher," *Rhetoric Society Quarterly* 36 (2006): 377–398; Sara Hayden, "Reversing the Discourse of Sexology: Margaret Higgins Sanger's 'What Every Girl Should Know,'" *Southern Communication Journal* 64 (1999): 288–306; Lisa S. Hogan and J. Michael Hogan, "Feminine Virtue and Practical Wisdom: Elizabeth Cady Stanton's 'Our Boys,'" *Rhetoric & Public Affairs* 6 (2003): 415–436; Susan S. Huxman, "Perfecting the Rhetorical Vision of Woman's Rights: Elizabeth Cady Stanton, Anna Howard Shaw, and Carrie Chapman Catt," *Women's Studies in Communication* 23 (2000): 307–336; Kristy Maddux, "When Patriots Protest: The Anti-Suffrage Discursive Transformation of 1917," *Rhetoric & Public Affairs* 7 (2004): 283–310; Angela G. Ray, "What Hath She Wrought? Woman's Rights and the Nineteenth-Century Lyceum," *Rhetoric & Public Affairs* 9 (2006): 183–213; Amy R. Slagell, "The Rhetorical Structure of Frances W. Willard's Campaign for Woman Suffrage, 1876–1896," *Rhetoric & Public Affairs* 4 (2001): 1–23; and Martha Solomon Watson, "Mary Church Terrell vs. Thomas Nelson Page: Gender, Race, and Class in Anti-Lynching Rhetoric," *Rhetoric & Public Affairs* 4 (2009): 65–89. For

examples of recent books, see Jacqueline Bacon, *The Humblest May Stand Forth: Rhetoric, Empowerment, and Abolition* (Columbia: University of South Carolina Press, 2002); Nan Johnson, *Gender and Rhetorical Space in American Life, 1866–1910* (Carbondale: Southern Illinois University Press, 2002); Carol Mattingly, *Appropriate[ing] Dress: Women's Rhetorical Style in Nineteenth-Century America* (Carbondale and Edwardsville: Southern Illinois University Press, 2002); and Jacqueline J. Royster, *Traces of a Stream: Literacy and Social Change Among African American Women* (Pittsburgh, PA: University of Pittsburgh Press, 2000). As these examples indicate, the work within the recovery project has been overwhelmingly Americanist, a characteristic that feminist public address scholarship shares with public address scholarship generally. A small amount of scholarship has focused on the discourse and activities of British suffragists. See, for example, Cheryl R. Jorgensen-Earp, *The Transfiguring Sword: The Just War of the Women's Social and Political Union* (Tuscaloosa: University of Alabama Press, 1997); and Donna M. Kowal, "One Cause, Two Paths: Militant vs. Adjustive Strategies in the British and American Women's Suffrage Movements," *Communication Quarterly* 48 (2000): 240–255. For a very rare example of work on Asian women's public discourse, see Shinobu Suzuki, "Hiratsuka's 'Editor's Introduction to the First Issue of Seito': Where 'Feminine Style' Intersects High-Context Communication," *Women's Studies in Communication* 23 (2000): 182–208.

22　The liberal and radical branches of the second wave were the most visible and influential (and have received the most attention in public address scholarship), but, at different points, the movement included Marxist, socialist, and cultural feminist factions as well. For a useful primer on varieties of second-wave feminism, see Josephine Donovan, *Feminist Theory: The Intellectual Traditions of American Feminism*, 3rd ed. (New York: Continuum, 2000).

23　Karlyn Kohrs Campbell, "The Rhetoric of Women's Liberation: An Oxymoron," *Quarterly Journal of Speech* 59 (1973): 74–86.

24　Campbell, "Consciousness-Raising," 45.

25　See, e.g., Celeste Condit [Railsback], "The Contemporary American Abortion Controversy: Stages in the Argument," *Quarterly Journal of Speech* 70 (1984): 410–424; Sonja K. Foss, "Equal Rights Amendment Controversy: Two Worlds in Conflict," *Quarterly Journal of Speech* 65 (1979): 275–288; Brenda Robinson Hancock, "Affirmation as Negation in the Women's Liberation Movement," *Quarterly Journal of Speech* 58 (1972): 264–272; Diane Hope Schaich, "Redefinition of Self: A Comparison of the Rhetoric of the Women's Liberation and Black Liberation Movements," *Today's Speech* 23 (1975): 17–25; and Martha Solomon, "The 'Positive Woman's' Journey: A Mythic Analysis of the Rhetoric of STOP ERA," *Quarterly Journal of Speech* 65 (1979): 262–274.

26　Bonnie J. Dow, "Reading the Second Wave," *Quarterly Journal of Speech* 91 (2005): 89–107.

27　See, for example, Wendy Atkins-Sayre, "The Emergence of 'Ms.' as a Liberatory Title," *Women & Language* 28 (2005): 8–16; Bonnie J. Dow, "Feminism, Miss America, and Media Mythology," *Rhetoric & Public Affairs* 6 (2003): 127–160; Bonnie J. Dow, "Fixing Feminism: Women's Liberation and the Rhetoric of Television Documentary," *Quarterly Journal of Speech* 90 (2004): 55–80; Bonnie J. Dow, "Spectacle, Spectatorship, and Gender Anxiety in Television News Coverage of the 1970 Women's Strike for Equality," *Communication Studies* 50 (1999): 143–157; Tasha N. Dubriwny, "Consciousness-Raising as Collective Rhetoric: The Articulation of Experience in the Redstockings Abortion Speak-Out of 1969," *Quarterly Journal of Speech* 91 (2005): 395–422; Charles Kimber Pearce, "The Radical Feminist Manifesto as Generic Appropriation: Gender, Genre, and Second Wave Resistance," *Southern Communication Journal* 64 (1999): 307–315; Kyra Pearson, "Mapping Rhetorical Interventions in 'National' Feminist Histories: Second Wave Feminism and Ain't I a Woman," *Communication Studies* 50 (1999): 158–173; Sally Perkins, "The Rhetoric of Androgyny as Revealed in 'The Feminine Mystique,'" *Communication Studies* 40 (1989): 69–80; Kristan Poirot, "Mediating a Movement, Authorizing Discourse: Kate Millett, Sexual Politics, and Feminism's Second Wave," *Women's Studies in Communication* 27 (2004): 204–235; and Ashli Quesinberry Stokes, "Constituting Southern Feminists: Women's Liberation Newsletters in the South," *Southern Communication Journal* 70 (2005): 91–108.

28   Karrin Vasby Anderson and Jessie Stewart, "Politics and the Single Woman: The 'Sex and the City Voter' in Campaign 2004," *Rhetoric & Public Affairs* 8 (2005): 595–616; Natalie Fixmer and Julia T. Wood, "The Personal is *Still* Political: Embodied Politics in Third Wave Feminism," *Women's Studies in Communication* 28 (2005): 235–257; Lisa Maria Hogeland, "Against Generational Thinking, or, Some Things that 'Third Wave' Feminism Isn't," *Women's Studies in Communication* 24 (2001): 107–121; Valerie R. Renegar and Stacey K. Sowards, "Liberal Irony, Rhetoric, and Feminist Thought: A Unifying Third Wave Philosophy," *Philosophy & Rhetoric* 36 (2003): 330–352; and Stacey K. Sowards and Valerie R. Renegar, "The Rhetorical Functions of Consciousness Raising in Third Wave Feminism," *Communication Studies* 55 (2004): 535–552.

29   Barbara Biesecker, "Coming to Terms with Recent Attempts to Write Women into the History of Rhetoric," *Philosophy & Rhetoric* 25 (1992): 142.

30   Biesecker, "Coming to Terms," 144.

31   Biesecker, "Coming to Terms," 148.

32   Karlyn Kohrs Campbell, "Biesecker Cannot Speak for Her Either," *Philosophy & Rhetoric* 26 (1993): 153–159.

33   Ryan, "Recasting Recovery," 32. Examples of anthologies that offer this mediated perspective, according to Ryan, include: Lunsford, *Reclaiming Rhetorica*; Ritchie and Ronald, *Available Means*; and Wertheimer, *Listening to Their Voices*. Ryan's happy narrative about the blending of recovery and gender critique would probably please Campbell more than Biesecker. Indeed, in a 2002 essay, Campbell maintained that "the most productive theorizing seems to be grounded in the discursive practices of specific women," a perspective that fits well with Ryan's conclusions. See Campbell, "Consciousness-Raising," 59. Ryan seems to interpret Biesecker's 1992 essay as a generalized call for theorizing for the purpose of interrogating rhetorical traditions rather than taking seriously the ways in which Biesecker's use of poststructuralism, as expressed in her 1992 essay, makes her perspective incommensurate with the kind of recovery-based theorizing that Ryan identifies.

34   See E. Michele Ramsey, "Addressing Issues of Context in Historical Women's Public Address," *Women's Studies in Communication* 27 (2004): 252–276, for a comprehensive discussion of the problems of agent-centered public address criticism and the possibilities of employing broader notions of context in feminist public address scholarship.

35   See, e.g., Judith Butler, *Gender Trouble: Feminism and the Subversion of Identity* (New York: Routledge, 1990); Judith Butler, *Bodies that Matter: On the Discursive Limits of "Sex"* (New York: Routledge, 1993). For early discussions of the uses of Butler's work for feminist rhetorical studies, see, e.g., Bruner, "Producing Identities," and Condit, "In Praise of Eloquent Diversity."

36 Susan Zaeske, *Signatures of Citizenship: Petitioning, Antislavery, and Women's Political Identity* (Chapel Hill: University of North Carolina Press, 2003), 2, 4, 66.

37 For a useful discussion of the ways that attention to "intersections of race and gender illuminate, challenge, and expand theoretical and critical approaches to discourse," see Jacqueline Bacon, "The Intersections of Race and Gender in Rhetorical Theory and Praxis," in *The Sage Handbook of Gender and Communication*, ed. Dow and Wood, 215–230.

38 Stormer, "A Vexing Relationship," 247.

39 For additional examples of criticism that emphasize the constitutive function of rhetoric around the topic of women's reform activities, see Roseanne Mandziuk and Suzanne Pullon Fitch, "The Rhetorical Construction of Sojourner Truth," *Southern Communication Journal* 66 (2001): 120–138; Maegan Parker, "Desiring Citizenship: A Rhetorical Analysis of the Wells/Willard Controversy," *Women's Studies in Communication* 31 (2008): 56–78; Angela G. Ray, "The Rhetorical Ritual of Citizenship: Women's Voting as Public Performance, 1868–1875," *Quarterly Journal of Speech* 93 (2007): 1–26; Angela G. Ray and Cindy Koenig Richards, "Inventing Citizens, Imagining Gender Justice: The Suffrage Rhetoric of Virginia and Francis Minor," *Quarterly Journal of Speech* 93 (2007): 375–402; and Belinda A. Stillion Southard, "Militancy, Power, and Identity: The Silent Sentinels as Women Fighting for Political Voice," *Rhetoric & Public Affairs* 10 (2007): 399–418.

40 See, e.g., Jennifer J. Borda, "The Woman Suffrage Parades of 1910–1913: Possibilities and Limitations of an Early Feminist Rhetorical Strategy," *Western Journal of Communication* 66 (2002): 25–52; Catherine H. Palczewski, "The Male Madonna and the Feminine Uncle Sam: Visual Arguments, Icons, and Ideographs in 1909 Anti-Woman Suffrage Postcards," *Quarterly Journal of Speech* 91 (2005): 365–394; E. Michele Ramsey, "Inventing Citizens during World War I: Suffrage Cartoons in *The Woman Citizen*," *Western Journal of Communication* 64 (2002): 113–147; and E. Michele Ramsey, "Driven from the Public Sphere: The Conflation of Women's Liberation and Driving in Advertising from 1910–1920," *Women's Studies in Communication* 29 (2006): 88–112.

41 For example, in recent work noteworthy for its attention to the role of gender in presidential discourse, gender still means women. In a 2002 essay, Vanessa Beasley examines three US presidents' rhetoric about woman suffrage before 1920 in order to delineate their visions of women's civic identity. See Vanessa B. Beasley, "Engendering Democratic Change: How Three US Presidents Discussed Female Suffrage," *Rhetoric & Public Affairs* 5 (2002): 79–103. In a chapter of her book, *You, the People: American National Identity in Presidential Rhetoric* (College Station: Texas A&M University Press, 2004), she focuses on a larger swath of presidential discourse to discuss the "ways that presidential discussions of American national identity might have changed as women's political roles and behaviors changed from 1885 through 2000" (122). This chapter, although titled "Gender and Presidents' Rhetoric of Shared Beliefs," largely equates gender with women, although it does note, at points, the ways that presidents "imagined the idealized American citizen to be male" (130).

42 James Jasinski's analysis of Henry Highland Garnet's "Address to the Slaves" is an exception to the general inattention to the role of masculinity in historical public address scholarship. Jasinski analyzes Garnet's steering of a middle course between feminized notions of the child-like "suffering slave" and hyper-masculine notions of the slave as an "uncontrollable savage brute." Importantly, however, Jasinski does not address the ways in which Garnet neglects the subject position of the female slave, nor

does he discuss the implications of the equation of submission and childishness with femininity. See James Jasinski, "Constituting Antebellum African American Identity: Resistance, Violence, and Masculinity in Henry Highland Garnet's (1843) 'Address to the Slaves,'" *Quarterly Journal of Speech* 93 (2007): 27–57. Other work that has addressed masculinity in relation to presidential rhetoric (although not from a feminist perspective) includes Leroy G. Dorsey, *We Are All Americans, Pure and Simple: Theodore Roosevelt and the Myth of Americanism* (Tuscaloosa: University of Alabama, 2007); Davis W. Houck, "Reading the Body in the Text: FDR's 1932 Speech to the Democratic National Convention," *Southern Communication Journal* 63 (1997): 20–36; and John M. Murphy, "The Heroic Tradition in Presidential Rhetoric," *Rhetoric & Public Affairs* 3 (2000): 466–470. Although they study a fictional text rather than presidential rhetoric per se, Trevor Parry-Giles's and Shawn Parry-Giles's book *The Prime-Time Presidency: The West Wing and US Nationalism* (Urbana: University of Illinois Press, 2006) comes closest to a feminist analysis of the strong links between masculinity and presidential power.

43   Butler, *Gender Trouble*, 13.

44   This conclusion does not hold true for scholars of classical rhetoric, whose treatment of masculinity's relationship to rhetorical theory and practice has been much more thorough than that of public address scholars. For a useful discussion of this work, see Cheryl Glenn and Rosalyn Collings Eves, "Rhetoric and Gender in Greco-Roman Theorizing," in *The Sage Handbook of Gender and Communication*, ed. Dow and Wood, 231–245.

45   Karlyn Kohrs Campbell, "The Rhetorical Presidency: A Two Person Career," in *Beyond the Rhetorical Presidency*, ed. Martin J. Medhurst (College Station: Texas A&M University Press, 1996), 180.

46   Karrin Vasby Anderson, "Hillary Rodham Clinton as 'Madonna': The Role of Metaphor and Oxymoron in Image Restoration," *Women's Studies in Communication* 25 (2002): 1–24; Diane M. Blair, "'No Ordinary Time': Eleanor Roosevelt's Address to the 1940 Democratic National Convention," *Rhetoric & Public Affairs* 4 (2001): 203–222; Tasha N. Dubriwny, "First Ladies and Feminism: Laura Bush as Advocate for Women's and Children's Rights," *Women's Studies in Communication* 28 (2005): 84–114; and Molly Meijer Wertheimer, ed., *Inventing a Voice: The Rhetoric of American First Ladies of the Twentieth Century* (Lanham, MD: Rowman & Littlefield, 2004).

47   Shawn J. Parry-Giles and Diane M. Blair, "The Rise of the Rhetorical First Lady: Politics, Gender Ideology, and Women's Voice, 1789–2002," *Rhetoric & Public Affairs* 5 (2002): 567.

48   Karrin Vasby Anderson, "A Site of 'American Womanhood,'" in *Inventing a Voice*, ed. Wertheimer, 18. For other examples of this strain of scholarship, see Karrin Vasby Anderson, "'Rhymes with Rich': 'Bitch' as a Tool of Containment in Contemporary American Politics," *Rhetoric & Public Affairs* 2 (1999): 599–623; Kristy Maddux, "Feminism and Foreign Policy: Public Vocabularies and the Conditions of Emergence for First Lady Rosalynn Carter," *Women's Studies in Communication* 31 (2008): 29–55; and Shawn J. Parry-Giles, "Mediating Hillary Rodham Clinton: Television News Practices and Image-Making in the Postmodern Age," *Critical Studies in Media Communication* 17 (2000): 205–226.

49   Karlyn Kohrs Campbell, "The Discursive Performance of Femininity: Hating Hillary," *Rhetoric & Public Affairs* 1 (1998): 15.

50 Anna Cornelia Fahey, "French and Feminine: Hegemonic Masculinity and the Emasculation of John Kerry in the 2004 Presidential Race," *Critical Studies in Media Communication* 24 (2007): 132–50. See also Shawn J. Parry-Giles and Trevor Parry-Giles, "Gendered Politics and Presidential Image Construction: A Reassessment of the 'Feminine Style,'" *Communication Monographs* 63 (1996): 337–353. Importantly, these studies examine contemporary presidential politics, thus the general point that feminist scholars tend not to study masculinity in historical public address texts remains.

51 Karrin Vasby Anderson, "From Spouses to Candidates: Hillary Rodham Clinton, Elizabeth Dole, and the Gendered Office of the US President," *Rhetoric & Public Affairs* 5 (2002): 106.

52 Anderson, "From Spouses to Candidates," 126.

53 Rhetorical scholars have a bias toward the national rather than the regional, and the relative paucity of work on women candidates for offices other than the presidency reflects it. For a review of recent scholarship treating women's strategies as political candidates at various levels, see Vanessa B. Beasley, "Gender in Political Communication Research: The Problem with Having No Name," in *The Sage Handbook of Gender and Communication*, ed. and Wood, 201–214.

54 See, e.g., Jennifer Young Abbott, "The Positive Functions of 'Negative' Rhetoric: Feminists' Expository Campaign Against the Promise Keepers," *Women's Studies in Communication* 30 (2007): 1–33; Celeste M. Condit, *Decoding Abortion Rhetoric: Communicating Social Change* (Urbana: University of Illinois Press, 1990); Mary M. Lay, "Midwifery on Trial: Balancing Privacy Rights and Health Concerns after *Roe v. Wade*," *Quarterly Journal of Speech* 89 (2003): 60–78; Phaedra C. Pezzullo, "Resisting 'National Breast Cancer Awareness Month': The Rhetoric of Counterpublics and their Cultural Performances," *Quarterly Journal of Speech* 89 (2003): 345–365; Caroline Joan (Kay) Picart, "Rhetorically Reconfiguring Victimhood and Agency: The Violence Against Women Act's Civil Rights Clause," *Rhetoric & Public Affairs* 6 (2003): 97–125; Kristina Schriver, "Rhetorical Pathologies and Gender Difference: An Ideological Examination of Cultural Discourse in *Faulkner v. The Citadel*," *Women's Studies in Communication* 26 (2003): 27–59; Gordon Stables, "Justifying Kosovo: Representations of Gendered Violence and US Military Intervention," *Critical Studies in Media Communication* 20 (2003): 92–115; Patricia A. Sullivan and Lynn H. Turner, "The Zoe Baird Spectacle: Silences, Sins, and Status," *Western Journal of Communication* 63 (1999): 413–432; and Mary Douglas Vavrus, *Postfeminist News: Political Women in Media Culture* (Albany: State University of New York Press, 2002).

55 Shannon L. Holland, "The Dangers of Playing Dress-Up: Popular Representations of Jessica Lynch and the Controversy Regarding Women in Combat," *Quarterly Journal of Speech* 92 (2006): 28–29.

56 For examples of scholarship that examine photographs as a form of public address, see Cara A. Finnegan, *Picturing Poverty: Print Culture and FSA Photographs* (Washington, DC: Smithsonian Institution Press, 2003); and Robert Hariman and John Louis Lucaites, *No Caption Needed: Iconic Photographs, Public Culture, and Liberal Democracy* (Chicago: University of Chicago Press, 2007). For examples of feminist analysis of visual rhetoric, see Dana L. Cloud, "'To Veil the Threat of Terror': Afghan Women and the 'Clash of Civilizations' in the Imagery of the US War on Terrorism," *Quarterly Journal of Speech* 90 (2004): 285–306; Greg Dickinson and Karrin Vasby Anderson, "Fallen: O. J. Simpson, Hillary Rodham Clinton and the Re-Centering of White

Patriarchy," *Communication and Critical/Cultural Studies* 1 (2004): 271–296; and Marita Gronnvoll, "Gender (In)Visibility at Abu Ghraib," *Rhetoric & Public Affairs* 10 (2007): 371–398.

57 Gronnvoll, "Gender (In)Visibility at Abu Ghraib," 394, 377.

58 The CBS News footage from March 9, 11, and 13, 1970, that is used in this analysis was obtained from the Vanderbilt University Television News Archives in Nashville, Tennessee. All quotations from that footage in this chapter are taken from transcripts created by the author.

59 Patricia Bradley, *Mass Media and the Shaping of American Feminism, 1963–1975* (Jackson: University Press of Mississippi, 2003), 75.

60 Susan Douglas, *Where the Girls Are: Growing Up Female with the Mass Media* (New York: Random House, 1994), 188.

61 See Laura Mulvey, "Visual Pleasure and Narrative Cinema," in *Feminist Film Theory: A Reader*, ed. Sue Thornham (New York: New York University Press, 1999), 62–63. Mulvey explains, "In a world ordered by sexual imbalance, pleasure in looking has been split between active/male and passive/female. The determining male gaze projects its fantasy onto the female figure, which is styled accordingly. In their traditional exhibitionist role women are simultaneously looked at and displayed ... so that they can be said to connote *to-be-looked-at-ness*" (emphasis in original).

62 See, for example, Douglas, *Where the Girls Are*, and Dow, "Spectacle, Spectatorship, and Gender Anxiety."

63 Dow and Condit, "The State of the Art," 460.

15

The Problem of Race in Public Address Research
W. E. B. Du Bois and the Conflicted Aesthetics of Race

Eric King Watts

It is no longer ironic to say that the commonplaces for ideological research in public address have been constitutive of absences and voids. Traditional public address research has concerned the invention and performance of speech on some occasion of significance and for the appreciation of an audience. Scholars of public address have traditionally explored the ways in which the speaker treats the situation and the materials available to her to produce attitudinal and behavioral change in the audience, typically favorable to the speaker's cause. The speaker, the audience, the materials, the situation are each "objective" elements. And of course sitting here, discussing these "objective" elements from the point of view of early twenty-first-century public address research, we know that these elements are historical and cultural – that potent values are constituted and distributed through the mass circulation of "normal" and "ordinary" words and deeds.[1] Many readers might find this assertion somewhat common-sensible, and that is good; but I do not wish for the irony of this common sense to be forgotten. For much of its modern American history, research in public address has been invested in studying intended effects and, like the motives of "pure aesthetics," dedicated itself to assessing the formal relations among empirically observable elements. These assessments, separated from social and ethical spheres of life, were misconstrued as de facto nonideological; in this context, the ethos of public address scholarship was seen as, ironically, both political and "natural" – the product of the universally reasoning subject.[2]

This narrative is now well known. Martin J. Medhurst, in *Landmark Essays on American Public Address*, has become one of the field's principal storytellers concerning the mythologies of tradition.[3] One of the quasi-myths that Medhurst dispels centered on the role that Edwin Black's influential work, *Rhetorical Criticism: A Study in Method*, played in loosening the neo-Aristotelian hold on the critical practices in public address scholarship. Widely considered as the work that announced the need for critical and ethical inquiry in public address research, Black's monograph, published in 1965, dissected the limitations of immediate effects-based judgments rendered through a narrow conception of reason and deliberation. Medhurst, however, calls attention to an intellectual milieu dating to 1955, when scholars like Thomas R. Nilsen and Albert J. Croft advocated that public address research ought to underscore the ethical and social work performed by public discourse. Moreover, Medhurst points out that the decade preceding Black's book laid the foundation for public address inquiry into the various ways in which ideas are historical and sociological (rather than metaphysical) and are appro- priated and reinterpreted for specific audiences.[4] As a doctoral student at Northwestern University learning about how some facets of the public address tradition discouraged inquiry into the ethics of public speech, I was intrigued by the ruptures fostered by Nilsen, Croft, and Black. Yet it was a debate among public address scholars about the norms and abuses of presidential rhetoric that inspired in me a fuller "ideological turn."[5]

President Richard M. Nixon's address to the nation on November 3, 1969, pro- vided the occasion for multiple public address scholars to study and assess the speech using diverse critical protocols. When Forbes Hill concludes his "traditional approach" to evaluating Nixon's speech on the Vietnam War by chastising Karlyn Kohrs Campbell and Robert P. Newman for employing methodologies that vio- lated the basic assumptions of neo-Aristotelian criticism, he provokes a response from Campbell that changed how I conceived of researching race in public address scholarship.[6] Campbell's essay contends that Nixon was not telling the truth in his account of how the war began and that he relies upon a vision of a "mythical America" to warrant his Vietnamization scheme. The subsequent debate brought into sharp relief what sort of labor neo-Aristotelian methodology performed in the field of research in public address. It reduced the critic's tasks to that of taking inventory of techniques marshaled by the speaker to advance his or her aims; it deferred to the speaker's judgment of the proper goals of rhetorical practice; and it advocated a detachment from the political implications of the speaker's choices. It was precisely the kind of anti-intellectual practice later dismissed by Philip Wander,[7] who argues that, "To be political is to raise questions about what is hap- pening, to undertake an interrogation of sides and choices."[8] Campbell's analysis examines the side Nixon chose to support and the dubious manner in which he defended his choices. Moreover, she illuminates what ethical considerations were shadowed by Nixon's rhetoric: "*Non*mythical America supports totalitarian gov- ernments all over the world. *Non*mythical America is engaged in a war in South Vietnam in which it is systematically destroying the civilian population and the agricultural capability of the country it is ostensibly defending. *Non*mythical America practices a racism that makes a mockery of its mythic principles."[9]

As we look into our rearview mirrors, it is clear that Campbell's act of demysti- fication was constitutive of a new and keen interest in what speakers, previously ignored by neo-Aristotelians, were saying about nonmythical America.[10] Public address scholars were "going further" than raising questions about choices and sides; they were involved in "an effort to articulate voids – a speech void, a speaker void, and an audience void."[11] Because of civil disturbances occurring on college campuses and city streets from the 1950s through the early 1970s, spectacles of dissonance and protest were broadcast into living rooms and made to seem more real and urgent. Public address research was transformed in part by these turbulent political realities, which inspired studies of civil rights, Black Power, and other forms of rage that had always seethed beneath the surface of mythical America.

This burgeoning body of work on race relations in late twentieth-century America is what observers typically point to when discussing the role of race in public address research.[12] I will first review this scholarship and articulate its assumptions, critical strategies, and goals. It will become clear that although this work on civil rights, abolitionism, Black Power, and nationalism ushered in new ways to think about public address and public speaking, it left largely unexamined the basic character of "race" as a political/economic discursive formation and an unstable trope. There are two analytical tendencies responsible for a neglect of "race." First, due to contemporary political realities, black speech was considered an urgent phenomenon in need of assessment. This impulse drew our attention toward how black speakers sought to change social life and constitute black communal consciousness. Second, particular claims by black speakers were subjected to universalizing effects regarding "race." That is, anxious to study discourses calling for social change, scholars tended to understand "race" in terms of its most prominent signifier – "blackness" – and comprehend "race" as a unitary sign designating something universally shared among black people. Indeed, segregation and other forms of discrimination heightened these effects. Thus, even as black speech was foregrounded in public address scholarship, the complex and radically contingent operations that make (and unmake) "race" were backgrounded.

This chapter offers a case study of a speech delivered by W. E. B. Du Bois during a critical juncture of the Harlem Renaissance that demonstrates how the concept of voice may help public address scholars contend with the instabilities constitutive of the trope of "race." I conceive of voice as an endowment that occurs when a public acknowledges the ethical and affective dimensions of speech. I argue that voice is produced when speech provokes an aesthetic experience that makes the hearer attuned to ethical and affective investments of speech. Voice also draws us toward the particular historical and social moment of "racial" identification and the specific forms of affect that help bond and dissolve these identifications. Finally, I will conclude with a consideration of how new and sometimes conflicting conceptions of "race" might encourage fresh approaches in public address research.

Investigating Black Speech and Neglecting "Race"

In this section, I survey several significant works prompted in part by the imperative arising from social struggles and enlivened by a call for critical pluralism. I emphasize the idea that by framing black speech as constitutive of unique "racial" contexts, public address scholarship overlooked the general discursive operations formulating "race." Importantly, given the social and intellectual circumstances of much of this work, I find this predicament to be understandable and productive of some healthy scholarly habits. I intend, therefore, to construct an intellectual history warranting our recognition of "race" as a radically contingent trope with peculiarly impressive affective force. Such recognition presupposes the need for alterations in our approaches to public address research regarding "race."

With the cloistered effects of neo-Aristotelian criticism dissipating, public address scholarship about race relations underwent creative change. Between the years 1968 and 1972, several studies appeared that examined the rhetorical practices propelling people into the streets. Not surprisingly, these initial forays into the context of black speech needed to contend with the fluid structure of social movements, the psychological make-up of the passionate protester, and the often non-instrumental character of protest rhetoric itself. Parke G. Burgess, in "The Rhetoric of Black Power: A Moral Demand?," clarified the impulses behind the rhetoric of Black Power. Rather than limit themselves to appeals to "civil rights" or to the civic obligations of white America, activists like Stokely Carmichael leveled charges that white racism violated basic human rights.[13] Similarly, Robert L. Scott and Donald K. Smith, in "The Rhetoric of Confrontation," demonstrated that a focus on persuasive effects ignored the fact that Black Power advocates were also concerned with constituting the ethical authority to challenge the agents and systems of oppression.[14] Richard B. Gregg, in "The Ego-Function of the Rhetoric of Protest," was even more focused on the self-reflexive character of black public address, arguing that the "failure" of some speech acts to bring about material change masked the revolution underway concerning the black self.[15]

It is important for students of public address to recognize a point made by Aaron David Gresson III, in "Minority Epistemology and the Rhetoric of Creation." Gresson argues that dominant world-views make micro-shifts to account for the previously unaccounted for; hence, public address scholars could be expected to reweave black perspectives into existing ways of knowing.[16] A case in point is the "postscript" to *The Rhetoric of Black Power*, edited by Scott and Brockriede, where these researchers posited that Lloyd Bitzer's "Rhetorical Situation" was a reliable way of making sense of black public address since Bitzer's framework calls for a sincere appreciation of the specificity of speaking contexts. As such, the struggles for black liberation in the United States could be perceived as constituting racially "unique situations." My intention here is not to knock the efforts of Scott and Brockriede; indeed, their postscript is both insightful and humble, calling for a long-overdue assessment of black public speech and for rhetorical scholars to "criticize criticism."[17] Rather, we are obliged to recognize that this idea proposed that race relations and struggles, protests and movements, advances and regresses, could (and should) be articulated through terms like "exigency," "remedy," "constraint," "rhetorical audience," and "fitting response." In this web of terminology, "blackness" stood for controlling "racial" problems, dominating "racial" constraints, and/or as a chief "racial" element conditioning rhetorical responses. We are encouraged to pay attention to the "racial" character of audiences and speakers, to try to comprehend their attitudes about "race," and to sketch cultural histories about it. In this way, "race" in public address research was conceived in terms amenable to the Burkean ratio of "scene-agency,"[18] where a "racial" context determined assessments of problems, acts, and responses and presumed a "racial" function rather than illuminating one. Implicit in this presumption, which worked to ground black speech in distinct "situations," is the idea that "race" exists as an "objective" exigence. Despite efforts to debunk the "objectivity" myth in relation to rhetorical exigence, this conceptualization has had lasting effects on "race." This is so in part because of the positivism associated with the rhetorical situation. It is also because "race" has traditionally been treated as if it is empirical; conventional wisdom held that "race" could be seen and its "truths" unlocked "scientifically." There was an unintentional collusion, therefore, between the healthy and responsible desire to better appreciate black speech and include black speakers in public address inquiry and the flawed epistemologies of "race."[19] This development in research about "race" in public address was arguably a necessary one and ushered in diverse investigations into black public speech.

There are too many examples of this sort of work in recent years to mention here (although there are far too few in general); therefore, a sketch of the diversity of methods and goals will have to suffice. Treating "race" as a constraint, Trevor Parry-Giles studies the congressional confirmation debate on the nomination of Thurgood Marshall to the Supreme Court. For Parry-Giles, Marshall's racial identity tests the nation's ideological commitment to "civil rights" and shapes both the rhetoric of opposition and support.[20] In terms of a rhetorical audience, Todd McDorman views the Dred Scott case as an impetus for the "African American community to (re)assert their personhood." Here we see black agents mobilizing black collective agency.[21] Kirt H. Wilson turns his attention to how prudence as a discursive space was the object of contestation during the nineteenth-century civil rights debate. Of special import here is Wilson's inclusion of black congressional voices during an era that set the stage for the legitimation of the "separate but equal" doctrine.[22] Scholars not only perceive of public spaces as the site of struggle over meaning, they also examine how iconic terminologies structure oppositional readings. Celeste Michelle Condit and John Louis Lucaites, in *Crafting Equality: American's Anglo-African Word*, employ an ideographic analysis to illustrate that, for example, Martin Luther King, Jr. and Malcolm X were often not referring to the same idea when using the term "equality."[23] Similarly, Gary Selby explicates Frederick Douglass's use of parody to reveal to white abolitionists how the Bible, as a polysemous theological text, could be made to subvert the arguments for holding slaves.[24]

Even as public address scholarship diversifies its critical protocols for comprehending various acts of black public speaking, scholars also bring our attention back to the traditional heart of public address: the great orator. Karlyn Kohrs Campbell examines the rhetoric of "early feminists" specifying how the public address of black women helped shape the nineteenth-century suffrage movement. Focusing on Ida B. Wells in particular, Campbell highlights the manner in which Wells's anti-lynching rhetoric was sophisticated, argumentatively sound, and eschewed a feminine style for public speech.[25] Mark Lawrence McPhail investigates the rhetoric of controversial Nation of Islam leader Louis Farrakhan as an example of how putative counter-hegemonic discourse can be "complicit" in reifying dominant racial ideologies regarding difference, division, and hierarchy.[26] Characterizing him as chiefly an orator, Robert E. Terrill contextualizes the radical genius of Malcolm X within a fluid field of discourse through which he fabricated new forms of political judgment.[27] Victoria J. Gallagher examines a speech that Stokely Carmichael delivered at the University of California at Berkeley in 1966 as an instance in which a black orator encouraged a white audience to reflect upon the impact that "whiteness" has on the evolution of American racial consciousness.[28] And revisiting what has been judged the most significant speech of the twentieth century, Mark Vail seeks to explain the rhetorical power of Martin Luther King, Jr.'s "I Have a Dream" in terms of its resemblance to, and manipulation of, the "dynamic spectacle" that was the March on Washington.[29]

What I am disclosing in the above survey is the largely unrecognized fact that critical attention paid to a black speaker does not necessarily translate into a coherent conception of "race" in public address research. A recent encounter with a student further demonstrated the ways in which public address research on black orators can be misapprehended as analyses of "race." A young black male student of mine wished to do a study on how black speakers orchestrate "race" in public address and wished to study the rhetoric of Senator Barack Obama. He was very excited about this new "star" in national politics. After doing some searching, he brought to me an article by Robert C. Rowland and John M. Jones on Barack Obama's Keynote Address at the 2004 Democratic National Convention. But he was dismayed when I alerted him to the fact that this fine study was not an exploration of "race" per se; the work was more about the rhetorical transformation of a traditionally "conservative" narrative – the American Dream – into a liberal vision.[30] This eager young student perked up, however, when I pointed out that Obama's words and deeds (and his very body) are constitutive of certain "problems" of racial identity, and that the general omission of discourse about race in his speech can and has been discussed as another unfortunate "void," a displacement of important features of American racist ideology.[31] My point to him then – and my contention here now – is that research about "race" in public address can begin (again) in earnest; that an examination of a black speaker is not a sufficient engagement of the rhetoric of "race"; indeed, it never was, but our field was trying urgently to fill in the holes of critical inquiry about black public address and rightly turned to "protest" speech. Scholars also sought to display a synthetic appreciation for vocabularies not usually associated with public address. These two motives are largely responsible for the "void" I am addressing above.

The predicament of Barack Obama is peculiarly instructive regarding the issues that public address scholarship faces in terms of "race": He is a biracial person who is at once (perhaps too) "black" and not "black" (enough). He is the first president of the United States with a Kenyan father, yet he ran as the candidate of change who just "happens" to be a person of color. He is thus subject to being both raced and erased by what Paul Gilroy anxiously calls a discourse of "raciology."[32] He cannot (and does not want to) "escape" his "blackness," but he resists being reduced to it. He understands that "race" must be a resource for (not a prohibition to) the change he wants to bring, and yet "blackness" inevitably "colors" the change of which he speaks. He needed your vote, but not *because* of black pride; nor did he want a guilty ballot – one cast by a white voter who wished to "purify" her own soul by being self-consciously *for* a black man seeking the presidency. I suspect that Obama aspired to master the multiple positionalities that Michele Wallace claims for herself: the power of being at home both nowhere and everywhere.[33]

The fluidity and contingency of "racial" identification demand from public address scholarship creative protocols and alterations in some philosophical assumptions about the publicity of "race." The tight contest between Obama and Senator Hillary Rodham Clinton for the Democratic presidential nomination was marked by events instructive for us now. For example, after a fierce exchange during a debate sponsored by the Congressional Black Caucus, each camp pledged to "stick to the issues," as if the decisions that a president must make regarding the "issues" – the political/economic policies and institutional practices coordinated by specific interests and investments – were somehow "pure" judgments of reason. The notion that "race" (or gender, or class, or sexuality) could be, by mutual decree, set aside is constitutive of the philosophy that understands "race" as a concept that can be apprehended in its entirety external to "us." From this (wrong) perspective, we presume to know what "race" already means (indeed, that it *does* already mean something), that it always means the same thing (whatever that thing is), and that we can thus (in the same manner) remove it from our social calculus. This presumption is made possible by ignoring the manner in which "race" is reinterpreted by particular speakers as they draw upon the sensations and gratifications cultivated by experiences of "race" in their lives. It overlooks the idea that hermeneutic practices are historical, sociological, cultural, geographical, and anthropological. It simplifies the way auditors make sense of "race" conceptually, aesthetically, and differentially. It has historically confused "blackness" (or "otherness") with "race" and, thus, could not account for the ways in which all persons, communities, and nations can potentially be "raced." Worst of all, this presumption, which functions to stabilize "race" and dull our sensitivity to its metabolism, undermines our capacity to invent and perform antiracist public address.

To apprehend the advantages and pitfalls of a potentially "post-racial" speech context, public address research needs to extend the kind of work that Kirt H. Wilson performs in, for example, "The Racial Politics of Imitation in the Nineteenth Century." In that essay, Wilson argues that "imitation" is a humanistic characteristic with a complex Western philosophical history; imitation has been pitted against "originality" in ways that privilege white intellectualism and creativity, while defining black social action that necessarily has to appropriate Western ways of knowing as inferior due to its putative "imitation."[34] The pliability of languages of "race" is also on full display in A. Cheree Carlson's work about how vision is unreliable in determining one's racial identity, and how discourses of domination invent a calculated rhetoric to "fix" race into place.[35] A similar dialectical process is featured in

James Jasinski's essay, "Constituting Antebellum African American Identity: Resistance, Violence, and Masculinity in Henry Highland Garnet's 1843 'Address to the Slaves.'" Jasinski demonstrates how "race" is constitutive of discursive and affective relations among tropes of "manhood" and rebellion.[36] Michelle Hall Kells explicates the manner in which the inscription of "racial" subordination must be coordinated with discourses of American citizenship, labor rights, and geography. Her analysis of the rhetoric of Hector P. Garcia spells out the conditions in which "racial" mobility for migrant workers can be achieved and denied.[37] For my part, I too have thought about how dialectics like "black/not-black" and "white/not-white" participate in a network of tropes regarding "race."[38] In an essay entitled "African American Ethos and Hermeneutical Rhetoric," I argue that Alain Locke's essays in an influential anthology about Harlem's "New Negro" should be understood as pragmatic aesthetic practices geared toward refashioning "race" as a trope that sutures together African philosophies, American black folk "spirit," and modern black ingenuity.[39] What these diverse approaches share is the understanding that "race" is deployed in public address as one of many coordinates of discourse imbricated in social, cultural, and institutional habits and rituals. Involving more than the understanding of "race" as a socially constructed representation, these works, to varying degrees, treat the fluid articulations and uses of "race" as a matter of politics; they also suggest that we must uncouple "race" from its conventional associations – culture, nation, and family – so that new forms may emerge. There is, thus, a proliferation of lines of inquiry into "race," and these lines intersect and diverge.[40] Public address research into "race" does not merely reflect social change already happening; it should and does produce alterations in our sense of the significance of "race" in social life. I will now turn to the case study involving the oratory of W. E. B. Du Bois. My analysis will show how an increased sensitivity to competing and contradictory ethical imperatives and affective characteristics allow us to apprehend the specific manner in which "race" is subject to historically and socially contingent relations.

W. E. B. Du Bois's "Criteria of Negro Art"

In his autobiography, *The Big Sea*, Langston Hughes characterized the Harlem of the 1920s and 1930s as a time and a place where "the Negro was in vogue."[41] The Harlem Renaissance's importance as an era of black artistic creativity and political activity is well documented.[42] Scholars have both praised and faulted the "New Negro" Renaissance on differing grounds and for various reasons over the years. Of importance here is the recognition that a "new" racial confidence – championed in the 2007 film *The Great Debaters* – was a source of rhetorical invention; that proponents of the Harlem Renaissance deliberately spoke of the "movement" in terms of historical inevitability, obscuring the fact that it was "artifice imitating likelihood."[43] One of the chief causes of both the celebration and denigration of this "new" black art was the fact that New Negro writers and intellectuals, making a case in art for "race" rights, were challenged to conceive of aesthetic practices in a social context where they were pressured to produce "pure" art and "black" art. On the one hand, the constraints placed on writers came from late Victorian Romantic Modernism, which conceived of "beauty" as rising above social contexts and political activities like "civil rights." From this point of view, "low-class" black life was deemed as most "authentic" because such folk were "natural." On the other hand, black activists like James Weldon Johnson, Alain Locke, and Walter White desired aesthetic practices that were shaped under the weight of fighting race prejudice and would express the explicit beauty of blackness. When black art was perceived as doing the latter, like Jessie Fauset's novel *There is Confusion* (1924), it was often condemned as "propaganda." It did not take long for W. E. B. Du Bois to recognize the dilemma: If one tried to conform to the criteria for "pure" art, one was expected to transcend politics or to go slumming through tropes of wild, "savage," promiscuous "blackness." By denying discourse about the politics of aesthetics, "pure" art reified stereotypes and muted black intellectual voices about the manufacture and manipulation of "blackness."

There have been few African American thinkers, writers, and orators more concerned with this sort of rhetorical conundrum than W. E. B. Du Bois. As a cofounder of the National Association for the Advancement of Colored People (NAACP) and as editor of its journal, *The Crisis*, Du Bois worked tirelessly during the height of the New Negro Renaissance to put black art in the service of civil rights.[44] By 1926, Du Bois sensed that the dictates of "pure" art were having too much sway over black youth. After having stayed on the sidelines during a nine-month-long debate in *The Crisis* about the ethos of black art,[45] Du Bois delivered the "Criteria of Negro Art" during the Spingarn Medal Award night at the annual meeting of the NAACP in Chicago on June 29. For the remainder of this chapter, I explore this address as an attempt to constitute "race" as a form of mediation between "pure" art and "propaganda." First, Du Bois constituted distinct norms of African American aesthetic practice, affiliating them with the ethical capacity to name the civic good. Second, Du Bois argued that black culture made available alternative aesthetic understandings to American social knowledge. He also linked them to the capacity for an American polity to deliberate on social justice. Lastly, Du Bois critiqued specific aesthetic practices of the art world, exposing them as impediments to the public deliberation necessary for the constitution of the civic good. In sum, Du Bois reinvented a "race" that at once authorized black art as a form of public address, and posited it as an expression of "universal" ideals of democracy. This analysis helps to endow Du Bois's voice by acknowledging the ethical and affective dimensions of his speech. Voice is useful to public address studies of "race" because it encourages an assessment of the aural character of public address; it reminds us of the hating and loving relations often conditioning "racial" identifications; and it illustrates how these relations coordinate fearful and lustful communities. In addition, it emphasizes that the power and prestige of "race" must be appreciated in terms of its capacity to stimulate and translate these affects into ways of knowing and living.

Beauty, blackness, and the civic good: Why "turn aside to talk about Art"?

During *The Crisis* debate, the arguments about the proper role and character of black art were framed so as to make the whole affair seem like a dispute over literary license and decorum. Despite some irreconcilable differences, the question of race art remained principally a question of artistic judgment. To Du Bois, the distinction between aesthetics and ethics was not dissolved by the participants. As he rose to take the podium in June 1926, he immediately collapsed the Kantian dichotomy:

> I do not doubt but there are some in this audience who are a little disturbed at the subject of this meeting, and particularly at the subject I have chosen. Such people are thinking something like this: "How is it that an organization like this, a group of radicals trying to bring new things into the world, a fighting organization which has come up and out of the blood and dust of battle, struggling for the right of black men to be ordinary human beings – how is it that an organization of this kind can turn aside to talk about Art? After all, what have we who are slaves and black to do with Art?" Or perhaps there are others who feel a certain relief and are saying, "After all it is rather satisfactory after all this talk about rights and fighting to sit and dream of something which leaves a nice taste in the mouth." Let me tell you that neither of these groups is right.[46]

In this opening passage, Du Bois rehearsed his themes of racial exclusion, racial exploitation, and social justice. In a satirical tone, he mimicked the voices from both sides of the equation. On the one hand, "some in this audience" supposedly were anxious about his speech, thinking that the "blood and dust of battle" hurt "art" and, therefore, should be left to those persons better suited to its pursuit – those unencumbered by racial struggle. These members of the audience thought "art" should be shielded from the debilitating effects of polemics. They also suffered from a racist psychosis, asserting that "we who are slaves and black" cannot be artists, Du Bois implied, because they saw nothing (purely) beautiful about blackness. On the other hand, there were others who felt "a certain relief," happy to put the topic of civil rights aside and "sit and dream" of the pleasures of consuming exotic and racy blackness. Pure art and propaganda (race rhetoric) were alluded to here as serving the motives of people who promoted nonpolitical (pure) art and who believed that black protest corrupts art. Some folks thought that the NAACP denigrated art, while other folks believed that questions of aesthetic judgment marked a complete departure from the civil rights agenda. But, according to Du Bois, "neither of these groups" was right.

Having bluntly declared that these presumptions were false, Du Bois enfolded black art into "the great fight we are carrying on." Moreover, he invested both the art and the civil rights struggle with a progressive spirit captured in a visual arc. Du Bois argued: "You and I have been breasting hills; we have been climbing upward; there has been progress and we can see it day by day looking back along blood-filled paths."[47] Du Bois sought here to make initial rhetorical use of the taken-for-granted notion of the perfectibility of society so ingrained in progressivism.[48] Accordingly, he argued: "But when gradually the vista widens and you begin to see the world at your feet and the far horizon, then it is time to know more precisely whither you are going and what you really want. What do we want?"[49]

This question created a void in the text, robbing progressivism of its idealistic energies and opening up presumptions of American virtue to critical reflection. This contemplative pause compelled Du Bois's audience to consider another's perspective. "What is the thing we are after?" he asked. "Do we want simply to be Americans?"[50] For Du Bois the answer was no. To be simply an "American" would represent a retreat from the sort of critical reflection he sought to enact. To Du Bois, the typical American suffered from a sort of pathology brought on by an infatuation with the "tawdry and flamboyant," an utterly materialistic craving that "maddens humanity."[51] But if Americans were spiritually corrupted, black folk, "pushed aside as we have been in America,"[52] had the capacity to make available a kind of cure to American society. At this point, at least two questions logically arose. First, what did social illness have to do with beauty? Second, what properties did black art possess that qualified it as remedial?

In this speech, Du Bois's answer to the first question was oblique. In general, Du Bois believed that Western forms of modernity were nonaesthetic. The affiliation of oppression with ugliness, however, probably dates back, as Arnold Rampersad speculates, to Du Bois's Calvinist upbringing. As a social theology, Calvinism pits the hideousness of sin against the beauty of the civic good.[53] In this context, the presence of injustice signifies the negation of beauty. In the speech, Du Bois argued that persons living in this "civilized" world, due to widespread oppression, had "their lives distorted and made ugly."[54] Ugliness and beauty were thus antithetical aesthetic judgments necessary for the quality of civic life.

Questions still remained, however, about the capacity for black art to make the world beautiful. "Who shall restore to men the glory of sunsets and the peace of quiet sleep," Du Bois asked. In the speech, Du Bois invoked the spirit of the "New Negro" to answer the question. He asserted: "We black folk may help for we have within us as a race new stirrings ... of the beginning of a new appreciation of joy, of a new desire to create, of a new will to be."[55] Black folk could help to make the world beautiful because the "New Negro" was progressive and sought in art "universal truth." But the "truth" of civic beauty was not disclosed through transcendence; rather, it was disclosed in aesthetic practices and artifacts. In many essays of this period, Du Bois referenced as beautiful and virtuous some distinct African American cultural norms. For example, in "The Essence of African Culture," Du Bois complimented the African village system for offering a sociological balm for the irritation associated with the mechanization of modern cities. He also argued that African children were nurtured as self-conscious citizens with a healthy "reverence for authority."[56] A primitivist desire for black culture was predicated on white psychological trauma.[57] In "Criteria," however, this trauma was transfigured into an ethical predicament. Thus, the racial difference of black folk culture did more than soothe the angst of white folk over self-alienation in an industrializing world; its distinctiveness also offered a "new [social] determination for all mankind."[58]

To this point, Du Bois had portrayed American society as "ugly" due not only to racial prejudice, but also to the nonaesthetic practices of "civilization." The forms of social order to which Du Bois alluded satisfied the needs of a privileged few; however, the "mass of human beings" were being "choked away" from beauty. Du Bois asked: "Who shall right this well-nigh universal failing?"[59] The answer to this question was fairly clear by now. If beauty was negated by injustice, then racial oppression negated the beauty of blackness in particular. But it wasn't just black folk who suffered. The negation of a black critical voice brought on by the transcendence of "race" or the "naturalization" of it within "pure art" signaled a "universal failing." It was at once a failure of a "universal" construct and a failure felt by all Americans. The capacity for America to imagine the civic good was "distorted and made ugly." Thus, the coherence and the performance of a distinct African American aesthetic in public venues became essential requirements for the reinvention of the (beautiful) civic good.

Yet Du Bois forestalled an idealistic closure that presumed all speakers had an equal opportunity to name the beautiful. What chance did a black speaker really have to speak the civic good? In the address, Du Bois put the query this way: "After all, *who* shall describe Beauty?"[60] If he didn't know it beforehand, Du Bois learned in this decade that it was futile to affirm the civic good in principle if one lacked the authority to enact it in practice. For black intellectuals, the problem of public speaking was compounded by the history of Western aesthetics privileging the cult of observation – the "truth" values associated with "proper" sight, perspective, or judgment. In the next section of this analysis, I examine Du Bois's rearticulation of these requirements for seeing (and speaking) the civic good.

"We who are dark can see"

Du Bois suspended the trajectory of American perfection with the question, "What do we want?"

> Do we want simply to be Americans? Once in a while through all of us there flashes some clairvoyance, some clear idea, of what America really is. We who are *dark can see* America in a way that white Americans can not [*sic*]. And seeing our country thus, are we satisfied with its present goals and ideals?[61]

In this part of the speech, Du Bois appropriated the authority of aesthetic vision and used it to sanction an African American perspective on the civic good. Traditionally, the value of distant surveillance has rested upon the presumption of a unilateral epistemological link between knower and known; the knower sees the known and speaks its "truths." Du Bois performed a narrative about history and culture that troubled the presumption that current aesthetic judgments of "truth" were universally correct. He created a transformative space where the judgments about the worth of blackness could be reenvisioned. Du Bois's rhetorical strategy was constitutive of a public dialogue that had intensified during the New Negro movement regarding the significance and value of a black perspective on social life. Such a strategy featured two complementary facets – dark and light. The virtual absence of African American voices in American public address strengthened the notion that there was no black thought of public value. Metaphorically, light connotes sight and spoken "truth," while darkness signifies their absences.[62] It is this taken-for-granted relation that Du Bois reconstituted so that "dark can see" and light (whiteness) must listen. Indeed, this rhetorical strategy contained both antiracist and anti-elitist dimensions. Inverting the truth-values associated with light and dark, Du Bois recognized how Platonic idealism affected thinking about "race." The enlightenment, embodied by the guardians of the cave in Plato's famous allegory, was depicted as a form of aesthetic understanding maintained by domination.[63]

Du Bois also argued that art is constitutive of life's ethical dilemmas. I have already discussed how Du Bois conceived of beauty as a value associated with the quality of social life. The myth of "pure art," however, was also maintained by a refusal to recognize the relationship between literature and the worldly contexts that gave rise to it. Thus, Du Bois had to address the character of the service beauty performed for social justice and knowledge:

> What has Beauty to do with the world? What has Beauty to do with Truth and Goodness – with the facts of the world and the right actions of men? "Nothing," the artists rush to answer. They may be right. I am but an [*sic*] humble disciple of art and cannot presume to say. I am one who tells the truth and exposes evil and seeks with Beauty and for Beauty to set the world right. That somehow, somewhere eternal and perfect Beauty sits above Truth and Right I can conceive, but here and now and in the world in which I work they are for me *unseparated and inseparable.*[64]

This passage is strongly reminiscent of Plato's resistance to any notion of artistic autonomy. Du Bois appropriated this philosophical legacy in his argument against pure art. Both Plato and Du Bois subjected art to ethical critique, but for slightly different reasons. Plato was concerned with how the poetic corrupted Reason through a powerful evocation of aesthetic pleasure. Artistic vision, then, was both dangerous and inferior to philosophical insight and needed to be controlled by intellectual or political elites.[65] Du Bois's own perspective on art was no less ambivalent. He shared Plato's desire to bring the poetic into the ethical and social world. But Plato prized above all the status of the transcendent even as he recognized his sinful love of art. Du Bois, on the other hand, worked to invent "race" in sociological and cultural terms and understood that the poetic could effectively do this work for precisely the reasons that Plato disparaged. As we shall see shortly, Du Bois was skeptical of Platonic idealism and exerted great energy explicating the political economics of aesthetic judgment.

At this point in his speech, however, the intimacy between art and life allowed Du Bois to introduce black history into art. The reason that beauty has everything to do with the "facts of the world" was clarified when Du Bois associated literary material with history. Black folk, said Du Bois, had been compelled by aesthetic judgments of white supremacy to forget Africa and black history:

> We thought nothing could come out of that past which we wanted to remember; which we wanted to hand down to our children. Suddenly, this same past is taking on form. ... We are remembering that the romance of the world did not die and lie forgotten in the Middle Age; that if you want romance to deal with you must have it *here and now and in your own hands*.[66]

Du Bois proposed that the aesthetic experiences of one's life supply the content for aesthetic practices like literature. But, the experiences of black folks' lives were dimly perceived because of the racist presumptions of white folk. The confidence that whites had in the power of their own observations helped corrupt their aesthetic vision of black life. By recounting specific episodes of racial injustice and racial heroism, Du Bois destabilized the confidence of the white observer and dramatized the rational infusion of art and life. Consider Du Bois's sad tale of the consequences of racial passing:

> I once knew a man and woman. They had two children, a daughter who was white and a daughter who was brown; the daughter who was white married a white man; and when her wedding was preparing the daughter who was brown prepared to go and celebrate. But the mother said "No" and the brown daughter went into her room and turned on the gas and died. Do you want Greek tragedy swifter than that?[67]

Here Du Bois posited for public deliberation the material tragedy of black experience, misperceived and misunderstood by white observers. Du Bois also informed his audience of previously negated historical dramas, like that of the 40,000 black men who "fought and won and lost German East Africa" in World War I.[68] Du Bois retrieved the particularity of black living from within the transcendent action of "pure art." He articulated its negation as an ethical concern within a deliberative forum to arouse a genuine rhetorical audience. To Du Bois, the problem with the "souls of white folk" was constitutive of the very same social relation that cultivated black folk "clairvoyance." The irresistibility of white authority moves us "more and more, day by day, to making the statement 'I am white,' the one fundamental tenet of our practical morality," Du Bois asserted.[69] The tendency for white intellectuals to presume to know – and thus claim to speak – the "truth" about black folk aggravated Du Bois for many years, prompting him to demand a more sensitive ear. In *Dusk of Dawn*, Du Bois articulated the surest path to the resuscitation of genuine public dialogue: "It will not be easy to accomplish all this, but the quickest way to bring the reason of the world face to face with this major problem of human progress is to listen to the complaint of those human beings today who are suffering most."[70]

Thus, "Criteria" embodied Du Bois's continuing efforts to get white folk to recognize and to hear a black public voice. Du Bois sought to establish as presumptive the need for "authentic" and diverse cultural expression in American public address. Du Bois's authority to say so was itself derived from his rhetorical performance. "Who shall describe Beauty?" Du Bois's answer was African Americans like himself:

> I remember tonight four beautiful things: The Cathedral at Cologne, a forest in stone, set in light and changing shadow, echoing with sunlight and solemn song; a village of the Veys in West Africa, a little thing of mauve and purple, quiet, lying content and shining in the sun; a black and velvet room where on a throne rests, in old and yellowing marble, the broken curves of the Venus of Milo; a single phrase of music in the Southern South – utter melody, haunting and appealing, suddenly arising out of night and eternity, beneath the moon.[71]

The montage of sights and sounds making up Du Bois's "four beautiful things" captured Plato's sense of the panoply of universal values that compose the transcendent realm. Scholars have made much of Du Bois's own expressive transcendence of the material world;[72] perhaps Du Bois's vision was an appellation of universal beauty. If so, it also deformed modern notions of universal beauty by invoking African and black folk culture as requisite elements. This reading also returns us to classical teachings, since Plato held that ideal forms necessarily took on varying shapes in the historical world.[73] But what is most important in this speech is not Du Bois's gesture toward the heavens. Rather, it is his examination of the kinds of political, cultural, and psychological work that "pure art" performed in "normal life."[74]

Du Bois "remembers tonight" not objects or places in the past; instead, he recalled a perspective on how to conceive of an aesthetic judgment of the civic good that did not yet exist. Du Bois's "four beautiful things," then, referred to a range of creative possibilities that could come true, but only if black and white folks were critical of the aesthetic experiences and practices of "race" that communities encountered during the activity of *sensus communis*. The cathedral, the village, and the Venus of Milo were ancient and timeless reservoirs of beauty – each contributing equally to Du Bois's mosaic. Historically, however, European foundations of "civilization" conflicted with African communalism.[75] This discord could be measured in terms of European colonialism in Africa, but it also could be heard in the American sorrow songs of the South.[76] Indeed, the Southern melody owed its spirituality to the unhappy acquaintance of Africa and Europe. But this "utter melody, haunting and appealing," also drew some of its emotional depth from black folk suffering in Jim Crow America. The "universal" quality of the sorrow songs could only be "truly" apprehended as a function of its localized practice in "normal life." By attending to the historicity of its utterance, we could hear its melody "suddenly arising out of night and eternity." Far from a transcendent synthesis of forms, Du Bois's collage exhibited the enduring character of history; it orchestrated the sights and sounds of cultural dissonance and harmony – giving rise to new voices and new visions of the civic good. "Such is Beauty," Du Bois announced, referring to the creative tension seized in this imagery. "Its variety is infinite, its possibility is endless."[77]

With his authoritative public interpretation of diverse beauty, Du Bois constituted persons like him as legitimate public black intellectuals. His authority was generated by the invention and orchestration of "racial" aesthetic experiences, practices, and values that were indivisible from American social relations. But this dynamism also set in motion the modern quest for stability.[78] And so, as the manifold features of an eternal and perfect beauty (momentarily) appeared before the audience, Du Bois voiced skepticism about any finalized notion of beauty, including the progressive idealism suggested by his own portrait. He did this by revealing the pernicious dominating tendencies of "pure art."

Contesting cultural politics: "All Art is propaganda"

Du Bois articulated the promises of a beautiful society as potentially redeemable if black aesthetics reconditioned what counted as Beauty. However, the "unhappy consciousness" of Southern sorrow songs and the brute force of white supremacy alerted him to the unscrupulous operations of cultural politics.[79] To fully understand Du Bois's argument, I must quote him at length:

> With the growing recognition of Negro artists in spite of the severe handicaps, one comforting thing is occurring to both white and black. They are whispering, "Here is a way out. Here is the real solution of the color problem. The recognition according Cullen, Hughes, Fauset, White and others shows there is no real color line. Keep quiet! Don't complain! Work! All will be well!" I will not say that already this chorus amounts to a conspiracy. Perhaps I am naturally too suspicious. But I will say that there are today a surprising number of white people who are getting great satisfaction out of these younger Negro writers because they think it is going to stop agitation of the Negro question. They say, "What is the use of your fighting and complaining; do the great thing and the reward is there?" And many colored people are all too eager to follow this advice; especially those who are weary of the eternal struggle along the color line, who are afraid to fight and to whom the money of philanthropists and the alluring publicity are subtle and deadly bribes. They say, "What is the use of fighting? Why not show simply what we deserve and let the reward come to us?"[80]

At this juncture in the address, Du Bois explicated the premises on which the dominating action of "pure art" rested. The public recognition of some black artists warranted the claim that race prejudice was being eroded. Publicly defined as pure artists, not propagandists, their success served as legitimate evidence of a decreased need for Du Bois's brand of "agitation." The more that this transaction was encouraged by white patronage, the more artists themselves would assent to its logic. But, for Du Bois, therein lay the "deadly" rub. If white aesthetic tastes dictated the development of black culture, the "authentic" historicity of black life would be forever lost. Du Bois demonstrated that the movement toward satisfying white aesthetic desires was not an emancipated impulse of "pure art," but rather was steered by the material imperatives of the culture industry.

Du Bois asserted that the positive public awareness of selected black artists over-shadowed the normative practice of racial exclusion. As Du Bois explained: "There is in New York tonight a black woman molding clay by herself ... because there is not a single school of sculpture in New York where she is welcome." And her pre-dicament was typical: "There was Richard Brown. If he had been white he would have been alive today instead of dead of neglect. ... There is a colored woman in Chicago who is a great musician. She thought she would like to study at Fountainebleau. ... But the application blank of this school says: 'I am a white American.'" Young black writers routinely faced the argument that their literature about the subjects they "knew best about" had to be mangled, made into hideous caricatures of the original to be published because "white publishers catering to white folk" wanted "Uncle Toms, Topsies, good 'darkies' and clowns."[81]

In terms of the values articulated in Du Bois's rhetoric, this cultural milieu was anything but beautiful. Du Bois understood that "a few recognized and successful Negro artists" would be able to rise out of obscurity,[82] but the normative racist practices he outlined denied the cultivation of true beauty. It is tempting to suggest that Du Bois believed that there was no way to transcend racial oppression. But this pessimism would be wrong. Du Bois was laboring not to kill the Beautiful, but to clarify the conditions under which it could provide hope for life. This is why, in the face of the severe odds, he aligned against himself – he could turn to make a pro-vocative moral charge: "Thus it is the bounden duty of black America to begin this great work of the creation of Beauty, of the preservation of Beauty, of the realiza-tion of Beauty." This task was essential to "Truth" and "Goodness," and could not in good conscience be ignored. As Du Bois noted: "The apostle of Beauty thus becomes the apostle of Truth and Right not by choice but by inner and outer com-pulsion. Free he is but his freedom is ever bounded by Truth and Justice; and slavery only dogs him when he is denied the right to tell the Truth or recognize an ideal of Justice."[83]

Du Bois once again appropriated Platonic idealism and constituted a pious trin-ity made up of the life struggles of black folk (Truth), artistic expression (Beauty), and social justice (Goodness). Contrary to the subordinate role Plato assigned art, aesthetic practices functioned in Du Bois's alignment as modes of ethical discourse because they could name the civic good – "an ideal of Justice." But since all forms of discourse were subject to censure in the service of domination, and the artist, "not by choice," took up a localized perspective on the world "ever bounded by Truth and Justice," art was always already in the main contingent. The artist as an "apostle" served this piety by recognizing that her "freedom" was constitutive of social obligations; black artists, in particular, were compelled by the specter of "slavery." Penitence was achieved through a devotion to the pursuit of "Truth" and "Goodness" – the political and ethical ideals of democracy. This is the effect of Du Bois's announcement that "all Art is propaganda and ever must be, despite the wailing of the purists. I stand in utter shamelessness and say that whatever art I have for writing has been used always for propaganda for gaining the right of black folk to love and enjoy."[84] By transfusing art and propaganda, Du Bois showed that aesthetic practices, removed from public interrogation by claims of philosophical perfection, reinvigorated forms of domination. It was the public deliberation of such operations of power that redeemed the possibility of eternal beauty.

Du Bois's moral romanticism was sweeping, but his skepticism was equally resolute. He argued that the younger artists needed to be released from the implacable paradox of "pure art," and that black audiences needed to make aesthetic judgments of a work not with the criteria of white publishers, but "by our own free and unfettered judgment." He then repeated his warning about the way that dominant discourses appropriated potentially disrupting influences: "Just as soon as true Art emerges; just as soon as the black artist appears, someone touches the race on the shoulder and says, 'He did that *because he was an American, not because he was a Negro.* ... He is just human; it is the kind of thing you ought to expect.' "[85] In an important way, Du Bois brought us full circle. We have returned to the troubles of a black public voice and the place of "race" in public deliberations of civic good. The bright and shining semblance of "American" again cast its long, ugly shadow over the accomplishments of African Americans. The metabolism of the text preserved the energies of Platonic idealism, holding in creative tension the potential for a better world and the doggedness of social injustice. In the end, the muting capacities that metaphysics generated for the material world were mediated by the disputatious activity of the materiality of "race." Du Bois enacted a deliberative process in which the aesthetic experiences and practices conditioning human beliefs and actions were exposed and subjected, time and again, to critique by interested others in order to sustain the possibility of perfect beauty.

Conclusion

This extended example of how "race" matters to public address research is designed to highlight three interrelated issues. First, public address research into "race" should be sensitive to the radical historical contingency of "race." During the New Negro Renaissance, Du Bois significantly altered his assertions regarding "race" and "propaganda" as the constraints of the culture industry and shifting alliances among New Negro artists and intellectuals shaped the Harlem debate over black aesthetics. Such a recontextualization coordinates the biographies of speakers, the demographies of communities, and the psychologies of an era. Du Bois and his contemporaries grappled with the meaning and uses of "race" at a moment and place in time when "race" was being unhinged from biological determinism, yet was invested with alternative and competing understandings of modern aesthetic. If public address scholarship is to advance our understanding of how "race" is constitutive of dynamic public discourses, it must be able to recognize how distinct and diverse histories may be appropriated in order to locate and dislocate "race." It must assess how specific circumstances constitute or dissolve a particular articulation of "race." And it must be skeptical of memories of "race" haunting these histories and appreciate their attendant pleasures or terrors.

Second, public address research into "race" must locate specific deployments of racial tropes in relation to tropes of class, sex, gender, and religion – as contingent upon the intersectionality that structures identification and difference. Part of Du Bois's task was to publicize the manner in which "whiteness" was imbricated in metaphysics and, thus, was not open to interrogation and revision. The constitution of a black aesthetics required the recognition of how the acts by the agents of New York City's "art world" orchestrated the complex and fluid discursive operations already making "race." If "race" is to be understood as, in part, a trope of biopower, public address scholarship needs to take stock of the hegemonic relations inciting particular forms of racial identification. Recent debates in social theory have focused on a "general rhetoric"[86] in which identities emerge through "tropological substitution" occurring "within the horizon of an ensemble of institutional practices."[87] I am sympathetic with the project of knowing "race" as an effect of hegemony. These important conversations, however, should benefit from public address scholarship because while much social theory references "rhetoric," it is largely ignorant of the power of speech. In particular, the human agent is generally not considered a key element in the explanation of why identification happens or why commitments to identifications dissolve.[88] By endowing Du Bois's voice, we are reminded of the ethical and affective dimensions inscribed in speaking choices and actions and of the risks human beings take or evade in social life.

Third, public address research into "race" must better account for how its "structure" has (and is) constitutive of the human senses. In my work on "race," I turn to aesthetics only in part because the case studies to which I devote myself involve public address as "creative expression." More importantly, I treat "race" as an unstable aesthetic understanding, articulated through a web of tropes of identification, and arising out of aesthetic experiences of social relations already conditioned by affects of "race." In *How Race is Made*, Mark M. Smith illustrates that the meanings and forms of "race" are productive of long-term aesthetic practices in America that cannot be accounted for by sight alone. As Smith argued, "In this regard, Jim Crow called into question Enlightenment, modernist authority and replaced it with 'lower,' even premodern, senses of hearing, smell, and touch." Once a social system trusts the aesthetic realm as a space for cohering "race," he continued, "[i]nnate racial characteristics spilled out, revealing themselves in behavior, dress, disposition – what was called 'taste' – all apparently quite evident to the white ear, nose, and skin." In short, "race" has been made through the coordinated experiences of all the senses.[89] Rather than solely focusing on the work performed by optical topoi, public address scholarship must generate ways of understanding how "race" is sensual, aural, and discursively remade within the animated terminologies of rhetorical performance. Although there are rationalities of "race" – reasons for why it is or should not be – "race" itself is largely a nonrational phenomenon.[90] It coheres through the coordinated efforts of the sensorium and is deployed in the service of particular interests. Public address needs to go beyond arguments and images of "race" and work to become immersed in the phenomenology of "race." This will undoubtedly be seen as a tall order. I, however, prefer to hear it as a call from (to) our well-being.

Notes

1   Michel Foucault, *Archeology of Knowledge*, trans. A. M. Sheridan (New York: Pantheon, 1972).

2   Immanuel Kant, *The Critique of Judgment*, trans. J. H. Bernard (New York: Prometheus, 2000), 34–38.

3   Martin J. Medhurst, "The Academic Study of Public Address," in *Landmark Essays on American Public Address* (Davis, CA: Hermagoras Press, 1993), xi–xliii.

4   Medhurst, "The Academic Study of Public Address," xxix–xxxi. See also Edwin Black, *Rhetorical Criticism: A Study in Method* (Madison: University of Wisconsin Press, 1978).

5   I take this term from Philip Wander's important essay, "The Ideological Turn in Modern Criticism," *Central States Speech Journal* 34 (1983): 1–18.

6   See Robert P. Newman, "Under the Veneer: Nixon's Vietnam Speech of November 3, 1969," *Quarterly Journal of Speech* 56 (1970): 168–178; Karlyn Kohrs Campbell, "An Exercise in the Rhetoric of Mythical America," in *Critiques of Contemporary Rhetoric*, ed. Karlyn Kohrs Campbell and Thomas R. Burkholder (Belmont, CA: Wadsworth, 1972), 50–57; and Forbes Hill, "Conventional Wisdom – Traditional Form: The President's Message of November 3, 1969," *Quarterly Journal of Speech* 58 (1972): 373–386.

7   I call this practice "anti-intellectual" because it arbitrarily and formalistically defined a host of critical questions as inappropriate for a scholar to ask of public address. This predicament put critics into the position of perhaps affirming the work of the "bullshit artist" as good speech. See Harry G. Frankfurt, *On Bullshit* (Princeton, NJ: Princeton University Press, 2005).

8   Philip Wander, "Marxism, Post-Colonialism, and Rhetorical Contextualization," *Quarterly Journal of Speech* 82 (1996): 403. See also, Wander "The Ideological Turn."

9   Campbell, "An Exercise in the Rhetoric of Mythical America," 56.

10 As Black makes plain, neo-Aristotelian criticism presumed that speakers and audiences were rational; this presumption unduly biased scholars against forms of public address that seemed to violate demonstrative form. See *Rhetorical Criticism*, 7–23.

11 Wander, "Marxism," 403.

12 See Stephen E. Lucas, "The Renaissance of American Public Address: Text and Context in Rhetorical Criticism," in *Landmark Essays*, ed. Medhurst, 179–202.

13 Parke G. Burgess, "The Rhetoric of Black Power: A Moral Demand?" *Quarterly Journal of Speech* 54 (1968): 122–133.

14 Robert L. Scott and Donald K. Smith, "The Rhetoric of Confrontation," *Quarterly Journal of Speech* 55 (1969): 1–8.

15 Richard B. Gregg, "The Ego-Function of the Rhetoric of Protest," *Philosophy & Rhetoric* 4 (1971): 71–91. This time period also ushered in many important anthologies and collections of black speech. See Molefi K. Asante [Arthur L. Smith] and Stephen Robb, eds., *The Voice of Black Rhetoric: Selections* (Boston: Allyn and Bacon, 1971); Molefi K. Asante [Arthur L. Smith], ed., *Language, Communication, and Rhetoric in Black America* (New York: Harper and Row, 1972); James L. Golden and Richard D. Rieke, eds., *The Rhetoric of Black Americans* (Columbus, OH: C. E. Merrill, 1971); Robert L. Scott and Wayne Brockriede, eds., *The Rhetoric of Black Power* (New York: Harper and Row, 1969); Haig A. Bosmajian and Hamida Bosmajian, eds., *The Rhetoric of the Civil Rights Movement* (New York: Random House, 1969); and Ernest

G. Bormann, ed., *Forerunners of Black Power: The Rhetoric of Abolition* (Englewood Cliffs, NJ: Prentice Hall, 1971).

16 Aaron David Gresson III, "Minority Epistemology and the Rhetoric of Creation," *Philosophy & Rhetoric* 10 (1977): 244–262. See also Gresson's *America's Atonement: Racial Pain, Recovery Rhetoric, and the Pedagogy of Healing* (New York: Peter Lang, 2004).

17 See Scott and Brockriede, "Postscript," in *The Rhetoric of Black Power*, 202–203; and Lloyd F. Bitzer, "The Rhetorical Situation," *Philosophy & Rhetoric* 1 (1968): 1–14.

18 Kenneth Burke, "Dramatism," in *International Encyclopedia of the Social Sciences*, vol. 7, ed. David L. Mills (New York: Macmillan, 1965), 445–451.

19 See Audrey Smedley, "Social Origins of the Idea of Race," in *Race in 21st-Century America*, ed. Curtis Stokes, T. Melendez, and G. Rhodes-Reed (East Lansing: Michigan State University Press, 2001), 3–23; Alan H. Goodman, "Six Wrongs of Racial Science," in *Race in 21st Century America*, ed. Stokes, Melendez, and Rhodes-Reed, 25–47.

20 Trevor Parry-Giles, "Character, the Constitution, and the Ideological Embodiment of 'Civil Rights' in the 1967 Nomination of Thurgood Marshall to the Supreme Court," *Quarterly Journal of Speech* 82 (1996): 364–382. See also Trevor Parry-Giles, *The Character of Justice: Rhetoric, Law, and Politics in the Supreme Court Confirmation Process* (East Lansing: Michigan State University Press, 2006).

21 Todd McDorman, "Challenging Constitutional Authority: African American Response to *Scott v. Sandford*," *Quarterly Journal of Speech* 83 (1997): 193, 192–204.

22 Kirt H. Wilson, "The Contested Space of Prudence in the 1874–1875 Civil Rights Debate," *Quarterly Journal of Speech* 84 (1998): 131–149. See also Wilson's extended treatment of these debates, *The Reconstruction Desegregation Debate: The Politics of Equality and the Rhetoric of Place, 1870–1875* (East Lansing: Michigan State University Press, 2002).

23 Celeste Michelle Condit and John Louis Loucaites, *Crafting Equality: America's Anglo-African Word* (Chicago: University of Chicago Press, 1993).

24 Gary Selby, "Mocking the Sacred: Frederick Douglass's 'Slaveholder Sermon' and the Antebellum Debate over Religion and Slavery," *Quarterly Journal of Speech* 88 (2002): 326–341.

25 Karlyn Kohrs Campbell, *Man Cannot Speak for Her*: *A Critical Study of Early Feminist Rhetoric* vol. 1 (Westport, CT: Praeger, 1989), 145–156.

26 Mark Lawrence McPhail, "Passionate Intensity: Louis Farrakhan and the Fallacies of Racial Reasoning," *Quarterly Journal of Speech* 84 (1998): 416–429. See also McPhail, "The Politics of Complicity: Second Thoughts about the Social Construction of Racial Equality," *Quarterly Journal of Speech* 80 (1994): 343–357.

27 Robert E. Terrill, *Malcolm X: Inventing Radical Judgment* (East Lansing: Michigan State University Press, 2005). See also Terrill, "Colonizing the Borderlands: Shifting Circumference in the Rhetoric of Malcolm X," *Quarterly Journal of Speech* 86 (2000): 67–85.

28 Victoria J. Gallagher, "Black Power in Berkeley: Postmodern Constructions in the Rhetoric of Stokely Carmichael," *Quarterly Journal of Speech* 87 (2001): 144–157. For a discussion of Carmichael's rhetoric within the context of the Black Power movement, see Charles J. Stewart, "The Evolution of a Revolution: Stokely Carmichael and the Rhetoric of Black Power," *Quarterly Journal of Speech* 83 (1997): 429–446.

29 Mark Vail, "The 'Integrative' Rhetoric of Martin Luther King Jr.'s 'I Have a Dream' Speech," *Rhetoric & Public Affairs* 9 (2006): 51–78.

30 Robert C. Rowland and John M. Jones, "Recasting the American Dream and American Politics: Barack Obama's Keynote Address to the 2004 Democratic National Convention," *Quarterly Journal of Speech* 93 (2007): 425–448.

31 See David A. Frank and Mark Lawrence McPhail, "Barack Obama's Address to the 2004 Democratic National Convention: Trauma, Compromise, Consilience, and the (Im)possibility of Racial Reconciliation," *Rhetoric & Public Affairs* 8 (2005): 571–594.

32 Paul Gilroy, *Against Race: Imagining Political Culture Beyond the Color Line* (Cambridge, MA: Harvard University Press, 2000), 21.

33 Michele Wallace, "The Politics of Location: Cinema/Theory/Literature/Ethnicity/Sexuality/Me," in *Dark Designs and Visual Culture* (Durham, NC: Duke University Press, 2004), 167–178. In this essay, Wallace resists the tendency in black studies to claim a specific theoretical territory as a kind of "home" from which to perceive the world and her relation to it. Thus, she contends that "homelessness" is a fruitful way to think about thinking. Paul Gilroy makes a similar point when he promotes "Diaspora" as a constructive metaphor for Black Atlantic studies. See Gilroy, *The Black Atlantic: Modernity and Double Consciousness* (Cambridge, MA: Harvard University Press, 1993).

34 Kirt H. Wilson, "The Racial Politics of Imitation in the Nineteenth Century," *Quarterly Journal of Speech* 89 (2003): 89–108.

35 A. Cheree Carlson, "'You Know It When You See It': The Rhetorical Hierarchy of Race and Gender in *Rhinelander v. Rhinelander*," *Quarterly Journal of Speech* 85 (1999): 111–128. See also Stephen Browne, "Remembering Crispus Attucks: Race, Rhetoric, and the Politics of Commemoration," *Quarterly Journal of Speech* 85 (1999): 169–187.

36 James Jasinski, "Constituting Antebellum African American Identity: Resistance, Violence, and Masculinity in Henry Highland Garnet's 1843 'Address to the Slaves,'" *Quarterly Journal of Speech* 93 (2007): 27–57.

37 Michelle Hall Kells, "Questions of Race, Caste, and Citizenship: Hector P. Garcia, Lyndon B. Johnson, and the Polemics of the Bracero Immigration Labor Program," in *Who Belongs in America? Presidents, Rhetoric, and Immigration*, ed. Vanessa B. Beasley (College Station: Texas A&M University Press, 2006), 183–205.

38 Eric King Watts, "The Ethos of a Black Aesthetic: An Exploration of Larry Neal's *Visions of a Liberated Future*," in *The Ethos of Rhetoric*, ed. Michael J. Hyde (Columbia: University of South Carolina Press, 2004), 98–117.

39 Eric King Watts, "African American Ethos and Hermeneutical Rhetoric: An Exploration of Alain Locke's *The New Negro*," *Quarterly Journal of Speech* 88 (2002): 19–32.

40 For example, the field of whiteness studies has birthed new conceptions of how the image and value of "whiteness" has behaved like a magnetic field that acts on the historical vocabulary of "Otherness." See Richard Dyer, *White* (New York: Routledge, 1997); George Lipsitz, *Possessive Investment in Whiteness: How White People Profit from Identity Politics* (Philadelphia, PA: Temple University Press, 1998); Robyn Wiegman, "Whiteness Studies and the Paradox of Particularity," *boundary* 2 (1999): 115–150; David Roediger, *Working Toward Whiteness: How America's Immigrants Became White* (New York: Basic Books, 2005); Thomas K. Nakayama and Judith N. Martin, eds., *Whiteness: The Communication of Social Identity* (Thousand Oaks, CA: Sage, 1999); and Eric King Watts, "Border Patrolling and Passing in Eminem's *8 Mile*," *Critical Studies in Media Communication* 22 (2005): 187–206. Similarly, there have been important conversations among scholars who study "blackness" and queer theory. See

Ian Barnard, *Queer Race: Cultural Interventions in the Racial Politics of Queer Theory* (New York: Peter Lang, 2004); Eric King Watts, "Queer Harlem: Exploring the Rhetorical Limits of a Black Gay Utopia," in *Queering Public Address: Sexualities in American Historical Discourse*, ed. Charles E. Morris III (Columbia: University of South Carolina Press, 2007), 174–194; and Bryant Keith Alexander, *Performing Black Masculinity: Race, Culture, and Queer Identity* (Lanham, MD: AltaMira Press, 2006).

41 Langston Hughes, *The Big Sea: An Autobiography* (New York: Hill and Wang, 1940), 223.

42 There are dozens of critical and historical assessments of the Harlem Renaissance and of some of its central figures. See, for example, Cary D. Wintz, ed., *Harlem Speaks: A Living History of the Harlem Renaissance* (Naperville, IL: Sourcebooks Inc., 2007); J. Martin Favor, *Authentic Blackness: The Folk in the New Negro Renaissance* (Durham, NC: Duke University Press, 1999); Cary D. Wintz, *The Politics and Aesthetics of "New Negro Literature"* (New York: Garland Press, 1996); James de Jongh, *Vicious Modernism: Black Harlem and the Literary Imagination* (Cambridge: Cambridge University Press, 1990); Houston A. Baker, Jr., *Afro-American Poetics: Revisions of Harlem and the Black Aesthetic* (Madison: University of Wisconsin Press, 1988); Arna Bontemps, *Harlem Renaissance Remembered* (New York: Dodd, Mead, 1972); and Nathan Irving Huggins, *The Harlem Renaissance* (New York: Oxford University Press, 1971).

43 David Levering Lewis, *When Harlem Was in Vogue* (New York: Oxford University Press, 1979), 120.

44 See, for example, Amy Helene Kirschke, *Art in Crisis: W. E. B. Du Bois and the Struggle for African American Identity and Memory* (Bloomington: Indiana University Press, 2007).

45 "The Negro in Art: How Shall He Be Portrayed, A Symposium," *The Crisis* 31–32 (March–October 1926).

46 W. E. B. Du Bois, "Criteria of Negro Art," *The Crisis* 32 (October 1926): 290.

47 Du Bois, "Criteria," 290.

48 By "progressivism" I refer to a general belief in the early twentieth century in the ability to "perfect" society perpetuated in part by the rise in political economic "expertise." See Adolph L. Reed, Jr., "Du Bois's 'Double Consciousness': Race and Gender in Progressive-Era American Thought," *Studies in American Political Development* 6 (1992): 93–139.

49 Du Bois, "Criteria," 290.

50 Du Bois, "Criteria," 290.

51 W. E. B. Du Bois, "Parting of the Ways," in *W. E. B. Du Bois: A Reader*, ed. David Levering Lewis (New York: Henry Holt, 1995), 330.

52 Du Bois, "Criteria," 292.

53 Arnold Rampersad, *The Art and Imagination of W. E. B. Du Bois* (Cambridge, MA: Harvard University Press, 1976), 6.

54 Du Bois, "Criteria," 292.

55 Du Bois, "Criteria," 292.

56 W. E. B. Du Bois, "The Essence of African Culture," *Forum* (February 1925): 7–9, in W. E. B. Du Bois Collection, University of Massachusetts.

57 See Marianna Torgovnick, *Gone Primitive: Savage Intellects, Modern Lives* (Chicago: University of Chicago Press, 1990).

58 Du Bois, "Criteria," 292.

59 Du Bois, "Criteria," 292.

60 Du Bois, "Criteria," 292 (emphasis added).

61 Du Bois, "Criteria," 290 (emphasis added).

62 Michael Osborne, "Archetypal Metaphor in Rhetoric: The Light–Dark Family," *Quarterly Journal of Speech* 53 (1967): 115–126.

63 Du Bois reinvented Plato's cave allegory in a number of his writings. See "Of the Coming of John," in *The Souls of Black Folk* (New York: Library of America, 1986, 1903), 165–179.

64 Du Bois, "Criteria," 292 (emphasis added).

65 See "Ion," in *Great Dialogues of Plato*, trans. W. H. D. Rouse (New York: Penguin Books, 1956); also Stephen Halliwell, *Republic 10: Plato: With Translation and Commentary* (Warminster: Aris and Phillips, 1988).

66 Du Bois, "Criteria," 292 (emphasis added).

67 Du Bois, "Criteria," 292.

68 Du Bois, "Criteria," 294.

69 Du Bois, *Darkwater: Voices From Within the Veil* (New York: Washington Square Press, 2004, 1919), 34.

70 Du Bois, *Dusk of Dawn: An Essay Toward an Autobiography of a Race Concept* (New York: Harcourt, Brace & Co., 1945), 172.

71 Du Bois, "Criteria," 292.

72 See James Darsey, "'The Voice of Exile': W. E. B. Du Bois and the Quest for Culture," in *Rhetoric and Community: Studies in Unity and Fragmentation*, ed. J. Michael Hogan (Columbia: University of South Carolina Press, 1998), 93–110.

73 Halliwell, *Republic 10*, 7–9.

74 Du Bois, "Criteria," 292.

75 See W. E. B. Du Bois, "Social Origins of American Negro Art," *Modern Quarterly* 3 (1925): 53–56.

76 See "Sorrow Songs," in *The Souls of Black Folk*.

77 Du Bois, "Criteria," 292.

78 Stephen Toulmin, *Cosmopolis: The Hidden Agenda of Modernity* (Chicago: University of Chicago Press, 1990), 92.

79 Shamoon Zamir, *Dark Voices: W. E. B. Du Bois and American Thought, 1888–1903* (Chicago: University of Chicago Press, 1995), 143.

80 Du Bois, "Criteria," 294.

81 Du Bois, "Criteria," 294–296.

82 Du Bois, "Criteria," 296.

83 Du Bois, "Criteria," 296.

84 Du Bois, "Criteria," 296.

85 Du Bois, "Criteria," 296 (emphasis added).

86 Ernesto Laclau, "Identity and Hegemony: The Role of Universality in the Constitution of Political Logics," in *Contingency, Hegemony, Universality: Contemporary Dialogues on the Left*, ed. Judith Butler, Ernesto Laclau, and Slavoj Žižek (New York: Verso, 2000), 64.

87 Laclau, "Identity and Hegemony," 78.

88 See Judith Butler's critique of Laclau's inability to make sense of why identifications erode and of his general structurational approach to rhetoric. Butler seeks to highlight "performativity" and "parody," focusing on the body and the figurative. Thus, she too cannot adequately discuss the allure and mystery of voice ("Competing Universalities," in *Contingency, Hegemony, Universality*, ed. Butler, Laclau, and Žižek, 136–181).

89   Mark M. Smith, *How Race is Made: Slavery, Segregation, and the Senses* (Chapel Hill: University of North Carolina Press, 2006), 69, 176.

90   This understanding does not lead us to any absolute evaluation of the significance or value of "race." Rather, we are encouraged to be simultaneously skeptical of the oppressive characteristics of what Paul Gilroy calls "raciology" and of claims of a post-racial context; in order to have a post-, we must come to a determination of what we are breaking from; such a break impossibly freezes "race."

16

Sexuality and Public Address
Rhetorical Pasts, Queer Theory, and Abraham Lincoln

Charles E. Morris III

In contemplating "handbooks," I think of Whitman's *Leaves of Grass*, which Rufus W. Griswold characterized as "such a mass of stupid filth," or Edward Carpenter's *Ioläus*, commonly referred to as the "bugger's bible," or Noel I. Gard's *Jonathan to Gide: The Homosexual in History*, described by Michael Bronski as "the klondike of historical faggotry."[1] I think of "McK"'s illicit underground photography during the World War II era; I think of the AIDS Quilt.[2] I do not reach for my dusty copy of *The Joy of Gay Sex*. In other words, I am drawn to those archives and landmarks which historically have provided inducement to imaginative mapping, a sense of frisson and defiance, anticipation and consummation of taboo engagements, articles/fragments/traces/effects of faith, desire, identity, community, difference, affirmation, trauma, fantasy, shame – if only one possessed a sense of wanderlust and hermeneutic will to read between the lines and against the grain. Never, let me underscore, do I imagine simply a grand narrative, a lit review, a banal manual in how to. What I have in mind is Frederick Douglass devouring Caleb Bingham's *Columbian Orator*, or the disruptiveness of Elizabeth Cady Stanton's *Woman's Bible*, or Abraham Lincoln in bed with Billy Greene enmeshed in Samuel Kirkham's *English Grammar*, or the tragedy of Newton Arvin's cache[3] – with an emphasis here on the devouring and disruption, the bed, the crossing and consequences of sexual, racial, class, and gender boundaries and prohibitions. In short, I think of delicious and harrowing and even embarrassing encounters with historical discourse that unsettles archival, textual, and methodological "regimes of the normal."[4] I think of historical discourse in its own traction and as an inventional resource for present contingencies and for future world-making. My contribution to this handbook, in other words, is meant to be queer.

GLBTQ issues constitute a still-emergent area of research in rhetorical studies generally, and public address specifically. The founding premise of this work is that sexuality constitutes a key domain in the constitution and constraint of human experience, identity, knowledge, values, community, social organization, culture, politics – of being, "truth," and power.[5] Drawing on David Halperin's rich conceptualization, sexuality "knits up desire, its objects, sexual behavior, gender identity, reproductive function, mental health, erotic sensibility, personal style, and degrees of normality or deviance into an individuating, normativizing feature of the personality." It functions as a "social apparatus" comprised of "heterogeneous discourses, practices, mechanisms, structures, agencies … form[ing] a vast and complex network, the formation of which correspond[s] to a dominant strategic function (which Foucault called 'bio-power,' the administration of life)."[6] Sexuality's specificities and complexities must be understood contingently throughout the history of the United States, of course, but there is no gainsaying its ubiquity and relevance. One cannot speak of rhetorical culture without speaking of sexuality.

Yet the acknowledgment that sexuality matters in the study of rhetorical discourse has been slow in coming. More alarming, there is some powerful evidence that for many the queer "turn," hardly invisible in the field, and well established for two decades in the academy writ large, has been ignored altogether.[7] Sexuality does not appear to be integrally positioned with and among theoretical or methodological frameworks and practices governing rhetorical scholarship despite steady publication for more than a decade in flagship journals, the appearance in 2007 of *Queering Public Address*, and other queer monographs in established rhetoric book series.[8] We would do well to reflect upon and respond accordingly to Gust Yep's observation that heteronormativity is a "symbolically, discursively, psychically, psychologically, and materially violent form of social regulation and control."[9] We would also do well to reflect upon and respond accordingly to heteronormativity's constraint on rhetorical studies and public address. In other words, there is still much queering to do.[10]

In what follows I briefly explore a number of queer historiographical and critical trajectories that have been developed in recent years. These trajectories provide frameworks for addressing sexuality in historical public discourse and the discourse of rhetorical pasts, which is to say rhetorics of history, historiography, and memory – public address, broadly conceived. This is by no means a comprehensive survey of queer trajectories into rhetorical pasts, which represent existing, some long-standing, complex conceptualizations and debates about queer historicism, and continue to mutate and multiply in ongoing GLBTQ scholarship. Indeed, within the limits of this chapter, my modest aim is to stimulate further exploration and expertise regarding the approaches and discourses I discuss. By way of illustrating these queer trajectories, I also sketch a number of queer historical-critical trajectories for engaging sexuality as a framework of analysis for the constitutive discourses by and about Abraham Lincoln.

Queer Trajectories into Rhetorical Pasts

Queer historical consciousness and criticism begins with the archive, requiring that we become what I have called "archival queers."[11] Although there are copious texts and fragments already culled and anthologized by scholars in other fields,[12] the project of recovery must be ravenous and perpetual. As Martin J. Medhurst has argued, "the task of rhetorical archaeology – that is, digging up from the residues of the past rhetorical artifacts that have been lost, misplaced, unrecognized, or never catalogued – ought to be a first-order priority for scholars of rhetoric and public affairs."[13] Or put differently, our mantra should echo the words of Edward Carpenter, who wrote in his preface to *Ioläus: An Anthology of Friendship*: "But it must be confessed that the present collection is only incomplete, and a small contribution, at best, towards a large subject."[14] Our mode should be akin to promiscuous cruising, an insatiable desire for endless moments of electric (mis)recognition and (dis)embodied potentialities, consummations, hauntings.[15]

Although by now it should go without saying, archival queers are not looking to supplement the existing pantheon of "great speeches" with "representative" texts from GLBT history. This is not a call for Nietzsche's "monumental history," which in homosexual terms, as John Champagne bitingly describes it, "might seek to establish a link between great homosexuals of the past and present fags and dykes, animating the poverty of present buggery with inspiring examples from days gone by."[16] Put more affirmatively, this familiar essentialist construction of the gay past through its figures and texts is known as liberation history, described by the late activist Jim Kepner as "an obligation to rescue [our rich cultural] heritage for all humanity and to share it with pride." Kepner's *From the Closet of History: A Heritage of Pride*, for example, offered brief biographies of more than 70 influential historical gays and lesbians; the portraits of some were "held aloft and carried throughout our 1980 Los Angeles Gay Pride Parade."[17] Critiques of such historicism are well known,[18] yet we must acknowledge how powerful, how resonant, how persistent history's relationship to identity can be.[19]

Instead, archival queers need to seek out the broadest diverse array of material texts, performances, and spaces, vernacular and elite, urban and rural, outlaw and institutional, anecdotal and official, ordinary and extraordinary. Thus, queer gossip should be taken as seriously as legal statutes, movement manifestoes, and literature.[20] We should also bear in mind, with Jennifer Terry, that, "Because the subaltern subject is in this textual sense produced by the dominant historical account, it cannot be understood independent of documentary evidence of the elite." Nor can we seek out only "gay" texts in making sense of queer discourse, as Donna Penn underscores: "An application of queer theory to the historical investigation of lesbianism need not require sources that are explicitly about lesbianism for them to shed light on the operation of the normal."[21] Being an archival queer means that we proceed with an understanding that, as Judith Halberstam observes, "The archive is not simply a repository; it is also a theory of cultural relevance, a construction of collective memory, and a complex record of queer activity. In order for the archive to function it requires users, interpreters, and cultural historians to wade through the material and piece together the jigsaw puzzle of queer history in the making."[22]

In moving from queer archival cruising to modes of queer rhetorical/historical labor, we should underscore from the outset the pressing particularities constitutive of "text/context" dynamics, past and present. In other words, we must be mindful of the multiple contingencies of sexuality at the historical locus of our critical analysis, as well as the multiple contingencies of sexuality constituting our contemporary scene as critics. Indeed, we need to comprehend the unpredictable effects of such approximations and appropriations when past and present "touch."[23] Influenced as it is by Foucault's genealogical perspective, queer historicism assumes that:

> [S]ex is heterogeneous and indeterminate – not the view that we can never know what really happened sexually in past cultures because their immediacy is lost, but the view that sex … is at least in part contingent on systems of representation, and, as such, is fissured and contradictory. Its meaning or significance cannot definitively be pinned down without exclusivity or reductiveness, and such meanings and significances shift, moreover, with shifts in context and location.[24]

Accordingly, let me sketch a number of useful purviews and approaches to queer historicism. Jennifer Terry has described "an interventionist strategy" she labels "deviant historiography," derived from Foucault's concept of "effective history": "[A] strategic awareness of points of emergence or 'possibilities' existing at particular moments in the formation of particular discourses. It traces the conditions whereby marginal subjects apprehend possibilities for expression and self-representation in a field of contest." This approach examines dominant discourses that constitute and discipline deviant subjectivity and, simultaneously, the ways in which reverse or counter-discourses deploy deviant subjectivity against such marginalization and oppression. In other words, through deviant historiography, "we can map the techniques by which homosexuality has been marked as different and pathological, and then locate subjective resistances to this homophobia."[25]

In an effort to push deviant historiography further, Martha Umphrey extends beyond what she calls "a politics of identity and resistance" toward an understanding of "the fluidity and contingency of deviance, a broad category of outlawry that is defined in relation to the 'normal' in any specific historical moment, rather than a positive identity in itself." This would allow, for instance, queer historicism to extend well beyond the demarcated "invention of homosexuality" into the widest possible historical field of sexual normalcy and its discontents. Umphrey labels this approach "queered history," and she conceives of it as "a history of scandal and its consequences: a history of rumor; a history of blackmail; a history of lust and its particular inscriptions in medico-legal discourses; a history of excess and its masquerades."[26]

As a corollary, we should consider William Spurlin's queer rhetorical hermeneutics: exploring the cultural conditions that invited and inflected specific audience responses, interpretations, and arguments regarding queer texts. Spurlin takes the case of *Time* magazine's 1963 feature on James Baldwin, which was situated within a broader story of racial violence and protest in Birmingham. From this queer critical angle, Spurlin suggests:

> It is important to remember that this article was written a year after the publication of Baldwin's novel *Another Country*, which frankly depicts gay issues and desires. … *Giovanni's Room*, published in 1956, would also have been part of Baldwin's critical reception in the early 1960s; but while several early reviews of *Giovanni's Room* often

glossed over its homosexual content ... by the time *Another Country* appeared, it became increasingly more difficult not to read either of these works in a gay context. But the important issue at stake here ... is not so much Baldwin's own (homo)sexuality, but that he was read and interpreted as gay by critics and by the media, and how readings of gay desire and gay identity in his work and in him made use of and extended dominant social practices, cultural conversations, and institutional discourses on homosexuality at a particular historical moment, in this case the early 1960s.[27]

Here too we might explore the oppressive, collusive, and convulsive silences that answered such queer instantiations.[28]

More recently, the scholarly focus on queer historicism has shifted from effective history to affective history, which is to say that the focus concerns not only sexuality in its own time but also how those pasts are taken up contingently across time. It also features the motivational dimensions of those historical engagements and configurations by varied agents, audiences, and communities. In exploring lesbianism in early modern England, for example, Valerie Traub has sought "not to recover the *lesbian* as a being with a discrete origin and stable meaning, but rather to examine the conditions of intelligibility whereby female–female intimacies gain, or fail to gain, cultural signification."[29] Traub engages in what she calls "strategic historicism" – "a mode of historical inquiry attuned simultaneously to continuity and rupture, similarity and difference."[30] As she explains:

> Why do certain figures of eroticism (and gender) become culturally salient at certain moments? Why do suspicions of deviant behavior sometimes seep into the most innocuous-seeming of friendships and why at other times are such friendships immune from suspicion? ... Emerging at certain moments, silently disappearing from view, and then reemerging in another guise as particularly relevant (or explosively volatile), these recurrent explanatory logics seem to underlie the organization, and reorganization, of erotic life. Nonetheless, the forms these axes take, their specific manifest content, the discourses in which they are embedded, and the angles of relations between them are all subject to change.[31]

Similarly, Christopher Nealon conceptualizes what he calls "affect-genealogy," "the activity of reception ... [as] a kind of organic historiography," and "homosexuality as a kind of historiographical-theoretical labor, produced in and through feeling."[32] In his work on "foundling texts" of the early to mid-twentieth century, he reclaims seemingly "naïve" discourses – Hart Crane's poetry, Willa Cather's novels, muscle magazines, and lesbian pulp fiction – caught between the isolation of the invert model and the community of the ethnic model of homosexuality, between pathology and politics in the standard historical narrative. Disrupting that narrative, Nealon discovers in these liminal texts a particular sort of historical consciousness, affect, and vision – "an overwhelming desire to *feel historical*":

> Through the lens of the foundling imagination, in other words, we can see homosexuality in twentieth-century US literature and culture, not as an early stage in the

formation of an autonomous sexual-political "identity" that has "liberated" itself over the past seventy years, but as a historiographical struggle: specifically, a struggle to find terms for historical narration that strike a balance between the unspeakability of desire, especially punishable desire, and group life. ... [These foundling texts] extend our idea of "the historical" to include the desire for its conditions.

From this vantage, Nealon draws our attention to the "relationship between historical fantasy and historical 'experience.' "[33]

Extending this scholarship, Heather Love elucidates "affective historiography," which focuses on "queer cross-historical relations" and asks questions such as "Why do we care so much if there were gay people in the past?" Or perhaps: "What relations with these figures do we hope to cultivate?"[34] Here we might examine a wide range of attachments and emotions toward the past, including desire, identification, nostalgia, idolatry, pride, pleasure, love – what Carolyn Dinshaw has conceptualized as a "queer historical impulse" toward identity and community building across time.[35] Such engagements can achieve affirmation, solidarity, the "fantasy of permanence" and "historical continuism," and sometimes the "psychic distance needed to return to old haunts, revive memories, and connect present to former states of mind."[36] Consider too the significance of negative emotions, disidentifications, dissociations regarding the past. Dinshaw observes that, "pleasure can be taken in the assertion of historical difference as well as similarity."[37] And pain is an equally meaningful negative affective engagement. As Love writes, "The relation to the queer past is suffused not only by feelings of regret, despair, and loss but also by shame of identification ... negative or ambivalent identifications with the past can serve to disrupt the present. Making connections with historical losses or with images of ruined or spoiled identity in the past can set in motion a gutting 'play of recognitions,' another form of effective history."[38]

Finally, we might consider Scott Bravmann's "queer cultural studies of history." Bravmann conceptualizes "gay and lesbian historical imaginations" and the relationships between "queer fictions of the past" and "queer fictions of the present" as a perspective that "takes individual, collective, and popular memory practices seriously as cultural and political interventions into everyday life."[39] Bravmann's approach entails a thoroughgoing genealogy of history's rhetoricity within a particular contemporary scene. As he explains,

> My interest in regarding gay and lesbian historical imaginations as hermeneutically and politically charged sites for constructing, maintaining, and contesting queer identities, however, is intended to problematize the construction of meanings, answers, and signposts by insisting that historical understandings are subject to questions of interpretation, representation, authority, textuality, and narrative.[40]

Bravmann further argues that "queer fictions of the past need to be regarded as performative rather than literal or descriptive retellings of history."[41] We should also query with John Howard the compelling claim by George Chauncey that gay male worlds of the early twentieth century are "almost entirely forgotten in popular memory": "How can we account for this social amnesia? Is it possible to speak of a queer collective memory? If so, how did it fail us? Or did it? And who are among the 'us' to which I refer? For whom are the acts of reclamation important today?"[42]

Bravmann's approach is powerful in critiquing historiography as "a privileged system of signification for representing the past" – as a regime of the normal. He insists on continual interrogation of historiography as a structure and process of power that mediates, distorts, and elides queer pasts and perpetuates heteronormativity through the marrow of historical consciousness, "resisting the cultural power historiography ascribes to itself through its concealed codes of representation."[43] One powerful variation of this is found in Gavin Butt's articulation of the risks in writing about queer gossip:

> Inevitably, as I cast my attention to such a widely derogated form of communication, I flirt with the dangers of not being taken seriously by the guardians of those who would claim to know the value of "proper" historical work. But this risk is the lot of almost anyone who writes historically of homosexuality. ... Indeed to write of homosexuality *at all* is to run the risk of being taken as a gossip.[44]

Butt's larger project of "queering the evidential" powerfully intervenes in the infrastructure of historiography by experimenting with "writing a history which works against the very logic of conventional, archivally sanctioned historical practice ... address[ing] head-on the vexing problem of the limits of our knowledge of intimate life, and how the epistemological uncertainties which come to attend the subject of sexuality might come to affect the status of interpretive discourse, of history."[45]

Bravmann's cultural analysis of the politics and productions of queer history is invaluable because it is not reducible to a model of dominance and resistance. Indeed, his trenchant analysis of Stonewall as "*the* emblematic event in gay and lesbian history" reveals that "the powerful 'common sense' fiction that 'we' share at least some common goals – goals that are symbolically represented by the resistance during the riots – is one centrally problematic way Stonewall erases and creates historical memory, in regard to relations between gay men and lesbians as well as racial and political differences."[46] Drawing on diverse texts across the nearly 40 years of Stonewall memory (among them Fred McDarrah's photograph in the *Village Voice*, lesbian-liberation writings such as *Sappho Was a Right-On Woman*, freedom-day parades and anniversary media coverage, Stonewall 25 events, and Martin Duberman's oral history, *Stonewall*), Bravmann critiques its various "comic emplotments." Fictions of Stonewall, he argues, "sustain a false sense of racial cooperation and displace critical reflection on race matters," obfuscate the meaningful gender limitations and tensions in "queer heterosociality," and reduce its political legacy to a liberal-pluralist emphasis on visibility, a "paradoxical spectacle of identity and difference [in which] the multiple differences between and among historical subjects are rendered equivalent" and "robbed of their ability to make critical interventions into specific historical relations and concrete social circumstances."[47] The trouble with Stonewall memory, Bravmann concludes, is that "[w]hile annual public celebrations of the riots and various institutional structures claiming Stonewall's legacy for themselves help to assert the queer nation of the late twentieth century, the highly salient points of social rupture in gay and lesbian political practices that disappear in comic readings of Stonewall persist nearly three decades after the riots."[48]

These efforts described here – just a few among many emergent in recent years – constitute a powerful conceptualization and critique of how time itself has been and continues to be constructed in relation to sexuality and public discourse. They show how rhetorical constitutions of past and present in various spheres have been constrained by and resisted heteronormativity and homophobia (or what has been called "straight time"), as well as the valuable "undoing" of reified narratives of gay and lesbian history and the ways in which queer theory itself productively and problematically engaged in (a)historicism.[49] Queer temporality, entailing among other things the rethinking of familiar notions of historicism, as well as ahistoricism and anachronism, offers new ways of thinking about the interplay of historical rhetoric and rhetoric of history that is at the heart of public address. Insofar as public address has from its inception almost exclusively focused on historical discourses in their own time, the value of queer historicism comes not only from its insistence on sexuality's relation to public discourse, but in its mandate that we as historical critics and rhetorical historians place ourselves in time, and consider how desire and other motives shape our readings of historical discourse. As a way of further illustrating the impulses, perspectives, and modes I have offered, I now turn to a sketch of critical trajectories I am charting in an ongoing effort to queer Abraham Lincoln.

Queering Abraham Lincoln

It is altogether fitting and proper to focus on Abraham Lincoln in the queering of public address. By virtue of his eloquence and national mythos, he has always been, and undoubtedly will continue to be, a keystone of public address scholarship and pedagogy. Moreover, David Zarefsky has rightly observed that "the field is hardly exhausted,"[50] by which he suggests that Lincoln's rhetorical corpus represents an ongoing boon of intellectual and political engagement. I take Zarefsky's comment doubly, understanding Lincoln as an inexhaustible wellspring in another important sense, namely by virtue of his enigmatic qualities, his peculiarities and passions, his vexations, his contradictions – all of which is to say, his queerness. It is worth noting at the outset that, like most historians who do not openly declare their feelings, I have fallen for Lincoln. A passage from Whitman beautifully expresses my sentiments: "31st Oct Called at the Presidents house, on John Hay – saw Mr. Lincoln standing, talking with a gentleman, apparently a dear friend. Nov 1st – his face & manner have an expression & are inexpressibly sweet – one hand on his friends shoulder the other holding his hand. I love the President personally."[51] In sketching here the possibilities for queer historicist projects on Lincoln, I am answering Michael Leff's charge to "open new ground for studying the rhetoric of our most rhetorically astute president."[52]

Let's begin by expanding the conventional archive of Lincoln discourse, beyond that which has comprised the Lincoln canon in public address. There are, in fact, texts that the queer historical critic in the mode of deviant historiography might read within and against the revealed contextual specificities of sexual norms and prohibitions of Lincoln's time. What should we make, for instance, of Lincoln's naughty 1829 poetic satire, "The First Chronicles of Reuben," a revenge text against his late sister's in-laws, the entire lot of whom he blamed for her death? The poem ends with what must be among the earliest articulations in US public discourse of same-sex marriage, that between Billy and Natty Grigsby; as the poem suggests, the Grigsby boys consummated that union. Where do we place this narrative within the epithetical and erotic economies of that era's rhetorical culture? What should we make of the poem's nearly perfect history of censorship after William Herndon published it in his 1889 *Life of Lincoln*?[53] Have we exhausted our understanding of the ways in which that text might have circulated surreptitiously throughout Lincoln's career and beyond, despite such efforts at erasure? This text, on its face and in its obfuscation, might constitute the origin of a queer genealogy of Lincoln, one ripe for what Umphrey calls "queered history."

Then there are the letters Lincoln wrote to Joshua Speed during 1841–1842. Beginning in 1837, Lincoln and Speed shared the same bed for four years in Springfield, Illinois, and were otherwise inseparable during this formative period of their lives. When in 1841 Speed returned to his family home in Kentucky and soon thereafter became engaged – after his own recently aborted engagement to Mary Todd and a famous breakdown – Lincoln wrote intimate letters expressing anxieties about women and marriage, and conveying the depth and contours of their friendship. Both men married, and despite being "something like soulmates," grew apart. But those letters constitute an important trace, perhaps a testament, in the intertwining personal and political emergence of Lincoln.[54]

Historians protective of Lincoln's heterosexual ethos take these letters seriously as exculpatory evidence; their overwrought insistence that the letters are merely conventionally cordial is evidence enough that these texts, like Lincoln's bed, in fact refuse pat interpretation and constitute a hermeneutical battleground. Skeptics regarding the relevance of this discourse might consider Jeremy Engels's recent study, which argued for the significance of Jefferson's love letters to Maria Cosway as evidencing his "patterns of thought," "a key for decoding his psychology," a "performance of self-regulation," and "an explanation of Jefferson's fantasy for orderly public affairs in the United States."[55] Or note that David Zarefsky in a recent review mentioned both David Herbert Donald's *"We Are Lincoln Men"* and Doris Kearns Goodwin's *Team of Rivals*, but conspicuously not C. A. Tripp's *The Intimate World of Abraham Lincoln*, as examples of "interpersonal persuasion," implying the relevance of such a genre for public address.[56] Given historians' recent surge in interest in Lincoln's legendary yet elusive "courtship" with Ann Rutledge, queer historical critics have much to offer in the developing conceptualization of texts of private life and their public influences and meanings.[57]

It is also with Lincoln's bed and letters in mind that we might revisit the hegemonic understanding of affective bonds between men in the United States prior to the "invention of homosexuality" late in the nineteenth century as, at its most fervent, nonsexual manifestations of "romantic friendship."[58] I am reminded here of Terry Castle's critique of such desexualized narrative/theory in the history of lesbianism: "What did women do who happened to desire one another before the crucial nomenclature appeared? According to the most extreme proponents of the sexological model, they mainly sat around doing needlework, pressing flowers into albums, and writing romantic letters to one another. If they ever got into bed together, it was strictly platonic; a matter of a few cuddles and 'darlings' and a lot of epistemic confusion."[59]

One more intriguing text: Lincoln's 1861 condolence letter to the parents of Elmer Ellsworth. Ellsworth was a dashing and gifted young soldier whom Lincoln had admired and befriended in Springfield, Illinois, between 1859 and 1861. Upon taking the presidency, Lincoln brought Ellsworth with him to Washington, DC, rapidly and pointedly arranging for his placement in the office of the chief clerk of the War Department, then a month later his promotion to Adjutant and Inspector General of Militia for the United States. In the first days of the war, Ellsworth knew that a Confederate flag flying over a hotel in Alexandria, Virginia, distressed Lincoln, who could see it from across the Potomac. While on a nearby mission on May 24, 1861, Ellsworth took his men into the hotel to seize the flag and was killed in the action. Lincoln's grief was severe, so severe in fact that more than once he began sobbing while conducting official business. He twice visited Ellsworth's body at the Naval Yard, and he arranged for funeral services to be held at the Executive Mansion. Ellsworth's death was also precipitous militarily, as David Donald observes: "Up to this point Lincoln had favored delay, but he now ordered an advance against the Confederate army." Here again the personal and political are textually imbricated, voiced in generic discourse rendered eloquent, revelatory of the contexts of nationalism, sentimentality, and masculinity – *eros* and/or *philia* – that animated it.[60] We might also contemplate public discourse related to Lincoln's adoration of Ellsworth in relation to circulating gossip during the same period that Lincoln occasionally shared his bed in the absence of his wife with Captain David Derickson.[61]

Let me offer now a different queer vantage on Lincoln's love of men. What can be said of affectional and erotic energy among men as a material context and animating motive in the invention of public discourse? In response, consider male homosociality, which designates a continuum of nonsexual and sexual relations among men, including friendship, mentorship, rivalry, and love, among others, that shape more broadly economic, social, political, and cultural – in fact, all power – dynamics.[62] More than simply saying that male acquisition and maintenance of power are sought and achieved in bonds with other men, homosociality implies that the process of dominance, and its rewards, are deeply forged by male erotic desire, or the fear of it, and functions, according to Eve Sedgwick, as "the affective or social force, the glue, even when its manifestation is hostility or hatred or something less emotively charged, that shapes an important relationship."[63] The male homosocial continuum, unlike its female counterpart described by Carroll Smith-Rosenberg,[64] is necessarily and particularly influenced by homophobia and misogyny, producing explicitly and implicitly the fragile, sometimes fractional, and often materially and symbolically disruptive distinctions between homosexuality and homosociality. In the United States, then, the affective, indeed erotic, energy productive of fruitful intercourse among men historically has been guarded in its mystery, as Kenneth Burke might call it,[65] by means of its concomitant assault on women and homosexuals and African Americans – whoever constitutes the embodied outlaw of masculinity in historically specific contexts in the United States.

In seeking the intersection of male homosociality and rhetorical action I turn to invention,[66] not only as a rhetorical process that I conceive metaphorically as a form of same-sex intercourse, but as a site of rhetorical production infused with male desire. Rhetorical invention might be understood in this context as an act of homosocial *collaboration* among men, an act that Jeffrey Masten has labeled "textual intercourse,"[67] which produces public discourse. The heteronormative metaphor of sexual intimacy and procreation at work is suggestive at once of both the intensity of homosocial bonds and the gendered and sexual anxieties and politics that attend them. I am broadening the meaning of collaboration here to mean more than the double-authorship that Wayne Koestenbaum has explored,[68] to include a variety of rhetorical practices ranging from "shop-talk," to draft reading and editing, to rehearsal, to the surrogacy of ghostwriting. However, I retain his sense (especially in certain historical periods) of collaboration as being "a sublimation of erotic entanglement," which manifests a variety of "desires and dreads … hysterical discontinuity, muteness, castratory violence, homoerotic craving, misogyny, a wish to usurp female generative power."[69] This characterization is consonant with the meaning of homosociality itself: an erotically charged male colloquy productive of rhetorical power typically at the expense of those it models.

I want to emphasize that the texture and resonance of this construct, however broad I believe its applicability, is historically contingent. To speak of homosocial bonds before or after the emergence of the terms homosexuality and heterosexuality, for instance, bears on the nature and scope of the bonds as they shaped invention, the politics of exclusion and secrecy, and so forth.[70] Moreover, situating historically the relationship between homosociality and rhetorical invention reveals its particular inflections by race, class, and gender.

As a case in point, reflect on one of the central rhetorical relationships of the Lincoln presidency, namely the intimate colloquy of Lincoln and his bachelor secretary, John Hay.[71] Much has been made of "fraternal love" among nineteenth-century men,[72] a concept that, according to Donald Yacovone, designates the effusive affection that was commonplace in male relationships of every personal and public stripe.[73] As Whitman described it,

[I]mportant as they are in my purpose as emotional expressions for humanity, the special meaning of the Calamus cluster of LEAVES OF GRASS, (and more or less running through that book, and cropping out in Drum-Taps,) mainly resides in its Political significance. In my opinion it is by a fervent, accepted development of Comradeship, the beautiful and sane affection of man for man, latent in all the young fellows, North and South, East and West – it is by this, I say, and by what goes directly and indirectly along with it, that the United States of the future, (I cannot too often repeat,) are to be most effectually welded together, intercalated, anneal'd into a Living Union.[74]

Lincoln embodied this "romantic manhood," as Robert Wiebe argues in accounting for his "particular kind of compassion": "Lincoln's democracy was a fraternity."[75] I am particularly interested in the intersection between this so-called "fraternal" context and Lincoln's eloquence.

Public address scholars would not be conventionally inclined to explore the seemingly extraneous observations that young assistant secretary John Hay was a "trusted and intimate friend of Lincoln's who probably lived nearer to that good man's heart during the years of the civil war, than any other man."[76] The exceedingly charming, boyishly handsome, articulate, and cosmopolitan Hay – variously described as foppish, dandyish, or as a "ladies' man" who "might with due change of garb have passed creditably as a lady's maid" – was often Lincoln's companion to the Capitol, the War Office, the Soldiers Home, the Smithsonian, and the theater.[77] Historians clumsily describe their relationship as akin to father/son or teacher/pupil (ignoring – perhaps willfully so – the complications of a paternal language frequently adopted by those with same-sex feelings prior to the category "homosexual"),[78] failing to interpret their deep homosocial bond and its influence on Lincoln's presidential rhetoric.

Of note, Hay served as a ghostwriter for a significant amount of Lincoln's discourse. Lincoln often read aloud to Hay, especially Shakespeare, whose eloquence offered occasion for much good-natured critical debate over textual and performative meaning. It is enticing to consider the possible intersection of homosociality and rhetorical invention in Hay's reminiscence of late-night meetings with "Tycoon."

> What a man he is. Occupied all day with matters of vast moment, deeply anxious over the fate of the greatest army in the world, with his own plans and future hanging on the events of the passing hour, he yet has such a wealth of bonhommie [*sic*] and good fellowship that he gets out of bed and perambulates the house in his shirt to find us, that we may share with him the fun of poor Hood's queer little conceits.[79]

Homosociality, in other words, arguably had much to do with Lincoln's rhetorical invention, which is to say that Lincoln's rhetorical bonds with Hay and other men were expressive of desire, and that desire and invention were significant reciprocal terms in conceiving of Lincoln's public discourse. Neither Yacovone nor Wiebe is willing to say that fraternity and *eros* could be joined. Yacovone, who prefers a Platonic model and the term *agape*, denies potentially erotic desire. By contrast, I would contend that the complexities of homosocial desire in the nineteenth century might account significantly for Lincoln's misogyny, his passion for the word, and the men that mediated both. In asking about Lincoln's "adhesiveness," to borrow Whitman's apt term,[80] we might extend our historical exploration of those libidinal currents that contingently charged the collaborative invention of public discourse.

In turning to the possibilities provided by queer affective historiography and queer cultural studies of history, we must begin by observing that the domain of Lincoln analysis within public address must be expanded beyond the meanings and functions of his discourse in its own time. In other words, Lincoln's discourse and discourses of "Lincoln" have had a rich rhetorical afterlife, with far-reaching cultural and political influence. Horace Greeley memorably and rightly predicted that, "Mr. Lincoln's reputation will stand higher with posterity than with the mass of his contemporaries – that distance, whether in time or space, while dwarfing and obscuring so many, must place him in a fairer light – that future generations will deem him undervalued by those for and with whom he labored."[81] Greeley's "prescience" says as much about public memory, history, and historiography as it does Lincoln's legacy: the extent to which reputation and posterity are a rhetorical – meaning hermeneutic, cultural, and political – and genealogical process of lighting and obscuring in time and space. There is no figure in American history who has been forged into more subject positions, more fictions.[82] Some of those Lincoln histories and memories have been queer, though their seemingly utter absence among the historiographical and popular record renders such a claim outrageous at first blush. Only recently have those engaged in the culture war over Lincoln's sexuality staked a major claim and begun to out the strategic operations by which his heterosexuality, thus US heteronormativity, has been constituted, entrenched, perpetuated – butched up and fiercely straightened across time.[83]

The recent historicist battle precipitated by Larry Kramer and C. A. Tripp has received significant and often dramatic attention in popular and academic press, but I should venture much farther back to begin genealogies of Lincoln's queer public memory. As a prime case, take Walt Whitman's largely neglected Lincoln commemoration, including not only his poetic tributes – "When Lilacs Last in the Dooryard Bloom'd," "O Captain! My Captain!," "Hush'd Be the Camps Today" – but Whitman's eulogy on Lincoln delivered numerous times as a public lecture in the decade before the bard's death.[84] If we accept Barry Schwartz's persuasive argument that first-generation attempts at Lincoln hagiography failed in their immediate aims but were indispensable in furrowing the national landscape for the apotheosis of Lincoln in the twentieth century,[85] then we might argue that Whitman was at the heart of that symbolic transformation, and consequently, more radically, that Lincoln's national memory was pink at its roots, indelibly queer. Unwittingly, Merrill Peterson said a mouthful when he observed, "What made Whitman's lecture memorable was not the content … but the rhapsodic sympathy between 'the good gray poet' and Abraham Lincoln."[86]

We might also extend a conceptualization of the vernacular in Cara Finnegan's insightful work on the relationship among "image vernaculars," an unearthed daguerreotype of a youthful Lincoln published in *McClure's* (1895), and the *fin-de-siècle* crisis of US nationalism. According to Finnegan, image vernaculars shaped "those interpretations of the photograph [and thus of Lincoln] that embodied contemporary tensions about the nature of America and Americans, the uniqueness of the national character, and boundaries of national morality."[87] The vernacular extension I have in mind concerns the scene, a decade earlier, of Whitman circulating among his boy friends the famous *carte de visite* entitled "Apotheosis," depicting Lincoln and Washington entwined in each other's arms as they ascended into heaven.[88] Finnegan identifies dominant cultural protocols for reading Lincoln's face, and thus his (and the nation's) character. Others not among the mainstream, especially queers, might have read Lincoln's face differently, influenced as they were by protocols – image vernaculars – of sexual alterity. Whitman remarked, "None of the artists or pictures has caught the deep, though subtle and indirect expression on this man's face. There is something else there. One of the great painters of two or three centuries ago is needed."[89]

Or consider the "Calamus photographs" of Whitman himself that circulated underground during the same time period as *McClure's* Lincoln photograph. As Ed Folsom argues, "Public photos of such marginalized territory could not exist, because once such images became public they could be co-opted and tamed by the heterosexual majority (just as for decades the dominant readings of 'Calamus' were simply as friendship poems). This sequestered life escaped exhibition except to the initiated few, for whom the Calamus photos – rare and intimate – became talismans."[90] Here we find an image vernacular of a very queer sort, with Lincoln and Whitman entwined. It is also worth observing that the *McClure's* photograph of Lincoln circulated in the year of Oscar Wilde's trial, the spectacle of which ushered into public discourse the category of the homosexual.

Lincoln's queer memory continued to circulate throughout the twentieth century, at various moments and in varied forms and with increasing visibility and contestation that reveal questions ripe for queer historical critics. Yet, at the same time, the manifestation has been rare enough that the archival queer should be roused in relentless pursuit of as yet undiscovered or forgotten traces. I cannot elaborate here, but offer some queer fragments to fathom. In the same year (1926) that Carl Sandburg wrote in *Abraham Lincoln: The Prairie Years* (with the now-famous passage about Lincoln and Speed sharing "streaks of lavender and spots soft as May violets"), Ernest Hemingway's *The Sun Also Rises* offered a conversation in which Bill Gorton says to Jake Barnes (by way of compensating for mentioning Jake's genital wound received during the war!): "Lincoln was a faggot." Or consider gay artist Marsden Hartley's well-known Lincoln folk portraits of the 1940s. Or consider Lincoln's appropriation within gay liberation discourse, including Jack Baker's campaign for gay marriage at the University of Minnesota in the early 1970s.[91] In each of these cases, Lincoln's sexuality circulates through elite and vernacular discourses, reflecting sexual norms and struggles against them, and as a means of unsettling heteronormativity, or constituting queer community, or enacting homophobic discipline.

In the past decade especially there has been a robust effort to reclaim a "gay" Lincoln, most especially by Larry Kramer in his 1999 lecture "Our Gay President" and by C. A. Tripp in his posthumously published 2005 book, *The Intimate World of Abraham Lincoln*. These efforts suggest that liberation history (i.e., history as identity politics) has resounded despite the meaningful and incisive critiques within the academy. These reclamations – these queer fictions, to borrow Bravmann's term – have also provided rich fodder for fierce public debate across popular and scholarly media, raising the ante and deepening the engagement with queer and heteronormative meanings and modes of history, historiography, and memory.

My own work only begins to examine these controversies in critiquing historiography generally, and the Lincoln establishment specifically, as a regime of the normal. By means of gay activist Larry Kramer's explosive appropriation of Lincoln, I interrogate the heteronormative if not homophobic discourse of putatively apolitical, "objective" historians who sought to discredit Kramer and preserve Lincoln's heteronormative reputation. Stricken by panic in the wake of Kramer's disclosure, Lincoln scholars dramatically enacted their custodianship of Lincoln's mutable memory by attempting what I call "mnemonicide," or the assassination of (counter-) public memory. This disclosure of "academic" investments in the queer culture war, and the intermingling rhetorical labor of academic and popular – institutional and vernacular – memory, is as significant here as the question of Lincoln's sexuality and its stake in American national identity.[92]

I have extended my queer cultural study of Lincoln's recent history by considering the discursive field that emerged in response to Tripp's *Intimate World*, the latest battle in an ongoing cold war over Lincoln's sexuality.[93] The copious response to Tripp's book reveals that an evidentiary struggle over Lincoln's sexuality is illusory, one that masks the heteronormative presumption undergirding and protected by the rhetorically constructed material status of evidence itself. As such, the vexations of Lincoln's corpus provide the ground for a queer refiguring of our understanding of the past as "mirror" and/or "lamp." And in keeping with Gavin Butt's project of "queering the evidential," the project offers a displacement of "so-called verifiable truths from their positivistic frames of reference to render them instead … as projections of interpretive desire and curiosity."[94] Instantiated through this interrogation of evidentiary materiality is a queer critical politics of revelatory inducement, not historical adducement, and an exhibition of desire as a material force in rhetorical productions of the past.

Tripp's idiosyncratic readings of same-sex desire in Lincoln's discourse, the discourse of oral testimony accounting for that desire, and their implications for the discourse of historiography provide invaluable circumstantial evidence of the importance of manifest desire in the rhetorical constitution of memory, history, and historiography. Its value is as much political as historical: In the presence of such methodological excess, one witnesses what others *make* of it. This case should also serve as an inducement to revisit, by means of critical juxtaposition and queering the evidential, the constitution and boisterous defense of Lincoln's heterosexuality by luminaries of the Lincoln establishment.[95]

A Final Queer Inducement

I close with a lamentation – not my own – that reflects the dying wail of history and memory as a regime of the normal in the United States. In his 2003 essay, "Lincoln at the Millennium," Barry Schwartz grieves the diminishment of Lincoln's memory in the second half of the twentieth century, claiming that we find ourselves culturally in the midst of a "memory crisis."[96] The seriousness of the crisis is evident in terms of the damage done to the past, and Lincoln specifically, by what Schwartz calls "the acids of postmodernism" and "the acids of multiculturalism." Drawing on Robert Nisbet, Schwartz shouts in the wilderness, " 'The instinct to mock the great, the good, and the wise is built into this age.' Such is the post-heroic mentality of our generation."[97] Lincoln's "fall," and the demise of this particular version of history generally, Schwartz blames on the contemporary context of "depthlessness, derision, and deteriorating moral authority."[98]

I share Schwartz's passion for the past: "Here, precisely, resides the peril: as Americans cease to believe in the sanctifying fullness of the past, they lose sight of the existential link between their present life and the transformations wrought by their forebears; they lose sight of themselves as historical beings, forget that they have inherited, not created, the most valuable of their possessions."[99] However, I would put it differently, queerly. In Bravmann's words:

> The importance of history to gay men and lesbians goes beyond the lessons to be learned from the events of the past to include the meanings generated through retellings of those events and the agency those meanings carry in the present. Lesbian and gay self-representation – queer fictions of the past – help construct, maintain, and contest identities – queer fictions of the present. For this reason, we need to look at how the images of the gay and lesbian past circulating among us animate the present and to read lesbian and gay historical self-representation as sites of ongoing hermeneutic and political struggle in the formation of new social subjects and new cultural possibilities.[100]

From my vantage, and by means of the particular persuasion I have been enacting for this *Handbook*, queer inducements and interrogations constitute not the end of history and memory, but an impetus to queer world-making that must ultimately be deepened by its ineluctable and intractable historicity. This is the charge of my chapter on "Sexuality and Public Address." This is what it means to queer public address.

Notes

1 Griswold quoted in *Calamus Lovers: Walt Whitman's Working-Class Camerados*, ed. Charley Shively (San Francisco: Gay Sunshine Press, 1987), 9; "bugger's bible" quoted in George Chauncey, *Gay New York: Gender, Urban Culture, and the Making of the Gay*

Male World, 1890–1940 (New York: Basic Books, 1994); and Michael Bronski, "Who's Out? And Who Stays in the Closet," www.guidemag.com (February 2005), 60.

2   See Thomas Waugh, *Hard to Imagine: Gay Male Eroticism in Photography and Film from Their Beginnings to Stonewall* (New York: Columbia University Press, 1996), 331–333, 439 n.57; and Charles E. Morris III, ed., "Special Issue: The AIDS Quilt at 20: Commemoration and Critique of the Epidemic Text," *Rhetoric & Public Affairs* 10 (2007): 557–721.

3   Frederick Douglass, *Narrative Life of Frederick Douglass, An American Slave: Written by Himself*, ed. John W. Blassingame, John R. McKivigan, and Peter P. Hinks (New Haven, CT: Yale University Press, 2001), 35; Elisabeth Griffith, *In Her Own Right: The Life of Elizabeth Cady Stanton* (New York: Oxford University Press, 1984), 210–213; C. A. Tripp, *The Intimate World of Abraham Lincoln*, ed. Lewis Gannett (New York: Free Press, 2005), 47–49, 53; and Barry Werth, *The Scarlet Professor, A Literary Life Shattered by Scandal* (New York: Anchor, 2001).

4   See Michael Warner, ed., "Introduction," in *Fear of a Queer Planet: Queer Politics and Social Theory* (Minneapolis: University of Minnesota Press, 1993), vii–xxxi.

5   For an excellent overview, see Gust A. Yep, "The Violence of Heteronormativity in Communication Studies: Notes on Injury, Healing, and Queer World-Making," in *Queer Theory and Communication: From Disciplining Queers to Queering the Discipline(s)*, ed. Gust A. Yep, Karen E. Lovaas, and John P. Elia (New York: Harrington Park Press, 2003), 11–59.

6   David M. Halperin, *How to Do the History of Homosexuality* (Chicago: University of Chicago Press, 2002), 29, 87.

7   Given its size and scope, with 32 chapters and nearly 700 pages, *The Sage Handbook of Rhetorical Studies* embodies this striking neglect. GLBTQ scholarship does not appear anywhere in the table of contents or the index of this massive volume. How should one read this absence? If one is being fair, what rationales for this silence, this erasure, would you allow? Andrea A. Lunsford, Kirt H. Wilson, and Rosa A. Eberly, eds., *The Sage Handbook of Rhetorical Studies* (Los Angeles: Sage, 2009). Likewise, AmericanRhetoric.com, arguably the leading archive for public address pedagogy, is conspicuous for its ongoing omission of texts from GLBT history. The scope and depth of that archive, which houses copious numbers of texts canonical to trivial, renders the absence of GLBT discourse political in implication if not intent.

8   Charles E. Morris III, ed., *Queering Public Address: Sexualities in American Historical Discourse* (Columbia: University of South Carolina Press, 2007).

9   Yep, "The Violence of Heteronormativity in Communication Studies," 18.

10 For conceptualizations of queering, see Michael Warner, "Introduction"; Lisa Duggan, "Making It Perfectly Queer," *Socialist Review* 22 (1992): 11–31; Eve Kosofsky Sedgwick, *Tendencies* (Durham, NC: Duke University Press, 1993), 8–9; Judith Butler, "Critically Queer," *GLQ: A Journal of Lesbian and Gay Studies* 1 (1993): 17–32; John Howard, *Men Like That: A Southern Queer History* (Chicago: University of Chicago Press, 1999); E. Patrick Johnson, "'Quare' Studies: or (Almost) Everything I Know About Queer Studies I Learned from My Grandmother," *Text and Performance Quarterly* 21 (2001): 1–25; Halperin, *How to Do a History of Sexuality*; Yep, Lovaas, and Elia, eds., *Queer Theory and Communication*; Judith Halberstam, *In a Queer Time and Place: Transgender Bodies, Subcultural Lives* (New York: New York University Press, 2005); Morris, ed., *Queering Public Address*; Erin J. Rand, "An Inflammatory Fag and a Queer Form: Larry Kramer, Polemics, and Rhetorical Agency," *Quarterly*

Journal of Speech 94 (2008): 297–319; and Jeffrey A. Bennett, *Banning Queer Blood: Rhetorics of Citizenship, Contagion, and Resistance* (Tuscaloosa: University of Alabama Press, 2009).

11 Charles E. Morris III, "Archival Queer," *Rhetoric & Public Affairs* 9 (2006): 145–151. See also Ann Cvetkovich, *An Archive of Feelings: Trauma, Sexuality, and Lesbian Public Cultures* (Durham, NC: Duke University Press, 2003); and Kelly Jacob Rawson, "Archiving Transgender: Affects, Logics, and the Power of Queer History" (PhD Diss., Syracuse University, 2010).

12 See Jonathan Ned Katz, *Gay American History: Lesbians and Gay Men in the USA* (New York: Thomas Crowell, 1976); Lillian Faderman, *Chloe plus Olivia: An Anthology of Lesbian Literature from the Seventeenth Century to the Present* (New York: Viking, 1984); Karla Jay, ed., *Out of the Closets: Voices of Gay Liberation*, 20th anniversary edition (1972; New York: New York University Press, 1992); Jonathan Ned Katz, ed., *Gay/Lesbian Almanac* (New York: Carrol and Graf, 1994); Mark Blasius and Shane Phelan, eds., *We Are Everywhere: A Historical Sourcebook of Gay and Lesbian Politics* (New York: Routledge, 1997); Chris Bull, ed., *Witness to Revolution: Advocate Reports on Gay and Lesbian Politics, 1967–1999* (Los Angeles: Alyson Books, 1999); and Robert Ridinger, ed., *Speaking for Our Lives: Historic Speeches and Rhetoric for Gay and Lesbian Rights (1892–2000)* (New York: Harrington Park Press, 2004).

13 Martin J. Medhurst, "The Contemporary Study of Public Address: Renewal, Recovery, and Reconfiguration," *Rhetoric & Public Affairs* 4 (2001): 504.

14 Edward Carpenter, ed., *Ioläus: An Anthology of Friendship* (1902; London: Allen and Unwin, 1929), v.

15 See Helen Freshwater, "The Allure of the Archive," *Poetics Today* 24 (2003): 729–758; James A. Knapp, "'Ocular Proof': Archival Revelations and Aesthetic Response," *Poetics Today* 24 (2003): 695–727; Barbara A. Biesecker, "Of Historicity, Rhetoric: The Archive as Scene of Invention," *Rhetoric & Public Affairs* 9 (2006): 124–131; and Heather Love, *Feeling Backward: Loss and the Politics of Queer History* (Cambridge, MA: Harvard University Press, 2007).

16 John Champagne, *The Ethics of Marginality: A New Approach to Gay Studies* (Minneapolis: University of Minnesota Press, 1995), 135. See also Friedrich Nietzsche, "On the Uses and Disadvantages of History for Life," in *Untimely Meditations*, trans. R. J. Hollingdale (Cambridge: Cambridge University Press, 1983).

17 Jim Kepner, *From the Closet of History: A Heritage of Pride* (Hollywood, CA: National Gay Archives, 1984), ONE National Gay and Lesbian Archives. Heather Love conceptualizes (and critiques) this as "affirmative historiography" (*Feeling Backward*, 105). See also Rictor Norton, *The Myth of the Modern Homosexual: Queer History and the Search for Cultural Unity* (London: Cassell, 1997).

18 Within this critique, Dana Cloud notes an interesting disciplinary challenge: "Scholars of every historically marginalized and oppressed group, including feminist scholars, have argued that the integration of new groups into scholarly canons and academic theory goes through several stages, beginning with the discovery and recovery from the past of 'great' representatives of the oppressed category. Recovery movements then traverse the stages of distinguishing the voices of marginalized groups from dominant voices and criticizing the ways in which such distinctions are produced culturally and politically. Work in contemporary queer theory demonstrates that this sequence is collapsed in our case: studies of famous gay people in history appear alongside work exploring the possibilities of agency in regimes of heteronormative distinctions"

(Cloud, "The First Lady's Privates: Queering Eleanor Roosevelt for Public Address Studies," in *Queering Public Address*, ed. Morris, 23–44).

19   Valerie Traub observed: "I resist the temptation to make historical inquiry culminate in a politics of identity. This is not to say that identity politics have no place in contemporary *lesbian* activism. As long as the lives of lesbians are constructed and destroyed by silences, misinformation, and hatred, the articulated self-presence and political agitation under the banner of identity will remain a crucial political strategy. Nonetheless, the politics of identity can operate as a stranglehold, limiting the questions one asks and thus the answers one finds ... for such identifications effectively quarantine individuals from complex and interdependent systems of erotic affect and practice (not the least of which is heterosexuality) as well as isolate erotic systems from other social formations, such as race" (Traub, *The Renaissance of Lesbianism in Early Modern England* [Cambridge: Cambridge University Press, 2002], 27).

20   Ono and Sloop wrote, "But if we limit our attention to such documents available to the widest possible audience, documents that shaped the 'history' of our society, then we are missing out on, and writing 'out of history,' important texts that gird and influence local cultures first and then affect, through the sheer number of local communities, cultures at large" (Kent A. Ono and John M. Sloop, "The Critique of Vernacular Discourse," *Communication Monographs* 62 [1995]: 19). See George Chauncey, *Gay New York*; José Esteban Muñoz, "Ephemera as Evidence: Introductory Notes to Queer Acts," *Women and Performance* 16 (1996): 5–16; Constance Jones, ed., *The Love of Friends: An Anthology of Gay and Lesbian Letters to Friends and Lovers* (New York: Simon and Schuster, 1997); David Román, *Acts of Intervention: Performance, Gay Culture, and AIDS* (Bloomington: Indiana University Press, 1998); John Ibson, *Picturing Men: A Century of Male Relationships in Everyday American Photography* (Washington, DC: Smithsonian Institution Press, 2002); Sophie Fuller and Lloyd Whitesel, eds., *Queer Episodes in Music and Modern Identity* (Urbana: University of Illinois Press, 2002); Richard Meyer, *Outlaw Representation: Censorship and Homosexuality in Twentieth-Century American Art* (New York: Oxford University Press, 2002); Thomas Waugh, *Out/Lines: Underground Gay Graphics from Before Stonewall* (Vancouver: Arsenal Press, 2002); John M. Sloop, *Disciplining Gender: Rhetorics of Sex Identity in Contemporary US Culture* (Amherst: University of Massachusetts Press, 2004); Gavin Butt, *Between You and Me: Queer Discourses in the New York Art World, 1948–1963* (Durham, NC: Duke University Press, 2005); Daniel Brouwer, "Counterpublicity and Corporeality in HIV/AIDS Zines," *Critical Studies in Media Communication* 22 (2005): 351–371; Claire Bond Potter, "Queer Hoover: Sex, Lies, and Political History," *Journal of the History of Sexuality* 15 (2006): 355–381; Isaac West, "Debbie Mayne's Trans/scripts: Performative Repertories in Law and Everyday Life," *Communication and Critical/Cultural Studies* 5 (2008): 245–263; Julie Abraham, *Metropolitan Lovers: The Homosexuality of Cities* (Minneapolis: University of Minnesota Press, 2009); and Scott Herring, "The Hoosier Apex," *Southern Communication Journal* 74 (2009): 243–251.

21   Jennifer Terry, "Theorizing Deviant Historiography," *differences: A Journal of Feminist Cultural Studies* 3 (1991): 58; and Donna Penn, "Queer: Theorizing Politics and History," *Radical History Review* 62 (1995): 35.

22   Halberstam, *In a Queer Time and Place*, 169–170.

23   Carolyn Dinshaw writes, "Since I contend that queer histories are made of affective relations, I aim to make such histories manifest by juxtaposition, by making entities past

and present touch" (Dinshaw, *Getting Medieval: Sexualities and Communities, Pre-and Postmodern* [Durham, NC: Duke University Press, 1999], 12).

24 Dinshaw defines "sex" as "sex acts, sexual desire, sexual identity, sexual subjectivity, sexuality, all of which I shall analyze as inflected by other cultural phenomena" (Dinshaw, *Getting Medieval*, 12). On Foucault's genealogy, see Michel Foucault, *The Archaeology of Knowledge and the Discourse of Language*, trans. A. M. Sheridan Smith (New York: Pantheon, 1972); "Nietzsche, Genealogy, History," in *The Foucault Reader*, ed. Paul Rabinow (New York: Pantheon Books, 1984), 76–100; *Power/Knowledge: Selected Interviews and Other Writings, 1972–1977*, ed. Colin Gordon, trans. Colin Gordon, Leo Marshall, John Mepham, and Kate Soper (New York: Pantheon, 1980).

25 Terry, "Deviant Historiography," 56, 57, 58. See also Jennifer Terry, *American Obsession: Science, Medicine, and Homosexuality in Modern Society* (Chicago: University of Chicago Press, 1999).

26 Martha M. Umphrey, "The Trouble with Harry Thaw," in *Queer Studies: An Interdisciplinary Reader*, ed. Robert J. Corber and Stephen Valocchi (Malden, MA: Blackwell, 2003), 26, 27–28.

27 William J. Spurlin, "Rhetorical Hermeneutics and Gay Identity Politics: Rethinking American Cultural Studies," in *Reconceptualizing American Literary/Cultural Studies: Rhetoric, History, and Politics in the Humanities*, ed. William E. Cain (New York: Garland, 1996).

28 Blanche Wiesen Cook, "The Historical Denial of Lesbianism," *Radical History Review* 20 (1979): 60–65; Martin Bauml Duberman, " 'Writhing Bedfellows': Two Young Men from Antebellum South Carolina Share 'Extravagant Delight,' " in *About Time: Exploring the Gay Past* (New York: Gay Presses of New York, 1986), 5–22; John D. Wrathall, "Provenance as Text: Reading the Silences around Sexuality in Manuscript Collections," *Journal of American History* 79 (1992): 165–178; Estelle B. Freedman, " 'The Burning of Letters Continues': Elusive Identities and the Historical Construction of Sexuality," in *Modern American Queer History*, ed. Allida M. Black (Philadelphia: Temple University Press, 2001), 51–68; Charles E. Morris III, "Passing by Proxy: Collusive and Convulsive Silence in the Trial of Leopold and Loeb," *Quarterly Journal of Speech* 91 (2005): 383–404.

29 Traub, *The Renaissance of Lesbianism*, 28.

30 Traub, *The Renaissance of Lesbianism*, 28.

31 Traub, *The Renaissance of Lesbianism*, 359.

32 Christopher Nealon, "Invert-History: The Ambivalence of Lesbian Pulp Fiction," *New Literary History* 31 (2000): 747. See also Heather K. Love, " 'Spoiled Identity': Stephen Gordon's Loneliness and the Difficulties of Queer History," *GLQ: A Journal of Lesbian and Gay Studies* 7 (2001): 487–519.

33 Christopher Nealon, *Foundlings: Lesbian and Gay Historical Emotion Before Stonewall* (Durham, NC: Duke University Press, 2001), 8–9, 13, 18.

34 Love, *Feeling Backward*, 31–32. Nealon's reflection on the novels of Willa Cather is insightful: "But what is important here is … the way they [queer theorists] find themselves trying to understand the historical possibilities for Cather's lesbianism because they care about her characters … struggling to use theoretical insights to bring them closer to what they love. This attempt at claiming, at bringing close, is also deeply political, of course: not everyone is going to want to hear that Cather's literary value is utterly related, at every level, to her being a lesbian. But the politics involved are not merely some kind of 'special interest' politics, designed to tally one more lesbian on the new, post-modern roster of achievement to Western civilization. These politics are bigger-hearted: they are

an attempt to understand, through an identification with an ancestor, how history works, what it looks like, what possibilities it has offered in the past, and what those possibilities suggest about our ineffable present tense" (Nealon, *Foundlings*, 96).

35 Dinshaw, *Getting Medieval*, 1.

36 Love, *Feeling Backward*, 36; Louise O. Fradenburg and Carla Freccero, "Introduction: Caxton, Foucault, and the Pleasures of History," in *Premodern Sexualities*, ed. Louise O. Fradenburg and Carla Freccero (New York: Routledge, 1996), xiii–xxiv; Mysoon Rizk, "Constructing Histories: David Wojnarowicz's *Arthur Rimbaud in New York*," in *The Passionate Camera: Photography and Bodies of Desire*, ed. Deborah Bright (New York: Routledge, 1998), 180; David Deitcher, *Dear Friends: American Photographs of Men Together, 1840–1918* (New York: Harry N. Abrams, 2001), 14; and Chauncey, *Gay New York*, 285–286. In a moving example, Dinshaw relates one reader's response to John Boswell's path-breaking *Christianity, Social Tolerance, and Homosexuality*: " 'Whereas I have often felt intellectual "friendships" across the centuries – historical thinkers with whom I have felt such strong affinities that I feel I know them and that we speak for one another, I had never felt – until I read your book – that I had gay friends across the centuries.' For this reader, history becomes a source – directly, itself – of gay community, a community of affinities, of friends, even perhaps (given this letter's impassioned tone), of lovers" (Dinshaw, *Getting Medieval*, 28).

37 Dinshaw, *Getting Medieval*, 35.

38 Love, *Feeling Backward*, 32, 45.

39 Scott Bravmann, *Queer Fictions of the Past: History Culture, and Difference* (New York: Cambridge University Press, 1997), 24.

40 Bravmann, *Queer Fictions of the Past*, 31.

41 Bravmann, *Queer Fictions of the Past*, 31.

42 John Howard, "The Talk of the County: Revisiting Accusation, Murder, and Mississippi, 1895," in *Queer Studies*, ed. Corber and Valocchi, 146; and Chauncey, *Gay New York*, 1. Questions of collective memory and social amnesia must also be considered within larger contexts of heteronormativity and homophobia that I discuss above. See Christopher Castiglia, "Sex Panics, Sex Publics, Sex Memories," *boundary 2* (2000): 156–159; Christopher Castiglia and Christopher Reed, " 'Ah, Yes, I Remember It Well,' Memory and Queer Culture in *Will and Grace*,' " in *Sexualities & Communication in Everyday Life: A Reader*, ed. Karen E. Lovaas and Mercilee M. Jenkins (Thousand Oaks, CA: Sage, 2007), 217–218; Patrick Moore, *Beyond Shame: Reclaiming the Abandoned History of Radical Gay Sexuality* (Boston: Beacon Press, 2004); Charles E. Morris III, "Hard Evidence: The Vexations of Lincoln's Queer Corpus," in *Rhetoric, Materiality, and Politics*, ed. Barbara Biesecker and John Lucaites (New York: Peter Lang, 2009), 185–214.

43 Bravmann, *Queer Fictions of the Past*, 25, 30.

44 Butt, *Between You and Me*, 4.

45 Butt, *Between You and Me*, 8–9.

46 Bravmann, "Queer Fictions of Stonewall," in *Queer Fictions of the Past*, 85.

47 Bravmann, "Queer Fictions of Stonewall," 75–94.

48 Bravmann, "Queer Fictions of Stonewall," 96.

49 See Valerie Rohy, "Ahistorical," *GLQ: A Journal of Lesbian and Gay Studies* 12 (2006): 61–83; Scott Herring, *Queering the Underworld: Slumming, Literature, and the Undoing of Lesbian and Gay History* (Chicago: University of Chicago Press, 2007).

50 David Zarefsky, "The Continuing Fascination with Lincoln," *Rhetoric & Public Affairs* 6 (2003): 368.

51 Walt Whitman, *Notebooks and Unpublished Prose Manuscripts*, ed. Edward F. Grier (New York: New York University Press, 1984), 539. For Whitman and Lincoln, see Daniel Mark Epstein, *Lincoln and Whitman: Parallel Lives in Civil War Washington* (New York: Ballantine Books, 2004); and William E. Barton, *Abraham Lincoln and Walt Whitman* (Indianapolis: Bobbs-Merrill, 1928).

52 Michael Leff, "Introduction," in "Special Issue on Abraham Lincoln's Rhetorical Leadership," ed. Michael Leff, *Rhetoric & Public Affairs* 3 (2000): 3.

53 Tripp, *Intimate World of Abraham Lincoln*, 39–43, 249–251.

54 Tripp, *Intimate World of Abraham Lincoln*, 125–151, 253–271; Charles E. Morris III, ed., "My Old Kentucky Homo: Abraham Lincoln, Larry Kramer, and the Politics of Queer Memory," in *Queering Public Address*, ed. Morris, 93–120; Jonathan Ned Katz, *Love Stories: Sex Between Men Before Homosexuality* (Chicago: University of Chicago Press, 2001), 1–25; David Herbert Donald, *"We Are Lincoln Men": Abraham Lincoln and His Friends* (New York: Simon and Schuster, 2003), 35–51; and Charley Shively, "Big Buck and Big Lick: and Lincoln and Whitman," in *Drum Beats: Walt Whitman's Civil War Boy Lovers* (San Francisco: Gay Sunshine Press, 1989), 71–88.

55 Jeremy Engels, "Disciplining Jefferson: The Man within the Breast and the Rhetorical Norms of Producing Order," *Rhetoric & Public Affairs* 9 (2006): 413–415.

56 David Zarefsky, "Review of Ronald C. White Jr., *The Eloquent President* and John Channing Briggs, *Lincoln's Speeches Reconsidered*," *Rhetoric & Public Affairs* 10 (2007): 539.

57 See Lewis Gannett, "The Ann Rutledge Story: An Evidential Lapse in Lincoln Studies?" *Journal of Abraham Lincoln Association* (forthcoming); Lewis Gannett, "Scandal Brewing in Lincoln Country," *The Gay and Lesbian Review Worldwide* 11 (2004): 13–18; and Lewis Gannett, "'Overwhelming Evidence' of a Lincoln–Ann Rutledge Romance? Reexamining Rutledge Family Reminiscences," *Journal of the Abraham Lincoln Association* 26 (2005): 28–41.

58 See E. Anthony Rotundo, *American Manhood: Transformations in Masculinity from the Revolution to the Modern Era* (New York: Basic Books, 1993).

59 Terry Castle, *The Apparitional Lesbian: Female Homosexuality and Modern Culture* (New York: Columbia University Press, 1993), 8.

60 Abraham Lincoln, "To the Father and Mother of Col. Elmer Ellsworth," in Tripp, *Intimate World of Abraham Lincoln*, 121–122; and David Herbert Donald, *Lincoln* (New York: Random House, 1995), 306. See also Tripp, *Intimate World of Abraham Lincoln*, 109–124; Ruth Painter Randall, *Colonel Elmer Ellsworth: A Biography of Lincoln's Friend and First Hero of the Civil War* (Boston: Little, Brown, 1960); and Ronald F. Dorr, "Loss, Love, and Renewal: Abraham Lincoln's Letters of Condolence," *MidAmerica: Yearbook for the Study of Midwestern Literature* 21 (1994): 23–38.

61 Tripp, *Intimate World of Abraham Lincoln*, ch. 1.

62 Eve Kosofsky Sedgwick, *Between Men: English Literature and Male Homosocial Desire* (New York: Columbia University Press), 1985.

63 Sedgwick, *Between Men*, 2.

64 Carroll Smith-Rosenberg, "The Female World of Love and Ritual: Relations Between Women in Nineteenth-Century America," in *Feminism and History*, ed. Joan Wallach Scott (New York: Oxford University Press, 1996): 366–397.

65 Kenneth Burke, *A Rhetoric of Motives* (New York: Prentice Hall, 1950), 115–123.

66 Karen LeFevre, *Invention as a Social Act* (Carbondale: Southern Illinois University Press, 1987).

67   Jeffrey Masten, *Textual Intercourse: Collaboration, Authorship, and Sexualities in Renaissance Drama* (New York: Cambridge University Press, 1997).

68   Wayne Koestenbaum, *Double Talk: The Erotics of Male Literary Collaboration* (New York: Routledge, 1989).

69   Koestenbaum, *Double Talk*, 4.

70   See Eve Kosofsky Sedgwick, *Epistemology of the Closet* (Berkeley: University of California Press, 1990); and Chauncey, *Gay New York*.

71   See John G. Nicolay and John Hay, eds., *Abraham Lincoln: A History*, 10 vols. (New York: Century Co., 1890); John G. Nicolay and John Hay, eds., *Complete Works of Abraham Lincoln*, 12 vols. (New York: Francis D. Tandy, 1905); John Hay, *Letters of John Hay and Extracts from Diary*, 3 vols. (New York: Gordian, 1969); Michael Burlingame and John R. Turner Ettlinger, eds., *Inside Lincoln's White House: The Complete Civil War Diary of John Hay* (Carbondale: Southern Illinois University Press, 1997); Michael Burlingame, ed., *At Lincoln's Side: John Hay's Civil War Correspondence and Selected Writings* (Carbondale: Southern Illinois University Press, 2000); Henry B. Van Hoesen, "Lincoln and John Hay," *Books at Brown* 18 (October 1960): 141–180; Ward H. Lamon, *Life of Abraham Lincoln* (Boston: Osgood and Co., 1872); William H. Herndon and Jesse W. Weik, *Herndon's Lincoln: The True Story of a Great Life*, 3 vols. (Chicago: Belford, Clark, and Co., 1889); and Donald, *Lincoln*.

72   See Mark C. Carnes and Clyde Griffen, eds., *Meanings for Manhood: Constructions of Masculinity in Victorian America* (Chicago: University of Chicago Press, 1990); Rotundo, *American Manhood*; Vincent J. Bertolini, "Fireside Chastity: The Erotics of Sentimental Bachelorhood in the 1850s," *American Literature* 68 (1996): 707–738; and Caleb Crain, *American Sympathy: Men, Friendship, and Literature in the New Nation* (New Haven, CT: Yale University Press, 2001).

73   Donald Yacovone, "'Surpassing the Love of Women': Victorian Manhood and the Language of Fraternal Love," in *A Shared Experience: Men, Women, and the History of Gender*, ed. Laura McCall and Donald Yacovone (New York: New York University Press, 1998), 195–221.

74   Walt Whitman, *Leaves of Grass: Facsimile Edition of the 1860 Text*, ed. Roy Harvey Pearce (Ithaca, NY: Cornell University Press, 1961), 753.

75   Robert Wiebe, "Lincoln's Fraternal Democracy," in *Abraham Lincoln and the American Political Tradition*, ed. John L. Thomas (Amherst: University of Massachusetts Press, 1986), 11, 19.

76   Quoted in Michael Burlingame, ed., *Lincoln's Journalist: John Hay's Anonymous Writings for the Press, 1860–1864* (Carbondale: Southern Illinois University Press, 1998), xxvi.

77   Quoted in Burlingame, *Lincoln's Journalist*, xxvii; and Van Hoesen, "Abraham Lincoln and John Hay," 157.

78   Michael Lynch, "'Here is Adhesiveness': From Friendship to Homosexuality," *Victorian Studies* 29 (1985): 92.

79   Quoted in Van Hoesen, "Abraham Lincoln and John Hay," 158.

80   See Lynch, "'Here is Adhesiveness.'"

81   *New York Tribune*, April 19, 1865, 4.

82   See Roy P. Basler, *The Lincoln Legend: A Study in Changing Conceptions* (1935; New York: Octagon Books, 1969); Merrill D. Peterson, *Lincoln in American Memory* (New York: Oxford University Press, 1994); and Barry Schwartz, *Abraham Lincoln and the Forge of National Memory* (Chicago: University of Chicago Press, 2000).

What Michael Leff says about Lincoln's "strategic use or emulation" among nineteenth-century orators can be generalized across the history of Lincoln memory: "Lincoln emerged as a complex, composite figure who could be interpreted and invoked in many different ways. There were, of course, limits to the range of this activity, but they were broad, and depending on circumstances and the interests of the orator, Lincoln could be constructed and adapted to fit a variety of political purposes and ideological agendas" (Michael C. Leff, "Lincoln Among the Nineteenth-Century Orators," in *Rhetoric and Political Culture in Nineteenth-Century America*, ed. Thomas W. Benson [East Lansing: Michigan State University Press, 1997], 135).

83 See Katz, *Love Stories*; Tripp, *The Intimate World of Abraham Lincoln*; Lewis Gannett and William A. Percy III, "Lincoln, Sex, and the Scholars," *The Gay and Lesbian Review Worldwide* 13 (2006): 18–22; Morris, "My Old Kentucky Homo"; and Morris, "Hard Evidence."

84 Walt Whitman, "When Lilacs Last in the Dooryard Bloom'd," "O Captain! My Captain!," "Hush'd Be the Camps Today," in *Leaves of Grass* (1891–1892; New York: Vintage Books, 1992), 459–468; and Walt Whitman, "Death of Abraham Lincoln," in *Specimen Days & Collect* (1883; Mineola, NY: Dover, 1995), 306–315.

85 Schwartz, *Abraham Lincoln and the Forge of National Memory*, ch. 2.

86 Peterson, *Lincoln in American Memory*, 139.

87 Cara A. Finnegan, "Recognizing Lincoln: Image Vernaculars in Nineteenth-Century Visual Culture," *Rhetoric & Public Affairs* 8 (2005): 51.

88 Shively, "Big Buck and Big Lick," 88.

89 Quoted in Basler, *The Lincoln Legend*, 283.

90 Ed Folsom, "Whitman's Calamus Photographs," in *Breaking Bounds: Whitman and American Cultural Studies*, ed. Betsy Erkkila and Jay Grossman (New York: Oxford University Press, 1996), 207.

91 Carl Sandburg, *Abraham Lincoln: The Prairie Years* (New York: Blue Ribbon Books, 1926), 1: 166–167; Ernest Hemingway, *The Sun Also Rises* (New York: Charles Scribner's Sons, 1926), ch. 12; Randall R. Griffey, "Marsden Hartley's Lincoln Portraits," *American Art* 15 (2001): 34–51; and Dudley Clendinen and Adam Nagourney, *Out for Good: The Struggle to Build a Gay Rights Movement in America* (New York: Simon and Schuster, 1999), 71.

92 Morris, "My Old Kentucky Homo."

93 Morris, "Hard Evidence."

94 Schwartz, *Abraham Lincoln and the Forge of National Memory*, 141, 251–255; and Butt, *Between You and Me*, 7.

95 See Allen Guelzo, Edward Steers, Jr., Joan L. Flinspach, John Y. Simon, Lucas E. Morel, Daniel W. Stowell, and Michael Burlingame, "The Lincoln Bedroom: A Critical Symposium," *Claremont Review of Books* (2005), www.claremont.org/writings/crb/summer2005/symposium.html (accessed December 7, 2006).

96 Barry Schwartz, "Lincoln at the Millennium," *Journal of the Abraham Lincoln Association* 24 (2003): 1–31.

97 Schwartz, "Lincoln at the Millennium," 24.

98 Schwartz, "Lincoln at the Millennium," 26.

99 Schwartz, "Lincoln at the Millennium," 31.

100 Bravmann, *Queer Fictions of the Past*, 4.

17

Public Address and the Revival of American Civic Culture

J. Michael Hogan

In their introduction to *American Voices: An Encyclopedia of Contemporary Oratory*, Bernard K. Duffy and Richard W. Leeman recall the classical conception of oratory and lament that the "grandiloquence" of nineteenth-century public address has given way to a "vernacular style" – a rhetoric of "image" and emotion – in our modern, mass-mediated society. Waxing nostalgic, they recall the golden age of American oratory, when "virtuosos" like Daniel Webster demonstrated their "prudence and erudition" from the public platform and people flocked to hear serious oratory on the Chautauqua and Lyceum circuits. Today, in contrast, speakers appeal to the "lowest common denominator," and audiences tend to be interested not in their ideas but their "quirks and mannerisms, their habits, lifestyles, and personal narratives and confessions." Like others before them, Duffy and Leeman blame television, suggesting that the tube has dumbed down the citizenry and transformed "intimacy, narrative, and self-reference" into "the unchallenged norms of political discourse."[1]

Duffy and Leeman have a point. Not only have the great orators disappeared, but so too have the street-corner conversations and community meetings where Americans used to engage in the business of everyday democracy. Strident, even shrill voices dominate the public airwaves, while ordinary citizens have been rendered indifferent, irrelevant, and silent. Meanwhile, our politicians duck the really tough issues, chasing red herrings or pandering to the masses with "quantifiably safe" speeches.[2] No wonder so many young people have dropped out of politics, refusing to vote and concluding that the "political process is both morally bankrupt and completely insulated from public pressure."[3]

Now President Barack Obama has called for a "new era of responsibility,"[4] an era in which we embrace not only the rights but the responsibilities of citizenship. If that vision is to be realized, we need a concerted effort to rediscover the democratic values and practices that have served us well in the past, and we need to invent new ways to reinvigorate our democracy. We need to find ways to use new technologies to strengthen rather undermine democratic values, and we need an educational renaissance emphasizing the habits and skills of engaged democratic citizenship. Above all, we need a renewed commitment to an old idea: that ordinary citizens, if properly educated and empowered, are capable of governing themselves. That is what David Matthews, president of the Kettering Foundation, has in mind when he imagines a "deliberative public democracy" – a democracy in which ordinary citizens "choose and act, not instead of government, but along with it."[5]

How might students of rhetoric and public address contribute to this revival of deliberative public democracy? As Duffy and Leeman suggest, we can begin by reminding our students of the "critical role" that speech plays in the "discourse and decision-making of the American polity."[6] Beyond that, we can help them understand what it means to be a "good citizen" and provide them with the knowledge and skills they need for civic life. We also can teach important lessons about the key rhetorical issues in democratic theory, including the limits of free speech and the threats posed by demagoguery in a free society. Finally, we can rediscover that sense of mission that defined the land-grant movement of the late nineteenth century. Resurrecting the civic and ethical foundations of the rhetorical tradition, we can recapture a spirit of public service and rededicate ourselves to making a difference in people's lives.

In this chapter, I elaborate on these and other ways public address scholars might contribute to a revival of American civic culture. My approach is, on the one hand, historical and traditional; it is grounded in the same traditions of rhetoric and civic republicanism that inspired the great democratic reformers of the early twentieth century – during the so-called Progressive era. At the same time, I take account of the growing diversity of our political culture and the impact of new communication technologies. In the spirit of the Progressive reformers, my emphasis is not on the rights but the *responsibilities* of citizenship, and I stress the need for an *ethical* conception of engaged democratic citizenship. If we hope to revitalize our civic culture, we need to recapture the normative spirit of the classical tradition – its emphasis on "civic virtue." At the same time, we must recognize that we live in very different times and that a democratic rhetoric for our age must reflect the social and technological realities of a rapidly changing world.

I begin by reviewing some of the latest developments in the ongoing debate over the health and vitality of America's civic institutions and traditions. I then discuss the relationship between America's civic crisis and the character and quality of our public discourse. Finally, I discuss some specific ways that students of rhetoric and public address might contribute to a revival of civic culture. As I have argued elsewhere,[7] I believe that the most promising solutions to the democratic crisis in America lie in a revival of rhetoric and public address as the core of a liberal education. More specifically, I argue for research and pedagogy that emphasizes the communicative skills of democratic citizenship, upholds higher rhetorical standards in the public sphere, and looks for ideas and inspiration for reviving our civic culture in the history and traditions of American public address.

The Crisis of Democracy in America

The publication of Robert Putnam's *Bowling Alone* in 2000 began a remarkable national debate over the health and vitality of America's civic culture.[8] Synthesizing an enormous body of data, Putnam documented declines in virtually every measure of civic engagement over the preceding half century, painting a portrait of a democracy in crisis. Much of Putnam's data was already familiar, of course. We already knew that voter turnout in presidential elections had dropped from over 60 percent in 1960 to under 50 percent in the 1990s, for example, despite greatly relaxed voter registration requirements, "motor voter" laws, and massive "get-out-the-vote" campaigns.[9] Yet other, less familiar measures of civic engagement had shown equally dramatic declines, including attendance at community meetings, religious participation, and membership in civic and charitable associations. In addition, there were significant declines in the number of people working for political parties, signing petitions, writing letters to their elected representatives and local newspapers, and giving speeches at political meetings and rallies. By the mid-1990s, some 32 million fewer Americans were involved in these sorts of activities than had been the case just two decades earlier. As Putnam summarized the bad news, fewer and fewer Americans were taking part "in the everyday deliberations that constitute grassroots democracy. In effect, more than a third of America's civic infrastructure simply evaporated between the mid-1970s and the mid-1990s."[10]

Not surprisingly, these signs of civic decay and political withdrawal were most pronounced among young people. Among voters between the ages of 18 and 24, for example, turnout had declined from about 50 percent in 1972 (the year 18-year-olds first became eligible to vote) to only about 32 percent in the 1996 election. In addition, the number of people under 35 who read a newspaper daily had dropped from about two-thirds to one-third between 1965 and 1990.[11] Some speculated that young people were simply turning to "new media," but as David Mindich argued, young people actually were "tuning out" the news altogether, including Internet sources of news and political information.[12] Indeed, many young people had completely lost faith in our democratic system. As political scientist Michael X. Delli Carpini concluded in 2000, younger Americans were not only "less knowledgeable about the substance or processes of politics," but also less trusting of their fellow citizens and less likely to participate in any sort of political activity. Not only did young people vote in lower numbers, but they were also less likely to join with others in their community to "address public problems through collective action or the formal policy process."[13]

Not all of Putnam's data pointed toward a crisis of democratic citizenship. The number of nonprofit organizations in America actually doubled between 1968 and 1997 (from 10,299 to 22,901),[14] and Americans were donating *more* money to political and civic causes than ever before. Self-help and issue-advocacy groups also were prospering, and volunteering – especially among young people – was on the rise.[15] According to Everett Carll Ladd, among others, these data suggested that civic engagement was not on the decline, but rather was being "renewed and extended," with Americans finding new outlets for their political expression and forming new associations to replace traditional civic groups like the PTA, the Lions Club, or the League of Women Voters.[16] Others pointed to the proliferation of Internet chat rooms and weblogs as evidence that civic engagement was not declining but merely assuming new forms. As early as 1996, for example, Richard Stengel noted that while Americans were going to fewer political meetings, they were nevertheless politically engaged, "discussing politics in the Internet equivalent of smokefilled rooms."[17]

Some even celebrated these trends as manifestations of a new "lifestyle politics." According to W. Lance Bennett, for example, there was no "crisis of democracy" in America, just "a shift away from old forms" of politics to "new forms of political interest and engagement." Civic culture was taking on "new identities," as people abandoned "traditional institutional politics" in favor of new, "more sensitive and expressive forms" of civic engagement. Reflecting changing economic realities and the impact of new technologies, this "liberation" from traditional politics reflected not only the "personal spirit of the times," but also helped to explain – even justify – the growing incivility of our political discourse. Generation X had gotten a "bad rap" for what was merely a new *style* of politics, Bennett concluded: "Incivility begins at home: Lifestyle issues are highly personal, leading to direct and even confrontational personal solutions over governmental ones."[18]

However one interpreted the data, it became clear by the end of the twentieth century that the United States had become a nation of *spectators* rather than *participants* in civic life. For more and more Americans, "getting involved" meant writing a check or participating in politics "virtually" via the Internet. Increasingly, the political landscape was dominated not by ordinary citizens but paid professionals – "hired guns" if you will – who raised and spent money promoting special interests. Some of these groups came *disguised* as "grassroots" movements, sounding populist themes and claiming broad-based support. But most were what sociologists have labeled "professional" or "astroturf" movements, consisting of small groups of fund-raising and public relations specialists.[19] Ordinary citizens supported such groups by donating money or signing online petitions, but they had no say in how their money was spent, nor were they participating in the deliberative or decision-making processes of those groups.

The rise of Internet politics only exacerbated the problem. The Internet opened up exciting new possibilities for citizen participation and engagement in civic life, yet thus far "virtual" politics has proven a poor substitute for the face-to-face interaction of a school board meeting or a town hall debate. Not only do people gravitate toward sites that confirm their existing beliefs, but the anonymity of the online environment seems to have encouraged an epidemic of "flaming" and other sorts of rhetorical excess. Lacking the personal accountability of face-to-face politics, the "virtual" political world has become a refuge for hatemongers, conspiracy theorists, and assorted other political crackpots and extremists. In the "virtual" political world, we have countless new sources of political information and opinion. Yet absent the "gatekeepers" of traditional media, it has become increasingly difficult to distinguish credible information from rumor, disinformation, and propaganda.

Since 2001, of course, there have been hopeful signs of civic revival in America. As Putnam himself noted, the 9/11 terrorist attacks apparently produced a "spike" in political awareness and participation, particularly among young people. In the wake of the attacks, the downward trend in "political consciousness and engagement" was at least "interrupted," and the public's interest in political affairs rose to levels "not seen in at least three decades."[20] This increase in civic participation was clearly evident in the 2004 and 2008 national elections, as many commentators have noted. In 2004, some 15 million *more* Americans turned out to vote than in 2000,[21] and in 2008, voter turnout hit a 40-year high as a record 131 million Americans went to the polls. That represented 61.6 percent of the nation's eligible voters, according to George Mason University political scientist Michael McDonald – a level of civic engagement not seen since the 1960s.[22] There also is some evidence that young people are rediscovering civic life. The most recent survey of incoming freshmen by the Higher Education Research Institute at UCLA found the highest level of political interest since the survey began in 1966,[23] and a recent study by the Center for Information and Research on Civic Learning and Engagement (CIRCLE) also found that young people are becoming increasingly involved in civic affairs. While many young people remain "turned off" by the "spin" and "polarized debate" of traditional politics, the so-called "Millennial Generation" is neither as cynical nor as selfish as the generation that preceded it, and many young people today care deeply about issues like the genocide in Darfur and the war in Iraq.[24]

Thus, there are reasons for optimism. At the same time, there are troubling signs that the nation's "civic health" continues to decline and that young people in particular remain largely disengaged from politics. In a major study released in September of 2006, for example, the National Conference on Citizenship (NCC) concluded that while the 9/11 attacks sparked a renewed "sense of community," there was no evidence of "the deeper civic transformation for which many had hoped." Charitable giving, volunteering, and political engagement all increased after the 9/11 attacks, but most of the NCC's 40 indicators of "civic health" (including measures of civic knowledge, trust in government, and faith in political institutions) soon resumed the downward trend of the past half century.[25] Two years later, the NCC's report on the nation's "civic health" was a bit more upbeat, noting that Americans were "actively engaged" in that year's presidential election and that there were encouraging signs that young people and others not previously engaged in civic affairs were getting more involved. Yet that same report also noted that more people described themselves as "frustrated" rather than "excited" by the election, and fewer than 20 percent expected to even "talk about" the issues once the election was over. The report also noted that the majority of young people – the Millennial Generation – remained "not very engaged," and that "levels of conventional community participation and connectedness" remained "low compared to 20 or 30 years ago."[26]

Perhaps Bennett is right: We have entered a new era of "lifestyle politics," with "new patterns of communication and civic engagement" that are "closer to home, less conventionally organized, and more likely to be defined in terms of struggles over evolving notions of rights, morals, and lifestyle values."[27] But so too is Harvard political scientist Theda Skocpol right when she says that we live in a "diminished democracy" – a democracy governed not so much by the people as by "professionally managed advocacy groups and institutions."[28] What can we do to reclaim our democracy from the special interests and the professional activists? In an age of "lifestyle" politics, is it even possible to change the "tone" of our politics, as President Obama has suggested, and engage in "vigorous debate" without "demonizing" those with "strongly held convictions on the other side"?[29] These are, at bottom, what Edwin Black dubbed *rhetorical* questions – questions about citizenship, social identity, and democratic deliberation that "tempt rhetorical interpretation."[30] In the next section of this chapter, I explore these issues at greater length, reflecting on the decline of our civic culture and its connections to the character and quality of our political discourse.

Civic Discourse and the Challenges of Ordinary Democracy

In his campus bestseller, former vice president and Nobel Prize winner Al Gore lamented the "assault on reason" that has corrupted our "market of ideas" and threatens our democratic way of life. "It is simply no longer possible to ignore the strangeness of our public discourse," Gore wrote in a reflection on the "systematic decay of the public forum" in America. This "assault on reason" is seen not only in superficial public argument and image-based campaigns, but also in the politics of fear and the willingness of some politicians to simply lie to the American people. Citing examples from the Bush administration, Gore, of course, had a political axe to grind. Yet his larger point remains valid: The "rules" of reasoned debate no longer hold sway in America, and the "superficial, emotional, and manipulative" rhetoric that now dominates our public forums is "not worthy of American democracy."[31]

The problem runs deeper than the deceptions of the Bush administration. With the proliferation of professional advocacy groups, the rhetoric of slogans and sound bites has displaced the collective voice of ordinary people deliberating over matters of public importance. Principled leadership has given way to appeals shaped by polling and focus groups, and we see more and more of the techniques of the propagandist and the demagogue in our mainstream political talk. During election campaigns, what Bill Clinton famously called the "politics of personal destruction" prevails, while in our legislative assemblies negotiation and compromise have given way to ideological posturing and gridlock. On radio and TV "debate" shows, speakers shout each other down, distort each other's positions, and hurl personal accusations and insults. No wonder so many young people are "turned off" by politics. For them, "politics" has become a meaningless "game," an exercise in verbal combat designed only to boost ratings.

One need not search hard for evidence of this coarsening of our public discourse. From Ann Coulter and Shawn Hannity on the right to Keith Olberman and Michael Moore on the left, advocates of all political stripes resort to name-calling, appeals to bigotry and fear, and outright deception as rhetorical strategies of first resort. After Coulter called Democratic presidential nominee John Edwards a "faggot" during a speech to the Conservative Political Action Committee, Democratic National Committee Chairman Howard Dean responded that there was "no place in political discourse for this kind of hate-filled and bigoted comments."[32] Yet this was the same Howard Dean who stereotyped Southerners as "guys with Confederate flags in their pickup trucks" and later called the Republicans "pretty much a white Christian Party" – a statement that some labeled "political hate speech."[33] From both sides of the political spectrum – and not just on the extremes – we hear angry, hateful speech, and the explanation seems obvious: Not only do the news media refuse to hold such speakers accountable, they actually *reward* them for bad behavior. By today's media standards, demagoguery is more "newsworthy" than well-reasoned speech.

Political scientist Morris P. Fiorina is right: Our political system has been hijacked by a "polarized political class" that is far more strident and polarized than the rest of us.[34] The pundits tell us that we are "split right down the middle, bitterly divided about national issues," but the truth is "more nearly the opposite": Most ordinary Americans are, in fact, ambivalent or uncertain about many political issues, and they "instinctively seek the center while the parties and candidates hang out on the extremes."[35] This is particularly true of younger people – those under the age of 30. According to CIRCLE, young people are turned off by the "spin" and "polarized debates" of today's mass-mediated politics; they are looking for more "authentic opportunities for discussing public issues."[36] Seeking the middle ground with regard to both policies and political parties, they do *not* embrace the rhetoric of confrontation, as implied by theorists of "lifestyle politics."[37] To the contrary, they actively resist the efforts of politicians, political activists, and the media to manipulate them, and they consider "open conversations" with a diversity of voices more "authentic" than the rhetoric of partisan combat.[38]

So who is to blame for the sorry state of public discourse in America today? Obviously, the "hired guns" of the special interest groups bear much of the blame. Competing for media attention and accountable only to the "true believers" who fund them, these specialists in high-tech demagoguery exploit divisive, highly emotional issues to demonize their "enemies" in what they view as a zero-sum "game" of politics. In their political world, winning is everything, and that means destroying the opposition, not finding common ground or solving our nation's problems. Indeed, we have had to invent new verbs to describe the methods of these rhetorical "hit men": To "Bork" or to "Swiftboat" the opposition means to win through character assassination.[39]

Journalists and political pundits, of course, must share in the blame. Over the past century, as political scientist Larry Sabato has noted, journalists have evolved from "lapdogs" to "watchdogs" to "junkyard dogs,"[40] and many now exhibit a corrosively cynical attitude toward our political leaders and institutions. With a special taste for personal failures and scandals, journalists who once boasted of their objectivity now trade in rumors, speculation, and personal attacks, fearful of being "scooped" by the tabloids or some anonymous blogger. Drawn to the most extreme and polarizing voices, even the mainstream media encourage rhetorical excess by rewarding public figures for their outrageous statements. Meanwhile, highly paid commentators and talk show hosts – dubbed the "punditocracy" by Eric Alterman[41] – traffic in gossip and innuendo and stage phony "debates." No wonder so many Americans have lost faith in the media.[42] For many of today's journalists, politics is not about important public policy issues, but about "competition, conflict, performance and artifice, hidden motivation, and self-interest."[43]

Finally, higher education must shoulder its part of the blame for our civic malaise. Instead of leading efforts to revive and reinvigorate our deliberative democracy, colleges and universities have stifled free speech on campus and have failed to provide students with the knowledge and skills they need for engaged citizenship. On many campuses, investments in math and science programs have come at the expense of the humanistic disciplines that educate for citizenship, and higher education in general has lost that *spirit* of engagement and public service that defined the land-grant movement of the late nineteenth century. As historian Thomas Bender has noted, the American research university at one time combined specialized research with education for citizenship, producing not just "scholars alone" but also "educated civic leaders and journalists" – including such towering figures as Theodore Roosevelt and Woodrow Wilson.[44] Over time, American universities lost that sense of mission, as David D. Cooper has argued, and today even the humanities have been corrupted by an "academic meritocracy" and a "clamber for display, recognition, self-promotion, and fame" that has undermined both the teaching and the civic mission of the research university.[45] As the late Ernest Boyer of the Carnegie Foundation summarized the situation in the mid-1990s: "Higher education is suffering from a loss of overall direction, a nagging feeling that it is no longer at the vital center of the nation's work."[46]

In recent years, a variety of educators, charitable foundations, and civic groups have launched new initiatives to promote civic engagement. After publishing *Bowling Alone*, for example, Robert Putnam founded the Saguano Seminar, which is an ongoing program of the John F. Kennedy School of Government at Harvard University dedicated to developing "far-reaching, actionable ideas to significantly increase Americans' connectedness to one another and to community institutions."[47] At the University of Texas, the Annette Strauss Institute for Civic Participation has a similar mission: (1) to conduct "cutting-edge research on the ways in which civic participation and community understanding are undermined or sustained," and (2) to "develop new programs for increasing democratic understanding among citizens."[48] Another initiative, Project Pericles, provides funding to colleges across the nation to improve their community-service efforts and to "make civic engagement a part of the curriculum in every department."[49] And at the more than 1,100 colleges and universities affiliated with Campus Compact, literally millions of students have been involved over the past 20 years in a variety of civic and community-service projects.[50]

A handful of these initiatives have focused specifically on public discussion and deliberation. The National Issues Forum (NIF), for example, promotes "locally sponsored public forums for the consideration of public-policy issues."[51] These forums range from large, town-hall meetings to smaller "study circles," and many of them have had encouraging results. After a series of NIF forums on immigration, for example, an assessment study concluded that the deliberations had encouraged participants to "think in broader, national terms," to acknowledge the "hopes and dreams" of immigrants, and to reject the fear appeals of some politicians and special interests. As they "worked through" the issue, participants became better informed and "less polarized," and they ultimately came together on the need for "some kind of practical, middle-ground solution" to the problem.[52]

Yet not all NIF forums have had such positive results. After a forum on the public's role in American politics, participants generally agreed that "something" was "dreadfully off track" in our political system, and many left still feeling "alienated from politics and community affairs – and powerless to do much about them." As the deliberations progressed, a few "made connections" between their own lives and national political affairs, but others left "feeling as cynical and dispirited as when they came in." Some even left "stewing," apparently more convinced than ever that the public had no real say in American politics. In the end, the deliberations produced a "strong but inchoate sense" that the nation was "on the wrong track," yet participants were unable to arrive at shared solutions and many "left the forums feeling as pessimistic as when they came in," doubtful that "things would change" no matter how the public acted.[53]

Other experiments in public deliberation have been equally disappointing. In a test of a well-known proposal for a national "Deliberation Day,"[54] a group of researchers convened 63 citizens – some from the "liberal" city of Boulder, Colorado, and the rest from the more "conservative" city of Colorado Springs – and asked them to discuss what the researchers dubbed three of the "most contested issues" of our time: global warming, affirmative action, and civil unions for same-sex couples. Supposedly replicating the "voluntary self-sorting" of people in the real world, the citizens of each city deliberated among themselves, and the results were perhaps predictable: Reinforced by like-minded neighbors, citizens from both cities actually became *more* extreme and *less* diverse in their opinions on these issues. Instead of increasing empathy for opposing points of view or a greater willingness to compromise, the experiment produced what the researchers labeled "ideological amplification," or the exaggeration of "preexisting tendencies."[55]

Why do some deliberations seem to inspire and motivate, while others only seem to polarize and exacerbate the differences among us? What *sorts* of procedures and deliberative forums work best, and how might citizens be better prepared to deliberate effectively? All of these questions invite further research, but history and common sense suggest some preliminary answers. First, for deliberations to work, they must be *authentic* and *meaningful*; that is, they must involve issues that genuinely matter to the participants, and the participants must have reason to believe that they can make a difference.[56] Second, deliberations must include a diversity of views, testing those differing perspectives in the give-and-take of open debate. Deliberations among like-minded people (e.g., the Deliberation Day experiment) are not really deliberations at all. Third, citizens must be taught *how* to deliberate; they not only need to learn about the issues to be discussed, but also how to communicate effectively and "work through" an issue (to use the NIF's terms).[57] Finally, public deliberations, if they are to be productive, require at least some basic level of historical and civic literacy. In order to deliberate effectively, citizens need at least *some* understanding of their nation's history and institutions and an *ethical* commitment to deliberating "in good faith."

In the remainder of this chapter, I discuss just a few of the ways that research and teaching in rhetoric and public address can contribute to more robust and productive democratic deliberation. At a time when the whole idea of debate and deliberation has become tainted, we first need to define – or *redefine* – what it *means* to deliberate. We need to articulate new rules and ethical standards for democratic deliberation, and we need to teach people *how* to deliberate. We also need to uphold higher standards of public discourse and teach citizens to be more critical consumers in the "marketplace of ideas." Finally, we need to rediscover America's rich heritage of democratic deliberation, using scholarship and teaching in the history of American public address to promote historical awareness, civic literacy, and engaged democratic citizenship.

The Rhetorical Tradition and the Art of Democratic Deliberation

"For democracy to work," as Patricia Roberts-Miller has written, people "have to talk," and "the ability of the general public to make appropriate decisions depends to a large degree on the quality of public discourse." If democratic deliberation is to produce sound collective judgments, people must look beyond their own "self-interest and limited points of view" and join with others in promoting the "general interest" or the "common good." Moreover, there must be rules to guide public deliberations, lest they degenerate into "name-calling, confrontation, or even coercion and violence." Roberts-Miller is right: we *need* "rules" of public deliberation and some shared conception of what constitutes "good public discourse."[58]

For most of our nation's history, of course, the "rules" for "good public discourse" have been drawn from the classical rhetorical tradition. At the time of our nation's founding, for example, classical rhetoric "lay at the heart of [a] ... liberal education," as historian Gordon Wood has noted, and the ability to deliver an eloquent oration was "regarded as a necessary mark of a gentleman and an indispensable skill for a statesman, especially for a statesman in a republic."[59] Over the next century, America's most renowned speakers continued to draw upon that tradition, forging a "golden age" of American oratory in the antebellum era and a "second oratorical renaissance" at the turn of the twentieth century – in the so-called Progressive era.[60] As the new century began, spellbinders like William Jennings Bryan reached out to mass audiences as never before, and Roosevelt and Wilson transformed the presidency into a "mighty platform for oratorical leadership."[61] Yet even as our political leaders addressed an expanding and more diverse democratic public, they remained bound by the artistic and ethical rules of the neoclassical rhetorical tradition. As Wilson himself expressed that commitment, the true "orator statesman" was committed to reason rather than "sophistry" and was a person of good character, distinguished by his "clearness of vision," courage in his convictions, and a certain "earnestness of purpose."[62]

As the twentieth century unfolded, science, technology, and the continuing expansion of the democratic public raised new challenges to the classical or neoclassical tradition. During World War I, Wilson's own Committee on Public Information pioneered new techniques of mass persuasion and propaganda that began to undermine faith in the public's collective judgment, and after the war, that new "science" of persuasion gave rise to modern advertising and public relations. Over the next half century, first radio and then television again redefined the conventions or "rules" of public talk, as a "cooler," more conversational style of speech replaced the metaphors of "fire and battle" in the discourse of American politics.[63] In the 1960s and 1970s, of course, the rhetoric of social movements once again inspired students of public address to rethink both the "rules" of public discourse and the canon of "great" speeches. Concerned that the neoclassical ideals of rationality, civility, and decorum might silence the voices of dissent and serve as "masks for the preservation of injustice,"[64] scholars sympathetic to the great movements for social change in the 1960s looked for alternatives to the dominant neo-Aristotelian paradigm and found them in theories of dramatism and the "ego-functions" of protest rhetoric.[65]

Today, rhetorical scholars continue to rethink and revise the "rules" of public speech and democratic deliberation. Some, like Roberts-Miller, continue to worry that "rules" of "good public discourse" might exclude marginalized groups by condemning "the very kind of rhetoric most likely to effect social change by or on behalf of the oppressed"[66] – the passionate, even confrontational rhetoric of populist social movements. Others reject rules altogether, insisting that any such rules inevitably silence or marginalize some voices.[67] Yet without *any* rules or standards distinguishing the good from the bad, public discourse inevitably becomes impoverished or worse – it devolves, as Roberts-Miller suggests, into demagoguery and coercion. In short, we *need* rules of "good public discourse." The trick is to strike the right balance between order and dissent, between reason and passion, between our need for rules and our commitments to diversity, inclusion, and free speech.

How can we uphold rules of "good public discourse" without marginalizing some voices or silencing dissent? In the remainder of this chapter, I offer some preliminary answers to this question by reflecting upon three major areas of research and teaching in rhetoric and public address: (1) public speaking and debate, where the basic skills and ethics of democratic deliberation are taught; (2) rhetorical crit-icism, or scholarship and teaching *about* the character and quality of public dis-course; and (3) the history of American public address, where we study the American rhetorical tradition and the "lessons" to be learned from the past. In each of these areas, I suggest directions in research and teaching that might help reinvigorate democratic deliberation and contribute to a broader revival of American civic culture.

Public speaking, debate, and the ethics of democratic deliberation

At first glance, most of today's public speaking textbooks reflect the classical roots of our discipline. Treating the *mechanics* of public speaking much as the ancients did, most still divide the subject into the five classical "canons" and distinguish among Aristotle's three "modes of proof." A few now incorporate findings from modern social scientific research, and some even mention contemporary theories of narrative, dramatism, or cultural myth. For the most part, however, the basic public speaking course is still wedded to the classical or neoclassical tradition. We still teach our students to adapt to their audiences, make reasoned arguments, and avoid emotional or stylistic excesses that might alienate or offend listeners.

There is, however, one sense in which today's public speaking textbooks diverge radically from those of a hundred or even 50 years ago: They say virtually nothing about the role of public speaking in a democracy, nor do they say much about the personal *character* of the speaker or the *ethics* of speech. Most pay lip service to mundane ethical issues, such as plagiarism or citing one's sources. But they say little about the rights and responsibilities of citizenship, the limits of free speech, or the ethics of advocacy in a democracy. They have nothing even remotely resembling Quintilian's portrait of the ideal speaker – the "good man skilled at speaking" – with its emphasis on ethics, citizenship, and devotion to the common good. Instead, today's public speaking textbooks are typically grounded in one of two very different ethical paradigms: a business or corporate ethic that upholds per-sonal advancement as the highest ideal, or an ideological ethic grounded in femi-nist, multicultural, or even postmodern theory.[68]

In the business model of public speaking – a model that I have elsewhere labeled the "Dale Carnegie approach" to public speaking[69] – the emphasis is on personal advancement, not the responsibilities of citizenship. It is all about showmanship and "winning," not disinterested leadership, civic engagement, or the "common good." Upholding the manipulation of others as the measure of "success," this approach teaches public speaking not as a liberal art but as a skill that one needs to "beat the competition."[70] Needless to say, this only exacerbates some of the worst tendencies in our already polarized and degraded public discourse.

The ideological approach, on the other hand, emphasizes personal identity and cultural diversity. Many of these books still treat the *mechanics* of public speaking in the language of the classical tradition.[71] Yet they imply a very different portrait of the ideal orator, and the personal and political values they celebrate are very different. Rejecting what historian Arthur M. Schlesinger, Jr., once described as "the historic theory of America as one people" – the theory that has "thus far managed to keep American society whole" – they promote not collective unity but "the fragmentation, resegregation, and tribalization of American life."[72]

Of course, public speaking textbooks must change with the times, and even Schlesinger concedes that multicultural education has helped Americans develop a "more complex and invigorating sense of the world – and of themselves."[73] That broader cultural awareness will become even more important in the years to come. Our textbooks need to acknowledge the challenges of public deliberation in a diverse, multicultural society, and we also need to take account of globalization and new information technologies. But that does not mean that we cannot uphold democratic ideals or a model of the ideal orator – a speaker with "civic virtue" and a devotion to the "common good." Nor does it mean that we can no longer aspire to some larger vision of our common purposes and values as a nation.

That is the idea behind at least one new public speaking textbook, *Public Speaking and Civic Engagement*.[74] In some respects, our book differs little from other textbooks; it treats the basic skills of public speaking like all those grounded in the classical tradition. It differs radically, however, in its emphasis on the role of speech in a democratic society and the responsibilities – not just the rights – of citizenship. Devoting an entire chapter to the ethics of speech, the book draws not only from the ancient rhetorical tradition but also from more contemporary theories of democratic deliberation. Throughout the book, we reflect on what it means to deliberate "in good faith,"[75] and the chapters on persuasion emphasize the distinction between effective and ethical speech and discuss at length the limits of free speech and the threat propaganda and demagoguery pose to our democracy. Even the chapter on ceremonial speaking reflects a concern with ethics and the responsibilities of citizenship, as we reflect upon the politics of epideictic discourse and treat such speeches not as an afterthought (as most textbooks do), but as an important mechanism for "defining and sustaining our civic culture."[76]

At the same time, *Public Speaking and Civic Engagement* has a strong emphasis on the speaker's responsibility to respect cultural differences, avoid stereotyping, and consider the role of race, gender, ethnicity, education, and class in all phases of the speech-making process. We also acknowledge the importance of dissent – even radical, militant, or confrontational speech – in the American rhetorical tradition. Noting that passionate political activists have "played an important role in American history, giving voice to the powerless and calling attention to injustices long ignored,"[77] we introduce students to a number of principled dissenters who have helped shape the American democratic experience: Angelina Grimké, Wendell Phillips, Eugene Debs, César Chávez, and Martin Luther King, Jr., to name just a few. In other words, we strive for a balance between upholding rules for "good public discourse" and acknowledging the role of protest and dissent in the American rhetorical tradition.

Reviewers have praised *Public Speaking and Civic Engagement* for incorporating the theme of civic engagement "into the very core" of the text and for effectively "weaving" together the "skills" of public speaking and the theme of civic engagement.[78] Yet it's not enough to talk about ethics and citizenship in our basic public speaking courses. We need to educate for citizenship in all of our courses, including advanced public speaking, speechwriting, argumentation and debate, and group communication. At Penn State, for example, we are experimenting with linked sections of the basic speech and writing courses, with students reading a common book on rhetoric and democracy, and we're now developing a new introductory course for honors students combining instruction in writing, speaking, visual communication, and digital media. With these and other curriculum initiatives, we hope to return rhetorical studies to the core of the liberal arts.

Beyond curriculum reform, perhaps the time has come to stand up to those who have corrupted extracurricular debate and forensics. At one time, of course, debate and forensics served as a "laboratory for the democratic process and an important training ground for future policy makers."[79] Such programs were also good public relations, attracting the university's best and brightest to our field and creating networks of loyal alumni. Now, however, so-called policy debate in particular has lost touch with reality, becoming a public embarrassment and draining our resources into an elitist, narcissistic activity that neither advances the discipline nor educates for citizenship. Some debaters "spew" arguments so rapidly that they can barely catch a breath (much less be understood), while others stage dramatic "performances," jumping up and down while passionately declaiming from their own personal diaries or denouncing the "white supremacy" inherent in the norms of debate.[80] At the 2008 national tournament of the Cross-Examination Debate Association (CEDA), one round even culminated in an obscenity-laden shouting match, during which a faculty coach dropped his pants to "moon" a judge. The coach, William Shanahan III of Fort Hayes State University, was fired for his actions, yet – amazingly – the debate community rallied to his defense, depicting him as some sort of martyr. In the strange and insular world of intercollegiate policy debate, Shanahan's firing apparently symbolized the threat posed by outsiders who just "don't get" the new "style" of debate grounded in "postmodern theory."[81]

Perhaps policy debate can be saved by a more stringent Code of Professional Conduct, as CEDA seems to think.[82] Or perhaps we simply need to steer students toward parliamentary debate or individual events that still involve competition but at least demand that participants communicate and behave like normal human beings. Yet there are other, better alternatives to traditional debate and forensics – extracurricular speech and debate activities that cultivate many of the same skills yet encourage collaboration and public service rather than narcissistic competition. At Ripon College, for example, Professors Jody Roy and Steve Martin have created the Ripon College Speakers Bureau, which trains students in public speaking and sends them into the community to advocate on behalf of local and national nonprofit groups. Since its inception in 2006, speakers from the Speakers Bureau have advocated on behalf of Students Against Violence Everywhere (SAVE), a national nonprofit association promoting conflict management and good citizenship in the schools, and the Huntington's Disease Society of America, which raises awareness of that devastating degenerative brain disorder. Other student speakers have helped rally public support for animal shelters and public libraries, among other local organizations. One graduate of the program has even made a career out of speaking, traveling around the country telling the tragic story of his own father's downward spiral into alcoholism and suicide. Shawn Karsten, whose father Adrian was an Emmy Award-winning sports reporter for ESPN, offers inspirational talks to other young people coping with alcoholic parents or family tragedies, and he even counsels adults in alcohol and addiction recovery programs. His speech about living with an alcoholic parent, "What It Feels Like To Be Your Kid," has helped a number of addicted parents to stay sober.[83]

A revival of our civic culture must begin with the basics: teaching young people about the *ethics* of public advocacy and the responsibilities of citizenship. In our introductory public speaking courses, we need to revive the neoclassical emphasis on "civic virtue," and in all of our courses we ought to cultivate the practical skills of engaged citizenship. If we are to support extracurricular debate and forensics, we should insist that such programs educate for citizenship, and we should continue to develop alternatives that better complement what we teach in the classroom. In our increasingly complex, culturally diverse, and technologically advanced society, it is not enough that we teach students how to communicate effectively. We also need to teach them what it means to deliberate "in good faith."

Rhetorical criticism, public scholarship, and the scholarship of teaching

What does it mean to be a "rhetorical critic"? What is it that we do, and what is our mission as scholars and teachers? Historically, as others have noted, the answers seemed clear, as the pioneers of our discipline articulated a rationale for creating departments of speech and founded a scholarly tradition of academic rhetorical criticism. For the first half century, our subject matter was oratory, which focused not on the timelessness or the beauty of great fiction, but was "intimately associated with statecraft," as Herbert Wichelns declared. Hence, the rhetorical critic had to not only study the classical rhetorical tradition, but also be a "careful student of history" and politics.[84]

The subsequent history of the field is likewise well known: the dominance of the neo-Aristotelian paradigm, the liberating influence of Edwin Black's *Rhetorical Criticism*, and the emergence over the last three decades of a more mature, more sophisticated, book-oriented discipline – a period that some dubbed the "renaissance" in American public address.[85] But where does that leave us now? And where is the field headed in the twenty-first century? Perhaps we now enjoy a better reputation as a scholarly enterprise. But are we doing a better job of teaching our students? Are we making important contributions to society?

If rhetoric and public address is to prosper in the twenty-first century, we need to be sensitive to larger trends in the humanities and to broader debates over the character and mission of the modern university. Especially in times like these, we need to do a better job explaining how we contribute to society; the humanities in general, as literary scholar Mark Bauerlein has suggested, need to do more than crank out arcane scholarly books that nobody reads.[86] This is not to say that we should pander to the consumer mentality of some students, nor does it mean that public opinion ought to dictate every detail of our scholarly and pedagogical agenda. But it does mean we have an obligation to produce socially useful knowledge, and it means that we should rededicate ourselves to teaching and service. If we expect society to continue investing in higher education, we need to reflect seriously on our mission and contributions.

Stanley N. Katz of the Woodrow Wilson School of Public and International Affairs at Princeton has made the point powerfully. Reacting to two recent surveys on the public's attitudes toward higher education, Katz writes that it "matters deeply what the public thinks of us. Ours is a public profession. We serve society both by training its young (and, increasingly, its old) and by creating socially necessary knowledge." Professors talk a lot about "academic freedom," but with those rights come responsibilities – to our students, to our universities, and to our larger communities. Chief among those is the "duty to teach," which should be the "core of our mission." We also have a responsibility to reform doctoral education, which has become so specialized that it can "neither support broad-based research or train postsecondary teachers." Finally, we have a responsibility to serve not just our disciplines but our local institutions, our communities, and our nation. As professors, Katz concludes, "our duty is to profess," and that means embracing our "calling" to be dedicated teachers and good citizens as well as accomplished researchers.[87]

As rhetorical critics, what do we "profess"? What sorts of socially useful knowledge do we produce, and what are our responsibilities to our students and fellow citizens? David Zarefsky has suggested one answer: As students of rhetoric, we can help our fellow citizens make sense of complex public policy debates. We also can help them to distinguish between the "two faces of democratic rhetoric" – the "benign" face that represents an "invitation to deliberate," and the "threatening" face that seeks to "engineer consent." Beyond that, Zarefsky urges us to promote the habits and attitudes of what Walter Lippmann called the "public philosophy" – the philosophy that acknowledges uncertainty and controversy over difficult public issues, recognizes and appreciates diverse points of views, and subjects those views to critical scrutiny. In short, we can help citizens function as members of a "deliberating and decision-making public."[88] And that means not only defending free speech and the right of minority voices to be heard, but also speaking out against demagoguery and propaganda, whatever the source. As rhetorical critics, we might fashion ourselves consumer "watchdogs" in the "marketplace of ideas," serving society by upholding higher standards of public discourse.

My own work as a rhetorical critic has ranged over a broad terrain, from critiques of presidential rhetoric and electoral campaigns, to studies of congressional foreign policy debates, direct mail campaigns, television news, political films, and documentaries. I have published exposés of K-12 curricula that mislead and indoctrinate children,[89] and I have written a number of critiques of what I call the "rhetoric of polling" – a pseudo-scientific discourse that oversimplifies complex issues, silences minority voices, closes off public debate, and routinely misrepresents the "will of the people."[90] What defines my work, then, is not a particular medium (like oratory) nor subject matter (like presidential rhetoric), but rather a *spirit* of critical intervention in the deliberative process. Generally, I am drawn to discourses that strike me as *designed* to deceive or manipulate, and I view my mission as exposing *how* those discourses work.

We can infuse this same spirit of critical intervention into our teaching as well. Through the scholarship of teaching, we can help our students become more informed, more thoughtful citizens, equipped with the knowledge and skills they need to be "citizen critics," as my colleague Rosa Eberly might put it.[91] Most Americans still think a college education should prepare students for a career, but some 85 percent of the public also consider it "important" or "very important" that we teach college students to be "responsible citizens."[92] That represents a pivotal opportunity for students of rhetoric and public address. We should be pushing for *more* general education courses in rhetorical and media criticism – courses that teach critical thinking, the ethics of public advocacy, and Lippmann's "public philosophy." At Penn State, for example, we have a popular general education course, "Persuasion and Propaganda," which emphasizes the rights and responsibilities of free speech in a democratic society and the distinctions between legitimate persuasion in a democratic society and the techniques of the propagandist and the demagogue. Examining everything from World War I propaganda posters to hate rhetoric and conspiracy theories on the Web, the course equips students to critically engage a wide variety of rhetorical texts with heightened sensitivity to the ethics of persuasion.

No less than virtuous and skilled public speakers, a deliberative public democracy requires both professional rhetorical critics and citizens educated to be more discerning and critical themselves. Through our scholarship, we can hold all who communicate in public to higher standards, and we can help our fellow citizens guard against deceptive and manipulative rhetorical techniques. Beyond that, we can emphasize the links between rhetoric and democracy in our scholarship of teaching, and we can teach our students about the rights *and* the responsibilities of free speech in America. If we hope to restore the balance between the two faces of democratic rhetoric, as Zarefsky has urged, we must "further the goals of deliberative democracy" in all of our scholarship and teaching.[93]

Recovering the spirit and traditions of American public address

Finally, why study the history of American public address? What can we learn by studying dead orators, or dead issues like slavery or woman suffrage? How might historical studies in public address contribute to a revival of American civic culture? According to Kenneth Burke, of course, we study demagogues like Adolf Hitler in order to better understand how such "medicine men" concocted their deadly brew, so that we know "what to guard against, if we are to forestall the concocting of similar medicine in America."[94] Yet there are other, more positive lessons to be learned from the history of public address as well. By studying the great speakers, speeches, political campaigns, and social movements of the past, we can discover ways to promote a revival of robust and productive public deliberation in America.

Much of my own historical work has focused on the so-called Progressive era,[95] a period in which our nation faced many of the same challenges we face today: rapid technological change, economic inequality, environmental degradation, racial tensions, loss of community, and political disaffection. As I have argued elsewhere,[96] Progressive reformers did not address these problems simply by passing new laws or implementing governmental programs. Rather, they sought ways to promote more public deliberation and looked for solutions to their problems in the collective wisdom of the people. For many Progressives, the essential challenge of the era was what John Dewey would later call "the problem of the public": the need to educate the masses in "the methods and conditions of debate, discussion, and persuasion."[97] In an increasingly complex world, Progressives feared that powerful special interests had supplanted the "voice of the people," and they sought ways to revitalize or even reinvent the public sphere.

This concern with public deliberation was at the heart of the reform efforts of that great Progressive crusader, Robert La Follette.[98] It also inspired a wide variety of initiatives designed to encourage more public discussion and debate. Progressives launched a "social centers" movement that opened school buildings to town meetings and public debates, and they founded many of the civic and voluntary associations that still exist today. Progressives staged community forums in settlement houses, and they revived the Chautauqua movement to educate farmers and other rural folk. In small Midwestern cities, they appointed "Civic Secretaries" to organize public meetings and debates, and they invented school newspapers and student governments to teach young people about politics. Meanwhile, debate and forensics clubs flourished in colleges and universities, and the University of Wisconsin even established a Department of Debating and Public Discussion to promote off-campus public debates on the income tax, woman suffrage, and other issues.[99]

By participating in such activities, citizens of the Progressive era "learned the necessary skills of a democratic public: how to listen, how to argue, and how to deliberate."[100] In response to waves of new immigrants and the changing role of women, they also learned some painful lessons about the challenges of democratic deliberation in an increasingly diverse society. Finally, they learned what Woodrow Wilson taught as a professor of politics and government: that true eloquence does not merely consist of "a good voice and a few ringing sentences," but rather must reflect the "character, spirit, and thought" of the nation.[101] In Wilson's view, citizens needed at least *some* understanding of "the history and leading conceptions" of the nation's political institutions and traditions,[102] and they needed to learn how to distinguish between charlatans and what Wilson called "orator-statesmen" – leaders who were not only eloquent but devoted to the common good.[103]

By studying the Progressive era, we can learn important lessons about promoting public deliberation. We can create twenty-first-century equivalents of the Chautauqua or the Civic Secretaries of that era, and we can imagine new spaces and forums for public deliberation. We can learn ways to nurture the habits and skills of engaged democratic citizenship, and we can find new ways to accommodate the wide range of views and interests in our increasingly diverse society. We can learn how to cultivate a renewed appreciation for the well-crafted argument and the eloquent speech, and we can help replenish our common store of civic and historical knowledge. In short, we can learn ways to promote more "serious speech," as E. J. Dionne, Jr. has put it – speech "in search of truth"; speech designed not just to defeat political adversaries, but to aid citizens in their "common search for understanding"; speech that *engages* citizens in "a continuous and ongoing effort to balance worthy but competing values, to mediate conflicts, to resolve disputes, to solve problems."[104]

Other periods in the history of American public address also have important lessons to teach. For profiles in rhetorical courage, we can look to the abolitionists or the women's rights activists of the nineteenth century. For lessons in presidential leadership, we might study the rhetoric of Abraham Lincoln, Theodore Roosevelt, or Franklin D. Roosevelt. To better understand the techniques of the demagogue, we might look first to Joseph McCarthy, then to a long list of others who have made a career out of deceiving and manipulating others. And for lessons in breaking down racial or gender barriers, we need look no further than the presidential campaign of 2008 – a campaign that produced a number of "firsts" for both African Americans and women.

By studying the great speeches and debates of the past, the next generation can carry on America's tradition of democratic deliberation. And that is the idea behind *Voices of Democracy: The US Oratory Project* (*VOD*), a new online curriculum resource funded by the National Endowment for the Humanities.[105] With a multimedia archive of significant speeches, along with curricular materials specific to each speech, *VOD* helps bring history to life for students, allowing them to study the actual words of people who have made a difference by "speaking out." It also teaches important lessons about the nation's history and civic traditions, and it promotes critical sensitivity to the rhetorical strategies and ethical choices of a variety of speakers. Finally, *VOD* may well inspire young people to "speak out" themselves. As students of rhetoric and public address, we cannot solve all the problems of our nation's democracy. But with projects like *VOD*, we *can* make a difference as part of a broader movement to revive American civic culture.

Conclusion

The American people have not yet given up on higher education. Indeed, public confidence in American colleges and universities remains "strong and steady," although recent surveys show growing concerns over a number of issues, including the "liberal bias" of faculties, the cost and accessibility of a college education, and the overemphasis on big-time sports. The public also wants to see universities focus less on their economic development and research missions and "more on the basics: general education, adult education, leadership and responsibility, and teacher training."[106] For students of rhetoric and public address, that means more *public* scholarship and a renewed commitment to teaching and service. It also means clarifying what we "profess" and becoming more actively engaged in ongoing debates over curriculum reform and the mission of higher education.

Public address scholars also have a broader social responsibility to speak out against the assault on reason that continues to threaten our "marketplace of ideas." As the debate over health care reform has demonstrated, that threat has grown even worse, as propagandists on both the left and right have launched well-funded campaigns deliberately designed to scare, deceive, and manipulate the public. When town halls degenerate into near riots and members of Congress act like spoiled children during presidential speeches, perhaps the time has come for a serious national debate over debate itself. As a coalition of deliberative democracy advocates put it in a recent statement, "Joe the Citizen" has been "squeezed out" of the health care debate by ideologues on both sides. The town halls offered little to the "millions of Americans who see the tough trade offs that need to be addressed," or who were "simply confused" and wanted "an open, fair discussion to help them make up their minds." Those town halls pointed to the need for new spaces where people with "honest questions" could "explore tough policy issues, hear one another, and productively work things through to find common ground." This is more than a matter of simply "encouraging more civil behavior," the statement concluded: "What we urgently need is a vibrant, inclusive democracy where people from different views and backgrounds can routinely meet, hear each other out in productive ways, and find ways to move forward."[107]

As scholars of public address, we need to stand up to the demagogues and propagandists in the public sphere, as well as the cynical celebrity journalists and the strident, uncompromising special interests whose "grammar of hostility" fuels the contemporary "culture wars."[108] And we need to teach our students and our fellow citizens to be more critical consumers of public discourse themselves. Perhaps new technologies can help provide those "new spaces" where the voices of ordinary citizens can be heard.[109] But new technologies alone cannot solve all our problems. We also need an *ethical* revival, a renewal of the democratic spirit of the classical tradition and a commitment to empowering *all* citizens in our increasingly diverse society. Students of rhetoric and public address have important contributions to make to that revival of civic culture in America – if only they have the will and the courage of their convictions.

Notes

1   Bernard K. Duffy and Richard W. Leeman, eds., *American Voices: An Encyclopedia of Contemporary Oratory* (Westport, CT: Greenwood Press, 2005), xi–xxv.
2   See Wynton C. Hall, "The Invention of 'Quantifiably Safe Rhetoric': Richard Wirthlin and Ronald Reagan's Instrumental Use of Public Opinion Research in Presidential Discourse," *Western Journal of Communication* 66 (2002): 319–346.

3   David T. Z. Mindich, *Tuned Out: Why Americans Under 40 Don't Follow the News* (New York: Oxford University Press, 2005), 6.

4   Barack Obama, "President Barack Obama's Inaugural Address," January 21, 2009, *The White House*, www.whitehouse.gov/blog/inaugural-address/ (accessed September 11, 2009).

5   David Matthews, *Politics for People: Finding a Responsible Public Voice*, 2nd ed. (Urbana: University of Illinois Press, 1999), 1–2.

6   Duffy and Leeman, *American Voices*, xxiii.

7   See J. Michael Hogan, "Rhetorical Pedagogy and Democratic Citizenship: Reviving the Traditions of Civic Engagement and Public Deliberation," in *Rhetoric and Democracy: Pedagogical and Political Practices*, ed. Todd F. McDorman and David M. Timmerman (East Lansing: Michigan State University Press, 2008), 75–97. Portions of this chapter are taken from this earlier study or extend and elaborate upon arguments made in that study.

8   Robert D. Putnam, *Bowling Alone: The Collapse and Revival of American Community* (New York: Simon and Schuster, 2000).

9   Putnam, *Bowling Alone*, 31–32.

10   Putnam, *Bowling Alone*, 43.

11   Putnam, *Bowling Alone*, 36.

12   Mindich, *Tuned Out*, esp. 18–33.

13   Michael X. Delli Carpini, "Gen.com: Youth, Civic Engagement, and the New Information Environment," *Political Communication* 17 (2000): 341–343.

14   Putnam, *Bowling Alone*, 49.

15   See Peter D. Hart and Mario A. Brossard, "A Generation to be Proud Of," *Brookings Review* 20 (Fall 2002): 36–37.

16   Everett Carll Ladd, "The American Way – Civic Engagement – Contrary to Cynical Conventional Wisdom, US Citizens are Not Increasingly Bowling Alone," *Christian Science Monitor*, March 1, 1999, 9.

17   Richard Stengel, "Bowling Together," *Time*, July 22, 1996, 35–36.

18   W. Lance Bennett, "The Uncivic Culture: Communication, Identity, and the Rise of Lifestyle Politics," *PS: Political Science and Politics* 31 (1998): 741–761.

19   See John D. McCarthy and Mayer N. Zald, "The Trend in Social Movements in America: Professionalized Movements and Resource Mobilization," in *Social Movements in an Organizational Society*, ed. Mayer N. Zald and John D. McCarthy (New Brunswick, NJ: Transaction Press, 1987); and Samantha Sanchez, "How the West Is Won: Astroturf Lobbying and the 'Wise Use' Movement," *The American Prospect* 25 (March–April 1996): 37–42.

20   Robert Putnam, "Bowling Together," *The American Prospect*, February 11, 2002, 20–22.

21   Committee for the Study of the American Electorate, "President Bush, Mobilization Drives Propel Turnout to Post-1968 High," News Release, November 4, 2004, www.fairvote.org/reports/CSAE2004electionreport.pdf (accessed August 4, 2009).

22   "Turnout in Presidential Elections Hit 40-Year High," *Politico*, December 15, 2008, www.politico.com/news/stories/1208/16576.html (accessed March 13, 2009).

23   Eric Hoover, "Freshman's Views: Politics, Admissions, and Marijuana," *Chronicle of Higher Education*, January 30, 2009, A18.

24   Abby Kiesa, Alexander P. Orlowski, Peter Levine, Deborah Both, Emily Hoban Kirby, Mark Hugo Lopez, and Karlos Barrios Marcelo, *Millennials Talk Politics: A Study of*

College Student Political Engagement (College Park, MD: Center for Information and Research on Civic Learning and Engagement, 2007).

25 Noting that America's overall "civic health" has shown "steep declines over the last 30 years," the NCC study concluded on a decidedly pessimistic note: "We find it alarming that a nation that is economically prosperous, relatively secure, and full of social opportunity and civil liberty evinces serious signs of civic weakness at a time when it most needs civic strength" (National Conference on Citizenship in Association with CIRCLE and Saguaro Seminar, *Broken Engagement: America's Civic Health Index* [Washington, DC: National Conference on Citizenship, 2006], 4–5, 10).

26 National Conference on Citizenship, *2008 Civic Health Index: Beyond the Vote* (Washington, DC: National Conference on Citizenship, 2008), 4–5.

27 W. Lance Bennett, "Introduction: Communication and Civic Engagement in Comparative Perspective," *Political Communication* 17 (2000): 308.

28 Theda Skocpol, *Diminished Democracy: From Membership to Management in American Civic Life* (Norman: University of Oklahoma Press, 2003), 174.

29 Barack Obama, "Remarks by the President in Commencement Address at the University of Notre Dame," May 17, 2009, *The White House*, www.whitehouse.gov/the_press_office/Remarks-by-the-President-at-Notre-Dame-Commencement/ (accessed June 8, 2009).

30 Edwin Black, *Rhetorical Questions: Studies of Public Discourse* (Chicago: University of Chicago Press, 1992), 23.

31 Al Gore, *The Assault on Reason* (New York: Penguin, 2007), 16, 104.

32 "Coulter Under Fire for Anti-Gay Slur," *CNN.com*, March 4, 2007, www.cnn.com/2007/POLITICS/03/04/coulter.edwards/index.html (accessed August 10, 2009).

33 Carla Marinucci, "Democrat Leaders Discount Comments by Dean on GOP," *San Francisco Chronicle*, June 9, 2005, A4.

34 Morris P. Fiorina, *Culture War? The Myth of a Polarized America* (New York: Pearson Education, 2005), 5.

35 Fiorina, *Culture War?*, ix.

36 Kiesa et al., *Millennials Talk Politics*, 4.

37 See, for example, Bennett, "The Uncivic Culture," 749.

38 Kiesa et al., *Millennials Talk Politics*, 24–27.

39 See William Safire, *The Right Word in the Right Place at the Right Time* (New York: Simon and Schuster, 2004), 175; and Frank Rich, "The Swift Boating of Cindy Sheehan," *New York Times*, August 21, 2005, www.nytimes.com/2005/08/21/opinion/21rich.html?ex=1282276800&en=54836c41c1bcb990&ei=5088&partner=rssnyt&emc=rss (accessed August 10, 2009).

40 Larry J. Sabato, *Feeding Frenzy: How Attack Journalism Has Transformed American Politics* (New York: Free Press, 1993), 49.

41 Eric Alterman, *Sound and Fury: The Making of the Punditocracy* (Ithaca, NY: Cornell Paperbacks, 1999).

42 See Mark Gillespie, "Media Credibility Reaches Lowest Point in Three Decades," in *The Gallup Poll: Public Opinion 2004*, ed. Alec M. Gallup and Frank Newport (Lanham, MD: Rowman and Littlefield, 2006), 387–388.

43 Joseph N. Cappella and Kathleen Hall Jamieson, *Spiral of Cynicism: The Press and the Public Good* (New York: Oxford University Press, 1997), 57.

44 Thomas Bender, "Then and Now: The Disciplines and Civic Engagement," *Liberal Education* 87 (2001): 6.

45 David D. Cooper, "Academic Professionalism and the Betrayal of the Land-Grant Tradition," *American Behavioral Scientist* 42 (February 1999): 776–777.

46 Ernest L. Boyer, "Creating the New American College," *Chronicle of Higher Education*, March 9, 1994, A48.

47 "The Saguano Seminar: Civic Engagement in America," www.hks.harvard.edu/saguaro/ (accessed August 10, 2009).

48 See "Our Purpose," in *The Strauss Report: A Publication of the Annette Strauss Institute for Civic Participation*, 2004–2005 edition, n.p.

49 Jeffrey R. Young, "Persuading Students to Care: Eugene Lang's Program Aims to Prod Colleges into Encouraging Civic Involvement," *Chronicle of Higher Education*, April 11, 2003, A47.

50 See Campus Compact, "About Us," www.compact.org/about/ (accessed March 25, 2009).

51 John Doble, Janay Cody, and Laura Kelsky, *Public Thinking About Democracy's Challenge: An Analysis of Results from the 2005–2006 National Issues Forums* (Dayton, OH: Kettering Foundation, 2006), 43.

52 John Doble Research Associates, *Public Thinking About the New Challenge of Immigration: An Analysis of Results from the 2003–2005 National Issues Forums* (Dayton, OH: Kettering Foundation, 2005), 3–6.

53 Doble, Cody, and Kelsky, *Public Thinking About Democracy's Challenge*, 1–2, 27–28.

54 See Bruce Ackerman and James S. Fishkin, *Deliberation Day* (New Haven, CT: Yale University Press, 2004).

55 David Schkade, Cass R. Sunstein, and Reid Hastie, "What Happened on Deliberation Day?" *California Law Review* 95 (June 2007): 915–940.

56 This, of course, speaks to the essential design flaw of the Deliberation Day experiment. The issues the researchers dubbed the "most contested" of our time actually register hardly at all in surveys of the most important issues on the minds of ordinary Americans. Poll after poll has shown that Americans are not particularly concerned about same-sex marriage, global warming, or affirmative action, but rather are most concerned with issues like the economy, the war against terrorism, health care, illegal immigration, and gasoline prices. Furthermore, the participants had no real stake in the outcome of their deliberations; they were not faced with some pressing community problem, nor were they given any reason to think that their deliberations might make some difference. In other words, they had no reason to believe that their deliberations really *mattered*. For a summary of polling data on the public's actual priorities, see "Problems and Priorities," *PollingReport.com*, www.pollingreport.com/prioriti.htm (accessed August 10, 2009).

57 The NIF publishes an occasional guide on the history, theory, and methods of demo-cratic deliberation, but they provide no formal training in deliberation for participants in their forums. See, for example, National Issues Forum, *Making Choices Together: The Power of Public Deliberation* (Dayton, OH: Kettering Foundation, 2003).

58 Patricia Roberts-Miller, "Democracy, Demagoguery, and Critical Rhetoric," *Rhetoric & Public Affairs* 8 (2005): 459–460.

59 Gordon S. Wood, "The Democratization of the American Mind," in *Leadership in the American Revolution: Papers Presented at the Third Symposium, May 9 and 10, 1974* (Washington, DC: Library of Congress, 1974), 70.

60 See Robert Alexander Kraig, "The Second Oratorical Renaissance," in *Rhetoric and Reform in the Progressive Era*, ed. J. Michael Hogan (East Lansing: Michigan State University Press, 2003), 1–48.

61 Kraig, "The Second Oratorical Renaissance," 1.

62 Woodrow Wilson, *Congressional Government: A Study in Politics*, in *The Papers of Woodrow Wilson*, ed. Arthur S. Link et al., 69 vols. (Princeton, NJ: Princeton University Press, 1966–1994), 4: 55–118.

63 Kathleen Hall Jamieson, *Eloquence in an Electronic Age: The Transformation of Political Speechmaking* (New York: Oxford University Press, 1988), 45.

64 Robert L. Scott and Donald K. Smith, "The Rhetoric of Confrontation," *Quarterly Journal of Speech* 55 (1969): 8.

65 See Richard B. Gregg, "The Ego-Function of the Rhetoric of Protest," *Philosophy & Rhetoric* 4 (1971): 71–91.

66 Roberts-Miller, "Democracy, Demagoguery, and Critical Rhetoric," 460.

67 See, for example, Nancy Fraser, "Rethinking the Public Sphere: A Contribution to the Critique of Actually Existing Democracy," in *Habermas and the Public Sphere*, ed. Craig Calhoun (Cambridge, MA: MIT Press, 1992), 126.

68 Textbooks with feminist or multicultural themes already have captured a small but significant portion of the public speaking textbook market, and the first postmodern public speaking textbook, entitled *Public Speaking in Postmodernity*, is reportedly in the works. See Josh Gunn, "Public Speaking in Postmodernity," *The Rosewater Chronicles*, October 8, 2008, www.joshiejuice.com/blog/?p=650 (accessed August 14, 2009).

69 Hogan, "Rhetorical Pedagogy and Democratic Citizenship," 84.

70 See, for example, Gary Hankins, *The Power of the Pitch: Transform Yourself Into a Persuasive Presenter and Win More Business* (Chicago: Dearborn Trade Publishing, 2005).

71 In *Invitation to Public Speaking*, for example, Cindy L. Griffin reflects the feminist view that public speaking should be an "invitational" rather than a persuasive or strategic art, yet the books is still structured around the Aristotelian "canons" of rhetoric. The table of contents of the book differs little from traditional texts, with chapters on developing one's topic, audience analysis, research, supporting materials, reasoning, organization, style, and delivery. See Cindy L. Griffin, *Invitation to Public Speaking* (New York: Wadsworth, 2004).

72 Arthur M. Schlesinger, Jr., *The Disuniting of America: Reflections on a Multicultural Society* (New York: W. W. Norton, 1992), 16, 18.

73 Schlesinger, *The Disuniting of America*, 156.

74 J. Michael Hogan, Patricia Hayes Andrews, James R. Andrews, and Glen Williams, *Public Speaking and Civic Engagement* (Boston: Pearson/Allyn and Bacon/Vango Books, 2008).

75 That is, with a commitment to truth, reasoned argument, and respectful disagreement. Deliberating "in good faith" also implies a willingness to change one's own mind in response to compelling arguments and to compromise in the interests of the "common good." See Hogan et al., *Public Speaking and Civic Engagement*, esp. 379–380, 501.

76 Hogan et al., *Public Speaking and Civic Engagement*, 439.

77 Hogan et al., *Public Speaking and Civic Engagement*, 33.

78 Kristen Treinen, Daniel Cronn-Mills, and Christa Brown, review of *Public Speaking and Civic Engagement*, *American Communication Journal* 10 (2008): n.p., www.acjournal.org/holdings/vol10/02_Summer/reviews/treinen_etal.php (accessed August 14, 2009).

79 Jeffrey R. Young, "Colleges Call Debate Contests Out of Order," *Chronicle of Higher Education*, October 3, 2008, A1.

80 See Young, "Colleges Call Debate Contests Out of Order," A20.

81 Young, "Colleges Call Debate Contests Out of Order," A20. Also see "FHSU, Shanahan Sever Relationship: President Also Suspends Debate Program Because Current Practices Fall Short of Educational Standards," News Release, Fort Haynes State University, August 22, 2008, www.fhsu.edu/currentevents/display_event. php?id=3604 (accessed August 14, 2009); and Bill Schackner, "College Debate Turns Cheeky," *Pittsburgh Post-Gazette*, August 15, 2008, www.post-gazette.com/ pg/08228/904458-53.stm (accessed August 14, 2009).

82 See "Proposed Amendment to Article 15 of the Bylaws: 'Clarify Organizational Policy for Professional Conduct and Establish Procedures for Enforcing Violations of Organizational Ethics,'" *Cross-Examination Debate Association*, www.cedadebate.org/ files/Prof_Conduct_Amendment.pdf, n.d. (accessed July 28, 2009).

83 "Bookings, Flight Schedules, and Network News Interviews: Speakers Bureau Scrambles to Keep Up with Demand," *The Proof: Department of Communication Newsletter*, Ripon College (Winter 2009), 5; Students Against Violence Everywhere, www.nationalsave.org/ (accessed July 9, 2009); and "Shawn Karsten: Transformed by Tragedy – Speaking to Survive," www.ShawnKarsten.com (accessed July 9, 2009).

84 Herbert A. Wichelns, "The Literary Criticism of Oratory," in *Readings in Rhetorical Criticism*, ed. Carl R. Burgchardt (State College, PA: Strata, 1995), 4.

85 See Stephen E. Lucas, "The Renaissance of American Public Address: Text and Context in Rhetorical Criticism," *Quarterly Journal of Speech* 74 (1988): 241–260.

86 Mark Bauerlein, "Diminishing Returns in Humanities Research," *Chronicle of Higher Education*, July 24, 2009, B4–B5.

87 Stanley N. Katz, "What Has Happened to the Professoriate?" *The Chronicle Review*, October 6, 2006, B8.

88 David Zarefsky, "Two Faces of Democratic Rhetoric," in *Rhetoric and Democracy*, ed. McDorman and Timmerman, 115–137.

89 See J. Michael Hogan and David Olsen, "The Rhetoric of Nuclear Education," in *Propaganda: A Pluralistic Perspective*, ed. Ted J. Smith III (New York: Praeger, 1989), 165–179.

90 See, for example, "George Gallup and the Rhetoric of Scientific Democracy," *Communication Monographs* 64 (1997): 161–179.

91 Rosa A. Eberly, *Citizen Critics: Literary Public Spheres* (Urbana: University of Illinois Press, 2000).

92 Annette Kolodny, "The Situation of the Humanities: How English Departments (and Their Chairs) Can Survive into the Twenty-First Century," *ADE Bulletin* 137 (Spring 2005): 10–17.

93 Zarefsky, "Two Faces of Democratic Rhetoric," 133.

94 Kenneth Burke, *The Philosophy of Literary Form* (Baton Rouge: Louisiana State University Press, 1941), 191.

95 See Hogan, ed., *Rhetoric and Reform in the Progressive Era*; and J. Michael Hogan, *Woodrow Wilson's Western Tour: Rhetoric, Public Opinion, and the League of Nations* (College Station: Texas A&M University Press, 2006).

96 Hogan, "Rhetorical Pedagogy and Democratic Citizenship," 89–92.

97 John Dewey, *The Public and Its Problems* (1927; Athens, OH: Swallow Press, 1991), 208.

98 As Peter Levine has noted, La Follette believed that the "surest way for voters to form wise judgments ... was for them to *deliberate* together about public affairs," and so he proposed a number of "practical measures to increase the quantity, quality, and

inclusiveness of public deliberation." See Peter Levine, *The New Progressive Era: Toward a Fair and Deliberative Democracy* (Lanham, MD: Rowman and Littlefield, 2000), xiii.

99   Hogan, "Rhetorical Pedagogy and Democratic Citizenship," 90.

100 Kevin Mattson, *Creating a Democratic Public: The Struggle for Urban Participatory Democracy During the Progressive Era* (University Park, PA: Pennsylvania State University Press, 1998), 45.

101 Woodrow Wilson, "The Making of a Nation," in *Papers of Woodrow Wilson*, 10: 233.

102 Woodrow Wilson, "University Training and Citizenship," in *Papers of Woodrow Wilson*, 8: 589.

103 See Hogan, *Woodrow Wilson's Western Tour*, 31–41.

104 E. J. Dionne, Jr., *They Only Look Dead: Why Progressives Will Dominate the Next Political Era* (New York: Touchstone Books, 1997), 261.

105 *Voices of Democracy: The US Oratory Project*, online at www.voicesofdemocracy.umd.edu.

106 Jeffrey Selingo, "What Americans Think About Higher Education," *Chronicle of Higher Education*, May 2, 2003, A10.

107 "Better Health Care Depends on a Stronger Democracy," A Statement from Everyday Democracy, AmericaSpeaks, Demos, and Professor Archon Fung of Harvard's Ash Institute for Democratic Governance and Innovation, August 13, 2009, *Everyday Democracy*, www.everyday-democracy.org/en/Article.1025.aspx (accessed September 11, 2009).

108 See James Davison Hunter, *Culture Wars: The Struggle to Define America* (New York: Basic Books, 1991), 143–156.

109 See, for example, Brock N. Meeks, "Better Democracy Through Technology," *Communications of the ACM* 40 (1997): 75–78; Jerry Berman and Daniel J. Weitzner, "Technology and Democracy," *Social Research* 64 (1997): 1313–1319; and Carolyn J. Lukensmeyer and Steve Brigham, "Taking Democracy to Scale: Creating a Town Hall Meeting for the Twenty-First Century," *National Civic Review* 91 (Winter 2002): 351–366.

Select Bibliography

Alexander, Bryant Keith. *Performing Black Masculinity: Race, Culture, and Queer Identity.* Lanham, MD: AltaMira Press, 2006.

Aly, Bower, ed. *Alexander Hamilton: Selections Representing His Life, His Thought, and His Style.* New York: Liberal Arts Press, 1957.

Aly, Bower. *The Rhetoric of Alexander Hamilton.* New York: Columbia University Press, 1941.

Aly, Bower, and Lucile Folse Aly, eds. *American Short Speeches: An Anthology.* New York: Macmillan, 1968.

Anderson, Judith, ed. *Outspoken Women: Speeches by American Women Reformers, 1635–1935.* Dubuque, IA: Kendall/Hunt, 1984.

Andrew, John A. *Address of His Excellency John A. Andrew, to the Two Branches of the Legislature of Massachusetts, January 18, 1864.* Boston: Wright and Potter, 1864.

Andrews, James R. ed. *Rhetoric, Religion, and the Roots of Identity in British Colonial America.* Volume 1 of *A Rhetorical History of the United States,* 10 vols. East Lansing: Michigan State University Press, 2007.

Andrews, James R. *The Practice of Rhetorical Criticism.* 2nd ed. New York: Longman, 1990.

Andrews, James R., and David Zarefsky, eds. *American Voices: Significant Speeches in American History, 1640–1945.* White Plains, NY: Longman, 1989.

Andrews, James R., and David Zarefsky, eds. *Contemporary American Voices: Significant Speeches in American History, 1945–Present.* White Plains, NY: Longman, 1992.

Arnold, Carroll. *Criticism of Oral Rhetoric.* Columbus, OH: C. E. Merrill, 1974.

Asante, Molefi K. [Arthur L. Smith]. *Language, Communication, and Rhetoric in Black America.* New York: Harper and Row, 1972.

Asante, Molefi K. [Arthur L. Smith]. *Rhetoric of Black Revolution.* Boston: Allyn and Bacon, 1969.

Asante, Molefi K. [Arthur L. Smith], and Stephen Robb, eds. *The Voice of Black Rhetoric: Selections.* Boston: Allyn and Bacon, 1971.

Auer, J. Jeffrey, ed. *Antislavery and Disunion, 1858–1861: Studies in the Rhetoric of Compromise and Conflict.* New York: Harper and Row, 1963.

Aune, James Arnt. *Rhetoric and Marxism.* Boulder, CO: Westview, 1994.

Aune, James Arnt, and Martin J. Medhurst, eds. *The Prospect of Presidential Rhetoric.* College Station: Texas A&M University Press, 2008.

Aune, James Arnt, and Enrique D. Rigsby, eds. *Civil Rights Rhetoric and the American Presidency.* College Station: Texas A&M University Press, 2005.

Bacon, Jacqueline. *The Humblest May Stand Forth: Rhetoric, Empowerment, and Abolition.* Columbia: University of South Carolina Press, 2002.

Bain, Alexander. *English Composition and Rhetoric: A Manual.* New York: American Book Co., 1866.

Baird, A. Craig, ed. *American Public Addresses, 1740–1952.* New York: McGraw-Hill, 1956.

Baird, A. Craig, ed. *College Readings on Current Problems.* Boston: Houghton Mifflin, 1925.

Baird, A. Craig, ed. *Essays and Addresses Toward a Liberal Education.* Boston: Ginn and Company, 1934.

Baird, A. Craig. *Rhetoric: A Philosophical Inquiry.* New York: Ronald Press, 1965.

Baird, A. Craig, and Lester Thonssen. "Methodology in the Criticism of Public Address." *Quarterly Journal of Speech* 33 (1947): 134–138.

Baker, George Pierce, ed. *The Forms of Public Address.* New York: Henry Holt and Company, 1904.

Baker, Houston A., Jr. *Afro-American Poetics: Revisions of Harlem and the Black Aesthetic.* Madison: University of Wisconsin Press, 1988.

Baker, William, and Kenneth Womack, comps. *Twentieth-Century Bibliography and Textual Criticism: An Annotated Bibliography.* Westport, CT: Greenwood Press, 2000.

Bal, Mieke. *Double Exposures: The Subject of Cultural Analysis.* New York: Routledge, 1996.

Barnard, Ian. *Queer Race: Cultural Interventions in the Racial Politics of Queer Theory.* New York: Peter Lang, 2004.

Barnett, Sylvan. *A Short Guide to Writing About Art.* 9th ed. Upper Saddle River, NJ: Pearson/Prentice Hall, 2007.

Barrett, Harold, ed. *Rhetoric of the People.* Amsterdam: Rodopi, 1974.

Barrett, Wendell. *English Composition.* New York: Charles Scribner's Sons, 1891.

Barwell, Graham. "Original, Authentic, Copy: Conceptual Issues in Digital Texts." *Literary & Linguistic Computing* 20 (2005): 415–424.

Baskerville, Barnet. "Must We All Be 'Rhetorical Critics'?" *Quarterly Journal of Speech* 63 (1977): 107–116.

Baskerville, Barnet. *The People's Voice: The Orator in American Society.* Lexington: University Press of Kentucky, 1979.

Basler, Roy P. *The Lincoln Legend: A Study in Changing Conceptions* (1935). New York: Octagon Books, 1969.

Beard, Mary R. *Woman as a Force in History: A Study in Traditions and Realities.* New York: Macmillan, 1946.

Beasley, Vanessa B., ed. *Who Belongs in America? Presidents, Rhetoric, and Immigration.* College Station: Texas A&M University Press, 2006.

Beasley, Vanessa B. *You, the People: American National Identity in Presidential Rhetoric.* College Station: Texas A&M University Press, 2004.

Bell, Susan Groag, and Karen M. Offen, eds. *Women, the Family, and Freedom: The Debate in Documents: Volume One, 1750–1880.* Stanford, CA: Stanford University Press, 1983.

Bell, Susan Groag, and Karen M. Offen, eds. *Women, the Family, and Freedom: The Debate in Documents: Volume Two, 1880–1950.* Stanford, CA: Stanford University Press, 1983.

Benson, Thomas W., ed. *American Rhetoric: Context and Criticism.* Carbondale: Southern Illinois University Press, 1989.

Benson, Thomas W., ed. *American Rhetoric in the New Deal Era, 1932–1945.* Volume 7 of *A Rhetorical History of the United States,* 10 vols. East Lansing: Michigan State University Press, 2006.

Benson, Thomas W., ed. *Landmark Essays on Rhetorical Criticism.* Davis, CA: Hermagoras Press, 1993.

Benson, Thomas W., ed. *Rhetoric and Political Culture in Nineteenth-Century America.* East Lansing: Michigan State University Press, 1997.

Benson, Thomas W., ed. *Speech Communication in the 20th Century.* Carbondale: Southern Illinois University Press, 1985.

Benson, Thomas W. *Writing JFK: Presidential Rhetoric and the Press in the Bay of Pigs Crisis.* College Station: Texas A&M University Press, 2004.

Benson, Thomas W., and Carolyn Anderson. *Reality Fictions: The Films of Frederick Wiseman.* Carbondale: Southern Illinois University Press, 1989.

Benson, Thomas W., and Brian J. Snee, eds. *The Rhetoric of the New Political Documentary.* Carbondale: Southern Illinois University Press, 2008.

Biesecker, Barbara. "Coming to Terms With Recent Attempts to Write Women into the History of Rhetoric." *Philosophy and Rhetoric* 25 (1992): 140–161.

Bitzer, Lloyd F. "The Rhetorical Situation." *Philosophy & Rhetoric* 1 (1968): 1–14.

Bitzer, Lloyd F., and Edwin Black, eds. *The Prospect of Rhetoric: Report of the National Developmental Project.* Englewood Cliffs, NJ: Prentice Hall, 1971.

Bitzer, Lloyd F., and Theodore Rueter. *Carter vs. Ford: The Counterfeit Debates of 1976.* Madison: University of Wisconsin Press, 1980.

Black, Edwin. "A Note on Theory and Practice in Rhetorical Criticism." *Western Journal of Speech Communication* 44 (1980): 331–336.

Black, Edwin. *Rhetorical Criticism: A Study in Method.* New York: Macmillan, 1965, 1978.

Black, Edwin. *Rhetorical Questions: Studies of Public Discourse.* Chicago: University of Chicago Press, 1992.

Black, Edwin. "The Second Persona." *Quarterly Journal of Speech* 56 (1970): 109–119.

Blasius, Mark, and Shane Phelan, eds. *We Are Everywhere: A Historical Sourcebook of Gay and Lesbian Politics.* New York: Routledge, 1997.

Boase, Paul H. *The Rhetoric of Christian Socialism.* New York: Random House, 1969.

Boase, Paul H., ed. *The Rhetoric of Protest and Reform.* Athens: Ohio University Press, 1980.

Bontemps, Arna. *Harlem Renaissance Remembered.* New York: Dodd, Mead & Co., 1972.

Booth, Wayne. *Rhetoric of Fiction.* Chicago: University of Chicago Press, 1961.

Boritt, Gabor. *The Gettysburg Gospel: The Lincoln Speech that Nobody Knows.* New York: Simon and Schuster, 2006.

Bormann, Ernest G. *The Force of Fantasy: Restoring the American Dream.* Carbondale: Southern Illinois University Press, 1985.

Bormann, Ernest G., ed. *Forerunners of Black Power: The Rhetoric of Abolition.* Englewood Cliffs, NJ: Prentice Hall, 1971.

Bormann, Ernest G. "Ghostwriting and the Rhetorical Critic." *Quarterly Journal of Speech* 46 (1960): 284–288.

Bosmajian, Haig A., and Hamida Bosmajian, eds. *The Rhetoric of the Civil Rights Movement.* New York: Random House, 1969.

Boulware, Marcus H. *The Oratory of Negro Leaders: 1900–1968.* Westport, CT: Negro Universities Press, 1969.

Bowers, John Waite, and Donovan J. Ochs. *The Rhetoric of Agitation and Control*. Reading, MA: Addison-Wesley, 1971.

Bowers, John Waite, Donovan J. Ochs, Richard J. Jensen, and David P. Schulz. *The Rhetoric of Agitation and Control*. Long Grove, IL: Waveland Press, 2009.

Braden, Waldo W. *The Oral Tradition in the South*. Baton Rouge: Louisiana State University Press, 1983.

Braden, Waldo W., ed. *Oratory in the New South*. Baton Rouge: Louisiana State University Press, 1979.

Braden, Waldo W., ed. *Oratory in the Old South*. Baton Rouge: Louisiana State University Press, 1970.

Bradley, Cornelius Beach. *Orations and Arguments by English and American Statesmen*. Boston: Allyn and Bacon, 1894.

Bradley, Patricia. *Mass Media and the Shaping of American Feminism, 1963–1975*. Jackson: University Press of Mississippi, 2003.

Bravmann, Scott. *Queer Fictions of the Past: History, Culture, and Difference*. New York: Cambridge University Press, 1997.

Brewer, David, ed. *The World's Best Orations: From the Earliest Period to the Present Time*. 10 vols. Chicago: F. P. Kaiser, 1899.

Brigance, William Norwood. *Classified Speech Models of Eighteen Forms of Public Address*. New York: F. S. Crofts & Co., 1928.

Brigance, William Norwood, ed. *A History and Criticism of American Public Address*. 2 vols. New York: McGraw-Hill, 1943.

Brigance, William Norwood. *Jeremiah Sullivan Black: A Defender of the Constitution and the Ten Commandments*. Philadelphia: University of Pennsylvania Press, 1934.

Brigance, William Norwood. "Whither Research?" *Quarterly Journal of Speech* 19 (1933): 552–561.

Brockriede, Wayne, and Robert L. Scott. *Moments in the Rhetoric of the Cold War*. New York: Random House, 1970.

Brooks, Cleanth. *Modern Rhetoric*. New York: Harcourt Brace, 1949.

Browne, Stephen H. *Angelina Grimké: Rhetoric, Identity, and the Radical Imagination*. East Lansing: Michigan State University Press, 2000.

Browne, Stephen H. *Jefferson's Call for Nationhood: The First Inaugural Address*. College Station: Texas A&M University Press, 2003.

Bruner, M. Lane. *Strategies of Remembrance: The Rhetorical Dimensions of National Identity Construction*. Columbia: University of South Carolina Press, 2002.

Bryant, Donald C. *Edmund Burke and His Literary Friends*. St. Louis: Washington University Press, 1939.

Bryant, Donald C. *Rhetorical Dimensions in Criticism*. Baton Rouge: Louisiana State University Press, 1973.

Bryant, Donald C. "Rhetoric: Its Functions and Its Scope." *Quarterly Journal of Speech* 39 (1953): 401–424.

Bryant, Donald C. "Some Problems of Scope and Method in Rhetorical Scholarship." *Quarterly Journal of Speech* 23 (1937): 182–189.

Bryant, Donald C., Carroll C. Arnold, Frederick W. Haberman, Richard Murphy, and Karl R. Wallace, eds. *An Historical Anthology of Select British Speeches*. New York: Ronald Press, 1967.

Bull, Chris, ed. *Witness to Revolution: Advocate Reports on Gay and Lesbian Politics, 1967–1999*. Los Angeles: Alyson Books, 1999.

Burgchardt, Carl, ed. *Readings in Rhetorical Criticism*. State College, PA: Strata, 1995.

Burgchardt, Carl. *Robert M. La Follette, Sr.: The Voice of Conscience*. New York: Greenwood Press, 1992.

Burgess, Parke G. "The Rhetoric of Black Power: A Moral Demand?" *Quarterly Journal of Speech* 54 (1968): 122–133.

Burke, Kenneth. *The Philosophy of Literary Form*. Baton Rouge: Louisiana State University Press, 1941.

Burke, Kenneth. *A Rhetoric of Motives*. New York: Prentice Hall, 1950.

Burke, Ronald K., ed. *American Public Discourse: A Multicultural Perspective*. Lanham, MD: University Press of America, 1992.

Burlingame, Michael, ed. *At Lincoln's Side: John Hay's Civil War Correspondence and Selected Writings*. Carbondale: Southern Illinois University Press, 2000.

Burlingame, Michael, ed. *Lincoln's Journalist: John Hay's Anonymous Writings for the Press, 1860–1864*. Carbondale: Southern Illinois University Press, 1998.

Burlingame, Michael, and John R. Turner Ettlinger, eds. *Inside Lincoln's White House: The Complete Civil War Diary of John Hay*. Carbondale: Southern Illinois University Press, 1997.

Butler, Judith, Ernesto Laclau, and Slavoj Žižek, eds. *Contingency, Hegemony, Universality: Contemporary Dialogues on the Left*. New York: Verso, 2000.

Butt, Gavin. *Between You and Me: Queer Discourses in the New York Art World, 1948–1963*. Durham, NC: Duke University Press, 2005.

Bytwerk, Randall L. *Julius Streicher: The Man Who Persuaded a Nation to Hate Jews*. New York: Stein and Day, 1983.

Cain, William E. *Reconceptualizing American Literary/Cultural Studies: Rhetoric, History, and Politics in the Humanities*. New York: Garland, 1996.

Calhoun, Craig. *Habermas and the Public Sphere*. Cambridge, MA: MIT Press, 1992.

Callaghan, Karen, and Frauke Schnell, eds. *Framing American Politics*. Pittsburgh, PA: University of Pittsburgh Press, 2005.

Camp, L. Raymond. *Roger Williams: God's Apostle of Advocacy*. Lewiston, NY: E. Mellen Press, 1989.

Campbell, Angus, Philip E. Converse, Warren E. Miller, and Donald E. Stokes. *The American Voter*. New York: Wiley, 1960.

Campbell, George. *The Philosophy of Rhetoric* (1841). Carbondale: Southern Illinois University Press, 1963.

Campbell, Karlyn Kohrs. "Biesecker Cannot Speak for Her Either." *Philosophy and Rhetoric* 26 (1993): 153–159.

Campbell, Karlyn Kohrs. *Man Cannot Speak for Her*. 2 vols. Westport, CT: Praeger, 1989.

Campbell, Karlyn Kohrs, ed. *Women Public Speakers in the United States, 1800–1925: A Bio-Critical Sourcebook*. Westport, CT: Greenwood Press, 1993.

Campbell, Karlyn Kohrs, ed. *Women Public Speakers in the United States, 1925–1993: A Bio-Critical Sourcebook*. Westport, CT: Greenwood Press, 1994.

Campbell, Karlyn Kohrs, and Thomas R. Burkholder. *Critiques of Contemporary Rhetoric*. 2nd ed. Belmont, CA: Wadsworth, 1997.

Campbell, Karlyn Kohrs, and Kathleen Hall Jamieson. *Deeds Done in Words: Presidential Rhetoric and the Genres of Governance*. Chicago: University of Chicago Press, 1990.

Campbell, Karlyn Kohrs, and Kathleen Hall Jamieson, eds. *Form and Genre: Shaping Rhetorical Action*. Falls Church, VA: Speech Communication Association, 1978.

Campbell, Karlyn Kohrs, and Kathleen Hall Jamieson. *Presidents Creating the Presidency: Deeds Done in Words.* Chicago: University of Chicago Press, 2008.

Cathcart, Robert. *Post Communication: Criticism and Evaluation.* Indianapolis: Bobbs-Merrill, 1966.

Ceccarelli, Leah. *Shaping Science With Rhetoric.* Chicago: University of Chicago Press, 2001.

Chapman, Nathaniel. *Select Speeches, Forensick and Parliamentary, with Prefatory Remarks.* 5 vols. Philadelphia: Hopkins and Earle, 1808.

Charland, Maurice. "Constitutive Rhetoric: The Case of the *Peuple Québécois.*" *Quarterly Journal of Speech* 73 (1987): 133–150.

Chauncey, George. *Gay New York: Gender, Urban Culture, and the Making of the Gay Male World, 1890–1940.* New York: Basic Books, 1994.

Chesebro, James W., ed. *Gayspeak: Gay Male and Lesbian Communication.* New York: Pilgrim Press, 1981.

Clark, Donald Lemen. *Rhetoric and Poetry in the Renaissance: A Study of Rhetorical Terms in English Renaissance Literary Criticism.* New York: Columbia University Press, 1922.

Clark, E. Culpepper. *The Schoolhouse Door: Segregation's Last Stand at the University of Alabama.* New York: Oxford University Press, 1993.

Cleary, James W., and Frederick W. Haberman, eds. *Rhetoric and Public Address: A Bibliography.* Madison: University of Wisconsin Press, 1964.

Clendinen, Dudley, and Adam Nagourney. *Out for Good: The Struggle to Build a Gay Rights Movement in America.* New York: Simon and Schuster, 1999.

Cohen, Herman. *The History of Speech Communication: The Emergence of a Discipline, 1914–1945.* Annandale, VA: Speech Communication Association, 1994.

Cohen, Jeffrey E. *Presidential Responsiveness and Public Policy-Making: The Public and the Policies that Presidents Choose.* Ann Arbor: University of Michigan Press, 1997.

Cohen, Philip, ed. *Devils and Angels: Textual Editing and Literary Theory.* Charlottesville: University Press of Virginia, 1991.

Condit, Celeste Michelle. *Decoding Abortion Rhetoric: Communicating Social Change.* Urbana: University of Illinois Press, 1990.

Condit, Celeste Michelle. "In Praise of Eloquent Diversity: Gender and Rhetoric as Public Persuasion." *Women's Studies in Communication* 20 (1997): 91–116.

Condit, Celeste Michelle, and John Louis Loucaites. *Crafting Equality: America's Anglo-African Word.* Chicago: University of Chicago Press, 1993.

Corber, Robert J., and Stephen Valocchi, eds. *Queer Studies: An Interdisciplinary Reader.* Malden, MA: Blackwell, 2003.

Coulter, John. *The American Orator: A Complete Encyclopedia of Elocution, Oratory, and Etiquette.* Chicago: Kuhlman, 1901.

Crain, Caleb. *American Sympathy: Men, Friendship, and Literature in the New Nation.* New Haven, CT: Yale University Press, 2001.

Crocker, Lionel, comp. *An Analysis of Lincoln and Douglas as Public Speakers and Debaters.* Springfield, IL: Thomas, 1968.

Crocker, Lionel, ed. *Harry Emerson Fosdick's Art of Preaching: An Anthology.* Springfield, IL: Thomas, 1971.

Crocker, Lionel. *Henry Ward Beecher's Art of Preaching.* Chicago: University of Chicago Press, 1934.

Darsey, James. "Must We All Be Rhetorical Theorists? An Anti-Democratic Inquiry." *Western Journal of Communication* 58 (1994): 164–181.

Darsey, James. *The Prophetic Tradition and Radical Rhetoric in America*. New York: New York University Press, 1997.

Denton, Robert E., Jr. *The Primetime Presidency of Ronald Reagan: The Era of the Television Presidency*. New York: Praeger, 1988.

Dewey, John. *The Public and Its Problems* (1927). Athens, OH: Swallow Press, 1991.

Dickey, Dallas C. *Seargent S. Prentiss: Whig Orator of the Old South*. Baton Rouge: Louisiana State University Press, 1945.

Dionne, E. J., Jr. *They Only Look Dead: Why Progressives Will Dominate the Next Political Era*. New York: Touchstone Books, 1997.

Dorgan, Howard. *Giving Glory to God in Appalachia: Worship Practices of Six Baptist Subdenominations*. Knoxville: University of Tennessee Press, 1987.

Dorgan, Howard. *The Old Regular Baptists of Central Appalachia: Brothers and Sisters in Hope*. Knoxville: University of Tennessee Press, 1989.

Dorsey, Leroy G., ed. *The Presidency and Rhetorical Leadership*. College Station: Texas A&M University Press, 2002.

Dorsey, Leroy G. *We Are All Americans, Pure and Simple: Theodore Roosevelt and the Myth of Americanism*. Tuscaloosa: University of Alabama Press, 2007.

Douglass, Frederick. *Narrative Life of Frederick Douglass, An American Slave: Written by Himself*. Ed. John W. Blassingame, John R. McKivigan, and Peter P. Hinks. New Haven, CT: Yale University Press, 2001.

Dow, Bonnie J. *Prime-Time Feminism: Television, Media Culture, and the Women's Movement Since 1970*. Philadelphia: University of Pennsylvania Press, 1996.

Dow, Bonnie J., and Julia T. Wood, eds. *The Sage Handbook of Gender and Communication*. Thousand Oaks, CA: Sage, 2006.

Drummond, A. M., ed. *Studies in Rhetoric and Public Speaking, In Honor of James Albert Winans*. New York: Century Co., 1925.

Drummond, A. M., and Everett Lee Hunt. *Persistent Questions in Public Discussion*. New York: Century Co., 1924.

Duffy, Bernard K., and Richard W. Leeman, eds. *American Voices: An Encyclopedia of Contemporary Orators*. Westport, CT: Greenwood Press, 2005.

Duffy, Bernard K., and Halford Ross Ryan, eds. *American Orators Before 1900: Critical Studies and Sources*. New York: Greenwood Press, 1987.

Duffy, Bernard K., and Halford Ross Ryan, eds. *American Orators of the Twentieth Century: Critical Studies and Sources*. New York: Greenwood Press, 1987.

Dumbrell, John. *The Carter Presidency: A Reevaluation*. New York: Manchester University Press, 1993.

Eadie, William F, ed. *21st Century Communication: A Reference Handbook*. Vol. 1. Thousand Oaks, CA: Sage, 2009.

Eagleton, Terry. *After Theory*. Cambridge, MA: Perseus Books, 2003.

Eberly, Rosa A. *Citizen Critics: Literary Public Spheres*. Urbana: University of Illinois Press, 2000.

Edwards, George C. III. *At the Margins: Presidential Leadership of Congress*. New Haven, CT: Yale University Press, 1989.

Edwards, George C. III. *On Deaf Ears*. New Haven, CT: Yale University Press, 2003.

Ellis, Richard. *The Union at Risk: Jacksonian Democracy, States' Rights and the Nullification Controversy*. New York: Oxford University Press, 1987.

Elshtain, Jean Bethke. *Public Man, Private Woman: Women in Social and Political Thought*. Princeton, NJ: Princeton University Press, 1981.

Enos, Theresa, ed. *Making and Unmaking the Prospects of Rhetoric*. Mahwah, NJ: Lawrence Earlbaum, 1997.

Erickson, Paul D. *The Poetry of Events: Daniel Webster's Rhetoric of the Constitution and Union*. New York: New York University Press, 1986.

Erickson, Paul D. *Reagan Speaks: The Making of an American Myth*. New York: New York University Press, 1985.

Eshbaugh-Soha, Matthew. *The President's Speeches: Beyond "Going Public."* Boulder, CO: Lynne Rienner, 2006.

Faderman, Lillian. *Chloe plus Olivia: An Anthology of Lesbian Literature from the Seventeenth Century to the Present*. New York: Viking, 1984.

Farrell, Thomas B. *Norms of Rhetorical Culture*. New Haven, CT: Yale University Press, 1993.

Favor, J. Martin. *Authentic Blackness: The Folk in the New Negro Renaissance*. Durham, NC: Duke University Press, 1999.

Finnegan, Cara A. *Picturing Poverty: Print Culture and FSA Photographs*. Washington, DC: Smithsonian Institution Press, 2003.

Fischer, David Hackett. *Liberty and Freedom: A Visual History of America's Founding Ideas*. New York: Oxford University Press, 2005.

Foner, Philip S., ed. *Mother Jones Speaks: Speeches and Writings of a Working-Class Fighter*. New York: Pathfinder, 1983.

Foner, Philip S., ed. *We, the Other People: Alternative Declarations of Independence by Labor Groups, Farmers, Woman's Rights Advocates, Socialists, and Blacks, 1829–1975*. Urbana: University of Illinois Press, 1976.

Foss, Sonja K. *Rhetorical Criticism: Exploration and Practice*. 3rd ed. Long Grove, IL: Waveland Press, 2004.

Foss, Sonja K., and Cindy L. Griffin. "Beyond Persuasion: A Proposal for an Invitational Rhetoric." *Communication Monographs* 62 (1995): 1–18.

Foucault, Michel. *Archeology of Knowledge*. Trans. A. M. Sheridan. New York: Pantheon, 1972.

Frankfurt, Harry G. *On Bullshit*. Princeton, NJ: Princeton University Press, 2005.

Friedenberg, Robert V. *"Hear O Israel": The History of American Jewish Preaching, 1654–1970*. Tuscaloosa: University of Alabama Press, 1989.

Frye, Northrop. *Anatomy of Criticism: Four Essays*. Princeton, NJ: Princeton University Press, 1957.

Fulton, Robert I., and Thomas C. Trueblood, eds. *British and American Eloquence*. Boston: Ginn and Company, 1912.

Gaines, Francis Pendleton. *Southern Oratory: A Study in Idealism*. Tuscaloosa: University of Alabama Press, 1946.

Gallagher, Victoria J. "Black Power in Berkeley: Postmodern Constructions in the Rhetoric of Stokely Carmichael." *Quarterly Journal of Speech* 87 (2001): 144–157.

Gamson, William A. *Talking Politics*. New York: Cambridge University Press, 1992.

Garland, Jasper Vanderbilt. *Public Speaking for Women*. New York: Harper and Brothers, 1938.

Gilroy, Paul. *Against Race: Imagining Political Culture Beyond the Color Line*. Cambridge, MA: Harvard University Press, 2000.

Glenn, Robert W., ed. *Black Rhetoric: A Guide to Afro-American Communication*. Metuchen, NJ: Scarecrow, 1976.

Goffman, Erving. *Frame Analysis: An Essay on the Organization of Experience*. New York: Harper and Row, 1974.

Golden, James L., and Richard D. Rieke, eds. *The Rhetoric of Black Americans.* Columbus, OH: C. E. Merrill, 1971.

Goodrich, Chauncey A. *Essays from Select British Eloquence.* Ed. A. Craig Baird. Carbondale: Southern Illinois University Press, 1963.

Gordon, Dexter B. *Black Identity: Rhetoric, Ideology, and Nineteenth-Century Black Nationalism.* Carbondale: Southern Illinois University Press, 2003.

Gottheimer, Josh, ed. *Ripples of Hope: Great American Civil Rights Speeches.* New York: Basic Books, 2003.

Graber, Doris A. *Processing the News: How People Tame the Information Tide.* 2nd ed. New York: Longman, 1988.

Gravlee, G. Jack, and James R. Irvine, eds. *Pamphlets and the American Revolution: Rhetoric, Politics, Literature, and the Popular Press.* Delmar, NY: Scholars' Facsimiles and Reprints, 1976.

Gray, Giles Wilkeson. "The Founding of the Speech Association of America." *Quarterly Journal of Speech* 50 (1964): 342–345.

Greenstein, Fred I. *The Hidden-Hand Presidency: Eisenhower as Leader.* New York: Basic Books, 1982.

Greetham, D. C. *Textual Scholarship: An Introduction.* New York: Garland, 1994.

Greetham, D. C. *Theories of the Text.* Oxford: Oxford University Press, 1999.

Gregg, Richard B. "The Ego-Function of the Rhetoric of Protest." *Philosophy and Rhetoric* 4 (1971): 71–91.

Gresson, Aaron David III. *America's Atonement: Racial Pain, Recovery Rhetoric, and the Pedagogy of Healing.* New York: Peter Lang, 2004.

Griffin, Cindy L. *Invitation to Public Speaking.* New York: Wadsworth, 2004.

Griffin, Leland M. "The Rhetoric of Historical Movements." *Quarterly Journal of Speech* 38 (1953): 184–188.

Griffith, Elisabeth. *In Her Own Right: The Life of Elizabeth Cady Stanton.* New York: Oxford University Press, 1984.

Gronbeck, Bruce E. "Rhetorical History and Rhetorical Criticism: A Distinction." *Speech Teacher* 24 (1975): 309–320.

Gross, Alan G., and William M. Keith, eds. *Rhetorical Hermeneutics: Invention and Interpretation in the Age of Science.* Albany: State University Press of New York, 1997.

Gunderson, Robert Gray. *The Log-Cabin Campaign.* Lexington: University of Kentucky Press, 1957.

Gunderson, Robert Gray. *Old Gentlemen's Convention: The Washington Peace Conference of 1861.* Madison: University of Wisconsin Press, 1961.

Haberman, Frederick W., ed. *Peace.* Amsterdam: Elsevier, 1972.

Habermas, Jürgen. *The Structural Transformation of the Public Sphere: An Inquiry into a Category of Bourgeois Society.* Trans. Thomas Burger. Cambridge, MA: MIT Press, 1989.

Hafbauer, Benjamin. *Presidential Temples: How Memorials and Libraries Shape Public Memory.* Lawrence: University Press of Kansas, 2005.

Haiman, Franklyn S. "The Rhetoric of the Streets: Some Legal and Ethical Considerations." *Quarterly Journal of Speech* 53 (1967): 99–114.

Hammerback, John C., and Richard J. Jensen. *The Rhetorical Career of Cesar Chavez.* College Station: Texas A&M University Press, 1998.

Han, Lori Cox, and Diane J. Heith. *In the Public Domain: Presidents and the Challenges of Public Leadership.* Albany: State University of New York Press, 2005.

Harding, Harold Friend, ed. *The Age of Danger: Major Speeches of American Problems.* New York: Random House, 1952.

Hardwicke, Henry. *History of Oratory and Orators: A Study of the Influence of Oratory on Politics and Literature.* New York: G. P. Putnam's Sons, 1896.

Hariman, Robert. *Political Style: The Artistry of Power.* Chicago: University of Chicago Press, 1995.

Hariman, Robert, ed. *Prudence: Classical Virtue, Postmodern Practice.* University Park, PA: Pennsylvania State University Press, 2003.

Hariman, Robert, and John Louis Lucaites. *No Caption Needed: Iconic Photographs, Public Culture, and Liberal Democracy.* Chicago: University of Chicago Press, 2007.

Harris, Jose. *Private Lives, Public Spirit: A Social History of Britain, 1870–1914.* Oxford: Oxford University Press, 1993.

Hart, Roderick P. *The Political Pulpit.* West Lafayette, IN: Purdue University Press, 1977.

Hart, Roderick P. *The Sound of Leadership: Presidential Communication in the Modern Age.* Chicago: University of Chicago Press, 1987.

Hart, Roderick P. *Verbal Style and the Presidency: A Computer-Based Analysis.* Orlando, FL: Academic Press, 1984.

Hatzenbuehler, Ronald L., and Robert L. Ivie. *Congress Declares War: Rhetoric, Leadership, and Partisanship in the Early Republic.* Kent, OH: Kent State University Press, 1983.

Hauser, Gerald A. *Vernacular Voices: The Rhetoric of Publics and Public Spheres.* Columbia: University of South Carolina Press, 1999.

Hellman, Hugo E. "The Greatest American Oratory." *Quarterly Journal of Speech* 24 (1938): 36–39.

Helly, Dorothy, and Susan Reverby, eds. *Gendered Domains: Rethinking Public and Private in Women's History.* Ithaca, NY: Cornell University Press, 1992.

Herring, Scott. *Queering the Underworld: Slumming, Literature, and the Undoing of Lesbian and Gay History.* Chicago: University of Chicago Press, 2007.

Hill, Adams Sherman. *The Principles of Rhetoric and Their Application.* New York: Harper and Brothers, 1878.

Hill, Forbes I. "Conventional Wisdom – Traditional Form: The President's Message of November 3, 1969." *Quarterly Journal of Speech* 58 (1972): 373–386.

Hill, Roy L., ed. *Rhetoric of Racial Revolt.* Denver, CO: Golden Bell, 1964.

Hillbruner, Anthony. *Critical Dimensions: The Art of Public Address Criticism.* New York: Random House, 1966.

Hillis, Newell Dwight. *The Battle of Principles: A Study of the Heroism and Eloquence of the Anti-Slavery Conflict.* New York: Fleming H. Revell Co., 1912.

Hinkley, Barbara. *The Symbolic Presidency: How Presidents Portray Themselves.* New York: Routledge, 1990.

Hochmuth, Marie Kathryn, ed. *A History and Criticism of American Public Address.* Vol. 3. New York: Longmans, Green, 1955.

Hockey, Susan. *Electronic Texts in the Humanities: Principles and Practice.* Oxford: Oxford University Press, 2000.

Hofstadter, Richard. *The Paranoid Style in American Politics and Other Essays.* Cambridge, MA: Harvard University Press, 1964.

Hogan, J. Michael. *The Nuclear Freeze Campaign: Rhetoric and Foreign Policy in the Telepolitical Age.* East Lansing: Michigan State University Press, 1994.

Hogan, J. Michael. *The Panama Canal in American Politics: Domestic Advocacy and the Evolution of Policy.* Carbondale: Southern Illinois University Press, 1986.

Hogan, J. Michael, ed. *Rhetoric and Community: Studies in Unity and Fragmentation.* Columbia: University of South Carolina Press, 1998.

Hogan, J. Michael, ed. *Rhetoric and Reform in the Progressive Era.* Volume 6 of *A Rhetorical History of the United States*, 10 vols. East Lansing: Michigan State University Press, 2003.

Hogan, J. Michael. *Woodrow Wilson's Western Tour: Rhetoric, Public Opinion, and the League of Nations.* College Station: Texas A&M University Press, 2006.

Hogan, J. Michael, Patricia Hayes Andrews, James R. Andrews, and Glen Williams. *Public Speaking and Civic Engagement.* Boston: Pearson/Allyn and Bacon/Vango Books, 2008.

Holland, DeWitte, Charles Stewart, and Jess Yoder, eds. *America in Controversy: History of American Public Address.* Dubuque, IA: W. C. Brown, 1973.

Holland, DeWitte, Hubert Vance Taylor, and Jess Yoder, eds. *Sermons in American History: Selected Issues in the American Pulpit.* Nashville, TN: Abingdon Press, 1971.

Holland, DeWitte, Jess Yoder, and Hubert Vance Taylor, eds. *Preaching in American History: Selected Issues in the American Pulpit, 1630–1967.* Nashville, TN: Abingdon Press, 1969.

Hollis, Patricia, ed. *Women in Public, 1850–1900: Documents of the Victorian Women's Movement.* Boston: G. Allen and Unwin, 1979.

Holmes, Barbara A., ed. *A Private Woman in Public Spaces: Barbara Jordan's Speeches on Ethics, Public Religion, and Law.* Harrisburg, PA: Trinity, 2000.

Holsti, Ole R. *Public Opinion and American Foreign Policy.* Rev. ed. Ann Arbor: University of Michigan Press, 2004.

Houck, Davis W. *FDR and Fear Itself: The First Inaugural Address.* College Station: Texas A&M University Press, 2002.

Houck, Davis W., and David E. Dixon, eds. *Rhetoric, Religion, and the Civil Rights Movement, 1954–1965.* Waco, TX: Baylor University Press, 2006.

Houck, Davis W., and David E. Dixon, eds. *Women and the Civil Rights Movement, 1954–1965.* Jackson: University Press of Mississippi, 2009.

Houston, Marsha, and Olga Idriss Davis, eds. *Centering Ourselves: African American Feminist and Womanist Studies of Discourse.* Cresskill, NJ: Hampton Press, 2002.

Howes, Raymond F., ed. *Historical Studies of Rhetoric and Rhetoricians.* Ithaca, NY: Cornell University Press, 1961.

Huggins, Nathan Irving. *The Harlem Renaissance.* New York: Oxford University Press, 1971.

Hunt, Everett Lee. *Plato and Aristotle on Rhetoric and Rhetoricians.* New York: Century Co., 1925.

Ivie, Robert L. *Democracy and America's War on Terror.* Tuscaloosa: University of Alabama Press, 2005.

Iyengar, Shanto. *Is Anyone Responsible? How Television Frames Political Issues.* Chicago: University of Chicago Press, 1991.

Iyengar, Shanto, and Donald R. Kinder. *News that Matters.* Chicago: University of Chicago Press, 1987.

Jamieson, Kathleen Hall. *Beyond the Double Bind: Women and Leadership.* New York: Oxford University Press, 1995.

Jamieson, Kathleen Hall. *Eloquence in an Electronic Age: The Transformation of Political Speechmaking.* New York: Oxford University Press, 1988.

Jamieson, Kathleen Hall. *Packaging the Presidency: A History and Criticism of Presidential Campaign Advertising.* New York: Oxford University Press, 1984.

Jamieson, Kathleen Hall, and David S. Birdsell. *Presidential Debates: The Challenge of Creating an Informed Electorate.* New York: Oxford University Press, 1988.

Jasinski, James. *Sourcebook on Rhetoric: Key Concepts in Contemporary Rhetorical Studies.* Thousand Oaks, CA: Sage, 2001.

Jay, Karla, ed. *Out of the Closets: Voices of Gay Liberation* (1972). New York: New York University Press, 1992.

Jensen, Richard J. *Reagan at Bergen-Belsen and Bitburg.* College Station: Texas A&M University Press, 2007.

Jensen, Richard J., and John C. Hammerback, eds. *The Words of Cesar Chavez.* College Station: Texas A&M University Press, 2002.

Johnson, Nan. *Gender and Rhetorical Space in American Life, 1866–1910.* Carbondale: Southern Illinois University Press, 2002.

Jones, Constance, ed. *The Love of Friends: An Anthology of Gay and Lesbian Letters to Friends and Lovers.* New York: Simon and Schuster, 1997.

Jorgensen-Earp, Cheryl R. *The Transfiguring Sword: The Just War of the Women's Social and Political Union.* Tuscaloosa: University of Alabama Press, 1997.

Jorgensen-Earp, Cheryl R. *In the Wake of Violence: Image and Social Reform.* East Lansing: Michigan State University Press, 2008.

Just, Marion R., Ann N. Crigler, Dean E. Alger, and Timothy E. Cook. *Crosstalk: Citizens, Candidates, and the Media in a Presidential Campaign.* Chicago: University of Chicago Press, 1996.

Keck, Margaret E., and Kathryn Sikkink. *Activists Beyond Borders: Advocacy Networks in International Politics.* Ithaca, NY: Cornell University Press, 1998.

Kendall, Kathleen E. *Communication in the Presidential Primaries: Candidates and the Media, 1912–2000.* Westport, CT: Praeger, 2000.

Kennedy, Patricia Scileppi, and Gloria Hartmann O'Shields, eds. *And We Shall Be Heard: Women Speakers in America.* Dubuque, IA: Kendall/Hunt, 1983.

Kernell, Samuel. *Going Public: New Strategies of Presidential Leadership.* Washington, DC: Congressional Quarterly Press, 1997.

Kiewe, Amos. *FDR's First Fireside Chat: Public Confidence and the Banking Crisis.* College Station: Texas A&M University Press, 2007.

Kimble, James J. *Mobilizing the Home Front: War Bonds and Domestic Propaganda.* College Station: Texas A&M University Press, 2006.

Kinder, Donald R., and Lynn M. Sanders. *Divided by Color: Racial Politics and Democratic Ideals.* Chicago: University of Chicago Press, 1996.

King, Andrew A. "Booker T. Washington and the Myth of Heroic Materialism." *Quarterly Journal of Speech* 60 (1974): 323–328.

Kirschke, Amy Helene. *Art in Crisis: W. E. B. Du Bois and the Struggle for African American Identity and Memory.* Bloomington: Indiana University Press, 2007.

Koestenbaum, Wayne. *Double Talk: The Erotics of Male Literary Collaboration.* New York: Routledge, 1989.

Kraditor, Aileen S., ed. *Up From the Pedestal: Selected Writings in the History of American Feminism.* Chicago: Quadrangle Books, 1968.

Kraig, Robert Alexander. *Woodrow Wilson and the Lost World of the Oratorical Statesman.* College Station: Texas A&M University Press, 2003.

Langland, Elizabeth. *Telling Tales: Gender and Narrative Form in Victorian Literature and Culture.* Athens: Ohio State University Press, 2002.

Lanham, Richard A. *A Handlist of Rhetorical Terms.* 2nd ed. Berkeley: University of California Press, 1991.

Larson, Barbara Ann. *Prologue to a Revolution: The War Sermons of the Reverend Samuel Davies, A Rhetorical Study.* Falls Church, VA: Speech Communication Association, 1978.

LeFevre, Karen. *Invention as a Social Act.* Carbondale: Southern Illinois University Press, 1987.

Leff, Michael C. "Interpretation and the Art of the Rhetorical Critic." *Western Journal of Speech Communication* 44 (1980): 337–349.

Leff, Michael C., and Fred J. Kauffeld, eds. *Texts in Context: Critical Dialogues on Significant Episodes in American Political Rhetoric.* Davis, CA: Hermagoras Press, 1989.

Leff, Michael C., and Andrew Sachs. "Word the Most Like Things: Iconicity and the Rhetorical Text." *Western Journal of Communication* 54 (1990): 252–273.

Lerner, Gerda. *The Majority Finds its Past: Placing Women in History.* New York: Oxford University Press, 1979.

Levine, Peter. *The New Progressive Era: Toward a Fair and Deliberative Democracy.* Lanham, MD: Rowman and Littlefield, 2000.

Linkugel, Wil A., R. R. Allen, and Richard L. Johannesen, eds. *Contemporary American Speeches: A Sourcebook of Speech Forms and Principles.* 2nd ed. Belmont, CA: Wadsworth, 1969.

Lipsitz, George. *Possessive Investment in Whiteness: How White People Profit from Identity Politics.* Philadelphia: Temple University Press, 1998.

Logan, Shirley Wilson, ed. *We Are Coming: The Persuasive Discourse of Nineteenth-Century Black Women.* Carbondale: Southern Illinois University Press, 1999.

Logue, Cal M., ed. *Eugene Talmadge: Rhetoric and Response.* New York: Greenwood Press, 1989.

Logue, Cal M. *Ralph McGill: Editor and Publisher.* Durham, NC: Moore, 1969.

Logue, Cal M., and Howard Dorgan. *A New Diversity in Contemporary Southern Rhetoric.* Baton Rouge: Louisiana State University Press, 1987.

Logue, Cal M., and Howard Dorgan, eds. *The Oratory of Southern Demagogues.* Baton Rouge: Louisiana State University Press, 1981.

Lomas, Charles Wyatt. *The Agitator in American Society.* Englewood Cliffs, NJ: Prentice Hall, 1968.

Lotman, Yuri M. *Universe of the Mind: A Semiotic Theory of Culture.* Trans. Ann Shukman. London: Tauris, 2001.

Lucas, Stephen E. *Portents of Rebellion: Rhetoric and Revolution in Philadelphia, 1765–76.* Philadelphia: Temple University Press, 1976.

Lucas, Stephen E. "The Renaissance of American Public Address: Text and Context in Rhetorical Criticism." *Quarterly Journal of Speech* 74 (1988): 241–260.

Lucas, Stephen E. "The Schism in Rhetorical Scholarship." *Quarterly Journal of Speech* 67 (1981): 1–20.

Lucas, Stephen E., and Martin J. Medhurst, eds. *Words of a Century: The Top 100 American Speeches, 1900–1999.* New York: Oxford University Press, 2009.

Lunsford, Andrea A., ed. *Reclaiming Rhetorica: Women in the Rhetorical Tradition.* Pittsburgh, PA: University of Pittsburgh Press, 1995.

Lunsford, Andrea A., Kirt H. Wilson, and Rosa A. Eberly, eds. *The Sage Handbook of Rhetorical Studies.* Thousand Oaks, CA: Sage, 2009.

Magoon, Elias Lyman. *Living Orators in America.* New York: Baker and Scribner, 1849.

Mailloux, Steven. *Rhetorical Power*. Ithaca, NY: Cornell University Press, 1989.

Mann, Barbara Alice, ed. *Native American Speakers of the Eastern Woodlands*. Westport, CT: Greenwood Press, 2001.

Masten, Jeffrey. *Textual Intercourse: Collaboration, Authorship, and Sexualities in Renaissance Drama*. New York: Cambridge University Press, 1997.

Mathews, David. *Politics for People: Finding a Responsible Public Voice*. 2nd ed. Urbana: University of Illinois Press, 1999.

Mattingly, Carol. *Appropriate[ing] Dress: Women's Rhetorical Style in Nineteenth-Century America*. Carbondale and Edwardsville: Southern Illinois University Press, 2002.

Mattson, Kevin. *Creating a Democratic Public: The Struggle for Urban Participatory Democracy During the Progressive Era*. University Park: Pennsylvania State University Press, 1998.

Mayer, Jane. *The Dark Side: The Inside Story of How the War on Terror Turned Into a War on American Ideals*. New York: Doubleday, 2008.

McBath, James H., and Walter R. Fisher, eds. *British Public Addresses, 1828–1960*. Boston: Houghton Mifflin, 1971.

McDorman, Todd F., and David M. Timmerman. *Rhetoric and Democracy: Pedagogical and Political Practices*. East Lansing: Michigan State University Press, 2008.

McGann, Jerome J. *A Critique of Modern Textual Criticism*. Chicago: University of Chicago Press, 1983.

McGee, Michael C. "In Search of the 'People': A Rhetorical Alternative." *Quarterly Journal of Speech* 61 (1975): 235–249.

McGee, Michael C. "The 'Ideograph': A Link Between Rhetoric and Ideology." *Quarterly Journal of Speech* 66 (1980): 1–16.

McKenzie, D. F. *Bibliography and the Sociology of Texts: The Panizzi Lectures 1985*. London: British Library, 1986.

McKerrow, Raymie. "Critical Rhetoric: Theory and Praxis." *Communication Monographs* 56 (1989): 91–111.

Medhurst, Martin J., ed. *Before the Rhetorical Presidency*. College Station: Texas A&M University Press, 2008.

Medhurst, Martin J., ed. *Beyond the Rhetorical Presidency*. College Station: Texas A&M University Press, 1996.

Medhurst, Martin J. "The Contemporary Study of Public Address: Renewal, Recovery, and Reconfiguration." *Rhetoric & Public Affairs* 4 (2001): 495–522.

Medhurst, Martin J., ed. *Landmark Essays on American Public Address*. Davis, CA: Hermagoras Press, 1993.

Medhurst, Martin J., and Thomas W. Benson, eds. *Rhetorical Dimensions in Media: A Critical Casebook*. Dubuque, IA: Kendall/Hunt, 1984.

Medhurst, Martin J., and H. W. Brands, eds. *Critical Reflections on the Cold War: Linking Rhetoric and History*. College Station: Texas A&M University Press, 2000.

Miller, Warren E., and J. Merrill Shanks. *The New American Voter*. Cambridge, MA: Harvard University Press, 1996.

Mohrmann, G. P., Charles J. Stewart, and Donovan J. Ochs, eds. *Explorations in Rhetorical Criticism*. University Park: Pennsylvania State University Press, 1973.

Montgomery, Bruce P. *Subverting Open Government: White House Materials and Executive Branch Politics*. Lanham, MD: Scarecrow, 2006.

Morrell, Caroline. *"Black Friday": Violence Against Women in the Suffragette Movement*. London: Women's Research and Resources Centre, 1990.

Morris, Charles E. III, ed. *Queering Public Address: Sexualities in American Historical Discourse.* Columbia: University of South Carolina Press, 2007.

Morris, Charles E. III, and Stephen H. Browne, eds. *Readings on the Rhetoric of Social Protest.* 2nd ed. State College, PA: Strata, 2006.

Murphy, John M. "The Language of the Liberal Consensus: John F. Kennedy, Technical Reason, and the 'New Economics' at Yale University." *Quarterly Journal of Speech* 90 (2004): 133–162.

Murphy, John M. "'Our Mission and Our Moment': George W. Bush and September 11th." *Rhetoric & Public Affairs* 6 (2003): 607–632.

Murphy, John M. "'A Time of Shame and Sorrow'": Robert F. Kennedy and the American Jeremiad." *Quarterly Journal of Speech* 76 (1990): 401–414.

Nakayama, Thomas K., and Judith N. Martin, eds. *Whiteness: The Communication of Social Identity.* Thousand Oaks, CA: Sage, 1999.

Newman, Robert P. "Under the Veneer: Nixon's Vietnam Speech of November 3, 1969." *Quarterly Journal of Speech* 56 (1970): 168–178.

Nichols, Marie Hochmuth. *Rhetoric and Criticism.* Baton Rouge: Louisiana State University Press, 1963.

Nicolay, John G., and John Hay, eds. *Complete Works of Abraham Lincoln.* 12 vols. New York: Francis D. Tandy, 1905.

Nilsen, Thomas R., ed. *Essays in Rhetorical Criticism.* New York: Random House, 1968.

Nix, S. Michele, ed. *Women at the Podium.* New York: Harper, 2000.

Norton, Rictor. *The Myth of the Modern Homosexual: Queer History and the Search for Cultural Unity.* London: Cassell, 1997.

Nothstine, William L., Carole Blair, and Gary A. Copeland. *Critical Questions: Invention, Creativity, and the Criticism of Discourse and Media.* New York: St. Martin's Press, 1994.

O'Connor, Lillian. *Pioneer Women Orators: Rhetoric in the Ante-Bellum Reform Movement.* New York: Vantage Press, 1954.

Oliver, Robert T. *Communication and Culture in Ancient India and China.* Syracuse, NY: Syracuse University Press, 1971.

Oliver, Robert T. *Four Who Spoke Out: Burke, Fox, Sheridan, Pitt.* Syracuse, NY: Syracuse University Press, 1946.

Oliver, Robert T. *History of Public Speaking in America.* Boston: Allyn and Bacon, 1965.

Oliver, Robert T. *Leadership in Asia: Persuasive Communication in the Making of Nations, 1850–1950.* Newark, NJ: University of Delaware Press, 1989.

Oliver, Robert T. *The Psychology of Persuasive Speech.* New York: Longmans, Green, 1942.

Oliver, Robert T. *Public Speaking in the Reshaping of Great Britain.* Newark, NJ: University of Delaware Press, 1987.

Oliver, Robert T., and Marvin G. Bauer, eds. *Re-establishing the Speech Profession: The First Fifty Years.* New York: Speech Association of the Eastern States, 1959.

Oliver, Robert T., and Eugene E. White, eds. *Selected Speeches from American History.* Boston: Allyn and Bacon, 1966.

Olson, Lester C. *Benjamin Franklin's Vision of American Community: A Study in Rhetorical Iconology.* Columbia: University of South Carolina Press, 2004.

Olson, Lester C., Cara A. Finnegan, and Diane S. Hope, eds. *Visual Rhetoric: A Reader in Communication and American Culture.* Thousand Oaks, CA: Sage, 2008.

O'Neill, Daniel J., ed. *Speeches by Black Americans.* Encino, CA: Dickinson, 1971.

O'Neill, James M. *Classified Models of Speech Composition*. New York: D. Appleton-Century Co., 1921.

O'Neill, James M. *Modern Short Speeches*. New York: Century Co., 1923.

O'Neill, James M., and Floyd K. Riley, comps. *Contemporary Speeches*. New York: Century Co., 1930.

Osborn, Michael. "Archetypal Metaphor in Rhetoric: The Light–Dark Family." *Quarterly Journal of Speech* 53 (1967): 115–126.

Page, Benjamin I., and Robert Y. Shapiro. *The Rational Public: Fifty Years of Trends in Americans' Policy Preferences*. Chicago: University of Chicago Press, 1992.

Palmer, Kathryn, and Stephen E. Lucas. "On Trial: Conflicting Versions of Emma Goldman's Address to the Jury." *Rhetoric & Public Affairs* 11 (2008): 47–88.

Parrish, Wayland Maxfield, and Marie Hochmuth, eds. *American Speeches*. New York: Greenwood Press, 1954.

Parry-Giles, Shawn J. *The Rhetorical Presidency, Propaganda, and the Cold War, 1945–1955*. Westport, CT: Praeger, 2002.

Parry-Giles, Shawn J., and Trevor Parry-Giles, eds. *Public Address and Moral Judgment: Critical Studies in Ethical Tensions*. East Lansing: Michigan State University Press, 2009.

Parry-Giles, Trevor. *The Character of Justice: Rhetoric, Law, and Politics in the Supreme Court Confirmation Process*. East Lansing: Michigan State University Press, 2006.

Parry-Giles, Trevor, and Shawn Parry-Giles. *The Prime-Time Presidency: The West Wing and US Nationalism*. Urbana: University of Illinois Press, 2006.

Pauley, Garth E. *LBJ's American Promise: The 1965 Voting Rights Address*. College Station: Texas A&M University Press, 2007.

Pearson, Paul M. *The Humorous Speaker: A Book of Humorous Selections for Reading and Speaking*. New York: Hinds, Noble, and Eldredge, 1909.

Perelman, Chaim, and Lucie Olbrechts-Tyteca. *The New Rhetoric: A Treatise on Argumentation*. Notre Dame, IN: University of Notre Dame Press, 1969.

Peters, John Durham. *Speaking Into the Air: A History of the Idea of Communication*. Chicago: University of Chicago Press, 1999.

Peterson, Carla L. *Doers of the Word: African-American Women Speakers and Writers in the North, 1830–1880*. New York: Oxford University Press, 1995.

Peterson, Merrill D. *Lincoln in American Memory*. New York: Oxford University Press, 1994.

Pfau, Michael William. *The Political Style of Conspiracy: Chase, Sumner, and Lincoln*. East Lansing: Michigan State University Press, 2005.

Phillips, Gerald M., and Julia T. Wood, eds. *Speech Communication: Essays to Commemorate the Seventy-Fifth Anniversary of the Speech Communication Association*. Carbondale: Southern Illinois University Press, 1990.

Phillips, Kendall R., ed. *Framing Public Memory*. Tuscaloosa: University of Alabama Press, 2004.

Pipes, William H. *Say Amen, Brother! Old-Time Negro Preaching: A Study in Frustration*. New York: William Frederick, 1951.

Popkin, Samuel L. *The Reasoning Voter: Communication and Persuasion in Presidential Campaigns*. Chicago: University of Chicago Press, 1992.

Portnoy, Alisse. *Their Right to Speak: Women's Activism in the Indian and Slave Debates*. Cambridge, MA: Harvard University Press, 2005.

Potter, David, and Gordon L. Thomas, eds. *The Colonial Idiom*. Carbondale: Southern Illinois University Press, 1970.

Prelli, Lawrence, ed., *Rhetorics of Display*. Columbia: University of South Carolina Press, 2006.

Rampersad, Arnold. *The Art and Imagination of W. E. B. Du Bois*. Cambridge, MA: Harvard University Press, 1976.

Ransom, John Crowe. *The New Criticism*. Norfolk, CT: New Directions, 1941.

Reid, Loren D., ed. *American Public Address: Studies in Honor of Albert Craig Baird*. Columbia: University of Missouri Press, 1961.

Reid, Loren D. *Charles James Fox: A Man for the People*. Columbia: University of Missouri Press, 1969.

Reid, Ronald F. *The American Revolution and the Rhetoric of History*. Falls Church, VA: Speech Communication Association, 1978.

Reid, Ronald F., ed. *Three Centuries of American Rhetorical Discourse: An Anthology and Review*. Prospect Heights, IL: Waveland Press, 1988.

Reid, Ronald F., and James F. Klumpp. *American Rhetorical Discourse*. 3rd ed. Prospect Heights, IL: Waveland Press, 2005.

Reilly, John E., ed. *American Public Opinion and Foreign Policy*. Chicago: Chicago Council on Foreign Relations, 1975, 1979.

Richardson, Marilyn, ed. *Maria W. Stewart, America's First Black Woman Political Writer: Essays and Speeches*. Bloomington: Indiana University Press, 1987.

Ridinger, Robert, ed. *Speaking for Our Lives: Historic Speeches and Rhetoric for Gay and Lesbian Rights (1892–2000)*. New York: Harrington Park Press, 2004.

Ritchie, Joy, and Kate Ronald, eds. *Available Means: An Anthology of Women's Rhetoric(s)*. Pittsburgh, PA: University of Pittsburgh Press, 2001.

Ritter, Kurt W., and James R. Andrews. *The American Ideology: Reflections of the Revolution in American Rhetoric*. Falls Church, VA: Speech Communication Association, 1978.

Ritter, Kurt W., and Martin J. Medhurst, eds. *Presidential Speechwriting: From the New Deal to the Reagan Revolution and Beyond*. College Station: Texas A&M University Press, 2003.

Roediger, David. *Working Toward Whiteness: How America's Immigrants Became White*. New York: Basic Books, 2005.

Rohler, Lloyd E., and Roger Cook, eds. *Great Speeches for Criticism and Analysis*. Greenwood, IN: Alistair Press, 1988.

Román, David. *Acts of Intervention: Performance, Gay Culture, and AIDS*. Bloomington: Indiana University Press, 1998.

Rose, Gillian. *Visual Methodologies: An Introduction to the Interpretation of Visual Materials*. Thousand Oaks, CA: Sage, 2001.

Rountree, Clarke. *Judging the Supreme Court: Constructions of Motives in Bush v. Gore*. East Lansing: Michigan State University Press, 2007.

Royster, Jacqueline J. *Traces of a Stream: Literacy and Social Change Among African American Women*. Pittsburgh, PA: University of Pittsburgh Press, 2000.

Rush, James. *The Philosophy of the Human Voice*. Philadelphia: J. Maxwell, 1827.

Ryan, Halford Ross. *Franklin D. Roosevelt's Rhetorical Presidency*. New York: Greenwood Press, 1988.

Ryan, Halford Ross, ed. *Oratorical Encounters: Selected Studies and Sources of Twentieth-Century Political Accusations and Apologies*. New York: Greenwood Press, 1988.

Sarkela, Sandra J., Susan Mallon Ross, and Margaret A. Lowe, eds. *From Megaphones to Microphones: Speeches of American Women, 1920–1960*. Westport, CT: Praeger, 2003.

Sauer, Beverly J. *The Rhetoric of Risk: Technical Documentation in Hazardous Environments.* Mahwah, NJ: Erlbaum, 2003.

Schiappa, Edward. "Second Thoughts on the Critiques of Big Rhetoric." *Philosophy and Rhetoric* 34 (2001): 260–274.

Schick, Frank L., Renée Schick, and Mark Carroll. *Records of the Presidency: Presidential Papers and Libraries from Washington to Reagan.* Phoenix, AZ: Oryx Press, 1989.

Schlesinger, Arthur M., Jr. *The Imperial Presidency.* Boston: Houghton Mifflin, 1973.

Schwartz, Barry. *Abraham Lincoln and the Forge of National Memory.* Chicago: University of Chicago Press, 2000.

Scott, Joan Wallach. *Gender and the Politics of History.* New York: Columbia University Press, 1999.

Scott, Robert L., and Bernard L. Brock. *Methods of Rhetorical Criticism: A Twentieth-Century Perspective.* New York: Harper and Row, 1972.

Scott, Robert L., and Wayne Brockriede. *The Rhetoric of Black Power.* New York: Harper and Row, 1969.

Scott, Robert L., and Donald K. Smith, "The Rhetoric of Confrontation." *Quarterly Journal of Speech* 55 (1969): 1–8.

Sears, Lorenzo. *John Hancock, The Picturesque Patriot.* Boston: Gregg Press, 1912.

Sears, Lorenzo. *John Hay, Author and Statesman.* New York: Dodd, Mead, and Company, 1914.

Sears, Lorenzo. *The History of Oratory from the Age of Pericles to the Present Time.* Chicago: S. C. Griggs and Co., 1895.

Sears, Lorenzo. *Wendell Philips: Orator and Agitator.* New York: B. Blom, 1909.

Sedgwick, Eve Kosofsky. *Between Men: English Literature and Male Homosocial Desire.* New York: Columbia University Press, 1985.

Sezzi, Peter. *Personal Versus Private: Presidential Records in a Legislative Context – A Bibliographic Exploration.* Lanham, MD: Scarecrow, 2005.

Shaw, Warren Choate. *History of American Oratory.* Indianapolis: Bobbs-Merrill, 1928.

Shillingsburg, Peter L. *Scholarly Editing in the Computer Age: Theory and Practice.* 3rd ed. Ann Arbor: University of Michigan Press, 1996.

Shoemaker, Robert B. *Gender in English Society, 1650–1850: The Emergence of Separate Spheres?* London: Longman, 1998.

Shurter, Edwin Du Bois. *The Complete Orations and Speeches of Henry W. Grady.* New York: Hinds, Noble, and Eldredge, 1910.

Shurter, Edwin Du Bois. *Masterpieces of Modern Oratory.* Boston: Ginn and Company, 1906.

Shurter, Edwin Du Bois. *The Modern American Speaker for School and College Students, Lawyers, Preachers, Teachers, and All Interested in the Art of Public Speaking.* Austin, TX: Gammel Book Company, 1901.

Shurter, Edwin Du Bois. *Oratory of the South, From the Civil War to the Present Time.* New York: Neale Publishing Company, 1908.

Shurter, Edwin Du Bois. *The Rhetoric of Oratory.* New York: Macmillan, 1909.

Shurter, Edwin Du Bois. *Woman Suffrage: Bibliography and Selected Arguments.* Austin: University of Texas Press, 1912.

Sloane, Thomas O., ed. *Encyclopedia of Rhetoric.* Oxford: Oxford University Press, 2001.

Sloop, John M. *Disciplining Gender: Rhetorics of Sex Identity in Contemporary US Culture.* Boston: University of Massachusetts Press, 2004.

Smith, Craig R. *Defender of the Union: The Oratory of Daniel Webster*. New York: Greenwood Press, 1989.

Smith, Craig R. *Freedom of Expression and Partisan Politics*. Columbia: University of South Carolina Press, 1989.

Smith, Ted J. III, ed. *Propaganda: A Pluralistic Perspective*. New York: Praeger, 1989.

Solomon, Martha. *Emma Goldman*. Boston: Twayne, 1987.

Stampp, Kenneth M., and Leon F. Litwack, eds. *Reconstruction: An Anthology of Revisionist Writings*. Baton Rouge: Louisiana State University Press, 1969.

Stange, Maren. *Symbols of Ideal Life: Social Documentary Photography in America, 1890–1950*. Oxford: Cambridge University Press, 1989.

Stanley, Liz, and Ann Morley. *The Life and Death of Emily Wilding Davison: A Biographical Detective Story*. London: Women's Press, 1988.

Stelzner, Hermann G. "The Quest Story and Nixon's November 3, 1969 Address." *Quarterly Journal of Speech* 57 (1971): 163–172.

Stewart, Charles J., Craig Allen Smith, and Robert E. Denton, Jr. *Persuasion and Social Movements*. Prospect Heights, IL: Waveland Press, 1989.

Straub, Deborah Gillan, ed. *Voices of Multicultural America: Notable Speeches Delivered by African, Asian, Hispanic, and Native Americans, 1790–1995*. New York: Gale, 1995.

Stuckey, Mary E. *Defining Americans: The Presidency and National Identity*. Lawrence: University Press of Kansas, 2004.

Stuckey, Mary E. *Jimmy Carter, Human Rights, and the National Agenda*. College Station: Texas A&M University Press, 2008.

Stuckey, Mary E. *Slipping the Surly Bonds: Reagan's Challenger Address*. College Station: Texas A&M University Press, 2006.

Sullivan, Patricia A., and Steven R. Goldzwig, eds. *New Approaches to Rhetoric*. Thousand Oaks, CA: Sage, 2004.

Sutton, Roberta Briggs. *Speech Index: An Index to 64 Collections of World Famous Orations and Speeches for Various Occasions*. New York: H. W. Wilson Co., 1935.

Tanselle, G. Thomas. *A Rationale of Textual Criticism*. Philadelphia: University of Pennsylvania Press, 1989.

Tanselle, G. Thomas. "Textual Criticism at the Millennium." *Studies in Bibliography* 54 (2001): 1–80.

Terrill, Robert E. *Malcolm X: Inventing Radical Judgment*. East Lansing: Michigan State University Press, 2005.

Thomas, John L., ed. *Abraham Lincoln and the American Political Tradition*. Amherst: University of Massachusetts Press, 1986.

Thonssen, Lester, and A. Craig Baird. *Speech Criticism: The Development of Standards for Rhetorical Appraisal*. New York: Ronald Press, 1948.

Thorpe, James. *Principles of Textual Criticism*. San Marino, CA: Huntington Library, 1972.

Tickner, Lisa. *The Spectacle of Women: Imagery of the Suffrage Campaign, 1907–14*. Chicago: University of Chicago Press, 1988.

Toulmin, Stephen. *Cosmopolis: The Hidden Agenda of Modernity*. Chicago: University of Chicago Press, 1990.

Towns, W. Stuart. *Oratory and Rhetoric in the Nineteenth-Century South: A Rhetoric of Defense*. Westport, CT, Praeger, 1998.

Trachtenberg, Alan. *Reading American Photographs: Images as History from Mathew Brady to Walker Evans*. New York: Noonday Press, 1989.

Trattner, Walter I. *Crusade for the Children: A History of the National Child Labor Committee and Child Labor Reform in America*. Chicago: Quadrangle Books, 1970.

Tripp, C. A. *The Intimate World of Abraham Lincoln*. Ed. Lewis Gannett. New York: Free Press, 2005.

Tulis, Jeffrey. *The Rhetorical Presidency*. Princeton, NJ: Princeton University Press, 1987.

Turner, Kathleen J., ed. *Doing Rhetorical History: Concepts and Cases*. Tuscaloosa: University of Alabama Press, 1998.

Turner, Kathleen J. *Lyndon Johnson's Dual War: Vietnam and the Press*. Chicago: University of Chicago Press, 1985.

Underhill, W. Robert. *The Truman Persuasions*. Ames: Iowa State University Press, 1981.

Van Leeuwen, Theo, and Carey Jewitt, eds. *Handbook of Visual Analysis*. Thousand Oaks, CA: Sage, 2001.

Veeser, H. Aram, ed. *The New Historicism*. New York: Routledge, 1989.

Veit, Fritz. *Presidential Libraries and Collections*. New York: Greenwood Press, 1987.

Waggenspack, Beth Marie. *The Search for Self-Sovereignty: The Oratory of Elizabeth Cady Stanton*. New York: Greenwood Press, 1989.

Walker, Robbie Jean, ed. *The Rhetoric of Struggle: Public Address by African American Women*. New York: Garland, 1992.

Wander, Philip. "The Ideological Turn in Modern Criticism." *Central States Speech Journal* 34 (1983): 1–18.

Warner, Robert M. *Diary of a Dream: A History of the National Archives Independence Movement, 1980–1985*. Metuchen, NJ: Scarecrow, 1995.

Watkins, William J., Jr., *Reclaiming the American Revolution: The Kentucky and Virginia Resolutions and Their Legacy*. New York: Palgrave Macmillan, 2004.

Watson, Martha S., and Thomas R. Burkholder, eds. *The Rhetoric of Nineteenth-Century Reform*. Volume 5 of *A Rhetorical History of the United States*, 10 vols. East Lansing: Michigan State University Press, 2008.

Weaver, Andrew Thomas. "Seventeen Who Made History – The Founders of the Association." *Quarterly Journal of Speech* 45 (1959): 195–199.

Welter, Barbara. *The Woman Question in American History*. Hinsdale, IL: Dryden Press, 1973.

Wertheimer, Molly, ed. *Listening to Their Voices*. Columbia: University of South Carolina Press, 1997.

White, Eugene E. *Puritan Rhetoric: The Issue of Emotion in Religion*. Carbondale: Southern Illinois University Press, 1972.

White, James Boyd. *When Words Lose Their Meaning: Constitutions and Reconstitutions of Language, Character, and Community*. Chicago: University of Chicago Press, 1984.

Wichelns, Herbert A. "The Literary Criticism of Oratory." *Studies of Rhetoric and Public Speaking in Honor of James Albert Winans*. Ed. A. M. Drummond. New York: Century Co., 1925.

Wichelns, Herbert A., Donald C. Bryant, Barnard Hewitt, and Karl R. Wallace, eds. *Studies in Speech and Drama in Honor of Alexander M. Drummond*. Ithaca, NY: Cornell University Press, 1944.

Widmer, Ted, ed. *American Speeches: Political Oratory from Abraham Lincoln to Bill Clinton*. New York: Library of America, 2006.

Williams, Jamye Coleman, and McDonald Williams, eds. *The Negro Speaks: The Rhetoric of Contemporary Black Leaders*. New York: Noble and Noble, 1970.

Williston, E. B. *Eloquence of the United States*. 5 vols. Middletown, CT: E. and H. Co., 1827.

Wills, Garry. *Lincoln at Gettysburg: The Words that Remade America*. New York: Simon and Schuster, 1992.

Wills, Garry. *"Negro President": Jefferson and the Slave Power*. Boston: Houghton Mifflin, 2003.

Wilson, Kirt H. *The Reconstruction Desegregation Debate: The Politics of Equality and the Rhetoric of Place, 1870–1875*. East Lansing: Michigan State University Press, 2002.

Wimsatt, W. K. *Explication as Criticism*. New York: Columbia University Press, 1963.

Winans, James A. *Public Speaking: Principles and Practice*. Ithaca, NY: Sewell Publishing Co., 1915.

Windt, Theodore Otto, Jr. *Rhetoric as a Human Adventure: A Short Biography of Everett Lee Hunt*. Annandale, VA: Speech Communication Association, 1990.

Wintz, Cary D., ed. *Harlem Speaks: A Living History of the Harlem Renaissance*. Naperville, IL: Sourcebooks Inc., 2007.

Wintz, Cary D. *The Politics and Aesthetics of "New Negro Literature."* New York: Garland Press, 1996.

Woodson, Carter Godwin. *Negro Orators and Their Orations*. Washington, DC: Associated Publishers, 1925.

Woolbert, Charles Henry. *The Fundamentals of Speech: A Behavioristic Study of the Underlying Principles of Speaking and Reading*. New York: Harper and Brothers, 1920.

Wrage, Ernest J. "Public Address: A Study in Social and Intellectual History." *Quarterly Journal of Speech* 33 (1947): 451–457.

Wrage, Ernest J., and Barnet Baskerville, eds. *American Forum: Speeches on Historic Issues, 1788–1900*. New York: Harper, 1960.

Wrage, Ernest J., and Barnet Baskerville, eds. *Contemporary Forum: American Speeches on Twentieth-Century Issues*. New York: Harper, 1962.

Yeager, Willard Hays. *Chauncey Mitchell Depew, the Orator*. Washington, DC: George Washington University Press, 1934.

Yep, Gust A., Karen E. Lovaas, and John P. Elia, eds. *Queer Theory and Communication: From Disciplining Queers to Queering the Discipline(s)*. New York: Harrington Park Press, 2003.

Zaeske, Susan. *Signatures of Citizenship: Petitioning, Antislavery, and Women's Political Identity*. Chapel Hill: University of North Carolina Press, 2003.

Zaeske, Susan. "'The South Arose as One Man': Gender and Sectionalism in Antislavery Petition Debates, 1835–1845." *Rhetoric & Public Affairs* 12 (2009): 1–28.

Zaller, John R. *The Nature and Origins of Mass Opinion*. Cambridge: Cambridge University Press, 1992.

Zarefsky, David. *Lincoln, Douglas, and Slavery: In the Crucible of Public Debate*. Chicago: University of Chicago Press, 1990.

Zarefsky, David. *President Johnson's War on Poverty: Rhetoric and History*. Tuscaloosa: University of Alabama Press, 1986.

Index